1

The Pilot's Manual

Flight Training

The Pilot's Manual

1

Flight Training

Second Edition

All the Flying and Practical
Knowledge for the Private and
Commercial Certificates

Trevor Thom

Graphics by Robert Johnson

Foreword by Barry Schiff

Aviation Supplies & Academics, Inc.
Renton, Washington

The Pilot's Manual 1: Flight Training

Aviation Supplies & Academics, Inc.
7005 132nd Place SE
Renton, Washington 98059-3153

Originally published by Center for Aviation Theory
© 1990–1993

Printed in the United States of America

99 98 97   9 8 7 6 5 4 3

ISBN 1-56027-184-1

ASA-PM-1

Acknowledgements

The Federal Aviation Administration (FAA), The National Ocean Service (NOS), Bendix/King, II Morrow, Inc., Cessna Aircraft Company, Piper Aircraft Corporation, Bruce Landsberg (Executive Director, AOPA Air Safety Foundation), Dora Muir (ASA—graphic art and design), Rob Fox (main cover picture), Bill Bennett, Fred Boyns, Robert G. Carter, Dale Castle, Bill Constable, Elizabeth Copping, Robyn Hind, Melonie James, Robert Lawson, Robert Loriente, Ola Rustenberg, Marc Vogel and Warren Yeates.
Also, to the many students and instructors whose comments have helped in developing and refining the material in this manual.

Contents

Phase One *Flying the Airplane*

		Personal Progress Table		
		Text	Review	Flying

Foreword

When it was time to take my private pilot written examination in 1955, my flight instructor handed me a pocket-size booklet. It was published by the Civil Aeronautics Administration (FAA's predecessor) and contained 200 true/false questions (including answers).

"Study these well," he cautioned with a wink, "because the test consists of 50 of these."

As I flipped through the dozen or so pages, my anxiety about the pending examination dissolved into relief. Nothing could be easier, I thought. One question, for example, stated—"True or False: It is dangerous to fly through a thunderstorm." Really. (I passed the test with flying colors—but so did everyone else in those days.)

The modern pilot, however, must know a great deal more to hurdle today's more-challenging examinations. This has resulted in a crop of books developed specifically to help pilots pass tests. Unfortunately, some do little else, and the student's education remains incomplete.

An exciting exception is "The Pilot's Manual"—a series of outstanding books written by Trevor Thom, a former flight and ground instructor and current airline captain. These voluminous manuals provide far in excess of that needed to pass examinations. They are also chock-full of practical advice and techniques that are as useful to experienced pilots as they are to students.

"The Pilot's Manual" is a refreshingly creative and clever approach that simplifies and adds spice to what often are regarded as academically dry subjects. Thom's extensive teaching background is reflected by the careful manner in which he explains complex subjects and concepts. Reading these books is like sitting with an experienced flight instructor who senses when you might be having difficulty with a subject and patiently continues teaching until confident that you understand.

Barry Schiff
Los Angeles

Barry Schiff has over 20,000 hours in more than 200 types of aircraft. As a twenty-one year veteran with Trans World Airlines, he currently flies the Boeing 767, and has received numerous honors for his contributions to aviation. He is well known to flying audiences for his many articles published in some 50 aviation periodicals, notably *AOPA Pilot,* of which he is a contributing editor.

This book is dedicated to Vice Admiral Donald D. Engen USN (Ret.) for his encouragement and contribution to the production of this series of training books for pilots, for his current role with the AOPA Air Safety Foundation, and in his previous roles ranging from naval aviator to Administrator of the FAA.

VICE ADMIRAL DONALD D. ENGEN USN (Ret.)

Chairman, Board of Visitors, and Immediate Past-President and Chief Executive Officer, AOPA Air Safety Foundation.

Former:
- Administrator, Federal Aviation Administration (FAA)
- Member, National Transportation Safety Board (NTSB)
- Executive, Piper Aircraft Manufacturing
- Deputy Commander-in-Chief of the US Atlantic Command and Atlantic Fleet
- Commanding Officer of the aircraft carrier USS America
- Engineering Test Pilot
- Naval aviator

Admiral Engen is a 7,000-hour pilot in nearly 250 aircraft types, and a current pilot.

About the Author

Trevor Thom. Current Boeing 757/767 captain on international operations, with time on Airbus A320, Boeing 727, DC-9, Fokker F-27 and the DC-4. He has represented pilots on many international technical committees, including the International Federation of Airline Pilots' (IFALPA) Aircraft Design and Operations Group (London), SAE S7 Flight Deck Design Committee (USA), the Australian Air Pilots' Technical Council, and the International Civil Aviation Organization (ICAO) in Montreal. Trevor holds B.Sc. and B.A. degrees, and a Diploma of Education. He has been a lecturer in physics and mathematics, and a ground and flight instructor.

Trevor is also the author of several series of popular pilot-training manuals in the United Kingdom and Australia, for which he received the inaugural Bicentennial Award for Aviation from the Guild of Air Pilots and Air Navigators (London 1988).

Editorial Team

Robert M. Johnson. Responsible for the production of this series; an experienced airline and corporate pilot, formerly a chief pilot on international operations of a Citation II-SP executive jet, a DC-3 and light aircraft, based in Switzerland; has also flown the DC-9, Lockheed Electra and Fokker F-27 in airline operations.

Madeline Mimi Tompkins. Experienced flight instructor, current Boeing 737-300/400 airline captain, crew resource management facilitator; well known for her part as copilot in an airliner emergency in Hawaii, about which a TV movie was made; has received many honors, including AOPA Air Safety Foundation's *Distinguished Pilot* award; a former FAA Designated Flight Examiner; currently an FAA Accident Prevention Counselor, Designated Written Test Examiner; also teaches CFI refresher courses.

Martin E. Weaver. An experienced flight and ground instructor in airplanes, helicopters and gliders; a former chief flight instructor and designated pilot examiner; has been closely involved with standardization procedures for the past 14 years; holds a B.S. from the University of Southern Mississippi; also currently a pilot in the Oklahoma Army National Guard.

Amy Laboda. Free-lance writer, editor, active flight instructor, member of the American Flyers Judith Resnik Scholarship committee; former editor at *Flying* magazine; has rotorcraft category, gyroplane rating, glider rating and multiengine ATP rating; holds a B.A. in Liberal Arts from Sarah Lawrence College.

Ian Suren. Former chief, Personnel Licensing and Training with ICAO in Montreal for 10 years, senior examiner in charge of Flight Crew License Examinations with the Australian Civil Aviation Authority, certificated pilot.

Richard James. Experienced flight instructor, charter pilot and air ambulance pilot; currently flying Boeing 767s on international operations; recently Boeing 747, DC-10 and Fokker F-50 pilot; has represented pilots on new-aircraft evaluation committees, the IFALPA Aircraft Design and Operation Study Group, and the ICAO En Route Obstacle Clearance Criteria Study Group.

Ronald G. Smith. Experienced flight instructor, ground instructor, charter pilot, air taxi service operator; member of International Wheelchair Aviators.

Abbreviations

For explanations, refer to the Pilot/Controller Glossary in the Airman's Information Manual.

ADF—automatic direction finder
A/FD—Airport/Facility Directory
AFM—Approved Flight Manual
agl or AGL—above ground level
AH—artificial horizon (see AI)
AI—attitude indicator
AIM—Airman's Information Manual
ALS—approach light system
ALT—altitude; altimeter
ASI—airspeed indicator
ASOS—automated surface observing system
ATC—Air Traffic Control
ATCRBS—ATC Radar Beacon System
ATIS—automatic terminal information service
AVASI—abbreviated VASI
AVGAS—aviation gasoline
AWOS—automated weather observing system
C—Celsius (formerly centigrade) degrees
C_D—coefficient of drag
CDI—course deviation indicator
CFI—certified flight instructor
CG—center of gravity
CHT—cylinder head temperature
C_L—coefficient of lift
CO—carbon monoxide
CO_2—carbon dioxide
CP—center of pressure
CTAF—common traffic advisory frequency
D—drag
DF—direction finder (in tower)
DG—directional gyro (replaced by HI)
DME—distance measuring equipment
DR—dead (deduced) reckoning
EFAS—en route flight advisory service ("Flight Watch")
ELT—emergency locator transmitter
ETA—estimated time of arrival
ETD—estimated time of departure
ETE—estimated time en route
F—Fahrenheit degrees
FAA—Federal Aviation Administration

FARs—Federal Aviation Regulations
FBO—fixed base operator
FL—flight level (hundreds of feet, e.g. FL210 is 21,000 feet)
fpm or FPM—feet per minute
FSS—Flight Service Station
ft or FT—feet (distance or altitude)
g or G—the gravity force
GMT—Greenwich Mean Time or "Z" zulu time (now UTC)
gph—gallons per hour
GPS—global positioning system
GS—groundspeed; glide slope
HAA—height above airport
HDG—heading
HI—heading indicator
HIRL—high intensity runway lights
HIWAS—hazardous in-flight weather advisory service
hPa—hectopascal (unit of pressure used internationally)
HSI—horizontal situation indicator
Hz—Hertz (cycles per second)
IAS—indicated airspeed
ICAO—International Civil Aviation Organization
IFR—instrument flight rules
ILS—instrument landing system
IMC—instrument meteorological conditions
in.Hg or "Hg—inches of mercury (measure of pressure)
ISA—international standard atmosphere
KCAS—knots calibrated airspeed
kHz—kilohertz (1,000 cycles per second)
KIAS—knots indicated airspeed
km—kilometer (1,000 meters)
kt—knots
KTAS—knots true airspeed
L—lift
L/D—lift/drag ratio
LDA—landing distance available
LIRL—low intensity runway lights
LORAN—long range navigation system
m or M—meters (distance)
°M—degrees magnetic
MAC—mean aerodynamic chord (in weight-and-balance)
MAYDAY (repeated three times)—international distress radio signal

mb—millibars (replaced by hPa)
MC—magnetic compass; magnetic course
MH—magnetic heading
MHz—megahertz (million cycles per second)
MIRL—medium intensity runway lights
MLS—microwave landing system
MLW—maximum certificated landing weight
MSA—minimum safe altitude
msl or MSL—mean sea level
MTOW—maximum certificated takeoff weight
MULTICOM—a self-announce radio frequency
MVFR—marginal VFR
NDB—non-directional radio beacon
nm or NM—nautical mile(s)
NOS—National Ocean Service (NOS charts)
NOTAM—Notice To Airmen
NTSB—National Transportation Safety Board
NWS—National Weather Service
OAT—outside air temperature
OBI—omni bearing indicator (on VOR cockpit instrument)
OBS—omni bearing selector (on VOR cockpit instrument)
OMNI—VHF omnidirectional radio range (same as VOR)
PAN-PAN (repeated three times)—international urgency radio signal
PAPI—precision approach path indicator
PATWAS—pilots' automatic telephone weather answering service
PCL—pilot controlled lighting
PIREP—pilot weather report
POH—Pilot's Operating Handbook
PVASI—pulsating VASI
QNH—international term for *altimeter setting*
RAIL—runway alignment indicator lights
RB—relative bearing
RBI—relative bearing indicator
RCLS—runway centerline light system
RCO—remote communications outlet
REIL—runway end identifier lights
RMI—radio magnetic indicator
RNAV—area navigation
rpm—revolutions per minute

RWY—runway
SAR—search and rescue
SFL—sequenced flashing lights
SIGMET—significant meteorological advisory alert
sm or SM—statute mile(s)
SSR—secondary surveillance radar
T—thrust
°T—degrees true
TACAN—military navigation station (see VORTAC)
TAS—true airspeed
TC—true course; turn coordinator
TDZL—touchdown zone lights
TE—tracking error
TPA—traffic pattern altitude
T-VASI—T-form VASI
TWEB—transcribed weather broadcast
UNICOM—aeronautical advisory radio communications unit (non-government)
UTC—coordinated universal time (previously GMT) or "Z" Zulu time (ATC reference to UTC)
V_A—design maneuvering speed
VASI—visual approach slope indicator
V_B—turbulence penetration speed
VDF—VHF direction finding station
V_{FE}—maximum flaps-extended airspeed
VFR—visual flight rules
V_{LO}—maximum speed, landing gear operating
VMC—visual meteorological conditions
V_{NE}—never-exceed airspeed
V_{NO}—normal-operating limit airspeed
VOR—VHF omnidirectional radio range
VORTAC—colocated and integrated VOR and TACAN* (*used for distance measuring)
V_S—stalling speed
V_{S1}—stalling speed clean
V_{S0}—stalling speed in landing configuration
VSI—vertical speed indicator
V_X—best angle-of-climb airspeed
V_Y—best rate-of-climb airspeed
Z—Zulu time (ATC reference to UTC)

Introduction

Becoming a Pilot

Every pilot begins as a student pilot whether the aim is to fly for a hobby or to fly for a career.

Learning to fly does not take long—within the first 20 hours of flight training you will have learned the basic skills. Since the training period is so short, good habits must be developed right from the start. Patterns formed in the first few hours will stay with you throughout your flying life and so, to gain the maximum benefit from each hour in the air and to develop good habits, you should be well prepared. This manual will help you to do this—our objective is to help you to win for yourself a *Private Pilot Certificate.*

A **commercial pilot,** as a professional, should have a higher level of knowledge and skill than a private pilot. The relatively small amount of additional knowledge is added as a supplement to the relevant chapter, and the additional flight maneuvers required have small sections of their own in Phase Three where you are sharpening your flying skills.

Private pilots are encouraged to reach a professional standard. By adding the relatively few additional commercial pilot requirements to our manual, this has been made easy.

An advanced formal education is not a requirement to become a pilot, although the English language is required for radio calls, and a knowledge of basic mathematics is useful. Beyond that, no special academic skills are required.

Learn correctly, right from the start.

The basic training airplane is simple in design and straightforward to operate. It has:
- **a control wheel** (or control column) to raise or lower the nose and to bank the wings;
- **a rudder** to keep the airplane coordinated so that the tail follows the nose and the airplane does not fly sideways; and
- **a throttle** to supply engine power.

The largest and fastest airliners have basically the same controls as your training airplane.

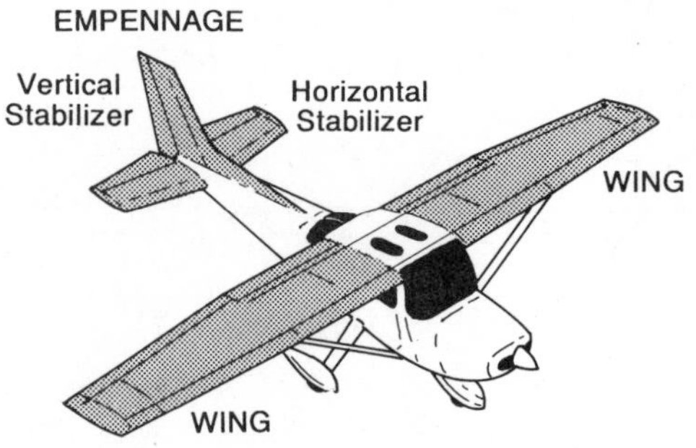

EMPENNAGE

Vertical Stabilizer

Horizontal Stabilizer

WING

WING

Figure 2. The main aerodynamic surfaces of a typical training airplane

How an Airplane Flies

When not in flight, an airplane is supported by the ground. When airborne, however, it must generate its own support. This it does by modifying the flow of the air over the wings and generating a force known as *lift*.

The lift generated by the wings supports an airplane in flight.

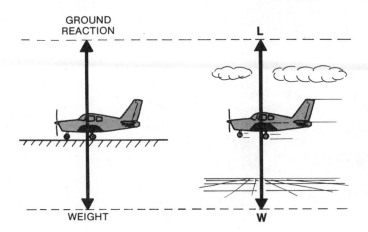

GROUND REACTION

L

WEIGHT

W

Figure 3. In flight, the airplane is supported by lift.

The air is made up of many molecules, all of which are moving at high speed and in random directions, even though the parcel of air itself might be stationary.

The molecules act like small tennis balls, bouncing off any surface that they come in contact with and exerting a force on it. The size of the force is greatest when the collision is head-on, and becomes less with glancing blows. All of these small forces, when added up over an area, exert a pressure on the surface. This is known as *static pressure*.

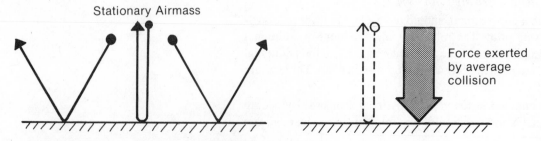

Stationary Airmass

Force exerted by average collision

Figure 4. Static pressure exerted by stationary parcel of air

If the parcel of air is moving relative to the surface, the collisions are more likely to be glancing blows rather than head-on, and so the pressure exerted on the surface will be less. **The faster the air flows** past the surface, **the lower the static pressure** that it exerts on the wing.

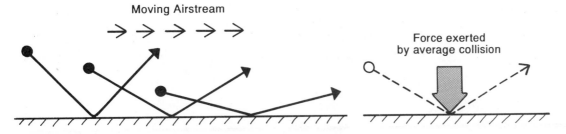

Moving Airstream

Force exerted
by average collision

Figure 5. Static pressure decreases with the speed of airflow.

A wing is shaped so that the airflow speeds up over its upper surface. This results in a lower static pressure above the wing than below it and so a lifting force is created.

Note: The decrease in static pressure with an increased speed of airflow is known in physics as **Bernoulli's principle.** It is usually stated as: *static pressure plus dynamic pressure* (which is related to speed) *equals a constant total pressure.*

The effect is the same when air flows past the wing as when the wing moves through the air—it is the **relative motion** of one to the other that is important.

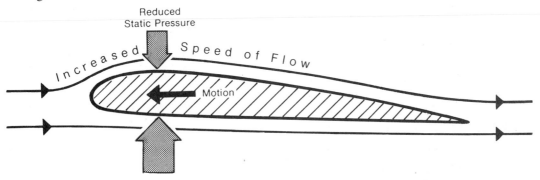

Reduced
Static Pressure

Increased Speed of Flow

Motion

Figure 6. The airflow is faster over a wing than under it, causing a lower static pressure to be generated.

The actual lift generated by a wing depends upon its shape and also upon the angle at which the wing is presented to the airflow. This angle between the wing chord line and the relative airflow is known as the *angle-of-attack.*

The greater the angle-of-attack, the faster the air will travel over the upper surface of the wing and the lower the static pressure will be—thus, **the greater the angle-of-attack, the greater the lifting ability of the wing.** The practical result is that sufficient lift to support the weight of the airplane can be generated at a lower airspeed.

Increasing the angle-of-attack of a wing increases its lifting ability.

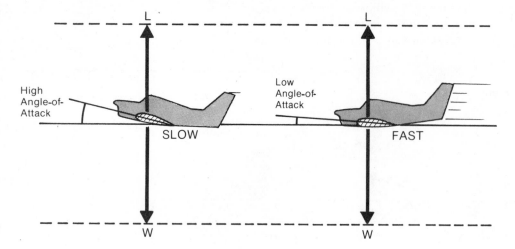

Figure 7. In level flight, the airplane can fly slower at high angles-of-attack.

The lifting ability of the wings at low airspeeds is limited however—when the airplane slows to a speed at which the angle-of-attack exceeds a critical value, the airflow separates from the upper surface of the wings, causing a drastic reduction in lift. The wings are then said to be *stalled*. Exercise 10a of this manual covers the recovery from a stall in detail.

The force that opposes the motion of the airplane through the air is called *drag*. In straight-and-level flight, the drag is counteracted by the thrust from the propeller. **The four main forces** acting on an airplane in steady straight-and-level flight are: **lift,** which is equal to **weight,** and **thrust,** which is equal to **drag.** Typically, lift and weight are 10 times greater than thrust and drag.

Control surfaces, operated from the cockpit by the pilot, can alter the airflow around the wings and the tail-section, varying the aerodynamic forces and allowing you to maneuver the airplane as desired.

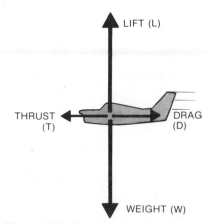

Figure 8. The four main forces that act on an airplane in flight

The Four Fundamental Maneuvers

You can achieve your desired flightpath by combining the four fundamental maneuvers as appropriate: **straight-and-level flight, turns, climbs,** and **descents.** If you train yourself to perform each of these maneuvers individually, and then learn to combine them, you are well on the way to becoming a competent pilot.

Your Flying Lessons

The cockpit is a difficult place in which to learn, so adequate preflight preparation is essential. For each training flight you should have a clear objective and be thoroughly prepared in order to achieve it. Ideally, the actual training flight should be an illustration of principles which you already understand, rather than a series of totally unexpected events.

Your objective is, with the guidance of your flight instructor, to achieve a standard where you:
- show good judgment and airmanship (common sense);
- apply your aeronautical knowledge;
- operate the airplane within its limits; and
- demonstrate mastery of the airplane at all times by confidently performing each maneuver or procedure smoothly and accurately.

The cockpit is not always an easy place to learn, so always be prepared for your flying lessons.

Airmanship is a term that embraces many things—skill in flying the airplane, thorough knowledge, qualities of common sense, quick reaction, awareness and experience. You should aim to achieve a high standard of airmanship during your pilot training course, and to maintain it throughout your flying career.

How to Use This Manual

For each stage of your training, this manual sets out:
- a clear objective;
- the principles and considerations involved;
- how to fly the maneuver;
- the actual *Airwork*—summarized graphically;
- any further points relevant to the exercise; plus
- review questions—to reinforce the main points.

This will prepare you well and help to minimize your training hours (and your expense). As your training progresses, the manual can also be used for revision. Earlier maneuvers can be revised simply by scanning the **side-notes** within the relevant chapter, referring to the *Airwork* pages (which act as a summary), and working through the Review questions again.

Your flight training will consist of various phases:

- **Phase 1—Flying the airplane:** upper airwork learning the four fundamental maneuvers (climbing, straight-and-level, turning and descending), with an introduction to stalling, and flying at critically slow airspeeds. Throughout this phase you will also be practicing starting and stopping the engine, and taxiing on the ground.

- **Phase 2—Takeoffs and Landings:** learning to make takeoffs, fly the airplane around the traffic pattern, and make approaches and landings; this leads on to your *first solo*.

- **Phase 3—Sharpening your Flying Skills:** advanced maneuvers and procedures, including steep turns, low flying, ground reference maneuvers and practice forced landings.

- **Phase 4—Expanding your Horizons:** cross-country navigation, basic instrument flying and night flying.

You will feel a great sense of achievement as you move through these phases toward your Private Pilot Certificate.

In the **Appendix—Specific Airplane Type:** there are questions that will help you to better understand your airplane type. You can apply this appendix not only to your own training airplane, but to any other type you may fly later on.

An Important Note to Pilots Regarding Flight Training

Our manual will allow you to be well-prepared for each flying lesson, which will make your flight training very efficient, and therefore less costly. The responsibility for your training rests with your own flight instructor, so his or her words have final authority.

We welcome written comments and suggestions for improvement of this manual, especially from flight instructors.

On the next page is a Note to Instructors.

A Note to the Instructor

First impressions are very important. Students seem to remember best what they learn first. Our manual has been designed so that correct understanding is possible the first time around. It is not just one book, but a collection of 20 booklets, each one standing alone and presenting everything that needs to be known for a specific flight lesson. The student need only read the chapter relevant to the flight lesson.

We aim to make the learning interesting and meaningful so that a student will assimilate it easily, and understand it well enough to be able to explain the main ideas in his or her own words.

New material is presented carefully, building on knowledge and experience already gained, but avoiding any confusion with previous material. (For instance, the distinction between a forward slip, used to steepen a zero-flap approach, and a sideslip, used to counteract drift in a crosswind touchdown, is carefully explained.) The main points in each chapter are expressed in different ways and repeated periodically throughout the text to reinforce the knowledge.

Active participation by the student in the learning process is encouraged by the review questions in each chapter.

The review questions will:
• actively involve the student;
• prepare the student for the particular flight lesson;
• consolidate the main points; and
• provide a means of revision after the flight lesson.

Some of the questions are quite easy, and are designed to reinforce the main points. Other questions are more demanding, and are designed to test depth of knowledge.

Each *Airwork* page is a graphic summary of the particular flight lesson.

Revision is made easy by reference to the "sidelines" that accompany the text, the airwork pages, and the review questions.

The flight instructor, expecially the very first flight instructor, plays a vital role in the life of a pilot. What the student learns first will stick. We wish you well with your students.

Trevor Thom

This manual is really 20 stand-alone booklets, each one dealing with one particular aspect of flying training.

Flying the Airplane Phase One

Phase One Completion Standards

In Phase One, you are learning the basic handling skills, both on the ground and in the air. On completion of this phase, you should be able to perform the following tasks within the required accuracy limits specified on the *Airwork* pages in each Exercise:

Phase One is learning how to handle the airplane.

- Be familiar with the Pilot's Operating Handbook (POH) for your airplane.
- Perform all normal checks, and use checklists without error.
- Understand all of the airplane controls, and use them correctly.
- Taxi safely with a correct technique, paying heed to airport markings and obtaining a taxi clearance at tower-controlled airports.
- Use standard radio procedures, both on the ground and in the air.
- Fly straight-and-level at speeds selected by your flight instructor, both clean and with flaps extended.
- Climb, level off, descend, level off—with descents in both low-drag (clean) configuration and high-drag (either flapped or forward slip) configuration.
- Perform turns in both directions at a constant altitude—shallow, medium, steep.
- Perform climbing turns, and descending turns clean and with flaps, in both directions.
- Stall the airplane in various configurations, and recover with a minimum loss of altitude.
- Recognize an imminent stall or spin, and take corrective action before a full stall or full spin develops.
- Handle emergency procedures and equipment malfunctions.
- Prepare the airplane to fly, and secure it after the flight.
- Ensure that the documentation prior to, and after, the flight is complete and signed off.

The Airplane

Features

The basic training airplane consists of a **fuselage** to which the **wings**, the **tail** or empennage, the **wheels** and an **engine** are attached. A **propeller,** driven by the engine, generates thrust to pull the airplane through the air. This enables the airflow over the wings to generate the aerodynamic force known as lift that is capable of supporting the airplane in flight. The airplane can fly without thrust if it is placed in a gliding descent.

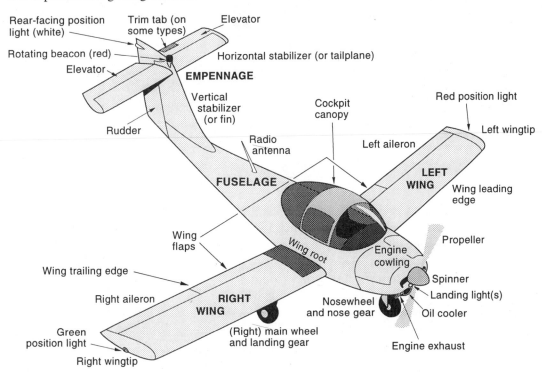

Figure 1-1. Features of a typical basic training airplane

The tail section (or empennage) of the airplane is situated some distance to the rear of the main load-carrying sections of the fuselage and provides a balancing or stabilizing force—much like the tail feathers on an arrow or a dart. The tail section consists of a **vertical stabilizer** (or fin) and a **horizontal stabilizer,** both of which are shaped to produce suitable aerodynamic forces.

The pilot and other occupants of the airplane are accommodated in the **cockpit** or cabin, usually seated side-by-side, with the pilot-in-command sitting on the left-hand side. Various controls and instruments are available in the cockpit to enable safe and efficient operation of the airplane and its systems.

The **main controls** used to fly the airplane are the **flight controls** and the **throttle.** The throttle—usually operated by the pilot's right hand—controls the power supplied by the engine/propeller combination. To open the throttle, push it forward—this increases the fuel/air supply to the engine, causing the engine to turn faster and develop more power. Pulling the throttle back, or closing it, reduces the power.

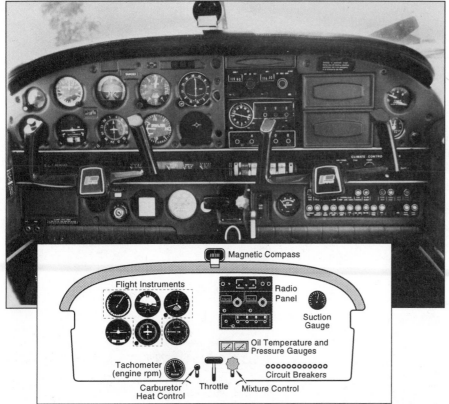

Figure 1-2. The cockpit and main controls of a typical training airplane

The **attitude** (or position in flight relative to the earth) of the airplane is controlled using the main **flight controls.** These are surfaces which, when deflected, alter the pattern of the airflow around the wings and the tail section, causing changes in the aerodynamic forces that they generate.

- The **elevator** (hinged to the trailing edge of the horizontal stabilizer) controls pitching of the nose up or down, and is operated from the cockpit with push-and-pull movements of the control column (or control wheel).
- The **ailerons** (hinged to the outer trailing edge of each wing) control rolling of the airplane, and are operated by left–right movements of the control column (or rotation of the control wheel).
- The **rudder** (hinged to the trailing edge of the vertical stabilizer) controls the yawing of the nose left or right, and is operated with the feet by pressing the base of the rudder pedals mounted on the floor under the instrument panel.

Other flight controls include:

- the **wing flaps** (situated on the inner trailing edge of each main wing)—used to change the shape of the wings and make slower flight possible; they are operated by a manual lever or electrical switch; and
- the elevator **trim tab** or similar device (situated on the trailing edge of the elevator)—used to reduce elevator control pressure on the pilot; usually operated by a trim-wheel or handle beside the pilot or above in the cabin roof.

There will be further controls in the cockpit to operate the **cabin heating** and **ventilation systems.**

Variations in Design

There are variations in design between different types, but the same basic principles apply to all airplanes.

Instead of a control column in the form of a stick, many airplanes are fitted with a control wheel, which serves exactly the same function. Moving the control wheel in or out operates the elevator, rotating it operates the ailerons. In this manual the term *control column* refers to both types.

Even though the aerodynamic sections of various airplane types serve the same basic functions, their actual location on the structure and their design can vary. For example, the wings may be attached to the fuselage in a high-, low- or mid-wing position; the horizontal stabilizer is sometimes positioned high on the vertical stabilizer, known as a T-tail, and the combined horizontal stabilizer and elevator is sometimes replaced by a **stabilator**, or all-flying tail.

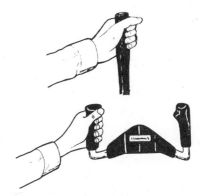

Figure 1-3. The control column and the control wheel

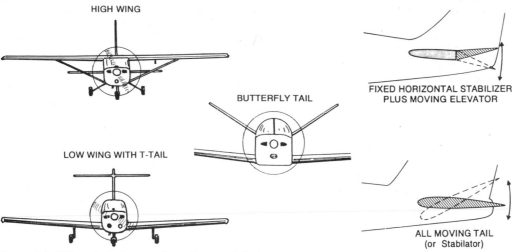

Figure 1-4. Different airplane configurations and designs

Most modern training airplanes have a tricycle **landing gear** assembly, consisting of two main wheels and a nosewheel, to provide support on the ground. Other aircraft have a tailwheel instead of a nosewheel. The nosewheel on most types is connected to the rudder pedals so that movement of the pedals will turn it, providing the primary means of directional control on the ground.

Most aircraft have **brakes** on the main wheels which are operated by pressing the top of the rudder pedals or by using a brake handle.

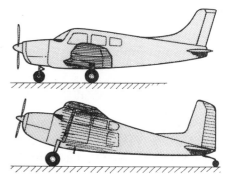

Figure 1-5. Tricycle and tailwheel landing gear designs

The Engine and Propeller

The typical training airplane has a horizontally opposed reciprocating engine that uses aviation gasoline (AVGAS). The engine revolutions per minute (rpm) are controlled by the **throttle**. Attached to the engine is a fixed-pitch **propeller** (one whose blade angle cannot be altered) that converts the power from the engine into thrust. A measure of the power being developed is the engine **rpm** which is indicated in the cockpit on the **tachometer.**

The fuel for the engine is usually stored in **wing tanks**—low-wing airplanes usually require a fuel pump to deliver fuel to the engine, high-wing airplanes usually rely on gravity feed. There are **fuel gauges** in the cockpit to indicate quantity, but it is good airmanship and just common sense to check the contents of the tanks visually prior to flight. It is also wise to confirm that the fuel is both of the correct grade (which is identified by its color) and that it is not contaminated—the most likely contaminant being water, which is denser than AVGAS and gathers at the low points in the fuel system.

The fuel check is performed by inspecting a small sample taken from **fuel drains** fitted at low points in the fuel system, for example from beneath each fuel tank, and from the **fuel strainer(s),** also known as gascolators, usually located under the engine compartment near the firewall—the barrier between the engine and the cockpit.

The fuel **tank selector** in the cockpit allows fuel to be supplied from each tank individually or possibly from all tanks. It is vital that a tank containing fuel be selected.

The fuel is mixed with air in a **carburetor** attached to the engine, and the fuel/air mixture passes through the induction system into the cylinders, where combustion occurs. The **mixture control,** situated near the throttle, is used to ensure that a suitable fuel/air mixture is provided to the engine by the carburetor.

The **carburetor heat control,** also located near the throttle, is used to supply hot air to protect the carburetor from ice.

Oil for lubricating and cooling the engine is stored in a sump in the engine compartment. Its quantity should be checked with a dipstick prior to flying. There are two cockpit gauges in the oil system, one of which registers **oil pressure** and one which registers **oil temperature** when the engine is running. These gauges are often color-coded, the normal operating range being shown as a green arc.

The engine has **dual ignition systems** which provide sparks to initiate the combustion process in the cylinders. The electrical current for the sparks is generated by two **magnetos** geared to the engine. The dual ignition systems provide more efficient combustion and greater safety in the event of one system failing.

An **ignition switch** in the cockpit is normally used to select BOTH magnetos, although it can select the LEFT or RIGHT systems individually, as well as having an OFF position. Most ignition switches have a further position, START, which connects the battery to an electric starter to turn the engine over.

When the engine starts, the ignition switch is returned to BOTH.

Note: The two magneto systems providing the sparks to the engine are totally separate from the electrical system—alternator/generator, battery, circuit breakers and fuses—that supplies power to various aircraft services.

The Electrical System

The **battery** is a source of electrical power to start the engine, and provides an emergency electrical backup supply if the engine-driven alternator (or generator) fails.

The electrical system will have an **alternator** or a **generator** to supply various aircraft services such as some flight instruments, the radios, cabin lights, landing lights, position lights, the wing-flap motor, pitot tube heater and stall warning system. It is important that airplanes fitted with an alternator have a serviceable battery so that the alternator can come on line.

The electrical system has an **ammeter** and/or **warning light** incorporated to enable the pilot to verify that electrical current is flowing. Each electrical circuit is protected from excessive current by a **fuse** or a **circuit breaker.**

One very useful electrical service is the **radio,** which is used for air/ground communications. It has an ON/OFF and volume control (usually combined in the one knob), a squelch control to eliminate unwanted background noise, a microphone for transmitting and speakers or headphones for receiving messages.

Fuel management is a high priority item for the pilot.

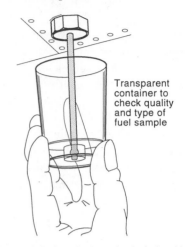

Transparent container to check quality and type of fuel sample

Figure 1-6. A typical method of checking the fuel

Figure 1-7. An ignition switch

Figure 1-8. Control panel of a typical communications radio

The Instruments

The panel in front of the pilot contains various instruments which can provide important information—the main groups being the **flight instruments,** which are directly in front of the pilot, and the **engine gauges,** which are usually situated near the throttle.

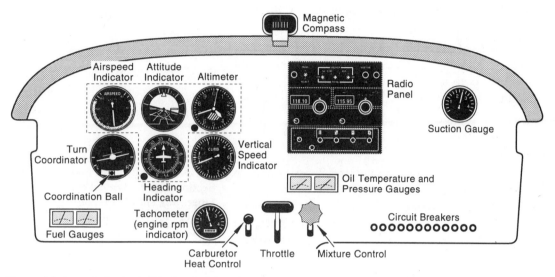

Figure 1-9. Layout of a typical instrument panel

The flight instruments include:
- an airspeed indicator (ASI);
- an attitude indicator (AI) to depict the airplane's attitude relative to the horizon;
- an altimeter to indicate the altitude;
- a vertical speed indicator (VSI) to show climb or descent rate;
- a heading indicator (HI); and
- a turn coordinator with an associated coordination ball.

The instruments related to airspeed and altitude are operated by air pressure obtained from the **pitot-static pressure system,** while those related to attitude, direction and turning are operated by internal spinning **gyroscopes** (with the exception of the magnetic compass).The gyroscope rotors may be spun electrically or by a stream of air induced by suction from the vacuum system. The **magnetic compass** is usually located well away from the magnetic influences of the instrument panel and radio.

The engine gauges include the **tachometer** (to read engine rpm), and the **oil pressure** and **oil temperature gauges.** Some aircraft also have a cylinder head temperature (CHT) gauge.

Other instruments may include an **ammeter** to monitor the electrical system and a **suction gauge** for the vacuum system.

Other Items

There may be a **fire extinguisher** provided in the cockpit, which should be checked for serviceability and security in its fitting. Light-aircraft fire extinguishers are normally of the halon or dry-chemical (powder) type, which are nontoxic. You should make yourself familiar with the operation of the type fitted to your training airplane.

Control locks may be used in the cockpit to lock the control column and/or externally on the actual flight controls. Their purpose is to prevent control-surface movement and damage from the wind when the airplane is parked. It is vital that they be removed prior to flight.

A **pitot cover** may be carried to protect the pitot head from blockage by insects and water while the airplane is parked. It must be removed prior to flight if the airspeed indicator is to read correctly.

Wheel chocks may be placed ahead of and behind the wheels when the airplane is parked as a precaution against movement. There may also be a tie-down kit containing ropes and wheel chocks to secure the airplane to the ground and prevent strong winds lifting the wings or tail.

A **first aid kit** may be carried.

Checklists

Written checklists are used to confirm that appropriate procedures have been carried out, for example, the Before-Takeoff checklist or the Engine Fire checklist. In earlier days, when airplanes were simpler, checks were usually memorized. Nowadays, in more complex airplanes and in a much busier operating environment, many checks are performed with the use of standard written checklists for that airplane.

Checklists are usually compiled in a concise and abbreviated form as ITEM and CONDITION (for example, Fuel—ON), where the item to be checked is listed, followed by a statement of its desired condition. Explanations for the actions are usually *not* included in the concise checklist, but may generally be found in the Pilot's Operating Handbook if required.

Emergency checklists, for instance the Engine Fire checklist, often have some items which should be memorized, since they may have to be actioned immediately, before there is time to locate the appropriate checklist and read it. These items are often referred to as memory items or *phase-one* items, and are often distinguished on checklists by **bold type** or by being surrounded with a box.

The method of using checklists may be one of:
• carrying out the items as the checklist is read; or
• carrying out the items in-full, followed by confirmation using the checklist.

The procedures for your training will be made quite clear by your flight instructor.

Remember: Checklists must be carried in the cockpit.

Normal checklists are found in Section 4 of the typical Pilot's Operating Handbook, and Emergency checklists are found in Section 3.

Vital checklists are best committed to memory so that they may be done quickly and efficiently, followed by confirmation using the printed checklist if required.

Emergencies

The **Pilot's Operating Handbook** for your particular airplane will specify the procedures to be followed in coping with certain emergencies, for example:

- engine fire on the ground;
- engine fire in flight;
- engine failure in flight followed by a forced landing;
- electrical fire or smoke;
- cabin fire; and
- a flat main tire.

The more serious emergencies are considered in detail in the appropriate chapter, however, since you are about to commence flight training, you should have a basic awareness of emergency procedures, even at this early stage.

Fire Emergencies

Fire is a hazard to aviation and is to be avoided at all costs. For a fire to occur, three things are required:

- fuel (AVGAS, oil, papers, fabric, seating, and so on);
- oxygen (present in the air); and
- a source of ignition (cigarettes, matches, electrical sparks, and so on).

The usual method of extinguishing a fire is to eliminate one or more of these items—for example, blanketing a fire with halon or dry chemical from a fire extinguisher to starve the fire of oxygen.

It is, of course, preferable that fire is prevented by keeping fuel and possible sources of ignition separate. For example, when **fueling** an airplane, ensure that there is **no smoking** in the vicinity, that the airplane and fueling equipment are adequately grounded to avoid the possibility of static electricity causing a spark, and that no fuel is spilled. As a precaution, have a fire extinguisher available. Know how to use it!

Engine Fire on the Ground

The best procedure if a fire occurs during engine start is to keep the engine turning with the starter, but move the mixture control to IDLE CUTOFF—or fuel selector to OFF—to allow the engine to purge itself and the induction system of fuel. The fire will probably go out. If not, take appropriate further action:

- Fuel—OFF;
- Switches—OFF;
- Brakes—ON;
- Evacuate, taking the extinguisher.

Engine Fire in Flight

If there is an engine fire in flight, shut down the engine and do not restart it. Maintain flying speed and plan for an immediate landing. If the flames are not extinguished following the emergency checklist, a maneuver known as a sideslip may keep the flames away from the cockpit and occupants. A fire in flight will probably be caused by a leakage of fuel or oil under pressure, so a typical procedure to stop the leakage is:

- Throttle—CLOSED;
- Mixture—IDLE CUTOFF, or fuel selector—OFF (so that fuel will be eliminated from the induction system and engine);
- Ignition switches—OFF; and
- Cabin heat—OFF (to avoid fumes from the engine entering the cockpit).

If any problem occurs in flight, the most essential task is to maintain flying speed and control the flight path of the airplane. The emergency must be handled in conjunction with this primary task.

During your *Preflight External check*, you should check the lower surfaces of the airplane structure, and the ground beneath, for any evidence of fuel leaks.

Electrical Fire

A peculiar smell is often the clue that the fire is electrical. Switch off any associated electrical circuits using appropriate switches and or circuit breakers. If required, a fire extinguisher can be used, but ensure that cabin ventilation is sufficient for safe breathing and the windows are open to remove smoke and toxic fumes from the cabin when the fire is out.

Whether or not to shut the engine down in flight is a command decision to be made by the pilot-in-command and will, of course, mean a forced landing without power.

A typical procedure for an electrical fire is:
- Master switch—OFF (to remove power from the electrical services);
- All other switches (except ignition)—OFF;
- Cabin heat—OFF;
- Fire extinguisher—use as required (and open fresh air vents to ventilate the cockpit);
- **On the ground**: shut down the engine and electrical system and evacuate;
- **In flight**: decide whether to keep the engine running and make an early landing or shut down the engine and make an immediate forced landing.

In the event of an electrical fire, an immediate landing is advisable. Do not reset any popped circuit breakers.

Cabin Fire

A cabin fire may be caused by such things as a cigarette igniting a seat or some other flammable material. The source of the fire should be identified and the fire eliminated using the fire extinguisher:
- **In flight**: maintain flying speed and a suitable flight path while putting out the fire;
- **On the ground**: consider an immediate evacuation after securing the airplane (shut down the engine; switches and fuel—OFF; brakes—ON).

A Flat Main Tire

A flat main tire may become apparent with an unusual sound from the tire and the aircraft veering off to one side during takeoff or landing. If known to have a flat tire in flight:
- Approach—NORMAL;
- Touchdown—GOOD TIRE FIRST; hold the airplane off the flat tire as long as possible with aileron control.

On the ground:
- Throttle—CLOSED;
- Steer away from other aircraft and obstacles;
- Apply the brakes to both wheels.

Brake Failure

If the brakes fail while taxiing, then:
- Throttle—CLOSED;
- Steer away from other aircraft and obstacles;

and, if a **collision** is imminent:
- Stop the engine (mixture control—IDLE CUTOFF);
- Fuel—OFF;
- Ignition—OFF;
- Master switch—OFF.

✍️ Review 1

To revise the material covered in this chapter, we recommend that you now complete the following *Review* questions. They will:

- prepare you for your flight lesson;
- consolidate the important points; and
- give you an idea of the type of questions you can expect from your flight instructor and when you take your practical test.

Some of the questions are very straightforward and have been included simply to refresh your memory about a significant point covered in the text. A good way to work through the questions is to cover the page with a blank piece of paper, then slide it down to reveal the first question, stopping at the gray arrowhead that precedes the answer. Then, when you have the (correct) answer in mind, you can check it with our answer shown just below the arrowhead.

1. Fill in the boxes below with the following items: fuselage; right wing; left wing; empennage; nosewheel; oil cooler; wing trailing edge; vertical stabilizer; elevator; propeller; rudder; left and right wingtips; wing root; wing flaps; spinner; wing leading edge; radio antenna; (right) main landing gear; cockpit canopy; rotating beacon (red); red position light; right aileron; elevator trim tab; green position light; engine cowling; rear-facing position light (white); landing light(s); engine exhaust; left aileron; horizontal stabilizer.

➤ *refer to figure 1-1 on page 9.*

The Airplane

2. Easing the control column toward you in normal flight will (raise/lower) the nose of the airplane.

➤ raise

3. Rotating the control column to the right in normal flight will cause the airplane to roll to the _____ .

➤ right

4. The rudder, which is located on the trailing edge of the vertical stabilizer, is operated by the rudder _____ .

➤ pedals

5. Moving the throttle in will (increase/decrease) engine power.

➤ increase

6. On the ground, wheel brakes can be operated by pressing the top of the _____ _____ .

➤ rudder pedals

7. The main division of instruments in the cockpit is into _____ instruments and _____ gauges.

flight instruments and engine gauges

8. Fuel is stored in fuel tanks located in the _____ .

➤ wings

9. The fluid that is used to lubricate and cool the engine is _____ .

➤ oil

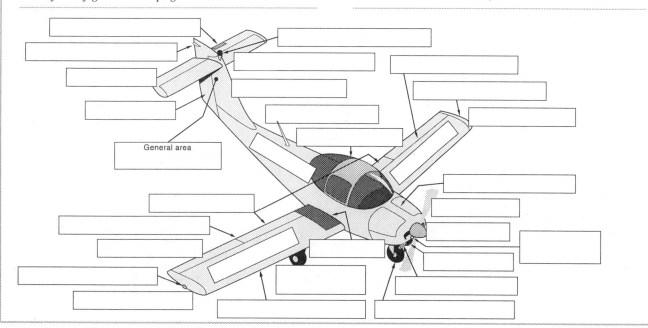

General area

10. Draw a circle around:
    (a) the flight instruments;
    (b) the engine gauges and controls;
    (c) the radio panel;
    (d) the magnetic compass.

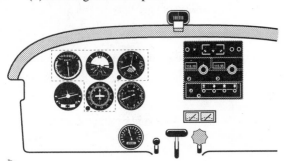

➤ *refer to figure 1-2, on page 10*

11. The fuel is mixed with air in the c_____ ; the ratio of the mixture is controlled by the pilot moving the m_____ c_____ , which adjusts the fuel/air mixture before it passes into the engine cylinders for combustion.

➤ carburetor, mixture control

12. The sparks that ignite the fuel/air mixture in the engine cylinders come from electrical current generated by two _____ incorporated in the engine. The dual ignition systems provide (more/less) efficient combustion in each cylinder and (more/less) safety in case of failure of one system.

➤ magnetos, more, more

13. Electrical power to start the engine by turning it over is usually supplied by the _____ .

➤ battery

14. Radios and other electrical services can be powered by the battery when the engine is not running. When the engine is running it drives an _____ which can power the radios, lights, and so on, as well as recharge the battery.

➤ alternator

15. Above is the (master/radio/ignition) switch.

➤ ignition

16. A concise and abbreviated list of items that a pilot should complete prior to a particular phase of flight is known as a _____ .

➤ checklist

17. A normal checklist, such as the Before-Landing checklist, is found in the Pilot's Operating Handbook, Section ____ , for _____ Procedures.

➤ Section 4, Normal Procedures

18. An Emergency checklist, such as the Engine Fire In Flight checklist, is found in the Pilot's Operating Handbook, Section ____ , for _____ Procedures.

➤ Section 3, Emergency Procedures

19. The item of equipment pictured above is a (navigation radio/communications radio/rpm indicator). The label "SQ" stands for _____ , which is used to remove unwanted _____ _____ .

➤ communications radio, squelch, background noise

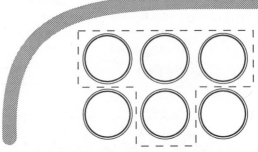

20. Label the six instruments on the above graphic: attitude indicator, heading indicator, airspeed indicator, turn coordinator, altimeter and vertical speed indicator; also label the coordination ball.

➤

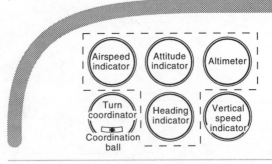

Am I Fit to Fly? 2a

Before each flight you must ask yourself, "Am I fit to fly? Do I feel well? Am I able to perform the physical and mental tasks that may be required of me as pilot-in-command?"

Physical Fitness

As a pilot, you should maintain a reasonable degree of physical fitness. It allows better physical and mental performance during flight and in the long term, and quite apart from flying, improves your chances of a long and healthy life.

Keeping fit is worth the effort.

Keeping fit takes some effort and this effort must be continuous for fitness to be retained, but it can also be good fun and very recreational. Walking, jogging, digging in the garden, cycling, swimming—in fact anything that steadily raises your pulse rate will improve your fitness.

If you are grossly unfit or obese, then allow yourself several diet-conscious months with moderate exercise that is gradually increased, and consider medical supervision. It might seem like a long haul, but the quality of life and your perception of yourself will improve along with your fitness. Physical activity also promotes a hunger for healthy foods as well as encouraging good sleeping patterns. Physical fitness also helps a pilot cope better with stress, tiredness, fatigue and the reduced availability of oxygen at higher levels in the atmosphere.

Mental Fitness

Flying an airplane involves physical activity but the main workload on a pilot is intellectual. Mental fitness is vital to safe flying, but it can be degraded by:

The main workload on a pilot is intellectual.

- medication;
- drugs, including alcohol and cigarettes;
- excessive demands on one's mental energy;
- personal or family problems;
- lack of sleep or poor eating habits; and
- fatigue or allowing oneself to get over-tired.

Illness and Drugs

A reasonably innocuous complaint on the ground (such as the common cold) may have serious effects under the demands of flying and high altitudes. Medical drugs taken to combat an illness may impair flying abilities and physical comfort in flight. "Recreational drugs", such as alcohol, marijuana and LSD, must *never* be mixed with flying, and a person dependent upon these may not be fit to hold a pilot's certificate.

Smoking also significantly decreases a pilot's capacity to perform by reducing the amount of oxygen carried in the blood, replacing it with the useless and potentially poisonous byproducts of cigarette smoke. A pilot does not have to be the active smoker to suffer the effects; smoke from any person in the cockpit will affect everyone.

The topic of *drugs* includes alcohol and smoking.

Medical Checks

Regular checks by an Aviation Medical Examiner are required to monitor your general health, both physical and mental. Major items in the medical test include checks of the central nervous system (including eyesight), the cardiovascular system (including heart and blood pressure), correct functioning of the kidneys (using a urine test), hearing ability and, finally, the respiratory system (ears, nose, throat and lungs), especially the eustachian tubes for their ability to allow pressures to equalize either side of the ear drums.

Medical checks verify your general health and fitness, but occasional bouts of sickness or injury may make you temporarily unfit to fly, particularly if medication is involved. **If in doubt** consult an Aviation Medical Examiner.

Pilots carry a heavy responsibility both to themselves and to the general community and so medical fitness is most important.

Medication

Until cleared by a doctor, it is safest to assume that any drug or medication will temporarily ground you. A list of common medications considered incompatible with flying includes:
- antibiotics (for example, penicillin) used to combat infection;
- tranquilizers, antidepressants and sedatives;
- stimulants (caffeine, amphetamines) used to suppress sleep or appetite;
- antihistamines, often used to combat colds and hay fever;
- drugs for the relief of high blood pressure;
- analgesics to relieve pain;
- anesthetics (used for local, general or dental purposes) usually require about 24 hours before returning to flight.

The use of drugs for recreational purposes is, of course, totally incompatible with flying.

It is also recommended that active pilots do not donate blood. While this is a worthwhile contribution to the community, it does reduce, at least temporarily, the ability to move energy-giving oxygen around the body.

Taking medicine or donating blood may ground you temporarily.

Alcohol

A pilot who has "had a drink" is obliged not to fly if under the influence of alcohol (or any drug which will impair his ability).

Alcohol and flying should never be mixed! Even small quantities of alcohol in the blood can impair one's performance, with the added danger of relieving anxiety so that the person thinks he is performing marvellously. Alcohol severely affects a person's judgment and abilities. High altitudes, where there is less oxygen, worsens the effect.

It takes time for the body to remove alcohol and, as a general rule, a pilot should not fly for at least 8 hours after drinking small quantities of alcohol,

ALCOHOL AND FLYING SHOULD NEVER BE MIXED!

Figure 2a-1. Alcohol is dangerous.

increasing this time if greater quantities are consumed. After heavy drinking, alcohol may still be in the bloodstream 30 hours later. Sleep will *not* speed up the removal process, in fact it slows the body processes down and the removal of alcohol may take even longer.

Persons who are dependent upon alcohol (alcoholics) should not hold a pilot certificate, and a drunk person should not be permitted on board an airplane as a passenger.

Upper Respiratory Tract Problems

The common cold, hay fever, sinusitis, tonsilitis or any similar condition can lead to blocked ears, which can mean trouble for a pilot. When air is unable to pass through the Eustachian tubes and equalize pressures either side of the ear drums (for example, with changes in altitude and therefore in pressure), great pain and ultimately permanent damage to the ear drums can be caused.

During a climb, atmospheric pressure on the outer parts of the body decreases. The differential pressure within the inner ear forces the ear drum out and also causes air to flow from the inner ear through the Eustachian tubes into the throat to equalize the pressures.

Most training airplanes only have a low rate of climb, allowing adequate time for pressure equalization to occur through the Eustachian tubes, which means that ear problems during the climb are generally not serious. During descent, however, difficulties with the ears may be more serious.

As atmospheric pressure on the outer parts of the body increases during a descent, it pushes the ear drums in. Ideally, some air will flow from the throat via the Eustachian tube into the inner ear and equalize the pressure.

The nature of the Eustachian tubes is such that air will not move into them as readily as it moves out and so any swelling or blocking can lead to problems. High rates of descent worsen the situation and the pain can be severe.

Problems can also arise in the sinuses, which are cavities in the head connected by narrow tubes to the nasal/throat passages. Blockages can cause great pain, especially during descent.

Blocked ears can sometimes be cleared by holding your nose and blowing, by chewing, swallowing or yawning.

Carbon Monoxide Poisoning

Carbon monoxide is a colorless, odorless and tasteless gas for which hemoglobin in the blood has an enormous affinity. The prime function of hemoglobin is to transport oxygen from the lungs throughout the body to act as fuel. If carbon monoxide molecules are present in the air breathed into the lungs, then the hemoglobin will transport them in preference to oxygen, causing the body and the brain to suffer oxygen starvation, even though oxygen is present in the air.

The performance of a pilot in an environment contaminated by carbon monoxide will be seriously impaired. Recovery, even on pure oxygen, may take several hours.

Carbon monoxide is produced during the combustion of fuel in the engine and is also present in cigarette smoke, both of which can sometimes be found in the cockpit.

Many cabin heating systems use warm air from around the engine and the exhaust manifold as their source of heat. Any **leaks in the exhaust system** can allow carbon monoxide to enter the cabin in the heating air and possibly through open windows and cracks. To minimize the effect of any carbon monoxide that enters the cockpit in this way, fresh air should always be used in conjunction with cabin heat.

If you have a cold, or any middle ear or sinus problem, do not fly!

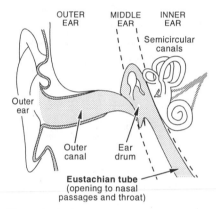

Figure 2a-2. The Eustachian tubes equalize pressure either side of the ear drums.

Carbon monoxide poisoning is serious and can be fatal!

Regular checks and maintenance are essential. Even though carbon monoxide is odorless, it may be assocated with other exhaust gases that do have an odor.

The symptoms of carbon monoxide poisoning may include headache, dizziness, nausea, deterioration in vision and slower breathing rate. If carbon monoxide is suspected in the cabin, shut off the cabin heat, stop all smoking, increase the supply of fresh air through the vents and windows and don oxygen masks if available.

Food Poisoning

Food poisoning may result from an improperly prepared meal and its onset may be almost immediate following consumption of the food, or it may not become evident for some hours but, even then, its onset may be sudden. The stomach pains, nausea, diarrhea, vomiting, and so on, that accompany food poisoning can make it physically impossible for a pilot to perform his duties.

It is a good practice, for the half day prior to flight, to avoid foods that are often associated with food poisoning, including shellfish, fish, mayonnaise, creams, over-ripe and thin-skinned fruits, uncooked foods such as salads and raw foods, and old food—for example, food that has been cooked and stored for some time. If you suspect that some effects of food poisoning are imminent from something bad that you have eaten, **do not fly!**

Avoid eating suspect food.

Eyesight and Glasses

If you are required by the Aviation Medical Examiner to wear glasses to correct your sight, then it is good airmanship to wear them as required. It is also compulsory to carry a spare pair of glasses whenever you are flying. If flying in bright sunlight, especially above clouds, it is good practice to wear a good set of sunglasses.

Wear sunglasses in bright light.

Smoking

Smoking is detrimental to good health, both in the short term and in the long term.

Avoid smoking in flight.

- **In the short term**—carbon monoxide which is present in cigarette smoke is absorbed into the blood in preference to oxygen. This reduces the body's ability to produce energy, including in the brain. The diminished supply of oxygen to the body and brain becomes noticeable at higher altitudes where cigarette smoke in the cabin can significantly decrease the pilot's performance, even if not actually smoking the cigarette!

- **In the long term**—it is now generally accepted that cigarette smoking plays a role in cardiovascular (heart) and other diseases. If you want to live a long and healthy life, then you should not smoke.

As a point of interest and worthy of note, cigarette smoking in the cockpit is banned by many airline captains, and, in some countries, smoking by everyone including passengers is banned in flight.

Fatigue and Sleep Deprivation

The nature of flying is such that you must train yourself to cope with moderate levels of these complaints, and to recognize when your **personal limits** are being approached. However, a deeply fatigued pilot should not be flying!

Fatigue can become deep-seated and chronic if psychological or emotional problems are not solved, resulting in deep rest or sleep not occurring over a prolonged period.

Chronic fatigue will be cured when the problems are solved, or at least being coped with, and the person can relax and unstress. You should prohibit yourself from flying until this is the case.

Fatigue, tiredness and sleep deprivation can lower your mental and physical capacity quite dramatically.

Short-term fatigue is caused by overwork, mental stress, an uncomfortable body position, a recent lack of sleep, living it up a bit too much, lack of oxygen or lack of food. Sleep and rest are essential!

To guard against fatigue that is detrimental to flight safety, a pilot should:
- have his psychological and emotional life under control;
- be reasonably fit;
- eat regularly;
- ensure he is not deprived of adequate sleep;
- ensure that cockpit comfort is optimized and that energy foods and drink are available on long flights; and
- exercise his limbs occasionally and land to stretch his legs at least every four hours, if practicable.

In-Flight Medical Factors

While fitness and good health are a good starting point for a pilot, you still must protect yourself against potential problems such as a lack of oxygen, an excess of oxygen, decompression sickness (the *bends* following scuba diving), food poisoning, fatigue and carbon monoxide poisoning.

Note: There is no need for you to study what follows here immediately, but you should refer to it in the course of your training.

Oxygen

The Atmosphere
The atmosphere surrounding the earth consists mainly of nitrogen (80%), oxygen (20%) and water vapor, with very small quantities of carbon dioxide and inert gases. The mixture is known familiarly as *air.*

The atmosphere is held to the earth by the force of gravity.

The great mass of air pressing down on the earth under the force of gravity causes air pressure and air density to be greater at the lower levels of the atmosphere. The atmospheric pressure pushing on our bodies is greatest at sea level, and our bodily tissues and fluids have adjusted to this and push back with the same pressure.

Air Pressure
As an airplane climbs, the air pressure drops and therefore less pressure is exerted on the human body. It will react to this lower pressure in various ways—for example, the Eustachian tubes will allow a small amount of air to flow through them to equalize the pressures on either side of the ear drums. Colds and other infections that cause blockages can prevent this from happening.

Air pressure decreases with altitude.

Air Density
At higher altitudes, the air density—the number of molecules per unit volume—will be less than at sea level, therefore each lungful of air will contain fewer oxygen molecules and the body and brain will have to function with less fuel (energy-giving oxygen).

Air density decreases with altitude, resulting in less oxygen per breath.

Air Temperature
On average the temperature falls about 4°F for every 1,000 feet (ft) gained in altitude. This will vary from place to place and from time to time, sometimes being greater and sometimes less, but in general, temperature decreases with altitude.

Air temperature decreases with altitude—*beware of hypothermia.*

The human body does not function all that well when it is extremely cold and, even though the temperature might be 60°F on the ground, it is likely to be well below freezing at 10,000 feet. Keep warm to avoid hypothermia.

Respiration

By muscular action of the diaphragm, the lungs are expanded and air is drawn in through the nose and mouth and into the lungs. The oxygen diffuses across the membranes in the millions of small air sacs in the lungs and becomes attached to hemoglobin in the red blood corpuscles.

The diffusion across the lung membranes depends upon the partial pressure of oxygen and when it is low—for example, at high altitudes—less oxygen enters the blood. The blood transports this oxygen throughout the body where it is used in a burning process to produce energy.

Carbon dioxide is produced as a waste product in the energy-production process and it is transported back to the lungs in the blood, where it is extracted and expelled in the breath. The concentration of waste carbon dioxide in the returning blood is sensed by the brain, which responds by altering the respiration (breathing) rate. If carbon dioxide is present in larger amounts than normal—for example, during strenuous exercise—the brain senses this and speeds up the rate of respiration.

The average capacity of the lungs is about five liters and the average breath when at rest is about one-half liter, using only a fraction of the lung capacity to provide about eight liters/minute. Strenuous activity may increase this to 60 liters/minute.

Respiration brings oxygen into the body and removes carbon dioxide.

Respiration at High Altitudes

At high altitudes, even though the percentage of oxygen in the air does not change greatly, the lower air pressure and lower partial pressure of oxygen will reduce the number of oxygen molecules that diffuse across the lung membranes and attach themselves to the hemoglobin in the red blood corpuscles. Less oxygen is then transported around the body and less energy is generated (including in the brain). In this condition a pilot is less able to think clearly and less able to perform physically.

Respiration at high altitudes brings less oxygen into the body.

Oxygen Deprivation—Hypoxia

Whereas food can be stored in the body, oxygen needs to be continually supplied.

Above 8,000 feet, the effects of oxygen deprivation may start to become apparent in some pilots, especially if the pilot is active or under stress. At 10,000 feet, most people can still cope with the diminished oxygen supply, but above 10,000 feet supplemental oxygen (oxygen supplied through a mask) is required to prevent a marked deterioration in performance.

At 14,000 feet, performance will be poor and at 18,000 feet the pilot may become unconscious—this will occur at lower altitudes if he or she is a smoker, unfit or fatigued.

The initial symptoms of hypoxia may hardly be noticeable to the sufferer, and in fact, they often include feelings of euphoria. The brain is affected quite early, so a false sense of security and well-being is present. Physical movements will become clumsy, but the pilot may not notice this.

Drowsiness, giddiness, a headache, deterioration of vision, a high pulse rate, blue lips and blue finger nails may all follow, ending in unconsciousness. Throughout all of this the pilot will probably feel that he is doing a great job.

The lack of sufficient oxygen to the body (and brain) is called *hypoxia*.

Pressurized Cabins

Advanced airplanes have pressurized cabins, which allow the cabin to hold air at a higher pressure than in the outside atmosphere. For instance, an airplane flying at 30,000 feet may have a cabin that is pressurized *(pumped up)* to the same pressure level found at 4,000 feet in the outside atmosphere, eliminating the need for the pilot and passengers to be wearing oxygen masks—a significant improvement in comfort and convenience.

This, of course, changes if the airplane depressurizes for some reason and the cabin air escapes, reducing the partial pressure of oxygen in the air available to the pilot. Supplementary oxygen then becomes vital and is usually obtained through a mask until the pilot descends to a lower altitude (below 10,000 feet) where there is sufficient oxygen available and the mask can be removed if desired.

Pressurized airplane cabins can lead to hypoxia if they depressurize.

Time of Useful Consciousness (TUC)

If a person is suddenly deprived of an adequate supply of oxygen, unconsciousness will follow. This is a very important consideration for a high-flying pressurized aircraft that suffers depressurization.

The time available for pilots to perform useful tasks without a supplemental oxygen supply is known as the *time of useful consciousness*, which gets shorter and shorter the higher the altitude. The pilots **must** get the masks on and receive oxygen well within this period, if flight safety is to be preserved.

Time of useful consciousness decreases with cabin altitude.

Altitude above sea level	Sudden Depressurization	
	Moderate Activity	Minimal Activity
22,000 feet	5 minutes	10 minutes
25,000 feet	2 minutes	3 minutes
28,000 feet	1 minute	1$\frac{1}{2}$ minutes
30,000 feet	45 seconds	1$\frac{1}{4}$ minutes
35,000 feet	30 seconds	45 seconds
40,000 feet	12 seconds	15 seconds

Figure 2a-3. Time of useful consciousness following failure of oxygen

Consciousness of the pilot is paramount, even if the passengers become unconscious for a short period. You must think of yourself first, since the safety of all on board depends upon your well-being.

How to Avoid Hypoxia

To avoid hypoxia it is best to be reasonably fit, to have no cigarette smoke in the cockpit, and to ensure that you use supplemental oxygen at the higher altitudes and most definitely above 10,000 feet cabin altitude.

Remember that lack of oxygen can lead to a feeling of euphoria and a lack of judgment (a similar effect perhaps to alcohol). Self-discipline should be used and the oxygen mask donned when the cabin altitude approaches 10,000 feet.

As a general guideline, consider using oxygen at cabin altitudes above 10,000 feet.

Note: Federal Aviation Regulations (FARs) Parts 91 and 135/121 specify requirements for the provision of supplemental oxygen at high cabin altitudes. These are less limiting than our 10,000-foot suggested guideline, however.

Hyperventilation

Hyperventilation occurs when the body "over-breathes" for some reason, such as fear, anxiety, excitement or in a mistaken attempt by a person trying to improve performance by forced breathing—for example, prior to an underwater swimming attempt.

The balance of oxygen and carbon dioxide in the body is upset, causing symptoms similar to those of hypoxia to occur—for example, giddiness, numbness, tingling sensations, increasing breathing rate and pulse rate. Hyperventilation may lead to blurred vision, muscle spasms and unconsciousness.

If these symptoms occur, it is essential to establish whether the problem is hyperventilation (too much oxygen) or hypoxia (too little oxygen) before it can be remedied.

Hyperventilation can be remedied by slowing down the breathing rate—talking is a good way of doing this—or by breathing into and out of a bag to increase the level of carbon dioxide in the blood back to more normal levels, but **if recovery is not evident**, then assume that hypoxia rather than hyperventilation is the problem and use oxygen.

Hyperventilation is an excess of oxygen.

Decompression Sickness

Scuba diving and flying do not mix very well. When the body is deep underwater it is subjected to strong pressures, and certain gases, such as nitrogen, are absorbed into the blood. The deeper and longer the diving, the more this absorption occurs.

If the pressure on the body is then reduced—for example, by returning to the surface from a great depth or, even worse, by flying in an airplane at high cabin altitudes—the gases may come out of the blood solution as bubbles. One sees this effect when the top is removed from gaseous drinks and bubbles of gas come out of solution.

Gas bubbles in the blood will cause great pain and immobilization in the shoulders, arms and joints. This serious complaint is known as *the bends*. The remedy is to return the body to a region of high pressure for a lengthy period of time—for example, in a decompression chamber—and gradually return it to normal pressures over a period of hours or days.

In an airplane, the best you can do if the presence of the bends is suspected is to descend to a low altitude or to land. Even landing may not provide a sufficient pressure increase to remedy the problem, in which case medical assistance should be sought without delay.

Diving at depths below 20 feet for long periods should **not** be considered prior to flying! Current *Diver's Alert Network* recommendations are to wait 12 hours between a single no-decompression dive and flying, and 24 hours or longer if you have done multiday or repetitive dives.

Decompression sickness can follow scuba diving.

Figure 2a-4. Scuba diving and flying don't mix very well.

Hypothermia

Low temperatures can decrease pilot performance, so it is important that the cabin temperature is kept comfortable. This applies when climbing to high altitudes, but it can also apply on the ground in cold climates.

Low temperatures can cause hypothermia.

Vertigo

Vertigo is generally experienced as a feeling of rotation, when in fact no rotation is actually occurring, or vice versa. Vertigo can be caused by disease, by accelerations that disturb the delicate balance mechanisms in the inner ear, and by sudden pressure changes in the inner ear. Strong blowing of the nose or sneezing can do this quite violently, and bring on a spell of dizziness.

Vertigo can be overcome by looking at the horizon (real or artificial).

If you wish to experience vertigo on the ground, you can bring it on by spinning around about 20 times with your head held low, and then trying to walk in a straight line. Similar forces can occur when an airplane is maneuvering, especially if high g-loads are being pulled in steep turns, spins, spiral dives, and so on. These can give rise to vertigo, especially if there is no visual reference to the horizon.

The effects of vertigo can often be overcome by looking out and referring to the natural horizon or, in instrument flying conditions, by referring to the flight instruments, especially the attitude indicator, also known as the artificial horizon.

Motion Sickness

Air sickness is generally caused by the balance mechanisms of the inner ear continually being over-stimulated by accelerations. This can be caused by turbulence, or maneuvers such as steep turns or spins, in which forces other than the normal **1g** (that the body is used to) will be experienced. A hot, smelly cockpit does not help!

Good ventilation can often prevent motion sickness.

Psychological aspects can also play a role in the onset of motion sickness—for example, a fear of flying or apprehension at seeing the horizon at different angles.

To avoid airsickness:
- fly the airplane smoothly and in balance;
- avoid maneuvers where unusual g-forces are pulled;
- ventilate the cabin with a good supply of fresh air;
- involve a potentially airsick passenger in the operation, especially if this involves looking outside the airplane and into the distance—for example, to help identify ground references;
- as a last resort, recline the passenger's seat to reduce the effect of the vertical accelerations and keep an airsickness bag handy.

Spatial Disorientation

Spatial disorientation is said to occur when you are unsure of your precise attitude in space—in other words, where is **up** and where is **down**. Dizziness due to vertigo need not necessarily be present although it may be.

Spatial disorientation can be prevented by referring to the horizon (real or artificial).

Spatial disorientation can occur when a non-instrument-rated pilot loses reference to the natural horizon by, for example, flying into cloud, or flying over sloping terrain or a sloping cloud layer, or when flying in restricted visibility. Flashing strobe lights or the sun flashing through the propeller can also have a destabilizing effect and cause a pilot to become disoriented or suffer vertigo.

To prevent spatial disorientation, a pilot should avoid flying in the above conditions, avoid looking directly at the sun or any strobe light, and should gain some basic expertise at flying on instruments. The flight instruments will allow you to orientate yourself spatially even when your normal sensory cues—sight and balance—obtained from the outside world are abnormal. Instrument training involves learning to trust your flight instruments.

✍ Review 2a

1. The responsibility for a pilot being fit to fly for each flight rests with the (pilot/flight school/flight instructor/doctor).

   ➤ pilot

2. Being physically fit (helps/does not help) a pilot to cope better with stress, tiredness, fatigue, and the reduced availability of oxygen at higher altitudes.

   ➤ helps

3. Mental fitness to fly (can/will not) be degraded by personal problems and fatigue.

   ➤ can

4. The lack of sufficient oxygen to the body and brain is called _____ .

   ➤ hypoxia

5. List the symptoms of hypoxia and how you can avoid it.

   ➤ *refer to our text, pages 24 and 25*

6. The ability of the blood to carry energy-producing oxygen around the body is (increased/not affected/degraded) by smoking cigarettes.

   ➤ degraded

7. Overbreathing, causing an excess of oxygen in the blood, is called _____ .

   ➤ hyperventilation

8. List the symptoms of hyperventilation and how you can remedy it?

   ➤ *refer to our text, page 26*

9. A blocked nose (may/will not) cause problems and pain when flying.

   ➤ may

10. Should a pilot fly when suffering an upper respiratory tract infection, or a middle ear or sinus problem?

    ➤ no

11. Engine exhaust contains the poisonous gas _____ _____ .

    ➤ carbon monoxide

Am I Fit to Fly?

12. Carbon monoxide (is/is not) colorless, (is/is not) odorless, (is/is not) poisonous.

    ➤ is, is, is

13. Smoking (increases/reduces) the amount of oxygen in the blood and so is (beneficial/harmful) to flying.

    ➤ reduces, harmful

14. The use of alcohol or drugs, including many medications, (is/is not) compatible with safe flying.

    ➤ is not

15. The blood alcohol level of a pilot (must/need not) be below a specified limit, and he must not have consumed even a small amount of alcohol within the previous _____ hours.

    ➤ must, eight

16. It (is/is not) permitted to carry a drunk person as a passenger.

    ➤ is not

17. An overstressed or fatigued pilot (may/should not) fly.

    ➤ should not

18. What steps can you take to avoid becoming fatigued?

    ➤ *refer to our text, page 23*

19. Climbing to altitude after scuba diving may cause _____ sickness, which is an excess of _____ in the form of bubbles in the blood.

    ➤ decompression, nitrogen

20. What steps can be taken to avoid a passenger suffering motion sickness?

    ➤ *refer to our text, page 27*

21. A person who becomes dizzy and is unsure of which way is up or down is said to be _____ disoriented.

    ➤ spatially disoriented

22. You can avoid, or recover from, spatial disorientation by taking note of (the flight instruments/your balance mechanisms in the inner ear).

    ➤ the flight instruments

Preparing to Fly 2b

Objective

To get ready to go and fly.

Considerations

The success of a flight depends largely on thorough preparation. In the course of your training, a pattern of regular preflight actions should be developed to ensure that this is the case. This includes planning the flight, and checking the airplane. These preflight actions must be based on the checks found in the **Pilot's Operating Handbook** (POH), or the **FAA-approved Airplane Flight Manual** (AFM) for your airplane.

Many airplanes also have an **Information Manual** which, at the time of issue, will normally be a duplicate of the official Pilot's Operating Handbook. It must be kept current to be valid.

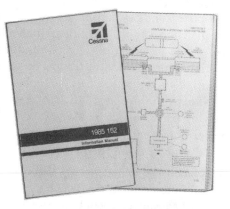

The typical Pilot's Operating Handbook contains the following numbered sections:

1. GENERAL—diagrams and description of the airplane, symbols, abbreviations and terminology.
2. LIMITATIONS—airspeed limitations, engine limitations, weight-and-balance limitations.
3. EMERGENCY PROCEDURES—airspeeds for emergency operations, engine failure, forced landings, fires, icing, flat tires, electrical malfunctions.
4. NORMAL PROCEDURES—normal airspeeds, checklists for normal operations.
5. PERFORMANCE—charts and/or tables for takeoff and landing distances, range and endurance, and so on.
6. WEIGHT-AND-BALANCE and EQUIPMENT LIST—loading data, plus a list of available equipment.
7. AIRPLANE AND SYSTEMS DESCRIPTIONS.
8. AIRPLANE HANDLING, SERVICE AND MAINTENANCE—procedures for ground handling, servicing and maintenance.
9. SUPPLEMENTS—usually quite a large section describing optional systems and operating procedures.

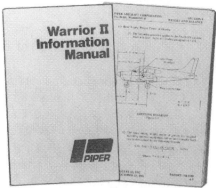

Figure 2b-1. Typical Information Manuals

Prior to each flight you, as pilot-in-command, are required to familiarize your-self with all the available information concerning the flight. Preparation for a flight commences well before you actually enter the airplane and consists of:

- satisfactory personal health and well-being;
- personal preparation;
- weather and NOTAM check;
- satisfying the preflight documentation requirements;
- confirming that the runway lengths available are adequate for the proposed takeoffs and landings, including those at possible alternate airports;
- calculating the amount of fuel required, allowing for known delays and possible diversions, and then ordering it from the fueler;
- the preflight inspection of the airplane;
- the checks associated with start-up and taxiing; and
- the Before-Takeoff check.

The pilot-in-command is responsible for determining that the airplane is airworthy prior to every flight. Use of authorized checklists facilitates this.

Personal Preparation for Flight

The pilot is the key person on any flight and must be properly prepared. If you are planning a flight, calm, unhurried and thorough **long-term preparation** a day or two ahead of time might be useful. Preparing the charts for a cross-country flight, for instance, or reading up on an imminent flight lesson will greatly contribute to the outcome of the flight.

Short term preparation involves such things as being properly equipped, arriving early enough at the airport for any briefing or flight preparation to proceed in an unhurried manner, and carrying out the required preflight checks of the airplane calmly and thoroughly.

A typical list of items to check before even leaving home should include:
- Am I fit to fly—physically and mentally?
- Have I consumed alcohol in the last eight hours, or is there any alcohol still in my bloodstream?
- Am I using pills, tablets, drugs, and so on, that could impair my abilities?
- Do I have a cold, blocked nose, blocked ears or any other upper respiratory complaint?
- Do I have the required equipment for this particular flight?
- Am I suitably clothed?—natural fibres and materials are generally best, such as a cotton shirt, wool slacks and leather shoes, as these allow the body to *breathe* as well as being somewhat fire-resistant.
- Do I have my **current Medical** and **Pilot Certificates** with me?
- Am I aware of the expiration date of my Medical, and the privileges and limitations of my Pilot Certificate?

Preflight Documentation

A high level of flight safety is maintained partly because of the thorough documentation required. Items that are recorded include the history of the airplane in terms of hours flown and maintenance carried out.

Each flight will be authorized by your flight instructor or flight school and will be recorded on a schedule. There may also be a book containing local rules and regulations appropriate to your training and which you should check prior to flying.

The Flight Plan, Weather and Fuel

It is not usual to compile a flight plan prior to a local training flight, but it is a consideration during your more advanced training when cross-country flights will be undertaken.

Weather is a consideration for every flight, and you should obtain a weather briefing or discuss the weather with your flight instructor each time you go flying. For a cross-country flight, you should obtain, read and analyze the available weather information, and then make a competent *go/no-go decision* based on this.

Based on weather and other considerations, make a go/no-go decision.

Notices To Airmen (NOTAMs) should be checked, to ensure that you are aware of items that may affect your flight, such as runway closures, unserviceability of airport equipment, and so on.

Always plan to carry sufficient **fuel** for the flight, plus sufficient in reserve— at least 30 minutes by day at normal cruise rate, and 45 minutes by night. Once you have decided how much you require, contact the fuel agent early enough so he has time to fuel the airplane and not delay your departure. Specify quantity and type of fuel, and be prepared to supervise the fueling if necessary:
- confirm correct grade and type of fuel;
- confirm fire extinguisher is handy;
- check that the airplane is grounded by a ground wire to equalize electrical potential; static electricity cannot be seen until it actually sparks, which is when it can ignite nearby fumes;
- check quantity;
- check purity;
- check fuel caps replaced firmly and ground wire removed.

If the fuel is contaminated by water, all of the water should be drained away; if the fuel is contaminated by dirt or other solid contaminants, the whole fuel system may have to be drained. Do not fly with contaminated fuel!

Weight-and-Balance

It is vital to the safety of every flight that no weight limit is exceeded, and that the load is arranged to keep the center of gravity within approved limits. The ability of the airplane to fly and remain controllable depends upon this. Generally heavy articles are best loaded forward.

The airplane must always be within weight-and-balance limitations.

Remember that an article weighing 100 pounds will, during a 2g maneuver such as a 60° banked turn, exert a force on the airplane structure equal to double its weight—to 200 pounds force. The effect of any overload is multiplied during maneuvers. Cargo and loose equipment must be secured.

Weight-and-balance documents, usually in the form of charts or tables, must always be available on board.

Most training airplanes are satisfactorily loaded with one or two persons on board, and so there may be no need to actually do a weight-and-balance calculation prior to every training flight. All the same, you should develop the habit of considering weight-and-balance before each and every flight.

Airworthiness Documents

It is a pilot's responsibility to check certain documents prior to flight to ensure the airplane is **airworthy.** You should know the significance of each document, and know where to locate them in the cockpit.

The documents important to the individual pilot are:
- the maintenance records (check every flight);
- the Pilot's Operating Handbook (POH) with aircraft limitations and placards (should always be in the airplane);
- the aircraft weight-and-balance data, and equipment list (which may be in the POH or Flight Manual);

- the Certificate of Airworthiness (shall always be in the airplane)—it shows that the airplane has met certain FAA safety requirements, and remains in effect if required inspections and maintenance has been performed;
- the Certificate of Registration (shall always be in the airplane)—it contains airplane and owner information—a new owner requires a new Certificate of Registration;
- the Radio Station License (shall always be in the airplane)—issued by the Federal Communications Commission, and lists the aircraft's radio transmission equipment.

The **maintenance records** should be checked prior to each flight, and any maintenance that you think is required should be specified after flight. Sometimes there will be *no* formal written maintenance release; however do not accept responsibility for the airplane if it has defects which may make it unacceptable for flight.

If in any doubt, discuss the matter with your flight instructor or with an aircraft mechanic. There are some simple maintenance actions which may be performed by a qualified pilot, such as topping up the oil, but certainly not anything that might affect the basic airworthiness of the airplane, such as working on the flight controls.

Aircraft and engine logbooks should be available, but it is not required that they be on board.

Takeoff and Landing Distances

You should confirm that the runway lengths available at the airports of intended use are adequate for your takeoff and landing requirements. This performance check is vital at unfamiliar airports, especially if the runways are short, with obstacles in the takeoff or landing path, or if the airport is high, or if the temperature is high.

Preparing the Airplane

The Pilot's Operating Handbook for your airplane will contain a list of items that must be checked during:
- the preflight inspection (external and internal);
- the preflight cockpit checks;
- the engine power check; and
- the before-takeoff check.

At first, these checks may seem long and complicated but, as you repeat them thoroughly prior to each flight, a pattern will soon form. It is vital that the checks are carried out thoroughly, systematically and strictly in accordance with your Pilot's Operating Handbook, so that you are organized in your preflight inspection and do not overlook any important item. Use of **written checklists,** if performed correctly, will ensure that no vital item has been missed.

The comments that follow are only general comments that will apply to most airplanes, however they may or may not apply to yours.

An easy way to remember the required documents is with the mnemonic ARROW:
A—Airworthiness Certificate.
R—Registration Certificate.
R—Radio Station License.
O—Operating Limitations (in Pilot's Operating Handbook, color coding on instruments, and speed decals in cockpit).
W—Weight-and-Balance—included in the POH or FAA-approved AFM, and sometimes found folded and stapled in the glove box or a seat pocket; weight-and-balance paperwork needs to be available on board the aircraft, but on many flights need not be filled in.
An equipment list should always be on board, and this is often found with the weight-and-balance information in the POH.

Check performance data applicable to your planned operations.

The External Inspection

This can begin as you walk up to the airplane and should include:
- the position of the airplane as being suitable for start-up and taxi (also, note the wind direction and the likely path to the takeoff point);
- the availability of fire extinguishers and emergency equipment in case of fire on start-up (a rare event, but it does happen).

Some of the vital items are:
- all switches OFF (master switch for electrics, magneto switch for engine), as a protection against the engine inadvertently starting;
- fuel check—quantity, and quality (drain into a clear cup);
- oil check; and
- structural check.

A list of typical *walk-around* items is shown below. Each item must be inspected individually, but do not neglect a general overview of the airplane.

Be vigilant for things such as buckling of the fuselage skin or popped rivets as these could indicate internal structural damage from a previous flight. Leaking oil, fuel forming puddles on the ground, or hydraulic fluid leaks from around the brake lines also deserve further investigation. With experience, you will develop a feel for what looks right and what does not.

The **walk-around inspection** starts at the cockpit door, and follows the pattern specified in the checklist provided by the aircraft manufacturer.

Cabin

Check the following:
- Parking brake—ON;
- Magneto switches—OFF;
- Landing gear lever (if retractable)—locked DOWN;
- Control locks—REMOVED;
- Master switch—ON (to supply electrical power);
- Fuel quantity gauges—check that there is sufficient fuel for the planned flight;
- Fuel selector valves—ON;
- Flaps—check operation; leave them extended for external inspection;
- Stall warning (if electrical)—check for proper operation;
- Rotating beacon (and other lights)—check, then OFF;
- Master switch—OFF;
- Primary flight controls—check for proper operation;
- Required documents on board—ARROW for aircraft; airman certificate and medical certificate for you, the pilot;
- Cabin door—securely attached, and latches working correctly;
- Windshield—clean.

Wing Area

- All surfaces, wingtip, leading and trailing edge—no damage or contamination; remove any frost, snow, ice or insects (on upper leading edge especially, since contamination here can significantly reduce lift, even to the point where the airplane may not become airborne);
- Wingtip position light—no damage;
- Flaps—firmly in position, actuating mechanism firmly attached and safety-wired;
- Aileron—remove aileron locks if fitted, check hinges, correct movement (one up, the other down) and controls safety-wired, mass balance weight on aileron secure (if used);

Always perform a thorough external inspection.

- Pitot tube—pitot cover removed, no damage or obstructions (otherwise airspeed indicator will not work);
- Fuel contents—checked in tanks, matches fuel quantity gauge indications, fuel caps replaced firmly and with a good seal (to avoid fuel siphoning away in flight into the low pressure area above the wing);
- Fuel drain from wing tanks and from fuel strainer into a clear container—correct color (blue for 100LL, green for 100 octane), correct fuel grade, correct smell (aviation gasoline and **not** jet fuel—kerosene), no water (being denser, water sinks to bottom), sediment, dirt or other contaminant (condensation may occur in the tanks overnight causing water to collect in the bottom of the tanks, or the fuel taken on board may be contaminated);
- Fuel port, or fuel vent (which may be separate or incorporated into the fuel cap)—clear (to allow pressure equalization inside and outside the tanks when fuel is used or altitude is changed—otherwise the fuel tanks could collapse as fuel is used and/or fuel supply to the engine could be stopped);
- Stall warning (if suction type)—check (if possible);
- Inspection plates—check that they are in place;
- Wing strut—check secure at both ends.

Fuselage
- All surfaces, including underneath—no skin damage, corrosion, buckling or other damage (corrosion appears as surface pitting and etching, often with a gray powdery deposit)—advise a mechanic if you suspect any of these;
- No fuel, oil or hydraulic fluid leaking onto the ground beneath the aircraft;
- Inspection plates—in place;
- Static ports (also called static vents)—no obstructions (needed for correct operation of airspeed indicator, altimeter and vertical speed indicator);
- Antennas—checked for security, no loose wires;
- Baggage lockers—check baggage, cargo and equipment secure, and baggage compartments locked;

Main Landing Gear
- Tires—check for wear, cuts, condition of tread, proper inflation, and security of wheel and brake disk;
- Wheel oleo strut—check for damage, proper inflation, and cleanliness;
- Hydraulic lines to brakes—check for damage, leaks, and attachment;
- Gear attachment to the fuselage—check attachment, and be sure there is no damage to the fuselage (buckling of skin, popped rivets);

Nose Section
- Fuselage—check for skin buckling or popped rivets;
- Windshield—clean;
- Propeller—check for damage, especially nicks along its leading edge, cracks and security (and for leaks in the hub area if it is a constant-speed propeller);
- Propeller spinner—check for damage, cracks and security;
- Engine air intake and filter—check for damage and cleanliness (no bird nests or oily rags);
- Nosewheel tire—check for wear, cuts, condition of tread, proper inflation, and security of nosewheel;
- Nosewheel oleo strut—check for damage, proper inflation (four to six inches is typical), security of shimmy damper and other mechanisms;

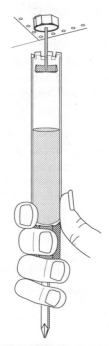

Figure 2b-2. Take fuel samples from the fuel system.

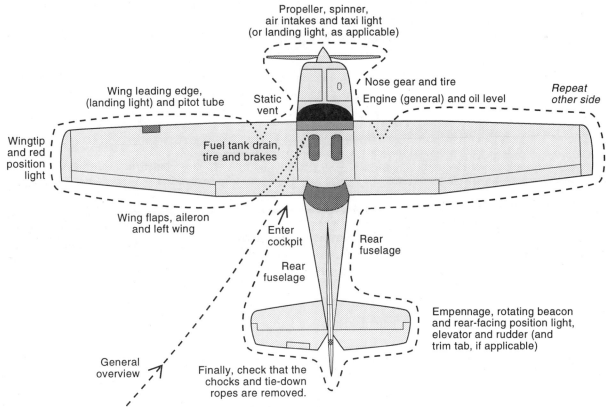

Figure 2b-3. A typical walk-around pattern for the external check

- Engine inspection panel—open; check engine mounts, engine, and exhaust manifold for cracks and security (to ensure that no lethal carbon monoxide in the exhaust gases can enter the cockpit—exhaust leaks may be indicated by white stains near the cylinder head, the exhaust shroud or exhaust pipes);
- Check battery, wiring and electrical cables for security (firmly attached at both ends);
- Check the oil level—top up if necessary (know the correct type and grade of oil to order); ensure that the dipstick is replaced properly and the oil cap is firmly closed to avoid loss of oil in flight; then
- close the inspection panel and check its security.

Other Side of Airplane

Repeat as appropriate.

Empennage

- Remove control locks if fitted;
- All surfaces—check for skin damage (vertical stabilizer and rudder, horizontal stabilizer, elevator and trim tab); remove any contamination such as ice, frost or snow;
- Control surface hinges—check for cracks, firmness of attachment, and safety-wiring, and check for correct movement.

Chocks and Tiedown Ropes

- Chocks and tiedowns—remove and stow (after checking that the parking brake is ON).

Overall View

Stand back and check the overall appearance of the airplane.

It cannot be emphasized too greatly just how important this preflight inspection by the pilot is. Even if you have no experience in mechanical things, you must train yourself to look at the airplane and notice things that do not seem right. Bring any items that you are unsure of to the attention of your flight instructor or a mechanic.

At this stage, you are now ready to seat yourself in the airplane and begin the **internal cockpit inspection.**

The Cockpit Inspection

The cockpit inspection involves preparing the cockpit and your personal equipment for flight. It should include:

Always perform a thorough cockpit inspection.

- Parking brake—SET (ON);
- Required documents on board—(**ARROW** items, listed on page 32);
- Flight equipment—organize and arrange your flight equipment and material in an efficient manner so that they are readily available in flight (flight bag, charts prefolded to show your route, computer, pencils, flashlight, and so on);
- Fuel—ON;
- Seat position and harness—comfortable and secure, with the seat definitely locked in position and rudder pedals (if adjustable) adjusted and locked into position so that full movement is possible;
- Ignition switch (magnetos)—OFF (so that the engine is not live);
- Master switch—ON (for electrical services such as fuel gauges);
- Flight controls—check for full and free movement (elevator, ailerons, rudder and trim wheel or handle).
- Trim—set to takeoff position;
- Engine controls—full and free movement (throttle, mixture control and carburetor heat control);
- Instruments—scan the instruments systematically from one side of the panel to the other for serviceability and correct readings;
- Circuit breakers and fuses—no circuit breakers should be popped nor fuses blown (for electrical services to operate);
- Microphone and/or headsets—plugged in (if you are to use the radio) and test intercom if used;
- Safety equipment (fire extinguisher, first aid kit, supplemental oxygen if planning to fly high, flotation equipment for overwater flights)—on board and securely stowed;
- Loose articles—stowed;
- Checklists—on board and available;
- Read the Preflight checklist, if appropriate.

Passenger Briefing

When the Preflight inspection is completed and you are comfortable in your seat, you should then **brief your passengers** on the use of their safety belts, and on any relevant emergency procedures.

Brief your passengers.

A typical briefing could be:

Seat Belts

- Remove any sharp articles from your pockets (such as keys, pocket knives, nail files, cigarette lighters);
- Position your seat and ensure it is locked in position so that it cannot move;

- To fasten your seat belt, lengthen the strap if necessary, insert the belt link into the belt buckle, and tighten the belt by pulling the free end until you have a snug fit across your hips. If it is too tight, you will be uncomfortable; if it is too loose you may not be held firm enough in your seat if we meet unexpected turbulence.
- To release your seat belt, pull upward on the top of the buckle.
- The shoulder harness can also be fitted into the buckle. It has an inertia reel that allows you lean forward, but will lock you firmly in position with any sudden deceleration.
- Your seat belt must be fastened for every takeoff and landing, but I recommend that it remain fastened throughout the flight.

Emergency Exits
- In the rare event of having to leave the aircraft quickly, the exit to use is ____ .
- Move away from the airplane, and keep well clear of the propeller at all times.

Smoking
- You must not smoke on the tarmac area, nor during takeoff or landing. I would prefer no smoking in flight, because we have nonsmokers also aboard and because it introduces an unnecessary risk of fire.

Radio
- If you wish to listen in to the flight radio, we can use the cockpit speaker or you may use a headset which should make the communications clearer. The volume control is here ____ , and we can also use the intercom *(test if possible)*.

Planned Route
- We will taxi out and use Runway__ , which means a takeoff into the (N, S, E or W), followed by a (right/left) turn.
- We will be tracking overhead ____ ____ and ____ to our destination ____ .
- The weather we expect en route is (good/may be a little bumpy).

Doors, Windows and Ventilation
- Ensure your seat belt is not hanging out, then close the door firmly and lock it.
- The window may be open for additional ventilation while taxiing.
- Normal vents are located ____ ____ , and you can adjust them by ____ .
- If you happen to feel unwell in flight, which I do not expect to be the case, advise me early on so that I can try to avoid any bumpy areas or tight maneuvers.

Now we are ready for engine start and radio communication.

— End of Passenger Briefing —

Crew Briefing

If you are operating in a two-pilot cockpit, you should give an operational briefing to your copilot, perhaps considering:

Brief any other pilots on board.

- taxi route to runway;
- takeoff procedures and route to follow;
- action in the case of an engine failure.

Good **crew coordination** begins on the ground.

If you are well prepared before you start the engine, which introduces a noise factor, and have your cockpit preparation and passenger briefing completed in a quiet atmosphere, then this shows good **cockpit management**.

✍ Review 2b

Preparing to Fly

1. Which personal documents should a pilot carry in flight?

   ➤ current medical and pilot certificates

2. Which aircraft documents should be on board?

   ➤ ARROW checklist, *see page 32 of our text*

3. Is it good airmanship to check relevant weather information prior to flight?

   ➤ yes

4. Is it good airmanship to check performance aspects prior to flight, such as whether the runways are long enough for takeoff and landing in the current weather conditions?

   ➤ yes

5. Should you cancel a flight if you feel the weather conditions or some other aspect of the flight is beyond your capabilities? This known as a _____/_____ decision.

   ➤ yes, go/no-go

6. Must an airplane remain within weight and center-of-gravity limitations throughout a flight?

   ➤ yes

7. The current maintenance status of an airplane (should/need not) be checked prior to flight.

   ➤ should

8. A thorough and systematic external check (should/need not) be made prior to each flight.

   ➤ should

9. Cargo and equipment (should/need not) be secured.

   ➤ should

10. Material and equipment to be used in flight is best prepared and organized so that they are readily available (during the cockpit preparation/in flight).

    ➤ during the cockpit preparation

11. Seat and rudder pedals should be adjusted and locked (during the cockpit preparation/in flight).

    ➤ during the cockpit preparation

12. The use of seat belts and safety harnesses (should/need not) be briefed.

    ➤ should

13. Write down and rehearse a suitable Passenger Briefing.

    ➤ *refer to our text (page 36) and your flight instructor*

14. Rehearse the Preflight checklist.

    ➤ *refer to our text (starting page 32) and your flight instructor*

Figure 2b-4. Carry out your preflight checks carefully.

Starting and Stopping the Engine 2c

Objective

To start and stop the engine.

Considerations

The engine of a light aircraft may be started by turning it over using:

- a **starter motor** attached to the engine and powered electrically by the **onboard battery** (usual method); or
- same starter motor but powered by an **external electrical power source;** or
- by turning the engine over by rotating the propeller manually, known as hand cranking or "hand-propping".

The usual method is using the starter motor and onboard battery, and this is the method we discuss first. The other two are supplementary procedures, and are discussed at the end of this exercise.

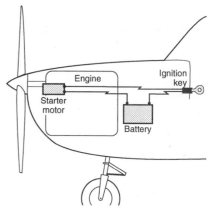

Figure 2c-1. Electric starter motor powered by onboard battery.

Prior to starting the engine, check that the surrounding area is suitable for start-up. The airplane should be on a surface suitable for taxiing, preferably in a clear area well away from any buildings, fuel storage areas and public areas. It should be parked facing in a direction that will not cause loose stones or gravel to be blasted back over other aircraft, or into open hangars, when the engine is running. Also, there should be no fuel spills in the vicinity, as this creates a fire risk.

The airplane should be manually moved to face into a strong wind prior to starting the engine. The **parking brake** should be ON prior to start to prevent any airplane movement during and after the start-up.

The engine then needs to be properly prepared for the start-up. In extremely cold weather, this may include preheating the engine. The correct procedure for this is found in your Pilot's Operating Handbook.

Use the specified **checklist,** and do not miss any items.

Ensure that no person is near the propeller by checking visually and by calling out "**clear**" loudly a few seconds before you engage the starter. It is important immediately the engine is started that you set the proper rpm and check the engine gauges for the desired indications, especially oil pressure to ensure that the engine is being lubricated and cooled adequately.

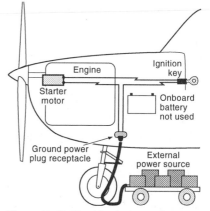

Figure 2c-2. Electric starter motor powered by external power source.

The Prestart and Starting Checklist

The Prestart and Starting checklist will include such items as:

- Seat—locked into position and secure;
- Doors—CLOSED and LOCKED, with no harness strap outside that could flap about in the airstream;
- Brakes—ON;

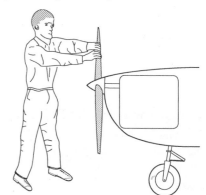

Figure 2c-3. Turning the engine over by hand cranking.

- Unnecessary electrical equipment—OFF: for example, radios;
- Master switch—ON (for electrical power);
- Fuel—ON, and suitable tank selected (some aircraft may also have an auxiliary electrical fuel pump to augment or boost the engine-driven fuel pump);
- Cowl flaps (if fitted)—OPEN;
- Carburetor heat control—COLD;
- Mixture—RICH;
- Throttle—CLOSED (or cracked one-quarter inch open);
- Fuel primer—LOCKED (one to three priming strokes to pump some fuel directly into the cylinders, if applicable; the priming pump may be manual or electrical);
- Rotating beacon—ON (as a warning to other people);
- Read the Preflight checklist if applicable;
- "**Clear**"—the area around the airplane, especially near the propeller, should be clear. The pilot is responsible for people around the airplane, so loudly call "CLEAR" to warn anyone that may be approaching the airplane;
- Starter—ENGAGE to crank the engine; then, when the engine has started, release the starter;
- Ensure that the airplane does not move—if it does, use the brakes; set the recommended rpm, and check normal indications on the engine gauges. Avoid using excessive engine rpm or creating an excessive engine temperature.

After starting, various items to be checked may include:
- Ensure airplane is remaining stationary;
- Oil pressure—sufficient pressure within 30 seconds of start-up (slightly longer in very cold weather—60 seconds maximum);
- Set the recommended rpm with the throttle—usually 1,000 to 1,200 rpm—to ensure adequate cooling;
- Ammeter—indicating charging of the battery following the drain on it during start-up;
- Suction gauge—check for sufficient suction to operate the gyro instruments;
- Gyroscopic flight instruments—erecting; when they have erected, align the heading indicator (HI) with the magnetic compass;
- Magnetos—check LEFT and RIGHT magnetos individually, as well as with the ignition switch in the usual BOTH position—the rpm should decrease slightly on each individual magneto and return to the previous value when the switch is returned to BOTH; but, if the engine stops, then a problem exists;
- Radios—ON, correct frequency selected, volume and squelch SET; it is a good idea to select the emergency frequency 121.5 MHz on the VHF-COM and check for inadvertent emergency locator beacon activation, before reselecting the local communications frequency;
- Lights: rotating beacon—ON, position lights and taxi light—SET as required;
- Electrical fuel pump (if fitted)—OFF, to check operation of the engine-driven fuel pump;
- Complete the After-Start checklist, if applicable.

The Before-Takeoff Check of the Engine

After you have taxied the airplane to the holding point or run-up area prior to entering the runway, bring it to a smooth stop and set the parking brake. Then carry out the Before-Takeoff check. One of these actions is a functional check of the engine. This is detailed in Exercise 12 of this manual, as part of the Standard Takeoff.

Shutting Down the Engine

There will be a shut-down procedure specified in the Pilot's Operating Handbook for your aircraft that will include such items as:

- Brakes—PARKED, with the airplane (ideally) heading into any strong wind;
- Engine—COOL; having taxied the airplane some distance, or having set 1,000 to 1,200 rpm for a minute or two, should be sufficient;
- Magnetos—CHECK; both magnetos should be checked individually; there should be a slight rpm drop as you go from BOTH to an individual magneto, and a return to the original rpm when the switch is returned to BOTH;
- Electrical equipment—OFF (lights, and so on);
- Radios and avionics—OFF; prior to switching the radios off it is a good idea to select the emergency frequency 121.5 MHz on the VHF-COM and check for inadvertent Emergency Locator Beacon activation.
- Mixture control—IDLE CUTOFF (fully out) to starve the engine of fuel and stop it running;
- After the engine stops, switch the Ignition OFF and remove the key;
- Master switch—OFF;
- Consideration should be given to switching the fuel selector valve OFF;
- If applicable, read the Engine Shutdown and the Securing Airplane checklists.

Problems during Start-Up

Most engine starts are uneventful if correct procedures are followed but, occasionally, a problem may occur. Refer to your Pilot's Operating Handbook which may contain checks similar to those following.

Use of the Accelerator Pump

Many aircraft engines are fitted with a carburetor which has an accelerator pump operated automatically by the throttle. Any rapid inward movement of the throttle will send an additional burst of fuel into the carburetor to provide a rapid and smooth acceleration of the engine.

If an engine is a little reluctant to start, a couple of quick pumps on the throttle will send extra fuel into the carburetor. This will richen the fuel/air mixture, and may assist the start-up.

Note: This *throttle-pumping* technique slightly increases the risk of a fire since the extra fuel goes to the carburetor, whereas the primer sends fuel directly to the cylinders, bypassing the carburetor.

Electric Fuel Pump

All aircraft engines have an *engine-driven* fuel pump that operates when the engine is rorating to ensure a continuous supply of fuel to the engine. Some aircraft also have an *electric* fuel pump fitted as a backup in case of failure of the engine-driven fuel pump or to provide a boosted fuel pressure.

You can check the function of the electric fuel pump, prior to starting the engine, by switching the pump on and:

- watching the fuel pressure rise on the gauge; and
- possibly hearing it operate (not possible when the engine is running).

After start-up, it is good technique to switch the electric fuel pump OFF to ensure that the engine-driven fuel pump is delivering fuel to the engine satisfactorily (better to find this out on the ground than in flight!), but then switch it back ON for takeoff and landing.

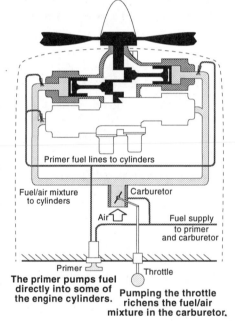

Primer fuel lines to cylinders

Fuel/air mixture to cylinders

Carburetor

Air

Fuel supply to primer and carburetor

Primer

Throttle

The primer pumps fuel directly into some of the engine cylinders.

Pumping the throttle richens the fuel/air mixture in the carburetor.

Figure 2c-4. Pumping the throttle to activate the accelerator pump.

Some airplanes, especially low-wing types, have an electric fuel pump to back up the engine-driven fuel pump.

Starting a Hot Engine

Starting an engine that has just been shut down, especially on a hot day, may require a special technique.

Hot engines can become flooded with excess fuel.

A hot engine often becomes flooded with excess fuel, with the resulting fuel/air mixture in the cylinders being too rich for a good start. The cylinders should be cleared of this excess fuel prior to start-up by either:

- cranking the engine through several revolutions using the starter motor; or
- by pulling the propeller through several times by hand, with the usual precautions for hand-propping having been taken.

No priming should be necessary. A normal start should now be possible.

Advanced Techniques

1. If you commence a start which you expect to be normal, but then realize that the engine is flooded with excess fuel, you can continue the start and move the throttle halfway to increase the airflow and help clear out the excess fuel—this should bring the over-rich mixture back into the normal range and allow the engine to start; then immediately after the engine starts, close the throttle to avoid excessively high rpm, along with unwanted thrust and noise.

2. If you are about to start an obviously flooded engine, use the technique described below.

A Flooded Engine

It is possible to flood an engine with too much fuel, making a start difficult and placing a strain on the battery which supplies electrical power to the starter motor. Sometimes the excess fuel can drain away naturally in about 5 minutes. If flooding is suspected **prior** to start-up, adopt the following procedure:

An advanced technique when clearing excess fuel from a flooded engine and starting it is:
- continue cranking and move the mixture control IN as the engine starts;
- close the throttle immediately the engine starts to avoid excess rpm and unwanted thrust and noise.

- Ignition switches—OFF;
- Throttle—FULLY OPEN (so that maximum airflow through the carburetor will help clear the excess fuel out of the cylinders);
- Fuel—ON, suitable tank selected, but electric fuel pump, if fitted—OFF (to avoid pumping in unwanted additional fuel);
- Mixture control—IDLE CUTOFF (no fuel is now being supplied to the engine);
- Crank the engine through several revolutions with the starter—this should clear the intake passages of excess fuel—or pull the propeller through several times by hand (taking suitable precautions).

Repeat the starting procedure without priming the engine.

Starting in Very Cold Weather

The oil in an engine that has been very cold for some time becomes thick and will not flow easily. This means it cannot properly perform its functions of:

Cold engines can be difficult to start.

- lubricating, cooling and cleaning the engine; and
- forming a seal between the piston rings and the cylinder wall to gain maximum power from the combustion.

Airplanes operating continually from cold airports often use a lighter grade of oil in winter than in summer—for instance, the thinner SAE 30 in winter, and the thicker SAE 50 in summer—or a multi-grade oil.

If the oil is suspected of being too cold and too thick, then the engine may be **pre-heated,** typically using an electric heater to blow hot air over the engine.

Another technique is to turn the engine over by hand by pulling the propeller through. This will loosen the oil and get it moving. Be sure to read the following paragraphs on hand-propping before you try this technique, to ensure that you do not accidentally start the engine (chocks in place, brakes—ON, throttle—CLOSED, mixture—IDLE CUTOFF, magnetos—OFF).

The technique used to start a very cold engine is:

1. First create a **rich** mixture—so prime the engine (using the manual or electric priming pump to send fuel directly into the cylinders), and consider pulling the propeller through a few times to loosen the oil and get it moving.

2. Follow the normal starting procedures and checklist, but be prepared to continue priming the engine, sending fuel directly into the cylinders, until the engine has warmed up. Then **lock the primer,** otherwise the mixture in the cylinders could be too rich causing the engine to run roughly or even stop.

3. Immediately apply carburetor heat after start-up to assist in warming the engine.

4. Allow the engine to idle for a few minutes, if necessary, until it warms up and the oil is at normal operating temperature and able to circulate normally through the engine and perform its functions.

Engine Fire on Start-Up

Engine fires are a rare event these days but they can still occur, possibly as a result of over-priming the engine with fuel. In such a case:

If the engine starts:
- Throttle—set about 1,700 rpm for a few minutes (to suck the fire through);
- Engine—shut down and inspect for damage.

When the fuel has been eliminated, the fire should stop. Release the starter.

If the engine fails to start:
- Starter, if still engaged—CONTINUE CRANKING (to suck flames and accumulated fuel through the carburetor and into the engine).
- Mixture control—IDLE CUTOFF (to stop fuel supply to the engine);
- Fuel selector—OFF;
- Throttle—OPEN (to allow maximum airflow through to purge the induction system and engine of fuel).

If the fire continues:
- Ignition switch—OFF;
- Master switch—OFF;
- Fuel shutoff valve—OFF or CLOSED;
- Brakes—ON;
- Evacuate, taking the fire extinguisher with you.

Supplementary Starting Methods

External Power Source

Some aircraft have a **ground service plug** receptacle that permits the use of an external electrical power source for:
- engine start (especially during very cold weather when difficult starts can really drain the battery);
- periods when lengthy maintenance work is being carried out on electrical and avionics equipment that requires electrical power.

The external power source should be suitable for your aircraft and should be plugged in to the ground service plug receptacle using correct positive/negative polarity. This normally disconnects the onboard aircraft battery from the aircraft circuitry.

Engine fires are rare, but they can occur.

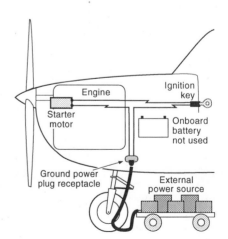

Figure 2c-5. An external battery cart connected to the ground service plug.

Using an external power source will preserve the charge of the aircraft battery.

Information regarding the use of an external power source will be found in the Pilot's Operating Handbook, Section 9 on **Supplements.** You should refer to your POH before using any external power source, since procedures and checklists to use before and after an external-power start-up vary between aircraft types.

Ensure that the external power source is removed and placed clear of the aircraft before taxiing away.

Hand Cranking

If not performed correctly, hand cranking (or "hand-propping") can be dangerous, either from the engine starting unexpectedly because of a loose or broken magneto groundwire, or by compression in the cylinders causing the propeller to kick back. A **briefing** from a flight instructor or mechanic on how to hand crank a propeller is absolutely essential.

Always have a pilot or mechanic in the cockpit and at the controls, and have a briefing of the required actions and callouts before starting the procedure.

Ensure that the parking brake is ON and that the wheels are CHOCKED, to prevent the airplane moving forward when the engine starts.

The hand cranking procedure is usually controlled by the person at the propeller. The technique is to move the propeller firmly in its normal direction of rotation (counterclockwise as seen from in front, clockwise as seen from the cockpit). Stand in front of and to the left of the propeller—in front of the down-going blade, with your right shoulder pointing toward the propeller hub, and with the fingers of both hands over the top of the propeller blade about midway between the hub and the propeller tip.

Your feet should be in a position close enough to the propeller arc so that you do not have to lean forward. Your weight should initially be on the right foot, so that after pulling the propeller blade down your weight will move back on to your left foot, and the natural motion of your body will be away from the plane of propeller rotation.

Another technique is to stand behind the right side of the propeller (as seen from the cockpit), so that if the airplane moves forward after the engine starts, it will move away from you.

Pull-Through if the Engine is Flooded. You may decide to pull the engine through several cycles to clean the cylinders of fuel before starting it, but always assume that the engine might inadvertently start.
- Call out and check:
    Brakes—ON.
    Switches—OFF (including magneto switches OFF so no sparks will occur in the engine cylinders).
    Throttle—OPEN (for maximum air movement through the engine to clean excess fuel away).
- Position your feet, and place your fingers over the down-going blade.
- Pull the blade through several times, moving away from propeller arc after each pull-through in case the engine fires.

Engine Start-Up.
- Call out and check:
    Brakes—ON.
    Throttle—CLOSED (or cracked slightly open, say one-quarter inch).
    Contact (magneto switches—ON).

Hand cranking means turning the engine over by *manually* rotating the propeller, rather than using the electric starter motor.

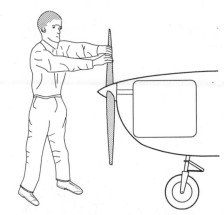

Figure 2c-6. Hand cranking (or hand-propping)

Do not consider hand-propping an airplane unless you have received expert instruction in the procedure.

- Position your feet, and place fingers over the down-going blade.
- Give the propeller a firm and strong downward movement, with your hands then moving away, your weight shifting back onto your left foot, and your body moving away from the propeller arc.
- If the engine does not start, wait a few seconds before moving back into position—in case it does start; then repeat the procedure.

Remember that, at 2,400 rpm, the propeller blade will be spinning at 40 revolutions per second. At idling speed, say about 800 rpm, it will be spinning at about 13 revolutions per second. It is lethal, and almost invisible!

In-Flight Restart

If the engine stops providing power in flight (possibly from fuel starvation caused by an empty tank or an iced-up carburetor, or by a faulty ignition system), then it may be possible to restart it if you can rectify the cause of the stoppage.

- **If the propeller has stopped rotating**, you can use the starter motor to turn the engine over.
- **If the propeller is windmilling in the airstream**, then there is no need to use the starter motor at all—just introduce fuel and ignition, and the engine should start.

This is covered fully in Exercise 17a.

Airmanship

Always perform each check thoroughly and read the appropriate checklist carefully. Do not just respond to a checklist item automatically, but actually check that the item has been accomplished or the switch position is correct before answering the checklist challenge. Reading checklist challenges and responses aloud is a good technique, especially when two pilots are in the cockpit.

Always be aware of any person standing near the propeller or moving toward it, even when the engine is stopped. Always treat the propeller, even when stationary, as a lethal weapon, and set a good example by never leaning against it. Never board or deplane passengers while the propeller is turning.

Airmanship is common sense and completing checklists thoroughly.

✍️ Review 2c

Starting and Stopping the Engine

1. It is preferable to position the aircraft on (loose stones/a smooth tarmac) for the engine start-up.

   ➤ a smooth tarmac

2. It is preferable to start the engine in a (clear/crowded) area.

   ➤ clear

3. Specify three ways in which an engine may be started on the ground.

   ➤ (1) starter motor and onboard battery
   (2) starter motor and external power source
   (3) by hand-propping

4. The parking brake should be (ON/OFF) for engine start-up.

   ➤ ON

5. For an engine start, you (should/need not) systematically follow the approved before-starting and starting procedures, and read the appropriate checklists thoroughly.

   ➤ should

6. Before starting the engine, you (should/need not) check outside for other people and (should/need not) loudly call out "CLEAR".

   ➤ should, should

7. Immediately after the engine starts, you (should/need not) check to ensure that the airplane is not moving forward.

   ➤ should

8. You (should/need not) check the engine gauges as soon as the engine starts, especially the _____ pressure, engine _____ , and engine _____ .

   ➤ should, oil, rpm, temperature

9. Oil pressure may take longer to rise in (hot/cold) weather.

   ➤ cold

10. For a normal start, the throttle should be (wide open/closed or slightly cracked open).

    ➤ closed or slightly cracked open

11. Using the priming pump sends fuel into the (carburetor/cylinders).

    ➤ cylinders

12. Pumping the throttle actuates the _____ pump, which sends a burst of fuel into the (carburetor/cylinders).

    ➤ accelerator pump, carburetor

13. To clear a flooded engine of excess fuel by turning it over using the starter motor, the mixture control should be in the (RICH/IDLE CUTOFF) position and the throttle should be (wide open/closed).

    ➤ IDLE CUTOFF, wide open

14. Information on using an external electrical power source for engine starts can usually be found in Section ____ , entitled _____ , of the Pilot's Operating Handbook.

    ➤ 9, Supplements

15. You (should never/may) hand-prop an airplane if you have not received expert instruction.

    ➤ should never

16. It is (safe/unsafe) to deplane passengers while the propeller is still turning.

    ➤ unsafe

17. It (is/is not) essential that all checklists, both normal and emergency, be followed precisely.

    ➤ is

18. For an in-flight restart of an engine that has stopped providing power but the propeller is still windmilling, the electric starter motor (is/is not) required.

    ➤ is not

Postflight Actions 2d

General Considerations

Postflight duties required of each pilot are to taxi the airplane to a suitable parking area—considering wind conditions and obstructions—stop the engine, secure the airplane and do the checklist. Then deplane the passengers safely, perform a postflight inspection, complete the postflight documentation, and **close the flightplan** with ATC or FSS if required.

A flight is not really completed until the engine is shut down and the airplane parked and secure. The postflight documentation must be finalized, since it is a **requirement** that certain records be kept and that any faults in the airplane be made known so that **maintenance** action will be taken.

An airplane has a life of its own in the sense that it passes continually from the command of one pilot to the command of another, the postflight check of one being followed by the preflight check of the other. To a certain extent, each pilot relies upon the fact that earlier pilots have performed their duties, even though we must all **accept individual responsibility.**

Securing the Airplane

The airplane should not be left unattended unless it is adequately secured against movement and possible damage.
- Park into the expected wind;
- Ensure that the parking brake is ON (if required) and that the wheel chocks are in place, in front of and behind the wheels;
- Consider releasing the brakes when the wheels are chocked to allow them to cool and to avoid freezing of moisture on them in cold climates; this will also allow ground staff to move the airplane without having to unlock the cockpit;
- Carry out a brief external inspection;
- Fit the pitot covers, control locks and tie down ropes if required;
- Secure the seat belts and shoulder harnesses;
- If yours is the last flight of the day, consider refueling to minimize overnight condensation of water in the fuel tanks;
- Complete the Securing-Airplane checklist (if applicable);
- Lock the door and return the key.

Tie Down

Attach ropes from permanent tie-down anchors or from pegs driven into the ground to the tie-down rings on the wings and on the tail.

The rope should have a little bit of slack in it to allow for shrinking if it rains (nylon rope is better than manila rope), but not so loose that a wind could lift the airplane over the chocks.

Figure 2d-1 on the next page illustrates this.

● Parked facing into the wind. ● Wings tied-down.
● Chocks prevent airplane moving back due to wind.
● Tail rope stops airplane moving forward.

Figure 2d-1. How to tie down the airplane

Postflight Documentation

- Record the engine time (or Hobb's gauge time) in the log;
- Report any airplane defects to your flight instructor or to a mechanic and, when appropriate, note them on the maintenance log to ensure that necessary maintenance will be attended to and that the following pilot will have a serviceable airplane;
- Complete your personal **logbook.**

DATE 1993	AIRCRAFT MAKE & MODEL	AIRCRAFT IDENT.	POINTS OF DEPARTURE & ARRIVAL		REMARKS, PROCEDURES, MANEUVERS	NO. INSTR. APP.	NO LDG.
			FROM	TO			
5/22	C172	54983	BFI	PWT	T/O – WHITE CTR – PILOTAGE To PWT VFR AND ADF		1
5/22	C172	54983	PWT	BFI	T/O A E TWIN PATTERN BASE CROSSWIND 13L (RWY DEBRIS)		1
5/29	C172	737TK	BFI – CLM – BFI		T/O BFI → PILOTAGE – APEX –X/W LDG SHORT-FLD T/O – CLM – FLT RULES PILOTAGE Alt management Climbs Descents Rob Patterson 526420358 CA X1190		3

AIRCRAFT CATEGORY				CONDITIONS OF FLIGHT						TYPE OF PILOTING TIME			TOTAL DURATION OF FLIGHT	
GS	AIRPLANE SEL	AIRPLANE MEL	CROSS COUNTRY	DAY	NIGHT	ACTUAL INSTR.	SIMULATED INSTR.	SYNTHETIC TRAINER	DUAL RECEIVED	PILOT IN COMMAND				
	O 6			O 6					O 6				O 6
	O 4			O 4					O 4				O 4
	2 1			2 1					2 1				2 1

Figure 2d-2. Part of your postflight actions is to complete your pilot's logbook.

During your training, a debriefing by your flight instructor will probably occur following the completion of your postflight duties. You can also re-read the appropriate chapter of this manual to consolidate what you have learned in the particular flight lesson and briefing.

✍ Review 2d   Postflight Duties

1. You should normally park the airplane so that the expected wind will blow from (ahead/behind/the side) and (close to/away from) obstructions.

   ➤ ahead, away from

2. You should complete the Shutdown checklist (before/after) you deplane any passengers.

   ➤ before

3. Any defect noted during or after the flight (should/need not) be made known to the flight instructor or a mechanic.

   ➤ should

4. When you tie the airplane down, rope tension should be (tight/a little slack/loose).

   ➤ a little slack

Your First Flight 3

This flight is not part of your formal instruction but rather an opportunity to get the feel of being airborne. Your flight instructor, an experienced and professional pilot, will use this flight to let you:
- become familiar with the cockpit;
- experience some of the more common sensations of flying an airplane; and
- to show you some of the landmarks and other features of the airport and the local area.

In the Cockpit

Sit comfortably in your seat and **relax.** Since you will be trained to become the captain of your airplane, you may as well start by sitting in the left-hand seat, the captain's seat by tradition and design. It needs to be positioned so that you can reach the appropriate controls comfortably with your hands and feet.

The **seatbelt** or harness should be firmly fastened. Even though this may be your first flight, it is important that your seat is positioned correctly, since the position of the natural horizon in the windshield is a vital element in assisting you to fly accurately.

Fresh air is available through vents, and directing these toward your face and body improves the cockpit environment considerably for you.

Communication in the cockpit is very important, so ensure that your headset is comfortable and that the intercom system is operating satisfactorily.

In the cockpit, make yourself comfortable and relax.

Leaving the Ground

While **taxiing out**, you can assist in maintaining a good **lookout** for other aircraft and for obstructions.

During the **takeoff** roll you should look well ahead. To best maintain a straight track down the runway and judge your altitude above it, keep your eyes focused about halfway down the runway.

Develop good habits right from the start! Even though the takeoff appears full of action, in reality it is a straightforward maneuver, which you will soon master.

As the airplane climbs, ground features take on a different perspective, being viewed more in plan than in profile—towns, roads, rivers, mountains and coastlines appearing as they would on a chart. The sensation of speed also diminishes with altitude and the airplane feels like it is traveling in slow motion.

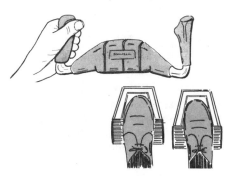

Figure 3-1. A light touch on the controls

Your first feel of the airplane controls.

In Flight

You will have the opportunity to follow your instructor on the flight controls by:
- placing your left hand lightly on the control wheel (or control column); and
- your right hand on the throttle or on your lap; and
- both feet lightly on the rudder pedals (with your heels on the floor to ensure that the toe brakes are not applied, and to keep your feet relaxed so that you can apply sensitive rudder pressures when required).

Control of the Airplane

During the course of your training, control will be passed from your instructor to you and then back again quite frequently.

Your flight instructor will say *"You have control"* (or words to that effect) when he wishes you to take control. Upon hearing this instruction, you should place your hands and feet on the controls lightly, but firmly, and, once you feel comfortable to take control, respond by saying *"I have control"*.

Each change of control should be preceded by an initial statement followed by a definite response from the other pilot.

Always be clear who has control.

Figure 3-2. Be clear at all times as to who has control.

Keep a Good Lookout

Visual flying requires that the pilot maintains a **high visual awareness of the environment outside the cockpit,** both to relate the attitude (or nose position) of the airplane to the natural horizon, as well as to **look out** for other aircraft, to check passage over the ground, and to remain clear of clouds.

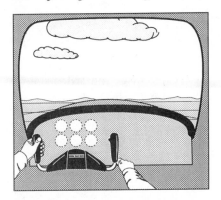 

Figure 3-3. The view from the cockpit while climbing and turning

A vital pilot duty is to maintain a good lookout for other aircraft, obstacles and bad weather, especially thunderstorms.

The most efficient means of scanning for other aircraft takes into account the fact that the eyes see better when they are stationary. Use a series of short, regularly spaced eye movements, moving the eyes about 10° each time, to position them to scan an area for about one second before moving on.

There is a **blind spot** under the nose of the airplane that a pilot cannot see, which you should periodically clear by making shallow turns that enable you to see this area out of the side window. Get to know the blind spots of your particular airplane, and periodically take action to clear the areas normally obscured.

Poor scanning habits will increase the risk of a collision. It is your responsibility to **see and avoid** other aircraft. A collision-risk exists if another aircraft remains at a fixed position in your windscreen and continues to increase in size.

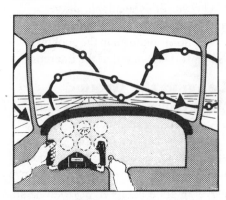

Figure 3-4. Scanning for other traffic

Note: The risk of a collision also increases as aircraft speeds increase, resulting in less time available to see and take avoiding action. It also increases with aircraft speed differential, with a faster aircraft catching up on a slow aircraft.

The **position of other airplanes** in relation to your own is best described by using the numbers of a clock, based on a horizontal clock face aligned with the airplane's heading or course. An airplane ahead of you, but higher, would be described as *"12-o'clock high"*, while one slightly behind and below you on the left-hand side would be at *"8-o'clock low"*.

Note any **landmarks** that can assist in your return to the airport and remain well clear of clouds at all times.

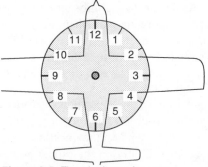

Figure 3-5. The clock numbers as aligned with the airplane

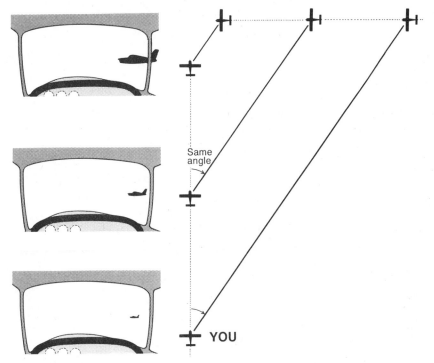

Figure 3-6. A potential collision situation

The Fundamental Maneuvers

The four fundamental flight maneuvers are: (1) the cruise straight-and-level; (2) climbing; (3) descending; and (4) turning.

Your instructor will guide you through these basic maneuvers, and soon you will be flying the airplane in three dimensions. The wings are kept level, or are banked, by rotating the control wheel (or left–right movements of the control column). This operates the ailerons at the end of each wing trailing edge. The nose position up or down relative to the horizon is controlled by push–pull movements of the control column, which operates the elevator at the tail of the airplane. The throttle controls engine power.

The most common in-flight attitude of the airplane is wings level with the horizon, with the nose positioned relative to the horizon so that level flight results. This is the **straight-and-level attitude.** It is virtually impossible to achieve perfect straight-and-level flight. In reality, straight-and-level flight is a series of minor corrections to recover from slight climbs, descents and turns. You will be surprised how quickly you can improve at flying straight-and-level with a little practice.

You may notice also that the faster you fly the more responsive the controls become. This is because of the increased airflow over the control surfaces. At low speeds, larger control movements are needed to achieve the same effect. An airplane also has inertia, so there may often be a slight delay between your movement of the controls and changes in the airplane's flight path.

The Instruments

The airplane has instruments which can provide useful information regarding attitude relative to the horizon, altitude, direction, airspeed and engine operation. The basic division is into **flight instruments** and **engine gauges.** An occasional glance at a particular instrument for one or two seconds is all that you require—your visual awareness of the world outside the cockpit must not suffer from this glance inside.

Occasionally check the instruments and gauges.

In **visual flight** (known as VFR), you relate the airplane's attitude to the external horizon. During **instrument flight** (IFR), the pilot relates the airplane's attitude to the artificial horizon bar in the attitude indicator.

Your Attention

As pilot, you must learn to divide your attention appropriately between internal **cockpit duties** (such as making power changes, checking the instruments, selecting new radio frequencies, and so on), and **visual scanning** outside the cockpit so that you see other aircraft and obstacles and can take timely action to avoid them.

Divide your time efficiently and effectively.

Returning to Earth

As the descent, approach and landing proceed, the pilot's workload increases. During the landing, you should again look about midway down the runway to allow better judgment in the flare and touchdown when you are making the landing. The approach and landing phase seems full of action, but it will not be long before you have mastered this maneuver! A flight is not complete until the airplane is parked and secured, and the **postflight duties** of the pilot completed.

Your first flight is now over, but a marvellous hobby or career awaits you. You should now prepare carefully for your next flying lesson, by reading the appropriate chapter of this manual (as determined by your flight instructor). This will ensure that you gain the maximum benefit from your next training flight.

Keep a good lookout as you return to the traffic pattern.

 Review 3

1. It is (vital/unnecessary/moderately important) for you to maintain a good lookout.

    ➤ vital

2. The most efficient means of scanning the sky for other aircraft is to (slowly and steadily move your eyes across the sky/use a series of short, regularly spaced eye movements).

    ➤ use a series of short regularly spaced eye movements

3. Your instructor says there is another aircraft at 10 o'clock. You would look ahead and (left/right).

    ➤ left

Your First Flight

4. Your instructor says there is another aircraft at 1 o'clock. You would look ahead and (left/right).

    ➤ right

5. What are the four fundamental flight maneuvers?

    ➤ straight-and-level, climbing, descending, turning

6. When the flight instructor says "you have control", you should take control and respond with the words "____ _____ _____".

    ➤ I have control

The Primary Effect of Each Main Flight Control 4a

Objective

To observe the primary effect of moving each main flight control.

Considerations

Airplane Movement

To describe an airplane's attitude or position in flight, three mutually perpendicular reference axes—the lateral, longitudinal and normal axes—passing through the center of gravity are used. Any change in airplane attitude can be expressed in terms of motion about these three airplane axes.

- Motion about the lateral axis is known as **pitch.**
- Motion about the longitudinal axis is known as **roll.**
- Motion about the normal axis is **yaw.**

Note: The word *normal* in geometry means perpendicular. We therefore refer to the yaw axis as the *normal axis,* because it is perpendicular to both the longitudinal axis and the lateral axis. It is preferable not to refer to it as the vertical axis, because it is only vertical when the airplane is in the cruise attitude. Whenever the airplane is banked, or the nose is pitched up or down, the normal axis is not vertical.

An airplane moves in three dimensions.

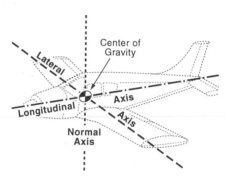

Figure 4a-1. Angular motion is described using three reference axes.

Motion about an axis can also be described as *motion in a plane.* For instance, the nose pitching up and down can be described as either rotation about the lateral axis, or motion in the pitching plane.

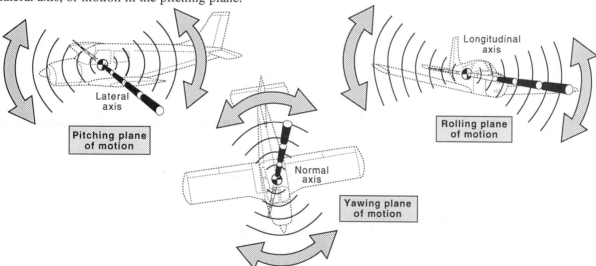

Figure 4a-2. Angular motion can occur in three planes of movement.

The Stability of an Airplane

Stability is the natural ability of the airplane to remain in its original attitude or to return to it following some disturbance, such as a wind gust, without any action being taken by the pilot.

Most training airplanes are reasonably stable in **pitch.** If correctly trimmed, they will maintain steady flight with the pilot flying hands-off. In other words, the nose position relative to the horizon will remain reasonably steady without too much attention from the pilot.

The stability of most airplanes in **roll** and **yaw**, however, is usually not as great as in pitch. If the wings are moved from their level position, say by a gust, the airplane will eventually enter a descending spiral turn unless the pilot actively does something about it—in this case by leveling the wings.

Stability is the natural ability of the airplane to stay in or return to its original attitude.

The Main Flight Controls

The pilot controls motion about the three axes with the main flight controls:
- the elevator controls pitch;
- the ailerons control roll; and
- the rudder controls yaw.

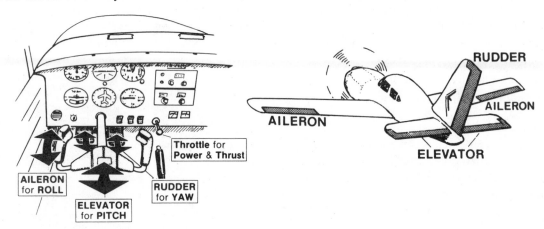

Figure 4a-3. The three main flight controls—elevator, ailerons and rudder

The Elevator

The elevator is operated by fore and aft movements of the control column and it controls pitch. The **conventional elevator** is a control surface hinged to the rear of the horizontal stabilizer. Some aircraft have a **stabilator,** or all-flying tail, which is a single moving surface acting as both the horizontal stabilizer and elevator. Either type has the same effect on the airplane when the control column is moved.

Deflecting the elevator with the control column alters the airflow around the horizontal stabilizer and changes the aerodynamic force generated by it.

Moving the control column back deflects the elevator up, causing an increased speed of airflow *beneath* the horizontal stabilizer and, consequently, a reduced static pressure in that area. This results in a downward aerodynamic force on the horizontal stabilizer which causes the airplane to pitch nose-up about its center of gravity. **The tail moves down and the nose moves up.**

Conversely, moving the control column forward deflects the elevator downward, causing an increased speed of flow *above* the horizontal stabilizer and a reduced static pressure in that area. This results in an upward aerodynamic force on the horizontal stabilizer, causing the airplane to pitch nose-down about its center of gravity. **The tail moves up and the nose moves down.**

The elevator controls pitch.

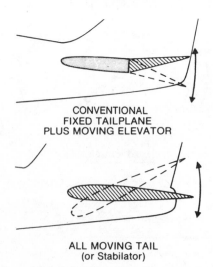

CONVENTIONAL
FIXED TAILPLANE
PLUS MOVING ELEVATOR

ALL MOVING TAIL
(or Stabilator)

Figure 4a-4. The separate horizontal stabilizer and elevator, and the stabilator

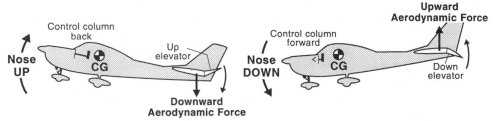

Figure 4a-5. The elevator controls pitch.

Forward and rearward movement of the control column is used to place the nose in the desired position relative to the horizon—that is, to set the **pitch attitude.**

The *rate* at which the pitch of the airplane changes will increase with larger elevator deflections.

The effectiveness of aerodynamic controls like the elevator also depends upon the speed of the air flowing over them—at normal flight speeds, the movement of the control column can be quite small and may feel more like pressure changes than actual movements; however, at slow speeds, larger elevator movements and larger control column deflections are required to produce the same effect.

The Ailerons

The ailerons are hinged control surfaces attached to the outboard trailing edge of each wing. The ailerons in some airplanes are controlled by rotation of the control wheel and in other airplanes by left–right movements of the control column. The control column (or control wheel) therefore serves two functions:
- fore-and-aft movement operates the elevator;
- rotation (or left–right movement) operates the ailerons.

As one aileron goes down and increases the lift generated by that wing, the other aileron goes up and reduces the lift on its wing, causing the airplane to roll. For example, moving the control column to the left causes a roll to the left by raising the left aileron and lowering the right aileron.

The ailerons control roll.

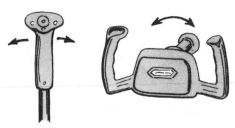

Figure 4a-6. A control column or a control wheel perform the same function.

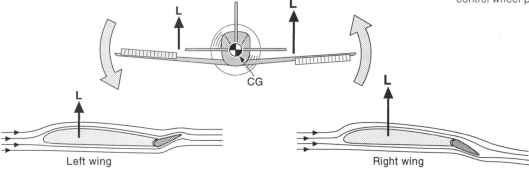

Figure 4a-7. A roll to the left

The airplane will continue to roll while the ailerons are deflected, the roll rate being determined by the amount of aileron deflection.

Holding the control column neutral (in the center position) places the ailerons in the neutral position and stops the roll.

The Rudder

The third (and final) main flight control is the rudder which is a hinged control surface at the rear of the vertical stabilizer (fin).

The rudder is controlled with both feet on the rudder pedals. These pedals are interconnected so that as one moves forward the other moves back.

The rudder controls yaw.

Moving the left rudder pedal forward deflects the rudder to the left. This increases the speed of airflow on the right hand side of the vertical stabilizer, reducing the static pressure there and creating an aerodynamic force to the right.

The airplane rotates about its center of gravity and so, with left rudder, the nose yaws left. Conversely, moving the right rudder pedal forward yaws the nose of the airplane to the right.

Yawing the airplane can be uncomfortable, and is aerodynamically inefficient because it causes drag to increase. It is neither a comfortable nor efficient means of turning an airplane in flight; a yawing turn falls into the same category as trying to round a corner on a bicycle without leaning it into the turn.

Although it can yaw the airplane, one of the main functions of the rudder is to **prevent adverse aileron yaw** (unwanted yaw) when the airplane is rolling as a result of deflected ailerons—for instance, when entering or exiting a turn. This function of the rudder is known as *maintaining coordinated flight,* and is indicated to the pilot by the small **coordination ball** on the instrument panel and also by the seat of your pants. If the airplane is uncoordinated, the ball moves out to one side (and the pilot, reacting in the same way as the ball, will feel pressed to the same side).

Coordinated flight can be restored by applying **same-side rudder pressure**—if the ball is out to the right, apply right rudder pressure (and vice versa).

Airplane Attitude and Control

The controls operate relative to the airplane's three axes.

The primary aerodynamic controls operate in the same sense **relative to the airplane** irrespective of the airplane's attitude in pitch or bank. For example, moving the control column forward will move the nose in a direction away from you, even if, taking an extreme case, the airplane is inverted.

Flying the Maneuver

Good flying requires the coordination of all three flight controls, however in this training exercise we will use them individually. It is a necessary step because the individual effects need to be appreciated before smooth coordination of the flight controls in normal flight is possible.

From straight-and-level flight, move each of the controls **individually** and relate the effects to the three axes. Repeat with the airplane banked.

Airmanship

You are training to be a visual pilot so develop good visual habits early. **Look out** of the cockpit most of the time, both to check the attitude of the airplane relative to the horizon and to look for other aircraft. Identify their position relative to the numbers on a clock.

Follow the correct *"You have control"—"I have control"* procedures, so that it is quite clear at all times who has control.

Hold the controls lightly and move them smoothly and fluently. Occasionally, large control movements are required to achieve the desired effect but, at normal flying speeds, **firm pressures** rather than large movements are all that is required.

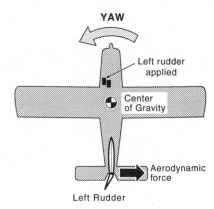

Figure 4a-8. Left rudder pressure yaws the nose left.

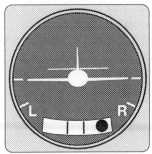

Figure 4a-9. Apply same-side rudder pressure to center the coordination ball. Right rudder pressure is required here.

Airmanship is common sense and awareness.

Airwork 4a
Primary Effect of Each Main Flight Control

Objective
To observe the primary effect of moving each main flight control during flight.

1. The Primary Effect of the Elevator is to Pitch the Airplane

(a) Establish the airplane in steady, straight-and-level flight; clear the area and maintain a good lookout.

(c) Smoothly and gently move the control column rearward—*the nose of the airplane pitches up toward you.*

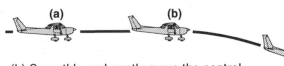

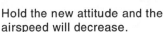

(b) Smoothly and gently move the control column forward—*the nose of the airplane pitches down away from you.*
Hold the new attitude and the airspeed will increase.

Hold the new attitude and the airspeed will decrease.

2. The Primary Effect of the Ailerons is to Roll the Airplane

(a) Establish the airplane in steady, straight-and-level flight; clear the area and maintain a good lookout.

(b) Initially hold the wings level. Then smoothly rotate the control column to the left—*the airplane rolls to the left in the same plane as the propeller.*

(c) Centralize the control column—*rolling ceases and a steady bank angle is maintained.*

Note: The secondary effect will be a yaw as the nose drops in the direction of bank angle, in this case left—this is covered in the next exercise.

(d) To roll out of the left turn, smoothly rotate the control column to the right—*the airplane rolls to the right.*

(e) When the wings are level centralize the control column.

(f) Repeat this sequence for rolls to the right and left using different amounts of control movement.

Continued

3. The Primary Effect of the Rudder is to Yaw the Airplane

(a) Establish the airplane in steady, straight-and-level flight; clear the area and maintain a good lookout.

(b) Select a reference point on the horizon.

(c) Smoothly apply left rudder pressure—*the nose of the airplane yaws left (and the coordination ball is thrown out to the right).*

(d) Centralize the rudder pedals (by removing left rudder pressure).

(e) Repeat using right rudder pressure and observe the reverse effects.

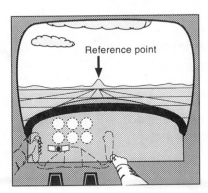

Left rudder—nose yaws left and coordination ball thrown right

4. The Controls Work the Same when the Airplane is not Flying Straight-and-Level

(a) Establish the airplane in steady straight-and-level flight; clear the area and maintain a good lookout.

(b) Bank the airplane with the ailerons, then operate the elevator:
  - *Forward pressure on the control column pitches the nose down and away from the pilot.*
  - *Aft pressure on the control column pitches the nose up and toward the pilot.*

(c) Set the airplane with a high nose attitude, then move the ailerons:
  - *Rotating the control column left causes the airplane to roll left.*
  - *Rotating the control column right causes the airplane to roll right.*

(d) Bank the airplane with the ailerons:
  - *Pushing the left rudder pedal causes the nose to yaw left relative to the pilot.*
  - *Pushing the right rudder pedal causes the nose to yaw right relative to the pilot.*

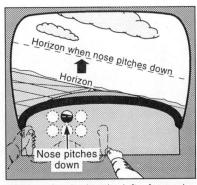

Airplane banked to the left—forward control-column pressure still pitches the nose down.

With a high nose attitude the airplane still responds to the aileron control—rolls to the right, as illustrated, and left.

Further Points

The Stabilator and Anti-Servo Tab

Because of their combined function, stabilators have a much larger area than elevators and so produce more-powerful responses to control input—that is, small movements of the control column can produce large aerodynamic forces. To prevent a pilot from moving the stabilator too far and overcontrolling—especially at high airspeeds—a stabilator often incorporates an *anti-servo tab*.

An anti-servo tab moves in the same direction as the stabilator's trailing edge and generates an aerodynamic force that makes it increasingly harder to move the stabilator further, as well as providing *feel* for the pilot.

Correct movement of the anti-servo tab can be checked during the preflight inspection by moving the trailing edge of the stabilator and noting that the anti-servo tab moves in the **same** direction as the trailing edge.

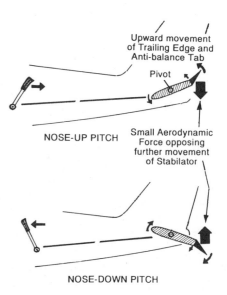

Figure 4a-10. The anti-servo tab opposes further stabilator movement and provides control *feel* for the pilot.

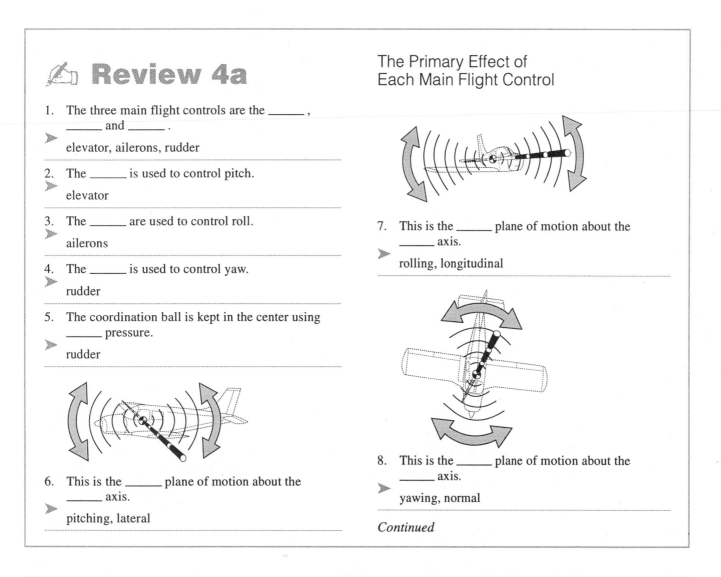

✍ Review 4a

The Primary Effect of Each Main Flight Control

1. The three main flight controls are the _____ , _____ and _____ .
    > elevator, ailerons, rudder

2. The _____ is used to control pitch.
    > elevator

3. The _____ are used to control roll.
    > ailerons

4. The _____ is used to control yaw.
    > rudder

5. The coordination ball is kept in the center using _____ pressure.
    > rudder

6. This is the _____ plane of motion about the _____ axis.
    > pitching, lateral

7. This is the _____ plane of motion about the _____ axis.
    > rolling, longitudinal

8. This is the _____ plane of motion about the _____ axis.
    > yawing, normal

Continued

---

9. Moving the elevator causes motion in the _____ plane, which is movement about the _____ axis.

> pitching, lateral

10. Moving the ailerons causes motion in the _____ plane, about the _____ axis.

> rolling, longitudinal

11. Moving the rudder causes motion in the _____ plane, about the _____ axis.

> yawing, normal (sometimes called vertical)

12. The rudder is generally used to (yaw the airplane/ prevent unwanted yaw).

> prevent unwanted yaw

13. Moving the right rudder pedal in will cause the nose to yaw (left/right) or prevent it from yawing (left/right).

> right, left

14. Moving the left rudder pedal in will cause the nose to yaw (left/right) or prevent it from yawing (left/right).

> left, right

15. Rotating the control column to the left will cause a roll to the (left/right).

> left

16. Rotating the control column to the right will cause a roll to the (left/right).

> right

17. This airplane has the control wheel rotated to the (left/right) and will roll to the (left/right).

> left, left

18. Rotating the control wheel to the left moves the left aileron (up/down) and the right aileron (up/down).

> up, down

19. Rotating the control wheel to the right moves the left aileron (up/down) and the right aileron (up/down).

> down, up

20. Moving the control column back will (raise/lower) the elevator and (raise/lower) the nose attitude.

> raise, raise

21. Moving the control column forward will (raise/ lower) the elevator and (raise/lower) the nose.

> lower, lower

22. Moving the left rudder pedal forward will move the trailing edge of the rudder to the (left/right).

> left

23. Moving the right rudder pedal forward will move the trailing edge of the rudder to the (left/right).

> right

24. To center the coordination ball on the instrument pictured above, you need to apply (left/right) rudder pressure.

> right

25. To center the coordination ball in this case, you need to apply (left/right) rudder pressure.

> left

26. The natural ability of an airplane to remain in, or return to, its original attitude is known as _____ .

> stability

27. At normal flying speeds, for the flight controls to be sufficiently effective (large movements/firm control pressures) are required.

> firm control pressures

28. One very important aspect of airmanship while flying maneuvers is to always maintain a good _____ for other aircraft.

> lookout

The Secondary Effect of Each Main Flight Control **4b**

Objective

To observe the secondary effect of moving each main flight control.

Considerations

Control Effects

Operating a single flight control can have more than one effect. When either the ailerons or the rudder are used individually, in addition to the primary effect there is a secondary—or *further*—effect.

Roll and Yaw

To roll left, the control wheel is rotated left, deflecting the right **aileron** down to produce more lift on the right wing, and the left aileron up to reduce lift on the left wing. Because of the down-deflected aileron, the right wing also produces more drag. The result is that the airplane rolls left, but yaws right. As this initial yaw is in the opposite direction to the roll, it is known as *adverse aileron yaw*.

When the control wheel is centered to stop the roll and maintain a steady bank angle, the ailerons are neutral, and the tendency for adverse aileron yaw ceases. The airplane is now banked, with the lift force tilted. A sideways component of the lift force now exists, causing the airplane to **slip** toward the lower wing. In this slip, the large keel surfaces behind the center of gravity (such as the vertical stabilizer and the fuselage) are struck by the airflow—this causes the airplane's nose to yaw in the direction of the slip. The nose will drop, and a spiral descent will commence (unless prevented by the pilot leveling the wings).

Roll causes yaw—the secondary effect of the ailerons.

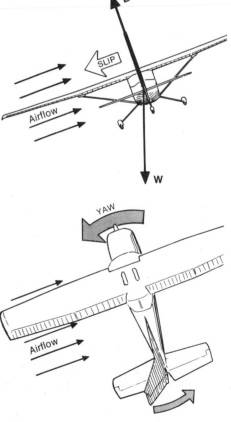

Figure 4b-1. Deflected ailerons cause adverse aileron yaw.

Figure 4b-2. Bank causes a slip followed by yawing.

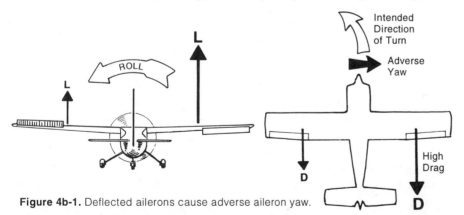

Moving the ailerons with left–right movements of the control column has two effects: (1) a roll followed by adverse yaw, and then (2) a yaw in the direction of bank when the ailerons are neutralized. Therefore the **primary** effect of the ailerons is to roll the airplane, and the **secondary** effect is to yaw the airplane.

Note: A pilot can counteract unwanted adverse aileron yaw caused by the deflected ailerons by using coordinated same-side rudder pressure—*left control wheel, left rudder pressure*—keeping the coordination ball in the center. When you have the desired bank angle and the ailerons are neutralized to stop further rolling, there will be no adverse aileron yaw and no need for same-side rudder pressure.

Yaw and Roll

Applying **rudder** will yaw the nose of the airplane—a yaw to the left if left rudder pressure is applied, a yaw to the right if right rudder is applied. As a result of the yaw, the outer wing will tend to rise because:

Yaw causes roll—the secondary effect of the rudder.

- it is moving faster than the inner wing and so generates more lift;
- the airplane will continue to move in its original direction because of its inertia, which causes the outer wing, if it has dihedral, to be presented to the airflow at a greater angle-of-attack, thereby generating increased lift. (*Dihedral* is the term for a wing that is angled up from the wing root toward the wingtip.)
- the inner wing will be somewhat shielded from the airflow by the fuselage and consequently will produce less lift.

Operating the rudder, therefore, causes **yaw followed by roll** and unless the pilot takes corrective action (by preventing unwanted yaw with opposite rudder or by leveling the wings) a spiral descent will result.

When rudder is applied:
- the primary effect is to yaw the airplane; and
- the secondary effect is to roll the airplane.

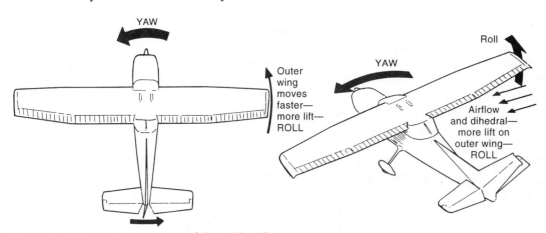

Figure 4b-3. The rudder causes yaw followed by roll.

Pitch and Airspeed

The primary effect of the elevator is to change the pitch attitude. For example, by moving the control column back the nose is raised.

The secondary effect of the elevator is an airspeed change.

Following a pitch change, the inertia of the airplane (its resistance to any change) will cause it to follow the original flight path for a brief period. The airflow will then strike the wings at a greater angle-of-attack and, as a consequence, the wings will generate a different aerodynamic force. Drag will increase, causing the airplane to slow down. Thus, raising the nose with the elevator will lead to an airspeed decrease.

Conversely, by moving the control column forward, the nose is lowered and the airflow will strike the wings at a reduced angle-of-attack, less drag will be created and so the airspeed will increase. Thus, lowering the nose with the elevator will lead to an airspeed increase.

When deflected by moving the control column, **the elevator has:**
- the primary effect of pitching the airplane; and
- the secondary effect of changing the airspeed.

SLOW **FAST**

Figure 4b-4. The secondary effect of the elevator is to change the airspeed.

Note: When the elevator changes the pitch attitude, the airplane will gradually settle at a new airspeed. Whether it climbs, descends or stays at the same level depends upon the **power** setting. The effect of power is discussed shortly—in particular, the coordinated use of power and pitch attitude.

Flying the Maneuver

Established in straight-and-level flight, observe the effects of moving each main flight control individually. Allow time after the initial effect for the further effect to become apparent. The effects should be related to the three airplane axes. Observing the effects of each of the main flight controls is a prelude to learning how to coordinate their use to achieve smooth, comfortable and efficient flight.

Airmanship

Always clear the area before a maneuver. Maintain a good **lookout,** both with respect to the horizon and landmarks, and looking for other aircraft.

    Be very clear at all times about who has control of the airplane. When you have control, exert gentle, but firm and positive pressures on the controls as required.

Airmanship is keeping a good lookout and flying the airplane confidently.

Airwork 4b
The Secondary Effect of Each Main Flight Control

Objective
To observe the secondary (or further) effect of moving each main flight control.

---

1. Roll Causes Yaw—the Secondary Effect of the Ailerons

(a) Establish straight-and-level flight; clear the area and maintain a good lookout.

(b) Remove your feet from the rudder pedals.

(c) Apply the ailerons by moving the control column—*while rolling, there may be adverse yaw in the opposite direction*—and while banked, with the ailerons neutral, the nose will drop (yaw) toward the lower wing (the nose drops into the turn).

Rolling—with possible adverse yaw

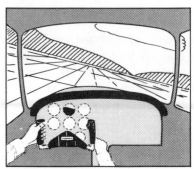

Banked—nose drops into turn

Possible adverse yaw

ROLL .... then .... YAW

2. Yaw Causes Roll—the Secondary Effect of the Rudder

(a) Establish straight-and-level flight; clear the area and maintain a good lookout.

(b) Take your hands off the control column, or hold it neutral.

(c) Apply rudder pressure—*the airplane yaws and then, because of the yaw, rolls in the same direction.*

Left Rudder applied

YAW .... then .... ROLL

> **Note:** The effects seen in steps 1 and 2 will also be the same when the airplane is banked, climbing, and descending.

Continued

---

3. Changing the Pitch Attitude Alters the Airspeed—the Secondary Effect of the Elevator

(a) Establish the airplane in straight-and-level flight; clear the area and maintain a good lookout.

(b) Ease the control column forward—*the nose pitches down and the airspeed increases.*

(c) Ease the control column back—*the nose rises and the airspeed decreases.*

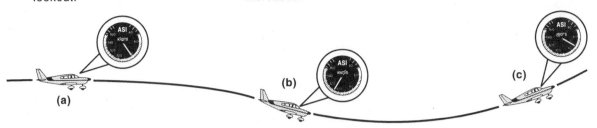

✍ Review 4b

1. Moving each of the three main flight controls causes a primary effect followed by a _____ effect.

   ➢ secondary

2. Rotating the control column to the left sends the left aileron (up/down) and the right aileron (up/down). The airplane will roll to the (left/right), but may show the secondary effect of a slight tendency to yaw to the (left/right)—known as adverse aileron yaw.

   ➢ up, down, left, right

3. Rotating the control column to the right sends the left aileron (up/down) and the right aileron (up/down). The airplane will roll (left/right), but may show the further effect of a slight tendency to yaw to the (left/right)—known as adverse aileron yaw.

   ➢ down, up, right, left

3. Adverse aileron yaw is caused by deflected (ailerons/rudder/elevator).

   ➢ ailerons

4. When the ailerons are neutralized, even when the airplane is banked, the tendency for adverse aileron yaw (ceases/increases).

   ➢ ceases

The Secondary Effect of Each Main Flight Control

5. In a banked turn with the ailerons neutralized, the nose will tend to (drop/rise) by yawing in the direction (of/opposite to) the turn.

   ➢ drop, of

6. Applying left rudder will yaw the nose to the (left/right), and will cause the secondary effect of a slight roll to the (left/right).

   ➢ left, left

7. Applying right rudder will yaw the nose to the (left/right), and will cause the secondary effect of a slight roll to the (left/right).

   ➢ right, right

8. Lowering the nose with the elevator will normally cause the airspeed to (increase/decrease/remain the same).

   ➢ increase

9. Raising the nose with the elevator will normally cause the airspeed to (increase/decrease/remain the same).

   ➢ decrease

10. You can counteract the adverse aileron yaw caused by deflected ailerons by using same-side _____ pressure to keep the coordination ball centered.

    ➢ rudder

The Art of Trimming 4c

Objective

To use the trim to relieve steady control pressures.

Considerations

The Need for Trimming

All training airplanes have an elevator trim that can relieve the pilot of sustained fore and aft pressures on the control column. Some airplanes also have a rudder trim to relieve steady pressures on the rudder pedals.

The trim is used to relieve control pressures in steady conditions of flight, such as straight-and-level, climbing and descending. The trim should generally *not* be altered in transient maneuvers, such as turning.

Using the trimming devices can reduce your workload tremendously, so the effect of trim and how to use it correctly should be clearly understood at an early stage.

Using the trimming devices can decrease your workload tremendously.

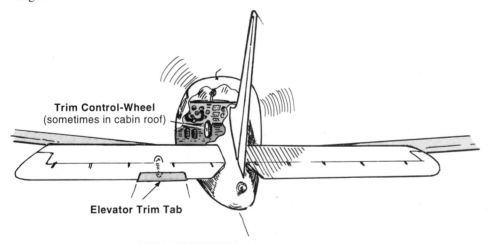

Trim Control-Wheel
(sometimes in cabin roof)

Elevator Trim Tab

Figure 4c-1. An elevator trim tab and trim wheel

Why Is Trim Needed?

The elevator is controlled by fore and aft movement of the control column and is used by the pilot to hold the desired pitch attitude. If this requires a **steady** pressure, then flight becomes quite tiring, making precision flight almost impossible.

Trim can be used to relieve this sustained pressure on the control column and, used precisely, can reduce it to zero, thereby making your task that much easier. Trim is **not** used to alter the attitude of the airplane; it is only used to relieve control column pressure.

Elevator Trim

Elevator trim in most airplanes is achieved by means of a small **trim tab** located on the trailing edge of the elevator. The trim tab is operated by a trim wheel (or handle) in the cockpit. The purpose of the trim tab is to hold the elevator displaced with an aerodynamic force, rather than a steady force that the pilot exerts via the control column.

If the trim tab is deflected downward, the airflow over the upper surface of the elevator speeds up, reducing the static pressure above the elevator. An aerodynamic force now exists to deflect the elevator upward.

If the trim tab is deflected upward, the airflow over the lower surface of the elevator speeds up, reducing the static pressure below the elevator. An aerodynamic force now exists to deflect the elevator downward.

The elevator trim on some aircraft is achieved by applying spring pressure from the trim-wheel to the elevator itself, instead of deflection of a trim tab.

On aircraft with a **stabilator,** moving the trim-wheel applies a bias to the anti-servo tab on its trailing edge.

Trimming Technique

A steady back pressure exerted by the pilot on the control column to hold the elevator up can be relieved by winding the trim wheel back, gradually releasing the pressure on the control column as the trim takes over.

Winding the trim wheel back deflects the trim tab down, reducing the static pressure above it. If the static pressure is sufficiently low for the elevator to remain deflected upward to the same degree, the pilot need not continue to hold steady back pressure on the control column. Flying now becomes less tiring.

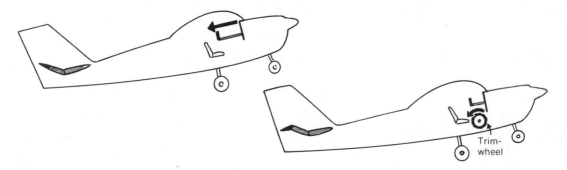

Figure 4c-2. Using the elevator trim to relieve steady pressures on the control column

Conversely, if you are exerting a sustained forward pressure on the control column to hold the desired attitude, wind the trim wheel forward, and gradually release the forward pressure without allowing the pitch attitude to change.

Retrimming

The demands placed upon the elevator change from time to time and so retrimming will be necessary:
- after a **new pitch attitude** is selected;
- after a **power change;**
- after a **configuration change** (for example, alteration of wing flap position);
- after a **change in the position of the center of gravity** (say, as fuel burns off, passengers move, baggage is shifted or parachutists depart).

Whenever you have to exert a sustained pressure on the control column to hold the desired attitude in steady flight, you should trim it off. After significant changes of power and/or attitude (for instance in a go-around), you may find it helpful to trim off the pressure in *two* stages—a rough or **coarse trim** to take the major control pressures off you and then, when the attitude and airspeed have stabilized, a **fine trim.**

Rudder Trim

Some aircraft, as well as an elevator trim, also have a rudder trim, which is useful for removing sustained rudder pressures, for instance in prolonged climbs and descents. The trimming technique is similar—trim the pressure off, but do not allow the airplane to yaw, and keep the coordination ball centered.

Rudder trim can hold the rudder deflected.

Flying the Maneuver

Elevator Trimming

Correct trimming is achieved if you move the trim wheel in a natural sense, gradually releasing the control pressure you were exerting. If you are holding back pressure on the control column, you should wind the trim wheel back, gradually releasing the pressure on the control column so that the pitch attitude does not change.

While you are trimming the airplane, the pitch attitude should not change.

Conversely, if you are holding forward pressure to maintain pitch attitude, you should wind the trim wheel forward until there is no steady pressure required on the control column.

Elevator and Rudder Trimming

In aircraft fitted with a rudder trim:
- first trim the elevator; and
- then trim the rudder—keep the wings level with aileron, and the coordination ball centered with rudder pressure—use the rudder trim to gradually remove this pressure, keeping the ball centered throughout. Do not allow the nose to yaw.

Airmanship

Always clear the area and maintain a good **lookout.**

Airmanship is keeping in trim.

Do not be reluctant to use the trim. If you feel a steady pressure then trim it off, but do not use the trim in transient maneuvers such as turns. Use the trim only to remove steady pressures. Do *not* use the trim to change the attitude of the airplane.

Trimming is an art. As you develop the skill of trimming an airplane, smooth and precise flying becomes much easier.

 Airwork 4c
The Art of Trimming
Objective
To use the trim to relieve steady pressures on the control column.

1. Trimming the Airplane Correctly

To trim the airplane correctly in pitch:

- Hold the desired pitch attitude with pressure on the control column; then
- Without looking, place your hand on the trim wheel and trim (in a natural sense) to relieve pressures so that the desired attitude is held without you exerting any pressure on the control column. If the load is high, trim quickly. As the load reduces, trim more finely. *Gradually, the pressure on the control column can be relaxed.*

This exercise involves use of the pitch trim-wheel or control.

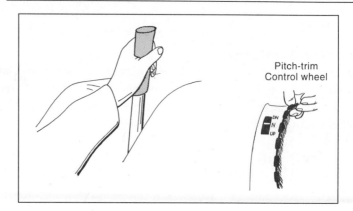

Pitch-trim Control wheel

2. Getting the Feel of Incorrect Trim

(a) To get the feel of incorrect trim, fly straight-and-level holding the desired pitch attitude with elevator control.

(b) Then, without letting the pitch attitude change, gradually wind the trim-wheel forward—*you will need considerable back pressure on the control column to hold the nose up in the level flight attitude.*

(c) Gradually wind the trim-wheel back until the control column back pressure is again reduced to zero.

(d) Repeat the procedure, winding the trim fully back this time, noting the considerable forward pressure required on the control column to maintain the level flight attitude.

Note: This is not a normal procedure. It is done only for you to experience the effect of incorrect trim, which makes flying almost impossible.

3. Common Situations Requiring Retrimming

Practice trim changes by holding a particular pitch attitude and then:

  (i)   adopt a new pitch attitude;
 (ii)   change the power setting, or
(iii)   change the aircraft configuration (lower some flaps).

After each change, hold the pitch attitude constant for a short period (10 or 20 seconds) and allow the airplane to settle into the new flightpath and/or airspeed before retrimming.

If a strong pressure is required on the control column then it is advisable to relieve most of it fairly quickly and then, after the airplane has settled down, trim more finely.

Note: Trim is used to relieve steady control pressure. It is not used to relieve control pressures that are only transient, such as those in a turn. For airplanes with rudder trim installed these exercises can be repeated. The same technique applies—use rudder trim to relieve steady pressures on the rudder pedals which are necessary to keep the coordination ball centered.

> The use of the word ***trim*** throughout the manual implies use of the elevator trim, and also use of the rudder trim, where installed.

✍ Review 4c

1. You can remove steady unwanted pressures on the control column by using elevator _____ .
   ➤ trim

2. While you are trimming the airplane, the pitch attitude (should not/can be allowed to) change.
   ➤ should not

3. Elevator trim should only be used to (remove unwanted pressure/alter the pitch attitude).
   ➤ remove unwanted pressure

4. As well as an elevator trim, some airplanes are also fitted with a _____ trim.
   ➤ rudder

5. If your airplane has a rudder trim, it should be adjusted to trim the airplane in yaw (prior to/after) trimming the airplane in pitch with the elevator trim.
   ➤ after

6. The trim should generally (be/not be) altered in transient maneuvers such as turning.
   ➤ not be

7. The elevator trim in most aircraft uses a (mechanical/aerodynamic) force to relieve the pilot of unwanted steady pressure.
   ➤ aerodynamic

8. You can relieve yourself of steady back pressure on the control column by winding the trim wheel (forward/back).
   ➤ back

9. You can relieve yourself of steady forward pressure on the control column by winding the trim wheel (forward/back).
   ➤ forward

10. As the trim takes effect, you should (gradually release/maintain) the steady pressure on the control column, and (allow the nose to pitch/hold the nose in the desired pitch attitude).
    ➤ gradually release, hold the nose in the desired pitch attitude

The Art of Trimming

11. Your aircraft has a small trim tab on the back of the elevator which you want to check in your pre-flight walk-around. The trim tab going down will hold the elevator (up/down) using a (mechanical/aerodynamic) force. This will tend to hold the nose of the airplane (up/down). You can achieve this by winding the trim wheel (forward/back).
    ➤ up, aerodynamic, up, back

12. Your aircraft has a small trim tab on the back of the elevator which you want to check in your pre-flight walk-around. The trim tab going up will hold the elevator (up/down) using a (mechanical/aerodynamic) force. This will tend to hold the nose of the airplane (up/down). You can achieve this by winding the trim wheel (forward/back).
    ➤ down, aerodynamic, down, forward

13. Normally trimming (is/is not) necessary after a new pitch attitude has been selected with the control column.
    ➤ is

14. Normally trimming (is/is not) necessary after the power has been changed.
    ➤ is

15. Normally trimming (is/is not) necessary after the flap position has been altered.
    ➤ is

16. Normally trimming (is/is not) necessary after a passenger passes a heavy brief case back to be stored behind the rear seat.
    ➤ is

17. Back pressure is usually required in a turn if a constant altitude is to be maintained. It is usual (to/not to) trim in a turn, because it is a transient maneuver.
    ➤ not to

The Pilot's Manual **Flight Training**

The Effect of Airspeed and Slipstream 4d

Objective

To observe the effect of a faster airflow over the control surfaces as a result of either higher airspeed or an increased propeller slipstream.

Considerations

Control Effectiveness

The effectiveness of the three main flight controls, and the rate at which the airplane moves in all three planes (pitch, roll and yaw), depends upon:
* the amount of control deflection; and
* the airflow over the control surface, which can be increased by a higher airspeed and/or an increased slipstream from the propeller.

Increased airflow increases control effectiveness.

Airspeed

The elevator, ailerons and rudder will all experience an increased airflow when the airplane is flying at a higher airspeed. Each one will feel firmer, and only small movements will be required to produce an effective response.

Conversely, at low airspeeds the airflow over each of the flight controls is less and their effectiveness is reduced. The elevator, ailerons and rudder will all feel sloppy, and large movements may be required to produce the desired effect.

All flight controls are more effective at higher airspeeds.

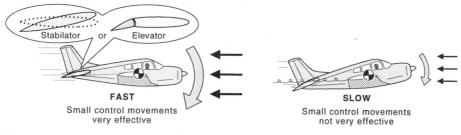

Figure 4d-1. The flight controls are more effective at high airspeeds.

The Propeller Slipstream

The slipstream increases rudder and elevator effectiveness. It flows rearward from the propeller around the airplane in a corkscrew fashion, increasing the airflow over the tail section and making the rudder and elevator more effective.

The ailerons, being outside the slipstream airflow, are not affected by it and will remain sloppy at low airspeeds irrespective of the power setting. The elevator on T-tail airplanes, such as the Piper Tomahawk, may also be well out of the slipstream, and therefore not affected by it to the same extent as the rudder.

The slipstream from the propeller flows back in a corkscrew pattern over the tail section, meeting the vertical stabilizer at an angle-of-attack. This generates a sideways aerodynamic force, which tends to yaw the nose of the airplane.

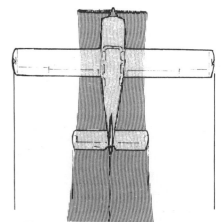

Figure 4d-2. The slipstream can increase elevator and rudder effectiveness.

You can counteract this yawing effect with rudder pressure. (Other propeller effects also cause a yawing tendency, and this is discussed in the next exercise.)

Slipstream effect is most pronounced under conditions of high power and low airspeed—for example, during a climb—when the corkscrew is tighter and its angle-of-attack at the vertical stabilizer is greater.

The direction of the yaw resulting from the slipstream effect depends upon the direction of propeller rotation. If the propeller rotates clockwise when viewed from the cockpit—as is the case for most modern training airplanes—the slipstream passes under the fuselage and strikes the vertical stabilizer on its left-hand side. This causes a tendency to yaw left (in most airplanes). Counteract this tendency, and keep the coordination ball centered, with right rudder pressure.

If the propeller rotates counterclockwise as seen from the cockpit, the slipstream passes under the fuselage and strikes the vertical stabilizer on the right-hand side. The nose will tend to yaw right, and will require left rudder to keep the coordination ball centered.

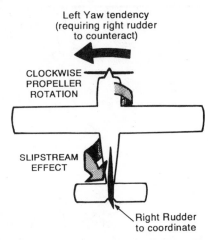

Figure 4d-3. The slipstream tends to yaw the airplane.

Offset Vertical Stabilizer

Many single-engine airplanes are designed with the leading edge of the vertical stabilizer slightly offset to the left. The normal airflow back over the airplane will strike the vertical stabilizer at an angle-of-attack, creating an aerodynamic force that counteracts the slipstream effect. The vertical stabilizer is offset so that the two forces counteract each other at cruise speed with cruise power, therefore requiring little or no rudder pressure on the cruise.

At low airspeed, and/or with high power, the slipstream effect wins out and tries to yaw the airplane nose-left, therefore right rudder pressure is required at low airspeed to keep the nose from yawing and the coordination ball centered.

At very high airspeed and/or with little power, say in a dive, the aerodynamic force from the offset vertical stabilizer wins out and tries to yaw the airplane nose-right—you can counteract this with left rudder pressure to keep the coordination ball centered.

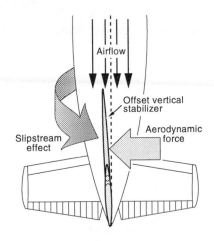

Figure 4d-4. An offset vertical stabilizer counteracts the slipstream effect in the cruise.

Flying the Maneuver

To observe the effect of airspeed on the flight controls, first establish a glide (to eliminate the slipstream effect) at a high airspeed and operate each of the three main flight controls. Each one will feel firm and be effective.

Then raise the nose to glide at a lower airspeed, and operate each of the three main flight controls. Each will feel sloppy and less effective than before.

Next apply climb power, maintaining the same low airspeed by raising the nose. This will introduce a strong slipstream effect, but will keep the airspeed effect constant. The elevator and the rudder, being in the slipstream, will feel firm and effective. The ailerons, which are outside the slipstream, will still feel sloppy and less effective.

Airmanship

Maintain a high visual awareness. Keep a good **lookout** for other traffic, and remain aware of the position of the airplane and the direction to be flown back to the airport.

Exert firm, positive, but smooth control over the airplane. Airspeed and power changes give you good practice in control coordination.

Airmanship is knowing where you are.

Airwork 4d
The Effect of Airspeed and Slipstream

Objective

To observe the effect of increased airflow over each of the main flight control surfaces as a result of:
- *airspeed; and*
- *slipstream.*

 Straight-and-Level ——— **(a)**

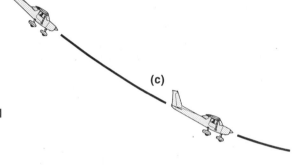

1. The Effect of Airspeed

(a) Begin a glide:
- Mixture—RICH.
- Throttle—CLOSED (carburetor heat—ON),
  to remove the effect of the slipstream.

(b) Glide at a high airspeed and operate each flight control:
- Elevator, ailerons, rudder each feel firm and resistant to movement.
- Small movements of each control produce a strong response.

(c) Glide at a low airspeed:
- Each of the primary controls feels sloppy.
- Large control deflections are easy to make against little resistance.
- The airplane is less responsive to movements of the controls and so large deflections may be required to produce the required response.

2. The Effect of Slipstream

Continuing directly on from sequence 1, above, with the airplane in a glide at low airspeed.

(d) Apply climb power (carb heat—COLD) and raise the pitch attitude to maintain same low airspeed.
- The ailerons, being outside the slipstream, still feel sloppy—*large aileron control movements are necessary to roll the airplane.*
- The elevator and rudder are firmer and more effective due to the higher airflow over them from the propeller slipstream.

- At the low airspeed and high climb power setting (and, therefore, strong slipstream)—*the airplane is responsive in pitch and yaw, but not in roll.*

The Effect of Airspeed and Slipstream

1. The effect of moving a flight control surface is greater with (greater/less) movement of the control.

    ➤ greater

2. The effect of moving a flight control surface is greater if the speed of the airflow over the surface is (greater/less).

    ➤ greater

3. The speed of airflow over the flight control surfaces is greater at (higher/lower) airspeeds.

    ➤ higher

4. With an increase in airspeed, which of the following flight controls feel firmer and are more effective: elevator, ailerons or rudder?

    ➤ all

5. When power is increased, the amount of air propelled rearward by the propeller is (greater/less).

    ➤ greater

6. The air propelled rearward by the propeller is called the propeller _____ .

    ➤ slipstream

7. The propeller slipstream flows back over the (wingtips/tail section/wingtips and tail section).

    ➤ tail section

8. With an increase in power while the airspeed is low, say in a steep climb, which of the following flight controls feel firmer and are more effective: elevator, ailerons, rudder?

    ➤ elevator, rudder (ailerons feel sloppy)

9. The elevator on T-tail aircraft may be (more/less) affected by the propeller slipstream than the rudder.

    ➤ less

10. The propeller slipstream flows rearward in a (corkscrew/straight) fashion.

    ➤ corkscrew

11. In conventional aircraft, the propeller rotates (clockwise/counterclockwise) as seen from the cockpit, and so the slipstream impinges on the (left/right) side of the vertical stabilizer. This causes a tendency for the nose to yaw (left/right).

    ➤ clockwise, left, left

12. To counteract the yawing effect of the propeller slipstream, so that little or no rudder pressure is required in cruising flight, the aircraft design may incorporate an _____ vertical stabilizer.

    ➤ offset

13. It is good airmanship to always maintain a good _____ for other aircraft.

    ➤ lookout

14. Another aspect of airmanship is always knowing where you are. (true/false)

    ➤ true

The Effects of Making Power Changes 4e

Objective

To observe the effects of applying and removing power, then to counteract any undesirable pitch/yaw tendencies resulting from power changes.

Considerations

Moving the throttle in, or forward—in other words, opening it—increases the power; this is indicated by increased rpm on the tachometer. This causes the propeller to rotate faster, generating increased thrust and a stronger slipstream. Pulling the throttle out or back (closing it) reduces power.

Throttle movements, to both increase and decrease power, should be smooth and not too fast.

Reducing Power

Most airplanes are designed so that, if power from the engine is lost, the airplane will automatically pitch nose-down and assume the glide attitude without action being taken by the pilot. This is a safety feature designed into the airplane to ensure that flying speed is maintained in case of engine failure.

Reducing power causes a pitch-down tendency.

The nose tends to drop because:
- the reduced slipstream over the horizontal stabilizer reduces the downward aerodynamic force generated by it; and
- the thrust–drag "couple" of forces, which causes a nose-up tendency, is reduced (see note which follows).

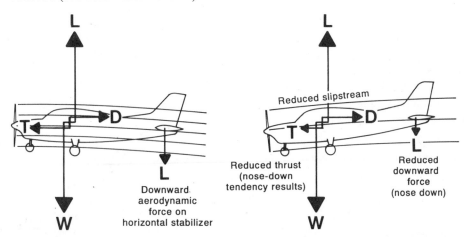

Figure 4e-1. Decreasing power causes a nose-down tendency—you can oppose this with elevator.

Note: A *couple* is two parallel opposing forces not acting through the same point, and so producing a rotating effect. Thrust and drag form a couple that tries to rotate most airplanes **nose-up** about the center of gravity; lift and weight form another couple that tries to rotate most airplanes **nose-down** about the center of gravity. The rotating effects are usually approximately equal and opposite, canceling each other out with the help of a small downward balancing force produced by the horizontal stabilizer. In normal flight, when the power is reduced with the throttle, the nose tends to pitch down—this can be counteracted with back pressure on the control column if you do not want the nose to drop.

Adding Power

When adding power, the nose will tend to pitch up because of:

- the stronger slipstream over the horizontal stabilizer increasing its downward aerodynamic force; and
- a stronger thrust–drag nose-up couple.

This can be counteracted with forward pressure on the control column.

Increasing power causes a pitch-up tendency.

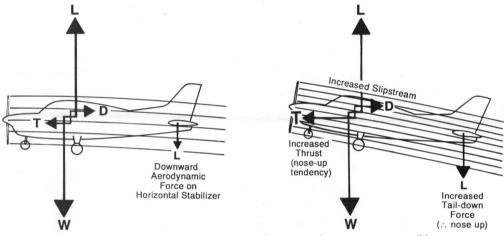

Figure 4e-2. Increasing power causes a nose-up tendency—again, you can oppose this by using elevator control.

Yawing

Adding power increases the slipstream effect on the vertical stabilizer, causing the nose to yaw to the left (for propellers rotating clockwise when viewed from the cockpit). This yawing tendency can be counteracted with right rudder pressure to keep the airplane coordinated (ball centered) and flying straight.

Conversely, **reducing power** reduces the slipstream effect on the vertical stabilizer, causing a yawing tendency in the other direction, which can also be counteracted with opposite rudder. It is very important for comfortable and efficient flight that you keep the coordination ball centered.

In prolonged operations with high or low power, holding the required rudder pressure to keep the coordination ball centered can become tedious.

Some aircraft are fitted with **rudder trim**, which can be used to trim off this steady pressure on the rudder pedals, for instance during steady climbs and descents.

Changing power also causes a yawing tendency.

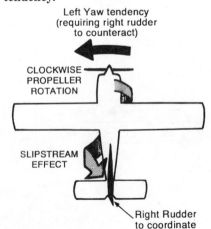

Figure 4e-3. Counteract the yawing tendency from the slipstream by using the rudder pressure.

Other Propeller Effects

The propeller rotating clockwise causes a **torque reaction** that tries to rotate the airplane counterclockwise and roll it to the left. This is easily controlled with the ailerons and rudder.

Two effects that are noticeable when flying at high angles-of-attack are **gyroscopic precession** and **P-effect** (also known as *asymmetric blade effect*). High angles-of-attack occur when flying at low airspeeds, and also early in the takeoff run of taildraggers while their tail is still on the ground.

Other propeller effects add to the yawing tendency.

The Mixture

Under certain conditions, the fuel/air mixture can be leaned using the mixture control. Opening the throttle to high power with the mixture lean can damage the engine, so have the mixture RICH prior to any significant power changes.

Set the mixture to RICH for significant power changes.

Carburetor Ice

When fuel is vaporized and mixed with air in the carburetor, the temperature of the resulting fuel/air is reduced. If any **moisture** is present in the air, ice can form in the carburetor, even if the outside air temperature is quite high (up to 70°F or even higher). Carburetor ice can restrict, or even totally block, the induction airflow to the engine cylinders and cause engine failure. Early indications of carburetor ice forming are **reducing rpm** followed by **rough running**.

When closing the throttle, protect yourself against carburetor ice.

The risk of carburetor ice forming is greatest at low power and so, if you intend to keep the throttle closed for long periods, first apply full carburetor heat.

Apply full carburetor heat at low power settings.

Flying the Maneuver

The Throttle

The engine has moving parts which should not be subjected to abrupt changes in their rate of movement, so always operate the throttle smoothly. Movement from idle power to full power should take approximately the same time as to count *"1–2–3"*. This also applies when closing the throttle.

Operate the throttle smoothly.

Pitch/Yaw

Increasing power will cause the nose of the airplane to rise and yaw left (for a standard clockwise-rotating propeller). This can be counteracted with:
- forward pressure on the control column to hold the desired attitude; and
- right rudder pressure to prevent the unwanted yaw and keep the ball centered.
- Control pressures can then be trimmed off.

Counteract any pitch/yaw tendency with elevator and rudder control.

Decreasing power will cause the nose of the airplane to drop and yaw right. This unwanted pitch/yaw tendency can be counteracted with:
- back pressure on the control column to maintain the desired attitude; and
- left rudder pressure to balance the unwanted yaw.
- Again, control pressures can then be trimmed off.

Airmanship

Maintain a high visual awareness. **Look out** for other aircraft and note landmarks so that you do not get lost. Make full use of the natural horizon when holding the desired pitch and bank attitude.

Have the mixture control in FULL RICH prior to any significant power changes. When about to reduce power, consider whether you need protection from carburetor ice. If so (and this is usually the case when reducing the power to idle), apply full carburetor heat before closing the throttle.

When changing power, consider the engine. It has lots of reciprocating and rotating parts moving at high speeds and any sudden shock to the system is not good for it. Move the throttle smoothly and handle the engine with care. Monitor the engine gauges, especially during the climb, when high power is set and there is reduced cooling because of the lower airspeed.

Handle the airplane smoothly, but firmly. Anticipate the effect of power changes—be prepared to hold the desired pitch attitude and prevent unwanted yaw with coordinated use of the controls.

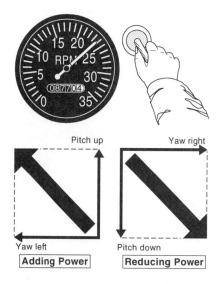

Figure 4e-4. Pitch/yaw tendencies with power changes

Airmanship is taking care of the airplane.

Airwork 4e
The Effects of Making Power Changes

Objectives
To observe the effect of changing power, and counteract undesirable tendencies resulting from power changes.

1. The Effect of Changing Power

(a) Trim the airplane to cruise straight-and-level, then remove your hands from the control column and your feet from the rudder pedals.

(b) Smoothly open the throttle to full power:
- *The nose pitches up; and*
- *Yaws.**

(c) Close the throttle smoothly:
- *The nose pitches down; and*
- *Yaws.***

*Left in most training airplanes

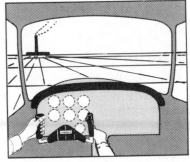

**Right in most training airplanes

2. The Correct Pilot Response when Changing Power

(a) When increasing power:
- Hold the desired nose attitude with elevator (forward pressure).
- Coordinate with rudder pressure.
- Trim.

(b) When reducing power:
- Hold the desired nose attitude with elevator (back pressure).
- Coordinate with rudder pressure.
- Trim.

A good means of practicing this process is to maintain the straight-and-level pitch attitude with the nose on a reference point on the horizon. Then, move the throttle smoothly from idle to full power and back again, anticipating the changes and holding the pitch attitude constant and preventing the unwanted yaw.

Note: Increasing airspeed (by lowering the nose) will cause an increase in engine rpm without any throttle movement.

 # Review 4e

The Effects of Making Power Changes

1. You (can/cannot) counteract the pitching and yawing tendencies caused by power changes by using elevator and rudder control.

   ➤ can

2. Adding power significantly will tend to (raise/lower) the nose and yaw it (left/right). This can be counteracted by (forward/back) pressure on the control column and (left/right) rudder pressure.

   ➤ raise, left, forward, right

3. Reducing power significantly will tend to (raise/lower) the nose and yaw it (left/right). This tendency when reducing power can be counteracted by (forward/back) pressure on the control column and (left/right) rudder.

   ➤ lower, right, back, left

4. Adding power, you will probably need to hold the nose (up/down) and apply (left/right) rudder pressure; reducing power will be (the same/opposite).

   ➤ down, right, opposite

The Effect of Using Flaps 4f

Objective

To observe the effect of altering the flap position and to control the airplane smoothly while you are changing the flap setting.

Considerations

The flaps are attached to the inboard trailing edge of each wing. They are operated from the cockpit—in some airplanes electrically by a switch and, in others, mechanically by a lever. They operate symmetrically on each wing, and extend downward only.

Flaps move symmetrically.

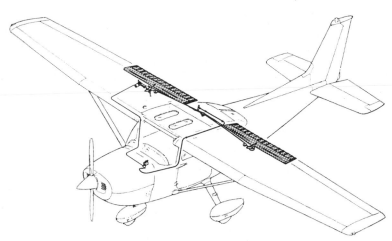

Figure 4f-1. Wing flap installation in a Cessna 172

The flaps alter the shape of the wings and the airflow around them. This changes the lifting ability of the wings, altering both the lift and drag generated. In a sense, flaps create new wings. They are used to:

Flaps increase the lifting ability of the wings by changing its shape.

- **generate the required lift at a lower speed** (allowing safe flight at low airspeeds as well as reducing takeoff and landing distances);
- **increase drag** and steepen the descent path on approach to land; and
- **improve the forward vision,** as a result of the lower nose attitude required.

The flaps may be used to serve various purposes simultaneously—for example, to steepen the descent path while at the same time allowing better forward vision and safe flight at a lower airspeed.

As the flaps are lowered the changes in lift and drag will cause a pitching tendency. This will result in the airplane ballooning, unless counteracted with pressure on the control column.

Conversely, when the flaps are raised, there will be a pitching tendency in the opposite direction and a tendency to sink.

When the attitude and power changes are complete, and the airspeed has stabilized at the desired value, these pressures can be trimmed off. In general, a **lower pitch attitude** is required to achieve the same airspeed when flaps are lowered compared to when the wings are clean, that is, flaps retracted.

A lower pitch attitude is required as flaps are lowered.

FLAPPED   Trailing-edge flaps extended, and the pitch attitude changed   **CLEAN**

Figure 4f-2. Flaps require a lower nose attitude.

The initial stages of flap extension are sometimes called *lift flaps* because the lifting ability of the wing is increased considerably, with only a small amount of extra drag created. Flaps allow the required lift to be generated at a lower speed—using a small flap setting for takeoff will enable the airplane to become airborne sooner, after a shorter takeoff ground run. A large flap setting is **never** used for takeoff because of the drag (air resistance) they cause.

The larger flap settings are sometimes called *drag flaps,* because they cause a marked increase in drag for only a small improvement in lifting ability. If the airspeed is to be maintained, the increased drag must be balanced by either additional thrust or a greater component of the weight force acting along the flight path, achieved by steepening the descent.

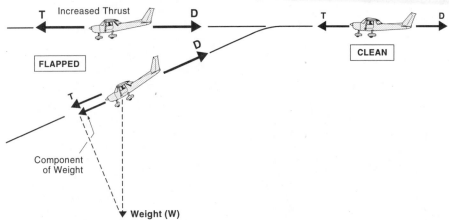

Figure 4f-3. Flaps require increased power or a steeper flight path if the airspeed is to be maintained.

Note: If additional thrust is applied, the increased slipstream over the tail will increase the rudder and elevator effectiveness.

The Flap Operating Speed Range

The flap operating range is shown on the airspeed indicator as a **white arc**.

Before lowering the flaps, ensure that the airspeed is less than the maximum speed allowed for flap extension, V_{FE}, to avoid overstressing the structure. This speed is specified in the Pilot's Operating Handbook and is shown on the airspeed indicator as the high speed end of the white arc.

Two straight-and-level stalling speeds (at maximum aircraft weight) are available on the airspeed indicator:

- V_{S0} with full flaps—the low-speed end of the white band;
- V_{S1} with a clean wing—the low-speed end of the green band.

They mark the approximate minimum flying speeds at which the airplane is capable of straight-and-level flight in each of these configurations. V_{S0} can be thought of as stall speed with flaps *OUT;* and V_{S1} as with flaps *IN.*

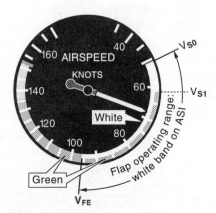

Figure 4f-4. The flap operating range on the airspeed indicator (ASI)

Flying the Maneuver

Raising or lowering large amounts of flaps in flight may cause large changes in pitch attitude, and in the trim required, so it is preferable to operate the flaps in stages, and to retrim after each selection.

Another reason to operate the flaps in stages, rather than all at the one time, is to allow for the (remote) possibility of a mechanical failure causing the flaps to move asymmetrically, which would give the airplane a strong rolling tendency.

Small changes would mean any asymmetry would (most likely) be small and give you a better chance of retaining control.

To operate the flaps:
- lower (or raise) one stage at a time;
- hold the desired pitch attitude with elevator and make any necessary power changes; and then
- trim off the pressure on the control column.

Move flaps in stages, and retrim.

Airmanship

Do not exceed the maximum flaps-extended speed (V_{FE}) with any setting of flaps extended and do not raise the flaps with the airspeed below the flaps-up stalling speed (V_{S1}).

Operate the flaps smoothly, and in small stages, holding the desired nose attitude with the control column, and then trimming.

Airmanship is operating the airplane within its limitations.

Airwork 4f
The Effect of Using Flaps

Objectives

1. To observe the effect of altering flap position.
2. To control the airplane smoothly while you change the flap setting.

---

1. Changing Flap Position Causes Pitch Change

(a) With the wing clean (flaps up), establish straight-and-level flight.

(b) Reduce the airspeed to within the flap operating range (white arc on ASI) and retrim; (higher nose attitude required to maintain altitude as the airspeed is reduced.)

(c) To illustrate the pitching tendency when extending the flaps, remove your hands from the control column (although normally you never do this).

Extend the flaps in stages (using a firm, steady movement if the flaps are manually operated).

Note the pitching tendency.

Then use the control column to place the nose in the desired altitude, and trim off any steady pressure.

(d) To illustrate the pitching tendency when retracting the flaps, once again temporarily remove your hands from the control column.

Retract the flaps fully in one selection (an incorrect procedure not used in normal operations).

Note the effect.

(There will most likely be a strong pitching tendency, with an altitude loss.)

Re-establish straight-and-level flight and retrim.

Note: In normal flap operations you will control any unwanted pitching tendency when the flap setting is changed with pressure on the control column.

---

2. The Flaps Increase Lifting Ability and Drag

(a) Fly straight-and-level; wings clean (flaps up), airspeed below V$_{FE}$ (high-speed end of the white ASI arc). Leave the power constant throughout the operation.

(b) Extend the first stage of flaps, holding the pitch attitude constant—*observe that the airplane gains some altitude (due to the wing's increased lifting ability), and slows down (due to the increased drag).*

(c) Lower the nose to maintain altitude and retrim—*note the lower nose position (improved vision) and the lower airspeed.*

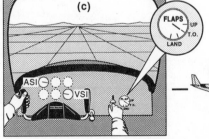

(d) Progressively extend the next stages of flaps and maintain altitude by lowering the nose; retrim after each flap selection—*note the lower airspeed as the extra drag slows the airplane.*

(e) Retract the flaps in stages and maintain altitude by raising the nose; retrim after each selection—*note the higher airspeed resulting from the reduced drag.*

---

3. Flaps Steepen the Descent Path

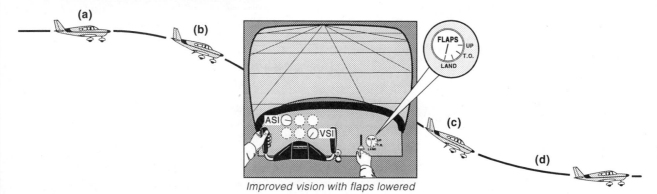

Improved vision with flaps lowered

(a) Fly straight-and-level with wings clean at a constant airspeed below V$_{FE}$. Again, leave the power constant throughout the maneuver.

(b) Extend the first stage of flaps, maintaining airspeed by holding a lower pitch attitude.

The airplane descends.

Trim.

(c) Repeat for each stage of flaps, until full flaps are extended.

*Observe:
the lower nose attitude required to maintain a constant airspeed;
the improved forward visibility; and
the increased rate of descent.*

This is similar to an approach to land.

(d) Raise the flaps in stages, retrimming after each selection.

Resume straight-and-level flight.

4. Using Flaps to Allow Safe Flight and Improve Forward Vision

(a) Establish straight-and-level flight at a speed less than V$_{FE}$, but within the green arc.

(b) Extend the flaps in stages, retrimming after each selection; maintain airspeed with elevator and altitude with power—*note the lower nose position and better forward vision flying straight-and-level with full flaps extended.*

(c) Reduce airspeed to the desired figure; maintain altitude with power—*observe that the airplane can fly quite comfortably at lower airspeeds with flaps extended compared to when the wing is clean.*

(d) Increase speed (by applying power) and retract the flaps in stages, retrimming after each selection.

Do not raise the final stage until you are above the clean stalling speed (low-speed end of green ASI arc).

(a) (b) (c) (d)

Review 4f

1. Wing flaps operate (symmetrically/
    asymmetrically), which is (like/unlike) the
    ailerons.

    ≫ symmetrically, unlike

2. The flaps extend (downward/upward).

    ≫ downward

3. Extending the flaps (increases/reduces/does not
    affect) the lifting ability of the wing.

    ≫ increases

4. Extending the flaps allows (faster/slower) flight.

    ≫ slower

5. A small stage of flaps is often used for takeoff
    because it increases the lifting ability of the wing,
    and gives a (small/large) increase in drag.

    ≫ small

6. Full flaps creates (little/a lot of) drag, and can be
    used to (steepen/flatten) a descent.

    ≫ a lot of, steepen

7. When the flaps are extended, the nose attitude of
    the airplane usually has to be (lower/higher) if
    airspeed is to be maintained. This provides
    (better/worse) forward and downward vision.

    ≫ lower, better

8. Full flaps are usually extended on approach to
    land because they allow a (steeper/flatter)
    approach path at a (higher/lower) airspeed, with
    (better/worse/the same) forward vision, and
    (shorter/longer) landing distances.

    ≫ steeper, lower, better, shorter

9. The flap operating range is shown on the airspeed
    indicator as a (white/green/yellow/red) band, with
    the full-flap stalling speed defining the (low-speed/
    high-speed) end of the band.

    ≫ white, low-speed

The Effect of Using the Flaps

10. The stalling speed with full flaps extended is
    called (V_X/V_Y/V_{S0}/V_{S1}) and is shown as the
    (high-speed/low-speed) end of the (white/green)
    arc on the airspeed indicator.

    ≫ V_{S0}, low-speed, white

11. It is a good technique to operate the flaps in (small
    stages/one large step), and to trim unwanted
    control pressure off (after each stage/only when
    full flaps are extended).

    ≫ small stages, after each stage

12. The initial stages of flaps often used for takeoff
    are referred to sometimes as (lift/drag) flaps.

    ≫ lift flaps

13. The larger stages of flaps that are used for landing
    are referred to sometimes as (lift/drag) flaps.

    ≫ drag flaps

14. It (is/is not) permitted to exceed the maximum
    flaps-extended speed, V_{FE}, with any flaps down.

    ≫ is not

15. Do not raise the flaps if the airspeed is
    (above/below) the clean stall speed, which is the
    (high/low) speed end of the (white/green) band on
    the airspeed indicator.

    ≫ below, low, green

16. Airmanship means (always/sometimes) operating
    the airplane within its limitations.

    ≫ always

Cockpit Controls 4g

Part (i)
Engine Controls:
The Throttle and Carburetor Heat

Objective

To operate the throttle and the carburetor heat control correctly.

Considerations

The Throttle

The throttle knob in the cockpit is connected to the carburetor, and regulates the amount of fuel/air mixture supplied to the engine. Power is increased by moving the throttle forward, and decreased by moving it back. In fixed-pitch propeller airplanes, a power increase is indicated by an rpm increase on the tachometer.

The throttle controls engine power output.

To achieve a good response from the engine, you should **move the throttle slowly,** with movement from idle to full throttle taking about the same time as to count slowly *"one–two–three"*. Moving it abruptly or roughly will **not** achieve a faster engine response, in fact the response may be poorer. The best throttle-handling technique is to move it slowly initially, and then increase the rate of movement until you have the desired power.

You should keep your hand on the throttle during critical maneuvers like takeoff and landing, but at other times you need not. Undesired creeping of the throttle, which can occur with aircraft vibration, may be prevented by lightly tightening the friction lock.

Keep your hand on the throttle during critical maneuvers.

Note: More advanced airplanes have a controllable-pitch propeller, rather than a fixed-pitch propeller. In these airplanes, there will be a propeller control knob (or pitch knob) situated beside the throttle.

Carburetor Heat

Vaporization of the fuel causes cooling of the fuel/air mixture in the carburetor, which may reduce the temperature to below freezing. If the air is sufficiently moist, ice may form in the induction system, partially or completely blocking the flow of fuel/air to the cylinders. Even very warm outside air (up to 20°C or 70°F, and even higher) may be cooled to below freezing in the carburetor, and in humid conditions carburetor ice will form.

Carburetor heat is used to prevent or remove ice that can form in the carburetor under certain conditions.

Indications of Carburetor Ice

Carburetor ice can occur at outside air temperatures of +20°C or more and affects engine power adversely, the noticeable effects including:

• a drop in rpm;
• rough running; and
• possible engine stoppage.

How Carburetor Heat Works

Heating the induction air before it enters the carburetor will prevent the formation of ice, and will melt any ice that has formed.

Most modern aircraft have a carburetor heat system that heats the induction air by ducting it close to the hot exhaust system, or obtains the induction air from around the exhaust system. The carburetor heat control, a knob situated near the throttle, is used to direct this hot induction air into the carburetor.

Being less dense than cold air, hot air lowers the mass of each fuel/air charge burned in the cylinders, reducing the maximum power available from the engine. Consequently, as carburetor heat is applied, the engine rpm will drop.

If ice is present, the rpm will rise (following the initial drop) as the ice is melted by the warm air.

As a precaution against the formation of carburetor ice when operating at low rpm, such as in a prolonged descent, it is usual to apply FULL HOT (or ON) carburetor heat prior to closing the throttle. This provides at least a brief period of strong hot air flow through the carburetor before the throttle is closed. Closing the throttle reduces the airflow, increases the cooling effect and increases the chance of ice forming in the carburetor.

Carburetor ice can form quickly, so it is better to have the heat before removing the power, rather than after.

The carburetor heat control is returned to FULL COLD (or OFF) when higher power is required (and if protection from carburetor ice is no longer required).

Carburetor heat can prevent or remove carburetor ice.

Taxiing

Usually taxi with carburetor heat OFF. In many airplanes, the hot air for carburetor heat is supplied from around the engine exhaust and is unfiltered (unlike the normal cold air, which is filtered in the engine air intake). For this reason, it is usual to taxi with the carburetor heat control in the FULL COLD position, to avoid introducing dust and grit into the engine, as this could seriously affect engine life.

As carburetor hot air is not filtered, taxi with carburetor heat OFF.

Airwork 4g, Part (i)
Use of Carburetor Heat

Objective
To learn the correct use of the throttle and carburetor heat.

---

1. If Carburetor Icing Is Suspected (Rough Running and/or RPM Decay)

- Apply FULL carburetor heat by pulling the carb heat control fully out;
- Note the drop in rpm (less dense air entering the engine cylinders).

- If carburetor icing was present and has been melted, a slight rise in rpm will occur following the initial drop.
- Return the carb heat control to FULL COLD. Note the rpm rise (denser air is now entering the cylinders).

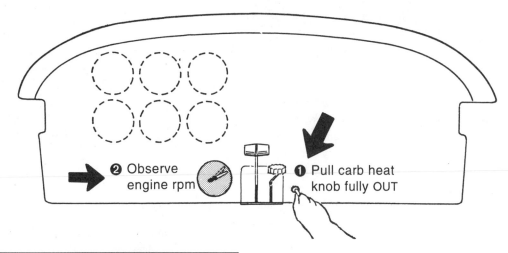

❷ Observe engine rpm   ❶ Pull carb heat knob fully OUT

2. Using Carburetor Heat as a Precaution

(Normal procedure on descent and approach to land.)

(a) When reducing power to idle:
- Select carb heat to FULL HOT (or ON).
- Throttle CLOSED.

(b) When about to increase power:
- Carb heat to FULL COLD (or OFF)—if hot air to the carburetor is no longer required.
- Apply power with the throttle, as required. Practice moving the throttle from idle to full power.

> **Note:** Your flight training organization's procedure for using carburetor heat as a precaution may differ from that given above, in which case you should follow it. (There may be variation in the order of operating the throttle and carburetor heat when both reducing and increasing power, perhaps due to manufacturer's recommendations.)
>
> If in doubt as to the correct procedure to follow, consult your flight instructor.

Part (ii)
Engine Controls:
The Mixture Control

Objective

To operate the mixture control correctly.

Considerations & Operation

The mixture control is usually a red knob situated near the throttle. Its two functions are:
- to lean the mixture in flight and achieve optimum fuel usage; and
- to cut off fuel to the carburetor and stop the engine.

Air density decreases with increasing altitude. This results in a lower weight of air being mixed with the same weight of fuel in the carburetor as an airplane climbs. Thus, the fuel/air mixture becomes richer as altitude is gained, and an increasing amount of fuel will remain unburned because of the reduced air available for the combustion process. This fuel is wasted in the exhaust.

The mixture is normally leaned out on the cruise to improve fuel economy and optimize range.

To avoid wasting fuel, and to get the maximum range out of a tank of fuel, it is normal to lean the mixture during cruise by moving the mixture control partially out—this reduces the amount of fuel available for mixing with the air in the carburetor.

As the fuel/air mixture is leaned and returns to its optimum value, the engine rpm will show a slight increase. Leaning the mixture past the optimum ratio will cause the rpm to fall, at which point the mixture control should be moved back in slightly on the rich side of optimum.

It is preferable to operate an engine slightly on the rich side, rather than too lean (when higher temperatures, and even detonation, may occur, causing damage to the engine). The excess fuel helps cool the cylinders, and little power is lost if the mixture is only slightly over-rich*.

It is preferable to operate an engine slightly on the rich side.

The mixture control should be left in the FULL RICH position (fully in) during climbs and descents. Furthermore, the Pilot's Operating Handbooks for many training aircraft recommend that leaning should only be used above a certain minimum altitude, and when the engine power is less than 75% maximum continuous power.

The mixture control should be fully in (RICH) for climb and descent.

If you have to apply carburetor heat for a long period on the cruise, the hotter and less dense air mixing with the same amount of fuel will result in a richer mixture. You should then re-lean the mixture for optimum fuel usage.

Moving the mixture control fully out to the IDLE CUTOFF position cuts off fuel flow within the carburetor completely. This is the safest way of shutting an engine down, since there will be no fuel left in the cylinders or induction manifold.

Shut the engine down by moving the mixture control to IDLE CUTOFF.

*Note: Range figures published by the manufacturer in the Pilot's Operating Handbook assume that you will be cruising with the mixture correctly leaned. If you forget to lean, you will not achieve the published range figures.

Airwork 4g, Part (ii)
Use of the Mixture Control

Objective
To operate the mixture control (red knob) correctly.

---

1. To Lean the Mixture at Altitude

(for improved range and fuel economy)

- Set the desired engine rpm (with the throttle).
- Slowly move the (red) mixture control knob OUT toward the lean position.
- Observe the rpm rise. If the rpm does not rise, return the mixture to FULL RICH.
- Continue moving the mixture control OUT until a slight drop in rpm occurs.

- Move the mixture control knob IN slightly to restore maximum rpm. Then move the mixture control slightly further in so that the mixture is slightly on the rich side (too-rich is preferable to too-lean), where the rpm will be slightly lower than the peak value.

Note: Whenever the power setting or cruise level is changed, or carburetor heat is applied for a prolonged period, repeat the above procedure.

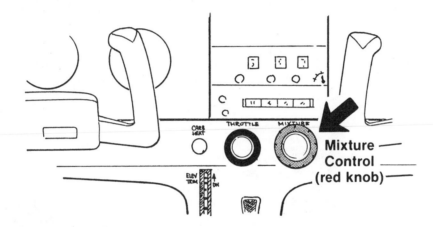

2. On Descent

Prior to beginning descent and reducing power:
- Select mixture to FULL RICH (fully in).

3. After Landing

To stop the engine:

- Set 1,000 rpm (or as recommended).
- Move the mixture control to IDLE CUTOFF by pulling it all the way out (this starves the engine of fuel).

- Complete other actions as per the procedure in your Pilot's Operating Handbook. Complete the checklist. It is good airmanship to remove the ignition key when leaving the aircraft.

Part (iii)
Using the Radio

Most airplanes are equipped with at least one high quality radio communications set which operates in the very high frequency (VHF) radio band. Such a set, which is known as a **VHF-COM,** is both a transmitter and a receiver (referred to as a *transceiver),* and is quite simple to operate. VHF transmissions provide high quality line-of-sight communications, and are the usual form of voice communications used in aviation.

Power is supplied to the radios via an electrical master switch, and possibly a separate avionics power switch. Many VHF-COM sets are combined in the same unit as a VHF radio navigation receiver—the whole unit being called a COM/NAV or **NAV/COM.** It is usual for the COM set to be on the left-hand side.

Connected to the radio are:
- a microphone for transmitting;
- speakers and/or headphones for reception; and
- an audio control panel (in some aircraft) to connect the radio set to the microphone and the speaker or headphones.

The VHF-COM provides good line-of-sight voice communications.

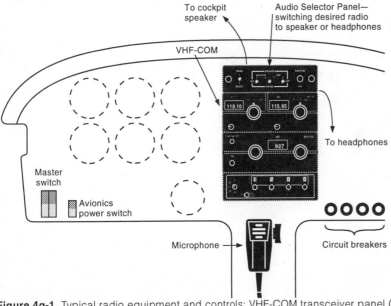

Figure 4g-1. Typical radio equipment and controls; VHF-COM transceiver panel (right).

Switching on the VHF-COM

1. Check the master switch is ON (and avionics power switch ON , if applicable).

2. Switch the radio ON.

3. Select the desired frequency.

4. Select audio for the appropriate radio set (speaker or headphones).

5. Adjust the volume to desired level, and adjust the squelch control (if the squelch is manually operated in your equipment) to cut out undesired background noise.

6. Check that the microphone is plugged in correctly.

7. Select the transmitter to the desired radio—for example, VHF No. 1.

Squelch

The function of squelch is to eliminate interference and unwanted weak signals that cause background noise (static or hash). Noise makes it difficult to hear the desired stronger signals. Some squelch controls are automatic and others are manual. Your flight instructor will advise you on your particular set.

To adjust the squelch manually:

- turn the squelch control up high (clockwise) until background noise or hash is audible; then
- rotate the squelch knob counterclockwise until the noise just disappears, or is at least at an acceptably low level. This suppresses the unwanted noise from weak signals, allowing only the strong signals to be heard.

Note: Turning the squelch down may also cut out the signal that you want to hear as well as the unwanted noise if you are not careful—**do not apply too much squelch.**

Eliminate unwanted hash with the squelch control.

Troubleshooting

Occasionally you may find that the set is not functioning correctly. If so then follow a simple fault-finding procedure:

1. Check correct switching, as specified above in *Switching on the VHF-COM;*
2. Check the circuit breakers or fuses;
3. Check that the squelch is not turned down (a common fault).

Hopefully the radio will now work. If not, speak with your flight instructor or a mechanic. If in flight, there are certain procedures to follow (which you will learn about later) including using your **transponder,** and also observing **light signals** from a control tower.

Before Transmitting

- Decide what you want to say; and
- listen on the frequency to be used, and do not interrupt other transmissions.

Who to Talk to

At a tower-controlled airport you will talk to air traffic controllers on a "ground" frequency (for example, "Miami Ground") when you are on the ramp and taxiways, or on the tower frequency ("Miami Tower") when you are on or about to enter the runway, and in flight. The relevant frequencies are found on charts and in the Airport/Facility Directory (A/FD), although you will become familiar with your local frequencies quickly.

At very busy controlled airports, there may also be a *departures* frequency and an *arrivals* frequency for in-flight use. For additional assistance, you are encouraged to identify yourself as a student pilot, for instance:

You can identify yourself as a student pilot so that the controller can assist you with the procedures, if necessary.

Pilot: *San Carlos Tower,*
 Cherokee Four Eight Three Seven Golf,
 Student Pilot.

At an airport without an operating control tower, you will talk mainly on the Common Traffic Advisory Frequency (CTAF) to advise others of your intentions, for which you are totally responsible since air traffic control is not operating. For instance, you would advise:

Pilot: *Frederick Traffic,*
 Piper Cub Nine Two Eight Sierra,
 On final for runway one niner, full stop Frederick.

The CTAF frequency is found on aeronautical charts and in the A/FD, and is usually either a:

- tower frequency, even though the tower is not operating;
- Flight Service Station (FSS) frequency, if an FSS is located at that airport— FSS is an FAA service used to provide briefings and advisories, and to accept and cancel flight plans—it is *not* a control service; you address an FSS on the radio as: *"(place name) Radio";*
- UNICOM frequency (operated by a Fixed Base Operator (FBO) at the airport, who can provide advice on refueling, and also on non-aviation matters such as ground transport—UNICOM may also be available for these private matters at tower-controlled airports); or
- MULTICOM frequency (122.9 MHz)—with no ground station involved.

When announcing your movements to other traffic you would address your call *"Frederick Traffic"*. When seeking information, you would address the station, for instance, *"Frederick UNICOM"* or *"Chicago Radio"* (an FSS).

Callsigns

Aircraft are identified by type and registration number, such as:

- "Cherokee Six Five Eight Two Tango"; or
- "Cessna Niner Three Zero One Foxtrot".

The Phonetic Alphabet

The international phonetic alphabet is used to ensure clear understanding in radio transmissions. You can practice it on registration numbers of airplanes and cars.

Character	Telephony	Phonic (Pronunciation)	Character	Telephony	Phonic (Pronunciation)
A	Alpha	Al-fah	S	Sierra	See-air-rah
B	Bravo	Brah-voh	T	Tango	Tang-go
C	Charlie	Char-lee *or* Shar-lee	U	Uniform	You-nee-form or Oo-nee-form
D	Delta	Dell-tah	V	Victor	Vik-tah
E	Echo	Eck-oh	W	Whiskey	Wiss-key
F	Foxtrot	Foks-trot	X	X-ray	Ecks-ray
G	Golf	Golf	Y	Yankee	Yang-key
H	Hotel	Hoh-tel	Z	Zulu	Zoo-loo
I	India	In-dee-ah	1	One	Wun
J	Juliett	Jew-lee-ett	2	Two	Too
K	Kilo	Key-loh	3	Three	Tree
L	Lima	Lee-mah	4	Four	Fow-er
M	Mike	Mike	5	Five	Fife
N	November	No-vem-ber	6	Six	Six
O	Oscar	Oss-cah	7	Seven	Sev-en
P	Papa	Pah-pah	8	Eight	Ait
Q	Quebec	Keh-bek	9	Nine	Nin-er
R	Romeo	Row-me-oh	0	Zero	Zee-ro

Types of Microphone

There are various types of microphone, each having its own operating characteristics. A **hand-held microphone** has a transmit switch incorporated on it. A **boom microphone** is attached to a headset worn by the pilot, and usually has its transmit switch situated in a convenient position on the control column.

Training airplanes may be equipped with both a hand-held microphone and headsets with a boom microphone.

When using a microphone the following basic rules generally apply:
- actuate the transmit switch before beginning to talk, and do not release it until after completion of your message;
- speak with the microphone one-quarter to one-half inch from your lips;
- speak slowly, confidently, and with authority;
- do not significantly vary the distance between your lips and the microphone;
- speak directly into the microphone and not to one side of it;
- do not look at the control panel when talking on the radio, but continue your normal scan outside.

The microphone is used like a telephone, except that:
- the transmit button must be depressed for you to transmit;
- while transmitting, most radio sets are unable to receive simultaneously;
- only one transmission from one station within range can occur on the frequency in use without interference. **While you are transmitting, no-one else can.**

Figure 4g-2. The hand-held and the boom microphone

Note: Your COM set will continue to transmit as long as the transmit switch is depressed, even if you are not speaking. This will block out other stations that may be trying to call on that particular frequency. So at the end of your transmission ensure that the transmit switch, or mike button, is released.

Radio communications in the vicinity of an airport are covered in Exercise 13c.

The Transponder

A transponder unit is fitted in most light aircraft, and when it is *squawking*, it enables an air traffic radar controller to identify the position of your airplane more easily on the radar screen. With *altitude reporting* (ALT), the controller also has a readout of your altitude.

Transponder requirements and operation are covered in the Airman's Information Manual (AIM).

There is no voice communication available through the transponder. Transponder code selection is accomplished by dialing in the required code with the knobs. The usual VFR transponder code is 1200 with altitude reporting, although ATC may ask you to squawk a specific code. Normally you select the transponder from STANDBY to ALT as you enter the runway for takeoff, and then return it to STANDBY on vacating the runway after landing.

When selecting a new code, avoid passing through the emergency codes (7700 EMERGENCY, 7600 RADIO FAILURE and 7500 HIJACK INTERFERENCE) when the transponder is ON, unless you really want to activate one of them.

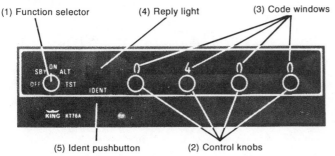

Figure 4g-3. A typical transponder control panel

Part (iv)
Cabin Heating and Ventilation

Your comfort and well-being is most important to flight safety, so maximize it with correct use of the cabin ventilation and heating systems as explained in the Pilot's Operating Handbook. Ventilation generally improves the cockpit environment quite significantly.

The hot air for cabin heating is usually taken from around the engine exhaust system. To protect the occupants of the airplane from any fumes escaping from a leaking exhaust system, it is good practice to **use the fresh air vents** in conjunction with cabin heating. Carbon monoxide, which is colorless, odorless and dangerous, is present in the exhaust gases, and ventilation provides good protection against it!

On hot days, you can also open the cockpit window on the ground for additional ventilation, but be careful that exhaust gases from your own or other aircraft do not enter the cockpit.

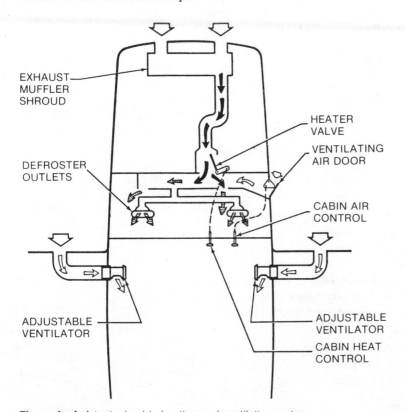

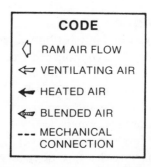

Figure 4g-4. A typical cabin heating and ventilation system

✍ Review 4g

Part (i)—The Throttle and Carburetor Heat

1. Power is increased by moving the throttle (forward/back), and reduced by moving it (forward/back).

   ➢ forward, back

2. Large throttle movements should be (fast/slow).

   ➢ slow

3. A loss of rpm on a warm, humid day in an airplane fitted with a fixed-pitch propeller could indicate _____ _____ .

   ➢ carburetor ice

4. The means of removing carburetor ice is to fully apply _____ _____ which introduces (hot/cold) air into the carburetor.

   ➢ carburetor heat, hot

5. As carburetor heat is applied, engine rpm will initially (rise/drop) because of the (more/less) dense air passing through the engine. If carburetor ice is present, and is melted by the hot air, engine rpm will then (rise/drop).

   ➢ drop, less, rise

6. When operating with low power, say during descent, it (is/is not) good airmanship to apply full carburetor heat as a precaution against the formation of carburetor ice.

   ➢ is

7. The hot air for carburetor heat (is/is not) filtered, and so it is usual to taxi on dusty surfaces with carburetor heat (HOT/COLD).

   ➢ is not, COLD

Part (ii)—The Mixture Control

1. The mixture control is usually a _____ -colored knob situated near the throttle, and its two functions are to _____ the mixture for optimum fuel usage at high altitudes, and, when pulled fully out, to _____ the engine.

   ➢ red, lean, stop

2. During climbs and descents the mixture control should normally be in the (FULL RICH/IDLE CUTOFF) position.

   ➢ FULL RICH

Cockpit Controls

3. When leaning the mixture at altitude, the mixture control should be moved slowly to achieve (peak/lowest) rpm, and then moved slightly (in/out).

   ➢ peak, in

4. The engine is usually shut down after parking the airplane by moving the mixture control to (FULL RICH/IDLE CUTOFF).

   ➢ IDLE CUTOFF

Part (iii)—Using the Radio

1. To use the radio both the master switch and the avionics power switch, if applicable, need to be (ON/OFF), and the particular radio switched (ON/OFF).

   ➢ ON, ON

2. The audio in most aircraft can be heard through either the cockpit s_____ or an individual set of h_____ .

   ➢ speaker, headphones

3. Unwanted background noise, known as static or hash, can usually be eliminated or reduced using the _____ control.

   ➢ squelch

4. While you have your microphone button pressed, others (can/cannot) use the radio frequency.

   ➢ cannot

5. For additional assistance from ATC, you can identify yourself as a _____ pilot.

   ➢ student

6. At a tower-controlled airport there is likely to be a _____ frequency and a _____ frequency.

   ➢ ground, tower

7. At airports without an operating control tower, you should announce your intentions to other traffic on the C_____ T_____ A_____ Frequency. This (is/is not) a control frequency.

   ➢ Common Traffic Advisory Frequency, is not

8. UNICOM is a (privately/FAA) operated frequency.

   ➢ privately

Continued

9. FSS is a (privately/FAA) operated frequency used for (control/advisory) purposes, and addressed as, for instance, Chicago _____ .

   ➤ FAA, advisory, Chicago Radio

10. MULTICOM is used for communications between a pilot and (other aircraft/a ground station). The usual MULTICOM frequency is ____ MHz.

    ➤ other aircraft, 122.9 MHz

11. The C____ T____ A____ F____ can be found in the A____ /F____ Directory.

    ➤ common traffic advisory frequency, Airport/Facility Directory

12. Using the phonetic alphabet, how would you express: Cessna 1830X?

    ➤ Cessna one eight three zero X-ray

13. Using the phonetic alphabet, how would you spell out the place name CONTA?

    ➤ Charlie Oscar November Tango Alpha

14. Using the phonetic alphabet, how would you identify Warrior 2957L?

    ➤ Warrior two nine five seven Lima

15. Using the phonetic alphabet, how would you spell out the name ASYUT?

    ➤ Alpha Sierra Yankee Uniform Tango

16. Using the phonetic alphabet, how would you spell out the name BEKTI?

    ➤ Bravo Echo Kilo Tango India

17. Using the phonetic alphabet, how would you spell out the name SWAMP?

    ➤ Sierra Whiskey Alpha Mike Papa

18. Using the phonetic alphabet, how would you spell out the name QUIRK?

    ➤ Quebec Uniform India Romeo Kilo

19. Using the phonetic alphabet, how would you spell out the name DIVEZ?

    ➤ Delta India Victor Echo Zulu

20. Using the phonetic alphabet, how would you spell out the name JULIO?

    ➤ Juliett Uniform Lima India Oscar

21. Using the phonetic alphabet, how would you spell out the name HUFOG?

    ➤ Hotel Uniform Foxtrot Oscar Golf

22. A "stuck mike" (will/will not) prevent others from communicating.

    ➤ will

23. What is the usual transponder code squawked by VFR aircraft?

    ➤ 1200

24. The transponder code to use in an emergency is ____ .

    ➤ 7700

25. The transponder code to use if an aircraft is being unlawfully interfered with by a person on board is ____ .

    ➤ 7500

26. The transponder code to use if suffering a communications failure in a radar environment is ____ .

    ➤ 7600

Part (iv)—Cabin Heating and Ventilation

1. The air used for cabin heating is usually warmed (as it flows over and around the exhaust system/by electric heaters).

   ➤ as it flows over and around the exhaust system

2. It (is/is not) good practice to use fresh air vents in conjunction with cabin heating.

   ➤ is

Advanced Airplanes

Advanced airplanes may have:
- rectractable landing gear;
- constant-speed propeller(s);
- two or more engines (piston or turbine), although there are high-performance single-engined airplanes (for example, the Cessna P210 and Piper Malibu, and Cessna Caravan single turboprop);
- leading-edge high-lift devices and wing- or fuselage-mounted spoilers—in addition to the trailing-edge flaps—and/or
- pressurized cabins.

Retractable Landing Gear

A retractable landing gear significantly reduces drag (air resistance) in flight and considerably improves climb performance and range capability. Most systems are electric and/or hydraulic, and operated by a landing gear lever or switch in the cockpit, usually with one or more green lights to indicate when the landing gear is down and locked.

Usually there is a **safety feature** to prevent the landing gear being inadvertently retracted on the ground, but never test this feature.

Always check that the landing gear lever is down before putting electrical or hydraulic power onto a parked airplane, and always carefully check "gear down with a green indicator light" in your Before-Landing checklist.

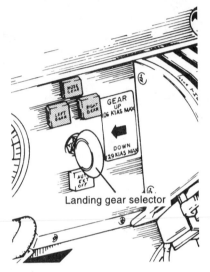

Figure 4h-1. Typical landing gear selector and gear-position indicator lights (Piper Turbo Lance).

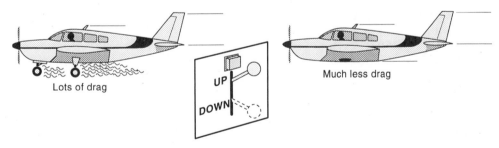

Figure 4h-2. A retractable landing gear reduces drag and improves performance.

Constant-Speed Propeller

The blade angle of a propeller which is controlled by a speed governor varies in flight to provide greater efficiency from the engine–propeller combination across a wide speed range.

Whereas with a fixed-pitch propeller you have only the throttle to control engine power and rpm (and consequently propeller rpm), with a constant-speed propeller there are two controls:
- the **propeller control** (or pitch knob) to control propeller rpm; and
- the **throttle** to control manifold pressure in the engine.

Some advanced engines have supercharging or turbocharging which forces more air through the engine and produces more power.

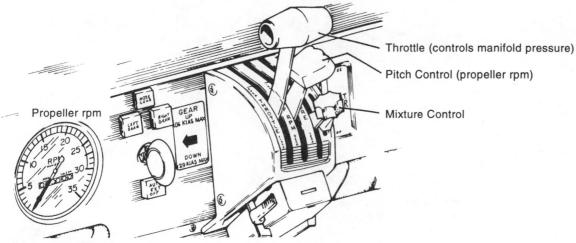

Propeller rpm

Throttle (controls manifold pressure)

Pitch Control (propeller rpm)

Mixture Control

Figure 4h-3. Typical arrangement of the controls for a constant-speed propeller

Two or More Engines

Having two or more engines is considered to increase safety in the event of engine failure, even though the performance with an engine failed is possibly not all that good. Having a constant-speed propeller that can be feathered—the angle of the blades rotated so that they have least resistance to the airstream—on a failed engine is critical to reducing unwanted drag from that propeller.

Advanced aircraft may have piston engines that run on AVGAS, or turbine engines that run on jet fuel (kerosene). Piston engines always require a propeller; turbine engines may have a propeller (turboprop), or may be a pure jet (usually a turbofan design) that provides thrust by ejecting air rearward.

Advanced piston engines may have a supercharger or turbocharger incorporated in the engine induction system to force more air through and so increase the power output of the engine.

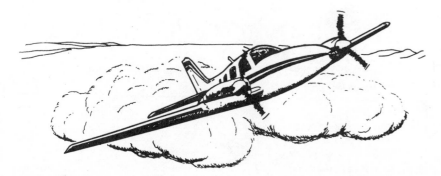

Figure 4h-4. The Beech Baron is a popular advanced piston-engine twin.

Leading-Edge Devices and Spoilers

Leading-edge devices extend from the leading edge of the wing to change its shape, giving it more curvature and greater lifting ability at low speeds. They may be operated from the cockpit by a separate lever in some aircraft, or by the flap lever in others. Some aircraft have leading-edge devices which extend automatically at low speeds.

Spoilers extend from the top of the wing to reduce lift and increase drag and act as air brakes. They are operated by a lever in the cockpit and are used to:
• slow the airplane down and/or increase the rate of descent;
• dump the weight of the airplane onto the wheels after touchdown for more effective wheel braking, by destroying the wing's lifting capability.

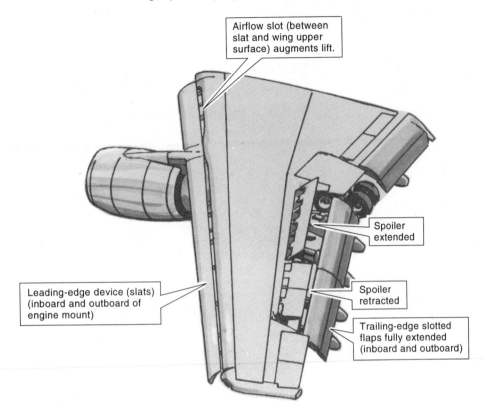

Figure 4h-5. Lift-augmenting and lift-dumping devices on the left wing of an airliner.

Pressurization

For the average person there is insufficient air pressure in the atmosphere above 10,000 feet above mean sea level (MSL) for satisfactory breathing over lengthy periods. At high altitudes you need to either wear an oxygen mask or be in a pressurized cabin, which is basically pumped up to provide a satisfactory pressure. Passenger jets flying at 41,000 feet may have their cabins pumped up to provide air pressure equivalent to only 8,000 feet MSL.

A danger in a pressurized cabin, of course, is the risk of depressurization through a structural failure, in which case:
• the pilots **must** immediately go onto **oxygen** and should commence an **emergency descent** to approximately 10,000 feet or below; and
• the passengers **should** go onto oxygen.

Cabin pressurization controls are in the cockpit.

Consider using oxygen when operating above a cabin altitude of 10,000 feet.

✍ Review 4h

Advanced Airplanes

1. A retractable landing gear reduces (lift/drag) and considerably (improves/reduces) climb performance and range capability.

   ➤ drag, improves

2. In your Before-Landing checklist, to ensure the landing gear is down you must check that (both/either) the landing gear is selected down and/or the gear indicator is showing down and locked.

   ➤ both

3. A constant-speed propeller has a (fixed/variable) pitch or blade angle, which makes the engine–propeller combination (more/less) efficient.

   ➤ variable, more

4. Multi-engine aircraft usually have propellers that can be _____ following an engine failure, to reduce drag.

   ➤ feathered

5. High-powered piston engines usually have a _____charger or a _____charger to boost power by forcing more air through the engine.

   ➤ supercharger, turbocharger

6. Piston engines run on (AVGAS/jet fuel); turbine engines run on (AVGAS/jet fuel).

   ➤ AVGAS, jet fuel

7. Flaps or slats that extend from the front of the wing are known as l_____-e_____ d_____ .

   ➤ leading-edge devices

8. Flaps that extend or lower from the rear of the wings are known as t_____-e_____ flaps.

   ➤ trailing-edge

9. Spoilers extend from the (upper/lower) surface of the wings.

   ➤ upper

10. Leading-edge devices (increase/reduce) lift; spoilers (increase/reduce) lift and (increase/reduce) drag.

    ➤ increase, reduce, increase

11. Consider using oxygen when operating above ____ feet cabin altitude.

    ➤ 10,000 feet

12. List six airplane features that are considered *advanced*.

    ➤ retractable landing gear, constant-speed propeller, two or more engines, leading edge devices, wing spoilers, cabin pressurization and oxygen

Taxiing an Airplane 5

Objective

To maneuver the airplane safely on the ground.

Considerations

Engine power is required to start the airplane moving; directional control is achieved using the rudder pedals, with the occasional assistance of differential braking if necessary; stopping is achieved by frictional drag on the wheels, assisted by brakes when necessary.

Aircraft wheels are usually chocked when the airplane is parked for long periods. The chocks must be removed prior to taxiing. Most aircraft have a parking brake that can hold them stationary without the use of chocks.

A reasonable taxiing speed is a **fast walking pace,** provided you are on a clear taxiway. In a confined space, such as an apron congested with parked aircraft, the taxiing speed should be much less.

To taxi an airplane means to move it about on the ground under its own power.

Plan your Taxi Path

To determine the active runway (also known as the runway in use), you can:
- listen to the Automatic Terminal Information Service (ATIS) if available, or otherwise call UNICOM or the Flight Service Station; or
- look at the wind direction indicator.

At simple, single runway airports, the best taxi path will be easy to determine. At more complicated airports, you may have to study an airport chart showing the taxiway and runway layout to determine the best route to take.

Runways are numbered by their magnetic direction, rounded off to the nearest 10°. For instance, a runway aligned with 264 degrees magnetic (°M) would be called Runway 26; in the opposite direction, 084°M, the runway would be known as Runway 8 or Runway 08.

If two runways are parallel, they will be designated *right* and *left,* as seen from the approach and takeoff direction—for example, 19L and 19R. At major airports there may even be a center runway—for example, Runways 3C and 21C at Detroit Metropolitan.

It is good airmanship to know where you are going to taxi before you actually start moving.

Study the airport chart prior to taxiing at an unfamiliar airport so that your taxi route from the parking area to the takeoff holding point follows the shortest and most expeditious route. The same applies when taxiing back to the parking area after landing. Some airports have a simple layout—for example, Santa Ynez, California; others are more complicated—for example, Las Vegas, Nevada, with the various taxiways designated by letters, such as *taxiway Bravo* and *taxiway Delta,* parallel runways, and the need for clearances to taxi and to cross runways.

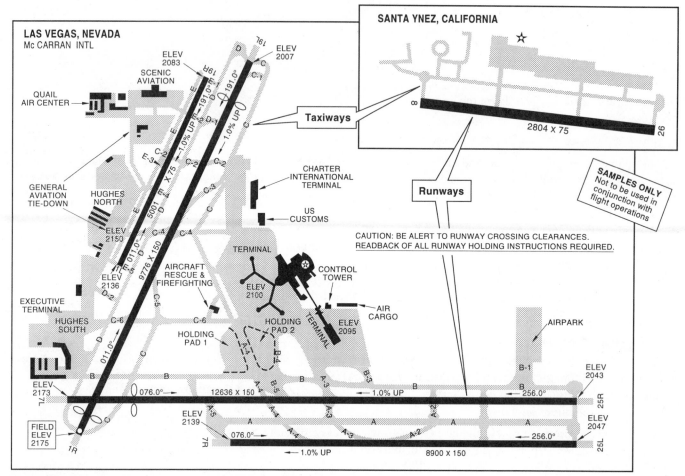

Figure 5-1. Taxiway and runway layout for Santa Ynez, CA and Las Vegas, NV.

In a two-pilot cockpit, it is good airmanship to give a clear briefing on your proposed taxi route. Plan on using the full length of the runway for takeoff, unless there is a good reason not to.

Also, after engine start-up, align the heading indicator (HI) with the magnetic compass. This will help you to maintain good directional orientation, and the HI will then be ready for when you check it during a turn on the ground.

Look Out

You must maintain a good lookout ahead and to the sides when you are taxiing—adequate wingtip clearance from objects such as buildings and other aircraft is essential.

The shadows that your wings throw onto the ground sometimes help. On a crowded tarmac area have an experienced person marshal you or provide wingtip guidance. In a very tight situation, you can even shut down the engine, complete the Shutdown checklist, then hand-maneuver the airplane.

Keep a good lookout when taxiing, especially in confined areas.

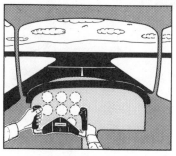

Nosewheel aircraft

Tailwheel aircraft

Figure 5-2. The view from the cockpit when taxiing

Taxi vision is usually good in a nosewheel aircraft, but it may be obstructed by the nose of a tailwheeler. In this case, you may have to zig-zag along the taxiway to give yourself a clear view of the area ahead by looking out the sides of the cockpit.

Steering

Most light airplanes are steered on the ground using the rudder pedals. The rudder pedals are connected to the rudder and, on most aircraft, to a steerable nosewheel.

Steer with your feet when taxiing.

The rudder pedals are moved with your feet, and are interconnected so that if you push the right pedal forward, the left pedal moves back. You should keep your heels on the floor when moving the rudder pedals, to avoid applying the toe brakes.

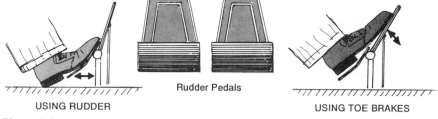

USING RUDDER   Rudder Pedals   USING TOE BRAKES

Figure 5-3. Using the rudder pedals and using the toe brakes

To turn to the right when taxiing, push the right rudder pedal forward with your right foot. The left rudder pedal, being connected to the right pedal, will move back. The nosewheel will turn to the right, causing the airplane to turn right. The rudder will be deflected so that it provides an aerodynamic force that will also turn the nose to the right—this force may be weak at typical taxiing speeds, but can be increased by applying power to increase the propwash airflow over the vertical stabilizer and rudder.

Airplanes that do not have nosewheel steering, such as those equipped with a tailwheel, may require occasional short bursts of power to increase the turning effect from the rudder. **Use only short bursts of power**—anything more than a short burst may lead to an unacceptable acceleration.

You can judge the amount of **rudder pedal movement** required according to the response of the airplane. How far to move the pedals depends on:
• the desired radius of turn;
• the nature of the ground surface;
• the wind direction and strength; and
• the strength of the propeller slipstream over the tail.

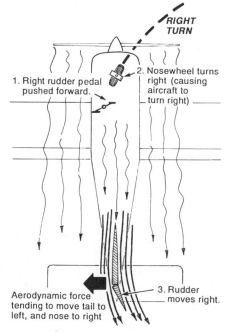

RIGHT TURN

1. Right rudder pedal pushed forward.

2. Nosewheel turns right (causing aircraft to turn right)

3. Rudder moves right.

Aerodynamic force tending to move tail to left, and nose to right

Figure 5-4. The rudder pedals, nosewheel and rudder in a right turn

If turning in a confined space, **differential braking** may be used to assist a turn. For instance, a touch of right brake would tighten up the right turn shown above.

When you have turned to the desired heading, centralize the rudder pedals to steer straight down the taxiway or runway. On a normal taxi with no crosswind, you will be continually making small corrections about this neutral position of the rudder pedals to maintain a straight path. In a strong crosswind, however, you may have to apply some rudder to counteract the weathercocking tendency. You can judge this simply from the response of the airplane.

Always have the airplane moving forward before you attempt to turn it. This avoids undue stress on the inside tire during a turn. It is good airmanship to decrease taxiing speed to a slow walking pace before turning—turning at too high a taxiing speed could cause the airplane to tip over.

Note: In the early stages of your training, the flight instructor may ask you to taxi with your hands off the control wheel to reinforce the fact that you steer the airplane on the ground with your feet.

Taxiing Speed

Power is used to commence taxiing an airplane; the effects of **wheel friction** and the **brakes** are used to stop it. Your aim should be to use the brakes as little as possible when taxiing, normally using them only to stop the airplane when slow, or to hold it in position, or to assist in a tight turn. Only use the brakes when you have to.

Use power and brakes to control taxiing speed.

Like all objects, an airplane has inertia and is resistant to change, so it requires more power to start moving than to keep moving. When the airplane is rolling at taxiing speed, however, the power can be reduced simply to balance the frictional forces and any air resistance, and not to provide an acceleration, so that a steady speed is maintained. Keep your hand on the throttle when taxiing.

On a straight and smooth taxiway with no obstructions, a **fast walking pace** is generally considered a safe taxiing speed. This can be judged by looking ahead and to the left of the airplane. In a confined area, the ideal speed is somewhat less. Your flight instructor will demonstrate a suitable taxiing speed on a smooth taxiway, away from other aircraft.

The amount of power required to maintain taxiing speed depends on the ground surface and its slope—a rough, upward-sloping grassy surface requires much more power than a flat, sealed taxiway. In general, soft surfaces or long grass will require more power to get the airplane moving than firm surfaces. **High power** may also be required to assist with turning the airplane, especially at low speeds.

To slow the airplane down, the power should be reduced. Friction may cause the airplane to decelerate sufficiently, otherwise the brakes can be used gently, but firmly. It is good airmanship to anticipate the need to slow down, and to reduce the power early, thereby minimizing the need to apply the brakes.

Brakes should be used gently so that the airplane responds smoothly—harsh braking being avoided except in an emergency. For a normal stop, a good technique is to relax the braking pressure—or perhaps even release it—just as the airplane comes to a halt. The resulting stop will be smooth.

Brakes should be used gently.

Toe brakes are situated on top of each rudder pedal. They are applied individually, using the ball of each foot. Normally you taxi with your heels on the floor and the balls of your feet on the rudder pedals, thereby avoiding inadvertent application of the toe brakes. When braking is needed, slide your feet up and, with the ball of each foot, apply the toe brakes as required. To stop the airplane while taxiing in a straight line, the brakes should be applied evenly; to assist in a tight turn, one brake can be applied differentially.

Generally speaking, power should not be used against brakes. It is a waste of energy and can lead to overheated brakes and increased brake wear. There are some aircraft, however, which have engines requiring a high idling rpm, and occasional braking may be required to prevent the taxi speed becoming excessive.

Power should not be used against brakes.

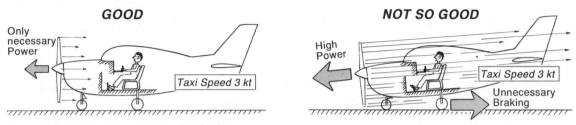

Figure 5-5. Avoid using power against brakes.

Differential braking is useful both for turning sharply (at low speed only) and for maintaining directional control when taxiing in a strong crosswind. You may have to use power and differential braking together when maneuvering in a confined space. The aircraft should be moving forward before you apply differential braking.

Be sure to test the brakes early. When taxiing has commenced from the parked position, the power should be reduced and the brakes tested, but in a manner that causes the airplane to respond smoothly.

Test the brakes as you begin to taxi.

During extended taxiing the brakes should be tested occasionally, and they should certainly be tested just prior to entering a congested tarmac area and when approaching a holding point. Always have an escape route in mind to avoid a collision in case the brakes fail to stop the airplane.

Allow for the fact that the wings of an airplane are wide and the tail section is well behind the main wheels. **Maintain a good lookout** ahead and to the sides. If the taxi path is obscured by the nose of the airplane, then turns slightly left and right as you taxi will permit a better view, but ensure that you remain within the confines of the taxiway.

Ensure that the taxi path is clear.

Should you unfortunately run into something while taxiing, stop the airplane, shut down the engine, set the parking brake, complete the Shutdown checklist, and investigate. **Do not fly!**

Surface Condition

The nature of the ground surface will affect your taxiing. Soft surfaces and long grass will require more power to be used than when taxiing on a hard and firm surface. Exercise caution when taxiing, especially in wet weather when taxiways and tarmacs can become slippery, to ensure that you have enough space in which to stop.

Be aware of the ground-surface condition when taxiing.

Ensure that propeller clearance will be adequate when taxiing in long grass or over rough or soft ground, especially if there are small ditches or holes, since striking grass or the ground can seriously damage the propeller. Holding the control column back (in suitable wind conditions) will help hold the propeller up. It is easier to keep an airplane taxiing on a soft surface than it is to get it moving, so keep it rolling if you can safely do so.

Loose stones or gravel picked up and blown back in the slipstream can damage both the propeller and the airframe. Damage may even be caused to other airplanes or persons quite some distance behind.

Taxiing on loose surfaces, avoid the use of high power as much as possible.

Avoid the use of carburetor heat when taxiing, since this would introduce unfiltered air into the engine which could be carrying dust and other particles blown up from the taxiway.

Small ridges or ditches should be crossed at an angle so that the wheels pass across the obstruction one at a time. This will minimize stress on the landing gear and avoid the nose pitching up and down excessively, which not only stresses the nosewheel but also puts the propeller at risk.

Large ditches or ridges should be avoided. If necessary, park the airplane and investigate on foot.

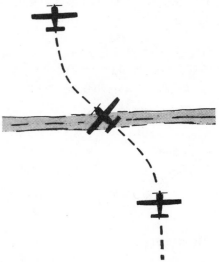

Figure 5-6. Cross small ridges and ditches at an angle.

Wind Effect

When taxiing, you should hold the flight controls in a position to avoid either the tail or a wing being lifted by a strong wind.

Taxiing into a **strong headwind,** hold the control column either neutral or back. This holds the elevator neutral or up, and the tail down, and takes some of the load off the nosewheel.

- For a **tricycle-gear** airplane, it is better to hold the control column neutral (elevator neutral) so that the weight carried by the nosewheel is neither too little (causing steering difficulties) nor too much.
- For a **tailwheel** airplane (or "taildragger"), it is better to hold the control column back (elevator up), causing the tailwheel to grip the ground firmly.

Taxiing with a **strong tailwind,** hold the control column forward to move the elevator down. This prevents the wind lifting the tailplane from behind.

A **crosswind** will try to weathercock the airplane into the wind because of the large keel surfaces behind the main wheels. This weathercocking tendency is greater in tailwheel airplane than in those fitted with a nosewheel.

The rudder pedals should provide adequate directional control to steer a straight path even in a strong crosswind, but, if not, then use differential braking to assist, especially if the airplane has nosewheel steering. The weathercocking tendency caused by a crosswind also makes it easier to turn the airplane upwind, and harder to turn it downwind.

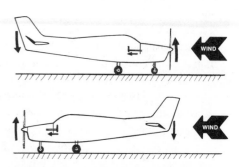

Figure 5-7. Taxi upwind with the control column neutral or back, and downwind with the control column forward.

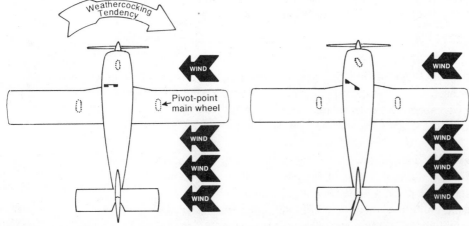

Figure 5-8. The weathercocking tendency—counteract it with rudder (and differential braking, if necessary).

- To avoid a **crosswind from *ahead*** lifting the upwind wing, raise its aileron by moving the control wheel or control column in the upwind direction. This also applies for a direct crosswind—move the control wheel into the wind.

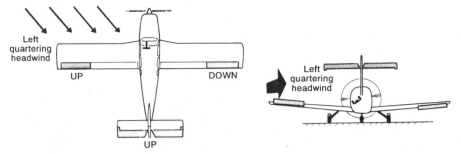

Figure 5-9. Taxiing with a left-quartering headwind

• To avoid a **crosswind from** *behind* lifting the upwind wing, lower its aileron so that the wind cannot get under it, by moving the control wheel out of the wind. A quartering tailwind from behind the airplane and to one side is the most difficult and hazardous taxiing condition. Hold the control wheel forward and out of the wind, and maintain directional control with the rudder pedals, using differential toe braking where necessary. Avoid any sudden braking or any sudden power increases.

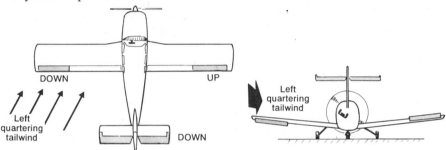

Figure 5-10. Taxiing with a left-quartering tailwind

Taxiway Markings

Taxiway markings are **yellow**. The taxiway centerline may be marked with a continuous yellow line, and the edges of the taxiway may be marked by two continuous yellow lines six inches apart.

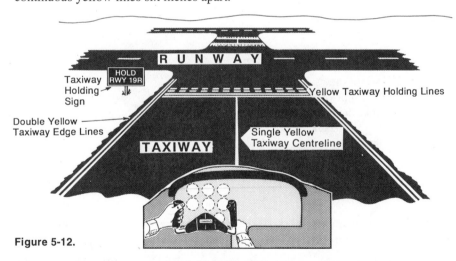

Figure 5-12.

Taxiway **holding lines**, across the width of the taxiway, consist of two continuous and two dashed yellow lines, spaced six inches between dashes. The two continuous lines are on the side from which an aircraft will approach a runway when taxiing, and if instructed to hold short of the runway or if not cleared onto the runway, then you should stop with no part of the aircraft extending beyond the holding line.

The propwash or jet blast of another airplane will produce the same effect as a wind, so always be cautious if you have to taxi close behind other aircraft, especially at an angle.

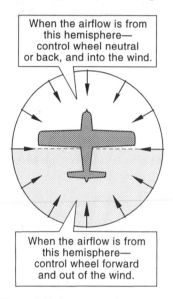

When the airflow is from this hemisphere—control wheel neutral or back, and into the wind.

When the airflow is from this hemisphere—control wheel forward and out of the wind.

Figure 5-11. Summary of the use of controls when taxiing in windy conditions

There may be **holding signs** at the edge of the taxiway, with white characters on a red sign face.

An aircraft exiting the runway after landing is not considered clear of the runway until all parts of the aircraft have crossed the holding line.

Taxi Clearances

At airports with an operating control tower, you should obtain a clearance to taxi to the takeoff runway. Your request for a taxi clearance should include:
- the station called;
- your callsign;
- your location on the airport;
- a request for taxi instructions;
- type of operation planned (VFR or IFR);
- destination or direction of flight.

Always obtain a taxi clearance when operating at a tower-controlled airport.

Example 1

Pilot: *Hagerstown Ground Control,*
Beechcraft three eight seven four Alpha,
At city ramp, ready to taxi,
Departing VFR northwest bound.

Tower: *Beechcraft seven four Alpha,*
Hagerstown Ground Control,
Wind calm, Altimeter two nine point nine five,
Taxi Runway Two,
Contact tower one two zero point three when ready for departure.

If you have a radio communications failure while taxiing at a tower-controlled airport, light signals from the tower mean:
- *steady red*—STOP
- *flashing red*—taxi clear of the runway in use
- *flashing green*—cleared for taxi (I would prefer to taxi back in and have the radio fixed)
- *steady green*—cleared for takeoff
- *flashing white*—return to starting point on airport
- *alternating red and green*—exercise extreme caution.

Some typical taxi clearances provided by ATC at other airports with operating control towers are:

Example 2

Tower: *Runway One Eight, taxi via Taxiway Echo.*

This clearance permits you to taxi along the designated taxi route to the assigned runway. You may cross other runways that intersect the taxi route, but you may **not** cross or enter the assigned runway.

Example 3

Tower: *Runway One Eight, taxi via Taxiway Echo, hold short of Runway Two Seven.*

This clears you to taxi along the designated taxi route toward the assigned takeoff runway (Runway 18), but only as far as the holding point prior to Runway 27. A further taxi clearance is required to proceed. It may take the form of something like: *"Cross Runway Two Seven without delay"*. Leave your radios tuned to the ground frequency until ready to enter the runway for takeoff.

Read back any "hold short of runway" instructions issued by ATC.

Taxi Intentions

At airports without an operating control tower (where a clearance to taxi is not required), you should advise your taxi intentions on the appropriate Common Traffic Advisory Frequency (CTAF).

At nontowered airports advise your taxi intentions.

Example 4

Pilot: *Vero Beach Radio,*
Cessna five one three six Delta,
Ready to taxi, VFR,
Departing to the southeast,
Request Airport Advisory.

Right-of-Way on the Ground

Taxiing frequently occurs on crowded tarmacs and taxiways. Five guidelines, understood and followed by all pilots when taxiing, make life easier for everybody.

1. Regardless of any ATC (Air Traffic Control) clearance it is the duty of the pilot to do all possible to avoid collision with other aircraft or vehicles.

2. Aircraft on the ground must give way to airplanes landing or taking off, and to any vehicle towing an aircraft.

3. When two aircraft are taxiing and approaching head on or nearly so, each should turn right.

4. When two aircraft are taxiing on converging courses, then the one that has the other on its right should give way and avoid crossing ahead of the other aircraft unless passing well clear.

5. An aircraft which is being overtaken by another should be given right-of-way, and the overtaking aircraft should keep well clear of the other aircraft.

If in any doubt—STOP!

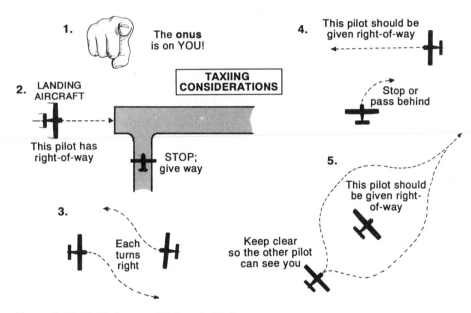

Figure 5-13. Right-of-way guidelines for taxiing

It is good airmanship to think of other pilots and avoid blocking taxiways or runways unnecessarily.

There are often **run-up bays** conveniently placed to allow you to carry out your engine run-ups and before-takeoff checks in a position that will not impede the progress of other aircraft. Position your airplane with adequate spacing so that it will not have debris blasted back over it in the propeller slipstream from another aircraft.

Always taxi and park in a manner that gives other pilots in the area confidence in your ability. Making your radio calls concise, efficient, and firm will also achieve this. Never taxi in a careless or reckless manner that could cause a hazard to persons or property, and never make weak or indecisive radio calls.

Marshaling

Although **the pilot is ultimately responsible** for the safety of the airplane on the ground, no matter who gives him guidance, taxiing guidance on a tarmac area may be given by a marshaler. Some of the basic signals are illustrated in figure 5-14, but you should only follow them if you consider it safe to do so.

On a crowded tarmac or in very strong winds, it may be preferable either to:
- obtain assistance from experienced personnel who can hold the wingtip down and walk beside the airplane as you taxi (known as *wingtip assistance);* or
- shut down the engine and move the airplane by hand or with a tow bar.

Brake Failure

If the brakes fail:
- close the throttle;
- steer away from other aircraft and obstacles and toward a high friction surface if possible (for example, grass).

If a collision is imminent:
- Mixture control—IDLE CUTOFF (to stop the engine by purging it of fuel);
- Fuel selector valve—OFF;
- Ignition—OFF;
- Master switch—OFF.

When stopped, chock the airplane.

Checks while Taxiing

Several items are checked prior to flight when clear of the tarmac area and moving along on a straight taxiway. The **rudder** should be checked for full-and-free movement, and the **directional flight instruments** should be checked for correct operation.

Turning left:
- the compass and heading indicator should decrease in heading;
- the turn coordinator or turn indicator should indicate a left turn; and
- the coordination ball should show a skid to the right.

You can refer to this as *"turning left—heading decreasing, skidding right"*. (The attitude indicator should remain level.) Figure 5-15a.

Turning right:
- the compass and heading indicator should increase in heading;
- the turn coordinator should indicate a right turn;
- the coordination ball should show a skid to the left.

"Turning right—heading increasing, skidding left" (attitude indicator level). Figure 5-15b.

When stopped, complete the prescribed Before-Takeoff checklist.

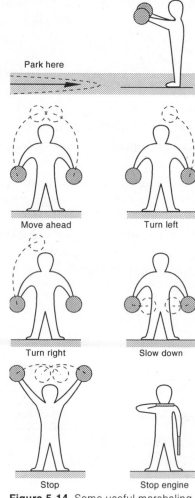

Park here

Move ahead

Turn left

Turn right

Slow down

Stop

Stop engine

Figure 5-14. Some useful marshaling signals

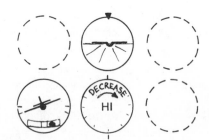

Figure 5-15a. Turning left—heading decreasing, skidding right

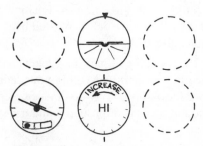

Figure 5-15b. Turning right—heading increasing, skidding left

The Maneuver

Before commencing to taxi, have a reasonable idea of the path that you will follow to the takeoff position, taking note of the surface and the position of other aircraft.

Align the heading indicator with the magnetic compass. At a tower-controlled airport obtain a taxi clearance from the tower by radio. At an airport without an operating control tower, advise your taxi intentions on the Common Traffic Advisory Frequency (CTAF).

Ensure that tie-down ropes and chocks have been removed before releasing the parking brake. Clear the area before moving and note the time you start taxiing (if relevant to your operation).

Test the brakes shortly after the aircraft starts to roll.

Maintain a suitable taxiing speed for the conditions and avoid using power against brakes (unless a high engine idling speed is required for better engine cooling). Cross ridges and small ditches at an angle, avoiding long grass and rough ground, and have an escape route in mind in case of brake failure. On the taxiing run, check the rudder and flight instruments for correct operation.

After a flight, park the airplane with the nosewheel straight to minimize stress on it and to make it easier to taxi away next time. When the airplane is stopped, the parking brake should be applied and the engine set to 1,000 rpm. Then shut down the engine and complete the Shutdown checklist.

After parking the airplane and chocking it, release the parking brake to avoid a buildup of pressure in the brake lines on hot days and a release of pressure on cold days or possible freezing.

Airmanship

Determine the runway in use before commencing taxiing. Obtain and acknowledge a taxi clearance, or make a taxiing call, as required at your airfield.

Always **clear the area** into which you will be taxiing. Maintain a good lookout ahead and to either side.

Airmanship is keeping a very good lookout and thinking of others.

Follow the accepted taxiing rules and do not blast debris back over your airplane, other airplanes or into hangars. Always check the brakes immediately you start moving forward, by reducing power to idle and gently applying the brakes. If you suspect a brake malfunction, shut down the engine and stop the airplane.

Operate the throttle and brakes smoothly so that there are no sudden stops, starts or turns. Do not use power against brakes, and anticipate the need to stop.

Maintain a radio listening watch on the appropriate frequency. Maintain an awareness of the position of other aircraft and vehicles along the taxi path, and in the traffic pattern. Do not be distracted when taxiing—for instance, avoid copying clearances or looking at charts until you are stopped.

Comply with markings, clearances and signals and complete the Before-Takeoff checklist, if there is one. And remember—**you** are in control!

Airwork (Groundwork) 5
Taxiing an Airplane

Objective
To maneuver the airplane safely on the ground.

1. To Commence Taxiing

- **Look out.**
- Survey the area around the airplane for obstructions and other airplanes. Consider the surface.
- Determine runway in use.
- After engine start, align the heading indicator with the magnetic compass.
- If *permission to taxi* is required at your airfield, obtain this by radio prior to taxiing.
- Loosen the throttle friction nut and reduce the power to idle.
- Release the parking brake.

Moving off:
- Parking brake released.
- Apply sufficient power with the throttle to start the airplane moving forward; then
- Reduce power to idle and gently test the brakes.
- Apply sufficient power to recommence taxiing; then
- Adjust power as necessary to maintain a safe taxiing speed (a fast walking pace or less).

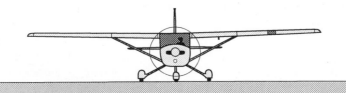

2. Taxiing the Airplane

Note: Steering is not possible until the airplane is rolling forward.

- Control direction with the rudder pedals and, if necessary, differential braking. An increased slipstream over the rudder may assist also.
- Gently test the brakes from time to time without bringing the airplane to a stop.

- Remember to allow plenty of clearance for the wingtips and tail.
- Hold the control column suitably to counteract any wind effect from the side or behind.

3. Stopping the Airplane

To stop the airplane:
- Anticipate by a few seconds.
- Close the throttle.
- Allow the airplane to roll to a stop with the nosewheel straight.
- If necessary, gently apply the brakes, releasing them just as the airplane stops, so that coming to a halt is smooth.

When completely stopped:
- Parking brake—ON;
- Use the throttle to set the correct engine rpm—usually 1,000 rpm.

Engine Shutdown:
- Shut down the engine and complete the Shutdown checklist.

✍ Review 5

Taxiing an Airplane

1. To assist in directional orientation you (should/should not) align the heading indicator with the magnetic compass before starting to taxi.

   ➤ should

2. Steering the airplane on the ground is achieved with the use of _____ _____ which can turn the nosewheel.

   ➤ rudder pedals

3. The rudder and the nosewheel can be moved by moving the (top/bottom) of the rudder pedals in and out, and on most aircraft differential brakes can be operated by pressing the (top/bottom) of the appropriate rudder pedal.

   ➤ bottom, top

4. The brakes (should/need not) be gently tested immediately after the airplane begins to move.

   ➤ should

5. Use the brakes (all the time/only when you have to) and (use/do not use) power against brakes.

   ➤ only when you have to, do not use

6. When the aircraft has started to move, it will probably require (more/less) power to keep moving.

   ➤ less

7. You should control the taxiing speed preferably with (power and frictional wheel drag/power and brakes).

   ➤ power and frictional wheel drag

8. A reasonable taxiing speed is (a fast walking pace/20 knots/1 knot).

   ➤ a fast walking pace

9. To turn left when taxiing, move the bottom of the (left/right) rudder pedal in, and to turn right move the bottom of the (left/right) rudder pedal in.

   ➤ left, right

10. You (should/need not) try to avoid taxiing over loose stones or through long grass.

    ➤ should

11. You will probably require a bit (more/less) power than usual when taxiing on a soft surface.

    ➤ more

12. Wet surfaces are usually (more/less) slippery than dry surfaces.

    ➤ more

13. In a two-crew cockpit, it shows good crew coordination if you (do/do not) brief the copilot on the proposed taxi path.

    ➤ do

14. When taxiing with the wind from ahead, hold the control column (forward/neutral or back) and (into the wind/out of the wind).

    ➤ neutral or back, into the wind

15. When taxiing with the wind coming from behind, hold the control column (forward/neutral or back) and (into the wind/out of the wind).

    ➤ forward, out of the wind

16. A crosswind will tend to weathercock the nose of a taxiing airplane (into/out of) the wind.

    ➤ into

17. The weathercocking effect of a crosswind on a taxiing airplane can be counteracted by using the _____ and, if necessary, d_____ b_____ .

    ➤ rudder, differential braking

18. Taxiway markings are usually colored _____ .

    ➤ yellow

19. You (should/need not) comply with clearances and markings when taxiing.

    ➤ should

20. Following a radio communications failure, you first of all receive a red light signal from the tower, followed some time later by a flashing green light signal. These mean _____ .

    ➤ stop, cleared to taxi

21. At a tower-controlled airport you (will/will not) require a taxi clearance.

    ➤ will

Continued

---

22. At an airport without an operating control tower, you (should/should not) advise your taxiing intentions on the C_____ T_____ A_____ F_____ , which (is /is not) a control frequency.

    should, Common Traffic Advisory Frequency, is not

23. When taxiing, the general right-of-way procedure is to give way to the (left/right).

    right

24. An airplane (taking off or landing/taxiing) has right-of-way.

    taking off or landing

25. A taxiing aircraft (has/does not have) right-of-way over a vehicle towing an aircraft.

    does not have

26. If two taxiing aircraft are approaching head-on, each should turn _____ .

    right

27. The ultimate responsibility for avoiding collisions between taxiing aircraft rests with (Air Traffic Control/the pilots).

    the pilots

28. When taxiing at a tower-controlled airport, you (must/need not) read back any "hold short of runway" instructions issued by ATC.

    must

29. Write the intended marshaling instructions which follow, under the appropriate diagrams—stop; slow down; park here; turn left; turn right; move ahead; stop engine.

    check your answers by referring to page 112

30. When taxiing, even with a marshaler, the onus is on _____ .

    the onus is on **You**, the pilot-in-command!

31. Vision when taxiing is better in a (nosewheel/tailwheel) airplane.

    nosewheel

32. Small ridges or small ditches are best crossed (at an angle/ head on) when taxiing. Large ridges or large ditches (can also/should not) be crossed.

    at an angle, should not

33. You (should/should not) taxi behind a large aircraft with its engines operating.

    should not

34. When taxiing in after a flight, you should taxi to a position where you can park the airplane on (a firm surface/a soft surface/loose stones).

    a firm surface

35. If you have to taxi over a gravel surface, or a surface with loose stones, you should try to use (low/high) power.

    low

36. When turning left during taxiing, the compass and heading indicator should (increase/decrease) in heading, the turn coordinator should show a (left/right) turn, and the coordination ball should be out to the (left/right).

    decrease, left, right

Flying Straight-and-Level at Constant Power 6a

Objective

To fly straight-and-level using a constant power setting.

Considerations

Flying **straight** means maintaining a **constant heading,** and this can be achieved by holding the wings level with the ailerons, and keeping the airplane coordinated with the rudder to prevent any yaw. Heading is displayed on the Heading Indicator and Magnetic Compass.

Flying **level** means maintaining a **constant altitude,** which can be achieved by having the correct **power** set and the nose held in the correct **attitude.** Altitude is displayed in the cockpit on the altimeter.

Steady straight-and-level flight, coordinated and in-trim, is desirable both for comfort and good airplane performance. Accurate straight-and-level flying is one sign of a good pilot.

The Forces on an Airplane

There are four main forces acting on an airplane:
- **weight;**
- **lift**—generated by the wings;
- **thrust**—from the propeller (using engine power); and
- **drag**—the resistance to the motion of the airplane through the air.

In steady straight-and-level flight, the airplane is in equilibrium, with no tendency to accelerate.
- The lift counteracts the weight; and
- the thrust counteracts the drag.

It is unusual for the four main forces to counteract each other exactly. Almost always, a small balancing force, either up or down, is required from the horizontal stabilizer and elevator.

Most airplanes are designed so that the horizontal stabilizer creates a downward aerodynamic force. This small balancing force is controlled by the pilot with the elevator. In normal flight, continual small adjustments of the elevator with the control column are required.

Airplanes are usually designed so that if the **thrust is lost** through engine failure (or the pilot reducing power to idle), the remaining forces will automatically lower the nose into the gliding attitude, allowing a safe flying speed to be maintained. In the situation illustrated in figure 6a-2, this is achieved by having the center of pressure (CP), through which the lift acts, located behind the center of gravity (CG), so that the lift–weight couple has a nose-down effect. In normal flight, this is counteracted by the thrust–drag nose-up couple. (A *couple* is a pair of parallel, opposing forces **not** acting through the same point, and therefore causing a tendency to rotate.)

The four main forces acting on an airplane are: lift, weight, thrust and drag.

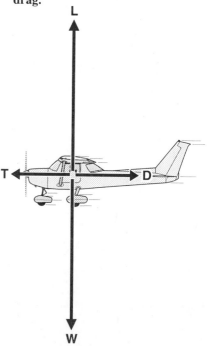

Figure 6a-1. The four main forces in steady straight-and-level flight

If the thrust is lost, the nose-up couple is diminished, the lift–weight nose-down couple wins out, and the nose drops into the gliding attitude. The same effect occurs when the pilot intentionally reduces power—the nose drops unless back pressure is exerted on the control column.

Also, if power is reduced and the propwash airflow over the horizontal stabilizer is reduced, then the downward aerodynamic force on the tail is less, and so the nose of the airplane will drop. (This effect does not apply to T-tail airplanes where the propeller slipstream passes beneath the horizontal stabilizer, rather than flowing over and under its surfaces.)

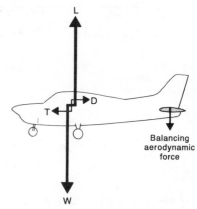

Figure 6a-2. The horizontal stabilizer provides a final balancing force.

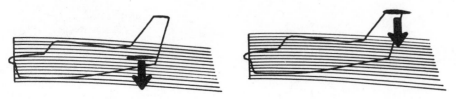

Figure 6a-3. A reduction in the propwash reduces the downward force on the horizontal stabilizer (except for T-tail airplanes).

Stability

Stability is the natural or built-in ability of an airplane to return to its original attitude following some disturbance, such as a gust, without the pilot taking any action.

An inherently stable airplane will return to its original condition unassisted after being disturbed, and so requires less pilot effort to control than an unstable airplane.

Longitudinal Stability In Pitch

If an air gust causes the nose to rise, then the horizontal stabilizer (or tailplane) is presented to the airflow at a greater angle-of-attack. It will therefore generate a greater upward, or less-downward, aerodynamic force that will raise the tail and lower the nose. The tail fins of a dart, in stabilizing its attitude and flight path, perform the same function as the horizontal stabilizer on an airplane.

The horizontal stabilizer provides longitudinal stability.

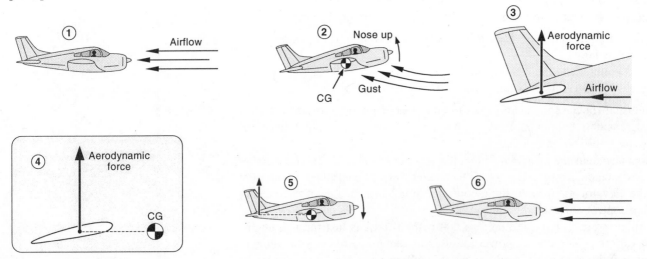

Figure 6a-4. Longitudinal stability following an uninvited nose-up pitch

A forward center of gravity (CG) makes the airplane more stable because of the greater restoring moment of the tail resulting from its greater leverage. If the airplane is loaded so that the **CG is too far forward:**
- the excessive stability will require stronger controlling forces from the elevator, which may become tiring for the pilot; and
- during the landing, the elevator will be less effective because of the low airspeed, and the nose-heavy moment may make it impossible to flare prior to touchdown.

If the airplane is loaded with the **CG too far rearward:**
- the airplane will be less stable at all airspeeds, and constant attention will have to be given to maintaining the pitch attitude; and
- the tail-heavy moment may cause a stall at low speeds when the elevator is less effective, and it may even be impossible to recover from stalled conditions.

Stability and control considerations make it imperative that an airplane is only flown when the **CG is within the approved range** (as stated in the Flight Manual). It is a pilot responsibility to ensure that this is **always** the case.

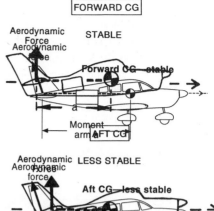

Figure 6a-5. Loading affects longitudinal stability and control.

Directional Stability In Yaw

If the airplane is disturbed from a straight path (a disturbance in yaw), then the vertical stabilizer is presented to the airflow at a greater angle-of-attack and generates a restoring aerodynamic force.

The vertical stabilizer provides directional stability.

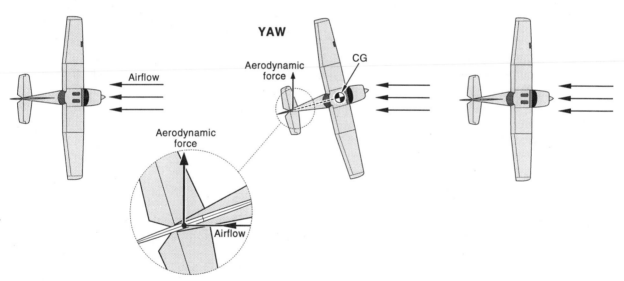

Figure 6a-6. Directional stability following an uninvited yaw

Lateral Stability In Roll

A disturbance in roll will cause one wing to drop and the other to rise. The lift force will be tilted, causing a **slip** sideways toward the lower wing. If the airplane has high keel surfaces, such as the vertical stabilizer and the side of the fuselage, then the airflow striking them in the slip will tend to restore a wings-level condition.

Lateral stability is provided by high keel surfaces and wing dihedral.

If the wings have **dihedral**—a design feature in which each wing is inclined upward from the wing root to the wingtip—the lower wing is presented to the airflow at a greater angle-of-attack in the slip sideways, thereby generating a greater lift force which tends to restore a wings-level condition.

Compared with stability in the pitching plane, the stability of the airplane is not as great in the rolling and yawing planes. The interrelationship between roll and yaw (as explained in Exercise 4b) is such that a disturbance in either roll or yaw will eventually lead to a spiral descent unless the pilot acts to level the wings and keep the coordination ball centered.

In general terms, however, the natural stability designed into the airplane will assist you in maintaining straight-and-level flight. If the airplane is in trim, you can more or less let it fly itself, with only a light touch on the controls being required.

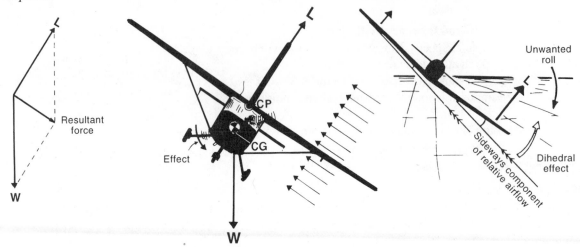

Figure 6a-7. High keel surfaces, such as the vertical stabilizer, and dihedral provide lateral stability.

Lift

The main wings are designed so that the airflow speeds up over their upper surface, creating a lower static pressure and an upward aerodynamic force. The vertical component is known as **lift** and the component parallel to the flight path is called induced drag (*induced* because it is the byproduct of the production of lift).

The wings generate lift.

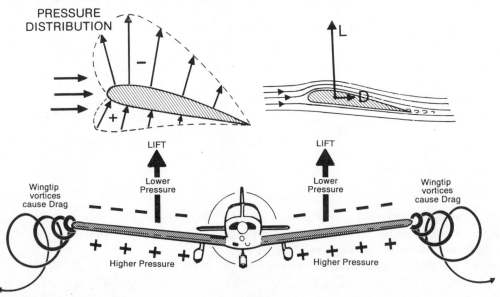

Figure 6a-8. The wings produce lift and, unfortunately, drag.

The lifting ability of a particular wing—known as the *coefficient of lift,* and abbreviated as C_L—depends on both the **shape** of the wing and its **angle-of-attack.** (The *angle-of-attack* is the angle at which the relative airflow strikes the wing.)

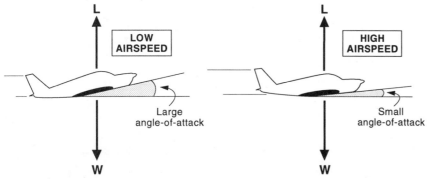

Figure 6a-9. The lifting ability of the wing depends on the angle-of-attack.

To fly straight-and-level and obtain the required lift to counteract the weight:
• **at low speed,** a high angle-of-attack is required; and
• **at high speed,** a low angle-of-attack is required.

Note: The angle-of-attack, which is related to the relative airflow, is not to be confused with the *pitch attitude,* which is related to the horizon.

Angle-of-Attack

Backward movement of the control column raises the nose of the airplane. Because of the airplane's inertia—its resistance to any change in the flight path— the airplane will continue in the same direction at the same airspeed for a brief period, but with an increased angle-of-attack. The wings will generate increased lift and the airplane will start to climb.

The pilot controls angle-of-attack with the elevator.

Conversely, moving the control column forward lowers the nose and decreases the angle-of-attack. Since the airspeed has not had time to alter, the wings will generate less lift and the airplane will lose altitude.

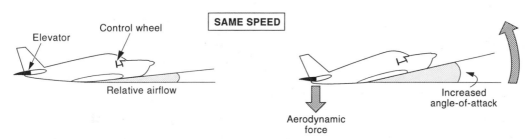

Figure 6a-10. The elevator controls the angle-of-attack.

The pilot cannot measure angle-of-attack in the cockpit, but can ensure that suitable angles-of-attack are being flown by choosing:
• a suitable **power setting;** and
• a suitable **pitch attitude.**

Performance

Power plus attitude determines the **performance** of the airplane in terms of:
- airspeed; and
- rate of climb (which is, of course, *zero* for straight-and-level flight).

Flying straight-and-level with constant power set, there will be a particular pitch attitude for straight-and-level flight. If the nose is too high, the airplane will climb; if the nose is too low, the airplane will descend. You know that you have set the correct pitch attitude because the airplane maintains altitude. You can observe this on the altimeter, with the vertical speed indicator serving as a backup instrument indicating any tendency to deviate from the altitude.

Power plus attitude determines the *performance* of the airplane.

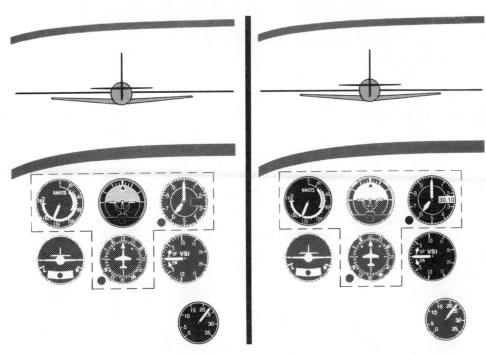

Figure 6a-11. Set the power and attitude; monitor the vertical performance.

Flying the Maneuver

Perhaps the most important point to make in flying straight-and-level is: keep the airplane in trim, and relax on the controls. Fingertip control should be sufficient. Aim for competence and confidence.

Keep the airplane in trim and relax on the controls.

Flying Straight

The essential elements in flying straight are to:
- **keep the wings level** with the ailerons; and
- **keep the ball in the center** with rudder pressure.

Wings Level

If the wings are not level, the airplane will tend to turn toward the lower wing—and applying opposite rudder to prevent the turn will mean uncoordinated flight with the ball not centered. This is uncomfortable and inefficient; it is called *flying with crossed-controls*—for instance, left aileron and right rudder—and should be avoided.

Keep the wings level.

The outside visual cue to the pilot of wings-level is the natural horizon being level in the windshield. If it is not level, then rotate the control wheel, or move the control column sideways, to remedy the problem.

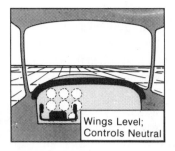

Left Wing Down

Right Aileron to correct

Wings Level; Controls Neutral

Figure 6a-12. Keep the wings level with the aileron control.

The position of the wingtips relative to the horizon can provide another cue to wings-level. If the left wingtip is below the horizon and the right wingtip is above the horizon, then obviously the airplane is banked left.

Use the ailerons to level the wings, so that both left and right wingtips have the same relationship to the horizon—equidistant **above** the horizon for high-wing airplanes, and equidistant **below** the horizon for low-wing airplanes (allowing for your seat position).

Coordination

Coordination is achieved by keeping the coordination ball centered with rudder pressure. If the ball is out to the left, more left rudder pressure is required; if it is out to the right, more right rudder pressure is required.

To achieve straight flight in visual conditions, an outside reference point ahead on the horizon should remain in the same position relative to the nose of the airplane as the airplane proceeds. In the cockpit, straight flight is indicated by a steady heading on the heading indicator and the magnetic compass. The turn coordinator will quickly show any tendency to turn. Aim to hold the heading as precisely as possible, even though a tolerance of plus or minus (±) 10° is acceptable.

If the airplane is deviating from straight flight, first of all stop the deviation by leveling the wings and centering the coordination ball. Then make a gentle turn back to the desired heading.

If a wing drops because of a gust, use coordinated aileron and rudder to lift it and then, when the wings are level, neutralize the controls.

Keep the coordination ball centered.

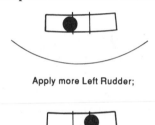

Apply more Left Rudder;

Apply more Right Rudder.

Figure 6a-13. Coordination ball indications and appropriate corrective responses

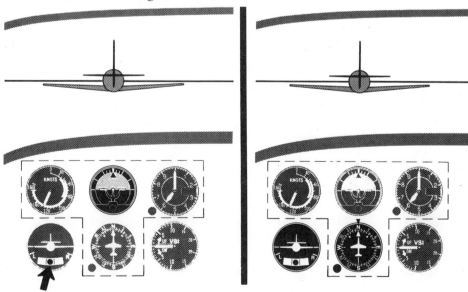

Figure 6a-14. Keep the wings level and ball centered to achieve straight flight.

Monitor the heading indicator and turn coordinator for heading performance.

Flying Level

The essential element in **maintaining altitude** is to establish the correct nose attitude for the power setting. The external reference is the natural horizon, which should appear at a particular position in the windshield relative to the nose cowl or to the top of the instrument panel.

The relationship between the horizon and the nose cowl will differ for different pilot eye-heights in the airplane, so you should establish a **comfortable seating position** that you use every flight. This will make it easier to commit to memory the correct attitude for normal cruise. Then, with cruise power set at cruise speed, you can place the airplane in this attitude and be reasonably certain that level flight will result.

Establish the correct nose attitude for the power setting.

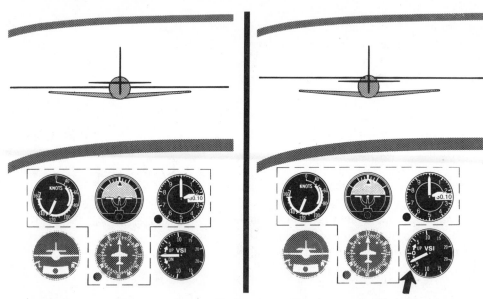

Figure 6a-15. In smooth air, the vertical speed indicator (VSI) indicates the pitch error well in advance of the altimeter.

Level flight can be confirmed on the **altimeter** and **vertical speed indicator** (VSI). The altimeter will indicate the altitude, and the VSI will indicate any tendency to deviate from this altitude.

Confirm that you are maintaining a constant altitude by referring to the altimeter and VSI.

• If the **pitch attitude is too high** and the airplane climbs, lower the nose slightly and regain the desired altitude.

• If the **pitch attitude is too low** and the airplane descends, raise the nose to regain the altitude. A satisfactory tolerance is to hold the altitude to within plus or minus 100 feet, however you should aim to hold it as precisely as possible—it is just as easy to fly precisely at 5,000 feet MSL (as indicated on your altimeter) as it is to fly 50 feet low at 4,950 feet. Do something about it—make a small correction with the elevator.

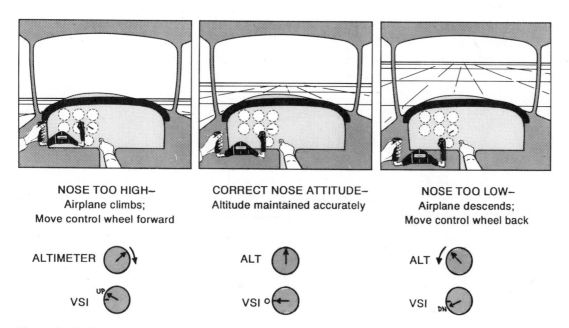

NOSE TOO HIGH–
Airplane climbs;
Move control wheel forward

CORRECT NOSE ATTITUDE–
Altitude maintained accurately

NOSE TOO LOW–
Airplane descends;
Move control wheel back

ALTIMETER

ALT

ALT

VSI

VSI

VSI

Figure 6a-16. With cruise power set, at cruise speed, maintain altitude with the elevator.

Accuracy

Steady straight-and-level flight at a constant altitude, with the airplane coordinated and properly trimmed, is desirable for comfort, for safety, and for good airplane performance.

Fly as accurately as possible.

In practice, however, it is almost impossible to hold altitude and heading perfectly. There will inevitably be some deviations, but these can be corrected so that the airplane flies very close to the target heading and altitude.

More comfortable flight is achieved by making small corrections frequently, rather than large corrections occasionally. It can be achieved in smooth air with small control movements; in rough air or windy conditions, however, the control movements required will be greater. The aim is to keep deviations from altitude and heading to a minimum—tolerances being within 10° of heading and 100 feet of altitude. If a particular airspeed is required, you should hold it to within 10 KIAS (knots indicated airspeed). See the next exercise.

Keep the airplane in trim to make accurate level flight easier.
• Hold the desired attitude with elevator control; and then
• trim off any steady control pressure.

The airplane should almost fly hands-off.

Do not fly with **crossed-controls.** It is possible to fly straight with one wing down and the airplane uncoordinated.

For example, if the left wing is down, right rudder can be applied to stop the airplane turning left. This is neither comfortable nor efficient and is known as a *slip* or *flying with crossed-controls* (since the ailerons and rudder oppose each other). It degrades performance by increasing drag, and results in a reduced airspeed and/or a higher fuel consumption.

Crossed-controls can be eliminated by leveling the wings with the ailerons and moving the coordination ball back into the center with rudder pressure.

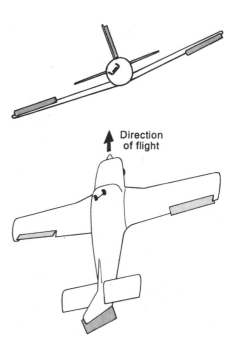

Direction of flight

Figure 6a-17. Crossed-controls are inefficient.

Recovering from Slightly Unusual Attitudes

If the airplane has some unintentional bank, level the wings with the ailerons. If the nose is too high or too low, ease it into the correct attitude with the elevator. If the speed is excessively high or low, or if large alterations to the altitude are required, some adjustment to the power setting may be necessary.

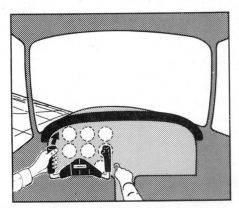 

Figure 6a-18. Nose high and turning left—lower the nose and level the wings.

Nose low and turning left—level the wings and raise the nose.

Airmanship

Your eyes should be out of the cockpit most of the time to:
- check the correct nose position relative to the horizon;
- check the reference point on the horizon; and
- **clear the area** for other aircraft above, below, ahead, and to either side—always **maintain a good lookout.**

An occasional glance into the cockpit, lasting one or two seconds only, is sufficient to cross-check relevant instruments. Only look at the instruments from which you need information.

Maintain firm, positive and smooth control over the airplane and keep it well trimmed. Fine-trimming will decrease your workload considerably. Do not allow large deviations from the desired flight path and airspeed to occur. Aim for perfect accuracy but stay within at least 10° of desired heading, 100 feet of desired altitude and 10 KIAS of desired airspeed. Small and subtle movements of the controls, made sufficiently early, will enable you to fly very accurately. Frequent small movements are preferable to occasional large corrections.

You will be a much smoother pilot if you are relaxed at the controls. Relax your muscles if you feel yourself tensing up, and avoid over-controlling.

Obey the basic **rules of the air** regarding right-of-way:
- An aircraft in distress has right-of-way over all other aircraft.
- Give way to less maneuverable aircraft, such as airships, gliders, balloons, and aircraft towing gliders or banners.
- Turn right if there is a danger of a head-on collision.

Appreciate the possible need for carburetor heat in humid conditions.

Remain well clear of clouds, and follow any ATC clearance or instruction, otherwise advise ATC immediately.

Airmanship is flying accurately and keeping a good lookout.

Airwork 6a
Straight-and-Level at Constant Power

Objective
To fly straight-and-level at a constant power setting.

- **Clear the area** and maintain a good **lookout**.
- Select a horizon reference point on which to keep straight.
- Keep the wings level with aileron.
- Maintain coordination with rudder pressure.

> **Accuracy:**
> - altitude ±100 ft
> - heading ±10°
> - airspeed ±10 KIAS
> - coordinated

1. With Cruise Power Set and at Desired Altitude

- Place the nose in the cruise attitude with elevator control, and with constant power set:
    cross-check the altimeter and vertical speed indicator; and
    make small attitude adjustments with elevator control.
- Allow the airspeed to settle:
    check the airspeed indicator for airspeed information;
    cross-check the altimeter and vertical speed indicator for attitude information; and
    trim off elevator pressure, while holding the new pitch attitude constant.

POWER plus ATTITUDE equals PERFORMANCE

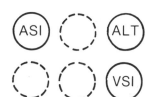
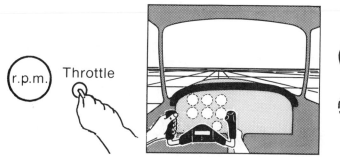
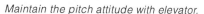

Maintain the pitch attitude with elevator.

2. The Correct Trimming Technique

- Hold the correct pitch attitude with elevator pressure.
- Trim to relieve the control pressure.

If rudder trim is fitted, trim off any steady rudder pressure while maintaining your heading and keeping the coordination ball centered.

Continued

Exercise 6a **Flying Straight-and-Level at Constant Power**

3a. If the Airplane Tends to Climb

- Regain the desired altitude with gentle movement of the elevator control.
- Hold the nose attitude slightly lower than previously with elevator:
    allow the airspeed to settle;
    check the altimeter and vertical speed indicator.
- Trim off any steady elevator pressure for the new attitude.

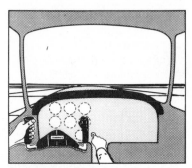

Initial attitude, climb tendency

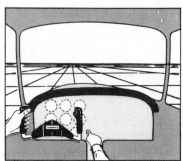

Regain altitude

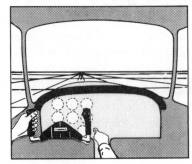

Slightly lower attitude; retrim

3b. If the Airplane Tends to Descend

- Regain the desired altitude with elevator control (adding power if necessary).
- Hold the nose attitude slightly higher than previously:
    allow the airspeed to settle;
    check the altimeter and vertical speed indicator.
- Trim off elevator pressure.

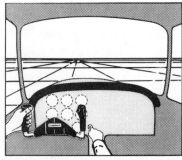

Initial attitude, descent tendency

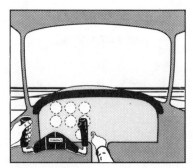

Regain altitude

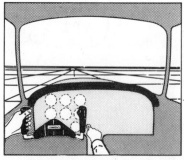

Slightly higher attitude; retrim

3c. If the Airplane Wanders Off Heading

- Gently bank the airplane toward the desired heading with aileron; and
- Apply same-side rudder pressure.
- Maintain altitude with elevator (fore or aft control-wheel pressure).

When on desired heading:
- Level the wings with aileron.
- Coordinate with the rudder.
- Maintain altitude with the elevator.

EXAMPLE –
Banking Left

Target
Heading

✍ Review 6a

Flying Straight-and-Level at Constant Power

1. In straight-and-level unaccelerated flight, lift is equal to (thrust/drag/weight), and thrust is equal to (lift/drag/weight).

   ➤ weight, drag

2. A final balancing force in pitch is provided by the (rudder/horizontal stabilizer and elevator).

   ➤ horizontal stabilizer and elevator

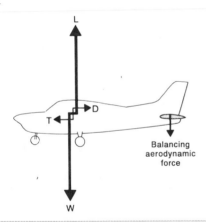

3. Label the four main forces, and the small balancing force.

   ➤

4. The angle-of-attack and the nose attitude are controlled by the (elevator/ailerons/rudder).

   ➤ elevator

5. Flying accurately is much easier if the airplane is (out of trim/in trim).

   ➤ in trim

6. The correct trimming technique is to (hold the desired attitude with elevator and trim off any steady pressures/change the attitude using trim).

   ➤ hold the desired attitude with elevator and trim off any steady pressures

7. The wings are kept level with the (elevator/ ailerons/rudder).

   ➤ ailerons

8. The coordination ball is kept centered with the (elevator/ailerons/rudder).

   ➤ rudder

9. The altitude is indicated in the cockpit on the _____ , and you should aim to hold the selected altitude accurately, but at least to a tolerance of within ____ feet.

   ➤ altimeter, 100 feet

10. The heading is indicated in the cockpit on the _____ _____ , which should be periodically aligned with the _____ _____ . Accuracy required is: specified heading plus or minus ____ °.

    ➤ heading indicator, magnetic compass, ±10°

11. If the airplane starts to climb, as shown on the _____ and the _____ _____ _____ on the instrument panel, when your objective is to fly straight-and-level, you should (lower/not change/ raise) the nose of the airplane.

    ➤ altimeter, vertical speed indicator, lower

12. Any required corrections to heading, as shown on the _____ indicator or magnetic _____ , should be made with (small coordinated/large uncoordinated) turns.

    ➤ heading indicator, magnetic compass, small coordinated

13. The performance capability of an airplane refers to its _____ capability and rate of _____ capability.

    ➤ airspeed, rate of climb

14. A high-performance airplane, compared with a low-performance airplane, has a greater _____ _____ and a greater _____ ___ _____ _____ .

    ➤ airspeed capability, rate of climb capability

15. P_____ plus a_____ determines performance.

    ➤ power plus attitude

16. The in-built natural ability of an airplane to return to its original condition following a disturbance is called _____ .

    ➤ stability

Exercise 6a Flying Straight-and-Level at Constant Power   **129**

17. Longitudinal stability in pitch is provided by the (horizontal/vertical) stabilizer.

➤ horizontal

18. Directional stability in yaw is provided by the (horizontal/vertical) stabilizer.

➤ vertical

19. Lateral stability in roll is provided by (high/low) keel surfaces and wing (dihedral/anhedral).

➤ high, dihedral

20. An airplane will be more stable longitudinally if it is loaded so that its center of gravity is well (forward/aft).

➤ forward

21. Loading heavy baggage in the rear locker, compared with securing it on the rear seat, will make an airplane (more/less) stable because it moves the CG (aft/forward).

➤ less, aft

22. The lift produced by a wing depends on its a_____-of-a_____ and the indicated a_____ .

➤ angle-of-attack, airspeed

23. To fly slowly at a constant altitude you need a (low/high) angle-of-attack.

➤ high

24. To fly with a high airspeed at a constant altitude you need a (low/high) angle-of-attack.

➤ low

25. For accurate flying you (should/need not) keep the coordination ball in the center.

➤ should

26. If the coordination ball is out to the right, you can center it by applying some (left/right) rudder pressure.

➤ right

27. Flying with left aileron and right rudder with the coordination ball well out of the center is known as flying with _____ controls.

➤ crossed-controls

28. Flying with crossed-controls is (efficient/inefficient) and (comfortable/uncomfortable).

➤ inefficient, uncomfortable

29. Tolerances when flying straight-and-level with a constant power setting are: within _____ feet of specified altitude and within ____° of heading, and with the coordination ball (centered/out of the center).

➤ 100 feet, 10°, centered

30. What is the right-of-way order of the following aircraft: glider, aircraft in distress, you operating normally?

➤ aircraft in distress, glider, you

31. If there is a danger of a head-on collision, you should turn _____ .

➤ right

32. The lift force and the weight force form a couple which has a (nose-up/nose-down) effect.

➤ nose-down

33. The thrust and the drag form a couple which has a (nose-up/nose-down) effect.

➤ nose-up

34. The (nose-up/nose-down) effect of the lift–weight couple is counteracted by the (nose-up/nose-down) effect of the thrust–drag couple.

➤ nose-down, nose-up

35. If thrust is lost in flight, the (lift–weight/thrust–drag) couple is weakened, and the nose will automatically (rise/drop).

➤ thrust–drag, drop

36. The small balancing force from the horizontal stabilizer and elevator is usually (a downward/an upward) aerodynamic force, which has the effect of helping to hold the nose (up/down).

➤ a downward, up

37. If the thrust is lost in flight, the propeller slipstream over the horizontal stabilizer and elevator is (increased/not changed/reduced). The small (upward/downward) balancing force is (increased/not changed/reduced), which causes the nose to (rise/drop).

➤ reduced, downward, reduced, drop

Flying Straight-and-Level at a Selected Airspeed **6b**

Objective

To fly the airplane straight-and-level at a selected airspeed.

Considerations

Straight-and-level flight can be maintained over a range of speeds—from a high-speed cruise to slow-speed flight just above the stalling speed.

A normal cruise or high-speed cruise is generally suitable for cross-country flying. Maneuvering in the traffic pattern in preparation for an approach and landing, however, may require a lower speed. Also, to sequence you in the traffic pattern at a tower-controlled airport, the tower controller might ask you to hold different speeds at different times. On other occasions, you may want to fly slowly to inspect a potential landing field. So there are several reasons why you should develop the skill of flying straight-and-level at a selected speed.

Accelerating and Decelerating

In the cruise, **thrust balances drag**—the source of the thrust being engine power. The drag results from the motion of the airplane through the air (parasite drag) and as the byproduct of the production of lift (induced drag).

If the desired airspeed is less than that being maintained then, by reducing power, the thrust will not balance the drag and consequently the airplane will slow down. If, however, the desired airspeed is somewhat greater than that being maintained then, by increasing power, the thrust will exceed the drag and the airplane will accelerate.

Power

When the airplane has accelerated or decelerated to the target airspeed, the power should be adjusted to maintain it. Subsequent adjustments to the power may be required for the selected speed to be maintained accurately.

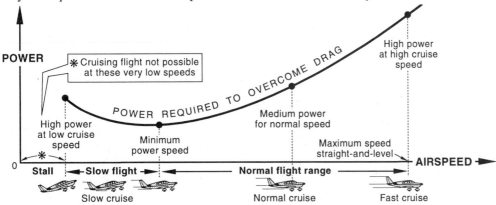

Figure 6b-1. Power requirements at different cruise speeds

Attitude

Since the lift generated by the wings depends on both the angle-of-attack and the airspeed, the lift will increase as the airspeed increases and, unless the nose is lowered, the airplane will begin to climb.

If the speed is decreasing, then the lift will also decrease and the airplane will lose altitude unless the nose is raised.

As the airspeed increases, the nose must be lowered to maintain altitude.

As the airspeed decreases, raise the nose to maintain altitude.

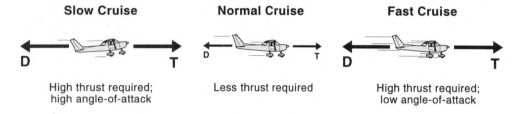

Slow Cruise

D ← → T

High thrust required; high angle-of-attack

Normal Cruise

D ← → T

Less thrust required

Fast Cruise

D ← → T

High thrust required; low angle-of-attack

Figure 6b-2. Maintain straight-and-level flight with power and attitude.

Flying the Maneuver

Prior to any significant power changes, the mixture control should be in the RICH position. Add power to increase airspeed or reduce power to decrease airspeed, while maintaining altitude with elevator.

Be prepared for the pitch/yaw tendency that occurs with power changes—nose-up and left yaw as power is added, nose-down and right yaw as power is reduced—counteracting it with appropriate control pressures.

When the desired airspeed is attained, adjust the power to maintain it. Then fine trim the airplane.

At very low airspeeds, where high power is required, close attention must be given to maintaining airspeed using power. Frequent, and sometimes large, power adjustments may be required. The reasons for this are considered in detail in Exercise 10b—Flight at Critically Slow Airspeeds—of this manual.

Satisfactory tolerances are: within 100 feet of altitude, within 10° of heading, and within 10 KIAS of the target airspeed—but you should aim for better accuracy than this.

Airmanship

Maintain a good **lookout**, continually clearing the area into which you are flying, ahead, above and below, and to either side. Be positive in achieving the desired airspeed and altitude. Maintain the altitude and airspeed by paying constant attention to power and attitude.

Coordinate the use of power and attitude to control the airspeed and/or flight path. Keep in trim, with fine-trimming whenever you find yourself having to exert a steady pressure on the controls. Use only fingertip-control on the yoke—*guide* the airplane rather than force it.

Airmanship is being positive in your control of the airplane.

Airwork 6b
Straight-and-Level at a Selected Airspeed

Objective
To fly straight-and-level at a selected airspeed.

---

1. To Increase Speed in Level Flight

- Increase power (coordinate with right rudder pressure).
- Lower the nose gradually to maintain level flight as the airspeed increases.
- Adjust power to maintain the desired airspeed.
- Trim off elevator pressure (nose-down).
- Make minor adjustments of **power, attitude** and **trim** as required.

> **Accuracy:**
> - altitude ±100 ft
> - heading ±10°
> - airspeed ±10 KIAS
> - coordinated

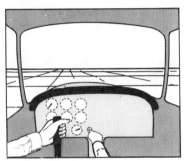
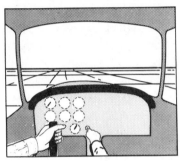

Add power   Lower nose attitude   Adjust power and retrim

---

2. To Decrease Speed in Level Flight

- Decrease power (coordinate with left rudder pressure).
- Raise the nose gradually to maintain level flight as the airspeed decreases.
- Adjust power to maintain the desired airspeed.
- Trim off any steady elevator pressure (nose-up).
- Make minor adjustments of power, attitude and trim as required.

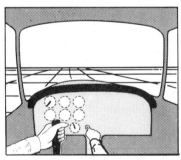

Decrease power   Higher nose attitude   Adjust power and retrim

---

Further Points

There are sound reasons for maintaining certain selected airspeeds. For example, one particular speed will provide the maximum range for a given quantity of fuel, while another particular speed will provide the maximum endurance for a given quantity of fuel.

Drag

Different airspeeds straight-and-level require different power settings. The thrust must balance the drag, which (like lift) depends on airspeed and angle-of-attack. At high airspeeds the drag is high; at medium speeds it is somewhat lower. This is because the **parasite drag** decreases as the airspeed decreases, the parasite drag being similar to the air resistance that you feel on a bicycle.

A bicycle is supported by the ground, but an airplane in flight must generate its own support, that is an airplane must generate its own lift. A byproduct of the production of lift by the wings is known as **induced drag;** it is greatest at the high angles-of-attack necessary at low airspeeds. As a result, the total drag is also high when the airplane is flying slowly.

Total drag is high at both high and low airspeeds, when compared with the total drag at normal cruising speeds. Therefore, a high power is required at both high and low airspeeds for the drag to be counteracted by the thrust. At intermediate speeds, the power requirement is lower.

Fuel Consumption

The rate at which fuel is consumed depends on the power setting, and will be greater at both high and low airspeeds.

Fuel consumption is a very important aspect in operating an airplane efficiently to obtain the maximum benefit from the fuel available—either the maximum time airborne (best endurance), or the greatest distance for a given amount of fuel (best range).

The Best-Endurance Airspeed

For minimum fuel consumption, fly at the **minimum power** airspeed. This will provide the maximum flight time for a given quantity of fuel. In-flight delays are sometimes encountered—for instance, when holding near an airport waiting for the weather situation to improve or traffic density to decrease.

Also, *time airborne* can be more important than *distance traveled* when flying a search pattern in a given area, or when fish-spotting for professional fishermen. Flying at the airspeed for **maximum endurance** provides the minimum fuel burn for a given flight time.

The best-endurance airspeed is specified in your Pilot's Operating Handbook.

The Best-Range Airspeed

A more common requirement is to achieve the maximum distance for a given quantity of fuel—the **maximum range.** Since most flights are over a fixed distance, another way of expressing best range is *minimum fuel burn to cover a given distance.* This occurs at the airspeed where the ratio of fuel/distance is least, and is known as the *best-range airspeed.*

The best-range airspeed is specified in your Pilot's Operating Handbook and is always a higher airspeed than that for maximum endurance. Note that the range distances published by the manufacturer assume **correct leaning of the mixture** when cruising at power less than 75% of maximum continuous power.

Total drag, and thrust required, vary with airspeed.

High drag at low speed

Minimum drag, medium speed

High drag at high speed

Figure 6b-3. Minimum drag occurs at an intermediate airspeed.

Correct leaning of the mixture is assumed in manufacturers' range figures.

Referring to the best-range airspeed as shown on the graph below, note that the rate of **fuel** consumption depends on the power.

The rate of covering **distance** is the speed. Therefore the ratio of fuel/distance will be the same as the ratio of power/speed, and so the minimum fuel consumption for a given distance—the best range—will occur at the point on the power-required curve where the power/speed ratio is least, as illustrated. The tangent to the power curve drawn from the origin has the flattest gradient, and where it touches the curve locates the *lowest* power/airspeed ratio.

Best range is achieved at the airspeed where the power/speed ratio is least.

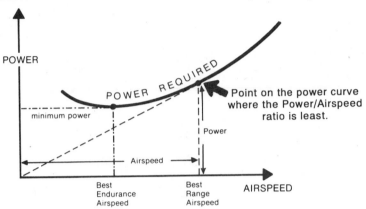

Figure 6b-4. Airspeeds for best endurance and best range

The line from the origin to any other point on the curve will have a steeper gradient, and therefore a greater power/speed ratio, and so more fuel per mile will be burned at these other speeds compared with the best-range airspeed.

Cruise performance is available to you in the Flight Manual and the Pilot's Operating Handbook, usually in the form of a table.

PRESSURE ALTITUDE FT	RPM	20°C BELOW STANDARD TEMP			STANDARD TEMPERATURE			20°C ABOVE STANDARD TEMP		
		% BHP	KTAS	GPH	% BHP	KTAS	GPH	% BHP	KTAS	GPH
2000	2400	- - -	- - -	- - -	77	102	6.3	73	101	6.0
	2300	73	97	6.0	69	97	5.7	66	96	5.4
	2200	65	93	5.4	62	92	5.1	58	91	4.9
	2100	58	88	4.9	55	87	4.7	52	85	4.5
	2000	51	82	4.5	48	81	4.3	45	79	4.2
4000	2450	- - -	- - -	- - -	78	104	6.4	74	103	6.0
	2400	78	102	6.4	74	101	6.0	70	101	5.8
	2300	70	97	5.8	66	97	5.5	62	96	5.2
	2200	62	92	5.2	59	91	4.9	55	90	4.7
	2100	55	87	4.7	52	86	4.5	49	84	4.4
6000	2500	- - -	- - -	- - -	78	106	6.4	74	105	6.1

Figure 6b-5. Cruise performance

Speeds on the Airspeed Indicator

There are various speed limits and speed ranges depicted on the airspeed indicator (ASI).

Normal speeds in the clean configuration (flaps-up) are in the **green band,** the upper limit being at the normal operating limit speed (V_{NO}) and the lower limit at the stall speed clean at maximum weight (V_{S1}). You should not normally operate in the yellow *caution* band—speeds greater than V_{NO}.

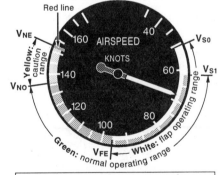

V_{SO}	Stalling speed at max weight, landing gear down, flaps down, power off
V_{S1}	Stalling speed at max weight, landing gear up (if retractable), flaps up, power off
V_{FE}	Maximum speed, flaps extended
V_{NO}	Maximum structural cruising speed (for normal operations)
V_{NE}	Never-exceed speed (max speed, all ops.)

Figure 6b-6. Indicated airspeed is what we read on the airspeed indicator.

	SPEED	KCAS	KIAS	REMARKS
V_{NE}	Never-Exceed Speed	205	208	Do not exceed this speed in any operation.
V_{NO}	Maximum Structural Cruising Speed	163	166	Do not exceed this speed except in smooth air, and then only with caution.
V_A	Maneuvering Speed 2,050 Pounds 1,900 Pounds 1,750 Pounds	106 99 94	108 101 96	Do not make full or abrupt control movements above this speed.
V_{FE}	Maximum Flaps-Extended Speed	101	100	Do not exceed this speed with flaps down.
	Maximum Window-Open Speed	145	148	Do not exceed this speed with windows open.

Figure 6b-7. A typical airspeed limitations table

Note: Knots indicated airspeed (KIAS) is important to you as a pilot since KIAS is what you can read on the airspeed indicator. Knots calibrated airspeed (KCAS), which is KIAS corrected for some errors, cannot be read in the cockpit.

Review 6b

1. High-speed cruise requires (high/low) power, with a (high/low) nose attitude.

   > high, low

2. Low-speed cruise just above the stall requires (high/low) power, with a (high/low) nose attitude.

   > high, high

3. To fly straight-and-level at very high speeds or at critically slow speeds requires (greater/less) power compared with that for normal cruise speed.

   > greater

4. Total drag at very high speeds or at critically slow speeds is (greater/less) than at normal cruise speed.

   > greater

5. Fuel consumption depends on (power/airspeed).

   > power

Flying Straight-and-Level at a Selected Airspeed

6. Cruising at very high speeds compared with normal cruise speed will (increase/not change/reduce) the rate of fuel consumption.

   > increase

7. V_{NE} is the _____ - _____ speed, and is shown on the ASI as a _____ line.

   > never-exceed, red

8. V_{NO} is the (maximum/minimum) structural cruising speed and is shown on the ASI as the (high-speed/low-speed) end of the green band.

   > maximum, high-speed

9. Tolerances when flying this maneuver are: altitude within ____ feet, heading within ____°, and selected airspeed within ____ KIAS, and with the coordination ball (out of center/centered).

   > 100 feet, 10°, 10 KIAS, centered

Cruising with Flaps Extended

Objective

To fly the airplane straight-and-level at a selected airspeed with flaps down.

Considerations

Flying along with a small amount of flaps extended (say 10° to 15°) is desirable when you wish to fly at a low speed, for example to inspect a prospective precautionary landing field, or when greater maneuverability is required.

Cruising with flaps extended provides:
- better forward visibility;
- a lower stalling speed;
- more responsive rudder and elevator; but
- increased fuel consumption.

Ballooning

Because the lifting ability of the wings is increased as flaps are extended, a lower nose attitude will be required to maintain altitude. If the nose is not lowered as the flaps are extended, the airplane will **balloon.**

Avoid ballooning when lowering the flaps.

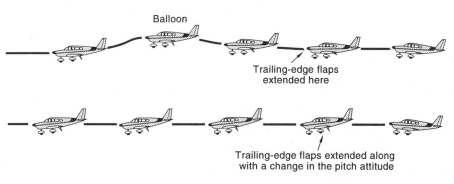

Figure 6c-1. A balloon can be avoided by lowering the nose as the flaps are extended.

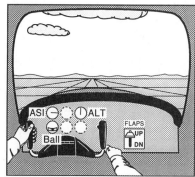

Flaps not lowered

Forward View

An advantage of the lower nose position required when flaps are extended is the **improved forward vision** from the cockpit—very useful, along with the low speed, when you want to inspect a potential landing field.

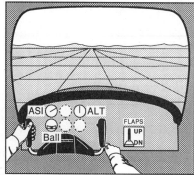

Flaps lowered

Figure 6c-2. Flaps improve the forward view.

Flap Speeds

The flaps should not be operated at high speeds, since this places unnecessary stress on the airframe. The maximum flap-extension speed (V_{FE}) is the high-speed end of the white band on the airspeed indicator.

Lower speeds are possible with flaps extended because of the increased lifting ability of the wings and the lower stalling speed. The stalling speed straight-and-level with flaps-extended (V_{S0}) is the low-speed end of the **white** band on the airspeed indicator; the stalling speed clean (V_{S1}) is the low-speed end of the **green** band.

Note: An easy way to remember which is which is: V_{S0} flaps *OUT*, and V_{S1} flaps *IN*.

Only extend flaps when the airspeed is in the flap-operating range.

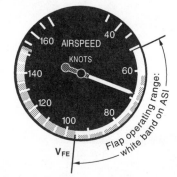

Figure 6c-3. The flap-operating speed range is marked on the ASI.

Power

Extending flaps increases the drag, so power must be added if the airspeed is to be maintained in straight-and-level flight. This increases the fuel consumption, making cruising with flaps extended less efficient than cruising clean.

On the positive side, the increased slipstream effect (from the extra power required when flying with flaps extended) provides you with a more responsive rudder and elevator.

Cruising with flaps extended requires more power and therefore more fuel.

Figure 6c-4. Extending flaps increases drag and fuel consumption.

Flying the Maneuver

As the flap position is changed, be prepared to make any necessary adjustments to power and attitude to achieve the desired performance.

- **Lowering the flaps** will require a lower nose position to avoid ballooning, and an increase in power to maintain airspeed. When adjustments are made, any steady control pressure should be trimmed off.
- **Raising the flaps** will require a higher nose position to avoid sinking, and an adjustment to power to maintain airspeed. Trim off any steady control pressures.

Do not operate the flaps at too high an airspeed—V_{FE} is the limit. Do not raise the flaps below the clean stalling speed—so have the airspeed in the green ASI band before raising the flaps completely.

When stabilized at the new cruise speed with flaps extended, you should maintain altitude to within 100 feet, heading within 10°, and airspeed within 10 KIAS.

Practice the maneuver with different stages of flaps lowered.

Airmanship

Maintain a good **lookout** and continually **clear the area** into which you will be flying, both above and below, and to the left and the right.

Airwork 6c
Cruising with Flaps Extended

Objective
To fly straight-and-level with flaps extended.

- Establish the airplane in straight-and-level flight clean (flaps fully retracted).
- Reduce power to reduce the airspeed, if necessary, and raise the nose to maintain altitude

1. To Lower the Flaps, Maintaining Straight-and-Level Flight

- Ensure that the airspeed is below the maximum flap-extension speed (V_{FE})—in other words, that it is in the white ASI band.
- Extend the flaps in stages, simultaneously lowering the nose progressively (to avoid *ballooning* and maintain altitude).
- Adjust power to maintain the desired airspeed.
- Trim off elevator pressure for each stage of flaps.

(1)   (2)

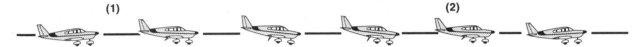

2. To Raise the Flaps

- Check that the airspeed is adequate (with ASI green band).
- Retract the flaps in stages, raising the nose to a higher attitude to prevent sink and maintain altitude.
- Adjust power to maintain the desired airspeed.
- Trim off elevator pressure.

Note: In a go-around situation, when you want to discontinue an approach, **apply full power first,** and establish a climb—or at least straight-and-level flight—before changing the flap position.

Accuracy:
- altitude ±100 ft
- heading ±10°
- airspeed ±10 KIAS
- coordinated

☞ Review 6c

Cruising with Flaps Extended

1. The flap-operating range is shown on the ASI as a _____ band.

  ➤ white

2. Cruising with flaps extended usually means a (higher/lower/the same) nose attitude and (more/less/the same) power compared with cruising clean.

  ➤ lower, more

3. Cruising with flaps extended allows you to fly (faster/slower), with a (poorer/better) forward and downward view.

  ➤ slower, better

4. As the flaps are lowered, the nose will have to be (raised/not changed/lowered) if a constant altitude is to be maintained. There is a tendency to b_____ .

  ➤ lowered, balloon

5. As the flaps are raised, the nose will have to be (raised/not changed/lowered) because there is a tendency to s_____ .

  ➤ raised, sink

6. The airspeed should be in the (green/white) range before lowering flaps, and in the (green/white) range before raising flaps.

  ➤ white, green

Climbing 7

Objective

To enter and maintain a steady climb on a constant heading, and to level off at a specific altitude.

Considerations

The Forces in a Climb

For an airplane to climb steadily the thrust must exceed the drag, otherwise it would slow down, and the nose would have to be lowered to maintain airspeed. The thrust in excess of that needed to balance the drag is called the *excess thrust*. The greater the excess thrust, the better the climbing performance of the airplane.

In a climb, the vertical component of the excess thrust supports a small part of the weight, and the lift generated by the wings supports the remainder—hence the surprising situation that **lift is slightly less than weight** in a steady climb. In the climb, a component of the weight acts in the direction opposite to the flight path and opposes the climb. The heavier the airplane, the poorer the climb performance.

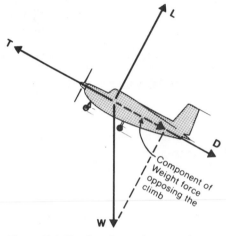

Figure 7-1. The four forces in a steady climb

Performance

Power plus attitude equals performance. The **power** applied and the **attitude** of an airplane determine its **performance** in terms of airspeed and rate-of-climb.

The normal climb attitude is higher than the normal cruise attitude, and can be held with elevator. The power in a climb is usually greater than that used for the cruise and, for many training airplanes, is in fact maximum power.

In the climb, **pitch attitude controls the airspeed.** Raising the nose will decrease airspeed; lowering the nose will increase airspeed. If the power and attitude are correct, then the climb performance will be as desired, and reference to the airspeed indicator need only be made to make fine attitude adjustments.

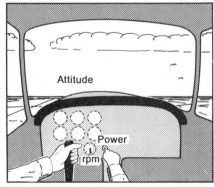

Figure 7-2. Climb power plus climb attitude provides climb performance.

Figure 7-3. The climb attitude is higher than the normal cruise attitude.

Climb performance can be measured in the cockpit on the flight instruments:
- **airspeed**—primarily on the airspeed indicator;
- **rate of climb**—on the vertical speed indicator and altimeter.

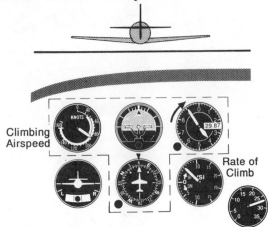

Figure 7-4. Monitor climb performance occasionally on the flight instruments.

Power Changes

Adding power has two effects on the nose position:
- it causes the nose to rise (by increasing the slipstream over the horizontal stabilizer and increasing its downward aerodynamic force, and also strengthens the thrust–drag nose-up couple);
- it causes the nose to yaw left (by increasing the slipstream effect on the vertical stabilizer—this yawing tendency is very pronounced at low airspeeds).

Power changes cause pitch and yaw changes.

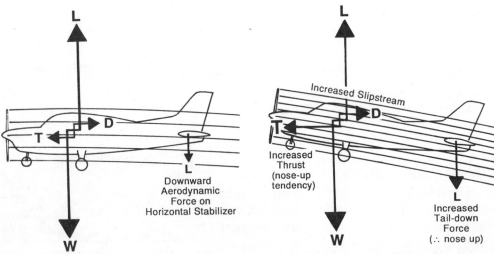

Figure 7-5. Increasing power causes a nose-up tendency; oppose this with the elevator.

You should hold the nose in the desired position with the controls—prevent the nose from pitching up with elevator control, and prevent the nose from yawing by keeping the coordination ball in the center with right rudder pressure. In a climb, the usual coordination rule applies—if the ball is out to the right, move it back into the center with right rudder pressure.

Since most training airplanes have a propeller that rotates clockwise when viewed from the cockpit, as climb power is applied, a coordinated increase in right rudder pressure will maintain the ball in the center. If the propeller rotates counterclockwise, left rudder pressure will be required for a power increase.

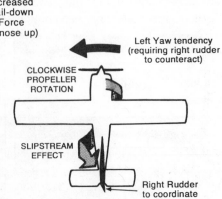

Figure 7-6. Counteract yawing tendency from the slipstream with rudder pressure.

Some airplanes have a rudder trim, which may be used to relieve steady foot pressures in the climb (and at any other time)—handle it the same as any other trim and use it, not to change the nose position of the airplane, but to remove steady control pressures (in this case rudder pressure).

Forward View in a Climb

The restricted view ahead during a climb could mean danger—other airplanes may be hidden by your nose cowl. It is good airmanship to make a small clearing turn left and then right, say 20° either side of heading, or even to lower the nose briefly, with every 500 feet gain in altitude to look ahead and clear the area obscured by the nose. A reference point on the horizon will assist you to return to the original heading.

Periodically make small clearing turns during a climb.

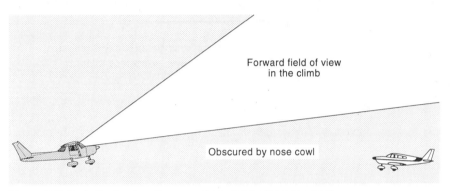

Forward field of view
in the climb

Obscured by nose cowl

Figure 7-7. Periodically clear the area obscured by the nose cowl.

The attitude in a normal climb will provide better forward vision than the higher nose attitudes required for the slower best-angle and best-rate climb speeds.

Engine Temperature

During a climb using high power, the engine is producing more heat energy than at lower power settings; additionally, the airspeed (being lower than the normal cruising airspeed) reduces the cooling airflow over the engine. There is therefore a risk of the engine overheating, so you must ensure that sufficient cooling is taking place. Excessively high engine temperatures can cause a loss of power, excessive oil consumption, and possible engine damage.

Ensure that the engine is adequately cooled in the climb.

It is usual to climb with the mixture fully RICH, because excess fuel, as it vaporizes, has a cooling effect in the engine cylinders.

Monitor the **engine instruments** periodically in the climb and, if the engine temperature is too high, increase the cooling effect by:
• increasing airspeed (to increase the airflow) or;
• opening the cowl flaps if fitted (to increase the airflow).

Climb Speeds

You can sacrifice some airspeed for a higher rate of climb (or vice versa). The choice of airspeed on the climb depends upon what you want to achieve. You can achieve (in order of increasing climb speeds):
• **a steep angle of climb** to clear obstacles (best-angle climb speed, V_X);
• **a rapid climb** to gain altitude in a short time (best-rate climb speed, V_Y);
• **a normal climb** (sometimes called a *cruise-climb)* which provides:
    faster en route performance;
    better airplane control due to the greater airflow over the control surfaces;
    better engine cooling; and
    a more comfortable airplane attitude.

There are various climb speeds to achieve different types of climb.

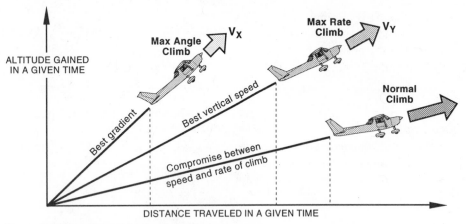

Figure 7-8. The different types of climb

The various climb speeds can be found in your Pilot's Operating Handbook. With climb power set, simply fly the airplane at the appropriate indicated airspeed to achieve the desired type of climb—the lower the nose attitude, the higher the climb airspeed. Remember, however, that engine cooling will be poorer at the lower airspeeds.

With climb power set, the climb performance will depend on the airspeed, which you select using pitch attitude. The accuracy required in the climb after takeoff is: within plus or minus 5 KIAS of your selected speed, except in the case of V_X which is quite slow and not far above the stall—in which case the tolerance is: plus 5 and minus zero—that is, no slower.

**V_X is max-gradient speed clean.
V_Y is max-rate speed clean.**

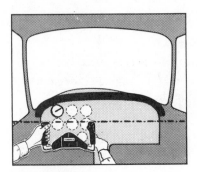
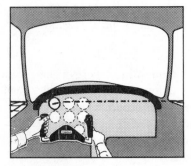
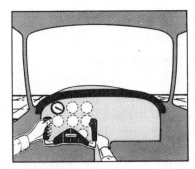

Best-Angle Climb—
for example, 55 KIAS

Best-Rate Climb—
for example, 65 KIAS

Normal Climb—
for example, 70 KIAS

Figure 7-9. The various climb attitudes

For the general en route climb well away from the ground, the accuracy required is: plus or minus 10 KIAS.

Climbing with Flaps Extended

If a small stage of flaps is used to shorten the takeoff ground roll, the steepest climb-out will be achieved at the speed noted for obstacle-clearance speed at 50 feet, found on the Takeoff Performance chart. Tolerance is the same as for V_X, plus 5 and minus 0 KIAS.

The obstacle-clearance speed is the max-gradient speed with takeoff flaps.

Headwind

Sometimes the flight path over rising terrain is very important—for instance, immediately after takeoff, or if operating in mountainous terrain. Climbing into a headwind will provide you with a steeper flight path over the ground than climbing downwind. Takeoffs are generally made upwind, rather than downwind, one of the advantages being to provide better obstacle clearance.

A headwind steepens the flight path over the ground.

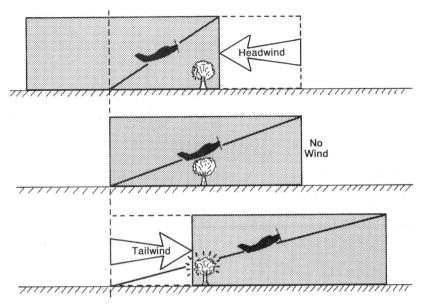

Figure 7-10. A steeper gradient over the ground is achieved by climbing upwind.

Flying the Maneuver

Prior to the Climb

Decide on the appropriate climb speed, select a reference point well ahead, look out and clear the area ahead into which you will be climbing. Check for any obstacles or airplanes ahead, above, below and to either side.

To Enter the Climb

Gently raise the nose to the climb **attitude.** The airspeed will start to reduce. Hold back-pressure on the control column to maintain the desired attitude and achieve the desired airspeed.

An easy way to remember the sequence of events when entering a climb is A–P–T: attitude–power–trim.

Increase **power**, first ensuring the mixture is RICH, by opening the throttle to climb power. Prevent the nose from yawing, and keep the coordination ball in the center, by applying right rudder pressure.

Trim—when you are established in the climb, trim off any steady control pressures with the elevator trim, and the rudder trim (if fitted). An out-of-trim airplane is difficult to fly accurately.

Note: Some pilots prefer to apply the power first, and then change the attitude; others prefer to apply the power and change the attitude simultaneously; others prefer to use the order we have described above. The actual order of using the controls in entering a climb is not that important, provided the end result is that you are in the **climb attitude** with **climb power** set.

To Maintain the Climb

Maintain the wings level with aileron, and the coordination ball centered with rudder pressure. Maintain the desired airspeed with elevator—the higher the nose, the lower the airspeed.

Do not immediately chase the airspeed after raising the nose into the climb attitude—allow time for the airspeed to settle before making any further changes in attitude. If the power and attitude are correct, then the climb performance will be as desired, and reference to the airspeed indicator need only be made to make fine adjustments.

Every 500 feet or so, either lower the nose or make clearing turns left and right to clear the area ahead. Periodically check engine temperatures and pressures, taking appropriate action if the engine is overheating such as opening the cowl flaps (if fitted), increasing the airspeed and/or reducing the power.

Leveling Off from a Climb

Since the cruise speed is higher than the climb speed, it is usual to gradually lower the nose as the intended cruise altitude is approached, leaving climb power set. Allow the airplane to accelerate until the cruise speed is attained, lowering the nose gradually to maintain altitude as the airspeed increases.

The sequence of events for leveling off is A-P-T: attitude–power–trim.

Anticipate reaching the cruise altitude by 20 feet or so and commence lowering the nose toward the cruise **attitude** before the cruise altitude is actually reached. This will make leveling off a smooth maneuver and avoid overshooting the altitude. The greater the rate of climb, the more you should anticipate the level-off altitude, say by 10% the rate of climb—for example, if climbing at 500 fpm (feet per minute), begin lowering the nose 50 feet before reaching the desired altitude.

As the cruise speed is reached, reduce to cruise **power,** keeping the coordination ball centered with rudder pressure. **Trim.**

When established in cruise, engine operation should be considered:

- mixture leaned as required;
- carburetor heat as required;
- cowl flaps (if fitted) possibly closed; and
- monitor the engine oil temperature and pressure from time to time.

Airmanship

Ensure that the engine is adequately cooled during the high power/low airspeed climb. The mixture should be RICH before the power is increased.

Airmanship is looking after the engine in a climb, and keeping a good lookout—especially under the nose.

Clear the area and maintain a continuous lookout. Clear the blind spot under the nose every 500 feet or so in the climb. Do not climb too close to clouds, and definitely do **not** fly into them (unless you are instrument rated and in a suitably equipped airplane).

Be aware of the nature of the airspace above you. For example, do not inadvertently climb into controlled airspace.

Exert firm, positive and smooth control over the airplane.

Airwork 7
The Climb

Objectives

1. To enter and maintain a steady climb on a constant heading, and
2. To level off at a specific altitude.

---

1. Prior to Entry

- Decide on an appropriate climb speed.
- Select a reference point well-ahead, slightly to the left of the nose.
- **Clear the area and look out**—ahead, above, below and to either side.

Accuracy:
- airspeed ±10 KIAS
- heading ±10°
- coordinated
- level-off altitude ±100 ft

2. Entry to a Climb

A—raise the nose to the climb **attitude.**

P—mixture RICH;
increase to climb **power**;
coordinate with rudder;
allow the airspeed to reduce and settle;
adjust the attitude to achieve the desired climb speed (check on the ASI).

T— **trim** off steady elevator pressure.

1. Select climb attitude with elevator.

2. Set climb power with the throttle.

Shallow clearing turn or lower the nose temporarily

In a climb maintain airspeed with elevator.

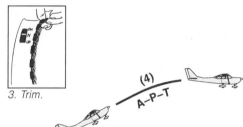

3. Trim.

Monitor the climb performance.

3. Maintaining the Climb

Maintain:
- Wings level with aileron.
- Coordination with rudder.
- **Airspeed with elevator.**
- Periodically check engine temperatures and pressures.

Look out for attitude reference and for other aircraft. Make shallow clearing turns 20° left and right every 500 feet or so, to clear the area ahead— or lower the nose temporarily.

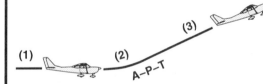

The Climb Speeds for your Airplane:

Normal climb speed = ... KIAS
Best-angle climb speed (V_X) = ... KIAS
Best-rate climb speed (V_Y) = ... KIAS

4. Leveling Off from the Climb

Clear the area and look out—anticipate the target level-off altitude.

A—gradually lower the nose to the cruise **attitude** (monitor the altimeter); allow the airspeed to increase to the cruise speed (monitor the ASI).

P—at cruise speed, reduce to cruise **power**— relax the rudder pressure for coordination.

T— **trim** off any steady elevator pressure.

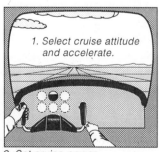

1. Select cruise attitude and accelerate.

2. Set cruise power.

3. Trim.

Further Points

Climb Performance

The curves below show the **power required** at a specific altitude for an airplane to maintain straight-and-level flight at various airspeeds, and the **power available** from the engine at those airspeeds.

If the engine can provide power *greater* than the power required (achieved by opening the throttle), then the airplane is capable of climbing at that airspeed.

Power is the rate at which energy is supplied, so the best **rate of climb** will be achieved at the airspeed at which maximum excess power is available—this occurs at the airspeed where the distance between the *power-required* and the *power-available* curves is greatest. This airspeed is known as V_Y, **the best rate-of-climb airspeed.**

Power is defined as the product of thrust × velocity so, for a given power output, the higher the velocity the lower the thrust. This explains why the "thrust curves" differ in shape from the "power curves".

The **angle of climb** depends on how much thrust is available over and above the drag—the excess thrust—and so the steepest climb (the best-angle climb) is achieved at maximum power and at the airspeed where maximum excess thrust occurs. The best angle-of-climb airspeed (V_X) is slightly lower than the best rate-of-climb airspeed.

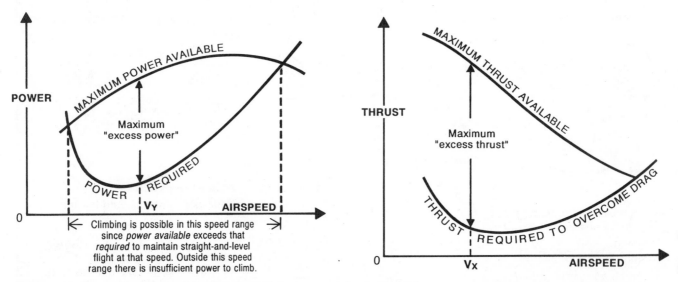

Figure 7-11. The power curve, and the thrust curve (also known as the drag curve)

Factors Affecting Climb Performance

Climb performance is less for an airplane carrying a heavy load compared with when it is light, because of the higher power-required curve.

Climb performance also decreases as the density altitude increases. Higher altitudes, higher temperatures, and more humid air all decrease the density of the air.

A decreasing air density means fewer air molecules passing through the combustion process in the engine, and therefore less power available. The higher the density altitude is, the lower the power-available curve.

Eventually an altitude will be reached above which the airplane will be unable to climb, and this is known as its *ceiling*.

Climb performance decreases with weight and density altitude.

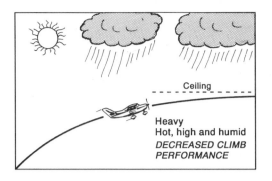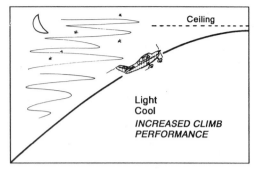

Figure 7-12. Heavy weights and low air density decrease climb performance.

Indicated Airspeed and True Airspeed

A decreasing air density affects not only the engine but also the airspeed indicator. Airspeed indicators are calibrated to read the true airspeed only under standard mean sea level conditions of pressure, temperature and density. Under other conditions, the indicated airspeed (IAS) will differ from the true airspeed (TAS). At density altitudes higher than standard conditions, the IAS will be less than the TAS.

A pilot flies the airplane according to the IAS.

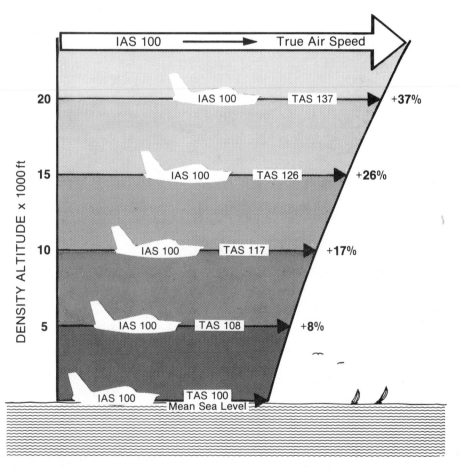

Figure 7-13. At a constant IAS (100 knots) the TAS increases with altitude.

Note: At 5,000 feet, the TAS exceeds the IAS by about 8%; and at 10,000 feet, TAS exceeds IAS by about 17%.

As an airplane climbs into less dense air, fewer molecules will be processed by the pitot-static system, and a lower IAS will be indicated, even though the actual true airspeed has changed little. If the nose is continually lowered to maintain a constant indicated airspeed, then the climb performance will deteriorate more than is necessary. To avoid this in climbs to high altitudes, maximum rate of climb tables will state the indicated airspeeds to use at various altitudes—the higher the altitude, the lower the recommended climbing IAS.

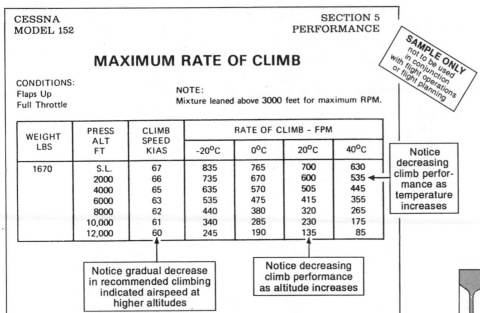

CESSNA
MODEL 152

SECTION 5
PERFORMANCE

*SAMPLE ONLY
not to be used
in conjunction
with flight operations
or flight planning*

MAXIMUM RATE OF CLIMB

CONDITIONS:
Flaps Up
Full Throttle

NOTE:
Mixture leaned above 3000 feet for maximum RPM.

WEIGHT LBS	PRESS ALT FT	CLIMB SPEED KIAS	RATE OF CLIMB - FPM			
			-20°C	0°C	20°C	40°C
1670	S.L.	67	835	765	700	630
	2000	66	735	670	600	535
	4000	65	635	570	505	445
	6000	63	535	475	415	355
	8000	62	440	380	320	265
	10,000	61	340	285	230	175
	12,000	60	245	190	135	85

Notice decreasing climb performance as temperature increases

Notice gradual decrease in recommended climbing indicated airspeed at higher altitudes

Notice decreasing climb performance as altitude increases

Figure 7-14. A typical maximum rate of climb performance table

Climbing with Flaps Extended

The takeoff is often made with some flaps extended, because flaps:
- allow the same lift to be generated at a lower airspeed, shortening the takeoff run;
- reduce the stalling speed, allowing slower flight; and
- may enable a steeper climb-out angle to be achieved (depending on the aircraft type).

With flaps extended, the nose position is lower than when clean.

Full flaps cause a large drag increase and significantly reduce the climb performance, so always ensure that only **recommended flap settings** are used for takeoff. This is typically the first stage, or 10° to 15°; on some airplanes it is zero flaps (check your Pilot's Operating Handbook).

Raising Flaps in the Climb-Out

When climbing out after takeoff, it is usual to raise the flaps when well clear of the ground (say 200 feet AGL). To avoid any tendency for the nose to pitch or for the airplane to *sink* as the flaps are raised:
- hold the nose in the normal attitude for a clean climb;
- allow the airspeed to stabilize at the desired airspeed;
- trim.

Check the airspeed indicator and adjust the nose attitude with the elevator if required (but do not chase the airspeed).

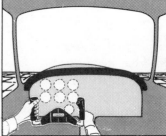

Normal Climb without Flaps

Climb with Takeoff Flaps Extended

Figure 7-15. Nose position in the climb is lower with flaps extended.

Climbing to High Altitudes—Use of Oxygen

If you are climbing to a cabin altitude above 10,000 feet MSL, it is advisable to use **supplemental oxygen.** Breathing additional oxygen will supplement the reduced amount available at high altitudes, and will prevent hypoxia—a lack of oxygen in the bloodstream. Hypoxia is dangerous to a pilot—it reduces your performance, even though you might feel euphoric.

While the use of supplemental oxygen is **recommended** above cabin altitudes of 10,000 feet MSL, it is **required** by the Federal Aviation Regulations for:
- all time in excess of 30 minutes above 12,500 feet MSL cabin altitude; and
- all time above 14,000 feet MSL cabin altitude.

Note: The term *cabin altitude* is used to describe the air in the cockpit that a pilot is breathing. A pressurized airplane flying at 31,000 feet may have the cabin pressurized to 8,000 feet, which means that the pilots have the same amount of oxygen to breathe as in an unpressurized airplane at 8,000 feet MSL. In this case, there is no need to use the oxygen masks. If, however, there was a sudden depressurization and the cabin air escaped, the pilots would require oxygen immediately.

Above 10,000 feet MSL it is advisable to use oxygen.

Review 7

Climbing

1. The power required for a steady climb is usually (greater/less) than that used when cruising straight-and-level.

   ➤ greater

2. For many training airplanes climb power is (maximum/cruise/minimum) power.

   ➤ maximum

3. To enter a climb from straight-and-level flight, you should apply _____ power and (raise/lower) the nose to the _____ attitude.

   ➤ climb, raise, climb

4. When settled in the climb, you (should/should not) trim off any steady control pressures.

   ➤ should

5. Climb performance is measured in terms of a_____ and rate of climb.

   ➤ airspeed, rate of climb

6. During a climb you should check the airspeed on the _____ _____ , and the rate of climb on the _____ _____ _____ and _____ .

   ➤ airspeed indicator, vertical speed indicator and altimeter

7. As you apply power to climb, the nose will tend to pitch (up/down) and yaw (left/right), which you can counteract with (forward/back) pressure on the control column, and (left/right) rudder pressure.

   ➤ up, left, forward, right

8. In a climb, with climb power set, the airspeed is controlled with small changes in (nose attitude/power/trim).

   ➤ nose attitude

9. If the climb airspeed is too low, you should (raise/lower) the nose.

   ➤ lower

10. If the climb airspeed is too high, you should (raise/lower) the nose.

    ➤ raise

11. It (is/is not) good airmanship to make small clearing turns in a prolonged climb so that you can clear the blindspot (above/below) the nose.

    ➤ is, below.

12. For the steepest climb-out with takeoff flaps extended, you should fly at the (obstacle-clearance speed/V_X/V_Y/normal climb speed) within a tolerance of plus _____ or minus ___ KIAS.

    ➤ obstacle-clearance speed, plus 5 or minus 0 KIAS

---

13. For the steepest climb-out with zero flaps, you should fly at (the obstacle-clearance speed/V_X/V_Y/the normal climb speed) within a tolerance of plus _____ or minus ___ KIAS.

➤ V_X, plus 5 or minus 0 KIAS

14. When clear of obstacles on a zero-flap takeoff, you could (lower/raise) the nose to achieve the best-rate climb speed of _____ , which you should fly to an accuracy of plus or minus ___ KIAS.

➤ lower, V_Y, plus or minus 5 KIAS

15. A tailwind will (flatten/steepen) the climb over the ground.

➤ flatten

16. A headwind will (flatten/steepen) the climb over the ground.

➤ steepen

17. The mixture should be set to (RICH/LEAN) for an en route climb.

➤ RICH

18. The accuracy for an en route climb is: airspeed within ___ KIAS, and heading within ___ °, and with the coordination ball (centered/out of center).

➤ plus or minus 10 KIAS, plus or minus 10°, centered

19. When leveling off from a climb you should hold the specified altitude to an accuracy of ___ feet.

➤ plus or minus 100 feet

20. The climb performance will (improve/decrease/not change) on hot days and (improve/decrease/not change) at higher altitudes.

➤ decrease, decrease

21. The climb performance will (improve/decrease/not change) at higher weights.

➤ decrease

22. The engine temperature will usually be (higher/lower) in the climb compared with in the cruise.

➤ higher

23. If the engine temperature is too high, engine cooling can be increased by (lowering the nose and increasing airspeed/raising the nose and reducing airspeed).

➤ lowering the nose and increasing airspeed

24. For a climb from a sea level airport the mixture control is usually in _____ .

➤ FULL RICH

25. Looking after the engine in a climb and keeping a good lookout is known as good _____ .

➤ airmanship

26. The climb performance of an airplane (improves/remains unchanged/decreases) as altitude is gained. The altitude above which the airplane is unable to climb is known as its _____ .

➤ decreases, ceiling

27. A pilot flies an airplane according to the (IAS/TAS) displayed on the _____ indicator.

➤ IAS, airspeed indicator

28. At high altitudes, the true airspeed will be (greater than/the same as/less than) the indicated airspeed.

➤ greater than

29. Airplane performance, engine performance, and human performance (increase/decrease) as the airplane climbs to high altitudes where the air is (more/less) dense.

➤ decrease/less

30. The use of supplemental oxygen is recommended at cabin altitudes above ___ feet MSL.

➤ 10,000 feet MSL

31. The use of supplemental oxygen is required by the FAA at all times the cabin altitude exceeds ___ feet MSL.

➤ 14,000 feet MSL

32. According to the FARs, a pilot may fly above a cabin altitude of 12,500 feet MSL for a period of ___ minutes before having to use supplemental oxygen, provided a cabin altitude of 14,000 feet MSL is not exceeded.

➤ 30 minutes

The Glide

Objective

To enter and maintain a steady glide, and to level off at a specific altitude.

Considerations

An airplane may descend in two ways.

1. In a **glide,** where engine power is **not** used and the pilot accepts the resulting rate of descent.

2. In a **powered descent**, where power is used by the pilot to control the rate of descent. The power-assisted descent allows you a lot of flexibility to maintain a particular rate of descent and any desired flight path, and so this is the descent technique normally used on approach to land.

A descent without power is called a glide.

The Forces in a Glide

If power is removed when the airplane is in level flight, the drag will be unbalanced. Only three forces will act on the airplane when the power is totally removed—drag (no longer counteracted by the thrust), lift and weight.

If you maintain altitude when the thrust is removed, by holding the nose up, the airplane will decelerate. To maintain flying speed, however, the nose must be lowered and a glide established when the thrust is removed. The drag, which always acts in the direction opposite to the flight path, now has a component of the weight counteracting it.

The nose must be lowered when thrust is totally removed to maintain flying speed.

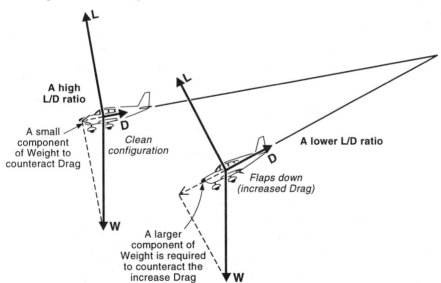

Figure 8a-1. The forces in a glide

A steady gliding speed will be achieved when the three forces (L, W and D) are in equilibrium. The greater the drag force, the steeper the flight path needed to counteract it—hence the drag-increasing methods used to steepen a descent, such as lowering the flaps, and the landing gear (if retractable), or "forward slipping" (used early in an approach before extending flaps, or in zero-flap approaches).

Steepness of the Glide

If the drag is increased more than the lift (say by lowering flaps, slipping or flying at an incorrect airspeed), a greater component of the weight is required to counteract it and maintain airspeed. A steeper flight path is the result.

High drag means a steeper glide.

The gliding range through the air depends upon the **lift/drag (L/D) ratio.** For instance, if the L/D ratio is six to one (6:1) then, for every 1,000 feet lost in altitude, the airplane will glide 6,000 feet (approximately one nautical mile); if the L/D ratio is 10:1 then, for every 1,000 feet of altitude, the airplane will glide 10,000 feet (1.7 nm). A typical L/D ratio for a training airplane is 9:1, so you can achieve approximately 1.5 nm progress for each 1,000 feet loss of altitude.

Gliding Range

The best gliding speed will be achieved when you fly the airplane at the angle-of-attack which provides the best lift/drag ratio. This can be related to an airspeed, the **best-glide airspeed,** which you can achieve by holding the correct pitch attitude.

The maximum gliding range is achieved at the speed for best lift/drag. Low drag means a shallower glide.

Changing the angle-of-attack with the control column changes the airspeed and the lift/drag ratio. This will have a significant effect on the glidepath. Flown at the wrong airspeed, the lift/drag ratio will be significantly reduced, and consequently the glidepath will be steeper. It may be that you have a L/D ratio of only 6:1 instead of 9:1, meaning that, for every 1,000 feet of altitude, you will achieve a range of only 1 nm (6,000 feet) instead of 1.5 nm (9,000 feet).

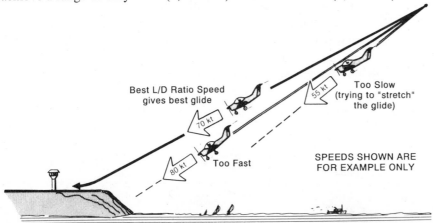

Figure 8a-2. Glide at the recommended speed to obtain the best still-air range.

Note: The *Pilot's Operating Handbook* specifies the best gliding speed when the airplane is at maximum weight. At lower weights, the best gliding speed is a little less but, since training airplanes do not have significant variations in gross weight, the one speed is generally acceptable at any weight. You should memorize this airspeed for your airplane.

If the airplane is gliding at an airspeed less than the recommended gliding speed, then, provided the airplane is still well above the terrain, it will pay to lower the nose and gain airspeed. While the glide angle will initially steepen, the final glide angle, when the correct speed is achieved and maintained, will be flatter, and so the airplane will glide further.

Establish the target gliding speed by setting the correct pitch attitude.

The Effect of Wind

At the normal gliding speed, a headwind will retard the airplane's passage over the ground; a tailwind will extend it. The rate of descent remains the same.

A headwind steepens the descent over the ground; a tailwind flattens it.

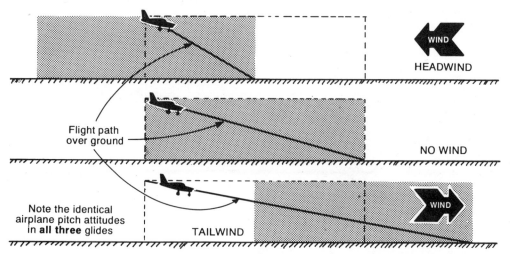

Figure 8a-3. Compared with a still-air glide, more ground is covered when gliding with a tailwind and less with a headwind.

In a tailwind, reducing the airspeed slightly below the recommended gliding speed may increase the range a little by decreasing the rate of descent, because it allows the airplane to remain airborne longer and be blown further by the wind.

Conversely, the effect of a headwind can be minimized by gliding at a slightly higher airspeed. The rate of descent will be increased, but the higher speed will allow the airplane to penetrate further into the wind and cover more ground. Increasing the airspeed could be an important technique to use if you are undershooting on a gliding approach to land in a strong headwind.

Estimating the Gliding Range

A practical means of estimating how far the airplane could glide at a constant airspeed is to note the ground feature which remains stationary in the windshield. In the situation illustrated below, it appears that the glide will reach the trees beyond the first road, but not as far as the second road.

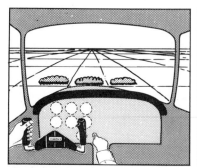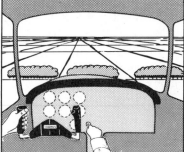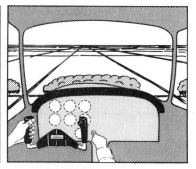

Figure 8a-4. Estimating the gliding distance

The airplane will not reach anything that moves steadily *up* the windshield, and will fly over anything that moves steadily *down* the windshield.

Note: Raising the nose in an attempt to reach the second field may have the reverse effect. If the speed falls significantly below the best gliding speed, the glidepath will steepen and fall well short of even the first road.

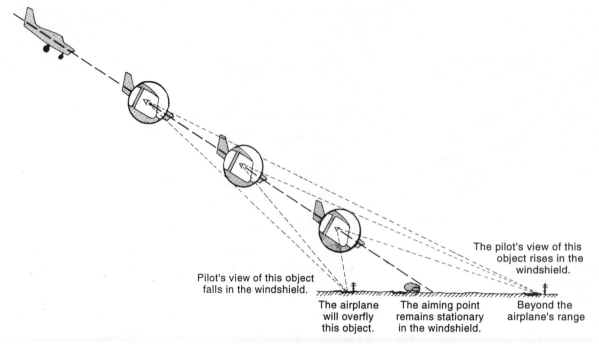

The pilot's view of this object rises in the windshield.

Pilot's view of this object falls in the windshield.

The airplane will overfly this object.

The aiming point remains stationary in the windshield.

Beyond the airplane's range

Figure 8a-5. The airplane can reach the point that remains fixed in the windshield.

Cockpit Controls

Mixture Control

It is usual to move the red mixture control to full RICH before establishing a descent, so that the mixture is not too lean when power is reapplied at a lower level where the air is denser. An excessively lean mixture can cause detonation, a process which is very damaging to an engine.

The mixture control should be moved to RICH for a glide.

Carburetor Heat

The usual clues of carburetor ice forming (reduced rpm and rough running) may not be evident because of the low engine speed. Consequently, during the glide the carburetor heat should be set to HOT to prevent the formation of carburetor ice (of course, being careful to ensure that it *is* the carburetor heat knob that is pulled right out and **not** the mixture control!).

Set carburetor heat to HOT for the glide.

Selecting the carburetor heat to HOT **prior** to closing the throttle is a good practice, so that some hot air passes through the induction system before the engine is reduced to idle. Done in the reverse sequence, there may be sufficient time after closing the throttle for carburetor ice to form before the HOT air is selected. In general, apply carburetor heat as the first item in establishing a glide, and remove it as the last item after reapplying power. *Discuss the correct technique for your airplane with your flight instructor.*

Power

With the mixture RICH and carburetor heat applied, the power can be reduced by smoothly pulling the throttle out. Full movement of the throttle should take about the same time as a slow *"1–2–3"* count. The reduced slipstream effect on the vertical stabilizer will require **left rudder** to keep the coordination ball centered and prevent the nose from yawing right.

Reduce power, controlling airspeed with elevator and coordination with rudder.

The tendency for the nose to drop too far, caused by the reduced thrust and the reduced slipstream over the horizontal stabilizer, will require **back pressure** on the control column.

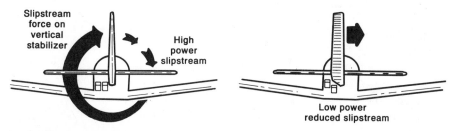

Figure 8a-6. Apply left rudder to prevent the airplane from yawing when the power is reduced.

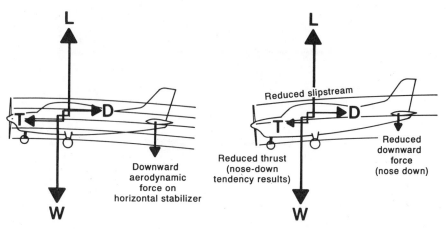

Figure 8a-7. The nose tends to drop when the power is reduced—counteract this with elevator back pressure.

Points to Note

1. Some airplanes have a rudder trim which may be used to relieve steady foot pressures in the descent. When you are established in the descent, feel free to use it.

2. The tendency for the nose to drop as power is reduced is a safety feature designed into an airplane to ensure that it will adopt a safe gliding attitude without any help from the pilot if the engine fails.

Warm the Engine

Every 500 feet or so on a prolonged descent, you should apply approximately 50% power for a few seconds to:

- keep the engine and oil warm;
- avoid carbon-fouling on the spark plugs; and
- ensure that the carburetor heat is still supplying heated air.

Warm the engine periodically during a prolonged descent.

Monitor Descent Rate

The rate of descent is a measure of how fast altitude is being lost (in feet per minute—fpm). It can be monitored on either:

- the vertical speed indicator (VSI); or
- the altimeter and clock combined.

A 500 fpm rate of descent shown on the VSI is equivalent to a loss of 250 feet in 30 seconds, or a loss of 125 feet in 15 seconds.

The Best Endurance Glide

Usually, the objective in a glide is to achieve the maximum range (the greatest distance over the ground) and this is the situation that we have addressed so far. Occasionally, **time** in flight, rather than distance covered, becomes important, say if the engine has stopped at 5,000 feet directly over an airfield and you want as long as possible to restart it.

The **best endurance glide** is achieved at the speed that results in the **minimum rate of descent** as indicated on the vertical speed indicator. Typically, it is some 25% less than the gliding speed used for maximum range.

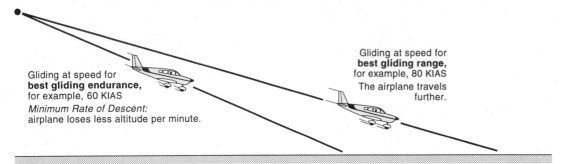

Gliding at speed for
best gliding endurance,
for example, 60 KIAS
Minimum Rate of Descent:
airplane loses less altitude per minute.

Gliding at speed for
best gliding range,
for example, 80 KIAS
The airplane travels
further.

Figure 8a-8. Select the best gliding speed for range or for endurance.

Flying the Maneuver

Prior to commencing the descent, decide on an appropriate gliding speed, select a reference point well ahead and **look out** to check all clear of other airplanes and obstacles ahead, below and to either side. A clearing turn to check under the nose may be advisable.

To Establish a Glide

Reduce the **power** by placing the mixture control to RICH, carburetor heat to HOT, and closing the throttle. This removes the thrust. Back pressure on the control column and left rudder pressure will be required to counteract the pitch/yaw tendencies as the power is reduced.

Hold the nose up and maintain altitude, allowing the airspeed to decrease. When at the target gliding speed, lower the nose slightly to the gliding **attitude** and maintain airspeed with fore and aft pressures, as required, on the control column. **Trim.**

An easy way to remember the sequence of events when commencing a descent is P–A–T, which stands for: **power–attitude–trim.**

To Maintain the Glide

To maintain a glide, hold the wings level with aileron and the coordination ball centered with rudder pressure. Control airspeed with elevator—a higher nose attitude for a lower airspeed.

Maintain a good lookout in the descent, possibly with clearing turns left and right every 500 feet to clear the area hidden by the nose. To enable you to maintain the original direction, select a reference point on the horizon or use the heading indicator and/or the magnetic compass. Another means of achieving a good lookout without changing heading is to lower the nose—but this will cause an increase in airspeed.

Warm the engine periodically, and remain aware of your altitude above the ground, and keep your target altitude MSL in mind. Ensure that the pressure window is set correctly so that the altimeter is in fact displaying altitude MSL.

To Level Off

Anticipate the level-off altitude by about 10% of the descent rate. For instance, at 400 fpm rate of descent, begin raising the nose when you are 40 feet above the target altitude, and start increasing the **power**—the mixture should already be set to RICH, smoothly move the throttle forward to cruise rpm. When the power is set, and provided conditions are suitable, move the carburetor heat to COLD.

Gradually allow the nose to rise to the cruise **attitude.** The yawing and pitching effects of adding power should be counteracted with right rudder pressure and forward pressure on the control column to stop the nose from rising too far. When cruise speed is reached, **trim.**

An easy way to remember this sequence is: P–A–T, **power–attitude–trim.** With some experience, you will be able to coordinate the use of power and attitude to make this a smooth procedure.

To Climb Away

Climbing away hardly differs from leveling off, except that you:

- smoothly apply **full power**—mixture RICH, carburetor heat COLD, and a silent *"1–2–3"* for correct timing to move the throttle fully in; there will be a greater *pitch/yaw* tendency which you can counteract with right rudder pressure and forward pressure on the control column;
- hold a higher pitch **attitude** for the climb, maintaining climb airspeed; and
- **trim.**

Note: You need **right** rudder pressure when power is applied in a conventional training airplane whose propeller rotates clockwise when viewed from the cockpit, but **left** rudder pressure in an airplane whose propeller rotates counterclockwise.

To climb away from a descent, such as in a go-around—P-A-T still applies.

Airmanship

Maintain a high visual awareness and clear the area under the nose every 500 feet or so in the descent. Maintain a listening watch on the radio if appropriate.

Remain aware of your altitude above the ground when descending. Set the altimeter pressure window correctly so that you can level off exactly at the target altitude, and make a positive effort to maintain this altitude accurately.

Airmanship is knowing exactly where you are in the air, and keeping a good lookout.

Airwork 8a
The Glide

Objective

To enter and maintain a steady glide on a constant heading and to level off at a specific altitude.

1. Prior to Descent

- Decide on a gliding speed.
- Select a reference point.
- **Clear the area** and **look out.**

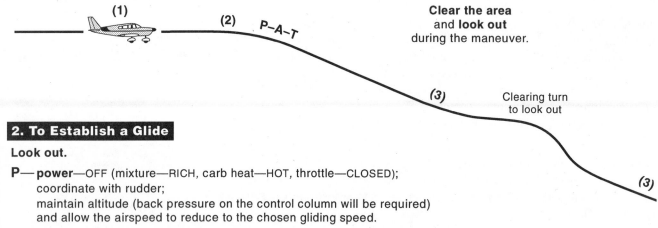

(1)

(2) P–A–T

Clear the area
and **look out**
during the maneuver.

(3)

Clearing turn
to look out

(3)

2. To Establish a Glide

Look out.

P—**power**—OFF (mixture—RICH, carb heat—HOT, throttle—CLOSED);
coordinate with rudder;
maintain altitude (back pressure on the control column will be required)
and allow the airspeed to reduce to the chosen gliding speed.

A—when the gliding airspeed is established, lower the nose to the glide **attitude;**
maintain airspeed with elevator.

T— **trim.**

1. Reduce power, maintain altitude.

2. Select the glide attitude.
3. Trim.

3. Maintaining the Glide

- **Look out**, making clearing turns if necessary. Maintain:
  - wings level with aileron;
  - coordination with rudder pressure; and
  - airspeed with elevator.
- Monitor engine instruments, and warm the engine periodically.

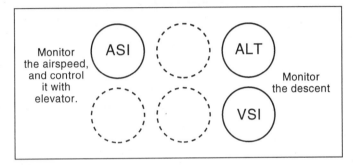

Monitor the airspeed, and control it with elevator.

Monitor the descent

4a. To Level Off

Clear the area and **look out**; anticipate reaching the target level-off altitude.

P—set cruise **power** with the throttle (carb heat—COLD); coordinate with rudder.

A—raise the nose to the straight-and-level **attitude**.

T—**trim**.

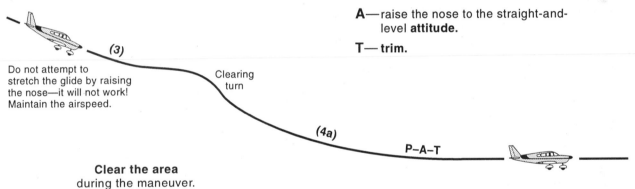

(3)

Do not attempt to stretch the glide by raising the nose—it will not work! Maintain the airspeed.

Clearing turn

(4a)

P–A–T

Clear the area during the maneuver.

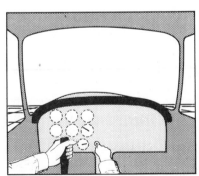

1. Set the power.
2. Set the attitude.
3. Trim.

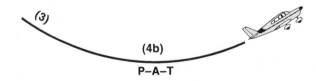

(3)

(4b)

P–A–T

4b. To Establish a Climb from the Glide

(for example, a go-around)

P—apply climb **power** *(as in item 4a above)*.

A—set the climb **attitude**.

T—**trim**.

✍ Review 8a

1. A descent without power is called a _____ .
   ➤ glide

2. Increased drag will (steepen/shallow) the glide.
   ➤ steepen

3. A clean airplane will glide (further than/not as far as) an airplane in a high-drag configuration—for instance, with landing flaps extended.
   ➤ further than

4. The drag that an airplane experiences (varies with airspeed/is not affected by airspeed).
   ➤ varies with airspeed

5. To glide the furthest, you should hold the pitch attitude for (a slow/a fast/the recommended best-glide) speed.
   ➤ the recommended best-glide speed

6. An airplane flying slower than the best gliding speed will glide (further/not as far) because it experiences (more/less) drag.
   ➤ not as far, more

7. An airplane flying faster than the best gliding speed will glide (further/not as far) because it experiences (more/less) drag.
   ➤ not as far, more

8. The airspeed in a glide is controlled by (power/nose attitude).
   ➤ nose attitude

9. In a glide, if the airspeed is too low, you should (raise/lower) the nose, and if the airspeed is too high, you should (raise/lower) the nose.
   ➤ lower, raise

10. When flying at the best-glide airspeed you (can/cannot) stretch the glide by raising the nose.
    ➤ cannot

11. A tailwind (steepens/flattens/does not affect) the glide path over the ground; it (reduces/increases/does not affect) the actual rate of descent.
    ➤ flattens, does not affect

The Glide

12. A headwind (steepens/flattens/does not affect) the glide path over the ground; it (reduces/increases/does not affect) the actual rate of descent.
    ➤ steepens, does not affect

13. A ground object that you will glide over and past will gradually move (up/down) the windshield.
    ➤ down

14. A ground object that you will not reach in your glide will gradually move (up/down) the windshield.
    ➤ up

15. For a glide, the mixture control should be (RICH/LEAN/IDLE CUTOFF) and the carburetor heat control in the (HOT/COLD) position.
    ➤ RICH, HOT

16. It (is/is not) good airmanship to periodically make a shallow turn during a descent to clear the area under the nose.
    ➤ is

17. Accuracy in a glide is: airspeed within ___ KIAS, heading within ____ °, and to level off within ____ feet of the target altitude.
    ➤ 10 KIAS, 10°, 100 feet

18. As you reduce power for a glide, you can expect the nose to yaw (left/right) and pitch (up/down), which you can counteract with (left/right) rudder pressure and (forward/back) pressure on the control column.
    ➤ right, down, left, back

19. It (is/is not) good airmanship to periodically warm the engine in a prolonged descent by _____ .
    ➤ is, adding power

20. If the engine fails in flight when it is supplying cruise power, the nose will want to (drop/rise); the airplane will automatically want to adopt the (glide/climb) attitude.
    ➤ drop, glide

The Powered Descent 8b

Objective

To control the rate of descent and the flight path using power, while maintaining a constant airspeed.

Considerations

The Forces in a Powered Descent

If power is applied in a descent, the resulting thrust will counteract some of the drag. Consequently, the component of weight acting along the flight path need not be as great for the same airspeed to be maintained. The pitch attitude will be higher and the rate of descent less, resulting in a shallower descent.

The pitch attitude for a powered descent is not as low as for the glide.

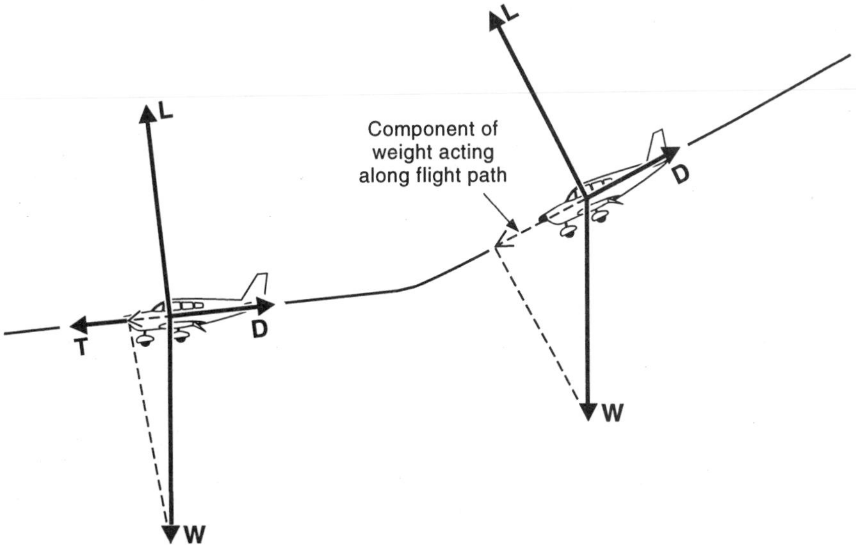

Figure 8b-1. Adding power flattens the descent.

Performance

Power plus attitude equals performance.

The performance achieved by an airplane depends both on the **power** selected and the **attitude.** To change the rate of descent and the flight path, while maintaining a constant airspeed, both power and attitude must be adjusted—power with the throttle and attitude with the control column. This is precisely what happens on a normal approach to land and on a cruise-descent.

The **cruise-descent** is used to save time, say at the end of a long cross-country flight—descent from cruise altitude is commenced some distance from the destination airport by reducing the power slightly and lowering the nose to maintain the same speed as on the cruise.

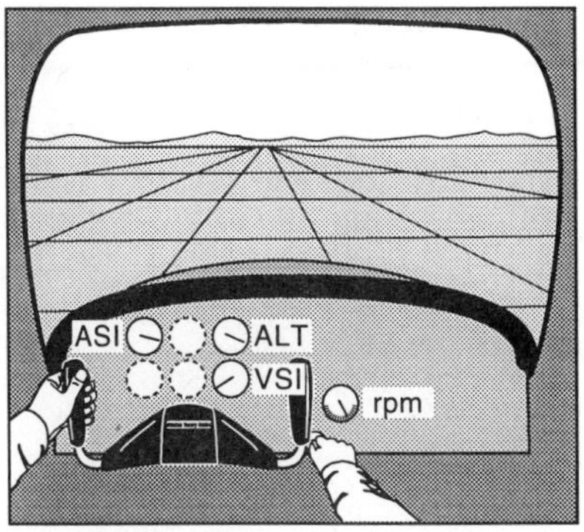

Figure 8b-2. Control the airspeed with elevator and rate of descent with power.

The Aiming Point

A practical means of estimating where the descent would reach the ground is to note the particular ground feature which remains **stationary** in the cockpit windshield while a constant nose attitude is maintained. This becomes particularly important when you are on an approach to land. You must adjust your flight path to arrive at the chosen aiming point on the runway.

The aiming point on the ground during descent stays fixed in the windshield.

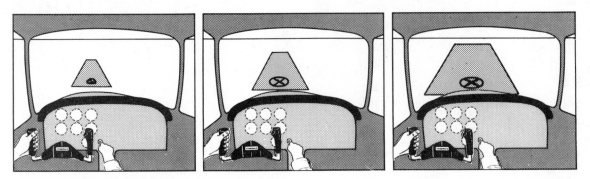

Figure 8b-3. The aiming point stays fixed in the windshield.

If you are **undershooting** the aiming point, then it will appear to move up the windshield. You should add power and raise the nose, ensuring that you hold the correct airspeed. This will flatten the descent path. Make power and attitude adjustments as required to achieve the desired flight path, indicated by your aiming point remaining stationary in the windshield.

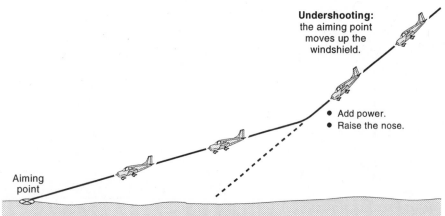

Figure 8b-4. Adjusting an undershoot

If you are **overshooting** the aiming point, then it will appear to move down the windshield. You should decrease power and lower the nose, ensuring that you hold the correct airspeed. This will steepen the descent path. Make power and attitude adjustments as required to achieve the desired flight path, indicated by your aiming point remaining stationary in the windshield.

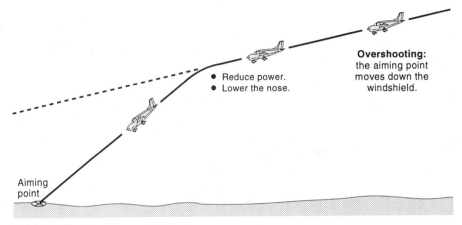

Overshooting:
the aiming point
moves down the
windshield.

• Reduce power.
• Lower the nose.

Aiming
point

Figure 8b-5. Adjusting an overshoot

Flying the Maneuver

If desired, you can monitor the rate of descent:
• on the vertical speed indicator; or
• with the altimeter and a clock.

To decrease the rate of descent and flatten the descent flight path:
• increase power;
• raise the nose to maintain airspeed;
• trim.

To increase the rate of descent and steepen the descent path:
• decrease power;
• lower the nose to maintain airspeed;
• trim.

The pitch/yaw tendency as power is altered should be counteracted with appropriate pressures on the rudder and control column—right rudder and forward pressure as you add power, left rudder and back pressure as you reduce power. (This applies to airplanes with a propeller that rotates clockwise when viewed from the cockpit, which is the conventional situation.)

On an approach to land, you can monitor the descent by constantly referencing the aiming point on the runway, estimating whether your flight path will take you there. If not, take positive action with power and attitude to ensure that it does.

Airmanship

Fly the airplane in a positive manner—use power and attitude to achieve the target airspeed and rate of descent. For an en route descent, the accuracy you should exceed is: within 10 KIAS of the target airspeed, within 10° of the specified heading, within 100 fpm of desired rate of descent (if specified), and you should level off within 100 feet of the target altitude.

If you are landing, control the airspeed and flight path precisely, and fly a stable approach path to the aiming point—**on slope** and **aligned with the extended runway centerline.** *You* should fly the airplane; do not let it fly you!

Consider the engine. Warm it periodically during a prolonged descent at low power, and use the carburetor heat as required.

Maintain a good visual awareness. Continually clear the area into which you are descending and maintain a **good lookout.**

**Airmanship is positively controlling
your flight path and airspeed.**

Airwork 8b
The Powered Descent

Objective
To control the rate of descent and the flight path using power, while maintaining a constant airspeed.

1. If the Descent Rate is Too High

- Add power with throttle—coordinate with rudder.
- Hold a higher nose attitude to maintain airspeed
  (monitor the airspeed indicator: *Power + Attitude = Performance*).
- Trim.

The rate of descent will decrease (monitor the VSI and altimeter), and the descent flight path will be shallower (a more-distant ground aiming point).

Attitude controls airspeed; power controls rate of descent.

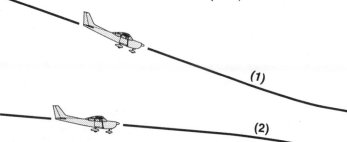

(1)

(2)

Accuracy:
- airspeed ±10 KIAS
- heading ±10°
- coordinated
- level-off altitude ±100 ft

2. If the Descent Rate is Insufficient

- Reduce power further.
- Coordinate with rudder.
- Hold a lower nose attitude to maintain airspeed (monitor the ASI).
- Trim.

The rate of descent will increase (monitor the VSI and altimeter), and the descent flight path will steepen (closer ground aiming point).

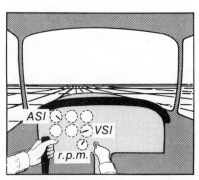

Descent attitude with higher power and lower rate of descent

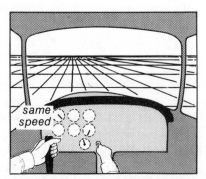

Descent attitude with less power and higher rate of descent

The Powered Descent

1. The pitch attitude for a powered descent is (lower than/not as low as) that for a glide.

   ➤ not as low as

2. To increase the rate of descent and steepen the flight path, you can (reduce/increase) power. The nose attitude will be (higher/lower).

   ➤ reduce, lower

3. To reduce your rate of descent and flatten the flight path, you can (reduce/increase) power; your nose attitude will be (higher/lower).

   ➤ increase, higher

4. If an airplane descends 100 feet in 15 seconds, the vertical speed indicator should read approximately ____ fpm rate of descent.

   ➤ 400 fpm

5. If an airplane descends 150 feet in 15 seconds, the vertical speed indicator should read approximately ____ fpm rate of descent.

   ➤ 600 fpm

6. If an airplane descends 150 feet in 20 seconds, the vertical speed indicator should read approximately ____ fpm rate of descent.

   ➤ 450 fpm

7. If the vertical speed indicator reads 300 fpm, the airplane will descend 100 feet in ____ seconds.

   ➤ 20 seconds

8. If the vertical speed indicator reads 200 fpm, but you desire 250 fpm, you should (add/reduce) power and (raise/lower) the nose.

   ➤ reduce, lower

9. If the vertical speed indicator reads 250 fpm, how long will it take to descend 1,000 feet?

   ➤ 4 minutes

10. If the vertical speed indicator reads 400 fpm, but you desire 300 fpm, you should (add/reduce) power and (raise/lower) the nose.

    ➤ add, raise

11. Tolerances on a powered descent are: to fly within ____ KIAS of the chosen airspeed, ____ ° of the heading, within ____ fpm of the descent rate, if specified, and to level off within ____ feet of the target altitude.

    ➤ 10 KIAS, 10°, 100 fpm, 100 feet

12. The point at which an airplane on descent would reach the ground (moves up/moves down/remains stationary) in the windshield.

    ➤ remains stationary

13. Your chosen aiming point on the ground moves up the windshield during your descent; you are (overshooting/undershooting), so you should (add/reduce) power and (raise/lower) the nose.

    ➤ undershooting, add, raise

14. Your aiming point on the ground moves down the windshield during your descent; you are (overshooting/undershooting), so you should (add/reduce) power and (raise/lower) the nose.

    ➤ overshooting, reduce, lower

15. Your aiming point in a powered descent is the approach end of the runway. In the figure below, you are (overshooting/undershooting); the remedy is to (add/reduce) power and (raise/lower) the nose.

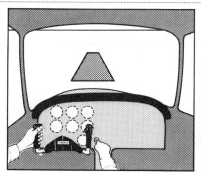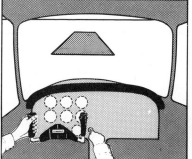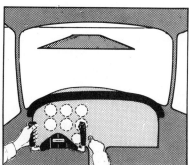

    ➤ undershooting, add, raise

Continued

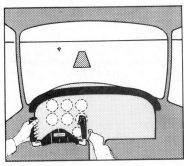 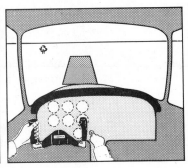 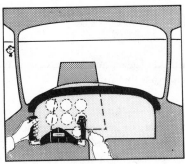

16. Your aiming point in a powered descent is the approach end of the runway. In the case illustrated above, you are (overshooting/undershooting); the remedy is to (add/reduce) power and (raise/lower) the nose.

overshooting, reduce, lower

Use of Flaps in the Descent   8c

Objective

To use flaps to steepen the descent.

Considerations

Flaps, Drag and Glide Angle

Extending the flaps causes a small increase in lift and a greater proportional increase in drag. Because drag increases more than lift as the flaps go down, the lift/drag ratio is decreased. To maintain a constant airspeed in the glide as the flaps are lowered, you will need to steepen the flight path or add power. The flight path will become progressively steeper with further flap extension.

Flaps increase drag and steepen the glide angle.

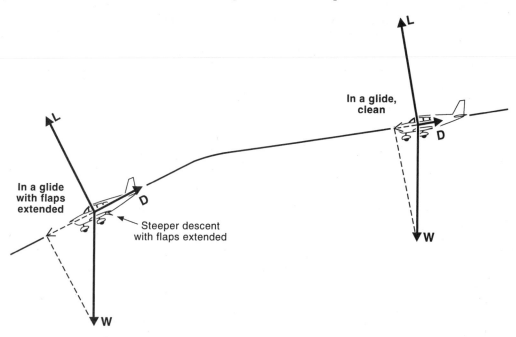

Figure 8c-1. Flaps steepen the glide.

Nose Attitude

The increased drag as the flaps extend requires a lower pitch attitude if airspeed is to be maintained in the glide. The lower nose position with flaps down affords a better view through the windshield than when the wings are clean (zero flaps). This is a significant advantage to a pilot, especially on an approach to land, and the greater the flap extension, the lower the nose position.

With flaps extended, a lower nose attitude is required.

You can maintain the specified airspeed by adjusting the pitch attitude with elevator, and then trimming off any steady control column pressure.

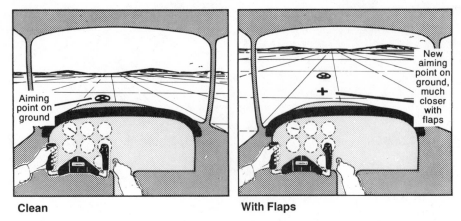

Clean　　　　　　　　　**With Flaps**

Figure 8c-2. A lower nose attitude is required to maintain speed with flaps extended.

Stall Speed

Extending the flaps changes the shape of the wing and increases its lifting ability. The stalling speed is reduced and so safe flight at a slightly lower airspeed is possible, while still maintaining an adequate safety margin above the stall.

Flaps lower the stalling speed.

Flap Extension and Retraction

As flaps are lowered, the changing shape of the wing and the changing aerodynamic forces produce extra stress on the airframe structure. For this reason, flaps should only be extended or raised when the airspeed is at or below the maximum flap operating speed, V_{FE}.

The allowable airspeed range for flap extension is shown on the airspeed indicator as a white band. V_{FE} is at the high-speed end of this white band; the stalling speed at maximum weight with full flaps extended and wings level (V_{S0}) is at the low-speed end.

Operate the flaps at a suitable airspeed, and be prepared for a pitch change.

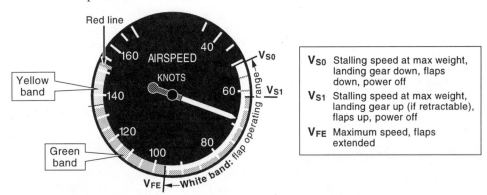

V_{S0}	Stalling speed at max weight, landing gear down, flaps down, power off
V_{S1}	Stalling speed at max weight, landing gear up (if retractable), flaps up, power off
V_{FE}	Maximum speed, flaps extended

Figure 8c-3. Useful flap speeds on the ASI

When you are raising the flaps to the clean position (zero flaps), you should be above the clean stalling speed (V_{S1}), which is the low-speed end of the green band on the ASI.

There may be a strong pitching tendency as the flaps are lowered or raised because the center of pressure, through which the lift force acts, moves fore or aft on the wings. You can oppose any unwanted pitch changes with pressure on the control column to hold the desired pitch attitude, and then trim off any steady control pressure.

Flying the Maneuver

Extending the Flaps

With the aircraft established in a normal descent, check that the airspeed is below V_{FE} (in other words, that it is in the white band). Extend the flaps in stages as required, holding the desired pitch attitude for each stage of flaps, and controlling the airspeed with elevator. Trim.

The greater the amount of flaps extended, the lower the required nose position. Re-trimming will be required after each stage of flaps is extended to relieve control column pressures. If the original airspeed is maintained, a higher rate of descent and a steeper flight path will occur. If the airspeed is reduced slightly (for example, on an approach to land), then the increase in the rate of descent will not be quite as much.

Raising the Flaps

As the flaps are raised, the loss of lift will cause the airplane to sink unless a higher nose attitude is set. Do **not** raise the flaps at speeds below the green band on the airspeed indicator; the lower end of the green arc is the stalling speed wings-level with a clean wing.

To raise the flaps, retract them in stages or degrees, holding the desired nose attitude for each configuration, and controlling the airspeed with elevator. Trim.

If flaps have been used for takeoff, then it is normal to raise them when established in the climb-out and at a safe altitude above the ground, say 200 feet AGL. Control the pitch to avoid sink and to maintain the specified airspeed, and then trim.

The flaps are generally used on an approach for a landing, so it is **not** a common procedure to raise the flaps in a continued descent, having lowered them, if the landing is to proceed.

In the case of a balked landing, the situation is different. Climb-out performance with landing flaps fully extended will be significantly degraded because of the high drag, so landing flaps should be raised to a more suitable position in a go-around. This is usually done in stages.

The strong pitch-up tendency as maximum power is applied for a go-around has to be resisted with forward pressure on the control column, if an appropriate attitude is to be held. The go-around is an important maneuver, and is covered in detail in a later exercise.

Airmanship

Do not exceed the maximum speed for flap extension (V_{FE}), and do not raise the flaps at airspeeds below the clean stalling speed (V_{S1}).

Airmanship is flying the airplane within its limitations.

Fly the airplane smoothly as the flaps are extended or raised; hold the desired pitch attitude, changing it smoothly as required when the flap position is changed.

Be aware of your airspeed.

Avoid ballooning as the flaps are lowered, and avoid sinking as the flaps are raised.

Airwork 8c
Use of Flaps in the Descent

Objective
To extend the flaps in a controlled descent.

To Lower the Flaps

- Check the speed—your airspeed must be at or below the maximum flap extension speed, V_{FE} (high-speed end of the white ASI band).
- Lower the flaps in stages or degrees.

- Hold a lower nose attitude and control the airspeed with elevator.
- Trim off any steady elevator pressure.

> *Note the increased rate of descent resulting from the extended flaps in the descent.*

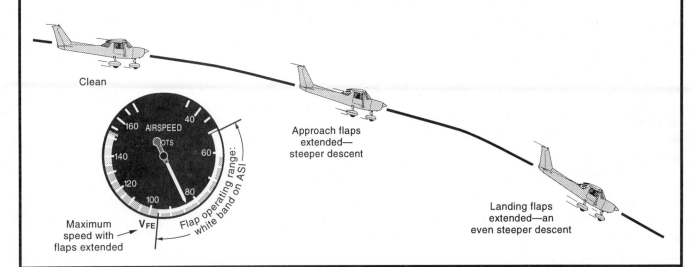

Clean

Approach flaps extended— steeper descent

Landing flaps extended—an even steeper descent

Maximum speed with flaps extended

V_{FE}

Flap operating range: white band on ASI

 # Airwork 8c

Use of Flaps in the Descent

1. The flaps can be used to (steepen/shallow) a descent path without any change in airspeed.

   > steepen

2. The nose attitude in a descent is (lower/higher) with flaps extended, thereby providing (better/worse) forward vision.

   > lower, better

3. The flaps should be operated in (stages/one complete movement).

   > stages

4. Lowering flaps will cause a tendency for the airplane to (balloon/sink) unless the nose is lowered.

   > balloon

5. After changing the flap setting, you (should/should not) adjust the trim to remove any steady pressure.

   > should

6. Raising the flaps will cause a tendency for the airplane to (balloon/sink) unless the nose is raised.

   > sink

7. Lowering the flaps (increase/reduces) the stalling speed

   > reduces

The Slip 8d

Objective

To slip the airplane sideways through the air using crossed controls—to either steepen the descent path, or to counteract the wind drift in a crosswind landing.

Considerations

What Is a Slip?

The slip is an uncoordinated flight condition with one wing lowered. It is uncoordinated because you use aileron and rudder in opposite senses—for example, left aileron to lower the left wing, with right rudder to stop the airplane turning left—and the coordination ball will *not* be centered. The longitudinal axis of the airplane will be at an angle to the airplane's path through the air.

A slip is flown with crossed-controls.

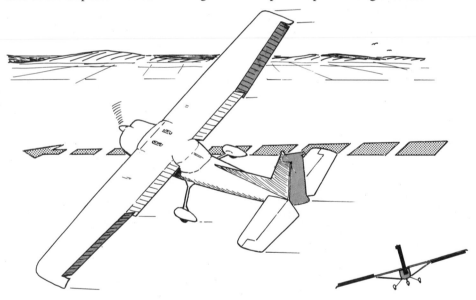

Figure 8d-1. The slip

Even though the airplane is in an uncoordinated condition during a slip maneuver, you can still make it feel comfortable by applying the aileron and opposite rudder smoothly, and with no dramatic changes in the pitch attitude.

There are two main purposes in knowing how to slip an airplane.
1. To steepen the descent during an approach to land, known as a **forward slip**; and
2. To counteract the wind drift during a crosswind landing, known as a **sideslip**.

Later in this chapter, the maneuver is divided into two parts which cover these two types of slip.

Aileron Control and Yawing

When an airplane is banked using the ailerons alone, it will slip through the air toward the lower wing, and the nose will want to yaw toward the lowered wing. This natural yawing tendency can be opposed by applying opposite rudder (sometimes referred to as *top rudder*). If the bank is to the left, right rudder should be applied.

The airplane will be uncoordinated, with the coordination ball not centered but out to the low-wing side. You will have crossed-controls—the control column one way and the rudder the other. This is a slip maneuver. The greater the bank angle and opposite rudder, the greater the slip, with the maximum slip possible usually being limited by the amount of rudder available.

The greater the bank angle, the greater the opposite rudder required.

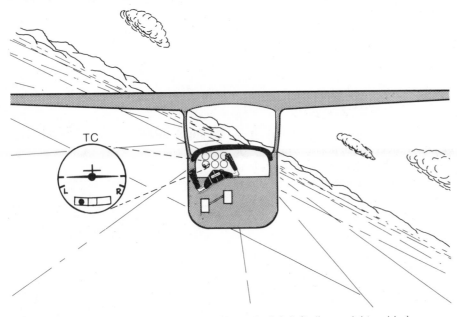

Figure 8d-2. Typical control positions in a slip to the left (left aileron, right rudder)

Forward Slip

The forward slip is mainly used to steepen the glide without gaining airspeed, and is generally used in airplanes *not* fitted with flaps. The forward slip is an especially valuable maneuver when you find yourself too high on an approach to land, and flaps are not available to steepen the descent. If you tried to steepen the descent by diving, the airspeed might increase unacceptably—slipping avoids this by virtue of the greatly increased drag.

The forward slip is used to steepen an approach to land.

Note: The importance of the forward slip maneuver in normal day-to-day flying has decreased because nearly all modern aircraft are fitted with flaps. However, it can still be a useful maneuver under certain circumstances, such as failure of the wing flap system, and so is still a worthwhile technique to practice and develop.

The forward slip steepens the descent by presenting the wing-down side of the airplane to the airflow, significantly increasing the drag. The lift/drag ratio is decreased, which causes the rate of descent to increase and the flight path to steepen. The greater the bank angle and amount of top rudder used, the greater the slip and the steeper the descent.

The power is usually at idle for a forward slip since the aim is to lose altitude quickly, and it would be contradictory to fly a forward slip maneuver using power at the same time.

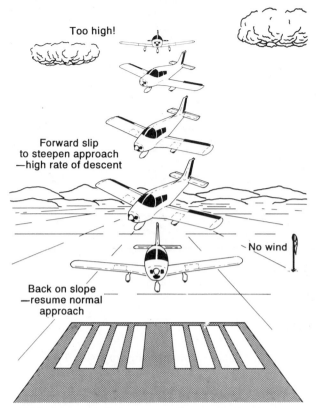

Figure 8d-3. A forward slip to steepen the approach

Pitch attitude and airspeed control in the forward slip can be maintained with pressure on the control column. Do not rely heavily on the airspeed indicator, since it may not give a reliable reading due to the disturbed airflow around the pitot tube and static ports in a slip. With practice, and guidance from your flight instructor, you will soon be able to judge airspeed fairly accurately from the attitude of the airplane, the air noise, and the feel of the flight controls.

If there is any crosswind on the approach, it is more effective to slip into the wind, rather than away from it. For instance, if you are high on approach with a crosswind from the left, then use left aileron and right rudder (a forward slip to the left).

During the forward slip maneuver, the longitudinal axis of the airplane will have been yawed away from the original direction of flight. The direction of travel, however, should be the same as as it was prior to you establishing the slip, the difference being that the airplane is now flying somewhat sideways. The steeper the slip, the greater the angle between the airplane's longitudinal axis and its flight path through the air.

If you are going to proceed with a landing, then the forward slip must be removed prior to the landing, both to align the longitudinal axis with the runway direction and to decrease the higher rate of descent. Some altitude is required to do this; your flight instructor will advise you on the altitude above the ground at which you should cease the forward slip.

A forward slip is useful when making an accurate approach to a short field (say during a forced landing) in an airplane without flaps. You can carry excess altitude early in the approach to ensure that you will definitely reach the field, and then slip off the extra altitude prior to the flare and touchdown.

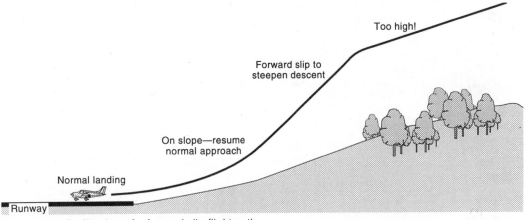

Figure 8d-4. Profile view of a forward slip flight path

The forward slip can also be used while turning, with more aileron than rudder being used to permit the airplane to turn. The slipping turn is considered in the next exercise.

Flaps and Forward Slips

The forward slipping maneuver is prohibited in some airplanes with flaps extended. This is to avoid excessively high rates of descent developing and/or situations where the elevator and rudder lose their effectiveness through blanketing of the airflow over them. If the fuel tanks are near-empty, a fuel port could be uncovered, causing an interruption of the fuel supply to the engine. The airplane Flight Manual or the Pilot's Operating Handbook will specify this restriction if it applies. There may also be a placard in the airplane itself.

Forward slipping with flaps extended is not an approved procedure in some airplanes.

Sideslipping and Wind Drift

For a good landing, the airplane should approach directly along the centerline of the runway, and touch down with its wheels aligned with the centerline. Any sideways drift when the wheels touch will cause an uncomfortable landing and place an undesirable side load on the landing gear.

Sideslip to counteract wind drift in a crosswind landing.

In crosswind conditions, an airplane aligned with the runway centerline and flying with its wings level will drift sideways. You can prevent this wind drift by lowering the upwind wing into the wind, and using opposite rudder to keep the airplane pointed straight down the runway. The result is a slip into the wind and, with practice, you will be able to judge the amount of slip so that it exactly counteracts the wind drift. This is called a **sideslip,** and will lead to a good touchdown in crosswind conditions.

If you are drifting to the downwind side of the runway, increase the sideslip by applying more bank and an appropriate amount of rudder to keep straight; if you are drifting to the upwind side of the runway, the sideslip is too great, so reduce the bank with aileron and adjust the rudder pressure to keep straight.

Most pilots like to get the airplane into the sideslipping condition prior to commencing the landing flare—more of this later, in the exercise on landings.

Note that, throughout the sideslip in a crosswind, the longitudinal axis of the airplane is aligned with the airplane's flight path over the ground, even though the airplane is slipping upwind. You will see airplanes of all sizes being landed in crosswinds using this technique, with the upwind wheel touching first, closely followed by the other main wheel and then the nosewheel.

Any restrictions on forward slipping your airplane during approach do **not** apply to using the sideslip technique for crosswind landings.

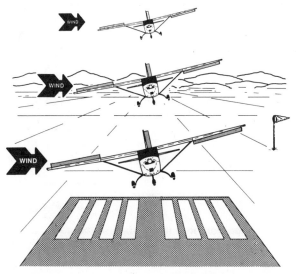

Figure 8d-5. Using a sideslip to align the airplane for a crosswind touchdown

Part (i)
The Forward Slip

Flying the Maneuver

To Enter a Forward Slip

Ensure that you have adequate altitude to recover, since a high rate of descent can be achieved in a slip. Close the throttle, establish an in-trim glide, then bank the airplane, and apply opposite rudder to stop the yaw. Hold the desired nose attitude with elevator to maintain the required airspeed. Do not trim, since slipping is a transient maneuver.

To Maintain the Slip

Maintain the bank angle with aileron and control the heading with opposite rudder. The greater the bank angle and rudder used, the steeper the flight path. The airspeed is controlled with elevator, but bear in mind that the airspeed indicator may be unreliable.

To Recover from the Slip

Level the wings with aileron and centralize the coordination ball by removing the excess rudder pressure. Resume a normal, coordinated descent at a suitable airspeed and rate of descent.

Airmanship

Maintain a good visual awareness of other aircraft and your proximity to the ground, because of the high descent rates. Do not slip in nonapproved configurations, and do not slip with near-empty fuel tanks.

Be in a glide with the throttle closed before establishing a forward slip—the purpose of a forward slip is to lose altitude quickly, and using power would decrease its effectiveness. Maintain a safe airspeed.

Airwork 8d, Part (i)
The Forward Slip

Objective

To increase the rate of descent in a glide, and steepen the descent flight path at a constant airspeed by forward slipping, using crossed-controls and without using the wing flaps.

1. To Establish a Forward Slip

From a normal glide (mixture—RICH, carb heat—HOT, throttle—CLOSED, flaps up):
• Apply bank in the direction of the slip with aileron control.
• Control the heading with coarse use of opposite rudder (uncoordinated flight—ball off-center).
• **Hold** the nose attitude and maintain the airspeed with elevator.

2. To Maintain the Forward Slip

• Maintain the bank angle with aileron—the steeper the bank angle, the greater the rate of descent.
• Control the heading with opposite rudder.
• Maintain airspeed with elevator.

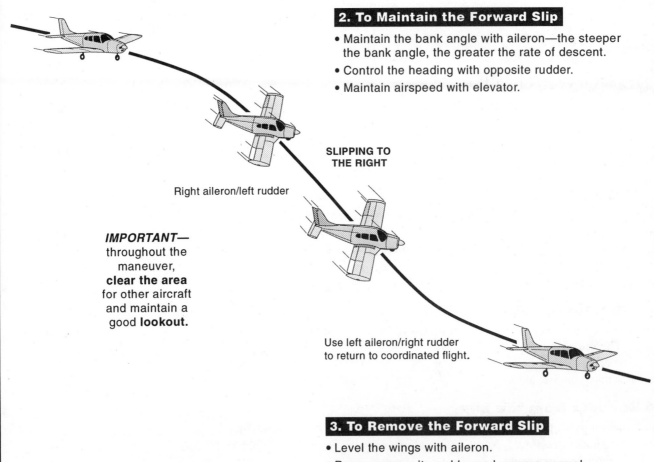

SLIPPING TO
THE RIGHT

Right aileron/left rudder

IMPORTANT—
throughout the
maneuver,
clear the area
for other aircraft
and maintain a
good **lookout.**

Use left aileron/right rudder
to return to coordinated flight.

3. To Remove the Forward Slip

• Level the wings with aileron.
• Remove opposite rudder and resume normal coordination.
• Maintain the desired airspeed with elevator.

Part (ii)
The Sideslip

Flying the Maneuver

Initially track along a line feature in a crosswind by **crabbing**—the usual method of maintaining a track over the ground and remaining in coordinated flight. The line feature on the ground could be a road, or it could be the runway centerline. The sideslip technique is normally used in a crosswind landing, but you can practice it while maintaining altitude using power.

During this practice, fly at a suitable altitude above the surface, as determined by your flight instructor.

To Establish a Sideslip in a Crosswind

To establish a sideslip, simultaneously yaw the nose into alignment with the line feature on the ground using rudder, and apply opposite aileron to bank the airplane upwind before any downwind drift develops.

To Maintain the Sideslip

Keep the nose aligned with the line feature using rudder.

If you are drifting downwind, increase the sideslip by increasing the bank angle and keeping straight with rudder; if you are drifting upwind, decrease the sideslip by reducing the bank angle, keeping straight with rudder. Control the airspeed with elevator, and the steepness of the descent path with power. (Your flight instructor may like you to practice this in level flight, which you can do by maintaining altitude with power.)

To Remove the Sideslip

You may not want to remove the sideslip. If you are using the sideslip technique to counteract wind drift in a crosswind landing, then you will want to keep the sideslip going right through to the touchdown. If, however, you do want to remove the sideslip, then simultaneously level the wings and centralize the rudder. Then apply a crab angle, if necessary for tracking, using a small coordinated turn.

 Airwork 8d, Part (ii)
The Sideslip

Objective
To counteract wind drift in a landing by using the sideslipping technique.

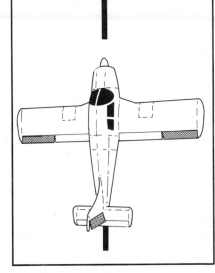

3. To Remove the Sideslip
(say if not landing)

Simultaneously:
- Level the wings and centralize the rudder.
- Apply crab angle necessary for tracking.

2. To Maintain the Sideslip

If drifting across the runway this way—**upwind:**
- Reduce bank with aileron.
- Keep straight with rudder.

2. To Maintain the Sideslip

If drifting across the runway this way—downwind:
- Apply more bank with aileron.
- Keep straight with rudder.

1. To Establish a Sideslip

On approach, simultaneously:
- Yaw the nose into alignment with the line feature using rudder; and
- Apply opposite aileron to bank the airplane into the wind before any downwind drift occurs.

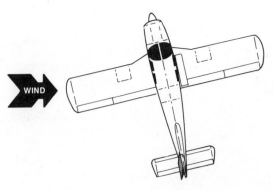

Maintaining course by crabbing into the wind

The Slip

1. In a slip, you use (same-side/opposite) controls, with the coordination ball (in/not in) the center.

    ➤ opposite, not in

2. A slip is flown with (coordinated/crossed) controls.

    ➤ crossed

3. You (should/should not) trim in a slip, because it is a transient maneuver.

    ➤ should not

4. The airplane illustrated below is performing a (forward slip/sideslip).

    ➤ forward slip

5. A forward slip can be used to (steepen/flatten) an approach.

    ➤ steepen

6. The airspeed indicator (will/may not) be accurate during a slip.

    ➤ may not

7. Forward slips are generally used to steepen the approach and lose unwanted altitude during an approach with (full/zero) flaps.

    ➤ zero

8. Forward slips with flaps extended (are/are not) a prohibited maneuver in some airplanes because of _____ the rudder, or the possibility of _____ the fuel ports.

    ➤ are, blanketing, uncovering

9. The airplane illustrated below is performing a (forward slip/sideslip).

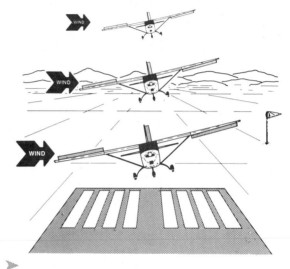

    ➤ sideslip

10. Any restriction regarding slipping with wing flaps extended applies to (forward slips only/sideslips only/both forward slips and sideslips).

    ➤ forward slips only

11. You (may/are not permitted to) use the sideslip technique during a crosswind landing with flaps extended.

    ➤ may

12. During a forward slip when making a zero-flap approach, the longitudinal axis of the airplane (will/will not) be aligned with the runway centerline.

    ➤ will not

13. Should the longitudinal axis of an airplane be aligned with the runway centerline on touchdown?

    ➤ yes

Continued

14. When using the sideslip technique in a crosswind landing, the longitudinal axis of the airplane (will/will not) be aligned with the runway centerline during the final stages of the approach.

➢ will

15. During a crosswind landing, the longitudinal axis of the airplane is aligned with the runway centerline before touchdown using the _____ .

➢ rudder

16. If the airplane is being carried downwind of the runway centerline by a crosswind just before touchdown, you should (lower/raise) the upwind wing.

➢ lower

17. If the airplane starts to move upwind of the runway centerline before touchdown in a crosswind landing, you have (too much/too little) wing down.

➢ too much

The Medium Constant-Altitude Turn 9a

Objective

To change the direction of the airplane's flight path by entering, maintaining and rolling out of a medium-bank-angle turn, using constant power and holding a constant altitude.

Considerations

What is a Medium Constant-Altitude Turn?

A medium constant-altitude turn is a turn performed with:
- a bank angle of 20° to 45°—less than 20° is shallow, more than 45° is steep;
- a constant power setting; and
- the airplane coordinated (coordination ball centered).

To achieve a good turn, coordinate the use of aileron, elevator and rudder.

Note: Apart from the medium constant-altitude turn (also known as the medium level turn) other turns which you will master in the course of your training are:
- climbing turns;
- descending turns;
- standard-rate turns (at 3° per second—for example, 2 minutes to turn 360°);
- steep turns (bank angle 45° or greater); and
- maximum-performance steep turns.

Figure 9a-1. A Beech Skipper in a medium constant-altitude turn to the right

Banking the Airplane

Banking the airplane tilts the lift vector. The horizontal component of the lift vector then provides a turning force (known as the *centripetal force*). Since there is no other horizontal force to counteract it, the airplane is no longer in equilibrium and will be pulled into a turn. The greater the bank angle, the more the lift force is tilted, and the greater the turning force.

A turn is accomplished by banking the airplane.

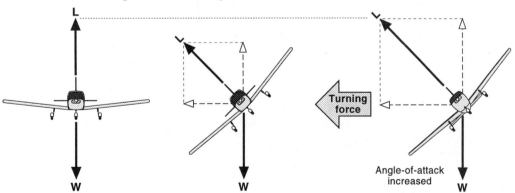

Figure 9a-2. Banking an airplane creates a turning force, and increasing the angle-of-attack increases the lift force.

Maintaining Altitude

Tilting the lift force reduces its vertical component, which will result in an altitude loss unless you increase the lift generated by the wings. You can do this by applying sufficient back pressure on the control column as the airplane is banked to retain a vertical component of the lift force sufficient to balance the weight.

To maintain altitude in a level turn, you must apply back pressure to increase the lift.

The Ailerons

To bank an airplane, you deflect the ailerons using the control column—one aileron goes down and the other aileron goes up. Deflecting an aileron down increases the lift from that wing, causing the wing to rise; conversely, the aileron deflected up on the other wing decreases its lift, causing it to descend. Hence the airplane rolls.

Rudder pressure is used to coordinate the turn.

Rudder Pressure

If the lift increases, so does the induced drag, which is the drag produced as a byproduct of the creation of lift. The rising wing in a turn suffers an increase in induced drag, since its aileron is deflected down to increase the lift and, consequently, causes an increase in induced drag.

The additional drag on the rising wing may cause the nose to yaw away from the direction of the roll. If you are rolling left, the nose may want to yaw to the right. This unwanted yaw (known as *adverse aileron yaw*) will throw the coordination ball left, to the inside of the roll, unless you do something about it.

The correct action is to **apply same-side rudder pressure** to keep the ball centered—left rudder pressure when rolling left; right rudder pressure when rolling right. Do this when you are rolling into, or out of, a turn. As you stop the rolling by neutralizing the ailerons, keep the coordination ball centered by simultaneously removing the additional rudder pressure.

Note: Many modern airplanes have design features, such as differential ailerons, to minimize adverse aileron yaw, and therefore require less same-side rudder pressure.

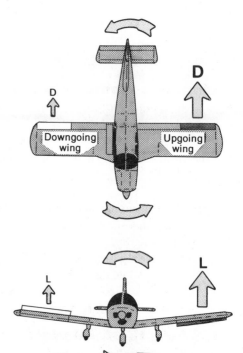

Figure 9a-3. Counteract adverse aileron yaw by using same-side rudder.

Airspeed

Airspeed tends to decrease in a turn.

To maintain altitude in a turn, lift is increased by applying some back pressure on the control column, thereby increasing the angle-of-attack. This results in increased induced drag from the wings. As a consequence of this **increased drag,** the airplane will tend to slow down, usually by five knots or so in a medium level turn.

At normal flight speeds, the small airspeed loss at medium bank angles is acceptable—the airspeed will be regained when you return the airplane to straight-and-level flight—so normally there is no requirement to increase power during a medium level turn.

Note: In steep turns (bank angles of 45° or greater) the airspeed loss would be significant and so additional power is applied to maintain airspeed. For this reason steep turns are sometimes referred to as *steep power turns.*

Normally there is no requirement to increase power during a medium level turn.

Wing Loading

The increased lift required to maintain altitude in a level turn means an increased loading on the wings, with each square foot of wing being required to produce more lift. At 30° bank angle, the lift that the wings need to produce is 1.15 times the weight of the aircraft; at 60°, it is double the weight. These are referred to as load factors of 1.15 and 2. The load factor in straight-and-level flight is 1.

The wing loading increases in a turn.

Stalling

The stall speed increases in a turn.

Because they have to generate additional lift in a turn, the wings are at a higher angle-of-attack than when the airplane is flying straight-and-level at the same speed. They carry an extra load, and so experience a **higher load factor.** The stalling angle will therefore be reached at a higher speed in a turn than when straight-and-level.

For example, the stall speed is about 7% higher in a 30° banked turn, increasing a straight-and-level stall speed of 50 KIAS to 54 KIAS. (The stalling angle is always the same—approximately 16° angle-of-attack for most wings.)

For medium level turns at normal flight speeds, there is still an adequate safety margin between actual airspeed and stall speed, despite the increased stall speed and despite the slightly reduced airspeed.

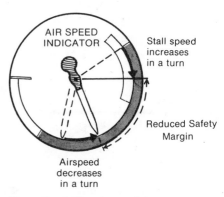

Figure 9a-4. The airspeed decreases and the stall speed increases in a level turn.

Bank Angle

A specific bank angle can be flown quite accurately by estimating the angle between the nose cowl of the airplane and the natural horizon. This is referred to as the **bank attitude.** It can be verified in the cockpit on the attitude indicator using either the angle between the miniature airplane and the artificial horizon, or by using the bank pointer at the top of the instrument.

Estimate the bank angle using the natural horizon.

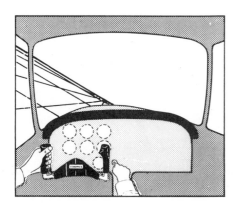

Figure 9a-5. Estimate the bank angle.

Pitch Attitude

Lift is increased in a turn by applying back pressure on the control column to increase the angle-of-attack. For this reason, the nose attitude of the airplane will be **higher** in a level turn than when flying straight-and-level.

The pitch attitude is higher in a level turn.

Estimating the correct pitch attitude against the natural horizon requires a little experience, especially if you are flying in a side-by-side cockpit as is the case in most modern training airplanes.

The pitch attitude for a given bank angle and airspeed will be correct if the airplane neither gains nor loses altitude.

Nose-Cowl and the Horizon

These remarks apply to a side-by-side cockpit.

In a left turn, the pilot in the left seat will be on the *low* side of the airplane's longitudinal axis, and the position of the center of the nose-cowl will appear to be higher relative to the natural horizon.

Conversely, **when turning right,** the center of the nose-cowl should appear lower against the horizon. After one or two turns left and right, you should have these attitudes fixed in your mind.

The nose-cowl/horizon relationship appears different in left and right turns.

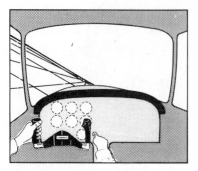 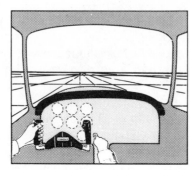 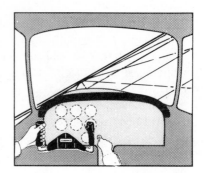

Figure 9a-6. Different nose positions for left and right turns

Turning Performance

The two aspects of turning performance are:
- the **rate** at which the heading changes; and
- the tightness of the turn—turn **radius.**

Bank Angle. The steeper the bank angle (for a constant airspeed), the better the turning performance—as the bank angle is increased, the rate of heading change increases and the radius of turn decreases.

Turning performance increases at steeper bank angles.

Airspeed. For the same bank angle, a lower airspeed will give a smaller radius of turn, and a greater rate of heading change.

Turning performance increases at lower airspeeds.

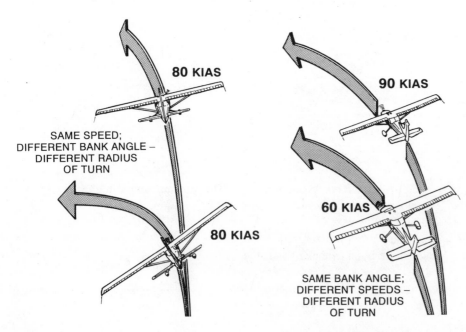

Figure 9a-7. A steep bank angle increases the turning performance.

Figure 9a-8. The turning performance is increased at low airspeeds.

Standard-Rate Turns

The *standard-rate* turn provides heading changes at a rate of **3° per second,** and is commonly used in instrument flying. At typical terminal-area maneuvering airspeeds, standard-rate turns are achieved with medium bank angles.

A standard-rate turn will cause a heading change of 180° in one minute, and 360° in two minutes. Most turn coordinators (or the older turn-and-slip indicators) have a marking to indicate standard rate, and are often labeled **2 MIN.**

The rate of turn achieved by an airplane depends upon its bank angle and its airspeed.

The higher the airspeed, the higher the bank angle required to achieve a given rate of turn. It has nothing to do with the size or weight of the airplane—a Boeing 747 will require the same bank angle as a Cessna to achieve the same rate of turn, provided that their airspeeds are the same.

To achieve a standard-rate turn at different airspeeds, different bank angles will be required. These are easily estimated using a simple rule-of-thumb:

> **Divide the airspeed by 10, and add one-half the answer.**

Figure 9a-9. Standard-rate left turn indications on the cockpit instrument—turn-and-bank (top) and turn coordinator

Examples
- **At 80 knots,** to achieve a standard-rate turn:
  bank angle = $^{80}/_{10}$ (which is 8) + one-half of 8 (which is 4) = 8 + 4 = 12°.
- **At 100 knots:**
  bank angle = $^{100}/_{10}$ (10) + one-half of 10 (5) = 10 + 5 = 15°.
- **At 120 knots,** required bank angle is (12 + 6 =) 18°.
- **At 150 knots,** required bank angle is 22°.

To enter a standard-rate turn, you can roll to your estimated target bank angle, and then verify if you are achieving a standard-rate turn by using either:
- the turn coordinator (indicating standard rate); or
- the heading indicator and clock combined (heading change at 3° per second).

If the turn is not quite standard rate, you can make minor adjustments to the bank angle.

Overbanking

The higher speed of the outer wing in a level turn will create extra lift on that wing, which tends to increase the airplane's bank angle. There is no need for you to be particularly conscious of this—simply maintain the target bank angle using the control column to "hold off" the overbanking tendency.

There is a tendency to overbank in a level turn.

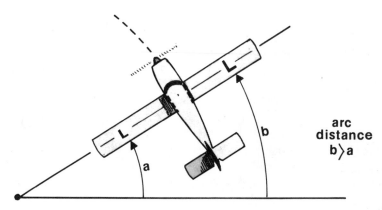

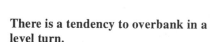

Figure 9a-10. In a turn, the faster-traveling outer wing develops more lift and tends to increase the bank angle.

Flying the Maneuver

Trim the Airplane

Unless an immediate turn is necessary, trimming the airplane properly for steady straight-and-level flight makes it easier to maintain altitude before and after the turn. There is no need to trim in the turn since a turn is only a transient maneuver.

Prior to applying bank, **check the altimeter and VSI** to ensure that you are maintaining the target altitude—the altimeter needle should be right on altitude and the VSI needle should be reading zero, or fluctuating about zero, indicating no tendency to either climb or descend. Also **check the ASI** to confirm that you are entering the turn at a reasonable airspeed.

There is no need to trim in a turn.

Scanning for Traffic

Develop a thorough scanning technique from side to side and both up and down before turning, remembering that airplanes, both yours and others, move in three dimensions. You should systematically focus on different segments of the sky for short intervals (one or two seconds) as a good means of detecting other aircraft.

Always look out and clear the area.

A good sky-scanning technique is:
- first look in the direction of turn, raising/lowering the wing to give you a view above and below;
- look in the direction opposite to the turn and as far behind as cockpit vision allows; then
- commence a scan, segment by segment, from that side of the windshield both up and down, until you are again looking well back in the direction of the intended turn.

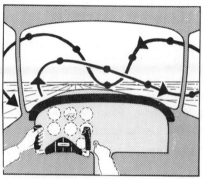

Figure 9a-11. A suitable scan before a left turn

Reference Point

While scanning for other aircraft, you can note visible landmarks helpful for orientation. Select a landmark as a reference point on which to roll out following the turn. Anticipate the target heading by commencing the roll-out about 10° prior to reaching it, since the airplane will continue turning as bank is removed (although at a decreasing rate) until the wings are level.

Select a reference point on which to roll out.

The Controls

Roll into the turn with a coordinated use of the control column and rudder. Apply bank with aileron and keep coordinated with same-side rudder pressure (keeping the ball in the center). Back pressure on the control column will be required to maintain altitude, which can be checked on the altimeter and VSI. Estimate bank angle against the horizon, checking it on the attitude indicator if desired.

The **roll-rate** at which the airplane rolls into the turn will depend upon how far you deflect the ailerons; the **steepness** of the bank angle will depend on how long you keep the ailerons deflected. To stop the roll in, you will have to neutralize the ailerons when you reach the target bank angle. Hold the specified bank angle to an accuracy of plus or minus 5°.

To maintain the turn, control the bank angle with aileron, coordinate with rudder, and maintain altitude with elevator. In *shallow* turns, the built-in stability of the airplane will try to roll the wings level—you may have to hold on bank.

In steep turns, the outer wing is traveling faster and creating more lift, and will want to steepen the bank angle further—you may have to hold off bank.

In medium turns, the two effects may cancel out, and the medium turn might continue with no aileron deflection.

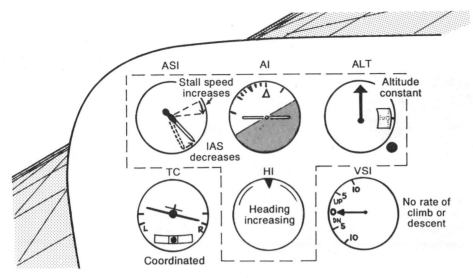

Figure 9a-12. Flight instrument indications in a medium level turn to the right

Do not forget to look out for other aircraft. Check the altimeter and VSI. **If gaining altitude,** either the bank angle is too shallow or the back pressure is too great—increase the bank angle and/or lower the nose. **If losing altitude,** either the bank angle is too steep or the back pressure is insufficient—decrease the bank angle and/or raise the nose.

Maintain coordination with same-side rudder pressure. Rolling right requires more right rudder pressure; rolling left requires more left rudder pressure. The coordination ball indicates the precise balance of the airplane—if the ball is out to the right, more right rudder is needed (or less left rudder if you already have left rudder applied); if the ball is out to the left, more left rudder (or less right rudder) is needed.

Aim to keep the ball centered throughout the whole turning maneuver—rolling in, maintaining the turn, and rolling out.

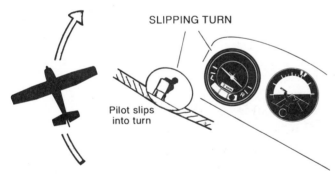

Figure 9a-13. Slipping turn: more right rudder is required.

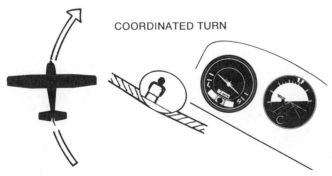

Figure 9a-14. A comfortable and coordinated turn

Exercise 9a **The Medium Constant-Altitude Turn**

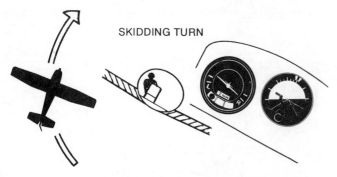

SKIDDING TURN

Figure 9a-15. A skidding turn: too much right rudder has been applied.

To roll out of a medium level turn, anticipate reaching the reference point by about 10° and commence removing bank with aileron, keeping coordinated with same-side rudder pressure. You should use rudder and aileron together. Gradually release the back pressure and lower the nose to the straight-and-level position.

You should aim to roll out well within 10° of your target heading. Stop the roll when the wings are approaching level by neutralizing the ailerons (and also rudder pressure). Having rolled out to the wings-level position, use small turns to make any minor adjustments to maintain your target heading as accurately as possible, and hold your altitude to within 100 feet.

Note: Steep Constant-altitude Turns, also known as Steep Power Turns, are considered in Exercise 15a. Turns Around a Ground Reference Point and S-turns Across a Road are considered in Exercise 16a which covers Flight Maneuvers with Reference to Ground Objects.

Airmanship

Remain aware of landmarks and keep yourself orientated with respect to the airfield—always know the way home. Your airplane will be changing heading in a turn, so maintain a good **lookout** for other aircraft.

Airmanship is scanning the sky before commencing a turn.

Since a constant power will remain set in the normal medium level turn, you can concentrate on placing the nose just exactly where you want it on the horizon, without having to worry too much about the airspeed and the throttle. Become familiar with the pitch attitudes for both left and right turns.

There is no need to trim in the turn since it is only a transient maneuver. Develop an awareness of coordination, and use rudder pressure to keep the ball in the center at all times. Aim for smoothly coordinated use of controls.

 Airwork 9a
The Medium Constant-Altitude Turn

Objective
To change the heading by entering, maintaining and rolling out of a medium level turn, using constant power and holding a constant altitude.

4. Rolling Out of the Turn
- **Look out**.
- Anticipate the roll-out reference point.
- Roll out of the bank with aileron.
- Coordinate with rudder pressure.
- Release the elevator back pressure.

Accuracy:
- altitude ±100 ft
- bank angle ±5°
- roll-out heading ±10°
- coordinated

Maintain altitude with elevator and accept the slight loss of airspeed.

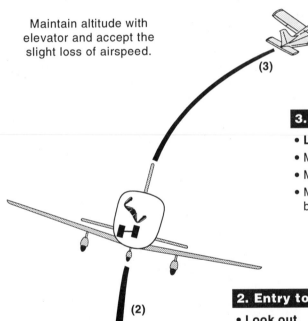

(4)

(3)

3. Maintaining the Turn
- **Look out**.
- Maintain the bank angle with aileron.
- Maintain coordination with rudder.
- Maintain altitude with the elevator, using back pressure on the control column.

(2)

2. Entry to a Medium Level Turn
- **Look out**.
- Roll into the bank with aileron.
- Coordinate with rudder pressure—
  (right rudder in this example).
- Exert back pressure on the control column to maintain altitude.

(1)

1. Prior to Entry
- Make sure you are at your chosen altitude and airspeed.
- Airplane in trim.
- **Look out** and clear the area for other aircraft.
- Select a reference point for the roll-out.

 START HERE

Note: Trim is not used during this maneuver.

1. An airplane is turned by _____ the lift force.

   ➤ tilting

2. An airplane is banked using the (ailerons/elevator/rudder).

   ➤ ailerons

3. Further banking is stopped by (reversing/neutralizing) the ailerons.

   ➤ neutralizing

4. The precise bank angle desired is maintained with (large/small) movements of the ailerons.

   ➤ small

5. The (horizontal/vertical) component of the tilted lift force pulls the airplane into a turn.

   ➤ horizontal

6. To keep the coordination ball centered while the control column is rotated to the left will probably require (left/right) rudder pressure.

   ➤ left

7. To keep the coordination ball centered while the control column is rotated to the right will probably require (left/right) rudder pressure.

   ➤ right

8. In a turn, you need to (increase/decrease/not change) the lift produced by the wings to maintain a constant altitude. This will cause drag to (increase/decrease/not change), and the airspeed will tend to (increase/decrease/not change).

   ➤ increase, increase, decrease

9. Compared with straight-and-level, the nose attitude in a turn is (higher/the same/lower).

   ➤ higher

10. You know that you have the right pitch attitude for a constant-altitude turn if (it looks right/the altitude remains constant).

    ➤ the altitude remains constant

11. The rate at which an airplane rolls depends on how (far/long) you deflect the ailerons.

    ➤ far

The Medium Constant-Altitude Turn

12. The steepness of the bank angle depends on how (far/long) you deflect the ailerons.

    ➤ long

13. You (should/should not) trim in a turn because it is a transient maneuver.

    ➤ should not

14. The load that the wings have to support in a turn (increases/decreases/does not change) with increased bank angle.

    ➤ increases

15. The stalling speed (increases/decreases/does not change) in a turn.

    ➤ increases

16. Increasing the bank angle will (tighten/widen) the turn, and (increase/decrease) the rate of turn.

    ➤ tighten, increase

17. A 30° banked turn at 60 KIAS, compared with a 30° banked turn at 100 KIAS, will be (tighter/wider/the same radius) and will take (the same time/longer/less time) to turn through a complete 360° heading change.

    ➤ tighter, less time

18. A standard-rate turn results in a heading change of _____ ° per second, which at 100 KIAS would require a bank angle of _____ °, and at 60 KIAS would require a bank angle of _____ °.

    ➤ 3°, 15°, 9°

19. A medium bank angle is considered to be between _____ ° and _____ °.

    ➤ 20° and 45°

20. Accuracy tolerances in constant-altitude turns are: altitude within _____ feet, nominated bank angle within _____ °, and nominated roll-out heading within _____ °. During the maneuver, the coordination ball should (always/occasionally) be centered.

    ➤ 100 feet, 5°, 10°, always

The Climbing Turn

Objective

To change heading while climbing at a constant airspeed.

Considerations

Forces in a Climbing Turn

The forces in a climbing turn are similar to those in a straight climb except that, because the lift force is tilted to turn the airplane, its contribution to supporting the weight is reduced. The result is a decreased climb performance if the airspeed is maintained.

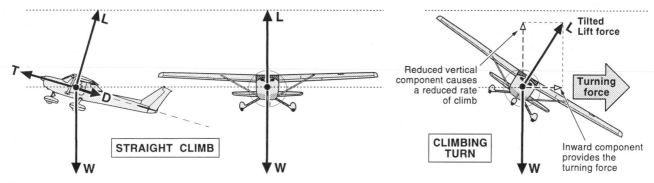

Figure 9b-1. A straight climb and a climbing turn

Rate of Climb

The **rate of climb** depends upon the excess power—that is, the amount of power available in excess of that required to overcome the drag. In a climbing turn, there is a reduction in the amount of excess power available compared with a straight climb, because of both the tilting of the lift force and an increase in the drag force. The result is a decreased rate of climb in a climbing turn, as indicated on the vertical speed indicator and the altimeter.

The rate of climb decreases in a climbing turn.

The steeper the bank angle in a climbing turn, the poorer the rate of climb. To retain a reasonable rate of climb, therefore, the bank angle in climbing turns should be limited to 15° to 20°. Remember this when making turns after takeoff.

Limit the bank angle in a climbing turn.

Airspeed

Climb performance depends upon the correct climb speed being flown with climb power set. For many training airplanes, climb power is maximum power, so the tendency to lose airspeed in the climbing turn cannot be overcome by adding extra power (since there is no more). To maintain the correct climb speed in a turn, it is therefore necessary to lower the nose.

Maintain airspeed in a climbing turn by lowering the nose attitude.

Figure 9b-2. Maintain airspeed in a climbing turn by lowering the nose.

There is a natural tendency for the nose to drop too far as bank is applied in a climbing turn, but this can be checked with slight back pressure on the control column. Hold the desired pitch attitude with elevator, and monitor the airspeed with an occasional glance at the airspeed indicator.

Slipstream Effect

Most airplanes are designed so that slipstream effect on the vertical stabilizer and rudder is balanced at cruise speed with cruise power set. Climbs are carried out with high power at an airspeed less than the cruise, with the result that steady right rudder pressure is usually required to counteract the slipstream effect.

Counteract the slipstream effect with the rudder.

The usual rules for maintaining coordination apply no matter what the maneuver is—move the coordination ball back into the center with "same-side" rudder pressure. The coordination ball tells you what rudder pressure is needed—if the ball is out to the left, increase left rudder pressure; if the ball is out to the right, increase right rudder pressure.

Overbanking

There is a tendency to overbank in a climbing turn. The higher speed and greater angle-of-attack of the outer wing in a climbing turn creates a tendency for the bank angle to increase—this overbanking tendency is greater than in a level turn. To hold the chosen bank angle, bank may have to be held off in a climbing turn using the control column, but you will do this naturally as you monitor the bank angle against the horizon.

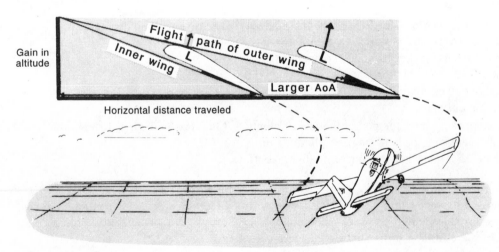

Figure 9b-3. The tendency is to overbank in a climbing turn.

Flying the Maneuver

To enter a climbing turn, establish the airplane in a straight climb at the desired airspeed and in trim. **Look out,** clear the area, and **select a reference point** on which to roll out.

Roll into the turn by applying bank in the direction of turn, using sufficient same-side rudder pressure to keep the ball in the center. Limit the turn to 15° to 20° bank angle and hold the nose in a slightly lower position (compared with the straight climb position) to maintain airspeed.

To maintain the climbing turn, control bank angle with aileron, coordinate with rudder pressure, and maintain the desired airspeed with nose attitude. Monitor the airspeed indicator. Keep a constant airspeed throughout the climbing turn with pitch-attitude adjustments, even though the rate of climb will decrease compared with climbing straight ahead. Maintain a steady lookout.

To roll out of a climbing turn, commence removing the bank some 10° before reaching your reference point. Roll off bank with aileron, coordinate with rudder pressure, and raise the nose to the normal climb attitude. Level the wings and keep the coordination ball centered, adjusting the heading and airspeed as required.

Airmanship

Limit the bank angle to between 15° and 20°, and maintain a constant airspeed with elevator.

Exert firm, positive and smooth control over the airplane. Maintain a good **lookout,** scanning the sky segment by segment.

Airmanship is keeping climbing turns shallow.

 Airwork 9b
The Climbing Turn

Objective
To change heading while climbing at a constant airspeed.

Throughout this maneuver maintain airspeed with elevator and accept the lower rate of climb.

(4)

Accuracy:
- bank angle 15°–20°
- heading ±10°
- airspeed ±5 KIAS
- coordinated

4. Rolling Out of the Climbing Turn
- **Look out.**
- Anticipate the roll-out reference point.
- Roll out of the bank with aileron.
- Coordinate with rudder pressure.
- Raise the nose to the straight climb position with elevator.

Practice the climbing turn in both directions.

3. Maintaining the Climbing Turn
- **Look out.**
- Maintain bank angle with aileron.
- Maintain coordination with rudder pressure.
- Maintain airspeed with elevator control.

(3)

Note: Trim is not used during this maneuver.

(2)

2. Entering a Climbing Turn
- **Look out.**
- Roll into the bank with aileron (20° maximum).
- Coordinate with rudder pressure.
- Lower the nose to maintain the climb speed (elevator).

 START HERE

(1)

1. Prior to Entry
- Airplane at correct climb speed, with climb power set.
- In trim.
- **Look out** and **clear the area** for other aircraft.
- Select a reference point for the roll-out.

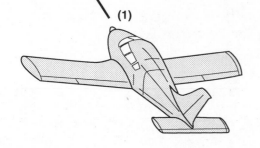

✍️ Review 9b

1. The lift force from the wings is (tilted/vertical) in a climbing turn.

   ➤ tilted

2. The turning force is provided by the (horizontal/vertical) component of the tilted lift force.

   ➤ horizontal

3. The weight of the airplane is counteracted to some extent by the (vertical/horizontal) component of the lift force.

   ➤ vertical

4. Because the lift force is tilted in a climbing turn, its contribution to supporting the weight of the airplane is (reduced/unaltered/increased).

   ➤ reduced

5. Climb performance (increases/decreases/is unchanged) in a climbing turn.

   ➤ decreases

6. Climb performance can be seen on two flight instruments. What are they?

   ➤ the vertical speed indicator, and the altimeter

7. If the rate of climb in a straight climb is 350 fpm, the rate of climb in a climbing turn at the same airspeed is likely to be (200/350/450) fpm.

   ➤ 200 fpm

8. The steeper the bank angle in a climbing turn, the (better/poorer) the climb performance.

   ➤ poorer

9. To preserve some climb performance at least, bank angle in a climbing turn is limited to approximately ____° to ____°.

   ➤ 15° to 20°

10. The airspeed is controlled in climbs, and climbing turns, using (power/nose attitude).

    ➤ nose attitude

The Climbing Turn

11. As you roll from a straight climb into a climbing turn, it is important that you maintain the same (vertical speed/airspeed/nose attitude).

    ➤ airspeed

12. To maintain the correct climb speed as you roll into a climbing turn, the nose attitude will have to be slightly (lower/higher).

    ➤ lower

13. In a climbing turn, you can maintain the desired bank angle using (elevator/aileron/rudder/power).

    ➤ aileron

14. In a climbing turn, you can maintain the desired airspeed using (elevator/aileron/rudder/power).

    ➤ elevator

15. In a climbing turn, you can maintain coordination using (elevator/aileron/rudder/power).

    ➤ rudder

16. During a climbing turn to the left, the coordination ball should be (out to the left/centered/out to the right)

    ➤ centered

17. If the ball is out to the left, you should apply (left/right) rudder pressure; if the ball is out to the right, you should apply (left/right) rudder pressure.

    ➤ left, right

18. The desired accuracy in a climbing turn is: bank angle between ____° and ____°, climbing airspeed plus or minus ____ KIAS, coordination ball (centered/out to one side), and then rolling out on the specified heading to an accuracy of plus or minus ____°.

    ➤ 15° and 20°, ±5 KIAS, centered, ±10°

19. You (should/should not) trim in a climbing turn because it is a transient maneuver.

    ➤ should not

20. It (is/is not) essential to always keep a good lookout, especially when turning or climbing.

    ➤ is

The Pilot's Manual **Flight Training**

Descending Turns **9c**

Part (i)
The Gliding Turn

Objective

To enter, maintain and roll out of a gliding turn, maintaining a constant airspeed.

Considerations

Forces in a Gliding Turn

The forces acting on an airplane in a gliding turn are similar to those in a straight glide, except that the airplane is banked, causing the lift force to be tilted. The **horizontal component** of the tilted lift force provides the centripetal force that pulls the airplane into the turn.

Banking the airplane to create a turning force:
- reduces the amount of lift available to counteract the weight, resulting in an **increased rate-of-descent** and a steeper glide angle; and
- increases the drag, causing a **tendency for the airspeed to decrease** (undesirable because the stalling speed increases in a turn).

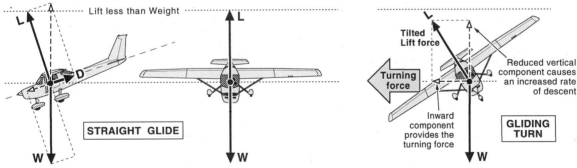

Figure 9c-1. The forces in a straight glide and in a gliding turn

Airspeed

The increased drag in a turn will tend to decrease the airspeed, so to maintain the target airspeed in a gliding turn the nose should be held in a lower attitude.

    As in all turns, there will be a tendency for the nose to drop, requiring back pressure on the control column to stop it dropping too far. Simply hold the attitude that gives the target airspeed. For side-by-side cockpits, the position of the nose-cowling relative to the horizon will differ for left and right turns.

Maintain airspeed in a gliding turn by lowering the nose.

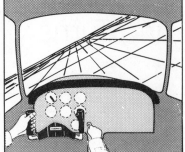

Figure 9c-2. Entering a gliding turn, lower the nose to maintain airspeed.

Rate of Descent

The tilted lift force and the lower nose position to maintain airspeed result in an increased rate of descent and a steeper flight path. The steeper the turn, the greater the effect, so be careful near the ground!

Limit the rate of descent in a gliding turn by restricting the bank angle. In a gliding approach to land, for instance, the turn to join final approach 500 feet above airport elevation should be flown at about 20° bank angle, and certainly should not exceed 30°.

The rate of descent in a glide increases in a turn.

Overbanking

Two effects tend to cancel each other out in descending turns, both when gliding and when using power. They are:

- an **overbanking** tendency due to the outer wing traveling faster; and
- an **underbanking** tendency due to the inner wing in a descending turn having a higher angle-of-attack.

There is no need to be conscious of this when flying—simply maintain the target bank angle with aileron.

There is less tendency to overbank in a descending turn.

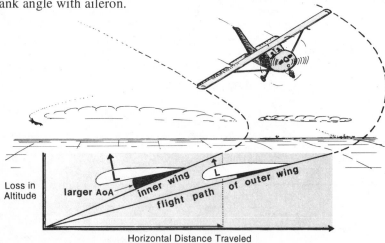

Figure 9c-3. The inner wing in a descending turn has a larger angle-of-attack.

Slipstream Effect

Most airplanes are designed so that they require no rudder pressure when cruising. However, in a glide (with no propeller slipstream effect), some rudder pressure may be required to keep the coordination ball in the center.

For an airplane with a propeller that rotates clockwise as seen from the cockpit, the lack of slipstream effect in the glide will require steady left rudder pressure to keep the ball centered. Normal coordination rules apply. If the ball is out the left, apply left rudder pressure. Left rudder pressure should be increased when rolling left in a descent and decreased when rolling right.

Counteract the lack of slipstream effect in a glide with rudder pressure.

Engine Temperature

As in a normal straight glide, apply power every 500 or 1,000 feet if the gliding turn is prolonged. This will keep the engine and its oil supply warm as well as clear any spark plug fouling that may have built-up while the engine was idling in the glide. Ensure that the carburetor heat is indeed supplying hot air to the carburetor in the descent to keep it clear of ice.

Keep the engine warm in a prolonged glide.

Flying the Maneuver

To enter a gliding turn, establish the airplane in a straight glide at the target airspeed and in trim. Look out to clear the area for other aircraft, scanning the sky segment by segment (especially below, since you will be descending), and select a **reference point** on which to roll out.

Roll into the turn with aileron, and apply sufficient rudder pressure to keep the coordination ball centered. A bank angle of 20° is usually sufficient for a gliding turn to avoid a high rate of descent developing, and you should hold it to an accuracy of plus or minus 5°. Do not unintentionally exceed a bank angle of 30°.

Lower the nose slightly to maintain airspeed (back pressure may be required to stop it dropping too far). Do not exceed a bank angle of 30°.

To maintain a gliding turn, control bank angle with aileron, coordinate with rudder pressure to keep the ball centered, and maintain the target airspeed with elevator—check the airspeed indicator. Hold the descent airspeed to an accuracy of plus or minus 5 KIAS. Accept the higher rate of descent, and keep a good **lookout,** especially below.

To roll out of a gliding turn, anticipate reaching the reference point by 10° or so and commence removing bank with aileron, coordinating with rudder pressure. Level the wings, and then make minor adjustments with small coordinated turns to achieve and maintain the target heading to an accuracy of plus or minus 10°. Hold the nose in the straight glide attitude (slightly higher than in the turn) to maintain airspeed.

Airmanship

Maintain a good **lookout**—especially important in any turn. Be aware of your altitude, since descent rates in descending turns can be high. Maintain airspeed with elevator, and exert firm, positive and smooth control over the airplane. There is no need to trim, since the turn is a transient maneuver.

Airmanship is keeping a good lookout in descending turns, and being very aware of altitude above the ground.

Airwork 9c, Part (i)
The Gliding Turn

Objective

To enter, maintain and roll out of a gliding turn, while maintaining airspeed.

Established
in a glide

(1)

(2)

1. Prior to Entry

- At desired descent speed.
- In trim.
- **Look out** and **clear the area** for other aircraft.
  Select a reference point for the roll-out.

Required accuracy:
- bank angle 20°, ±5°
- heading ±10°
- airspeed ±5 KIAS
- coordinated

2. Entry to a Gliding Turn

- **Look out.**
- Roll into the bank with aileron (30° maximum).
- Coordinate with rudder pressure.
- Lower the nose to maintain the descent speed (elevator).

(3)

3. Maintaining a Gliding Turn

- **Look out.**
- Maintain bank angle with aileron.
- Maintain coordination with rudder.
- Maintain airspeed with elevator.

4. Rolling Out of the Gliding Turn

- **Look out.**
- Anticipate the reference point.
- Roll out of the bank with aileron.
- Coordinate with rudder pressure.
- Raise the nose slightly to a straight-ahead descent position.

(4)

Practice in both directions

Throughout this maneuver maintain
airspeed with elevator and accept
the higher rate of descent.

Part (ii)
The Descending Turn Using Power

Objective

To change heading in a descent at a constant airspeed with a controlled rate of descent.

Considerations

Descent Performance

A descent may be either a glide with the throttle closed, or a powered descent in which power is used to control both the rate of descent and the flight path.

Descent performance is controlled by power and attitude. You can control **airspeed** with elevator, and the **rate of descent, and flight path,** with power. The nose attitude in a powered descent is higher compared with that in a glide at the same airspeed.

The rate of descent can be controlled with power.

Flying the Maneuver

Establish the aircraft in a powered descent at a steady airspeed and a specific rate of descent—for example, 300 fpm—using power as required, with the wings level and the airplane in trim.

Enter the turn normally, applying bank angle with aileron and coordinating with rudder. Add power to maintain the target rate of descent, and control the airspeed with elevator.

The steeper the bank angle in a descending turn, the greater the additional power required to maintain a constant rate of descent. You should be able to maintain the target rate of descent to an accuracy of within 100 fpm.

To reduce the rate of descent and flatten the descent path:
• add power; and
• raise the nose to a slightly higher attitude to maintain airspeed.

To increase the rate of descent and steepen the flight path:
• reduce power; and
• lower the nose to a slightly lower attitude to maintain airspeed.

To maintain a constant airspeed, the use of power and attitude should be coordinated.

Gradually reduce the power to maintain the target descent rate, and adjust the pitch attitude to maintain the airspeed when rolling out of the turn.

 Airwork 9c, Part (ii)
The Descending Turn Using Power

Objective
To change heading in a descent at a constant airspeed, with a controlled rate of descent.

---

1. Prior to Entry
- Set your desired airspeed.
- Trim.
- **Clear the area** and **look out** for other aircraft.
- Select a reference point for the roll-out.

Established in a powered descent

Maintain airspeed with elevator control and rate of descent with power.

(1)

(2)

2. Entry to a Descending Turn
- **Look out.**
- Roll into the bank with aileron (30° maximum).
- Coordinate with rudder pressure.
- Add power to maintain the desired rate of descent.
- Adjust the nose attitude with elevator to maintain airspeed.

Required accuracy:
- bank angle 20°, ±5°
- rate of descent as desired ±100 fpm
- heading ±10°
- airspeed ±5 KIAS
- coordinated

Practice in both directions

(3)

3. Maintaining a Descending Turn
- **Look out.**
- Maintain bank angle with aileron.
- Maintain coordination with rudder pressure.
- Maintain airspeed with elevator.
- Control the rate of descent with power.

(4)

4. Rolling Out of a Descending Turn
- **Look out.**
- Anticipate turn to reference point.
- Roll off bank with aileron.
- Coordinate with rudder pressure.
- Reduce power to maintain constant rate of descent.
- Adjust nose attitude to maintain airspeed with elevator.

Part (iii)
Descending Turn with Flaps

Objective

To change heading in a descending turn with flaps extended.

Flying the Maneuver

Turning with flaps extended is a common maneuver when making an approach for a landing. Flying with flaps extended:
- allows the required lift to be generated at a lower airspeed;
- reduces the stalling speed, making slower flight and shorter landing distances possible;
- requires a lower nose attitude for the same airspeed; and
- increases forward visibility.

A descending turn with flaps extended is flown exactly the same as a clean descending turn except that the **nose position is lower with flaps.**

   Because such maneuvers are made during the approach for a landing, it is important that suitable airspeeds and rates of descent are maintained. In general, do not exceed 30° bank angle at altitude—for turning to final approach, or when maneuvering near the ground, approximately 20° maximum bank angle is recommended.

As in all turns:
- maintain the bank angle with aileron;
- maintain coordination with rudder pressure;
- maintain airspeed with elevator; and
- (if desired) control the rate of descent with power.

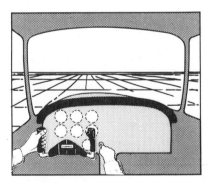

Clean

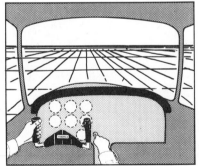

With Flaps

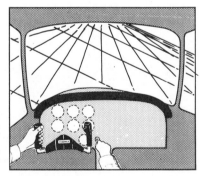

Descending Turn
with Flaps Extended

Figure 9c-4. With flaps extended, the nose position is lower.

Airwork 9c, Part (iii)
Descending Turn with Flaps Extended

The same procedure as in the previous exercise
(9c, Part ii) applies, except that the nose
attitude is lower with flaps extended.

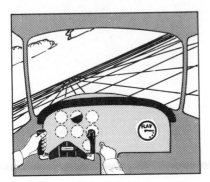

*Typical horizon view in a descending turn
clean.*

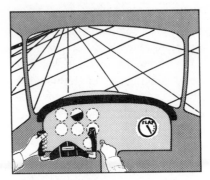

*Typical horizon view in a descending turn
with full flaps extended.*

Practice in both directions.

Accuracy:
- bank angle 20°, ±5°
- airspeed ±5 KIAS
- coordinated

Part (iv)
Slipping in a Descending Turn

Objective

To lose excess altitude in a gliding turn at a constant airspeed by slipping the airplane in the turn using **crossed-controls**.

Note: Refer to the Pilot's Operating Handbook to determine if forward slipping is an approved maneuver for your particular airplane type and, if so, in which configurations. Some airplanes are *not* to be slipped with flaps extended because of the disrupted airflow around the wings and empennage.

Considerations

Flight Path

The rate of descent and the steepness of the flight path can be increased dramatically by slipping, while the airspeed is kept constant. This maneuver is especially useful in an airplane not fitted with flaps when too high on a gliding approach for a landing.

Slipping can steepen the flight path.

The Importance of Slipping

The means of steepening the glide in most modern airplanes is to use the flaps, which will provide a steeper glide angle than a slip. The power of the rudder determines the amount of slip that a pilot can achieve and, since effective flaps have removed the need for the large and powerful rudder deflections required to slip the airplane, modern airplanes in general will not slip as well as some of the older types.

Slipping is not as important as it once was.

Forces

The forces in a slipping gliding turn are similar to the forces in a normal gliding turn, except that drag is increased dramatically to steepen the descent. This is achieved by applying significant rudder pressure opposite to the turn, causing the large keel surfaces of the airplane (the side of the fuselage and the vertical stabilizer) to be presented to the airflow. The slip can only occur in the direction of the turn—so, if turning left, apply right rudder to slip to the left.

Drag increases dramatically in a slipping, descending turn.

The airplane will not be coordinated in the slipping turn—indicated by the coordination ball being on the downside of the slip—that is, to the inside of the slipping turn. The lack of coordination can also be felt by the occupants of the airplane, who will feel pushed to the lower side on the inside of the turn. The rudder actually opposes the turn, and so the rate of turn will decrease unless the bank angle is increased.

The airplane is not coordinated in a slipping turn.

To maintain airspeed, the nose attitude in a slipping turn must be *lower* than in a straight descent. With a large keel surface presented to the airflow, there will probably be a tendency for the nose to drop, and so back pressure on the control column may be required to stop the nose dropping too far. Do not rely too greatly on the airspeed indicator, as the sideways airflow over the pitot tube and static vent may cause indication errors. A safe airspeed must still be maintained however.

The crossed-controls that you need to hold during a slipping maneuver could lead to a spin if you allow the stalling angle-of-attack to be approached—best guarded against by maintaining the correct airspeed. (Intentional spin entries and recoveries are discussed in detail in Exercise 11a.)

The result of a slip is an increased rate of descent at a constant airspeed, and a steeper descent angle. The greater the bank angle and rudder pressure, the steeper the flight path. It is not usual to use engine power during this maneuver since the purpose of a slip is to increase the steepness of the flight path.

The slip, and especially the slipping turn, are transient maneuvers, so **do not trim.**

Flying the Maneuver

Establish the airplane in a normal gliding turn, and maintain a good lookout for other aircraft.

To establish a slip in the gliding turn apply *top rudder,* control the bank angle with aileron, and maintain airspeed with nose position. The rate of descent and the steepness of the flight path can be increased by using a greater bank angle and more top rudder.

To stop the slip in the turn, centralize the coordination ball with rudder, maintain the target bank angle with aileron, and maintain the required airspeed with elevator.

Airmanship

Only slip in approved airplanes and configurations (refer to your Pilot's Operating Handbook).

Be aware that high rates of descent and steep flight paths can result from slipping, so allow sufficient altitude to recover coordinated flight at the end of the maneuver.

Airmanship is being aware of altitude above the ground.

Airwork 9c, Part (iv)
Slipping in a Gliding Turn

Objective

To lose excess altitude in a gliding turn at a constant airspeed by slipping the airplane in the turn using crossed-controls.

Note: Refer to the Pilot's Operating Handbook to determine if slipping is an approved maneuver for your particular aircraft type.

1. & 2. Enter a Gliding Turn

As per diagram 9c, part (i)

3. To Cause a Slip in the Gliding Turn

- **Clear the area** and **look out.**
- Apply top rudder.
- Maintain bank angle with aileron.
- Maintain airspeed with elevator (a lower nose attitude).
- Control rate of descent with bank angle and rudder.

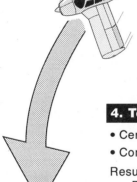

4. To Stop the Slip during the Turn

- Centralize the coordination ball with rudder.
- Control bank angle with aileron.

Resume a gliding turn, using the procedure as per Part (i).

During the slip, maintain airspeed with elevator, and control rate of descent with bank angle and uncoordinated rudder.

Practice in both directions.

Review 9c

Part (i)—The Gliding Turn

1. The lift force from the wings is (tilted/vertical) in a descending turn.

   ➤ tilted

2. Because the lift force in a descending turn is tilted, its contribution to supporting the weight of the airplane is (reduced/unaltered/increased).

   ➤ reduced

3. In a glide, the rate of descent will (increase/decrease/not change) as you increase bank angle.

   ➤ increase

4. The increased rate of descent can be seen on two instruments. What are they?

   ➤ vertical speed indicator, altimeter

5. The steeper the bank in a descending turn without power, the (greater/lower) the rate of descent.

   ➤ greater

6. The turn is caused by the (horizontal/vertical) component of the tilted lift force.

   ➤ horizontal

7. During a descending turn to the right, the coordination ball should be (out to the left/centered/out to the right).

   ➤ centered

8. During a descending turn to the left, the coordination ball should be (out to the left/centered/out to the right).

   ➤ centered

Part (ii)—Descending Turn Using Power

1. To maintain a constant rate of descent at constant airspeed as you roll into a descending turn, you will need to (increase/reduce/not change) power.

   ➤ increase

2. To maintain a constant rate of descent at constant airspeed as you roll out of a descending turn, you will need to (increase/reduce/not change) power.

   ➤ reduce

3. You should aim to hold the desired rate of descent to an accuracy of plus or minus ____ fpm.

   ➤ plus or minus 100 fpm

Descending Turns

4. Airspeed in a descent is maintained with (elevator/power).

   ➤ elevator

Part (iii)—Descending Turn with Flaps

1. The nose attitude in a straight descent with flaps extended is (higher than/the same as/lower than) when the wing is clean.

   ➤ lower than

2. The nose attitude in a descending turn with flaps extended is (higher than/the same as/lower than) when the wing is clean.

   ➤ lower than

3. What is the common situation when you fly a descending turn with flaps extended?

   ➤ turning to the final approach leg for landing

4. In a descending turn with flaps extended, the coordination ball should be (centered/to one side).

   ➤ centered

5. During a descending turn to the left with flaps extended, you would control airspeed with (elevator/power) and control rate of descent, if necessary, using (elevator/power).

   ➤ elevator, power

Part (iv)—Slipping in a Gliding Turn

1. Slipping in a descending turn will (increase/reduce) the rate of descent and (steepen/shallow) the flight path by (increasing/reducing) drag.

   ➤ increase, steepen, increasing

2. In a slip in a descending turn, (top/lower) rudder is applied to yaw the nose (into/away from) the direction of the turn.

   ➤ top, away from

3. The coordination ball in a slip is (centered/out to one side).

   ➤ out to one side

4. In a slipping turn to the left with (left/right) rudder applied, the coordination ball will be out to the (left/right).

   ➤ right, left

Turning to Selected Headings

Objective

To turn to a selected magnetic heading (MH) using:

1. The heading indicator (HI); or
2. The clock and the turn coordinator; or
3. The magnetic compass.

Flying the Maneuver

Reference Point

Whenever possible, select a distant reference point to turn to. This acts as a backup to the instrument indications as well as aiding you in orientation.

Select a visual reference point as a guide.

1. Using the Heading Indicator

The heading indicator (HI) is easier to use and more accurate in a turn than a magnetic compass, because the HI is a gyroscopic instrument and consequently does *not* suffer acceleration and turning errors. It must, however, be correctly aligned with the magnetic compass in steady wings-level flight for it to indicate the correct magnetic direction.

Figure 9d-1. The heading indicator

To turn to a specific heading using the heading indicator:

• Fly steady, straight-and-level to an accuracy of plus or minus 100 feet.

• Align the HI with the magnetic compass (so that your heading is indicated in degrees magnetic (°M)—the normal procedure).

• Decide the shorter way to turn—left or right—to reach the target heading—for example, to change heading from 090°M to 240°M, turn right 150°.

• **Look out** and clear the area.

• Carry out a normal turn, with occasional reference to the HI.

• Hold altitude to an accuracy of plus or minus 100 feet.

• Commence the roll-out approximately 10° prior to reaching the target heading on the HI, and roll out as closely as possible to the target heading—certainly within 10°.

• Make minor adjustments using small coordinated turns to maintain the target heading as accurately as possible.

Note: We write magnetic bearings either appended with °M (as above) or prefixed with MH for magnetic heading or MC for magnetic course, as appropriate. For example, **MH 240** is a magnetic heading of 240 degrees magnetic; **MC 175** means a magnetic course of 175 degrees magnetic.

2. Using the Clock and the Turn Coordinator

The turn coordinator allows you to turn at a constant rate in degrees per second, and the clock can be used to time the turn. A **standard-rate turn** (3° per second) for 30 seconds will alter the heading by 90°.

To turn to a specific heading using a standard-rate timed turn:

- Divide the change in heading by 3 to obtain the number of seconds—for example, from MH 090 to MH 240 is 150° to the right which, at 3° per second, will take 50 seconds.
- Carry out a normal standard-rate turn with reference to the turn coordinator (at say 120 knots, this will require a bank angle of $^{120}/_{10} + 6 = 18°$).
- Time the turn using the second hand on the clock (start the timing as you commence the roll-in, and then commence the roll-out when the calculated number of seconds has passed).

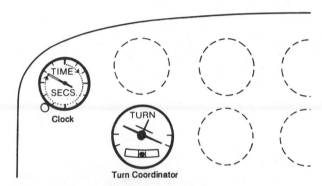

Example: From MH 090 to MH 240 is 150°, at standard rate (3° per second) = 50 seconds

Figure 9d-2. A timed turn using the clock and turn coordinator

3. Using the Magnetic Compass

This is the least-preferred method since the magnetic compass suffers considerable indication errors in a turn. It can, however, be used to verify the heading when the airplane has settled into steady wings-level flight and the compass oscillations have ceased.

The construction of a magnetic compass is such that, when an airplane is turning (especially through north or south), it will give false indications of magnetic heading. In the **northern hemisphere,** the allowances required when turning to particular headings using the magnetic compass are:

- when turning to northerly headings, roll out when the magnetic compass indicates approximately 30° **before** your target heading;
- when turning to southerly headings, roll out when the magnetic compass indicates approximately 30° **past** your target heading.

An easy way to remember this is *UNOS:*

- **U**ndershoot on **N**orth;
- **O**vershoot on **S**outh.

The above allowances should be reduced:

- when turning at less than standard rate; and
- when turning to headings well removed from North and South—in fact, when turning to East or West, no allowances need to be made.

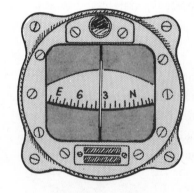

Heading 035° M

Figure 9d-3. The magnetic compass

The allowances described above only apply to the magnetic compass because of the turning and acceleration errors associated with it. They do *not* apply to the heading indicator, because it is a gyroscopic device which does not suffer from these errors and so is easier to use.

If the airplane has an unserviceable heading indicator, perform a timed standard-rate turn using the turn coordinator and the clock, with the magnetic compass as a back-up.

Note: In the **southern hemisphere,** the allowances when turning to particular headings using the magnetic compass are reversed.

(a) Turning to northerly headings, roll out when the magnetic compass indicates approximately 30° **past** your target heading.

(b) Turning to southerly headings, roll out when the magnetic compass has passed approximately 30° **before** your target heading.

✍ Review 9d

1. When turning to selected headings it is a lot easier to use the (heading indicator/magnetic compass).

   ➤ heading indicator

2. The heading indicator (does/does not) suffer turning and acceleration errors.

   ➤ does not

3. The magnetic compass only indicates accurately when the airplane is (turning/accelerating or decelerating/in steady wings-level flight).

   ➤ in steady wings-level flight

4. The heading indicator needs to be periodically aligned with the magnetic compass when the airplane is (turning/accelerating or decelerating/ in steady wings-level flight).

   ➤ in steady wings-level flight

5. When practicing turns to a selected heading in level flight you should aim to maintain desired altitude to an accuracy of plus or minus ____ feet, and roll out on the selected heading to an accuracy of plus or minus ____ °. You (should/need not) then make minor adjustments to achieve the desired heading perfectly.

   ➤ plus or minus 100 feet, plus or minus 10°, should

6. To turn from MH 010 to MH 170 the shortest way, you should turn (right/left).

   ➤ right

7. To turn from MH 010 to MH 340 the shortest way, you should turn (right/left).

   ➤ left

Turning to Selected Headings

8. To turn from MH 330 to MH 360 the shortest way, you should turn (right/left).

   ➤ right

9. To turn from MH 330 to MH 030 the shortest way, you should turn (right/left).

   ➤ right

10. To turn from MH 330 to MH 170 the shortest way, you should turn (right/left).

    ➤ left

11. To turn from MH 190 to MH 030 the shortest way, you should turn (right/left).

    ➤ left

12. To turn from MH 190 to MH 020 the shortest way, you should turn (right/left).

    ➤ left

13. To turn from MH 200 to MH 090 the shortest way, you should turn (right/left).

    ➤ left

14. To turn from MH 200 to MH 010 the shortest way, you should turn (right/left).

    ➤ right

15. To turn from MH 200 to MH 020 the shortest way, you should turn (right/left).

    ➤ either way

---

16. To turn from heading 360°M to 120°M, you should turn (left/right), and a standard-rate turn would take ____ seconds.

  ➤ right, 40 seconds

17. To turn from heading 360°M to 270°M, you should turn (left/right), and a standard-rate turn would take ____ seconds.

  ➤ left, 30 seconds

18. To turn from heading 190°M to 010°M, you should turn (left/right), and a standard-rate turn would take ____ seconds.

  ➤ left or right, 60 seconds

19. When turning to a northerly heading using the magnetic compass, you should roll out (before/when/after) the compass indicates your selected heading. You are in the northern hemisphere.

  ➤ before

20. When turning to a southerly heading using the magnetic compass, you should roll out (before/when/after) the compass indicates your selected heading. You are in the northern hemisphere.

  ➤ after

21. When turning to an easterly heading using the magnetic compass, you should roll out (before/when/after) the compass indicates your selected heading.

  ➤ when

22. When turning to a westerly heading using the magnetic compass, you should roll out (before/when/after) the compass indicates your selected heading.

  ➤ when

23. As in all turns, there is a tendency for the nose to (rise/drop) when turning to a selected heading.

  ➤ drop

24. When turning and wanting to maintain a constant altitude you can prevent the nose from dropping by using (elevator/aileron/rudder).

  ➤ elevator

25. You (should/should not) trim in a turn because it is a transient maneuver.

  ➤ should not

26. When turning to a selected heading at a constant altitude you can expect the airspeed to (rise/drop) a little if you retain constant power.

  ➤ drop

27. When turning to a selected heading in a descending turn, you can maintain airspeed with (elevator/aileron/rudder/power).

  ➤ elevator

28. When turning to a selected heading in a descending turn, you can maintain a constant rate of descent using (elevator/aileron/rudder/power).

  ➤ power

29. When turning to a selected heading in a climbing turn, you can maintain airspeed with (elevator/aileron/rudder/power).

  ➤ elevator

30. In all turns, you should control the bank angle with (elevator/aileron/rudder/power).

  ➤ aileron

31. One vital point of airmanship in all turns is to maintain a good _____ .

  ➤ lookout

Stalling 10a

Objective

To recognize the stall, and to recover from it with a minimum loss of altitude.

Considerations

The Stalling Angle

As the angle-of-attack of the wings is increased, the streamline flow over the wings breaks down and becomes more turbulent. This causes a buffeting (shaking or shuddering) of the airframe which is felt through the controls, and possible activation of any stall-warning device. At a critical angle-of-attack, the airflow will separate from the upper surface of the wings, causing:

- a marked decrease in lift, which results in a loss of altitude;
- rearward movement of the center of pressure (through which the lift acts), resulting in the nose dropping; and
- a marked increase in drag.

Stalling occurs at a critical angle-of-attack.

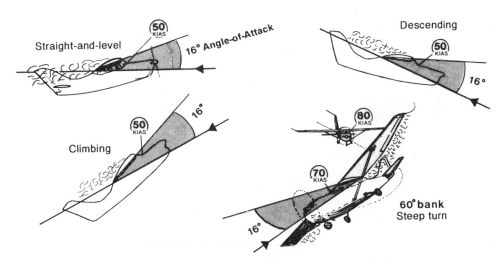

Figure 10a-1. Stalling occurs at the critical angle-of-attack.

The only way to recover from a stall is to decrease the angle-of-attack (by relaxing the back pressure and/or moving the control column forward).

You can increase the angle-of-attack (and reduce the airspeed) by bringing the control column back. This happens in many maneuvers such as:

- establishing slow flight;
- turning—especially steep turns;
- pulling out of a dive; and
- landing.

Stalling will occur whenever the critical angle-of-attack is exceeded, irrespective of the airspeed.

Furthermore, an upward gust of wind striking the wing will increase its angle-of-attack instantaneously. If the wing is already near the critical angle, the upward gust may be just enough to stall it; this is one reason why many pilots carry a little extra speed (with the wings at a slightly lower angle-of-attack) on final approach in gusty conditions.

What is the Stalling Speed?

The basic stalling speed is considered to be the speed at which the airplane stalls when it is at maximum weight, with the wings clean (that is, zero flaps), and flying straight-and-level with the power at idle. The straight-and-level power-off stall is made to occur by the pilot closing the throttle (carburetor heat ON), and progressively raising the nose.

The basic stalling speed is referred to as V_{S1}. It is published in the Pilot's Operating Handbook, and is represented on the airspeed indicator as the lower end of the green arc. V_{S1} should be memorized, as it is a valuable guide.

The stalling speed with full flaps extended (at maximum weight, straight-and-level, idle power and full flaps) is called V_{S0}. It is also found in the Pilot's Operating Handbook and on the airspeed indicator at the low-speed end of the white arc. The V_{S0} for your airplane should also be memorized.

Since stalling always happens at the same angle-of-attack, and not the same indicated airspeed, **listed stall speeds are only a guide**. Some advanced airplanes have an *angle-of-attack meter*, which is a better guide to an imminent stall than an airspeed indicator. The vast majority of airplanes, however, have only the airspeed indicator to help you.

Any maneuvering that increases the g-loading, such as a turn or pulling out of a dive, will increase the stalling speed, as will a weight-overload. Wing surfaces contaminated with frost, snow, insects, and so on, will disturb the smooth airflow and also increase the stalling speed. Reduced weights and high power will reduce the stalling speed.

Most airplanes have a **stall warning device** designed into the leading edge of the wing, such as:

- a small air inlet that detects the disturbed airflow that occurs at high angles-of-attack and pneumatically activates a whistle; or
- a small metal plate that is moved up by the airflow at high angles-of-attack, and electrically activates a horn or light in the cockpit.

Stall warning devices are usually set to operate at about 5 KIAS **before** the stall actually occurs, warning of an approaching (or imminent) stall.

The Flight Controls

Reduced airflow over the control surfaces will cause them to become less effective as your airspeed reduces and the stall is approached. Control pressures will decrease, and larger movements of the elevator and rudder will be required.

It is the main wing that stalls. The empennage remains unstalled (by design) so that during the stall the elevator and rudder remain effective. The ailerons may or may not remain effective during a stall depending upon the airplane type.

The Ailerons

A dropping wing can normally be picked up by moving the control column in the opposite direction. This causes the aileron on the dropping wing to deflect downward, increasing the angle-of-attack and producing more lift on that wing. If the wing is near the stalling angle, however, the aileron deflection could cause the critical angle to be exceeded on that wing and, instead of it rising, the loss of lift would cause the wing to drop further. With any yaw, a spin could develop.

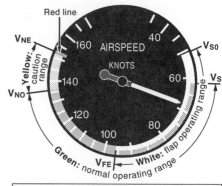

V_{S0}	Stalling speed at max weight, landing gear down, flaps down, power off
V_{S1}	Stalling speed at max weight, landing gear up (if retractable), flaps up, power off
V_{FE}	Maximum speed, flaps extended
V_{NO}	Maximum structural cruising speed (for normal operations)
V_{NE}	Never-exceed speed (max speed, all ops.)

Figure 10a-2. Color-coding on the ASI

The published stalling speeds are only a guide.

Most stall warning devices activate before the stall occurs.

The flight controls are less effective near the stall.

Be careful using the ailerons near the stall.

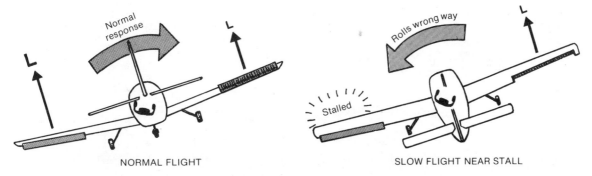

NORMAL FLIGHT   SLOW FLIGHT NEAR STALL

Figure 10a-3. Near the stall, use of the ailerons may not pick up the wing.

Modern training airplanes are designed so that the wing-root stalls first, and the ailerons remain effective right through the stall. This means that the coordinated use of aileron and rudder may be possible, even when the inner sections of the wings are stalled. Discuss this with your flight instructor.

The Rudder

Near the stall, any tendency for a wing to drop or for the airplane to yaw can be prevented with opposite rudder. If the right wing drops, or if the airplane yaws right, apply left rudder (and vice versa).

Flying the Maneuver

Practice this maneuver at altitude so that recovery is completed no lower than 1,500 feet AGL.

Figure 10a-4. Near the stall, prevent wing drop and further yaw with opposite rudder.

Stalling in Straight-and-Level Flight

Stalling is first practiced in straight-and-level flight by reducing power and raising the nose to maintain altitude. The angle-of-attack will gradually increase.

Warnings of an impending stall include:
- a reducing airspeed and air noise level, decreasing control effectiveness and a mushy feel;
- operation of a stall warning (such as a horn, buzzer, light or whistle);
- the onset of pre-stall buffet, felt in the airframe and the controls;
- a high nose attitude for the maneuver being flown.

The **actual stall** can be recognized by:
- the nose dropping (caused by the wing's center of pressure moving rearward); and
- a high rate of descent.

Stall Recovery

To recover from a stall, **reduce the angle-of-attack** by releasing the back pressure on the control column, lowering the nose. The aim is to restore a smooth airflow back over the top of the wing so it can produce lift.

    When the wings are unstalled, the buffeting ceases, the airspeed increases, and the airplane can be eased out of the slight dive back into normal flight. The altitude loss will be approximately 200 feet.

    Power can be added to regain or maintain altitude, otherwise flying speed should be maintained in a glide. (If the flaps are extended and you wish to bring them up, then do so in stages to avoid rapid attitude and angle-of-attack changes which could induce another stall.)

Stall recovery requires decreasing the angle-of-attack.

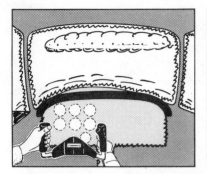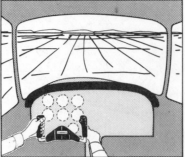

Figure 10a-5. Stall and recovery attitudes

Adding power is not required to recover from the stall, however altitude loss will be minimized if full power is applied as the back pressure is released and the nose is lowered. Recovery can be achieved with an altitude loss of less than 50 feet.

Altitude loss during a stall can be minimized with power.

After Stalling

The inertia of an airplane causes it to follow the original flight path for a brief time before the change in attitude, and resulting change in forces, moves it into a new flight path.

Pulling the nose up too sharply during the stall recovery may not give the airplane time enough to react and ease out of the dive, and could increase the angle-of-attack beyond the stalling angle again. A **secondary stall** will be induced, and a further stall recovery will be necessary. Rough handling in this second recovery could lead to yet another secondary stall.

Pulling out of a dive increases the g-loading (load factor) on the wings, which increases the airspeed at which the stalling angle is reached—this type of stall is known as an *accelerated stall*. They can also occur in steep turns where, for instance, 2g is pulled if the bank angle is 60°.

Avoid entering a secondary stall during the stall recovery.

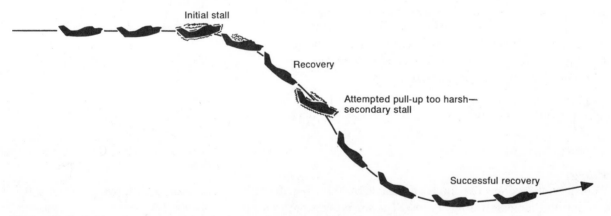

Figure 10a-6. Raising the nose too sharply during a stall recovery may induce a secondary stall.

The stall recovery can really be quite gentle, so do not run the risk of a secondary stall when performing a stall recovery. Ease the nose up after unstalling the wings and monitor the airspeed closely.

Stall with Flaps Extended

When the trailing-edge flaps are lowered, the effective angle-of-attack of the wings is increased; this allows the airplane to fly slower and have a lower nose attitude. The stall with flaps extended will now occur with a much lower nose attitude and a lower airspeed than when the wings are clean. With full flaps extended on an approach to land, for instance, the stall could occur with the nose well below the horizon.

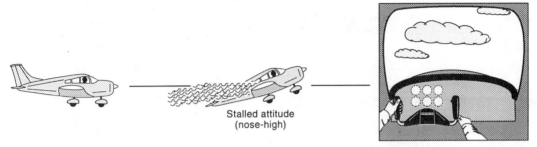

Stalled attitude
(nose-high)

Figure 10a-7. The clean stall

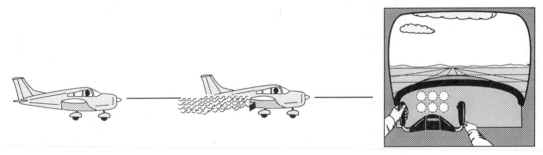

Figure 10a-8. The pitch attitude in a flapped stall—nose much lower

Clean Up after Stall Recovery

If you are recovering from a stall in the landing configuration, you would recover in the normal manner by simultaneously applying full power and lowering the nose to unstall the wings, and then climb away.

You would then clean up the airplane by raising the flaps in stages (and raising the landing gear, if retractable, to reduce drag) and establish a climb or resume straight-and-level flight, as desired.

Other Stalls
Stalling in a Turn

In a constant-altitude turn, you have to apply back pressure on the control column to maintain altitude by increasing the angle-of-attack to generate more lift. Too much back pressure may increase the angle-of-attack to the critical angle, causing a stall. Since the load factor is increased in a turn, the stall will occur at a higher speed than in straight-and-level flight—by how much higher depends on the g-loading, and this depends on the bank angle.

At a 60° bank angle, the pilot and airplane will experience a 2g force and the stalling speed will increase by about 40%. So, a straight-and-level stalling speed of 50 KIAS will increase to 70 KIAS in a 60° banked turn. The same effect occurs when pulling out of a dive.

Stalls at a higher speed than the normal straight-and-level stalls are called *accelerated stalls*.

Accelerated stalls—at a higher stalling speed than straight-and-level —can occur with the higher g-loading in maneuvers such as turns.

For a stall in a turn (level, climbing or descending), follow the standard recovery procedure of releasing the elevator back pressure and, when the **wings are unstalled,** use coordinated rudder and aileron to roll the wings level. Apply power as required to resume the desired flight path.

Recovery at the First Sign of a Stall

The warning of an imminent stall occurs from the stall warning device, onset of airframe buffeting, flight controls becoming mushy, and a low airspeed reading.

If an unwanted stall appears imminent, then **recover immediately.** This is especially applicable if the airplane is near the ground—for example, on takeoff, approach to land, going-around or low-level flying.

Recover immediately at the first sign of an inadvertent stall.

To recover at the first sign of a stall, simply:
- relax the back pressure on the control column (or move it forward);
- simultaneously: apply power smoothly, and use the controls normally—since the wings are **not** stalled.

When practicing this maneuver, you should get set up in the same way as when practicing full stalls. This means:
- at an altitude that permits recovery by at least 1,500 feet AGL;
- in the desired configuration;
- establish the appropriate pitch attitude to induce an imminent stall either on a constant heading to an accuracy of plus or minus 10°, or in a 20° banked turn to an accuracy of plus or minus 10°.

In the recovery, you should:
- recover before a full stall develops;
- avoid a secondary stall (so do not pull back too hard in easing out of any recovery dive);
- avoid excessive airspeed;
- avoid excessive altitude change;
- avoid entering a spin (which could occur if the flight controls are used in an uncoordinated manner); and
- avoid flight below 1,500 feet AGL.

Recovery from an Incipient Spin

The recovery from an incipient spin (the early stages of a spin) is really the same as for an *imminent stall with a wing-drop.* Simultaneously:
- ease the control column forward sufficiently to unstall the wings (ailerons neutral);
- apply sufficient rudder to prevent further yaw;
- apply maximum power; and
- when the airspeed increases as the wings become unstalled, level the wings with coordinated use of rudder and aileron, ease out of the descent and resume the desired flight path.

Note: The risk of dropping a wing in a stall (and, in an extreme case, entering a spin) is greatly increased if you are not in coordinated flight (ball is well off-center)—something that can occur when flying with crossed-controls. This situation could develop when turning to final approach if a careless pilot uses crossed-controls—it is discussed in Exercise 11b.

Airmanship

Unexpected stalls should never occur.

Ensure that stalling is only practiced at altitude, so that you will recover no lower than 1,500 feet AGL, and carry out the *HASELL* check (see below) immediately prior to practicing stalls and stall recovery. This includes keeping a good lookout.

Exert smooth, but firm and positive control over the airplane.

Be particularly conscious of any other aircraft in the vicinity, your altitude above ground level, and the area over which you are flying. Note landmarks, and keep in mind the direction to the airfield so that you do not get disoriented. Maintain a high visual awareness. It is your responsibility to **see and avoid.**

Airmanship is *never* allowing a stall to develop inadvertently—but knowing how to recover, just in case.

Pre-Aerobatic Checklist

Stalling is the first aerobatic-type maneuver that you will perform.

Prior to doing any aerobatics, it is usual to carry out a series of checks to ensure safe operation. The Pilot's Operating Handbook will contain a suitable check, which you should use, covering items such as those in the HASELL check suggested below, (so-called because the items it contains start with these letters).

H—Height: sufficient altitude to recover by **1,500 feet above ground level.**

A—Airframe: flaps and landing gear as desired; in trim.

S—Security: doors and harnesses (seat belts) secure; no loose articles in the cockpit, such as fire extinguishers, tie-down kits, and so on; gyros caged, if applicable.

E—Engine: check for normal engine operation; fuel contents and selection checked (fullest tank selected, fuel pump—ON, if appropriate); mixture—RICH and carburetor heat as required.

L—Location satisfactory: away from towns, active airports and other aircraft; your airplane located in visual conditions.

L—Look out: make an inspection turn of at least 180°—preferably 360°—to clear the area around and below you.

Begin the maneuver immediately upon completion of the clearing turn.

Be sure to realign the heading indicator with the magnetic compass following stalling practice.

Airwork

Stalls are covered in the following six parts:

- **Part (i)—The Basic Stall.**
- **Part (ii)—Stall, Power Off in a Turn.**
- **Part (iii)—Stall, Power On.**
- **Part (iv)—Stall, Climbing Turn.**
- **Part (v)—Stall, Descending Turn in the Landing Configuration.**
- **Part (vi)—Recovery at the First Sign of a Stall.**

This looks like a lot, but really isn't. The purpose is to show you how a stall can occur in different flight situations—but the stall recovery is basically the same.

Airwork 10a, Part (i)
The Basic Stall

Objective

To stall the airplane fully and then recover with a minimum loss of altitude.

1. Prior to Entry

*Pre-aerobatic HASELL check

H—Height: altitude sufficient to recover by 1,500 feet AGL.

A—Airframe: flaps—AS DESIRED; in trim.

S—Security: doors and harnesses secure; no loose articles; and gyros—CAGED (if applicable).

E—Engine: operating normally; fuel contents and selection checked (fuel pump—ON, if applicable); mixture—RICH and carb heat as required.

L—Location: satisfactory.

L—Look out: clearing turn to check for any other aircraft.

Commence the maneuver as soon as the area is clear.

2. Stall Entry

- Power—OFF (carb heat—HOT, throttle—CLOSED).
- Maintain altitude with elevator (±100 ft).
- Use rudder to keep straight and the wings level (selected heading ±10°).
- Ailerons neutral.
- Continue bringing the control column fully back.

3. Symptoms of an Approaching Stall

- Decreasing airspeed and noise level.
- Controls less firm and less effective.
- Stall warning (light, horn or buzzer).
- Shuddering airframe.
- A relatively high nose-up attitude.

(1)   (2)   (3)

Clear the area
and
look out.

> Recognize the actual stall:
> - Nose drop; • Sink rate.

During the stall
use rudder only to
prevent further yaw.

*Refer also to the expanded HASELL check on the previous page.

Practice stalls clean, and with flaps extended (which results in lower nose attitudes), and when flying straight-and-level, climbing, descending and turning.

Start practice at a suitable altitude so that recovery will be above 1,500 feet AGL.

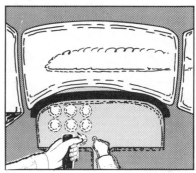
Stall

4a. Stall Recovery with Power

Simultaneously:

- Release the back pressure to lower the nose (see cockpit diagram).
- Add full power—throttle FULLY OPEN (carb heat—COLD).
- Regain flying speed.
- Use coordinated aileron and rudder to level the wings if necessary.
- Resume normal flight (desired attitude, power and airspeed if desired, bring the flaps up in stages).

Altitude loss approximately 50 feet

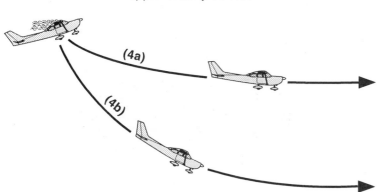

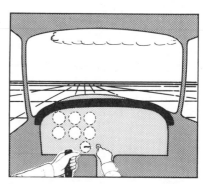
Recovery with power

4b. Stall Recovery without Power

- Release the back pressure and lower the nose (see cockpit diagram).
- Regain flying speed.
- Use coordinated ailerons and rudder to level the wings if necessary.
- Resume normal flight (desired attitude, power and airspeed—if desired, bring the flaps up in stages).

Altitude loss approximately 200 feet

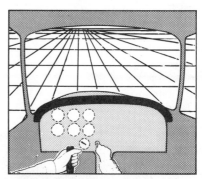
Recovery without power (lower nose attitude than with power)

Airwork 10a, Part (ii)
Stall, Power Off in a Turn

Objective

To stall the airplane fully in a banked turn, and then recover with a minimum loss of altitude.

1. Prior to Entry

- Complete the Pre-aerobatic HASELL check.
- **Look out** and **clear the area.**
- Enter a constant-altitude 20° banked turn at an airspeed about 20 KIAS above the normal straight-and-level stalling speed.

2. Stall Entry

- Power—OFF (carb heat—HOT, throttle—CLOSED).
- Maintain the 20° banked turn (±10°).
- Continue bringing the control column back to maintain altitude (±100 ft).

Stall entry; power—OFF, raising nose, in a right turn

3. Symptoms of the Stall

- Decreasing airspeed and noise level.
- Controls less firm and less effective.
- Stall warning (light, horn or buzzer).
- Shuddering airframe.
- A relatively high nose-up attitude, followed by a nose drop, high sink rate, and perhaps a tendency for either the left or right wing to drop—which wing depends upon airplane type, and whether the flight controls are coordinated or not.

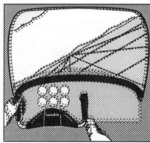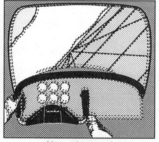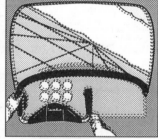

Nose drop

Nose drop and right (lower) wing drop

Nose drop and left (upper) wing drop

The stall in a right turn; shudder, stall warning, nose drop, sink rate and perhaps a wing drop

4. Stall Recovery

- Release the back pressure (and apply full power if desired, to minimize the altitude loss).
- Roll wings-level with coordinated controls, and lower the nose.
- Resume normal flight (and check carb heat —COLD).

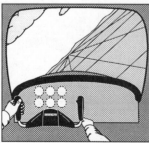

Release back pressure, and apply full power.

Roll wings-level, and lower the nose (if necessary).

Resume normal flight.

Airwork 10a, Part (iii)
Stall, Power On

Objective
To stall the airplane fully while power is applied, and then recover with a minimum loss of altitude.

1. Prior to Entry
- Pre-aerobatic HASELL check.
- **Look out** and **clear the area.**
- Maintain a nominated heading (±10°), or maintain a selected bank angle—20° bank is adequate (±10°).

2. Approach to Stall
- Leave the power applied.
- Maintain heading (±10°) or bank angle (±10°).
- Continue bringing the control column back to maintain altitude (±100 ft). The nose will be higher than in a power-off stall.

3. Symptoms of the Stall
- Decreasing airspeed (but decreasing slower than if no power was used) and decreasing air noise (engine noise is still present, as well as the propeller slipstream noise).
- The controls are less firm and less effective (although the propeller slipstream over the rudder and elevator may keep them effective, but the ailerons will certainly be mushy).
- Stall warning (light, horn or buzzer).
- Shuddering airframe.
- A very high nose attitude—followed by what could be a very sharp nose-drop with a high sink rate, and possibly a strong wing drop.

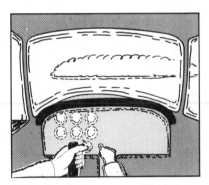

Stall with power on; nose attitude is very high

4. Recovery from a Power-On Stall
- Release the back pressure and ensure that *full* power is applied (to minimize altitude loss).
- Roll wings-level and lower the nose.
- Resume normal flight.

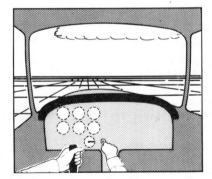

Recovery—use full power.

Airwork 10a, Part (iv)
Stall, Climbing Turn

Objective

To stall the airplane fully in a climbing turn with power applied, and then recover with a minimum loss of altitude.

Note: Practice at an altitude that allows recovery above 1,500 feet AGL. This maneuver is practice for an inadvertent stall on a poorly flown climbing turn after takeoff or on departure, which may be at a low altitude and which you should never allow to occur.

1. Prior to Stall Entry

- Complete the pre-aerobatic HASELL check.
- **Look out** and **clear the area.**
- Adopt the climb (or takeoff) attitude and airspeed, and then apply climb (or takeoff) power.
- Enter a climbing turn (15°–20° bank angle).

2. Stall Entry

- Increase control back pressure to try and achieve a steep climb (the climb will initially be steep, but keep the same shallow 15°–20° bank angle).

3. Symptoms

- Decreasing airspeed and air noise level.
- Controls less firm and less effective (especially the ailerons).
- Stall warning (light, horn or buzzer).
- Shuddering airframe.
- A relatively high nose attitude—followed by a nose drop, high sink rate, and perhaps a wing drop (especially if the coordination ball was not centered).

Climbing left turn; power on

Climbing left turn; power on; nose far too high

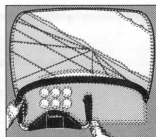
Stall, shudder, nose drop with possible wing drop (left or right)

Entry to stall in a climbing turn

4. Stall Recovery

- Release back pressure (and apply *full* power, if not already applied, to minimize altitude loss).
- Roll wings level with coordinated controls and lower the nose.
- Resume normal flight.

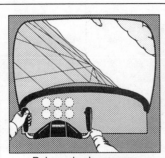
Release back pressure, and apply full power.

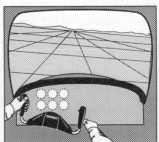
Roll wings-level, and lower the nose.

Resume normal flight.

Stall recovery

Airwork 10a, Part (v)
Stall, Descending Turn in Landing Config.

Objective

To stall the airplane fully in a gliding turn (power off), and then recover with a minimum loss of altitude.

Note: Practice at an altitude that allows recovery above 1,500 feet AGL. This maneuver is practice for an inadvertent stall on a poorly flown turn to final approach, which may be at a low altitude and which you should never allow to occur.

1. Prior to Stall Entry

- Pre-aerobatic HASELL checklist.
- **Look out** and **clear the area**.
- Reduce power (carb heat —HOT), establish the landing configuration with flaps extended, and establish a normal 30° banked gliding turn (±10°).

3. Stall Symptoms

- Decreasing airspeed and noise level.
- Controls less firm and less effective.
- Stall warning (light, horn or buzzer).
- Shuddering airframe.
- A relatively high nose attitude—followed by a nose drop, sink rate, and perhaps a wing drop, especially if the coordination ball was not centered.

2. Stall Entry

- Increase elevator back pressure to raise the nose; try and achieve the landing attitude or higher.

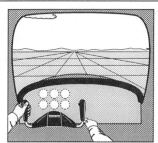
In a clean glide

In a flapped glide

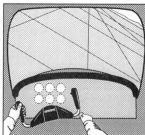
Flapped gliding turn to the left, with correct attitude and airspeed

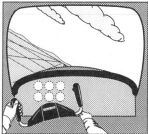
Nose attitude too high

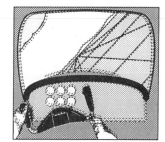
Stall—with nose drop, and possible wing drop (either left or right)

Entering the stall in a gliding turn

4. Stall Recovery

- Release elevator back pressure and apply full power (carb heat—COLD).
- Roll wings level with coordinated controls and lower the nose.
- Resume normal flight, and raise the flaps in stages if desired (check carb heat—COLD).

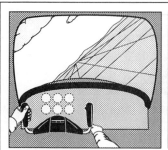
Release back pressure, and apply full power.

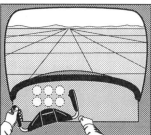
Roll wings-level, (with coordinated controls) and lower the nose.

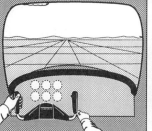
Flaps extended

Flaps up
└── Resume normal flight. ──┘

Airwork 10a, Part (vi)
Recovery at the First Sign of a Stall

Objective

To recognize the approach to a stall (that is, an imminent stall), and recover to normal flight before a full stall develops.

1. Prior to Entry

- Complete the pre-aerobatic HASELL check.
- **Look out** and **clear the area**.
- Maintain a specified heading (±10°), or (if you want to practice in a banked turn) maintain a chosen bank angle (±10°)—suggested bank angle 20°.

Approaching a stall in a right bank

2. Approach to the Stall

- Power—OFF (carb heat—HOT, throttle—CLOSED)
- Maintain heading (±10°) or chosen bank angle (±10°).
- Continue bringing the control column back to maintain altitude (±100 ft).

3. Symptoms of an Approaching (Imminent) Stall

- Decreasing airspeed and noise level.
- Controls less firm and less effective.
- Stall warning (light, horn or buzzer).
- Initial shudder of airframe (on the edge of a stall, but not yet fully stalled).

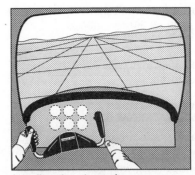

Leveling the wings after recovery

4. Recovery from an Imminent Stall

- Release the elevator back pressure (and apply full power if it is desired to minimize altitude loss).
- Roll the wings level and lower the nose (to the level flight attitude if power is used, otherwise lower the nose to the gliding attitude).
- Resume normal flight and set the carb heat to COLD.

> **Practice this maneuver:**
> - Straight-and-level.
> - In a banked turn.
> - With power off, then with power on.

Further Points

Wing Surface

If ice, frost, insects or any other contaminant is present on the wings, or if the wings are damaged (especially the upper leading edges) the airflow could separate from the upper surface of the wings at a lower angle-of-attack than normal. Stalling will then occur sooner and at a higher airspeed. **Always check the surface condition of the wings** (especially the upper leading edges) in your preflight inspection, and remove any contamination.

Contaminated or damaged wings increase stalling speed.

Stalls during Maneuvers

To turn, or to pull out of a dive, the wings must produce more lift than in straight-and-level flight. This is achieved by the pilot using back pressure on the control column to increase the angle-of-attack. The relative airflow striking the wings at a greater angle-of-attack causes the **stalling angle** to be reached at a higher indicated airspeed.

Stalling speed increases in maneuvers.

For example, the stalling speed increases by 7% at a 30° bank angle, and by 40% when pulling 2g in a 60° banked turn or in the recovery from a dive.

A stalling speed of 50 KIAS straight-and-level will increase to 54 KIAS in a 30° banked turn, and to 70 KIAS when pulling 2g in a 60° banked turn or in a dive recovery.

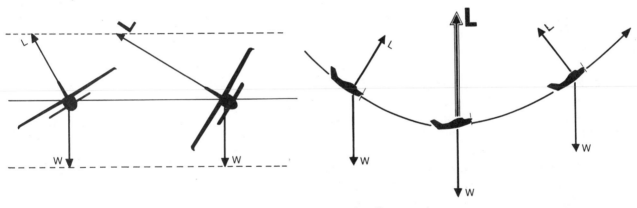

Figure 10a-9. An increased wing loading (g-factor) means an increased stalling speed.

You can physically recognize an increased load factor on the wings by the increased g-loading on your body, so any time your *apparent weight* is increased in maneuvers, the stall speed is increased.

When the airplane approaches a stall during maneuvers (say in a steep turn or pulling out of a dive), releasing control back pressure is usually sufficient to prevent the stall occurring.

The Effect of Flaps

The stall with flaps extended will differ somewhat from the clean stall. For a start, flaps increase the lifting capability of the wings, allowing the required lift to be generated at a lower speed. The stalling speed will be lower. Flying at the lower speeds may make the controls feel mushy.

Extending flaps lowers the stalling speed and affects the stall characteristics of the airplane.

The increased drag from the flaps will cause the airplane to decelerate more rapidly when power is reduced. Also, the changed distribution of lift on the wings may cause a greater tendency for a wing to drop.

With flaps extended, the nose attitude will be lower in each phase of flight, therefore stalling with flaps will occur at a lower pitch attitude than when clean.

The recovery from a stall with flaps extended is standard. Altitude loss can be minimized by applying full power as the nose is lowered, but be prepared to hold forward pressure on the control column—full power may produce a strong pitch-up moment. Use aileron to roll the wings level when they are unstalled.

If full flaps are used, a climb-away may be difficult unless some stage of flaps is raised when a safe speed is attained. Raise the flaps in stages to avoid any sink.

Stalling with flaps extended will occur at a lower pitch attitude than flaps up (clean).

Stalling On Final Approach

Initiate a recovery immediately if you suspect an impending stall on approach. Lower the nose and apply full power to minimize altitude loss.

It is worthwhile to practice the full stall in the approach configuration at altitude to familiarize yourself with it. This should ensure that you will never allow a stall to occur near the ground (unless of course you are doing a full-stall landing within about one foot of the ground—stalling anywhere between 1 foot and 1,500 feet AGL is strongly discouraged!).

A situation in which a stall *might* occur is an approach that gets out of hand—for example, full flaps extended and a tendency to undershoot, with the pilot raising the nose instead of adding power. The airspeed will decrease, and the undershoot will worsen. If the pilot continues to pull the control column back in an attempt to stretch the flight path, a stall could occur. With full flaps and possibly high power applied, the stall could be fairly sudden, and a wing could drop—especially if the coordination ball is not kept centered.

The standard recovery technique should be used. The control column may have to be moved well forward to unstall the wings, and care should be taken to avoid using the ailerons until the wings are unstalled. The substantial drag from full flaps may make a go-around difficult—gain speed in level flight or a slight climb, reduce the flaps in stages, and then climb away as desired.

On approach to land, the airplane is usually trimmed for a slow airspeed and low power condition with a reasonable amount of nose-up trim. A sudden application of full power, such as in a go-around, will cause the nose to rise. If this is not counteracted with forward pressure to hold the nose in the desired pitch attitude, an *elevator-trim stall* could occur. It is the main wings which stall, but the high angle-of-attack as power is added is encouraged by the nose-up elevator trim.

Do not stall on final approach.

Never allow a stall to occur near the ground.

In a go-around, beware of an elevator-trim stall.

Power-On Stall

With power on, the propeller creates a slipstream over the inner sections of the wings, and this may delay the stall, which will then occur at a higher nose position and at a lower airspeed. The slipstream makes the elevator and rudder more effective, but not the ailerons (see figure 10a-10).

The increased airflow may delay the stall on the inner sections of the wing—the stall occurring first on the outer sections, perhaps leading to a greater wing-dropping tendency.

Standard recovery technique is used—any further yaw being prevented with opposite rudder to prevent a spin from developing.

Power decreases the stalling speed.

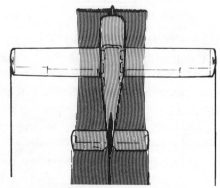

Figure 10a-10. Power reduces the stalling speed.

The Effect of Weight

The lighter the airplane, the less lift the wings must generate for straight-and-level flight, and so the smaller the required angle-of-attack at a given airspeed. Therefore, a lightly loaded airplane can be flown at a slower airspeed before the stalling angle-of-attack is reached.

The stalling speed decreases as weight decreases.

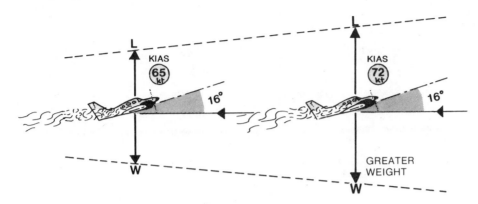

Figure 10a-11. Stalling speed is less at lower weights.

Center of Gravity Position

In many aircraft, the horizontal stabilizer generates a small downward force to balance the four main forces and prevent the airplane pitching. The upward lift from the main wings in straight-and-level flight will therefore have to support two downward forces—the weight plus this small downward aerodynamic force on the tail.

A forward center of gravity (CG) increases the stalling speed.

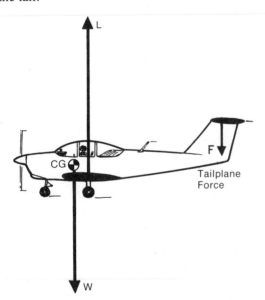

Figure 10a-12. The vertical forces in straight-and-level flight

The further forward the CG, the greater the downward tail force, and so the greater the lift required from the main wings. This requires a higher angle-of-attack at a given airspeed, therefore the stalling angle will be reached at a higher airspeed. This is one good reason why the airplane must be correctly loaded with the CG within approved limits.

Review 10a

1. A stall occurs when the (streamline/turbulent) flow over a wing breaks down and becomes (streamline/turbulent).

    ➤ streamline, turbulent

2. The stall occurs at a critical (angle-of-attack/ airspeed).

    ➤ angle-of-attack

3. Published stalling speeds are (always exact/ a guide) for your flight situation.

    ➤ a guide

4. The published stalling speeds are for (maximum/ minimum) weight (in a 30° banked turn/straight-and-level).

    ➤ maximum, straight-and-level

5. When flying at less than maximum weight, the actual stalling speeds will be (the same as/ lower than/higher than) those published.

    ➤ lower than

6. The stalling speed clean, straight-and-level at maximum weight, is shown on the airspeed indicator as the lower end of the (white/green/ amber) band.

    ➤ green

7. Run through the checklist you will use prior to practicing stalls.

    ➤ for example, HASELL *(refer to the text, page 221)*

8. Select an entry altitude when practicing stalls that will allow recovery to be completed no lower than ____ feet AGL. If the local terrain is 2,300 feet MSL, this means to recover by at least ____ feet MSL.

    ➤ 1,500 feet AGL, 3,800 feet MSL

9. List four warnings of an impending stall.

    ➤ *refer to our Airwork diagrams, pages 222–228*

10. The actual stall may be recognized by the nose (rising/dropping), and the airplane (climbing/ descending).

    ➤ dropping, descending

Stalling

11. The main point in any stall recovery is to (lower/raise) the nose and restore (smooth/ disturbed) airflow over the wings.

    ➤ lower, smooth

12. What is an imminent stall?

    ➤ the approach to a stall

13. Stall-warning devices usually activate (just before/ at) the stalling angle-of-attack.

    ➤ just before

14. Compared with a power-off stall, a stall with power on will occur with (a higher/a lower/the same) nose attitude, at (a higher/a lower/the same) airspeed and (a higher/a lower/the same) angle-of-attack.

    ➤ a higher nose attitude, at a lower airspeed, the same angle-of-attack

15. An airplane on final approach with flaps down and a low airspeed usually has a small amount of (nose-up/nose-down) trim. If full power is applied for a go-around, the nose will tend to pitch (up/down) and the pilot must hold it (up/down) in the desired go-around attitude, otherwise the main wings could stall—this is known as an _____-_____ stall.

    ➤ nose-up, up, down, elevator-trim stall

16. With the high g-loadings that occur in maneuvers, the stalling speed will be (higher/the same/lower); this is known as an _____ stall.

    ➤ higher, accelerated

17. What is a secondary stall?

    ➤ a stall that inadvertently occurs during a stall recovery

18. List the accuracies required during stall entry for heading, altitude, bank angle climbing, and bank angle descending.

    ➤ heading within 10°; altitude within 100 feet; climbing turn 15° to 20°; descending turn 30°, with tolerance of plus or minus 10°

Flight at Critically Slow Airspeeds 10b

Objective

To establish slow flight, develop an awareness of the airplane's handling characteristics at critically slow airspeeds, and to return the airplane to a safe flying speed.

Considerations

This exercise is designed to provide exposure to flight at abnormally low airspeeds, so that you can:

Slow Flying is an awareness exercise.

• recognize an inadvertent approach to the stall;
• experience how the airplane handles at an abnormally low airspeed; and
• take recovery action by returning the airplane to a safe flying speed.

You are flying the airplane slowly during takeoffs, landings, go-arounds, and during stalling practice, so it is important that you develop an awareness of how the airplane handles at low speed, and how effective (or ineffective) the controls become. In this exercise, we take it to an extreme by flying at high angles-of-attack just below the stall—at critically slow airspeeds.

Because you are flying near the stall, you should practice this exercise no lower than 1,500 feet AGL.

What is Slow Flight?

Slow flight is steady flight at a speed just above the stalling speed—if you fly any slower, or if you suddenly increase the angle-of-attack, you will stall. The objective of this exercise is for you to get a feel for when the airplane is approaching the stall, and to handle it smoothly at these critically slow airspeeds.

Indicated airspeed in itself is not the only clue that you are approaching a stall. Published stalling speeds are based on maximum gross weight; if you are lighter than this, then the normal, basic, straight-and-level 1g stalling speed will be a few knots lower.

Conversely, if you "pull g" in a maneuver, such as in a turn or a pull-out from a dive, the increased angle-of-attack will mean a much higher stalling speed than that published (40% higher in a 60° banked turn). Consequently, when flying at critically slow airspeeds, beware of the stall when maneuvering.

To maintain a steady airspeed at a constant altitude, engine power must produce enough thrust from the propeller to counteract the total drag. The *Power Required* curve is therefore similar in shape to the *Drag* curve. It shows that high power is required for steady flight at both high and low airspeeds, with minimum power occurring at a specific speed in between.

Minimum power will give minimum fuel consumption for a piston-engine, propeller-driven airplane, and consequently maximum endurance—so this speed is often listed as the *endurance speed* in the Pilot's Operating Handbook.

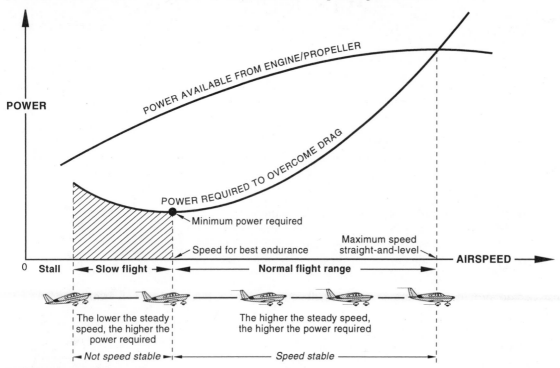

Figure 10b-1. The power curve

Flight at speeds less than the best endurance speed is *slow flight.* To maintain a constant speed in the slow flight range below minimum power speed requires more power the lower the steady slow speed you have established. This is known as *flying on the back side of the power curve.*

Flight at the minimum controllable airspeed is considered to be at about 5 KIAS above the stall. Any loss of speed, or any increase in angle-of-attack, will result in a stall—so you need to fly accurately and with sensitivity.

Flight at minimum controllable speed is considered to be at about 5 knots above the stall.

Power Handling

At normal cruising speeds, higher speeds require higher power settings. Also, any minor speed variations due to gusts will automatically correct themselves in the normal flight range— a slight increase in speed will cause a drag increase which will return the airplane to its original speed. (The total drag increase is due to the additional parasite drag that results from the increased speed.)

Conversely, a slight decrease in speed in the normal flight range reduces drag, allowing the airplane to regain speed. An airplane is *speed-stable* in the normal flight range.

In the slow flight range, however, the situation is reversed—the lower the speed, the higher the power required. This is because, at low speeds, a high angle-of-attack is needed to produce the required lift, greatly increasing the induced drag. The increase in total drag (due to the additional induced drag) will slow the airplane down unless power is applied.

The slower the steady speed you want to maintain, the more power you require.

The lowest steady airspeed that can be maintained by an airplane may be limited either by the maximum power the engine/propeller can deliver, or by the stall.

In the slow-speed range, the airplane is **not** speed-stable— an airspeed loss due to a gust will result in an increase in total drag which will slow the airplane down even further (and continue to do so), unless the pilot takes corrective action by adding power.

An airspeed *gain*, conversely, will reduce the total drag and the airplane will accelerate unless the pilot reduces power. For this reason, you have to be more active on the controls in the slow-flight range compared with the normal-flight range. Slow flight is not difficult to control, or dangerous, but it does require constant attention to airspeed, power, attitude, altitude and yaw.

At slow speeds, you need to be active on the controls.

The Left-Yawing Tendency

There are two reasons for the left-yawing tendency in slow flight.

- With high power set, the propeller creates a strong **slipstream** that flows back in spiral form over the airplane, striking the left side of the vertical stabilizer and tending to yaw the nose of the airplane to the left.

- At high angles-of-attack, with the airplane in a nose-high attitude, there will be an **asymmetric propeller blade effect,** also known as the **P-factor.** The downgoing blade on the right-hand side of the airplane will be taking a larger slice of the air than the upgoing blade on the left side, and so will be producing more thrust. This will also cause a tendency for the nose to yaw left.

At high-power, some right rudder may be needed to keep the coordination ball centered.

Figure 10b-2. Asymmetric propeller blade effect (P-factor)

You should anticipate the left-yawing tendency in slow flight as you apply high power, and counteract it with right rudder pressure to prevent the yaw and keep the coordination ball in the center. Conversely, you can expect to use left rudder as power is reduced.

Control Effectiveness

At low airspeeds, the flight controls will feel mushy and less effective—large control movements may be required to obtain the desired response. Since the elevator and rudder are in the propeller slipstream, they may be somewhat more effective when high power is set. The ailerons, however, will not be affected by the slipstream, and their effectiveness will be greatly reduced at low airspeeds.

Significant rudder deflection may be required to prevent the left-yawing tendency at high power settings and low airspeeds. At very low speeds and very high power, the large rudder deflection might require extra aileron movement to hold the wings level—thus you will have **crossed-controls.** Beware of a stall and wing-drop!

The effectiveness of the flight controls depends upon the airflow over them.

The feel of the airplane becomes important in slow flight. The low speed, the less effective controls, the high nose attitude, the high power required, and the large rudder deflection are all clues that the stalling angle is not far away.

Slow flight at 10 knots above the stall (and then possibly only 5 knots above) will be practiced. Stalling speeds straight-and-level at maximum weight are marked on the airspeed indicator: V_{S1} at the low-speed end of the green band (for a clean wing), and V_{S0} at the low-speed end of the white band (for full flaps).

Check the Flight Instruments

Frequent glances at the flight instruments are necessary in slow flight if you are to hold airspeed, altitude and pitch attitude accurately. Required accuracy is:
- selected altitude: plus or minus 100 feet (private pilot), plus or minus 50 feet (commercial pilot);
- selected heading in straight flight: plus or minus 10°;
- selected bank angle in turning flight: plus or minus 10° (private), plus or minus 5° (commercial);
- airspeed: at minimum controllable speed plus 5/minus 0 KIAS; at specified slow speed plus or minus 5 KIAS.

Although you need to check the airspeed and altitude frequently in slow flight, you must also keep a good **lookout** and maintain visual awareness of the outside environment (obstacles, other aircraft and wind effect).

Hold Airspeed Accurately

The airspeed needs to be monitored closely in slow flight. It should be controlled accurately with power and attitude changes because of the proximity of the stall. The tendency to lose speed in a turn should be counteracted with additional power. Do *not* attempt steep turns at slow speeds near the stall—the stall speed will increase to meet your actual airspeed because of the increased load factor!

At minimum controllable airspeed—say 5 KIAS above the stall—you need to fly at this speed or 5 KIAS faster, but certainly no slower, so the tolerance is plus 5/minus 0 KIAS. If you are flying at a nominated slow speed which is at least 10 KIAS above the stall, then the accuracy required is plus or minus 5 KIAS.

Configuration Changes

Extending flaps reduces the stalling speed, enabling you to fly even slower than when you are clean. You can practice this by reducing power, extending flaps as the airspeed reduces. Then add power to maintain the new, slower airspeed. Retrim. Lowering the landing gear (in a retractable-gear airplane) will require more power to maintain airspeed.

Conversely, when you want to raise the flaps, add power—full power in an emergency—and, as the speed increases, gradually retract the flaps in stages. Be prepared for the nose to drop and the airplane to sink, which you can counteract by holding the nose up to maintain altitude. Accelerate to the speed you have selected, and then reduce power to maintain it. Retrim. Raising the landing gear will require less power if the airspeed is to remain constant.

Attention

Flying at a critically slow airspeed, an inadvertent increase in angle-of-attack, reduction in power, loss of airspeed, or increase in g-loading could lead to a stall.

The workload is high during slow flight, yet your attention is often required elsewhere, say to inspect a potential landing surface while flying slowly just above it. Glance at the flight instruments frequently to check your airspeed and coordination. Each of these aspects is important to safe slow flight.

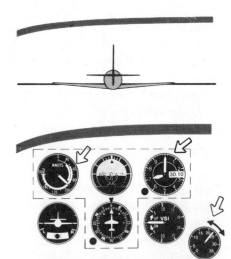

Figure 10b-3. Closely monitor airspeed and altitude in low-speed flight, and be prepared to adjust power frequently.

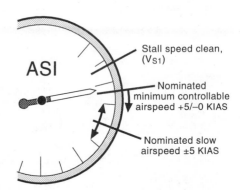

Figure 10b-4. Required accuracy in flight at critically slow airspeeds

With changes in configuration, adjust power to maintain the target airspeed.

Keep a good lookout, and frequently check the airspeed and coordination ball.

Flying the Maneuver

For reasons of safety, this maneuver should be practiced not below 1,500 feet AGL.

Divide your attention between inside and outside the cockpit:
- *inside* to check airspeed, altitude and coordination ball;
- *outside* to check for other aircraft and terrain or obstacles.

Slow flight is good practice for your coordination.

1. Attaining Slow Flight

To reduce airspeed to the selected value (initially 10 KIAS above the normal stalling speed and then, after some practice, only 5 KIAS above it):
- reduce power, and gradually raise the nose to maintain altitude;
- when the target airspeed is reached, increase power and continually adjust both power and attitude to maintain that speed;
- anticipate the need for right rudder to keep the coordination ball centered as power is added;
- retrim.

2. Maneuvering in Slow Flight

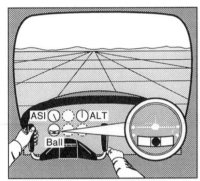

- Reduce power, keeping the coordination ball centered with left rudder pressure.

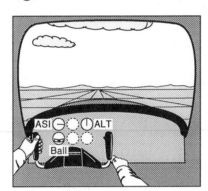

- Raise the nose to maintain altitude as the airspeed reduces.

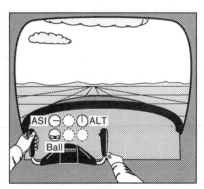

- Add power to hold the slow airspeed (keeping the ball centered).
- Monitor the airspeed, altitude, and coordination ball.
- Retrim.

Figure 10b-5. Attaining steady slow flight

To maintain airspeed and altitude accurately, be prepared to work the throttle vigorously and readjust the attitude as necessary. The longer you delay corrections, the greater they will have to be.

As always: **power + attitude = performance.**

To correct speed variations:
- if speed increases—raise the nose and reduce power;
- if speed decreases—lower the nose and add power;
- keep the coordination ball centered with rudder pressure.

To correct altitude variations:
- if the airplane climbs—reduce power and lower the nose;
- if the airplane sinks—add power and raise the nose;
- keep the coordination ball centered with rudder pressure.

The use of elevator, power, and rudder must be coordinated. Every time you change the power there will be a pitch/yaw tendency that you will have to counteract.

Climbing. To enter a slow-speed climb:
- simultaneously adjust the pitch attitude and slowly increase power to maintain airspeed;
- keep the coordination ball centered with rudder pressure;
- trim.

To level off from a slow-speed climb:
- lower the nose;
- simultaneously reduce power slowly to maintain airspeed and keep the coordination ball centered with rudder pressure;
- trim.

Descending. To establish a descent:
- reduce power;
- lower the nose to maintain airspeed;
- keep the coordination ball centered with rudder pressure;
- trim.

To level off from a descent:
- increase power;
- gradually raise the nose to the cruise attitude to maintain airspeed;
- keep the coordination ball centered with rudder pressure;
- trim.

Turning. To turn at a low airspeed: increase power to maintain speed as the bank angle is applied.

Maximum Performance Climb. To make a maximum performance climb away from a descent:
- open the throttle fully (and counteract yaw with right rudder);
- allow the nose to rise and hold it in the climb attitude;
- control airspeed with elevator;
- trim.

To avoid high load factors, do not exceed a 30° bank angle—20° is preferred. Remember that in steep turns at a 60° bank angle, the load factor doubles to 2g and the stall speed increases by 40%.

To Approach the Stall:
- raise the nose until a stall is imminent;
- recover by easing the control column forward and applying power.

Changing Configuration. To fly slower with flaps extended:
- reduce power, raising the nose as the speed washes off to maintain altitude;
- lower flaps (in stages as required) and hold the nose down to avoid gaining altitude;
- add power to maintain the new slow airspeed;
- retrim.

To accelerate and raise the flaps:
- add power, hold the nose down to maintain altitude;
- raise the flaps in stages as the speed increases and hold the nose up to avoid sinking;
- reduce power to maintain the new airspeed;
- retrim.

Sometimes the increased drag from the flaps will cause the speed to wash off, and there is no need for the initial power reduction.

Note: When about to raise the flaps, ensure that you have accelerated to at least 5 KIAS faster than the flaps-up stalling speed, otherwise the change in the wing profile could cause a stall.

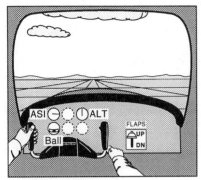 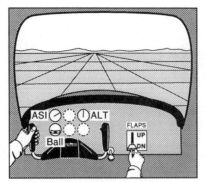 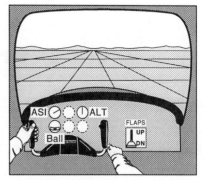

- Constant altitude, clean and slow
- Reduce power to slow down (if necessary).

- Lower the nose as the flaps go down to avoid ballooning (that is, gaining altitude).

- Add power to hold the new airspeed (keep ball centered).
- Monitor the airspeed, altitude, and coordination ball.
- Retrim.

Figure 10b-6. Lowering the flaps and flying even slower

3. Reverting to Normal Cruise Speed

To return to normal cruise speed:
- increase power;
- lower the nose to maintain altitude;
- keep the coordination ball centered with rudder pressure;
- adjust the power as the target airspeed is attained;
- trim.

These maneuvers should be practiced both clean and with flaps extended, in the takeoff and approach configurations.

Airmanship

Exert firm, positive and smooth control over the airplane, and be prepared to make large and prompt power changes when required. Keep your right hand on the throttle, except when you are using it to trim.

Maintain airspeed in slow-speed level turns with the use of additional power. Coordinate the use of power/elevator/rudder, and aim to keep the coordination ball centered with rudder pressure at all times.

Monitor the engine instruments to confirm adequate cooling of the engine at the high power and low airspeed.

Maintain a safe altitude above ground level and obstacles if the slow flying is carried out close to the ground. Remember that a continuing lookout is important in all phases of visual flight. Dividing your attention between cockpit duties and visual scanning to see-and-avoid is essential.

You should aim to achieve an accuracy of within 100 feet (50 feet for commercial pilots) of target altitude, within 10° of the target heading in coordinated flight (5° for commercial pilots), and hold your selected critically slow airspeed to an accuracy of plus 5/minus 0 KIAS. Avoid gaining or losing altitude, and **do not stall!**

Practice flying at critically slow airspeeds at altitudes no lower than 1,500 feet AGL.

Airmanship is flying the airplane accurately and positively, especially at the critically slow airspeeds, and keeping a good lookout.

Airwork 10b
Flight at Critically Slow Airspeeds

Objective

To establish slow flight, and then fly the airplane slowly at airspeeds just above the stall, without actually stalling.

Practice slow flying at or above 1,500 ft AGL.

FAST CRUISE (1) SLOW CRUISE (2)

1. Establishing Slow Flight, Flaps Up

To adopt a slow cruise:
- Reduce power.
- Raise the nose to reduce airspeed and maintain altitude.
- Keep the coordination ball centered with rudder pressure.
- Trim.

To maintain a slow cruise:
- Set power and attitude to maintain altitude and airspeed—be active on the throttle if necessary. Monitor the ASI.
- Keep coordinated with rudder pressure.

Note: The controls are less effective at low airspeed.

Clear the area and **look out.**

2. Maneuvering in Slow Flight

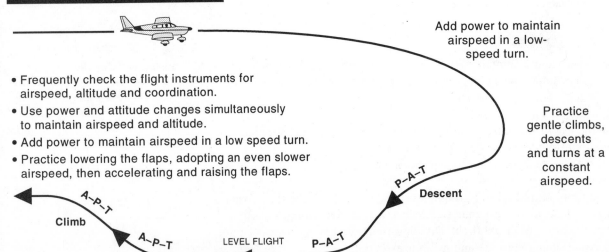

Add power to maintain airspeed in a low-speed turn.

- Frequently check the flight instruments for airspeed, altitude and coordination.
- Use power and attitude changes simultaneously to maintain airspeed and altitude.
- Add power to maintain airspeed in a low speed turn.
- Practice lowering the flaps, adopting an even slower airspeed, then accelerating and raising the flaps.

Practice gentle climbs, descents and turns at a constant airspeed.

A–P–T Climb
A–P–T
LEVEL FLIGHT
P–A–T
P–A–T Descent
P–A–T

3. To Return to Normal Cruise Speed
- Increase power.
- Lower the nose to maintain altitude.
- Keep the coordination ball centered.
- Trim.

Required Accuracy	Private	Commercial
Altitude	±100 ft	±50 ft
Airspeed	+5/–0 KIAS	+5/–0 KIAS
Heading	±10°	±10°
Bank angle	±10°	±5°

Note: Repeat the above procedure with flaps extended and in the takeoff and approach configurations. Try slow flight initially at 10 KIAS above the 1g stalling speed, then at only 5 KIAS above the 1g stalling speed.

1. Maintaining a steady airspeed that is slower than the minimum-power steady airspeed is known as flying on the (front/back) side of the power curve.

    ➤ back

2. The slower the speed you wish to maintain, the (higher/lower) the power required.

    ➤ higher

3. If the airflow over a flight-control surface is slow, the control will feel (firm/mushy) and be (more/less) effective.

    ➤ mushy, less

4. Flying at a slow airspeed at a high power setting, the airflow over the flight control surfaces which are *not in* the propeller slipstream will be (strong/weak). These controls will feel (mushy/firm and effective). Which control surfaces are they?

    ➤ weak, mushy, the ailerons

5. Flying at a slow airspeed at a high power setting, the airflow over the flight control surfaces which are *in* the propeller slipstream will be (strong/weak). These controls will feel (mushy/firm and effective). Which control surfaces are they?

    ➤ strong, firm and effective, the elevator and rudder

6. With high power and a low airspeed, you can expect to use a fair amount of (left/right) rudder to keep the coordination ball centered.

    ➤ right

7. Which three flight instruments are particularly important when flying at a critically slow airspeed if accuracy is required and a stall is to be avoided?

    ➤ airspeed indicator, altimeter, coordination ball

8. When flying at the minimum controllable airspeed, say 5 KIAS above the stall, the tolerance to aim for is: the target airspeed plus ____ KIAS and minus ____ KIAS. What are these speeds if the stall speed is 40 KIAS?

    ➤ plus 5/minus 0 KIAS, target speed 45 KIAS (V_S+5), and tolerance is 45 to 50 KIAS

9. Aircraft performance is determined by p_____ plus a_____ .

    ➤ power plus attitude

10. The slower the airspeed required, the (higher/lower) the nose attitude.

    ➤ higher

11. The higher the airspeed required, the (higher/lower) the nose attitude.

    ➤ lower

12. Describe how to transition from a fast cruise speed to a critically slow airspeed, maintaining straight-and-level flight.

    ➤ *refer to our text, page 237*

13. Describe how to accelerate from a critically slow airspeed to a fast cruising airspeed in straight-and-level flight.

    ➤ *refer to our text, page 239*

14. Describe how to transition from a fast clean cruise to critically slow flight with flaps extended, maintaining straight-and-level flight.

    ➤ *refer to our text, page 238*

15. Describe how to transition from critically slow flight with flaps extended to a normal fast clean cruise.

    ➤ *refer to our text, page 238–9*

16. Keeping the airplane in trim following any speed, power, or configuration change makes it (easier/harder) to fly accurately.

    ➤ easier

17. Practice-flying at critically slow airspeeds should be done at least ____ feet AGL. If the local terrain is 5,300 feet MSL, this means you must practice at or above ____ .

    ➤ 1,500 feet AGL, 6,800 feet MSL

18. The tolerances expected when you demonstrate flying at critically slow airspeeds are: altitude ____ , airspeed ____ , heading ____ , and bank angle ____ .

    ➤

	altitude	airspeed	heading	bank
private:	±100 feet	+5/–0 KIAS	±10°	±10°
commercial:	±50 feet	+5/–0 KIAS	±10°	±5°

19. At low airspeed with high power, (left/right) rudder pressure will be required to keep the coordination ball centered. What are the two reasons for this?

⮞ right, (1) the strong propeller slipstream due to the high power, and (2) the P-factor (also known as asymmetric propeller blade effect) due to the high nose attitude.

20. The basic stall speed clean is the (upper/lower) end of the (white/green/amber) arc on the airspeed indicator.

⮞ lower, green

21. The basic stall speed in the landing configuration is the (upper/lower) end of the (white/green/amber) arc on the airspeed indicator.

⮞ lower, white

22. At weights below maximum weight the actual stalling speed will be (higher than/lower than/the same as) the published stalling speed.

⮞ lower

23. In maneuvers where "g" is pulled, the actual stalling speed is (increased/reduced/not affected).

⮞ increased

24. In a 60° banked turn, 2g is pulled, so you will feel (your normal weight/twice as heavy), and the stalling speed will have increased by ____ %. Therefore, you (should/should not) use steep bank angles when flying at slow speeds.

⮞ twice as heavy, 40%, should not

25. In a 30° banked turn, the stalling speed is increased by ____ %.

⮞ 7%

26. If a stall inadvertently occurs due to lack of attention by the pilot, describe the recovery.

⮞ release back pressure and apply full power, level the wings and lower the nose, resume normal flight

27. Stall warning devices usually activate (just before/ at/just after) the stalling angle-of-attack is reached.

⮞ just before

28. When flying at critically slow airspeeds you (should/should not) allow a stall to occur.

⮞ should not

29. If you inadvertently approach a stall when flying at a critically slow airspeed, you should initiate a recovery (immediately at the imminent stall stage before the stall actually occurs/after the stall occurs).

⮞ immediately at the imminent stall stage before the stall actually occurs

30. It is good airmanship to (always/occasionally/ never) exert firm, positive and smooth control over the airplane.

⮞ always

31. It is (good/poor) airmanship to always maintain a good lookout.

⮞ good

Full Spins 11a

Objective

To enter, maintain and recover from a fully developed spin (provided it is an approved maneuver for your particular airplane).

Considerations

Spinning can be a comfortable and exciting maneuver if you have been taught well, and if the airplane is approved for spinning.

What Is a Spin?

A spin is a condition of stalled flight in which the airplane follows a spiral descent path.

In a spin the airplane is stalled, yawing, and one wing is producing more lift than the other—this results in a roll. Greater drag from the stalled lower wing results in further yaw, further roll, and so on. Pitching of the nose may also occur.

The airplane is in motion about all three axes. In other words, lots of things are happening in a spin! The airplane is:

- stalled;
- rolling;
- yawing;
- pitching;
- slipping; and
- rapidly losing altitude at a low airspeed.

In a spin the wings do not produce much lift, since they are stalled. You can keep the airplane in the spin by holding the control column fully back to keep the wings stalled. (If you release the back pressure, the wings will probably unstall and the airplane would be in a steep diving turn, or spiral, rather than a spin.)

The stalled and spinning airplane will accelerate downward until it reaches a vertical rate of descent where the greatly increased drag, now acting upward, counteracts the weight. The altitude loss will be rapid as the airplane spins downward around the vertical spin axis but, because of the high angle-of-attack and the stalled condition, the steady airspeed in the spin will be quite low.

Characteristics of a developed spin include a **low indicated airspeed** (which does not increase until recovery action is initiated), and a **high rate of descent.**

A vital part of the spin recovery is to unstall the wings by lowering the nose (which reduces the angle-of-attack), and to build up flying speed.

Spinning is an optional instructional exercise.

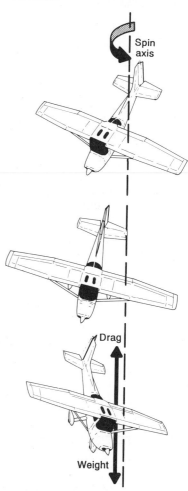

Figure 11a-1. The spin

A well flown spin will not stress a properly certificated airplane any more than a normal stall.

Autorotation

The two main features of the autorotation that occurs when a wing drops **in stalled flight** are:

- **auto-roll**—the more-deeply stalled dropping wing will generate even less lift, and so will want to keep dropping, causing the airplane to continue rolling; and
- **auto-yaw**—the dropping wing will generate increased drag, and want to yaw the nose of the airplane in the same direction as the roll.

If a wing drops in flight—because of a gust or perhaps intentionally by the pilot's actions—the relative airflow will strike the wing more from below, and so its angle-of-attack will be greater. The rising wing, conversely, will have its angle-of-attack temporarily reduced.

In normal flight, at fairly low angles-of-attack well away from the stall, the increased angle-of-attack of the dropping wing will cause it to develop more lift. Conversely, the reduced angle-of-attack of the rising wing reduces its lift. The natural tendencies of the airplane in normal flight will therefore be for the rolling motion to be damped, and for the wings to roll level.

The spin is caused by the dropping wing being more stalled, producing less lift, and having higher drag.

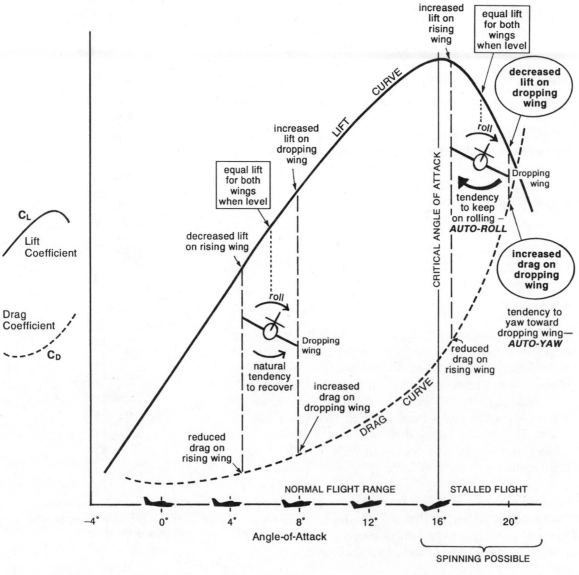

Figure 11a-2. Lift and drag effects on a dropping wing

In stalled flight, however, the increased angle-of-attack on the dropping wing will cause it to be even more stalled, and develop even less lift. The result is that **the dropping wing in a stalled condition will *continue* to drop,** and the rolling motion will tend to continue. This will occur without any movement of the ailerons, so this characteristic may be thought of as *auto-roll*.

The auto-roll effect can be illustrated on the familiar lift curve, which shows lift increasing with angle-of-attack, but only up to the critical stalling angle-of-attack, beyond which the lift decreases.

In normal flight, when the lift on a wing increases, so does the drag. In stalled flight, however, as we can see from the drag curve in figure 11a-2, a dropping wing that is stalled not only experiences **reduced lift**—causing it to continue rolling (auto-roll)—it also experiences **increased drag** which tends to yaw it in the direction of roll (auto-yaw). This effect can also be seen in the figure.

The yawing motion in the same direction as the roll will increase the rolling tendency, making the rolling–yawing cycle self-sustaining, or automatic, in the sense that the increasing rolling velocity sustains, or even increases, the difference in the angle-of-attack on the two wings, strengthening the rolling–yawing tendency.

This natural tendency to continue rolling and yawing in the same direction when stalled (because of the uneven lift and uneven drag on the left and right wings) is known as **autorotation.** Autorotation is the basis of the spin.

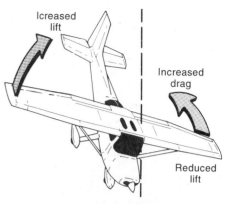

Figure 11a-3. When stalled, reduced lift and increased drag on a dropping wing causes autorotation.

A spin can occur with both wings stalled, as shown above; it can also occur with only one wing stalled (the dropping wing), with the rising wing unstalled and producing significant lift.

Spin Rotation

If the airplane adopts a higher nose attitude and the spin flattens:
- the rate of rotation will decrease; and
- the rate of descent will reduce (because of the increased drag from the higher angle-of-attack).

The flatness of the spin determines the rate of rotation.

A spinning ice-skater moves her arms in and out from her body to alter the rate of rotation. The same effect occurs in an airplane. In a steep nose-down attitude, the mass of the airplane is close to the spin axis and the rate of rotation is high. If the spin flattens, some of the airplane's mass is distributed further from the spin axis and the rate of rotation decreases.

If the nose pitches up and down in the spin, the rate of rotation will vary, becoming slower when the spin is flatter and faster when the nose position is steeper. Since the nose is purposely lowered in the recovery from a spin, you can expect a temporary increase in the rate of rotation until recovery is complete.

A rearward CG will encourage a flatter spin and it will be more difficult to lower the nose in the recovery. This is one important reason for ensuring that you never fly an airplane loaded outside its approved weight-and-balance limits.

Conversely, **a forward CG** normally results in a steeper spin with a higher rate of descent and a higher rate of rotation. It may make recovery much easier and, in fact, may even prevent a spin occurring.

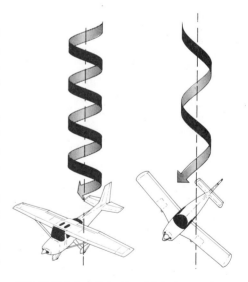

Figure 11a-4. A flat spin and a steep spin

Spiral Dives

A maneuver that must not be confused with a spin is the spiral dive, which can be thought of as a steep turn that has gone wrong. In a spiral dive the nose attitude is low, the wing is not stalled, the airspeed is rapidly increasing and the rate of descent is high—a spiral dive is really just a steep descending turn. It is a **low angle-of-attack/high airspeed** maneuver, whereas the spin is a **high angle-of-attack/low airspeed** maneuver.

Because the wings are not stalled, there is no need, in the recovery from a spiral dive, to move the control column forward. Spiral dives are considered in Exercise 15b on Recovery from Unusual Flight Attitudes.

Practicing Spins

During your first spin, you will probably be a little overcome by the sensations, and not really comprehend exactly what is happening. It feels like the nose is pointing straight down, but in fact this is not the case. After a few practice spins, however, you will become reasonably comfortable, and the whole maneuver will seem to slow down enough for you to recognize the characteristics, count the turns, recognize landmarks and so on.

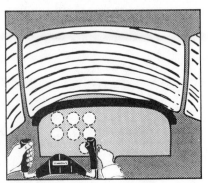
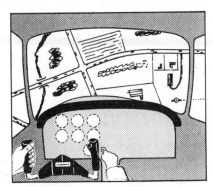

Figure 11a-5. The spin as you first see it, ... and as you will see it

The Three Stages

The spin maneuver can be considered in three stages:

1. The **incipient spin** (or the beginning of the spin), which is an unsteady maneuver where the entry path of the airplane is combined with the phenomenon called autorotation. The incipient stage may last five or six seconds, and take about two turns as the flight path changes from a straight-and-level stall into a descending spin.

2. The **fully developed spin** is the next stage. The airplane has settled into a comparatively steady rate of rotation, with a steady rate of descent at a low airspeed and a high angle-of-attack. The descent path will be almost vertical, with the airplane in a stalled attitude—about 30° off the vertical in a steep spin, and about 70° off the vertical in a flat spin. You may lose 300 to 500 feet of altitude per turn—each turn taking perhaps three to five seconds.

3. The **recovery from the spin** is the third stage. Spin recovery is initiated by the pilot who:
   - opposes the autorotation with rudder;
   - unstalls the wings with forward movement of the control column; then
   - eases out of the ensuing dive, and resumes normal flight.

Note: It may take one full turn or more after the recovery actions have been initiated for the spin rotation to stop.

Do not confuse a spin (stalled) with a spiral dive (not stalled).

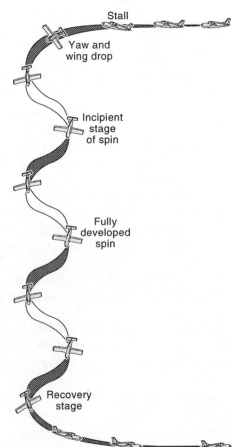

Stall

Yaw and wing drop

Incipient stage of spin

Fully developed spin

Recovery stage

Figure 11a-6. The flightpath in a spin

How a Spin Develops

A spin is a condition of stalled flight, so the first prerequisite is that the wings be at a high angle-of-attack. This is achieved by moving the control column progressively back, as in a normal **stall entry.**

A **wing drop** is essential to enter a spin, and this may occur by itself or (more likely) be induced by the pilot yawing the airplane with rudder, or misusing the ailerons on certain airplanes just prior to stalling.

Autorotation will begin as the dropping wing becomes further stalled, with a consequent decrease in lift and increase in drag. The airplane will roll and yaw in the same direction, a slip will develop and the nose will drop. If no corrective action is taken, the rate of rotation will increase and a spin will develop. It will be an unsteady maneuver with the airplane appearing to be very nose-down. The rate of rotation may increase quite quickly, and you will experience a change of g-loading.

Generally, the airplane will not go straight from the stall into a spin, but experience a transition period which may vary from airplane to airplane, typically taking two or three turns in the unsteady and steep autorotation mode, before settling into a fully developed and stable spin.

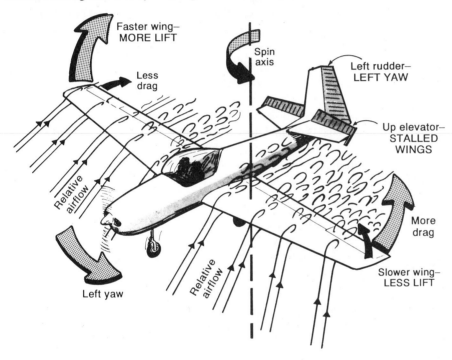

Figure 11a-7. The airplane controlled into a spin

Misuse of the Ailerons

Trying to raise a dropped wing with opposite aileron may have the *reverse* effect when the airplane is near the stall. If, as an aileron goes down, the stalling angle-of-attack is exceeded, instead of its wing rising it may drop quickly, resulting in a spin.

This is the spin entry technique used on some older aircraft types; modern aircraft designs, however, are required by the FAA to have ailerons that remain effective through a stall. (This can be achieved with design features such as washout, which results in the inner part of the wing near the fuselage stalling before the wingtip/aileron area.) Your flight instructor will brief you carefully on this point.

Misuse of ailerons can cause a spin.

Figure 11a-8. Inducing a spin with opposite aileron

Use of Power

At the early stage of a stall, having power on may cause a greater tendency for a wing to drop, which could lead to a spin. When the airplane is in a spin, power may destabilize it as the slipstream will tend to flow across the outer wing, increasing its lift and consequently increasing the rate of roll. If power is applied, the entire spin maneuver will be speeded up. It is essential, therefore, to **remove power** by closing the throttle either before or during the spin recovery.

Power may destabilize an airplane before and during the spin.

Wing Flaps

The flaps tend to decrease the control effectiveness of the elevator and rudder, and so should be raised either before or during the spin recovery. For many aircraft, practicing spinning with flaps down is not permitted, since the aerodynamic loads on the flap structure may cause damage.

The flaps should be raised for spinning.

Flying the Maneuver

Entering a Spin

About 5 to 10 knots prior to the airplane stalling, with the control column being progressively moved back, a smooth and firm large deflection of the rudder will speed up the outer wing and cause it to generate more lift. The inner wing will have slowed down, and will generate less lift.

It is usual to enter a spin by yawing with rudder just prior to the stall.

The airplane will begin to roll, the slower inner wing that is dropping will experience an increased angle-of-attack (which will cause it to stall or, if already stalled, become more deeply stalled), and a spin will develop.

The direction of the spin is determined by the direction of yaw, and the spin entry may require full travel of the rudder. If the left rudder pedal is pushed fully forward, the airplane will yaw and roll to the left, and a spin to the left will develop. If the right rudder is pushed fully forward, the airplane will yaw and roll to the right, and a spin to the right will develop. It may take two or three turns before the airplane actually settles into a steady, stable spin.

The direction of the spin is determined by the direction of yaw on entry.

Note: Some airplanes require a short burst of power just at the point of stall for a spin to occur (by making the rudder more effective). Other aircraft will not spin at all because they have been designed with a weak elevator that does not allow the nose to be raised to the stalling angle-of attack. The danger in these airplanes is that, if somehow a stall and spin does occur, the elevator might not have sufficient authority to unstall the wings and recover.

Maintaining the Spin

To allow a steady spin to develop and be maintained, continue to:
• hold the control column fully back (to keep the wing stalled);
• maintain full rudder (to keep yawing); and
• keep the ailerons neutral.

Recognizing a Spin

A pilot can recognize a spin by the following characteristics:
• a steep nose-down attitude;
• continuous rotation;
• buffeting (possibly);
• an almost constant low airspeed; and
• a rapid loss of altitude at a steady rate of descent (the VSI pointer may be off-scale, with typical rates of descent being 7,000 fpm in a steep nose-down spin and 5,000 fpm in a flat spin).

The instrument gyros may tumble in a spin, so information from the attitude indicator may be misleading. The gyroscopic flight instruments (such as the attitude indicator) on some aircraft need to be caged (locked) prior to performing any aerobatic maneuver, in order to protect them.

The precise spin recovery depends upon the **spin direction**. While practicing spinning you will, of course, know the direction of the spin you have induced. In an inadvertent spin, however, where the direction of spin may not be obvious, it can be obtained from the turn coordinator indicating left or right. Pay no attention to the coordination ball in a spin. Your outside view of the ground may also assist you, but the turn coordinator is the best clue to spin direction.

The turn coordinator is the best clue to spin direction.

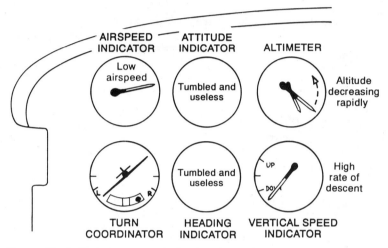

Figure 11a-9. Flight instrument indications in a spin

Recovery from a Spin

The technique is:
- check throttle closed and flaps up;
- verify direction of spin on the turn coordinator;
- apply full opposite rudder (to slow the rotation);
- pause (to allow the rudder to become effective and be able stop the yaw which turns a stall into a spin);
- ease the control column forward to unstall the wings (full forward if necessary);
- as soon as the rotation stops, neutralize the rudder (it may take one, two or more complete turns for the rotation to stop);
- level the wings and ease out of the ensuing dive;
- as the nose comes up through the horizon, add power and climb away to regain altitude.

Note: The purpose of the **pause** with full opposite rudder, but still with the control column back, is to avoid blanketing the rudder with the elevator; this could happen if the elevator was moved down (control column forward) too soon.

In the process of unstalling the wings, the nose attitude will become steeper and the mass of the airplane will move closer to the spin axis. The result may be a noticeable increase in the rate of rotation just before recovery.

Fly smoothly as you ease out of the ensuing recovery dive. Pulling back far too hard might induce a secondary stall and, if too much rudder is used and the coordination ball is well out of the center, another spin could be induced—possibly in the other direction. In this case, you would have to initiate a second spin recovery.

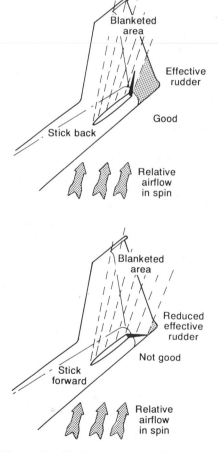

Figure 11a-10. Pause after applying full opposite rudder, to avoid blanketing the rudder with the elevator.

Potential Spinning Situations

Some situations where an inadvertent spin could be dangerous are:
- an uncoordinated climbing turn after takeoff—nose too high, airspeed too low, coordination ball not centered (too much rudder);
- an uncoordinated descending turn from base leg to final approach—nose too high, airspeed too low, coordination ball not centered (too much rudder).

Avoid getting into these situations by holding a suitable pitch attitude, and monitoring the airspeed indicator and the coordination ball.

Airmanship

Ensure that your airplane is certified for spins, and that the weight-and-balance is correct.

Ensure that you know the correct spin recovery technique for your airplane type (found in the Pilot's Operating Handbook).

The spin is an aerobatic maneuver, and so the pre-aerobatic HASELL check should be performed prior to practicing spins. A thorough **lookout** is essential, as a spin and recovery will consume a lot of altitude (possibly 500 feet per rotation). Begin your practice at an altitude that will allow you to **recover by 3,000 feet AGL.**

Exert firm control over the spin entry and recovery. You should fly the airplane—not vice versa! Never allow the airplane to enter a spin inadvertently!

When climbing away after each spin recovery, reorientate yourself using familiar landmarks.

Airmanship is knowing how to recover from a spin, even though you may never have to do it.

Airwork 11a
Full Spins

Objective

To enter, maintain and recover from a fully developed spin (provided it is an approved maneuver for the airplane).

Note: Recovery should be made by 3,000 feet AGL.

1. Complete the Pre-Aerobatic HASELL Check *(page 221)*

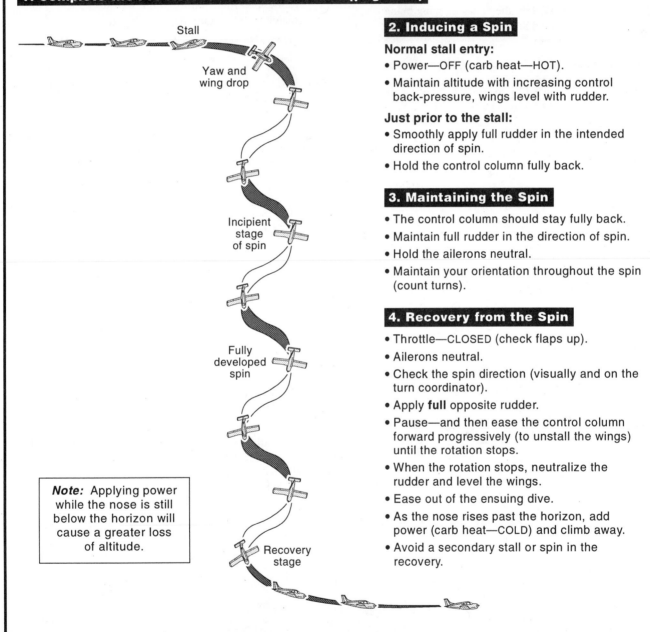

Stall

Yaw and
wing drop

Incipient
stage
of spin

Fully
developed
spin

Recovery
stage

Note: Applying power
while the nose is still
below the horizon will
cause a greater loss
of altitude.

2. Inducing a Spin

Normal stall entry:
- Power—OFF (carb heat—HOT).
- Maintain altitude with increasing control back-pressure, wings level with rudder.

Just prior to the stall:
- Smoothly apply full rudder in the intended direction of spin.
- Hold the control column fully back.

3. Maintaining the Spin

- The control column should stay fully back.
- Maintain full rudder in the direction of spin.
- Hold the ailerons neutral.
- Maintain your orientation throughout the spin (count turns).

4. Recovery from the Spin

- Throttle—CLOSED (check flaps up).
- Ailerons neutral.
- Check the spin direction (visually and on the turn coordinator).
- Apply **full** opposite rudder.
- Pause—and then ease the control column forward progressively (to unstall the wings) until the rotation stops.
- When the rotation stops, neutralize the rudder and level the wings.
- Ease out of the ensuing dive.
- As the nose rises past the horizon, add power (carb heat—COLD) and climb away.
- Avoid a secondary stall or spin in the recovery.

Note: The spin entry and recovery technique in the Pilot's Operating Handbook for your airplane may differ slightly from this procedure. Use the technique recommended for your airplane.

1. The spin is a condition of (stalled/unstalled) flight.

    ➤ stalled

2. In a spin, one wing is more stalled than the other. (True/False)?

    ➤ true

3. The spin is caused by the dropping wing being (more/less) stalled and having (more/less) drag than the other wing.

    ➤ more, more

4. The rotation caused by the dropping wing being more stalled, producing less lift and more drag than the other wing, is called _____ rotation.

    ➤ autorotation

5. Compared with an airplane loaded with a forward CG, a spin with a rearward CG will be (flatter/steeper), with a (faster/slower) speed of rotation, and a (higher/lower) rate of descent.

    ➤ flatter, slower, lower

6. A spin is a (high/low) angle-of-attack and a (high/low) airspeed maneuver.

    ➤ high, low

7. In a spin, the rotation is caused by (unequal/equal) lift and (unequal/equal) drag on the wings.

    ➤ unequal, unequal

8. The spin maneuver can be considered in three stages. They are _____ , _____ , _____ .

    ➤ the incipient spin, the fully developed spin, the recovery from the spin

9. The conditions for a spin to begin are: a (stalled/unstalled) wing and a w_____ d_____ , which (can/cannot) be induced by yawing the airplane with rudder.

    ➤ stalled, wing drop, can

10. On some older airplanes, misuse of the a_____ near the stall can lead to a spin developing.

    ➤ ailerons

11. In a spin recovery, you should apply full rudder in the direction (of/opposite to) the spin.

    ➤ opposite to

Full Spins

12. To avoid the rudder being blanketed by the elevator, you should (pause/not pause) before moving the control column forward to unstall the wings.

    ➤ pause

13. When the rotation stops you should (neutralize the rudder/continue holding full opposite rudder), and then level the wings and ease out of the ensuing dive.

    ➤ neutralize the rudder

14. In the spin recovery, the wings (must/need not) be unstalled by moving the control column (forward/back).

    ➤ must, forward

15. Name two situations during flight near the ground where low speed and misuse of the rudder could lead to a dangerous inadvertent spin.

    ➤ (1) a too-steep uncoordinated climbing turn after takeoff, and (2) a too-slow uncoordinated turn onto final approach

16. The entry altitude when practicing spins should be high enough to ensure that recovery is completed above _____ feet AGL. If the elevation of the local terrain is 1,800 feet MSL, this means that recovery should be completed by at least _____ feet MSL.

    ➤ 3,000 feet AGL, 4,800 feet MSL

17. Spinning is an (optional/compulsory) component of pilot training.

    ➤ optional

18. For stall training to be permitted, an airplane (must/need not) be specifically approved for stalling; (all/only some) airplanes are permitted to be stalled.

    ➤ need not, all

19. For spin training to be permitted, an airplane (must/need not) be specifically approved for spinning; (all/only some) airplanes are permitted to be spun.

    ➤ must, only some

20. A spiral dive is a (high/low) angle-of-attack and (high/low) airspeed maneuver, with the wings (stalled/unstalled). It (is/is not) a spin.

    ➤ low, high, unstalled, is not

Incipient Spins 11b

Objective

To recognize the onset of a spin, and recover before a full spin develops.

Considerations

The term **incipient spin** means the beginning or onset of a spin. It is, if you like, a recovery from a spin before the spin actually occurs—and with a minimum loss of altitude. An incipient spin is most likely to occur when the airplane approaches a stall and some yaw develops. This situation could occur near the stall if the pilot is using:

- crossed-controls—ailerons one way, rudder the other way;
- high power, and insufficient rudder to keep the coordination ball centered.

While spinning is not permitted in many training airplanes, the incipient spin is. Recovery should be made before the bank angle exceeds 90°.

An incipient spin is the beginning of a spin

Flying the Maneuver

An incipient spin can be induced from almost any flight condition by flying slowly, continually bringing the control column back and then, when almost at the stall, applying full rudder to generate yaw in the intended spin direction. It is the same entry as for the full spin; the only difference in this maneuver is that you recover before the spin has a chance to develop. This recovery is what you would do in practice if an inadvertent spin seemed imminent.

To recover from an incipient spin, simultaneously:

- ease the control column forward sufficiently to unstall the wings;
- apply sufficient rudder to prevent further yaw;
- apply maximum power (see note below); and
- as the airspeed increases, level the wings with coordinated use of rudder and aileron, ease out of the descent, and resume your desired flight path.

Airmanship

Avoid getting into a potential spin situation by monitoring airspeed and keeping the coordination ball centered.

Avoid unintentional spins.

Airwork 11b
The Incipient Spin

Objective

To recognize the onset of a spin and recover before a spin develops.

Note: Commence practice at an altitude sufficient to ensure recovery above 3,000 feet AGL.

1. To Induce an Incipient Spin

- Fly slowly, bringing the control column progressively back, maintaining altitude as the speed reduces.
- Just prior to the stall, apply full rudder in the desired spin direction.

2. Recovery Procedure

As the spin commences, simultaneously:
- Ease the control column forward sufficiently to unstall the wings.
- Apply sufficient rudder to prevent further yaw.
- Apply maximum power (see note below).
- As the airspeed increases when the wings are unstalled, level the wings with coordinated use of rudder and ailerons, ease out of the descent and resume your desired flight path.

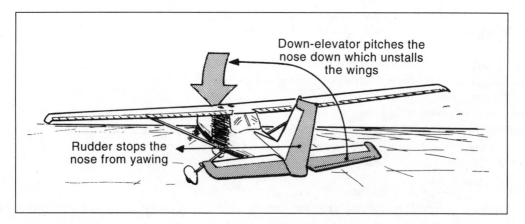

Note: If the nose has dropped below the horizon, do not apply power until after the recovery is complete and the nose rises above the horizon as you ease out of the dive.

Further Points

Stalls with Crossed-Controls

Crossed-controls means that the pilot is using aileron one way and rudder the other way. The coordination ball will be well out of the center, and you will feel yourself pushed against the same side of the airplane as the ball.

Crossed-controls are sometimes used intentionally (for example, during slips, and crosswind takeoffs and landings), but if used near the stalling angle, this condition can lead to a stall with a strong wing drop—an incipient spin.

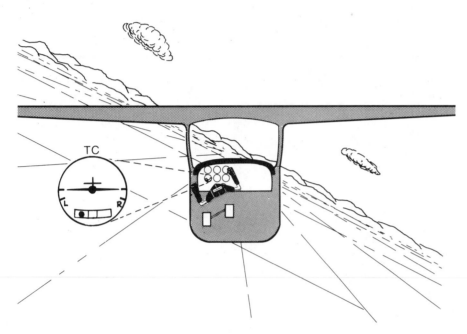

Figure 11b-1. Flying with crossed-controls (left ailerons/right rudder)

The airplane will be flying somewhat sideways through the air, in this case slipping. If too much top-rudder is used (in this case right rudder), the airplane will be flying even more sideways and the upper wing will be blanketed to a greater extent, possibly causing it to stall. This will be exacerbated if the control column is rotated further left, lowering the right aileron and bringing that wing closer to the stall.

Figure 11b-2. Slipping

Top-Rudder Stall

The result of too much top-rudder could be a top-wing stall, with the airplane rolling toward the top-wing (or what was the top wing). This is known as **top-rudder stall**, and can occur in poorly flown slips.

A *top-rudder stall* **can occur in poorly flown slips.**

Bottom-Rudder Stall

If too much bottom-rudder is used, the outside wing speeds up, increasing its lift, and the lower wing slows down, reducing its lift. If a stall occurs, the lower wing will stall first, and the airplane will roll toward the lower wing. This is known as a **bottom-rudder stall.**

This situation could occur when an inexperienced pilot is turning near the ground, say from base leg to final approach. The turn will be coordinated, with the ball in the center and probably not much aileron required when the turn is established.

A *bottom-rudder stall* **can occur when turning from base onto final approach.**

The pilot appears to be overshooting the extended centerline of the runway, but is reluctant to increase the bank angle to increase the turn, and instead tries to skid the airplane around by applying bottom rudder. The upper wing speeds up and tries to rise because of the increased lift.

To prevent this unwanted steepening of the bank angle, the pilot rotates the control wheel to the right, and now has left rudder and right aileron—**crossed-controls.**

The aileron on the inner, lower wing will now be down, bringing that wing closer to the stalling angle. If a stall occurs, the lower wing will stall first, and the airplane will roll toward it.

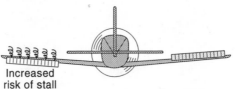

Increased
risk of stall

Nicely coordinated left turn
(but about to overshoot centerline)

Left rudder to skid tail around, and right
control wheel to stop bank increasing—
crossed-controls (left rudder/right aileron)

Figure 11b-3. Skidding around to final approach—a poor technique since it increases the risk of the lower wing stalling

The **correct technique** when on base leg and turning to final approach is to look out, but with quick glances in the cockpit to check the airspeed and that the coordination ball is centered.

If overshooting the turn onto final approach, you should **not** try to skid around, but either:
• increase the bank angle (to a maximum of 30°) to tighten the turn; or
• fly through the extended runway centerline at the current bank angle, maintain the turn and re-intercept final from the other side.

Do not fly with crossed-controls unless you really intend to—for example, in the last stages of a crosswind approach and landing.

Do not unintentionally fly with crossed-controls.

Additional Airwork

As a conclusion to Exercises 10a & b and 11a & b on Stalling and Spinning, you could practice recovering from approaching stalls and incipient spins in situations that occur in the traffic pattern—**but** practice them at altitudes that permit recovery by at least 1,500 feet AGL. Examples follow.

1. Takeoff and Departure Stalls:
- Takeoff configurations (takeoff flaps extended).
- Power-on.
- Climb attitude too steep.
- Straight ahead.
- In a climbing turn.

2. Approach-to-Land Stalls:
- Approach configuration (approach flaps extended).
- Power-off.
- Nose attitude too high.
- Straight ahead.
- In a descending turn.
- In a descending turn with crossed-controls.
- Go-around (full flaps, full power, nose attitude too high).

3. Accelerated Stalls:
- In maneuvers, such as turns with power on and off.

✍ Review 11b

Incipient Spins

1. An incipient spin is a (full/imminent) spin.

    ➤ imminent

2. A wing is most likely to drop in a stall if the pilot is flying (uncoordinated/coordinated) with the ball (way out of the center/centered).

    ➤ uncoordinated, way out of the center

3. The procedure to enter an incipient spin is _____ .

    ➤ *refer to our text*

4. Flying with right aileron and left rudder, or vice versa, is known as flying with _____-_____ .

    ➤ crossed-controls

5. If you are overshooting a turn onto final approach and try to skid the airplane around with lower rudder, you run the risk of stalling the (upper/lower) wing. This is known as a (bottom-rudder stall/top-rudder stall).

    ➤ lower, bottom-rudder stall

6. If you are rough on the controls during a slipping maneuver and apply too much top rudder, you could stall the (upper/lower) wing. This is known as a (top-rudder stall/bottom-rudder stall).

    ➤ upper, top-rudder stall

7. To avoid the risk of an incipient spin during turns onto final approach to land, you should periodically glance into the cockpit and check that the approach _____ is correct and that the _____ _____ is centered.

    ➤ airspeed, coordination ball

8. An example of where flying intentionally with crossed-controls is a correct procedure is during the final stages of a _____ _____ _____ .

    ➤ crosswind approach and landing

9. In a poorly flown slip, the airplane is likely to enter a (top-rudder/bottom rudder) stall.

    ➤ top-rudder stall

Takeoffs, Phase Two
Traffic Patterns
and Landings

Phase Two Completion Standards

On completion of Phase Two, you should be operating comfortably on the ground and in the traffic pattern at an airport, with the quality of your takeoffs, traffic patterns and landings steadily improving.

Phase Two introduces takeoffs, traffic patterns and landings, leading to your first solo flight.

You should be able to:

- Use correct radio procedures and phraseology at your airport.
- Perform all checks and checklists (including emergency checklists) without error.
- Take off upwind, fly a normal traffic pattern and land upwind, with emphasis on:

  Flying a rectangular traffic pattern using appropriate wind correction angles (WCA), on altitude and on speed.

  Alignment with the runway centerline on climb-out and approach.

  Making a stable approach, with no uncorrected tendency to balloon or sink.

  Safe control of the landing run, maintaining directional control along the runway centerline, and with use of wheel braking only when needed.

  Correct procedures for clearing the runway, and then the after landing checks.

  All checklists called out loud and performed precisely without error.

  Avoidance of wake turbulence from any large aircraft.

- Handle an unexpected engine failure after takeoff.
- Fly a go-around, with a positive transition from the approach to the climb-out, and correct radio procedures.
- Operate from a runway which has a signficant crosswind component.
- Land without flaps (using a forward slip if necessary to lose altitude).
- Operate from a short field (maximum performance takeoff and landing).
- Operate from a soft field.
- Perform some of the flight maneuvers referenced to ground objects.
- Perform all items in Phase One to a higher level of proficiency.

First solo may (or may not) occur in this phase, after you have successfully completed a pre-solo written test administered and graded by your flight instructor.

Takeoff and Climb to Downwind Leg **12**

Objective

To take off into the wind and climb away in the traffic pattern to downwind leg.

Considerations

This maneuver involves:
• accelerating on the runway to liftoff speed;
• flying the airplane off the ground and clearing any obstacles;
• a climb to traffic-pattern altitude; and
• positioning the airplane on the downwind leg.

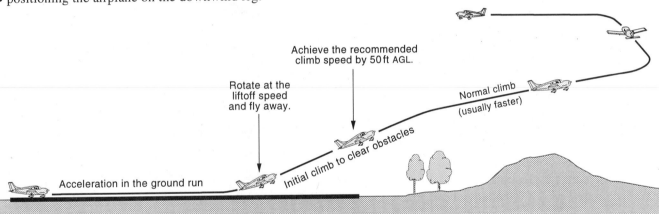

Figure 12-1. The various stages in the takeoff and climb-out

Before using any airport for takeoff or landing, you must evaluate:
• the wind direction;
• the takeoff and landing surface (length available and condition); and
• any obstacles or other hazards in the takeoff and approach paths.

The Takeoff

The takeoff and initial climb-out is one continuous maneuver, but it can be considered in three stages:
• the takeoff roll or ground run;
• the liftoff or rotation; and
• the intitial climb-out to a safe maneuvering altitude.

Take off upwind, if possible.

During the takeoff, the airplane must be accelerated to an airspeed at which it is capable of flying. Having a headwind component on a runway gives you airspeed even before you have started rolling. For example, a 10-knot headwind component gives you an additional 10 knots of airspeed over and above your groundspeed.

Taking off into the wind is good airmanship because it gives:
- the shortest ground run;
- the lowest groundspeed for the required takeoff airspeed;
- the best directional control, especially at the start of the ground run, when there is not much airflow over the control surfaces;
- no side forces on the landing gear;
- the best obstacle clearance because of the shorter ground run and the steeper flight path over the ground; and
- the best position in the climb-out from which to make an upwind landing straight ahead (or slightly to one side) in the case of engine failure immediately after takeoff.

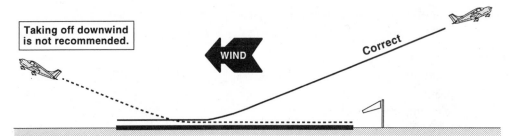

Figure 12-2. Always take off as much upwind as possible.

Wind Direction

The traffic pattern direction will normally be upwind, since this benefits both takeoffs and landings. Knowing the wind, you can choose the most suitable runway and work out what the traffic pattern will be. You can determine the wind direction:

Be aware of the surface wind direction.

- as you walk out to the airplane;
- from the wind direction indicator (which can be a windsock, tetrahedron, wind cone or wind-T);
- from other clues, such as smoke being blown away from a chimney;
- from the Automatic Terminal Information Service (ATIS), or by asking Air Traffic Control (ATC), who will advise you of the magnetic direction from which the wind is blowing and its strength—for example, **360/25** is a north wind at 25 knots.

Runway Distance

The Takeoff Performance chart should be consulted if you are not certain that the runway is adequate in all respects. High-elevation airports and high temperatures will increase the runway distances required, because of the decreased air density which degrades both engine and aerodynamic performance.

Ensure that the runway is adequate.

A decreased air density is also known as a **high density altitude.** Runway upslope and a tailwind component will also degrade the takeoff performance. So will moist air on days of high relative humidity— it also decreases air density, but, unlike each of the items mentioned above, it is not allowed for on the performance charts.

Flaps

Most training aircraft use either zero flaps or 10° to 15° of flaps for takeoff. Extending takeoff flaps increases the lifting ability of the wings, enabling the airplane to take off at a **lower airspeed** and with a **shorter ground run.** The airborne climb-out performance with takeoff flaps set, however, may be slightly degraded.

Use of takeoff flaps shortens the takeoff run.

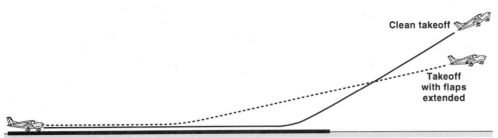

Figure 12-3. Flaps enable a shorter takeoff ground run.

Do not use landing flaps for takeoff, because the significant increase in drag will degrade the takeoff and climb-out performance. **Do not exceed the recommended flap setting for takeoff!**

Recommended Climb-Out Speeds

If flaps are used for takeoff, the Pilot's Operating Handbook will recommend an **obstacle-clearance climb speed** that should be achieved by 50 feet, and which, coupled with the shorter ground run, will provide the best clearance over obstructions in the takeoff path.

A typical speed schedule for a flaps-10° takeoff could be: lift off at 50 KIAS; initial climb-out at an obstacle-clearance speed of 54 KIAS. After the obstacles are cleared, and at a safe altitude, accelerate, raise the flaps and climb out at the normal climb speed clean.

If zero flaps are used for takeoff, the steepest climb-out will be achieved at speed V_X, the **best angle-of-climb speed.** This will provide the greatest gain of altitude in a given horizontal distance, when you use zero flaps and full power.

If obstacles are not a problem, then it is usual to climb out with a slightly lower nose attitude and a slightly higher speed, V_Y, the **best rate-of-climb speed.** This will provide the greatest gain of altitude in a given time, and the vertical speed indicator (VSI) will show the best-rate climb performance. You will reach the traffic-pattern altitude or your cruise altitude quicker at V_Y than at the slower speed V_X, but it will take more horizontal distance.

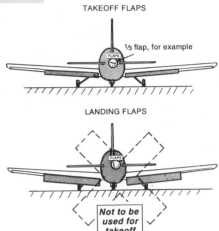

Figure 12-4. Flaps for takeoff are less than those used for landing.

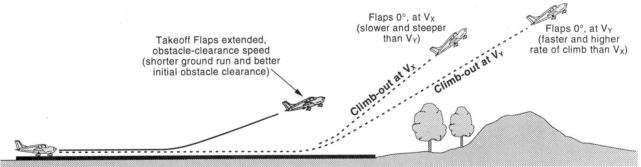

Figure 12-5. The effect of flaps and airspeed on the takeoff and climb-out

Takeoff Power

Best takeoff performance will be achieved with full power set. This can be done by applying full power with the brakes set, and then releasing them when full power is achieved—known as a **standing start;** or it can be applied while the airplane is rolling down the runway centerline—known as a **rolling start.**

Normally, the mixture is in FULL RICH for takeoff, but if the air is thin—as it would be at a high-altitude airport, say above 3,000 feet MSL on a hot day—you may have to lean the mixture to obtain maximum rpm in a full-throttle static run-up. Follow the **manufacturer's recommendations** in the Pilot's Operating Handbook.

Use maximum power for takeoff.

When airborne, with full power already set, you can only control the flight path and airspeed with changes in the pitch attitude. Lower the nose to increase speed in the climb, raise the nose to reduce speed.

Control the airspeed in the climb with pitch attitude.

The Standard Traffic Pattern

Aircraft are flown in a standard traffic pattern to maintain some form of safe and orderly flow of traffic at an airport, and to allow easy and safe access to the active runway. For good operational reasons, the preferred direction of takeoff and landing is upwind, therefore the same direction will generally be used by aircraft both taking off and landing.

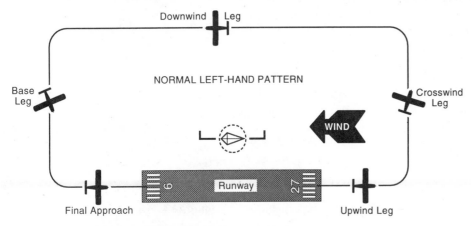

Figure 12-6. The traffic pattern is rectangular.

The traffic pattern is a rectangular ground path based on the runway in use. The **standard pattern is left-handed,** with all turns being made to the left. This gives a better view from the captain's seat than turns to the right. At some airports and on some particular runways, however, the patterns are **right-handed** to avoid built-up areas, high terrain, restricted airspace, and so on. This will be indicated by approved visual markings or lights, by instructions from the tower at a controlled airport, and in the A/FD airport listing.

The standard traffic pattern is left-handed.

Some airports have **parallel runways,** with a left-hand traffic pattern off Runway Left, a right-hand traffic pattern off Runway Right, and a no-transgression zone between the two patterns.

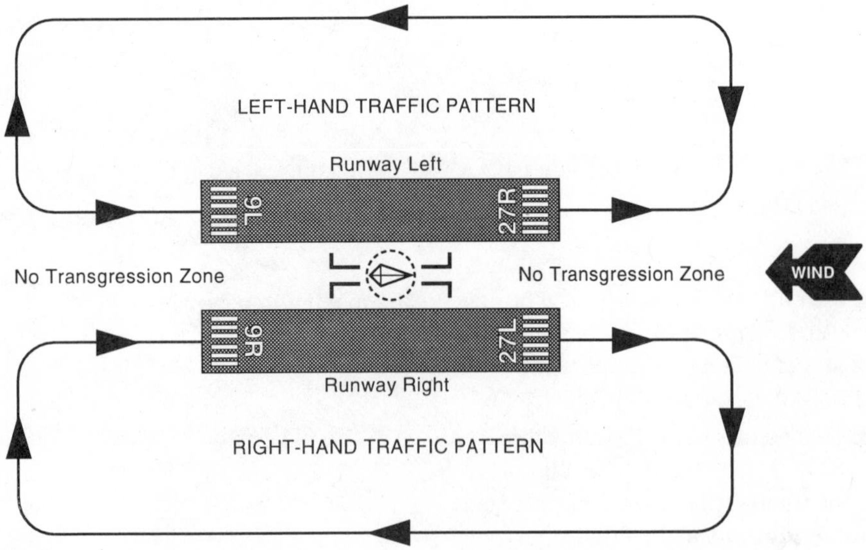

Figure 12-7. Left-hand and right-hand traffic patterns for parallel runways

The traffic pattern is referred to the runway on which it is based—for example, *left traffic for Runway 36* refers to the pattern based on Runway 36. The *36* indicates that the runway heading is somewhere in the range 355° to 360° to 005°.

Legs of the Traffic Pattern

After takeoff, climb straight ahead on the **upwind leg** until beyond the departure end of the runway and within 300 feet of pattern altitude. The upwind leg is an extension of the runway in the direction of takeoff and landing.

Within 300 feet of pattern altitude and beyond the end of the runway, begin a climbing turn to **crosswind leg.** The crosswind leg of the traffic pattern is a flight path at right angles to the runway in use and beyond its departure end. Continue the climb to the pattern altitude—typically **1,000 feet** above airport elevation—and then level off.

With the correct setting in the pressure window of the altimeter, pattern altitude is indicated when the altimeter shows the pattern altitude above the airport (say 1,000 feet) added to the airport's elevation (say 2,300 feet MSL) which is, in this case, 3,300 feet MSL on the altimeter.

Pattern altitudes at some airports may be different for various reasons—for example, to avoid high terrain or remain beneath certain airspace. Most will be in the range of 800 to 1,200 feet *above the airport elevation* (also referred to as *above ground level—AGL)*. You must maintain **visual contact with the ground** at all times and have a visibility of at least 3 statute miles (sm)—5 sm at night.

Having reached the pattern altitude, or when at a suitable distance from the runway, a turn is made to the **downwind leg.** This is a flight path parallel to the runway in the opposite direction to takeoffs and landings. On the downwind leg, the airplane is flown at traffic-pattern altitude parallel to the runway. The downwind leg is usually about one-half to one mile from the runway, depending on wind conditions and airplane speed—faster airplanes need more space to maneuver.

A "downwind" radio call is often made to alert other aircraft and Air Traffic Control of your position. Descent for landing may be commenced at any convenient point after passing abeam your intended touchdown point on the runway.

> Follow the prescribed legs of the standard traffic pattern.

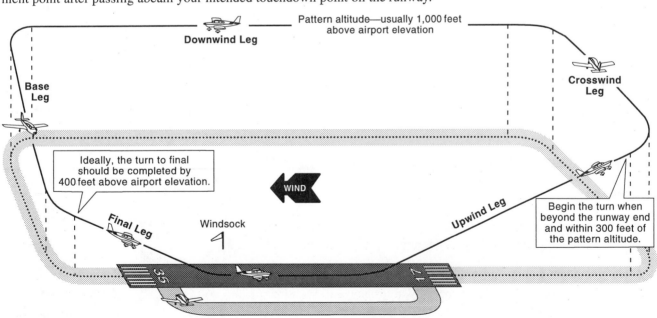

Figure 12-8. The normal traffic pattern—pattern altitude is usually 1,000 feet above the airport elevation.

At a suitable point at the end of the downwind leg, a turn to **base leg** is made, and the descent continued or started. The base leg of a traffic pattern is a flight path at right angles to the landing runway, and off its approach end, extending from downwind leg to the intersection of the extended runway centerline.

Ideally, a turn from base leg to **final approach** should be completed by 400 feet AGL.

Wind

While flying in the pattern, you should aim to fly a rectangular path over the ground. This means that, on any leg where there is a crosswind component, drift should be allowed for and a wind correction angle (WCA) applied to compensate for the wind effect. This is most easily achieved by selecting a reference point on the ground well ahead of the airplane, and making sure that the airplane tracks directly toward it.

Allow for wind effect in the traffic pattern.

The wind at pattern altitude may differ to that on the ground—simply adjust your heading so that the track over the ground is correct.

Throughout the pattern, the gyroscopic heading indicator provides useful heading information (more easily read than the magnetic compass, which experiences turning and acceleration errors).

Weather Conditions

To operate at an airport in controlled airspace (other than Class B), the **basic VFR minimums** required are:
- ceiling 1,000 feet AGL or more; and
- visibility 3 statute miles (sm) or more.

VFR minimum weather conditions in controlled airspace are: ceiling 1,000 feet AGL and visibility 3 sm.

As a student pilot to fly solo, you must retain **visual reference** to the surface and have a flight or surface visibility of at least **3 sm** (5 sm by night).

Flying the Maneuver

The takeoff and climb to downwind leg can be split into various stages:
- before-takeoff;
- line up to position on the runway;
- the takeoff roll;
- liftoff;
- initial climb-out; and
- climbing turn to crosswind leg, and a turn at pattern altitude to downwind leg.

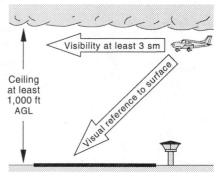

Figure 12-9. Minimum weather conditions for visual flight in Classes C, D & E airspace

Before Takeoff

Taxi toward the runway and position the aircraft clear of the runway (or in a run-up area if provided) to do your engine run-up and Before-Takeoff check.

Ensure that:
- you position the airplane so that it will not be in the propeller slipstream of other aircraft, and so that it will not restrict their movement;
- the slipstream from your propeller will not affect other aircraft;
- the nosewheel is straight and the brakes parked;
- a brake failure will not cause you to run into other aircraft or obstacles;
- loose stones will not damage the propeller or be blown rearward.

A suitable position is usually at 90° to the runway, giving you a good view in either direction, although it is better, especially in strong wind conditions, to be facing upwind. This ensures adequate cooling of the engine.

Taxi to a suitable position for the pretakeoff checks.

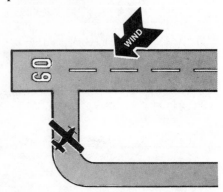

Figure 12-10. Position the airplane for the Before-Takeoff check, preferably upwind.

Set the parking brake, and set the engine rpm to 1,000. This allows the engine to continue warming up, yet be adequately cooled. Ensure that the oil temperature and pressure are within limits for the run-up. In a very cold climate, it may take a few minutes for the engine oil to warm up sufficiently.

At all times, **remain aware** of other aircraft near you and in the traffic pattern by dividing your attention between cockpit tasks and looking outside, and also listening to the radio communications on the airport frequency.

Vital Actions

Confirm that the parking brake is set, to ensure that the airplane will not inadvertently move forward, and complete the Before-Takeoff checklist.

The Before-Takeoff check contains vital actions.

You are just about to take the airplane off the ground and into the air, so it is vital that everything be as it should and the airplane is in a safe operating condition. The Before-Takeoff check should confirm this—**if not, do not fly!**

As a point of airmanship, it is good to say these checks aloud using concise and clear language, for the benefit of both yourself and your flight instructor.

A Typical Before-Takeoff Check

Use the Before-Takeoff check in your Pilot's Operating Handbook. It will probably contain such items as:

The mnemonic TMPFISCH covers the Before-Takeoff items well; but still read the checklist!

T—Trim: set for takeoff.

> **Throttle friction nut:** sufficiently tight to prevent the throttle slipping when it has been set, but not so tight that the throttle is difficult to move.

M—Mixture: RICH (or adjusted as recommended by the manufacturer at high-altitude airports).

> **Master switch:** ON (battery and alternator).

P—Primer: fuel primer in and locked (to avoid flooding the cylinders with excess fuel).

F—Fuel: correct fuel tank selected and contents sufficient for flight.

> **Fuel pump:** ON (if fitted—most likely in low-wing airplanes) and fuel pressure adequate.
>
> **Flaps:** set for takeoff.

I— Instruments: Flight instruments checked for correct settings and indications, and engine instruments checked for correct indications. Follow a systematic scan around the instrument panel.

> *Flight Instruments:*
> - **airspeed indicator:** indicating zero or well below the stalling speed;
> - **attitude indicator:** set the miniature airplane against the artificial horizon;
> - **altimeter:** set altimeter setting and check that correct elevation is indicated (or vice versa, set the known airport elevation and confirm that a reasonable altimeter setting is displayed in the pressure window).
> - **vertical speed indicator:** showing zero (neither a climb nor a descent);
> - **heading indicator:** align with the magnetic compass (which you also check);
> - **turn coordinator:** previously checked with left and right turns during the taxi (if it is driven electrically or by an engine-driven vacuum pump—if venturi driven, it cannot be tested prior to flight);
> - **ball:** tested during the taxi with left and right turns;
> - **clock:** wound (yes, the clock is a flight instrument!), check that the correct time is set—important for navigation, radio position reports, and to be aware of the onset of darkness.

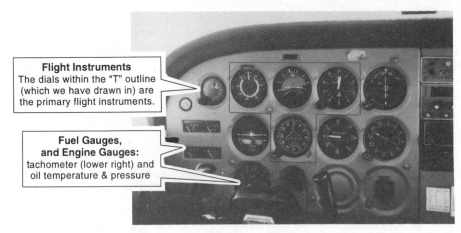

Flight Instruments
The dials within the "T" outline (which we have drawn in) are the primary flight instruments.

Fuel Gauges, and Engine Gauges:
tachometer (lower right) and oil temperature & pressure

Figure 12-11. Instrument panel of a typical training airplane

Engine and Other Gauges:

- **tachometer:** rpm remaining steady (at 1,000 rpm);
- **oil pressure:** normal;
- **oil temperature:** normal;
- **fuel pressure:** already checked if a fuel pump (or boost pump or auxiliary pump) is installed;
- **ammeter:** to indicate that the electrical system is charging;
- **suction gauge:** for correct suction from engine-driven vacuum pump (if vacuum-driven flight instruments are installed).

Note: This seems a lot but, if you work your way around the panel systematically, you will cover them all.

S—Switches:

Magneto Switches: confirm that there are no aircraft behind you, and then run the engine up (typically to 1,800 or 2,000 rpm). Ensure that the engine does not overheat, and check each of the two magneto systems, as follows.

- While at high rpm, the carburetor heat can be tested at HOT, which should cause the rpm to drop by about 100 rpm. This indicates that the system is working—the warm air entering the engine, being less dense, causes a drop in power. An rpm increase during the 10 seconds or so that you leave the carburetor heat on will indicate that carburetor ice *was* present and has been melted. At the end of this test, return the carburetor heat to COLD. The magnetos can now be checked knowing that the carburetor is free of ice. If you think carburetor ice may re-form prior to takeoff, then take appropriate action (see later).
- Switch from BOTH to LEFT and note the rpm drop—typically between 75 to 175 rpm drop, because the right magneto system is grounded and only the left-system spark plug in each cylinder is firing—then return the switch to BOTH, and the rpm should return to the original setting.
- Switch from BOTH to RIGHT and note the rpm drop—again, typically between 75 to 175 rpm drop, with the left magneto system now grounded, and only the right-system spark plug in each cylinder firing—then return the switch to BOTH, and again the rpm should return to the original setting.
- If there is no rpm drop, or if the engine stops firing, or if there is an imbalance of more than 75 to 100 rpm between the two drops, then there is a problem and you should not fly.
- Close the throttle and check the idle rpm (typically 600 to 700 rpm), then return to the normal idling speed of around 1,000 rpm.

If you inadvertently go to OFF when testing the magnetos, allow the engine to stop; an *experienced* pilot will be able to keep the engine going by moving the switch to L, R, or BOTH, but quick action is needed, otherwise possible exhaust system damage could occur. It is no problem to stop the engine and then start it again normally.

Other Switches: as required (including pitot heat and rotating beacon, if installed).

C—**Controls:** full-and-free movement in the correct sense.

Carburetor heat: COLD (or as advised by the Pilot's Operating Handbook if you are in conditions where the formation of carburetor ice is likely).

Cowl flaps: (if fitted) set for takeoff.

H—**Hatches:** doors and windows secure, and no loose articles in the cockpit.

Harness (seat belts): secure, seats locked in place, passengers briefed.

Hydraulics: (if appropriate) as required.

Note: TMPFISCH is only one mnemonic to help pilots remember the items in the Before-Takeoff check. Other items in more advanced airplanes may be included, such as *P for pitch* when checking the operation of a constant-speed propeller. There are other mnemonics such as TTMFGHH, and so on. The important thing is that you follow the check as described in your own Pilot's Operating Handbook. Use a written checklist, if recommended. **Checks are a vital part of safe flying.**

Be very thorough with the Before-Takeoff checklist.

The 10-Second Review

Having completed the Before-Takeoff checklist, and prior to lining up on the runway for takeoff, it is good airmanship to conduct a 10-second review of:

The 10-second review prior to takeoff sharpens your performance.

- the wind direction;
- takeoff performance airspeeds;
- the expected takeoff distance and liftoff point;
- the departure route if the takeoff is normal;
- relevant emergency procedures (for example, engine failure after takeoff); and
- any expected radio frequency change after takeoff.

A suggested review and briefing is included in the *Further Points* later in this chapter.

Line-Up

ATC and Radio Procedures

The category of the airport will determine whether takeoff clearances are required. **At nontowered airports,** clearances are not required, but you would advise other aircraft that you are about to enter the runway on the Common Traffic Advisory Frequency (CTAF). **At tower-controlled airports,** you do need a clearance to enter the active runway.

Consider ATC and radio procedures before lining up on the runway.

You may have to change from the ground control frequency to the tower frequency. Your radio call to the tower should include:

- the name of the station you are calling;
- your identification; and
- your position and intentions.

An example could be:

Pilot: *Hagerstown Tower,*
Cessna 2538 Papa,
Ready for departure Runway 27,
VFR, remaining in the traffic pattern.

Consider the clearance and other Air Traffic Control requirements before entering the runway, checking *all clear left* and *all clear right* along the runway and on final approach before you do.

Aircraft already taking off or landing have **right-of-way** over a taxiing airplane. Avoid taking off immediately after large aircraft because of the wake turbulence they create. *(This topic is covered in more detail later.)*

Turn the strobe lights on (if fitted) and the landing light(s) also, to make you more conspicuous to other aircraft and to birds. Turn on your transponder—usually Mode C altitude reporting—using the code given by the tower at a tower-controlled airport, or using 1200 otherwise for VFR flights.

Make yourself visible.

Straighten the Nosewheel

Make full use of the runway length available (within reason). One of the most useless things in aviation is runway behind you!

Line up and ensure that the nosewheel is straight.

The takeoff run should be along the centerline of the runway, and the easiest way to achieve this is to line up with one mainwheel either side of the centerline markings (if the runway has them). Roll forward a few feet, thereby ensuring that the nosewheel is straight (before applying brakes, if used) but do not waste runway length.

Have a good **look out.** Scan the runway and traffic pattern area for other aircraft that could conflict with you. Maintain an awareness of other traffic, both visually and aurally (by listening to the radio). It is a good habit to check the windsock just before you roll.

The Takeoff Roll

Select a reference point at the end of the runway (or beyond) on which to keep straight. You should view this reference point straight ahead (parallel with the longitudinal axis of the airplane), and **not** over the propeller spinner.

Select a reference point, release the brakes and open the throttle smoothly.

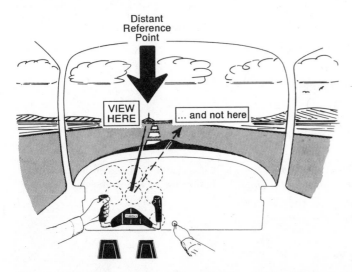

Figure 12-12. View the selected reference point straight ahead, not over the spinner.

Take note of any obstructions or other hazards in the climb-out path, and remain aware of the position of other aircraft. For instance, there could be one on short final that you noticed on approach before lining up, but you considered sufficient spacing was available—your decision at an uncontrolled airport, the tower's decision at a tower-controlled airport—but still, you should only line up if you feel spacing is adequate. As pilot-in-command you always have final responsibility for the safety of your aircraft.

Release the brakes, and smoothly apply full power. A mental count of *one–two–three* will occupy the time required to advance the throttle to full power. Have your heels on the floor with the balls of your feet on the rudder pedals to control steering (and **not** high enough to apply the toe brakes). Keep straight and accelerate smoothly in the first few seconds of the ground roll.

Keep straight and accelerate smoothly in the first few seconds of the ground roll.

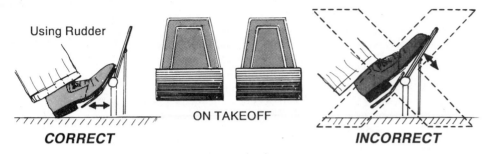

Figure 12-13. Heels on the floor (and *no* pressure on the brakes)

Glance at the tachometer early in the takeoff run to confirm that the correct rpm has been achieved. Quickly check oil pressure and temperature.

Rudder Control to Keep Straight

Even though you are focusing well ahead, the edges of the runway in your peripheral vision and the runway centerline disappearing under the nose provide supporting guidance. With the application of power, there may be a tendency to yaw because of the:

Use a reference point at or beyond the far end of the runway centerline to assist you in keeping straight.

- slipstream effect on the horizontal stabilizer; and
- torque reaction pressing one wheel down.

For an airplane whose propeller rotates clockwise as seen from the cockpit, the tendency is to yaw left. (If the propeller rotates counterclockwise, the tendency is to yaw right.)

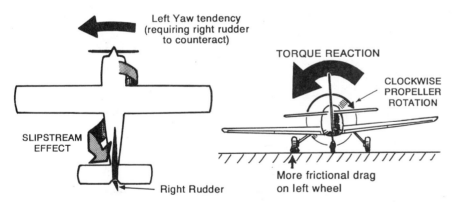

Figure 12-14. There is a tendency to yaw on the takeoff run.

Any yawing tendency should be counteracted with rudder. If yawing left, apply right rudder (and vice versa).

Large rudder pedal movements may be required early in the takeoff run but, as the airflow over the rudder increases and the rudder becomes more effective, smaller movements will be sufficient. Just look ahead and keep the airplane tracking straight down the centerline. Steer the airplane with your feet (and not your hands). **Keep straight with rudder.**

Figure 12-15. Keep straight using your feet.

Note: A brief mention of crosswinds (which are covered more fully in a later exercise) is made here in case an upwind runway is not available. Any significant crosswind will tend to lift one wing. The wings can be kept level by holding the control column sufficiently into the wind (by a large amount at the start of the takeoff run, reducing the amount as speed is gained and the ailerons become more effective). **Keep the wings level with aileron.**

Protect the Nosewheel

On the ground, the nosewheel carries a fair load, especially if the takeoff surface is rough or soft.

Protect the nosewheel by holding the weight off it.

During the normal takeoff roll of a tricycle-gear airplane, the pilot should hold a little back pressure on the control wheel. This takes some of the weight off the nosewheel and protects it somewhat. It also improves propeller clearance.

Back pressure also prevents **wheel-barrowing**—a situation in which the nosewheel is held on the ground after sufficient lift has been generated for flight. Wheel-barrowing is bad news for the nosewheel!

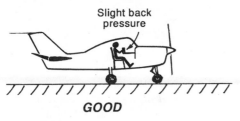
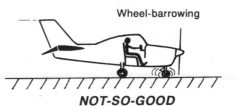

GOOD   **NOT-SO-GOOD**

Figure 12-16. Protect the nosewheel.

Check the Power

After maximum power has been set and tracking down the runway centerline is under control, glance at the engine gauges to check that full power is indeed being developed. Engine rpm should be as expected. The oil pressure and temperature should both be within limits. This glance should take no more than one or two seconds.

Check the power early in the takeoff run.

If you are not satisfied with engine performance or the rate of acceleration, then close the throttle and stop the airplane, using brakes as necessary. Your right hand should remain on the throttle throughout the takeoff run, until you are at a safe altitude where you can use your right hand to raise the flaps.

The Controls

Before the start of the takeoff roll, and with no airflow over the controls, the control wheel will feel quite sloppy. You should hold the control column in a neutral position (with the ailerons positioned into the wind to keep the wings level if there is a significant crosswind).

The controls will feel firmer as airspeed increases.

As power is applied and airflow over the controls increases as a result of the propeller slipstream and increasing airspeed, the control column will feel firmer. As the speed increases, you should keep the wings level with aileron, and exert a little back pressure on the control column to lighten the load on the nosewheel. Approaching liftoff speed, you should increase the back pressure to raise the nose to the takeoff attitude.

Liftoff

As the airspeed increases during the takeoff ground roll, the wings will generate more and more lift. When flying speed is reached, a gradual backward movement of the control column will allow the airplane to become airborne. Raising the nose to assist the airplane to lift off is called *rotating*.

Lift the airplane off the ground with elevator when you reach flying speed.

The transition from the ground roll to the climb-out should be a smooth liftoff with no dramatic pitch changes. You should apply back pressure, and rotate smoothly to your estimated pitch attitude for the liftoff, holding the wings level with aileron control. As the stabilizing effect of the nosewheel is lost as it leaves the ground, you may have to apply a little more right rudder to counteract the tendency for high power to yaw the nose left. Immediately after liftoff, you may need to relax the back pressure a little to hold the desired nose attitude.

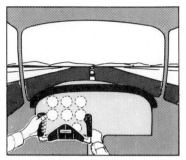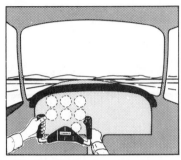

Figure 12-17. Gradually adopt the climb attitude with elevator.

If you raise the nose too soon, the additional drag will reduce acceleration and delay the liftoff.

If you lift off too soon, the airplane may not fly and will settle back onto the runway. If you lift off too late, the wheels and tires will have been subjected to extra stress, the airspeed will be excessive and the takeoff will have been unnecessarily lengthened; obstacle clearance might also be a problem.

The cushioning of **ground effect** when the airplane is flying close to the ground allows you to fly at lower speeds than when the airplane is well clear of the ground. It is important that the airplane accelerates to the correct climbing speed fairly soon after liftoff to avoid sinking.

If the airplane is properly trimmed, it may require some back pressure to hold the pitch attitude as the airplane accelerates to climb speed. The back pressure can gradually be released as the airspeed increases, but you may not be conscious of this as you concentrate on holding the desired nose attitude.

Note: In a strong and gusty wind, or in a strong crosswind, it is sometimes advisable to delay the liftoff by a few knots. This is to give you a small additional airspeed safety margin when airborne—in case of a sudden lull in the headwind, or some other significant windshear, that could briefly reduce your airspeed. The liftoff at this higher speed should be smooth and positive.

The Climb-Out

Initial Climb-Out

- **Look out,** both at the horizon to check your attitude and your tracking, and to look for other aircraft.
- Keep the wings level with the ailerons.
- Keep your right hand on the throttle to ensure FULL POWER is applied.
- Maintain coordination with rudder pressure (high power may require a little right rudder pressure)—any corrections to tracking in flight should be made with shallow coordinated turns.
- With the elevator, hold the nose attitude in the correct position relative to the horizon for the climb-out, glancing at the airspeed indicator to confirm that the target climb speed has been achieved. In the climb, airspeed is controlled with elevator; make small pitch changes as required.
- Trim.

When airborne and climbing, check airplane attitude and tracking, and look out for other traffic.

At a safe altitude (say between 100 and 200 feet AGL), raise the takeoff flaps, if used, hold the pitch attitude to avoid sinking, and accelerate to the desired climb speed—normally the published V_{Y,} for the quickest climb to pattern altitude. Retrim if necessary.

Established in the Climb-Out

After the airplane has settled into a steady climb, trim off any steady control pressure. Leave full power on until at least 500 feet above airport elevation. For some airplanes, you can then reduce to climb power; for others, you retain full power throughout the climb.

When the airplane is established in the climb, trim.

Check your reference point to confirm that you are tracking on the extended centerline of the runway and not drifting to one side. If necessary counteract any drift by applying a wind correction angle, with a shallow coordinated turn, and crab into the wind. Hold the normal climb speed to an accuracy of plus or minus 5 KIAS by altering the nose attitude if necessary.

Climb straight ahead, in line with the extended centerline of the runway, until you have reached a point beyond the end of the runway and within 300 feet of pattern altitude, where you commence a turn onto the **crosswind leg.**

Notes:

1. In airplanes with a **retractable landing gear,** raise the gear when a positive rate of climb is established after liftoff, when there is no risk of sinking back onto the runway. After liftoff on long runways, you could consider leaving the landing gear down a little longer if sufficient room remains for a landing in the rare case of engine failure; when insufficient runway ahead remains, raise the landing gear. Most training airplanes have fixed-gear and so this is not a consideration.

2. The procedure for aircraft that have a **fuel pump** switched on for takeoff is to switch it off at a safe altitude (say 500 feet), checking that the fuel pressure (now provided solely by the engine-driven fuel pump) remains satisfactory.

3. If your Pilot's Operating Handbook calls for an **After-Takeoff checklist** (flaps and fuel pump, for instance), perform this check when you are established in the climb-out (say at about 400 to 500 feet above the airport elevation).

Crosswind Leg

Before commencing the turn to the crosswind leg, scan the area toward which you will be turning. Select a new reference point to assist you in tracking correctly on this leg, which should be a path over the ground at right angles to the runway.

Then turn (usually left) to the crosswind leg using a normal climbing turn (bank angle 20° or less). Coordinate with rudder pressure and maintain the required climb speed with elevator. Roll out on the crosswind heading, which should be calculated by applying a wind correction angle to the crosswind course (90° off the runway direction) to allow for any drift due to wind effect.

As you continue the climb having turned to crosswind leg, look out to check your attitude and scan ahead, above and to either side.

Anticipate reaching pattern altitude and, as you approach it, start lowering the nose to the cruise attitude. To level off from a climb, use **A-P-T:**

A—Attitude: lower the nose to the straight-and-level attitude and allow the speed to increase to the desired airspeed.

P—Power: reduce power to maintain the desired airspeed.

T—Trim.

Downwind Leg

At (or approaching) pattern altitude, check *all clear* and turn to downwind leg, selecting a reference point well ahead on which to parallel the runway. Fly right on the pattern altitude at your selected airspeed, adjusting attitude and power as necessary. Accuracy required is within plus or minus 100 feet and 10 KIAS. Maintain your orientation with the runway by glancing frequently in its direction, and maintain a good lookout and radio listening watch for other aircraft.

The most efficient means of **scanning for other aircraft** is a series of short, regularly spaced eye movements, moving the eyes about 10° each time to scan that area for about one second before moving on. Remember that an aircraft in distress has right-of-way over all other aircraft.

The wind at altitude is often quite different to that on the ground, so make heading adjustments with shallow turns to achieve a straight downwind track over the ground parallel to the runway and about one-half to one mile from it.

You may be required to report *downwind* on the radio to inform the tower and/or other aircraft of your position.

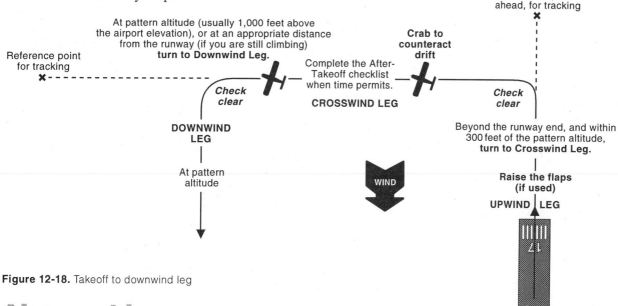

Figure 12-18. Takeoff to downwind leg

Airmanship

Maintain a good **lookout** while performing the Before-Takeoff check, as well as prior to entering the runway and in the traffic pattern area.

Using correct phraseology, obtain and acknowledge Air Traffic Control (ATC) clearances, or make an advisory call entering the active runway, as required at your field. Make sure that you understand all clearances totally, otherwise request clarification. Comply with any ATC instruction, but if unable to do so, inform ATC immediately.

The takeoff roll, liftoff and climb-out to pattern altitude is one continuous maneuver that you should endeavor to fly smoothly and with firm control over the airplane. Hold your heading accurately, and adjust the pitch attitude to hold the climb-out airspeed as closely as possible, but certainly within 5 KIAS.

The usual speed for the climb-out is that for best rate of climb (V_Y).

Fly an accurate traffic pattern at the correct altitude, and maintain the correct airspeeds (as recommended by your flight instructor).

Listen carefully to the radio when flying in the traffic pattern, and make required radio calls without cutting off any transmissions from other aircraft.

Airmanship is flying confidently, using the radio correctly, and keeping a good lookout.

Airwork 12
The Standard (upwind) Takeoff and Climb to Downwind Leg

Objective

To take off into the wind and climb out in the traffic pattern to downwind leg.

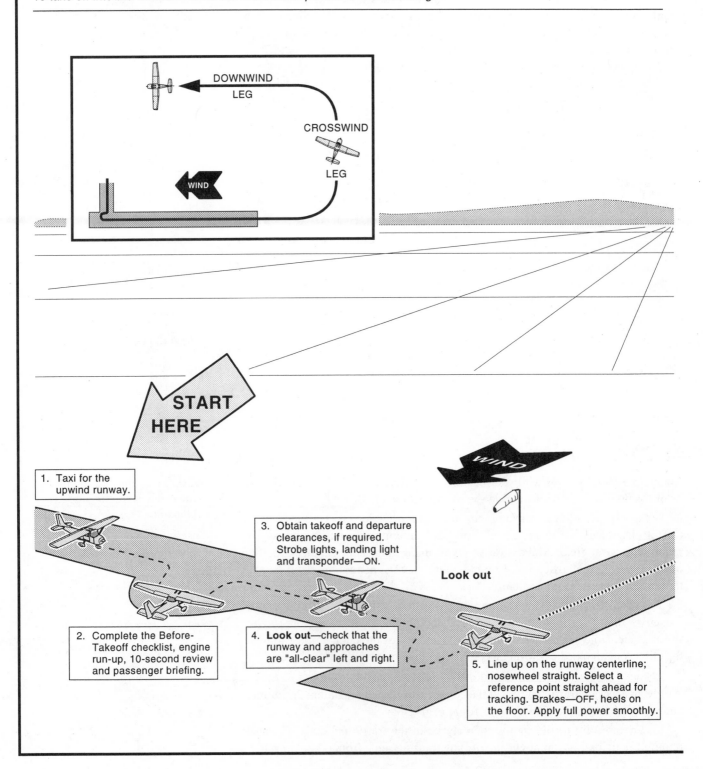

DOWNWIND LEG

CROSSWIND LEG

WIND

START HERE

WIND

1. Taxi for the upwind runway.

2. Complete the Before-Takeoff checklist, engine run-up, 10-second review and passenger briefing.

3. Obtain takeoff and departure clearances, if required. Strobe lights, landing light and transponder—ON.

Look out

4. **Look out**—check that the runway and approaches are "all-clear" left and right.

5. Line up on the runway centerline; nosewheel straight. Select a reference point straight ahead for tracking. Brakes—OFF, heels on the floor. Apply full power smoothly.

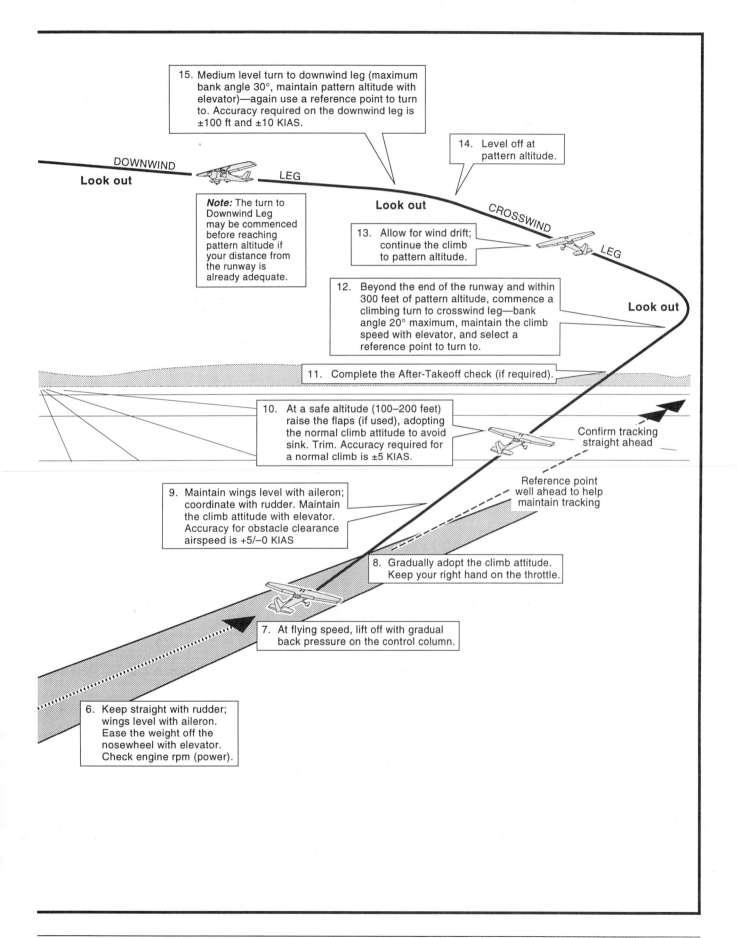

15. Medium level turn to downwind leg (maximum bank angle 30°, maintain pattern altitude with elevator)—again use a reference point to turn to. Accuracy required on the downwind leg is ±100 ft and ±10 KIAS.

14. Level off at pattern altitude.

DOWNWIND

Look out

LEG

Note: The turn to Downwind Leg may be commenced before reaching pattern altitude if your distance from the runway is already adequate.

Look out

CROSSWIND

13. Allow for wind drift; continue the climb to pattern altitude.

LEG

Look out

12. Beyond the end of the runway and within 300 feet of pattern altitude, commence a climbing turn to crosswind leg—bank angle 20° maximum, maintain the climb speed with elevator, and select a reference point to turn to.

11. Complete the After-Takeoff check (if required).

10. At a safe altitude (100–200 feet) raise the flaps (if used), adopting the normal climb attitude to avoid sink. Trim. Accuracy required for a normal climb is ±5 KIAS.

Confirm tracking straight ahead

9. Maintain wings level with aileron; coordinate with rudder. Maintain the climb attitude with elevator. Accuracy for obstacle clearance airspeed is +5/–0 KIAS

Reference point well ahead to help maintain tracking

8. Gradually adopt the climb attitude. Keep your right hand on the throttle.

7. At flying speed, lift off with gradual back pressure on the control column.

6. Keep straight with rudder; wings level with aileron. Ease the weight off the nosewheel with elevator. Check engine rpm (power).

Emergencies on Takeoff

There are two emergencies in the takeoff for which you should be prepared, even though they may never happen—and are less likely to happen if you are thorough with your Before-Takeoff checklist.

1. **Engine failure after takeoff** (uncommon these days).
2. **The discontinued takeoff** while still on the ground (pilot initiated).

Prior to opening the throttle on each and every takeoff, it is a good idea to run through both of these procedures in your mind as you do your 10-second review. Your passengers need not be aware of this, but it is one sign of a sharp pilot.

Be prepared for two emergencies on takeoff—engine failure and a discontinued takeoff.

Engine Failure after Takeoff

If engine power is lost in the climb-out following takeoff, the options open to you will vary according to how high the airplane is, the nature of the terrain ahead, the wind conditions, and so on. An event such as engine failure close to the ground will require prompt and decisive action.

No matter when the engine fails in flight, the first priority is to maintain safe flight. A controlled descent and landing, even on an unprepared surface, is preferable by far to an unwanted stall in the attempted climb-out. Close the throttle in case the engine comes back to life at an inopportune time.

Immediately lower the nose to the gliding attitude to maintain flying speed.

Do Not Turn Back to the Field

The altitude at which the failure occurs determines how you maneuver the airplane but, in general, you should plan to land approximately straight-ahead. Altitude is rapidly lost in descending turns and, from less than 500 feet AGL, it is doubtful if you would make the runway. **Look for a landing area ahead and within range.**

In your day-to-day flying, make yourself familiar with suitable emergency landing areas in the vicinity of your airport so that, in the event of engine failure, you already have a plan of action in mind.

Following engine failure and having established the glide, **quickly select the best landing area** from the fields available ahead and within approximately 30° either side of your heading, if possible—otherwise within 60°. Make only gentle turns (at a 15° to 20° bank angle).

Land straight ahead.

Gliding turns at low level can be dangerous because of:
• the high rates of descent; and
• the tendency for the pilot to raise the nose to stop a high rate of descent and inadvertently stall or spin the airplane.

Complete the emergency checks and transmit a MAYDAY call if time permits. Any attempt to change fuel tanks and/or restart the engine depends on having time. **Maintaining flying speed is vital**—more important than any radio call or even attempting to restart the engine.

If the selected field looks rough and you feel that damage could ensue and increase the risk of fire, then when committed to carrying out the landing:
• Mixture—IDLE CUTOFF.
• Fuel—OFF.
• Ignition—OFF.
• Flaps—AS REQUIRED (to control descent path and reduce touchdown speed).
• Master switch—OFF (after electrically driven flaps have been lowered).
• Doors—UNLOCKED (or as advised in the Pilot's Operating Handbook) to ensure that they can be opened if damage occurs.

After landing:
- Stop the airplane and set the parking brake;.
- Stop the engine (if it is still running).
- Check: fuel—OFF; ignition—OFF; electrical equipment and master switch—OFF.
- Evacuate, taking the fire extinguisher with you if possible.

After liftoff on a long runway, you may have sufficient runway remaining to land on. This is one reason why it is good airmanship to start such a takeoff using the full length of the runway. One of the most useless things in aviation is runway behind you!

One of the most useless things in aviation is runway behind you!

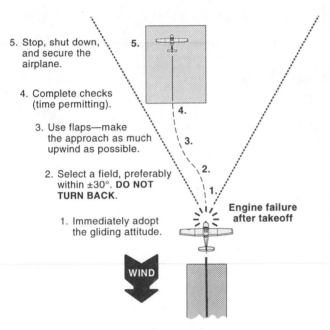

5. Stop, shut down, and secure the airplane.

4. Complete checks (time permitting).

3. Use flaps—make the approach as much upwind as possible.

2. Select a field, preferably within ±30°. **DO NOT TURN BACK.**

1. Immediately adopt the gliding attitude.

Engine failure after takeoff

WIND

Figure 12-19. Engine failure after takeoff

The Discontinued Takeoff

A discontinued takeoff is one that is begun and then halted. This maneuver is also known as *an aborted takeoff, a balked takeoff, an abandoned takeoff*, or *an accelerate–stop maneuver*. You may decide to abort a takeoff during the ground run for many reasons, such as:
- an obstruction that becomes apparent on the runway;
- engine failure or loss of power;
- an engine or fuel problem;
- faulty instrument indications;
- a doubt that the airplane is capable of flying;
- an unsecured seat that feels like it might slip backward;
- a command from the tower controller (possible conflict with another aircraft); or
- any other condition that may, in your opinion, make the takeoff inadvisable.

Aborting the Takeoff

You must make a firm and conscious decision to abort, and then act positively:
- Close the throttle fully;
- keep straight with rudder;
- apply firm braking (**immediate** maximum braking, if required), avoiding skidding or slipping while maintaining directional control; and
- stop the airplane, set the parking brake, and establish what is the problem.

Be positive in the aborted takeoff.

If necessary, shut down the engine (preferably clear of the runway) and complete the appropriate checklist. Also, notify the tower (if there is one), and seek assistance if required.

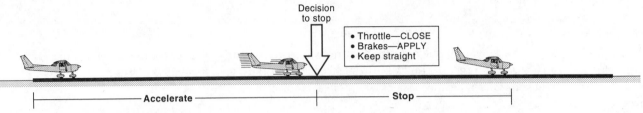

Figure 12-20. The aborted takeoff

Further Points

A Typical 10-Second Review

A typical 10-second review of the takeoff and departure made before lining up on the runway could sound something like this:

Normal Takeoff
- The wind is about 10 knots from straight ahead.
- Liftoff speed for this takeoff is 50 knots, obstacle-clearance speed is 54 knots, and, when the flaps are up, V_X is 60 knots and V_Y is 76 knots.
- I expect the ground roll to be 1,000 feet, so we should lift off about half way down the runway, and be climbing through 50 feet at the 1,800-foot point, so we will be well above all obstacles.
- I will climb straight ahead to 700 feet above the runway, which will be 1,400 feet on the altimeter, and then turn left onto the crosswind leg.
- We will be remaining in the traffic pattern, so I expect to remain on tower frequency.

Action in the Event of Engine Failure
- If I have an engine failure on the ground I will close the throttle, apply the brakes, and bring the airplane to a stop. I will set the brakes and carry out any emergency procedure and inform others by radio.
- If I have an engine failure in flight, I will land on the remaining runway if sufficient remains, otherwise I will land approximately straight ahead with only slight turns if necessary. There is a large field slightly left of those trees ahead that is suitable.

Variations on the Standard Takeoff

A restricted runway length, a soft surface, or a runway crosswind component, are all variables that require the pilot to adopt a slightly different technique on takeoff, compared with the basic method covered in this exercise.

To avoid interrupting the flow of learning to fly a standard traffic pattern by describing these variations here, they are covered in the next Section (13), within the relevant Exercises (13f, 13g and 13h).

Takeoff Performance

Takeoffs involve more than piloting skills—they involve careful planning and preparation, especially at unfamiliar airports. You must be certain, prior to every takeoff, that the runway is long enough and that the airplane is capable of climbing out above any obstacles. Airplane weight-and-balance, runway condition, and atmospheric conditions will affect this.

Poorer takeoff performance will occur with:
- high airplane weight;
- high airport elevation;
- high airport pressure altitude;
- high temperature; and
- high humidity.

The heavier the airplane, and the less dense the air, the poorer the takeoff performance.

Takeoff performance in terms of **ground roll distance** and **distance to clear a 50-foot barrier** will be shown in airplane information manuals, either in tabular or graphical form. Each of the above factors, except humidity, is considered in Performance charts.

A headwind will decrease both ground-roll and 50-foot distances (improved performance) and a tailwind will increase them (degraded performance).

A correctly loaded airplane (at or below the maximum weight limit and with the center of gravity within limits) is absolutely essential.

Note: The Performance charts on the next two pages are extracted from the Pilot's Operating Handbooks for the Cessna 172 and Piper Warrior, and are reproduced courtesy of Cessna and Piper. We emphasize that these are examples only and you should use the proper Performance charts for your particular airplane when involved in actual flight operations or flight planning.

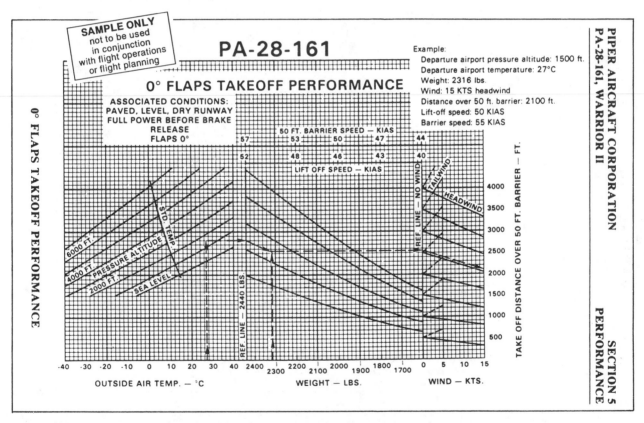

Figure 12-21a. Piper Warrior Takeoff Performance chart—takeoff climb to 50 feet above the runway

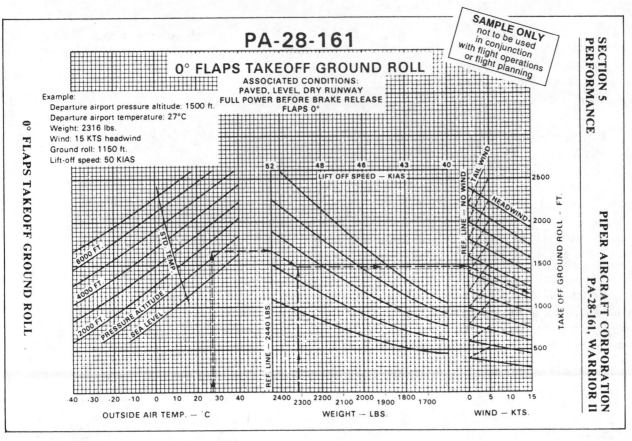

PA-28-161

0° FLAPS TAKEOFF GROUND ROLL

ASSOCIATED CONDITIONS:
PAVED, LEVEL, DRY RUNWAY
FULL POWER BEFORE BRAKE RELEASE
FLAPS 0°

Example:
Departure airport pressure altitude: 1500 ft.
Departure airport temperature: 27°C
Weight: 2316 lbs.
Wind: 15 KTS headwind
Ground roll: 1150 ft.
Lift-off speed: 50 KIAS

LIFT OFF SPEED — KIAS

OUTSIDE AIR TEMP. — °C   WEIGHT — LBS.   WIND — KTS.

0° FLAPS TAKEOFF GROUND ROLL.

Figure 12-21b. Piper PA-28 Warrior—takeoff ground roll

TAKEOFF DISTANCE

MAXIMUM WEIGHT 2400 LBS

SHORT FIELD

CONDITIONS:
Flaps 10°
Full Throttle Prior to Brake Release
Paved, Level, Dry Runway
Zero Wind

NOTES:
1. Short field technique as specified in Section 4.
2. Prior to takeoff from fields above 3000 feet elevation, the mixture should be leaned to give maximum RPM in a full throttle, static runup.
3. Decrease distances 10% for each 9 knots headwind. For operation with tailwinds up to 10 knots, increase distances by 10% for each 2 knots.
4. For operation on a dry, grass runway, increase distances by 15% of the "ground roll" figure.

WEIGHT LBS	TAKEOFF SPEED KIAS		PRESS ALT FT	0°C		10°C		20°C		30°C		40°C	
	LIFT OFF	AT 50 FT		GRND ROLL	TOTAL TO CLEAR 50 FT OBS	GRND ROLL	TOTAL TO CLEAR 50 FT OBS	GRND ROLL	TOTAL TO CLEAR 50 FT OBS	GRND ROLL	TOTAL TO CLEAR 50 FT OBS	GRND ROLL	TOTAL TO CLEAR 50 FT OBS
2400	51	56	S.L.	795	1460	860	1570	925	1685	995	1810	1065	1945
			1000	875	1605	940	1725	1015	1860	1090	2000	1170	2155
			2000	960	1770	1035	1910	1115	2060	1200	2220	1290	2395
			3000	1055	1960	1140	2120	1230	2295	1325	2480	1425	2685
			4000	1165	2185	1260	2365	1355	2570	1465	2790	1575	3030
			5000	1285	2445	1390	2660	1500	2895	1620	3160	1745	3455
			6000	1425	2755	1540	3015	1665	3300	1800	3620	1940	3990
			7000	1580	3140	1710	3450	1850	3805	2000	4220	---	---
			8000	1755	3615	1905	4015	2060	4480	---	---	---	---

Figure 12-22. Takeoff Performance chart for a Cessna 172P

Climb-Out Performance

The Takeoff Performance charts only consider the performance of the airplane up to the point where it has reached 50 feet above the runway. The recommended speed at the 50-foot point will be:

• the obstacle-clearance airspeed for the specified flap setting; and

• the maximum angle-of-climb airspeed for zero flaps.

A tailwind after takeoff will degrade the climb-out performance.

There still may be obstacles in the climb-out flight path for the airplane to clear and, if you climb into an increasing tailwind, the flight path over the ground will tend to flatten out. An increasing tailwind may occur if you take off in calm or tailwind conditions, or if **windshear conditions** exist, say at the boundary of an inversion layer. For this reason, you should **take off upwind.** Any increase in the strength of the headwind as you climb will tend to steepen your flight path over the ground, which is good.

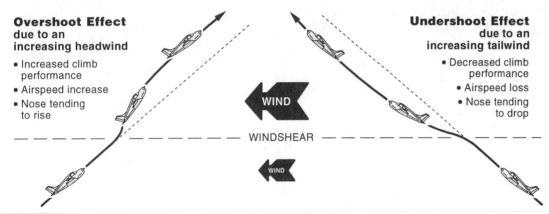

Overshoot Effect
due to an
increasing headwind

• Increased climb
  performance
• Airspeed increase
• Nose tending
  to rise

Undershoot Effect
due to an
increasing tailwind

• Decreased climb
  performance
• Airspeed loss
• Nose tending
  to drop

WIND

WINDSHEAR

WIND

Figure 12-23. Two possible windshear situations in the climb-out.

Ground Effect

Birds know all about ground effect, and it is quite common to see large birds flying leisurely just above a water surface. They may not understand the physics of ground effect, but they certainly know how to use it!

Ground effect is the interference of the airflow around the airplane by the ground surface.

Ground effect is the interference of the airflow around the airplane by the ground surface. It cushions the air beneath the wings of an airplane when it is close to the ground, within a height equal to about one wingspan.

Ground effect enables an airplane to fly more easily. The runway surface restricts the upwash and the downwash of the airflow around the wings, causing more lift. It also restricts the formation of wingtip and line vortices, thereby reducing drag.

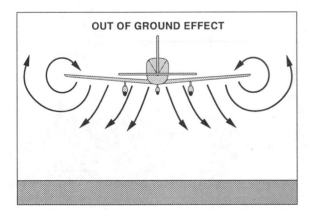

OUT OF GROUND EFFECT

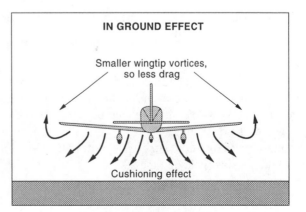

IN GROUND EFFECT

Smaller wingtip vortices,
so less drag

Cushioning effect

Figure 12-24. Ground effect occurs close to the surface.

When the airplane climbs out of ground effect, its performance decreases slightly—there is a decrease in lift and an increase in drag. In an extreme case, it is possible for a poorly performing airplane to fly *in* ground effect but be unable to climb out of it because of having insufficient power, insufficient airspeed, or excessive weight.

Performance decreases as you climb out of ground effect.

Wake Turbulence on Takeoff

When taking off behind a large airplane that has just taken off, commence your takeoff at the end of the runway. This will ensure that you become airborne in an area well before where the large airplane rotated—or to where you estimate that its vortices may have drifted. If in doubt, delay your takeoff to give the wake turbulence time to dissipate.

Avoid flying through the wake of a large airplane especially at low speed near the ground.

Do not use an intersection departure (less than the full runway length) behind a large airplane, as this may bring your flight path closer to its wake turbulence.

Maneuver to avoid the vortices in flight by climbing steeply (but not too slowly, as speed is a safety factor if you strike wake turbulence) or turning away from where you think the wake turbulence is.

When taking off after a heavy airplane has landed, plan to become airborne well past the point where it flared and landed.

If a large airplane has taken off on a different runway and you expect to be airborne prior to the intersection of the runways, check to ensure that it was still on the ground until well past the intersection, before you commence your takeoff.

Maneuver to Avoid Vortices

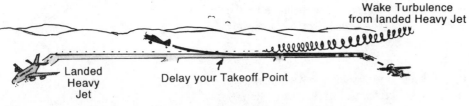

Wake Turbulence from landed Heavy Jet

Landed Heavy Jet

Delay your Takeoff Point

Figure 12-25. Avoid wake turbulence on your takeoff.

Always avoid flying through the wake of a heavy airplane, especially when it is flying at low speed near the ground.

Hydroplaning

At high groundspeeds on a wet or flooded runway, a film of water may exist between the tires and the runway. preventing direct contact between them. The frictional forces will be very low, making steering and braking difficult. Any crosswind will add to the difficulties.

Under extremely wet conditions, or if pools of water have formed on the runway, you should consider delaying the takeoff.

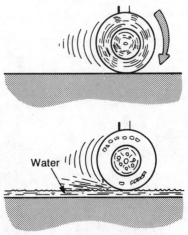

Water

Figure 12-26. Hydroplaning

Operations at Nontowered Airports

Some airports without an operating control tower have a **segmented circle** visual indicator system to assist pilots in determining the traffic-pattern direction. The segmented circle is located in a position on the airport affording good visibility to pilots in the air and on the ground, and may be associated with:

- a wind direction indicator (windsock, tetrahedron wind cone or wind-T);
- a landing direction indicator;
- landing strip indicators; and
- traffic pattern indicators.

AIRPORT OPERATIONS

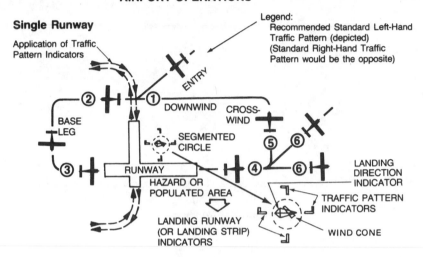

Key:

① Enter pattern in level flight, abeam the midpoint of the runway, at pattern altitude. (1000' AGL is recommended pattern altitude unless established otherwise).

② Maintain pattern altitude until abeam approach end of the landing runway, or downwind leg.

③ Complete turn to final at least ¼ mile from the runway.

④ Continue straight ahead until beyond departure end of runway.

⑤ If remaining in the traffic pattern, commence turn to crosswind leg beyond the departure end of the runway, within 300 feet of pattern altitude.

⑥ If departing the traffic pattern, continue straight out, or exit with a 45° left turn beyond the departure end of the runway, after reaching pattern altitude.

⑦ Do not overshoot final or continue on a track which will penetrate the final approach of the parallel runway.

⑧ Do not continue on a track which will penetrate the departure path of the parallel runway.

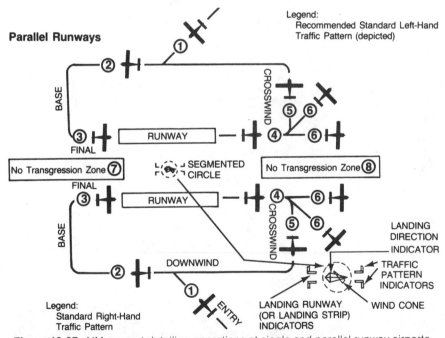

Figure 12-27. AIM excerpt detailing operations at single and parallel runway airports

Figure 12-28. Wind direction indicators

Departing the Traffic Pattern

If, following takeoff, you wish to depart the traffic pattern, you should continue straight out on the upwind leg, or exit with a 45° left turn beyond the end of the runway after reaching pattern altitude for a left-hand traffic pattern (a 45° right turn for a right-hand traffic pattern).

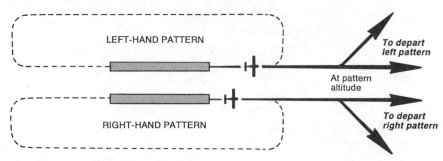

Figure 12-29. Departing the traffic pattern

✍ Review 12

Takeoff and Climb to Downwind Leg

1. What three items would you consider before using a runway for takeoff?

   ➤ (1) wind direction; (2) runway surface (length available and condition); (3) obstructions and other hazards in the takeoff and approach paths

2. As a general rule, it is good airmanship to take off from (the start of the runway/an intersection).

   ➤ the start of the runway

3. Taking off into the wind will provide the (shortest/longest) takeoff distance and (best/worst) climb-out over obstacles.

   ➤ shortest, best

4. Using a small flap setting for takeoff will (increase/reduce/not affect) the length of the ground roll, compared with a takeoff using zero flaps.

   ➤ reduce

5. The normal takeoff will use (full/reduced) power, with the mixture (rich/significantly leaned).

   ➤ full power, rich

6. The Before-Takeoff checklist (must/need not) always be performed before lining up for takeoff.

   ➤ must

7. Prior to takeoff, a 10-second review covering your planned actions after takeoff (will/will not) sharpen your performance.

   ➤ will

8. At a tower-controlled airport, a clearance (is/is not) required from the tower to enter the active runway.

   ➤ is

9. A clearance (is/is not) required to enter a runway at an airport where there is no operating control tower.

   ➤ is not

10. At a nontowered airport you (should/should not) advise others of your movements on the C_____ T_____ A_____ F_____ .

    ➤ should, Common Traffic Advisory Frequency

11. It (is/is not) vital that you check the approach path before entering a runway.

    ➤ is

12. Before lining up for takeoff, what items could you switch on to make yourself more visible, both visually and on a radar screen?

    ➤ landing light, strobe lights, transponder

Continued

---

13. You should (smoothly and positively/slowly and hesitantly) apply full power (before/when) you are aligned with the runway centerline, and (check/not check) the engine gauges.

    ➤ smoothly and positively, when, check

14. Keep straight in the ground roll using your (feet/hands), and keep the wings level using the (ailerons/rudder).

    ➤ feet, ailerons

15. At liftoff speed, you can raise, or r_____ , the nose to assist the airplane to fly away from the ground.

    ➤ rotate

16. During the ground roll, you should (take the weight off the nosewheel/hold the nosewheel firmly on the ground with forward pressure on the control column).

    ➤ take the weight off the nosewheel

17. With full power set, the nose will tend to yaw (left/right), so you can expect to use a little extra (left/right) rudder pressure.

    ➤ left, right

18. With zero flaps and full power, holding the pitch attitude that gives you V_X will ensure that you climb the greatest amount of altitude in the shortest (time/horizontal distance).

    ➤ horizontal distance

19. With zero flaps and full power, holding the pitch attitude that gives you V_Y will ensure that you climb the greatest amount of altitude in the shortest (time/horizontal distance).

    ➤ time

20. V_X is (slower/faster) than V_Y.

    ➤ slower

21. The pitch attitude for V_X is (higher/lower) than for V_Y.

    ➤ higher

22. The steepest climb-out gradient over obstacles will be achieved if you fly at the _____ airspeed for the specified takeoff flap setting, or at (V_X/V_Y) for flaps 0°, known as the best _____ airspeed.

    ➤ obstacle-clearance, V_X, best angle-of-climb

23. During the climb-out, you control the airspeed with (power/nose attitude).

    ➤ nose attitude

24. If flying at obstacle-clearance speed with takeoff flaps set, or at V_X with flaps 0° set, in order to climb out steeply over obstacles, the tolerance on airspeed is plus _____ KIAS to minus _____ KIAS.

    ➤ plus 5/minus 0 KIAS

25. Having accelerated to V_Y, known as the best _____ airspeed, to climb to altitude as (quickly/steeply) as possible, the tolerance on airspeed is _____ KIAS.

    ➤ rate-of-climb, quickly, plus or minus 5 KIAS

26. You may turn to crosswind leg (before/after) passing the far end of the runway and when within _____ feet of the pattern altitude, which for a 1,000 feet AGL traffic pattern would be at _____ feet AGL.

    ➤ after, 300 feet, 700 feet AGL

27. The standard traffic pattern is (left-handed/right-handed), with all turns being made to the (left/right).

    ➤ left-handed, left

28. If visual markings or light signals at an airport without an operating control tower indicate that turns should be made to the right, you should fly a (right-hand/left-hand) traffic pattern.

    ➤ right-hand

29. If you saw the following visual markings at an airport with crossing runways 9–27 and 36–18, you would interpret the runway in use to be _____ with a (left-hand/right-hand) traffic pattern.

    ➤ 27, left-hand

30. In the above case, the traffic pattern for Runway 9 is _____ -handed, for Runway 36 _____ -handed, and for Runway 18 _____ -handed. This could be designed to keep traffic away from a built-up area or high obstruction in the (NW/NE/SE/SW) sector.

    ➤ right, right, left, NW

Continued

31. Which aircraft has right-of-way: an airplane which is about to taxi out and line up for takeoff, or an aircraft on final approach to land?

   the aircraft on final approach to land

32. The Before-Takeoff checklist (must/need not) be completed prior to takeoff.

   must

33. If the airport elevation is 1,200 feet MSL, and traffic pattern altitude is 800 feet AGL, you could commence your turn after takeoff onto the crosswind leg when the altimeter indicates _____ feet MSL, which is _____ feet AGL . You would level off when the altimeter indicates _____ feet MSL, which is _____ feet AGL, and reduce power to stop the airplane from accelerating. What are the altitude and airspeed tolerances on downwind leg?

   1,700 feet MSL, 500 feet AGL, 2,000 feet MSL, 800 feet AGL, plus or minus 100 feet and 10 KIAS

34. A typical downwind leg is displaced _____ from the runway.

   one-half to one mile

35. Minimum weather conditions required for VFR flight at a tower-controlled airport are ceiling _____ feet AGL and visibility _____ statute miles.

   1,000 feet AGL, 3 sm

36. Given the following information, say aloud a 10-second review you might give to your flight instructor before lining up for takeoff:
   wind at 15 knots, straight down the runway, liftoff speed 50 KIAS, obstacle-clearance speed 55 KIAS, V_X 60 KIAS, V_Y 70 KIAS, ground roll 1,000 feet, 50-foot point by 1,600 feet, traffic pattern altitude 1,000 feet above the airport (airport elevation 800 feet), a clear field suitable for an emergency landing slightly to the right of the climb-out flight path, a nonstandard right-hand traffic pattern to avoid the town.

   refer to our text, page 280

37. To make your airplane more conspicuous in flight to other pilots and to birds, you could switch on your _____ light and your _____ _____ . To make you more conspicuous on radar screens, it is also usual to switch on your _____ prior to lining up.

   strobe, landing lights, transponder

38. Unless otherwise instructed by an air traffic controller, when flying VFR you should set your transponder to squawk code _____ (with/without) altitude reporting.

   1200, with

39. The best method to scan for other aircraft is to move your eyes (steadily/in a series of short movements).

   in a series of short movements

40. If the engine cuts out at 200 feet AGL just after takeoff, your first actions should be to (raise/lower) the nose and (land straight ahead/turn back to the field).

   lower, land straight ahead

41. Name three variables that are allowed for in a takeoff performance chart or table.

   aircraft weight, airport pressure altitude, outside air temperature

42. An airplane at less than about one wingspan above the ground will experience _____ effect, which will cause the airplane to fly (better/worse) because of _____ beneath the wings, and (less/more) drag because of (reduced/increased) wingtip vortices.

   ground effect, better, cushioning, less, reduced

43. Climbing into a headwind that increases with altitude will (increase/reduce/not affect) your climb performance over obstacles.

   increase

44. Climbing with a tailwind that increases with altitude will (increase/reduce/not affect) your climb performance over obstacles.

   reduce

45. When taking off after a large airplane has just taken off or landed, you (should/need not) avoid the wake turbulence caused by its wingtip vortices.

   should

46. During your takeoff ground roll, a dog runs onto the runway and into your takeoff path. Describe how you would abort the takeoff.

   throttle—CLOSE, brakes—APPLY, keep straight

The Traffic Pattern, Power-On Approach and Normal Landing

13a

Objective

To continue a normal traffic pattern for a powered approach and landing into the wind.

Considerations

Continuing from the previous exercise, this maneuver involves:
- flying an accurate traffic pattern based on the runway in use;
- making a powered descent, an approach; and
- a landing into the wind.

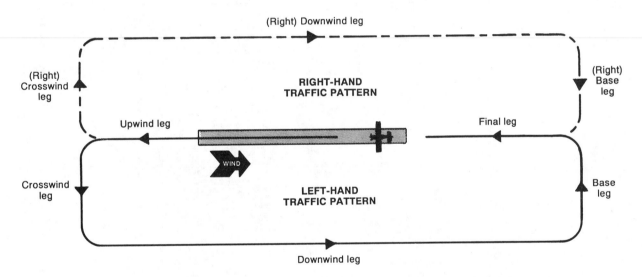

Figure 13a-1. The traffic pattern

Wind

Landing upwind is desirable because:
- for a given airspeed on approach, a headwind gives the lowest groundspeed and the lowest touchdown speed on the ground;
- there is no tendency to drift sideways in the flare and touchdown;
- it allows the best directional control both in flight and on the ground; and
- it requires less runway.

Land into a headwind if possible.

Landing Distance

If necessary, consult the Landing Distance chart to confirm that the runway is adequate for the conditions and for the airplane weight. High elevations and high temperatures decrease air density and increase the landing distance required, as does a tailwind component, a downslope, or a contaminated runway.

Ensure that the landing distance available is adequate.

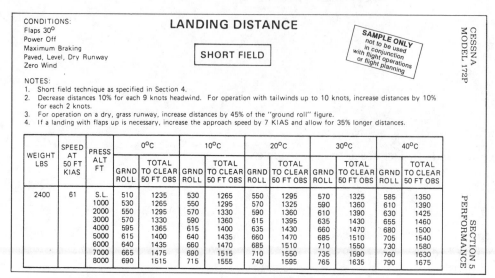

Figure 13a-2. Cessna 172 Skyhawk Landing Distance chart (sample extract, reduced)

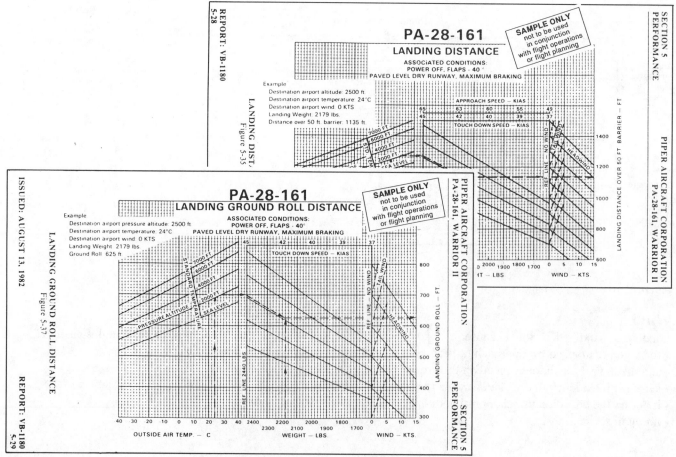

Figure 13a-3. Sample extracts of the Piper Warrior Landing Distance, and Landing Ground Roll Distance charts (reduced)

Early in your training, your flight instructor will take the responsibility for ensuring that you have **adequate runway length.**

Later in your training you will need to check NOTAMs (notices to airmen) to ensure that runway lengths have not been temporarily reduced, say because of works-in-progress to repair the runway surface or because of new obstructions in the takeoff or approach paths.

Ensure that you know whether the full length of the runway is available for landing or not. A **displaced threshold** showing the start of the landing portion of the runway will be indicated by arrows or chevrons to a thick solid line across the runway. If arrows are used, that part of the runway can be used for takeoff, but not for landing. If chevrons, rather than arrows are used, then that part of the runway is not available for any use.

Always check NOTAMs for changes to runway lengths or runway unserviceability.

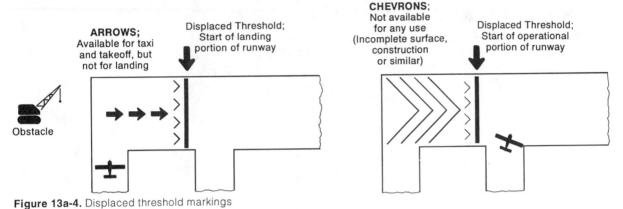

Figure 13a-4. Displaced threshold markings

If the runway is totally unusable, it will have a large cross (✕) at each end.

Figure 13a-5. Closed runway (or taxiway)

Approach Speed

Touching down at a low speed puts less strain on the landing gear and airplane structure, and uses less runway. For these reasons, the approach airspeed is usually $1.3V_{S0}$, which provides a 30% safety margin over the stall speed in the landing configuration, V_{S0}. This applies to aircraft of all sizes, from the smallest training airplane to the largest Boeing 747.

If your airplane stalls at 50 KIAS in the landing configuration, then your approach speed will be $1.3 \times 50 = 65$ KIAS. If the B747 stalls at 100 KIAS in the landing configuration, then its approach speed will be $1.3 \times 100 = 130$ KIAS.

You should aim to fly the chosen approach speed as accurately as possible (within one or two knots in steady wind conditions), and certainly within plus or minus 5 KIAS, down to the point at which you commence to flare. At this point you will make the transition to the landing attitude and remove the power, with the airspeed bleeding off prior to touchdown. The wheels will touch at a speed significantly less than the approach speed.

Note: In gusting winds, it may be advisable to carry a few extra knots in the approach to allow for gusts and lulls affecting the airspeed.

Approach at a slow, but safe, airspeed.

Power

A power-on approach is the normal procedure, since:
- you can use power to control the rate of descent and the approach flight path in varying winds;
- the engine is kept warm (ensuring power is available for a go-around); and
- the attitude change in the flare after a power-on approach is less compared with that for a power-off approach.

Use power in the approach and landing.

Flaps

Using flaps provides a:
- lower stalling speed, thus permitting a slower approach speed while still retaining an adequate margin over the stall;
- steeper flight path at a given airspeed, because of the increased drag;
- lower nose attitude at a given airspeed, providing a better view of the approach and landing path; and
- shorter flare and landing run because of the increased drag and lower airspeed.

Use flaps in the approach and landing.

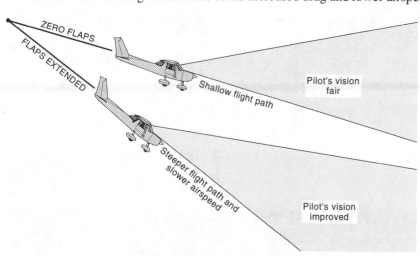

Figure 13a-6. Flaps allow a steeper approach at a slower speed, with better vision.

Note: The amount of flaps you use will depend upon the airplane itself and upon the prevailing wind conditions. In strong and gusty winds it may be preferable to use less than full flaps, or no flaps at all, for better controllability and better response to power changes. Your flight instructor will advise you. Also, refer to your Pilot's Operating Handbook for guidance.

Flying the Traffic Pattern

Fly an accurate traffic pattern and get set-up early for the approach and touchdown. Make a *"downwind"* radio call on your downwind leg at nontowered airports (airports where there is no tower or the tower is closed) and complete the Before-Landing checklist.

A good approach leads to a good landing.

Keep a good **lookout**, both for other aircraft and to check your position relative to the runway. Hold the pattern altitude as accurately as you can, and certainly within 100 feet; hold your selected airspeed to within 10 KIAS.

You may need to maneuver the airplane to maintain spacing from other traffic, typically by widening your pattern out a little, slowing down, or delaying the turn onto base leg if you are catching up on another aircraft. Do **not** make any unexpected maneuvers in the traffic pattern, such as a 360° turn, except in an emergency situation (or unless instructed to do so by the tower).

Remember that an aircraft in distress has priority over all other aircraft.

The Before-Landing Checklist

The Before-Landing check should be completed by about mid-point on the downwind leg so you can concentrate fully on your base turn, and approach to land.

The Before-Landing checklist should be completed on downwind leg.

The check will include items such as:
- Brakes—CHECKED and OFF.
- Mixture—RICH.
- Fuel—correct tank(s) selected, contents sufficient, fuel pump on (if fitted) and fuel pressure normal, fuel primer locked.
- Flaps—as required: consider what flap setting you will use for the landing, because this may affect where you turn onto base leg.
- Hatches (doors) and harnesses (seat belts)—SECURE.

Be methodical in flying the traffic pattern, and carrying out checks at the appropriate time.

Descent Position

If you have an unrestricted approach—if, for instance, you are number-one to land—then you can apply carburetor heat, and commence your descent on downwind leg by reducing power abeam your proposed touchdown point.

Begin your descent at an appropriate position to maintain spacing with other traffic.

You may decide to delay your descent to maintain spacing with other aircraft, or to position the airplane in a more suitable position for the descent from pattern altitude.

Base Leg

A medium turn from downwind leg to base leg is made when the touchdown point on the runway lies approximately 30° behind. This is the eight-o'clock position relative to the track of the airplane. In a strong wind, the turn should be established earlier to keep base leg closer to the airport boundary.

Allow for drift on base leg by crabbing into the wind, so that the wind does not carry the airplane too far from the field, and to maintain the rectangular traffic pattern over the ground. The amount of drift can assist you in estimating wind strength—the greater the crab angle required on base, the stronger the headwind on final. Make a *"base"* radio call at airports without an operating control tower.

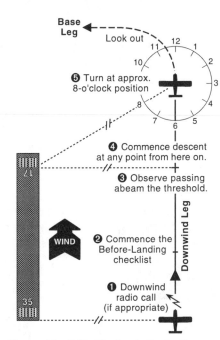

Figure 13a-7. Positioning in the traffic pattern and turning base

Judging the Descent

The descent should be judged so that you roll out on final no lower than 400 feet AGL. This means that the turn to final should be commenced not below 500 to 600 feet. With a little experience, you will get a feel for just where to begin descending to achieve this. Judgment develops with experience! The availability of power and flaps also gives you the ability to control your descent flight path as you wish.

Flaps for the approach and landing should be used as recommended in the Pilot's Operating Handbook and as advised by your flight instructor. It is typical to use partial flaps in the descent, and not to extend full landing flaps until established on final approach.

Final Approach

The turn to final is a medium descending turn in which you should:
- limit the bank angle to 30° or less (ideally about 20°), maintaining coordination with rudder pressure;
- aim to be lined up on final at or above 400 feet above the airport elevation;
- maintain flight path and airspeed with power and attitude.

Aim to be lined up on final at least 400 feet above the airport elevation.

The runway perspective as seen from the cockpit will indicate whether you are in line with the runway or not. If not, then do something about it!

Left of centerline

On runway centerline

Right of centerline

Figure 13a-8. Runway tracking perspectives on final approach

Steep turns near the ground should be avoided. If you overshoot the turn to final, rather than steepen the turn excessively, be prepared to fly through final and rejoin it from the other side without exceeding a medium bank angle.

Note: Many pilots have a tendency to fly with crossed-controls during the descending turn from base to final—for example, left control column and right rudder. This increases the risk of a stall with a wing drop, especially if the airspeed is allowed to fall. Avoid this by flying at the recommended airspeed, with the coordination ball centered. Monitor the airspeed and take positive action (power and/or attitude) to maintain it to an accuracy of plus or minus 5 KIAS throughout the approach.

Wind Effect

A tailwind on base leg will increase the airplane's speed over the ground, so the turn should be commenced early to avoid flying through final. Conversely, if there is a **headwind on base leg,** the turn to final can be delayed.

If there is any **crosswind** on final, then lay off drift using a crab angle so that the airplane tracks along the extended centerline of the runway, and keep the ball in the center to ensure that the airplane is coordinated.

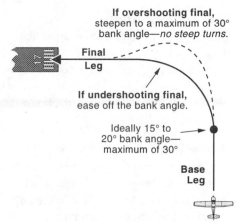

If overshooting final, steepen to a maximum of 30° bank angle—*no steep turns*.

Final Leg

If undershooting final, ease off the bank angle.

Ideally 15° to 20° bank angle—maximum of 30°

Base Leg

Figure 13a-9. Turning to final approach

Allow for the wind effect when turning final.

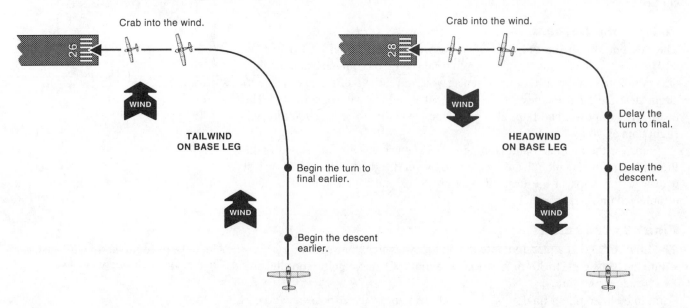

Figure 13a-10. Allow for the wind when turning to final approach.

Right-of-Way on Approach

- The aircraft at the **lower altitude** has right-of-way, but do not take advantage of this rule to cut in front of, or overtake, another aircraft on final approach.
- Give right-of-way to those aircraft that have it, but be prepared to give way even if *you* have right-of-way—the other pilot may not have seen you.
- Remember that an aircraft in distress always has right-of-way over all others.
- Do not make unexpected maneuvers such as 360° turns to avoid traffic, except in an emergency. Minor maneuvers, such as shallow S-turns on final as a delaying tactic, are acceptable however.

Windshear and Turbulence on Final

It is usual for the wind to change in strength and direction near the ground. A sudden reduction in the headwind component will cause a reduction in indicated airspeed, which can result in an increased sink rate. You can control this with attitude and power changes. **Turbulence** on final also causes airspeed and descent-rate fluctuations.

The wind often changes in strength and direction near the ground.

If a strong **wind gradient** is suspected—that is, strong wind changes with changes in altitude—then you should consider flying the final approach using a lower flap setting (or no flaps at all) and a higher approach speed than normal. The airplane will be more stable and more responsive compared with full flaps. Check with your flight instructor for advice.

Runway Perspective

The perspective of the runway seen on approach will depend upon the position of the airplane. If **too high,** then the runway will appear longer and narrower than usual, and a steep flight path will be required to arrive near the aiming point for the flare. If the airplane is **too low,** then the runway will appear shorter and wider than usual and the airplane will have to be "dragged in" with power.

Either of these situations can be remedied. Adjust the rate of descent and the flight path (using power and attitude) so that the runway assumes its normal perspective as soon as possible. This may require firm and positive action, but the sooner you do it, the better your approach will be, and the more likely you are to make a good landing.

Take positive action with *power* and *attitude* to stay on-slope and on-speed.

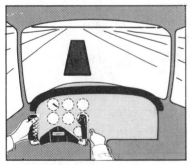
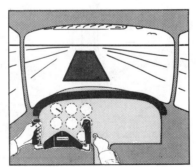
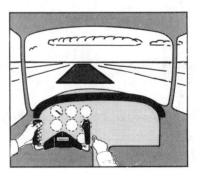

Too high   Just right   Too low

Figure 13a-11. Runway perspectives on approach

If a Visual Approach Slope Indicator (VASI) light system is available for slope guidance, then you may use it, although it is important that you develop the skill of judging the correct approach slope without any external assistance. You should not fly a shallow approach beneath the VASI slope unless absolutely necessary for a safe landing. Most light airplanes have an approach slope steeper than the typical 3° VASI slope.

Note: VASI light systems are covered in Exercise 20 on Night Flying.

Fly a Stabilized Approach

The approach path to the runway is three-dimensional. A good approach requires tight control of the flight path and airspeed—in other words, a stabilized approach—and this should set you up for a good landing.

A stable approach sets you up for a good landing.

Landing flaps should be selected by at least 300 feet AGL, and the airplane re-trimmed as necessary. As more flaps are lowered, the required nose attitude will be lower to maintain the required airspeed. Keep these attitude changes smooth. Good trimming technique will help you avoid jerky movements and enable you to fly positively, but smoothly.

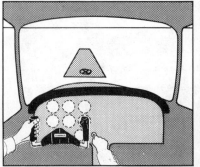 

Figure 13a-12. A stabilized approach is preferable.

Approach at the selected indicated airspeed (IAS) on a suitable approach slope, and maintain a flight path over the ground that is in line with the extended runway centerline. This will require positive and firm action on your part. The approach speed you choose will depend upon your landing-flap setting and the prevailing conditions—wind strength and direction, or the suspected presence of gustiness, windshear, turbulence or wake turbulence.

The Aiming Point

Ideally, the aiming point should remain fixed in the windshield—the runway appearing larger and larger as it is approached, without its perspective changing.

The aiming point should stay fixed in the windshield.

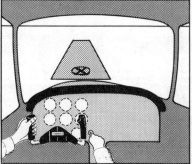

Figure 13a-13. Ideally, the aiming point remains fixed in the windshield on final approach.

If the aiming point moves progressively **up** the windshield, then the airplane is **undershooting**. Conversely, if the aiming point moves progressively **down** the windshield, then the airplane is **overshooting**.

In each case, you must take positive action to modify the approach path, so that the aiming point remains fixed in the windshield—points beyond the aiming point should gradually move up the windshield, and points short of the aiming point should gradually move down the windshield and out of view as you fly over them.

The sides of the runway abeam of the aiming point will expand outward as you approach.

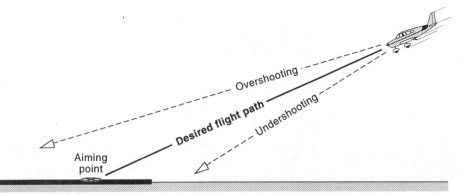

Figure 13a-14. Fly the airplane down the desired approach path.

Airspeed Control

Power plus attitude provides performance. Any change in power will require a change in pitch attitude if the same airspeed is to be maintained, so you will be coordinating the use of power and attitude to control airspeed and flight path.

Control airspeed with elevator and flight path with power.

• If power is added, raise the nose to maintain airspeed.

• If power is reduced, lower the nose to maintain airspeed.

Continually make corrections to the flight path as necessary, and hold the approach speed as closely as possible—within 1 or 2 KIAS in a steady wind, otherwise within plus or minus 5 KIAS.

Keeping the airplane in trim during the approach will make your task considerably easier.

Undershooting

If the actual approach path projects to a point short of the aiming point—indicated by the aiming point moving up the windshield and the runway appearing shorter and wider—then you are undershooting. Regain the desired flight path by adding power and raising the nose to maintain airspeed.

If undershooting, add power and raise the nose to regain the desired flight path.

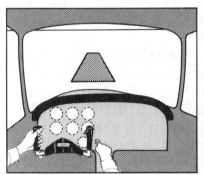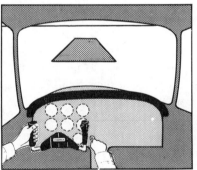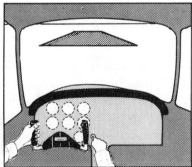

Figure 13a-15. Undershooting; to correct, add power and raise the nose.

Overshooting

If the actual approach path projects beyond the aiming point (indicated by the aiming point moving down the windshield and the runway appearing longer and narrower), then you are overshooting. Steepen the descent by:

If overshooting, steepen the descent.

• increasing flaps and adjusting the pitch attitude; or

• reducing power and lowering the nose to maintain airspeed.

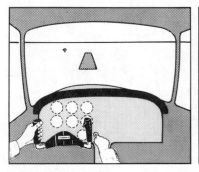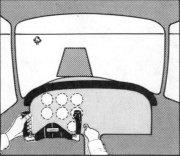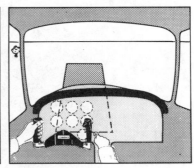

Figure 13a-16. Overshooting; to correct, reduce power and lower the nose, or increase the flaps.

Note: Some instructors prefer to say *power controls flight path;* others that *power controls airspeed.* It is **the coordinated use of power and attitude** that controls both the airspeed and the flight path, so either description is valid—although the combined statement *power plus attitude provides performance* is best in my opinion. This allows the instructor to explain how airspeed is controlled with attitude on a glide approach (when power is not being used).

Flightpath Corrections

Most flight paths on approach fluctuate between a slight overshoot and a slight undershoot, and continual minor corrections are required. Ideally, of course, a pilot will always be on the perfect slope, but I can't ever remember having achieved this all the way down final approach.

Ensure that the Before-Landing checklist has been completed. Pilots of advanced airplanes sometimes do a mental check of the vital items at about 200 feet AGL on final: propeller pitch control—FULLY IN, landing gear—DOWN, flaps—SET.

An accurate approach will enable you to touch down at or within 500 feet beyond your aiming point. (For commercial pilots, the accuracy required is at or within 200 feet beyond the specified point.)

Short Final

A good landing is most likely if you have made a good approach, so aim to be well established in a stabilized approach by the time you reach short final. For a training airplane this may be thought of as the last 200 feet of the approach. Do not allow significant deviations in the flight path—approach slope or tracking—or in the airspeed to develop and destabilize your approach.

Carburetor heat will normally be returned to COLD on short final, in case maximum power is required for a go-around—however if icing conditions exist, follow the guidance provided in your Pilot's Operating Handbook.

Throughout the final approach and landing, have your:
- left hand on the control column to control attitude; and
- right hand on the throttle to control power.

The Landing

The landing starts with a "flare" (or "round-out") commencing at about 20 feet above the runway and does not finish until the end of the landing run. When you begin to flare, forget your runway aiming point because you will fly over and well past it before the wheels actually touch down. It has served its purpose and you should now look well ahead.

You will make many corrections to the approach flight path.

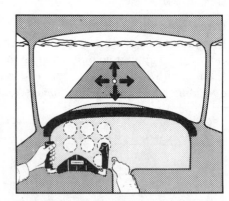

Figure 13a-17. As you approach, the aiming point should remain fixed, and other points expand.

A normal landing is similar to a power-off stall, with the touchdown occurring just prior to the moment of stall. This method of landing allows the lowest possible touchdown speed (significantly less than the approach speed) with the pilot still having full control.

Having commenced the flare, airspeed is no longer important and you should not look in the cockpit at the instruments at all—keep looking outside well ahead and to the left. The objective is to touch down at a fairly low airspeed (achieved by closing the throttle and raising the nose of the airplane) and at a low vertical speed (judged visually). Vision is the most important sense you have for landing. With a little practice, your actions on the controls during a landing will become almost instinctive in responding to what your eyes see.

The landing can be considered in three stages that should flow from one into the other.

1. **The flare** (or round-out) and holdoff period.
2. **The touchdown**.
3. **The landing run** (or roll-out).

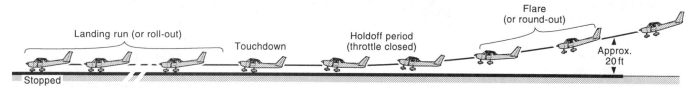

Figure 13a-18. The Landing

1. The Flare (or Round-Out)

During the flare, the power is reduced and the nose is gradually raised to break the rate of descent and make the transition to the landing attitude. The rate of sink can be "checked" with the control column, a high rate of sink requiring a greater backward movement to check it. **Ground effect**—caused by the air between the wing and the ground—will provide a natural cushioning effect and cause the airplane to float.

> **Break the rate of descent as you near the ground.**

Hold the airplane off close to the ground (within a foot or so). Close the throttle and ease the control column back progressively to keep the airplane flying level in the landing attitude with the wheels just off the ground. As the airplane slows, and the elevator loses its effectiveness, more and more back pressure will be required to keep the nose up.

> **Hold the airplane off for as long as possible, just above the runway.**

If sinking, apply more back pressure; **if climbing** away from the ground, relax the back pressure.

The airspeed will be decreasing to a very low figure while the airplane floats, but this is of no concern to you, even if the stall warning activates. You should be looking well ahead from the beginning of the flare until you touch down.

You need to ensure that the throttle is fully closed, so that the float is not prolonged unnecessarily. Any sideways drift caused by a slight crosswind can be counteracted by lowering the upwind wing a few degrees, and keeping straight along the runway with rudder.

Try to hold the airplane off the ground for as long as possible, responding to what your eyes see, rather than to the feel of the controls.

Figure 13a-19. Typical attitudes in the approach and flare

2. Touchdown

In the touchdown, the main wheels should make first contact with the ground (which will be the case following a correct flare). Keep the nosewheel off the ground with back pressure while the speed decreases.

Touch down on the main wheels.

Judgment. To assist in judging how much the wheels are above the ground and the rate at which the airplane is sinking, your eyes should remain **outside the cockpit** from shortly before establishing the flare (when airspeed is no longer important) until the end of the landing roll.

To achieve the best depth perception and to develop a feel for just where the main wheels are in relation to the ground, it is best to look at least 150 feet ahead and slightly to the left of the airplane's nose. If you look too close, the ground will be blurred as it passes by; too far, and your depth perception will suffer.

Avoid looking directly over the nose as this makes it difficult to raise the nose in the flare and still retain depth perception. It may also cause a tendency to fly the airplane into the ground, resulting in a heavy touchdown (possibly nose-wheel first) and even a bounced landing.

3. The Landing Run

During the landing run the airplane is kept rolling straight down the centerline using rudder, and the wings are kept level with aileron. Finally, lower the nosewheel to the ground gently before elevator control is lost.

Keep on the runway centerline during the ground roll using rudder, and keep the wings level with the ailerons.

You are still flying the airplane in the landing roll-out—using the rudder pedals for directional control, the elevator for weight distribution on the wheels, and the ailerons to keep the wings level.

Brakes (if required) may be used when the nosewheel is on the ground, but this is generally best avoided.

Do not try to turn off at the first taxiway if your speed is still high—roll past it and exit the runway when you have slowed down to a suitable taxiing speed.

The landing is not complete until the end of the landing run, when the airplane is stationary or at taxiing speed.

The After-Landing Check

When clear of the runway, stop the airplane, set idle rpm (1,000 or 1,200 rpm, as recommended) and complete the After-Landing check as specified in the Pilot's Operating Handbook. It will contain such items as:

- flaps—RETRACT;
- carburetor heat—check COLD (hot air may be unfiltered in your airplane);
- fuel pump (if fitted)—OFF;
- cowl flaps (if fitted)—OPEN.

At tower-controlled airports, you should exit the runway without delay at the first available taxiway after you have slowed down to a safe taxiing speed, or as instructed by the tower-controller (who will also advise you of the ground control frequency to call to obtain a taxi clearance, if necessary).

Airmanship

Never use a runway unless you have considered:

- the wind direction;
- the landing surface (length available and surface condition);
- obstructions and other hazards in the takeoff and landing paths.

Fly a precise traffic pattern, **on altitude** (plus or minus 100 feet) and **on speed** (plus or minus 10 KIAS around the pattern, plus or minus 5 KIAS on final). Complete the Before-Landing checklist on downwind leg.

Commence descent and the base turn to position the airplane for a turn onto final that will have you aligned with the runway at or above 400 feet above the airport. Use wing flaps as appropriate.

Fly a stabilized approach *on slope, on the extended centerline* and *on speed.* Maintain firm, positive and tight control of all three, with one hand on the control column and the other on the throttle.

Although you will be busy, remain aware of other aircraft. Keep a good **lookout**, not only ahead and to either side, but also above and below. Also, avoid wake turbulence from preceding heavy aircraft.

Aim to touch down at or within 500 feet of the selected aiming point on the runway, with the airplane's longitudinal axis aligned with the runway centerline and with no apparent sideways drift (200 feet for commercial pilots).

When the landing is complete, taxi clear of the runway at a moderate speed as soon as possible so that other pilots are not inconvenienced. The aircraft is not clear of the runway until it has passed the holding point entirely. Conform to taxiway marking aids and lights, and follow ATC instructions at tower-controlled airports.

> **Airmanship involves flying accurately and smoothly, and exercising good judgment.**

Airwork 13a
The Powered Approach and Normal Landing

Objective
To make an approach with power and land into a headwind.

21. Keep straight with rudder, and wings level with aileron.

22. **Stop**—using brakes as necessary.

20. Gently lower the nosewheel onto the runway.

19. Touch down on the main wheels and hold the nosewheel off, keeping straight with rudder.

18. Progressively raise the nose to hold the airplane off just above the runway.

 WIND

Windsock

(continued in panel)

Downwind Leg

LOOK OUT

1. Begin your Before-Landing checks (and complete if possible).

2. Abeam the runway threshold—descent may be started at any convenient point from here on, traffic permitting.

3. Descend when ready
   • Carb heat—HOT.
   • Reduce power.
   • Maintain altitude and reduce to the descent speed, then lower the nose and descend.

4. Lower first stage of flaps.

ABEAM POINT

PATH —— OVER —— THE —— GROUND —— —

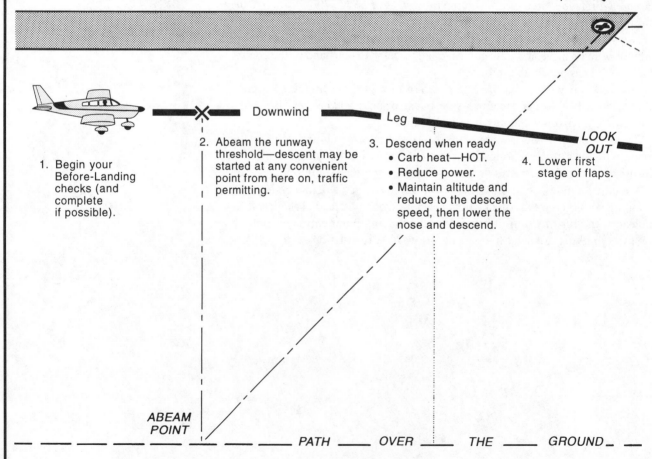

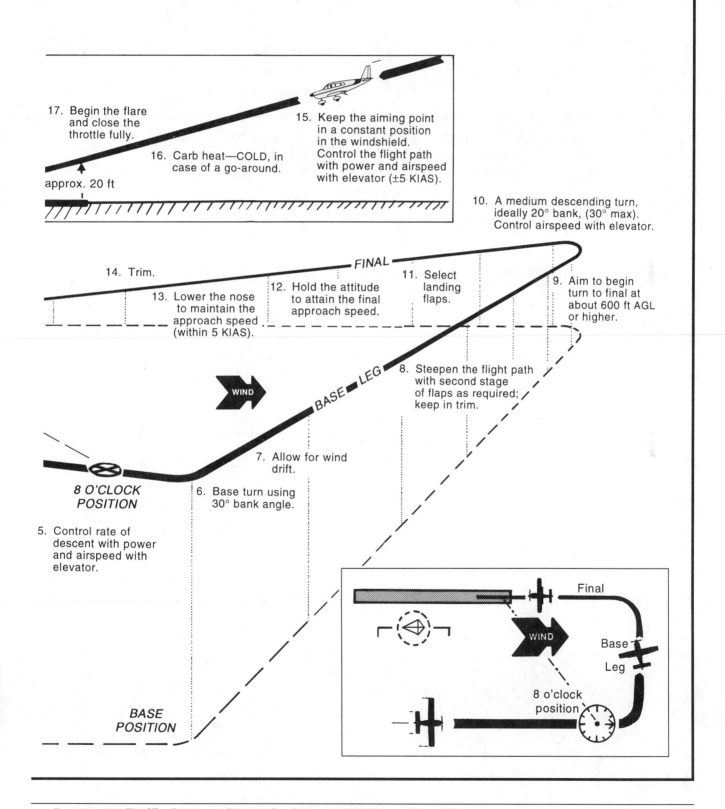

17. Begin the flare and close the throttle fully.

16. Carb heat—COLD, in case of a go-around.

15. Keep the aiming point in a constant position in the windshield. Control the flight path with power and airspeed with elevator (±5 KIAS).

approx. 20 ft

10. A medium descending turn, ideally 20° bank, (30° max). Control airspeed with elevator.

FINAL

14. Trim.

13. Lower the nose to maintain the approach speed (within 5 KIAS).

12. Hold the attitude to attain the final approach speed.

11. Select landing flaps.

9. Aim to begin turn to final at about 600 ft AGL or higher.

WIND

BASE LEG

8. Steepen the flight path with second stage of flaps as required; keep in trim.

7. Allow for wind drift.

8 O'CLOCK POSITION

6. Base turn using 30° bank angle.

5. Control rate of descent with power and airspeed with elevator.

BASE POSITION

Final

WIND

Base Leg

8 o'clock position

Further Points

Some Common Faults on Approach

1. Not Aligned with the Centerline

If your approach path is angled to the runway, then it will be difficult to achieve a good landing with all the juggling required to align the flight path at the last moment.

Stay on the extended runway centerline during the approach.

The remedy is to use some self-discipline and track directly along the extended centerline all the way down final. Make corrections as often as necessary to track correctly, especially for about the last 300 feet of altitude prior to touchdown.

2. Approaching Too Low, or Too High

If your approach slope is **too low**, you may compromise obstacle clearance before reaching the runway. To clear any close-in obstacles, a shallow approach path will require an initial aiming point a long way down the runway, wasting a lot of runway.

Stay on slope.

As all pilots know, one of the most useless things in aviation is the runway behind you! You could, of course, reduce power when you have passed over the obstacle, but this may destabilize your approach, causing you to *drop in* for a hard landing.

If you are **too low on approach**, do **not** try to stretch the glide by raising the nose alone—you will just fly slower and descend more steeply (or stall, in an extreme situation). **Add power!** Maintain the correct airspeed and then, when you have re-intercepted the desired flight path, reduce power and lower the nose slightly to maintain airspeed.

If your approach is **too high**, the flight path to the touchdown point on the runway will be very steep, and the rate of descent will be higher than normal, requiring a firmer and more positive flare into the landing attitude before touchdown.

The remedy for high or low approaches is to recognize the situation early, and immediately use power and/or attitude changes to adjust the approach flight path and maintain the desired approach speed. You should aim to be on a suitable approach slope by at least 300 feet AGL, so that the final stages of the approach are stable.

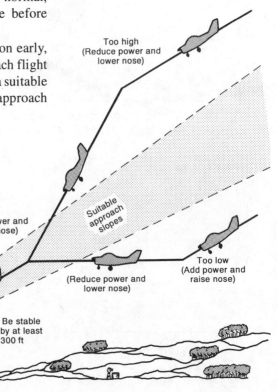

Figure 13a-20. Adjust your approach path as necessary.

As well as having to adjust your approach path periodically in steady wind conditions, you will find it a continuing task when there is windshear, or thermal effects such as rising hot air on final approach. Early small corrections are better than late large ones. The ability to *see* what is happening to your flight path and to make early corrections will develop with experience, and your first rather erratic approaches will soon smooth out.

3. Approaching Too Fast, or Too Slow

If you approach with the **airspeed too high,** then you will use excessive runway in the flare and holdoff period prior to touchdown—you might even run out of room at the far end of the runway! Excessive floating may require you to make a go-around. Also, a fast approach speed makes the control surfaces very effective, and the airplane very responsive, consequently it will be easy for you to flare too much and balloon away from the ground.

Stay on speed.

If you approach **too slowly,** you run the risk of a stall, and a hard landing (or worse!).

In both cases, control your airspeed with coordinated use of power and attitude. To reduce speed, reduce power and/or raise the nose; to increase speed, add power and/or lower the nose.

Common Faults in the Landing

Every pilot learns how to land through experience. It is inevitable that many landings will be far from perfect, but progress will be made when you have flown enough to recognize faults and correct them. Some common faults are:

Good approaches and landings take practice.

- flying into the ground without flaring;
- the balloon (when the airplane flies away from the ground before touchdown);
- the bounced landing (when the airplane leaves the ground again after touchdown—perhaps after several touchdowns);
- flaring and holding the airplane off too high; and
- wheelbarrowing when the wheels are on the ground.

It sounds like a lot can go wrong in a landing, but with a little guidance from your flight instructor and a bit of practice, you will soon be making consistently good landings.

1. The Balloon

A balloon can be caused by either:
- too much back pressure on the control column in the flare; and/or
- too much power left on; and/or
- too high an airspeed; and/or
- a gust of wind.

To correct for a small balloon:
- relax some of the back pressure on the control column;
- allow the airplane to begin settling (sinking) again;
- when approaching flare height again, continue the backward movement of the control wheel; and
- complete a normal landing.

Flare again and hold off normally.

Relax back-pressure on the control column.

Balloon

Figure 13a-21. Correcting for a small balloon

A Large Balloon. As you gain experience, it may be possible to reposition the airplane after a large balloon—using power if necessary—for the flare and touchdown, but this uses up lots of runway. The decision to attempt a recovery from a pronounced balloon will therefore depend upon the extent of your experience and on the runway length remaining. If there is any doubt about a safe landing, apply maximum power and go-around.

A large balloon during the landing may call for a go-around, certainly for inexperienced pilots!

2. Flying into the Ground without Flaring

Flying the airplane into the ground for a hard landing without flaring is usually caused by the pilot not looking far enough ahead—maybe looking just over the nose—and tending to not raise the nose for the flare and touchdown. **The remedy** is to look further down the runway before and during the flare.

3. The Bounced Landing

A bounce can occur because of:
- a failure to flare sufficiently;
- touching down on the nosewheel (possibly caused by looking over the nose);
- touching down too fast;
- excessive backward movement of the control column during or after touch-down; or
- flaring too high.

The bounce is really not so much a real bounce, but rather a fly-away caused by the nose bouncing up and creating a greater angle-of-attack on the wings, and hence more lift.

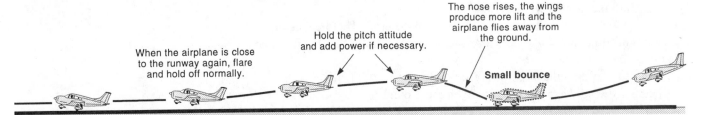

When the airplane is close to the runway again, flare and hold off normally.

Hold the pitch attitude and add power if necessary.

The nose rises, the wings produce more lift and the airplane flies away from the ground.

Small bounce

Figure 13a-22. Recovery from a bounced landing

An inexperienced pilot should consider an immediate go-around following a bounced landing. With experience, however, a successful recovery from a bounce can be made—provided that the runway length is adequate—by relaxing the back pressure and adding power if necessary, to reposition the airplane suitably for another landing.

Avoid pushing the nose down, as a second bounced landing may result. Also, avoid a second touchdown on the nosewheel—a series of "porpoises" down the runway is not a desirable way to land an airplane! Prior to touchdown, make sure that the airplane is in the correct nose-high attitude.

4. Flaring and Holding Off Too High

The period when you hold the airplane off is best accomplished within a foot or so of the runway—any more than this, and a landing somewhat heavier than usual will result.

If you recognize that you have flared too high and are sinking fast, add power—this will break the descent rate somewhat and allow a softer touchdown. When the wheels touch the ground, close the throttle so that the airplane will begin to slow down.

Holding off too high generally results from:

- not looking far enough into the distance, with the result that the ground rushing by is blurred and your depth perception is poor;
- a difficult runway surface which affects your depth perception (such as a snow or water covering);
- a second attempt to land following a balloon or bounce; or
- inexperience, and not knowing where the wheels are in relation to the ground.

5. Wheelbarrowing

If you do not bring the control column back far enough during the landing, the nosewheel may contact the ground too early. This will cause the airplane to "wheelbarrow" along the runway, with the main wheels only lightly loaded, and with a tendency for the airplane to pivot about the nosewheel.

Directional control will be more difficult to achieve, and braking through the main wheels will not be as effective.

Avoid wheelbarrowing by holding the control column back, and keeping the load off the nosewheel.

Figure 13a-23. Wheelbarrowing

The Go-Around or Balked Approach

If at any stage during the approach or landing you feel uncomfortable about the situation, carry out a go-around (also known as a *balked approach, overshoot* or *discontinued approach*). This maneuver is covered fully in the next exercise.

Touch-and-Go Landings

The number of practice traffic patterns per hour can be greatly increased by doing touch-and-go landings. This involves making a normal approach and landing and then, when established in the landing run and after the nosewheel has been gently lowered onto the ground, with sufficient runway length remaining and the airplane totally under control:

- move the flaps to a takeoff setting;
- move the trim to a position suitable for takeoff (if necessary);
- apply full power (carburetor heat—COLD), and perform a normal takeoff without stopping on the runway.

In a touch-and-go takeoff, the trim may not be set correctly for takeoff and there may be a reasonable amount of (forward) pressure required on the control column to hold the nose in the climb attitude. Hold the nose in the attitude that you want—do not let the airplane fly you, you fly it! When you are established in the climb, this pressure can be trimmed off.

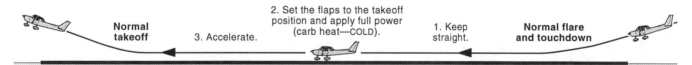

Normal takeoff — 3. Accelerate. — 2. Set the flaps to the takeoff position and apply full power (carb heat—COLD). — 1. Keep straight. — Normal flare and touchdown

Figure 13a-24. The touch-and-go landing

If you know where the controls are in the cockpit by feel, you can use them without disturbing your outside view too much in the landing and takeoff roll.

If the landing is misjudged and **excessive** runway is used, then bring the airplane to a stop as in a normal landing, rather than continue with a doubtful takeoff on possibly insufficient runway.

Turbulence and Windshear

Friction affects the air flowing over the earth's surface, so the wind at ground level may be different to that at traffic-pattern altitude and above. Any change in wind speed and/or direction is called **windshear,** and it can give rise to turbulence and to momentary airspeed changes.

Flying into a suddenly decreasing headwind or a downdraft could cause the airspeed to momentarily decrease, the nose to drop, and the aircraft to sink below the desired flight path. This is known as **undershoot effect,** or negative windshear. The remedy is to add power, and regain the desired airspeed and flight path. Do this positively and confidently, and be prepared for many such adjustments.

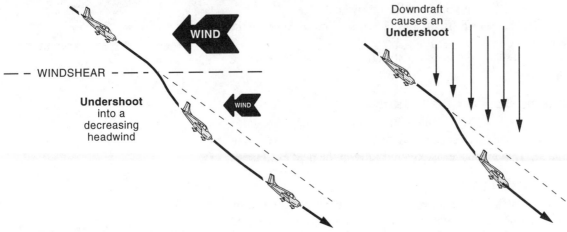

Figure 13a-25. Undershoot and downdraft

Conversly, a suddenly increasing headwind or an updraft will cause an **overshoot effect.** The remedy is to reduce power and regain the desired airspeed and flight path. Be prepared to add power again.

Uneven heating of the earth's surface will cause vertical convection currents also leading to turbulence. You will experience this as a bumpy ride with a fluctuating airspeed.

In turbulent conditions, it is advisable to carry a few extra knots on the approach to give you better controllability. A typical addition is half the gust factor—for a 12-knot gust, add 6 KIAS to your approach speed.

A zero-flap approach should be considered, since it will make the airplane more responsive to a power increase because you have lower drag. Your flight instructor will guide you on this.

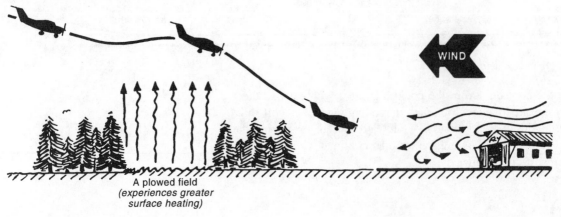

Figure 13a-26. Turbulence has various causes.

Wake Turbulence

Significant wake turbulence can form behind the wingtips of large airplanes flying at high angles-of-attack—for example, during their takeoffs and landings. The vortices that cause this type of turbulence drift downward and with the wind. **They are best avoided!**

You can avoid the wake turbulence of a large aircraft in flight by flying above its flight path and/or upwind of it, otherwise more than 1,000 feet below it.

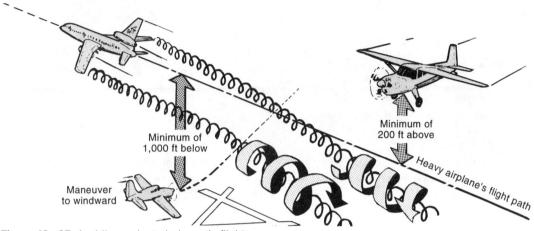

Figure 13a-27. Avoiding wake turbulence in flight

If you are on approach behind a large aircraft (a "heavy"), fly above its flight path, and land well beyond its touchdown point. This is usually possible, since large aircraft require long runways, and your training airplane probably does not. The **most dangerous conditions** are a light quartering tailwind, because:
- the tailwind can move the vortices of the preceding heavy aircraft into your touchdown area; and
- the slight crosswind can move the upwind vortex across onto the runway.

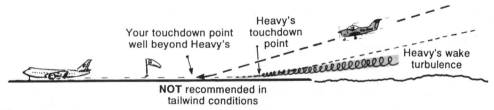

Figure 13a-28. Land long behind a landing heavy.

When landing on a runway from which a heavy has just taken off, make sure that you touch down well short of the heavy's liftoff point or where you think its vortices may have drifted to. Landing in the normal touchdown zone will usually ensure this.

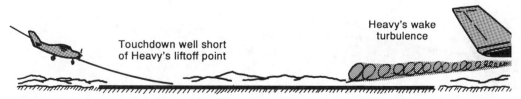

Figure 13a-29. Touch down short of a heavy's liftoff point.

If a preceding heavy has discontinued its approach and gone around, its turbulent wake will be a hazard to following aircraft. You should consider changing your flight path in these circumstances.

Never be afraid to delay a takeoff or approach if you suspect that wake turbulence from another aircraft could be a problem.

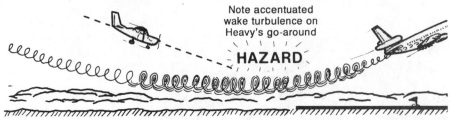

Figure 13a-30. Avoid the wake turbulence of a heavy that has gone around.

Visual Illusions on Approach

Most runways are of standard width and on flat ground.

If you are approaching a **sloping runway**, however, the perspective will be different. A runway that slopes **upward** will look longer, and you will feel that you are high on slope, when in fact you are right on slope. The tendency will be for you to go lower and make a shallower approach. If you know that the runway does have an upslope, you can avoid this tendency.

Visual illusions can dramatically affect your perception of the approach slope to the runway.

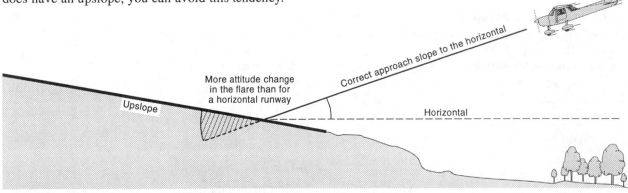

Figure 13a-31. An upward sloping runway creates an illusion of being too-high.

A runway that slopes **downward** will look shorter, and you will feel that you are low on slope, when in fact you are right on slope. The tendency will be for you to go higher and make a steeper approach. If you know that the runway does have a downslope, you can avoid this tendency.

Figure 13a-32. A downward sloping runway creates an illusion of being too low.

If you know the slope of the runway, you can allow for it in your visual estimation of whether you are high or low on slope.

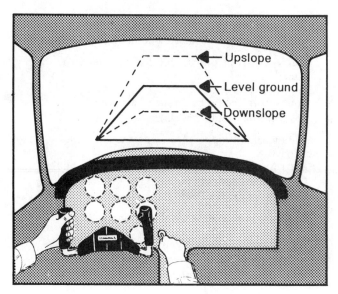

Figure 13a-33. How runways of different slope should appear at the same point on final.

A wide runway, because of the angle at which you view it peripherally in the final stages of the approach and landing, will cause an illusion of being too low, and you may flare and hold off too high as a result, dropping in for a heavy landing.

Conversely, **a narrow runway** will cause an illusion of being too high, and you may delay the flare and make contact with the runway earlier (and harder) than expected.

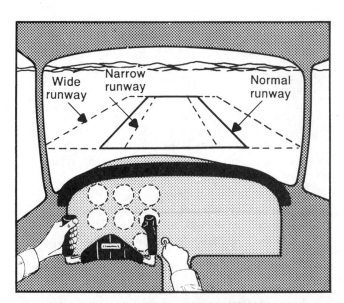

Figure 13a-34. How runways with different widths would appear at the same point on final.

If you know that the runway is wider or narrower than what you are familiar with, then you can compensate for this in your visual judgment of the flare and touchdown.

Review 13a

The Traffic Pattern, Power-On Approach and Normal Landing

1. Specify three items you would consider before landing on an unfamiliar runway.

    (1) wind direction; (2) landing surface (length available and condition); (3) obstructions and other hazards in the approach and takeoff paths

2. The shortest landing distance is achieved if you land (into a headwind/with a tailwind) and with (zero flaps/landing flaps).

    into a headwind, landing flaps

3. Flaps allow you to make a (steeper/shallower) approach to a landing at a (slower/faster) speed, and with (better/poorer) forward vision.

    steeper, slower, better

4. In the approach to land, you should positively control flight path and airspeed using _____ and

    _____ .

    power and attitude

5. A written Before-Landing checklist that you can read (will/will not) assist you to check the necessary items.

    will

6. The power-off stalling speed with the flaps in the landing position is the (high-speed/low-speed) end of the (white/green) arc on the airspeed indicator.

    low-speed, white

7. The stalling speed with power on is (greater/less) than with power off.

    less

8. In gusty wind conditions, you (may/must not) add a gust correction factor to your normal approach speed.

    may

9. A good landing is more likely if you fly a (stable/unstable) approach.

    stable

10. Try to fly your selected approach speed as accurately as possible, but certainly within an accuracy of plus or minus ____ KIAS.

    ±5 KIAS

11. You should try to touch down at or within ____ feet beyond a specified point on the runway.

    500 feet (private pilots), 200 feet (commercial pilots)

12. Touchdown should be on the (main wheels/nosewheel/all three wheels).

    main wheels

13. After touchdown on the main wheels, you should (lower the nosewheel onto the ground gently/force the nosewheel onto the ground).

    lower the nosewheel onto the ground gently

14. During the landing roll you should keep straight with (rudder/ailerons/elevator) and keep the wings level with (rudder/ailerons/elevator.

    rudder, ailerons

15. A preceding heavy jet airliner has touched down on the runway; you are on final approach to land, and the surface wind is a light quartering tailwind. This is (more/less) dangerous from the point of wake turbulence than a strong headwind. If the runway is extremely long, you should aim for (the runway threshold/well down the runway).

    more, well down the runway

16. A runway that slopes upward will look (longer/shorter) and give you the impression that you are (high/low) on slope. The risk is you may be influenced to make a (steep/shallow) approach.

    longer, high, shallow

17. A runway that slopes downward will look (longer/shorter) and give you the impression that you are (high/low) on slope. The risk is you may be influenced to make a (steep/shallow) approach.

    shorter, low, steep

18. A wide runway will give you the impression during the flare that you are too (high/low). The risk is you might flare (higher/lower) than normal.

    low, higher

19. A narrow runway will give you the impression during the flare that you are too (high/low). The risk is you might flare (higher/lower) than normal.

    high, lower

The Go-Around

13b

Objective

To discontinue an approach with flaps and climb away.

Considerations

The term *go-around* describes the maneuver of discontinuing an approach, and climbing away. The go-around maneuver is also known as *a missed approach, a discontinued approach*, *a rejected landing*, or *a balked landing*. It may be thought of as:

- stopping the descent; and
- climbing away.

The need to discontinue an approach and/or landing might occur at any point in the approach and landing phase, with the most critical go-arounds having to be made from a point close to the ground.

The go-around is a climb away from a discontinued approach to land.

Why Go Around?

It may be necessary to perform a go-around for various reasons.

- The runway is occupied by another airplane, a vehicle or animals.
- You are too close behind another airplane on final approach and it will not clear the runway in time for you to land.
- You are instructed to go around by the tower controller.
- The conditions are too severe for your experience—for example: turbulence, windshear, heavy rain, excessive crosswind, wake turbulence from a preceding heavy airplane, and so on.
- Your approach is unstable (in terms of airspeed or flight path).
- The airspeed is far too high or too low.
- You are too high at the runway threshold to touch down safely and stop comfortably within the confines of the runway.
- You are not mentally or physically at ease.
- You need to fly away from a balloon or a bounced landing.

Make a Positive Decision

The go-around can be achieved safely and comfortably if you make a quick positive decision, and initiate the procedure with firmness and skill. The earlier a decision is made and acted upon, the easier it is on you.

Act decisively!

As you gain more and more experience, you will be able to handle more difficult conditions and fly more stable approaches, and the need for so many go-arounds will gradually diminish. There may always be occasions, however, when a go-around is necessary. Aim to fly it as a precision maneuver—firmly applying full power and holding a suitable climb attitude.

The Effect of the Flaps

Full flaps cause a significant increase in drag. This has advantages in the approach to land—it allows a steeper descent path, the approach speed can be lower, and you have a better forward view.

Full flaps have no advantages in a climb—in fact establishing a reasonable rate of climb may not be possible with full flaps extended! For this reason, when attempting to enter a climb from an approach with flaps, raise the flaps early in the climb. They should be raised in stages as the climb is established, to allow a gradual increase in your airspeed without the airplane sinking.

You should read the go-around procedure in your Pilot's Operating Handbook which **may** recommend:

- an initial flap retraction to a takeoff setting (typically 20° or 10°) with an initial target speed of the recommended obstacle-clearance airspeed until all close-in obstacles are cleared; then
- acceleration to the best-angle climb airspeed, V_X (tolerance: plus 5/minus zero KIAS) with the flaps coming completely up; then
- acceleration to the best-rate climb airspeed, V_Y (tolerance: plus or minus 5 KIAS).

Full flaps makes a climb-out difficult, so reduce the flaps in stages as you climb away; avoid sinking.

Tracking

If you go around from a point close to the ground, then initially climb straight ahead. If you go around from a point in the approach where there could be aircraft beneath you either landing, taking off or going around, then you should move to the right of the runway when established in the climb (if the traffic pattern is to the left). Fly parallel to the runway so that the other aircraft can climb straight ahead, and so that you have a clear and unobstructed view of them.

For a right-hand pattern, you should move to the left of the upwind leg—that is, to the side away from the traffic pattern.

Go around straight ahead, or to the side away from the pattern.

Flying the Maneuver

Establish a Descent

Follow the usual descent procedures and lower an appropriate amount of flaps. Initially, it may be desirable to practice the go-around maneuver with only a small amount of flaps extended (or perhaps none at all), as would be the case early in the approach to landing.

A go-around with full flaps requires more attention and skill, because of the airplane's poorer climb performance.

Initiate a Go-Around

A successful go-around requires that a positive decision be made, and positive action taken. A sign of a good pilot is a **timely decision** to go around when the occasion demands it—the maneuver being executed in a firm, but smooth manner.

The procedure to use is similar to that already practiced when entering a climb from a clean descent—**P-A-T: power–attitude–trim.** The additional consideration is flaps, which should be raised when the descent is stopped and the climb is initiated, or when level flight is achieved if a climb is not possible.

To initiate a go-around, smoothly apply **full power** and move the carburetor heat control to COLD. The application of power can be coordinated with the **attitude change** required to establish a climb at the recommended airspeed.

Be prepared for a strong pitch-up and left-yaw tendency as the power is applied. These tendencies can be counteracted with forward pressure on the control column and right rudder pressure. Hold the nose in the appropriate climb **attitude** for the particular flap setting, and then **trim.** The initial pressure and trim required may be quite significant, especially with full flaps. You must hold the attitude that you want no matter how much control pressure is required.

The airplane may experience a stall caused by the nose-up elevator trim that is usually applied on approach (known as *an elevator-trim stall* or *a trim-stall),* unless you take positive action to hold the nose in the correct pitch attitude. **You must fly the airplane (and not vice versa)!** It may help to trim most of the pressure off immediately maximum power and go-around attitude have been set, and then fine-trim later when things have settled down a bit.

Climb Away

Full flaps create a lot of drag, and the initial climb performance might be poor. Level flight might be necessary while the flap setting is initially reduced. If less than full flaps are extended, a reasonable climb can probably be entered without delay. As the airplane accelerates to an appropriate speed, raise the flaps in stages and adjust the pitch attitude to achieve the required speeds and climb performance. Trim as required.

Keep the airplane straight and the wings level as you climb away.

A complete retraction of flaps from full down to completely up in one move may result in unwanted sink, especially if the airspeed is low. Typical stages of retraction are:

- from full down to a takeoff setting; target speed—obstacle clearance airspeed; and climb away over any obstacles;
- accelerate to the best angle-of-climb airspeed, V_X, and raise the flaps completely; the target speed is V_X plus 5/minus 0 KIAS;
- accelerate to the best rate-of-climb airspeed, for a normal climb to altitude.

Maintain a ground track aligned with the extended runway centerline, or to one side of it you feel that is safer. In a two-pilot cockpit, it is good to state your intentions clearly so that the other pilot does not think you are just carelessly drifting off the extended centerline.

Normally, climb at the best-rate-of-climb airspeed, V_Y, plus or minus 5 KIAS, when established in the go-around with the flaps retracted.

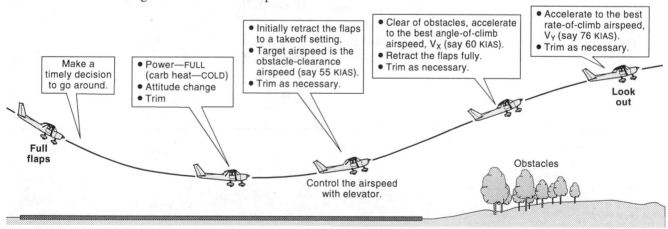

Figure 13b-1. The go-around.

When comfortably established in the climb-out, with everything under control, notify the tower and other aircraft by radio that you have gone around. Fly the airplane first—then communicate.

Communicate—when you are comfortable in the climb-out.

The Go-Around with Zero Flaps

There may be occasions when you want to go around before any flaps have been extended, in which case the procedure is quite simple:

- apply full power; and
- hold a suitable attitude to achieve the best angle-of-climb airspeed, V_X, to clear any obstacles—then lower the nose and accelerate to the best rate-of-climb airspeed, V_Y.

Retractable-Gear Airplanes

When performing a go-around in an aircraft fitted with retractable landing gear, the usual technique is to:

- apply full power;
- hold a suitable pitch attitude to stop the descent and commence a climb;
- raise the flaps immediately to a takeoff setting (to remove one cause of now-unwanted drag); and
- establish a positive rate of climb—as indicated on the altimeter and VSI—then raise the landing gear (to remove another major cause of drag).

Airmanship

Make a positive decision to discontinue the approach and then **perform the go-around decisively.** A go-around is *not* a sign of failure—it can be a sign of good airmanship.

Exert firm, positive and smooth control over the airplane. Firm pressure must be held on the control column and rudder pedals when the power is applied. Correct trimming will make things easier. Ensure that a safe airspeed is reached before each stage of flaps is raised.

It is usual, when established in the go-around, to move slightly to one side of the runway (the side away from the traffic pattern direction is preferred) so that you have a view of airplanes that may be operating off the runway and beneath you.

When comfortably established in the climb-out, advise the tower (and the other airplanes in the pattern) by radio that you are *going around.* Do not be concerned about making this call too early, as other airplanes nearby should be able to see you clearly, and you should be concentrating on flying the airplane. Flying the airplane accurately in the go-around is far more important than struggling with the microphone to make a radio call.

Following the go-around, delay turning onto crosswind leg until at least at the upwind end of the runway. This should avoid any conflict with other aircraft in the traffic pattern.

Airmanship is being decisive.

Airwork 13b
The Go-Around

Objective
To discontinue an approach with flaps and climb away.

With the Airplane Established in a Descent with Flaps

1. Make a firm decision to *go around.*

2. **P-A-T:**
   - **Power**—throttle OPEN FULLY (carb heat COLD).
   - **Attitude**—hold the nose in the appropriate pitch attitude to stop the descent and commence a climb.
   - **Trim.**

3. Raise the flaps slowly, in stages.
   Target speeds:
   - takeoff flap setting: obstacle-clearance airspeed;
   - clean: V_X +5/−0 KIAS initially, then V_Y ±5 KIAS for a normal climb-out.

4. Adjust the pitch attitude (higher as flaps are retracted) and maintain speed with elevator; avoid sinking.

5. Retrim for the climb-out.

6. Maintain your tracking, either along the extended runway centerline or to one side of it, for better vision of other traffic.

7. Continue in a normal traffic pattern.

Look out during the maneuver,
especially in a real go-around situation.

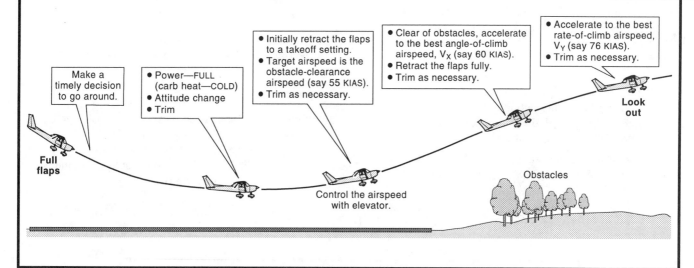

Make a timely decision to go around.

- Power—FULL (carb heat—COLD)
- Attitude change
- Trim

- Initially retract the flaps to a takeoff setting.
- Target airspeed is the obstacle-clearance airspeed (say 55 KIAS).
- Trim as necessary.

- Clear of obstacles, accelerate to the best angle-of-climb airspeed, V_X (say 60 KIAS).
- Retract the flaps fully.
- Trim as necessary.

- Accelerate to the best rate-of-climb airspeed, V_Y (say 76 KIAS).
- Trim as necessary.

Look out

Full flaps

Control the airspeed with elevator.

Obstacles

Review 13b

1. When making a decision to go around, you must be (positive/hesitant and indecisive).

   ➤ positive

2. Write down the recommended go-around procedure for your airplane.

   ➤ *refer to your POH or flight instructor*

3. Sketch a typical go-around and write down the main points of how to fly the maneuver.

   ➤ *refer to our text*

4. When you apply full power for a go-around, there will be a natural tendency for the nose to pitch (up/down). You (must/need not) hold it in the correct pitch attitude for the climb.

   ➤ up, must

5. With the application of full power, the nose will not only want to pitch up, but also yaw to the (left/right), which you can counteract with (left rudder/right rudder).

   ➤ left, right rudder

6. Trimming off unwanted elevator pressure in the climb-out (will/will not) make the go-around easier.

   ➤ will

7. Target speeds in the go-around are:
   • for a takeoff flap setting;
   • for a clean climb over obstacles; and
   • for a clean climb to altitude.

   ➤ obstacle-clearance airspeed plus 5/minus 0 KIAS; V_X plus 5/minus 0 KIAS; V_Y plus or minus 5 KIAS

The Go-Around

8. If you go-around because of an aircraft taking off just ahead of you, it is good airmanship to climb (straight ahead along/to one side of) the extended runway centerline.

   ➤ to one side of

9. During the go-around, it is more important to (fly the airplane/make an advisory radio call).

   ➤ fly the airplane

10. If the runway is occupied by another airplane, a vehicle or animals when you are on a short final you should (continue with the landing/go around).

    ➤ go around

11. If you are too close behind another airplane also on final approach that will not have cleared the runway in time for you to land, you should (continue with the landing/go around).

    ➤ go around

12. If you are too high over the runway threshold for a safe landing within the confines of the runway, you should (continue with the landing/go around).

    ➤ go around

13. If you find on final approach that conditions are too severe for your experience, you should (continue with the landing/go around).

    ➤ go around

14. If everything looks good on final approach—you are on speed, on flight path, aligned with the extended runway centerline, checklists completed, and no conflicting traffic—you should (continue with the landing/go around).

    ➤ continue with the landing

Departing and Entering the Traffic Pattern 13c

Objective

This chapter is aimed at making you familiar with standard procedures and considerations when:
- departing from the traffic pattern after takeoff on a flight to the training area or on a cross-country flight; and
- returning to the airport from outside the traffic pattern area, with the intention of joining the pattern for an approach and landing.

Considerations

The traffic pattern is designed to simplify the operations of aircraft in the vicinity of an airport. The standard traffic pattern is 1,000 feet above the airport elevation—often referred to as *above ground level (AGL)*—and with left turns. Some airports have other traffic pattern altitudes, perhaps because of controlled airspace above, or high obstructions below; these usually fall within the range of 600 feet to 1,500 feet AGL.

The standard traffic pattern is at 1,000 feet AGL with left-hand turns.

Where the traffic pattern altitude (TPA) differs from the standard 1,000 feet AGL, the nonstandard TPA is found in the Airport/Facility Directory (A/FD). For example, the A/FD listing for **Sycamore Strip,** Texas, elevation 760 feet, shows a TPA of "1560(800)". This indicates that the traffic pattern altitude is 800 feet AGL, which is (800 + 760 =) 1,560 feet MSL.

Nonstandard traffic patterns are published in the Airport/Facility Directory.

The traffic pattern is based on the runway in use, which is dictated by the tower at tower-controlled airports, and chosen by the pilot at nontowered airports. It is usual to take off and land on a runway which faces upwind.

All turns in traffic patterns at nontowered airports are normally to the **left**, giving the pilot in the left-hand seat a good view of the airport—unless the airport has approved traffic pattern indicators showing that right-hand turns are required. The A/FD also includes this information, with "Rgt tfc" (right-hand traffic pattern) noted beside the specific runway.

Much of your early training will be carried out away from the airport, which gives you a chance to develop good habits in departing from and re-entering the traffic pattern. It should be noted that procedures for pattern departure and pattern entry vary between countries and, if flying overseas, you should ask to be briefed on them. The procedures here refer to the United States.

For flights away from the traffic pattern area, you need to be confident of your:
- local area knowledge (landmarks and airspace restrictions);
- pattern departure and entry procedures for your particular airport;
- altimetry procedures ("vertical navigation");
- radio procedures;
- en route or regular checks to ensure satisfactory operation of the airplane; and
- ability to fly a particular heading using the magnetic compass.

Flying the Maneuver

Departing the Traffic Pattern

At a **tower-controlled airport**, follow the instructions given by Air Traffic Control, and make the necessary radio calls to obtain a taxi clearance and later a takeoff clearance. Follow any special procedures applicable to your airport.

Make appropriate radio calls.

If the tower is **not** active at your field, then you should plan a traffic pattern departure that will not conflict with other aircraft that are in the pattern or joining it. The recommended procedure for departing a **nontowered airport** is to either:

- extend the upwind leg as you climb out after takeoff and then, when clear of other pattern traffic, maneuver to set heading for the local training area (or the first leg of your cross country flight); or
- continue climbing out on the upwind leg and then, when at or above pattern altitude, turn 45° left and depart the pattern. (In a right-hand pattern, the turn would be 45° right.)

Plan your departure.

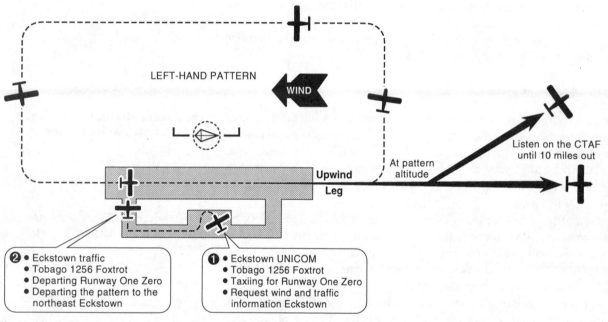

Figure 13c-1. Departing the traffic pattern

Ensure that the current altimeter setting is set in the pressure window so that the altimeter will read altitude above mean sea level (MSL). This enables you to determine accurately when you have reached the pattern altitude. If the airport has an elevation of 890 feet, and the pattern is to be flown at 1,000 feet above the airport elevation, then the traffic pattern altitude is reached when the altimeter indicates (890 + 1,000 =) 1,890 feet MSL.

The elevations of mountains, radio masts, and so on are shown as altitude MSL on charts, so it is important for your own protection that your altimeter indicates correctly.

Radio Calls Departing Nontowered Airports

When departing from an airport that does **not** have an active control tower, you should make **advisory radio calls** on the Common Traffic Advisory Frequency (CTAF). This call may be to a UNICOM, MULTICOM, or Flight Service Station—or it may be on the tower frequency, even though though the tower is not operating; the facility may respond. The calls may otherwise be "self-announce" calls to which there might be no response, depending upon who is listening.

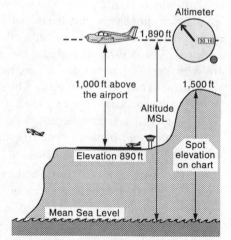

Figure 13c-2. The altimeter reads altitude MSL with the current altimeter setting in the pressure window.

The UNICOM and FSS frequencies may be manned, so you can request wind and runway advisories on them. There may be no one else listening on the MULTI-COM or tower frequency. Advisory radio calls should be made:
• before taxiing from the parking position; and
• before taxiing onto the runway for departure.

Some typical advisory calls departing a **nontowered airport:**

Example 1
Pilot: *Ocean City traffic,*
Queen Air 7155 Bravo,
At Hangar two, taxiing to runway two six, Ocean City.

Example 2
Pilot: *Ocean City traffic,*
Queen Air 7155 Bravo,
Departing runway two six, departing the pattern to the southwest,
Climbing to five thousand five hundred, Ocean City.

Radio Calls Departing Tower-Controlled Airports

Two-way radio communication between the pilot and the tower is *required* at tower-controlled airports, unless specially authorized or in the case of radio failure. When you are departing from a tower-controlled airport, you should:
• listen to the **ATIS** if available;
• contact **ground control** before taxi—transmit aircraft identification, position on field, request a taxi clearance, and specify flight status, direction of flight or destination, and ATIS identifier (if received);
• contact **tower** before takeoff—transmit aircraft identification, ready for departure, runway, and direction of flight.

Obtain permission to taxi and take off at a tower-controlled airport.

The next example shows some typical radio calls that would be made when about to taxi for departure from a **tower-controlled airport:**

Example 3
Pilot: *Hagerstown Ground Control,*
Cessna 5345 Alpha,
At city ramp, ready to taxi, departing VFR southeast bound.

Ground Control: *Cessna 5345 Alpha,*
Hagerstown Ground Control,
Wind calm, altimeter 30.05, taxi runway zero two,
Contact tower 120.3 when ready for departure.

Pilot: *Cessna 5345 Alpha.*

Read back any "hold short of runway" instructions from ATC. After you have taxied to a point near the runway and completed the engine run-up, change frequency and call the tower:

Pilot: *Hagerstown Tower,*
Cessna 5345 Alpha, ready for departure runway two,
VFR southeast bound.

Tower: *Cessna 5345 Alpha,*
Hagerstown Tower, cleared for takeoff.

Pilot: *Cessna 5345 Alpha.*

After takeoff, continue to monitor the tower frequency, and keep a good lookout for other traffic until well clear of the traffic area.

Joining the Traffic Pattern

You should always know the **elevation** of the airport you intend to use—found on charts and in the Airport/Facility Directory—so that you can fly toward it at an appropriate altitude. Ensure that the altimeter pressure window is set to the current altimeter setting, so that the altimeter reads altitude MSL.

Set the altimeter correctly.

If you are returning to an airport that has an Automatic Terminal Information Service (ATIS) broadcast on a specific VHF frequency, it is good airmanship to listen to the information broadcast when you are some 25 nm out to obtain the weather conditions and the runway in use.

When joining the traffic pattern at a tower-controlled airport, follow any ATC instructions that are given to you.

At an airport without an operating control tower, follow the standard recommended procedures that will avoid conflict with other aircraft. If possible, when at 10 miles out request an airport advisory (wind and runway in use) from UNICOM, FSS, or on the CTAF, so that you can plan an efficient traffic pattern entry. If no advisory is received, then fly overhead the airport at least 500 feet above traffic pattern altitude and check the windsock and segmented circle. **Traffic pattern indicators**, and the **landing direction indicator**, provide a visual indication to a pilot flying overhead as to the runway in use and the direction of the pattern. Then fly at least one-half mile outside the traffic pattern before descending to traffic pattern altitude.

Plan your entry into the traffic pattern.

Be at traffic pattern altitude at least one-half mile before reaching and entering the pattern from a 45° angle to the downwind leg.

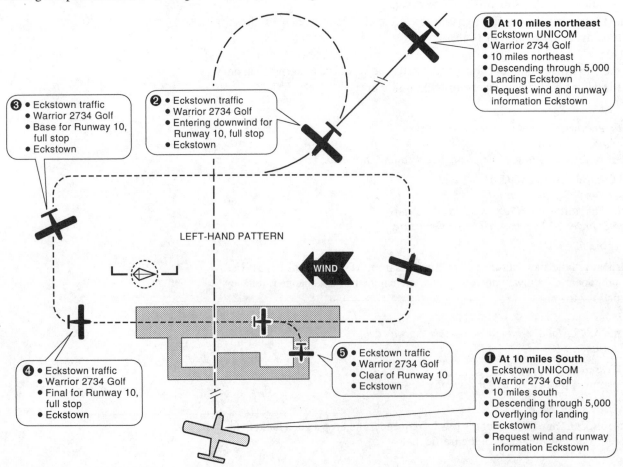

Figure 13c-3. Entering the pattern at a nontowered airport

Obey the right-of-way rules in the traffic pattern and keep adequate spacing from other aircraft. Make small S-turns to assist with spacing or widen out if necessary, but do not make any unexpected or drastic maneuvers such as a 360° turn (except in an emergency of course).

On downwind and base legs, keep an eye out for other aircraft in the landing sequence, especially those that might be making a straight-in approach, possibly an IFR (Instrument Flight Rules) aircraft following a let down through the clouds.

On approach, an aircraft at the lower altitude has right-of-way, but should not take advantage of this right to cut in front of or overtake another aircraft.

Radio Calls Arriving at Nontowered Airports

When you are in flight and approaching a nontowered airport, you should make **advisory radio calls**:
- 10 miles out;
- entering downwind leg;
- on base leg;
- on final; and
- on leaving the runway after you have landed.

Some typical advisory calls inbound to a **nontowered airport:**

Example 4

Pilot: *Ocean City traffic,*
Apache 225 Zulu, 10 miles south,
Descending through three thousand to enter downwind,
Runway one seven at Ocean City.

Pilot: *Ocean City traffic,*
Apache 225 Zulu,
Entering downwind runway one seven at Ocean City.

Pilot: *Ocean City traffic,*
Apache 225 Zulu, turning base runway one seven at Ocean City.

Pilot: *Ocean City traffic,*
Apache 225 Zulu, final runway one seven full stop at Ocean City.

Pilot: *Ocean City traffic,*
Apache 225 Zulu, clear of runway one seven at Ocean City.

Note: You can cancel a flight plan filed with FSS on the manned FSS frequency, but not on UNICOM or MULTICOM (which are non-FAA frequencies).

Radio Calls Arriving at Tower-Controlled Airports

When you are in flight and approaching a towered airport, you should:
- at 25 miles out, listen to the **ATIS,** and monitor the tower frequency;
- at 15 miles out, contact the **tower** with aircraft identification, position, altitude, and intentions—then respond to any instructions.

After landing and taxiing clear of the runway, you should contact **ground control** when directed, and advise "clear of the active". If you are unfamiliar with the airport, you should also request taxiing instructions.

Some typical radio calls with the tower controller at a **tower-controlled airport:**

Example 5

At 15 miles out:

Pilot: *Hagerstown Tower,*
Cessna 5345 Alpha,
Fifteen miles southeast at two thousand five hundred,
Landing Hagerstown.

Tower: *Cessna 5345 Alpha,*
Hagerstown Tower,
Runway two in use, wind calm, altimeter 30.04,
Enter left downwind, report turning left base.

You join on the downwind leg of the left traffic pattern, and then call as instructed when turning to base leg:

Pilot: *Hagerstown Tower,*
Cessna 5345 Alpha,
Turning left base runway two.

Tower: *Cessna 45 Alpha,*
Cleared to land.

Pilot: *Cessna 45 Alpha.*

You land, and then taxi straight ahead on the runway to the first safe taxiway, to clear the active runway. Clear of the runway, you change frequency and call *ground control* when directed to do so.

Pilot: *Hagerstown Ground Control,*
Cessna 5345 Alpha,
Clear of runway two,
Request taxi instructions to city ramp,
Unfamiliar with airport.

Ground Control: *Cessna 45 Alpha,*
Taxi to city ramp, continue straight ahead,
Turn right at the first intersection.

Pilot: *Cessna 45 Alpha.*

Airmanship

Use your rotating beacon, strobe lights, landing lights and position lights, as appropriate, to make your airplane as visible as possible to other aircraft in the vicinity of an airport. This will reduce the risk of conflict. When on the ground and clear of the runway, switch the strobe and landing lights off to avoid annoying other pilots.

Keep a particularly good lookout in the airspace around an airport—this is where most near-misses and mid-air collisions occur. Obey the right-of-way rules.

Always depart and enter the traffic pattern at a nontowered airport in accordance with the recommended standard procedures, or the procedures recommended for that airport. Announce your intentions in advance. At tower-controlled airports, follow the instructions given by ATC.

The preferred procedure for closing a flight plan filed with FSS is to contact an FSS by phone or radio and request that your plan be closed. You can also close a flight plan by requesting an ATC facility (tower or ground) to do so with the FSS designated on your flight plan.

It is good airmanship to make yourself visible.

Further Points

Orientation

In poor visibility you may not be able to see the airport from your local training area. To help you to continually know where you are, you should become familiar with all the local landmarks—for example, reservoirs, railroads, highways, towns, villages, churches, other airfields, radio towers—that will lead you to your home field, and you should also know the approximate magnetic heading to steer to return home.

The magnetic compass suffers errors when the airplane is turning or otherwise accelerating, and gives accurate headings only when the airplane is in straight flight at a steady airspeed. Therefore, to maintain an accurate magnetic heading, fly straight at a constant speed, making use of external reference points on the horizon if you can.

If a turn is needed, select a new external reference point and turn toward it. Allow the compass to settle down, and then check the heading. When you use the heading indicator (HI) on the lower center of your flight instrument panel, ensure that it is aligned with the magnetic compass during straight and steady flight. Being a gyroscopic instrument, the HI (when aligned correctly) is easier to use than the compass.

If you become uncertain of your position, you should ask for assistance from ATC or FSS.

Flying magnetic headings can assist your orientation in the vicinity of the airport.

Periodic Checks

While flying the airplane for long periods, either en route, in the local training area, or for prolonged periods in the traffic pattern area, periodic checks (say every 15 minutes or so) should be made of the various systems that are vital to safe flight.

In-flight checks of the airplane should be made regularly.

Your flight instructor will ensure that you perform the appropriate check, which will contain items such as those included in the following **FREHA** check:

F—*Fuel:* on and sufficient;
Fuel tank: usage monitored;
Mixture: rich or leaned as required;
Fuel pump: on (if fitted and if required) and fuel pressure checked.

R—*Radio:* frequency correctly selected, volume and squelch satisfactory, and make any necessary radio calls.

E—*Engine:* oil temperature and pressure, mixture set correctly, carburetor heat if required, check of other systems (ammeter for electrical system, suction gauge for air-driven gyroscopes if installed).

H—*Heading indicator:* aligned with magnetic compass (only realign the HI with the magnetic compass in steady straight-and-level flight).

A—*Altitude:* checked and correct current altimeter setting set in altimeter pressure window.

It is good airmanship to perform these checks at regular intervals on every flight and also just prior to entering the traffic pattern area (where your workload generally increases).

Emergency Radio Transmissions

As well as the more usual traffic-type radio calls, you may occasionally hear Distress or Urgency Signals. If you ever have to make an emergency call or a distress call, you should also squawk *7700* on your transponder. This will alert the radar controller.

In an emergency, squawk 7700 on your transponder, and make a *MAYDAY* call.

Example 6

MAYDAY MAYDAY MAYDAY,
   Cessna November One Three Two Papa Kilo,
   Engine has failed,
   Losing altitude,
   Intending to land five miles south of Honeygrove,
   Descending through two thousand feet,
   Heading two eight zero.

The use of the word MAYDAY (an anglicized version of the French *m'aidez* —"help me") signifies a **distress signal** and it takes priority over all other calls. This MAYDAY call informs ATC that the pilot of the airplane registered N132PK has the serious problem of a failed engine.

While ATC may offer helpful suggestions, you (the pilot in distress) must not be distracted from your main duty, which is to **fly the airplane** as safely as possible. Remember that an airplane does not need a radio to fly.

Another type of call that you may hear (or make) is the PAN-PAN call.

Example 7

PAN-PAN PAN-PAN PAN-PAN,
   Cessna November One Three Two Papa Kilo,
   Unsure of position in poor visibility east of Orange County,
   Maintaining two thousand feet,
   Heading two four zero.

The use of the term PAN-PAN signifies that this is an **urgency signal.** It informs ATC that the pilot of N132PK is requesting assistance, but the use of PAN-PAN indicates that the airplane is in **no immediate danger.** Squawk **7700** on your transponder to draw the attention of radar controllers to you. A PAN-PAN call is also appropriate if you wish to report that another airplane or a ship is in distress.

Hopefully, you will never have to make a distress or urgency call of this nature but, if you do, remember to **fly the airplane first and make radio calls second**. If you hear another pilot make such a call, then impose a temporary radio silence on yourself for a suitable period to avoid jamming these important transmissions and the ATC responses.

Radio Failure

If you ever experience two-way radio communications failure (a rare event), you must continue to fly the airplane carefully, then exercise **good judgment** in determining a suitable course of action.

Check Your Radio

- Correct frequency selected.
- Headphones and microphone still plugged in.
- Volume up; squelch adjusted.
- Change back to the previous frequency or another local frequency or to the emergency frequency 121.5 MHz and try to establish contact.

If you suffer a complete loss of radio communications while within a radar environment—that is, under the control of an ATC facility that has you identified on its radar screens—you can use the IFR transponder procedure of squawking 7600. This will draw the attention of the radar controllers to your predicament.

Note: Exercise best judgment in the use of this IFR procedure. It would be appropriate to use if, for example, you are operating on a VFR clearance in radar-controlled airspace. If the failure occurs outside of a radar environment, the appropriate procedure would be to remain outside this airspace. If you are in Class D airspace, then you would receive appropriate light signals from the control tower (see below), remaining outside the Class D Surface Area until you have determined the direction and flow of traffic. At a nontowered airport you would want to keep a good lookout.

Operating under radar control, squawk 7600 if you suffer a complete radio failure.

Remain VFR and Land

You can land at a nontowered airport at any time without a radio, and you may land at a tower-controlled airport without radio in an emergency.

Following a radio failure, remain in visual conditions, join the traffic pattern, and land.

If you have just taken off, then stay in the traffic pattern and return for a landing, keeping an eye on the tower for light signals at a tower-controlled airport. Transmit "blind", which means transmit the usual radio calls on the usual frequency, in case your transmitter is functioning but your receiver has failed.

If you are arriving at an airport, transmit blind, and establish the traffic pattern in use before entering it. This can be done by observing other aircraft or by overflying the airport at least 500 feet above the traffic pattern altitude and checking the windsock and traffic pattern direction indicator.

Then join the traffic pattern normally, making the usual radio calls blind, and keeping a good lookout for other aircraft and for light signals from an active control tower.

If your receiver is functioning, you will be able to hear messages. You can acknowledge radio messages or light signals from the tower by:
- rocking your wings in daylight (in flight);
- moving the ailerons or rudder in daylight (on the ground); and
- by blinking the landing light or position lights at night.

Light Signals

If radio contact cannot be maintained at a tower-controlled airport, the tower controller can pass instructions to the pilot by means of **light-gun signals.**

Light signals from the tower may be given following a radio failure.

On the Ground

When you are on the ground, the signals are:
- *flashing green*—cleared for taxi.
- *steady green*—cleared for takeoff.
- *steady red*—stop.
- *flashing red*—taxi clear of the landing area (runway) in use.
- *flashing white*—return to starting point on airport.
- *alternating red and green*—warning: exercise extreme caution.

In Flight

When you are in flight, the signals are:
- *steady red*—give way to other aircraft and continue circling.
- *flashing red*—airport unsafe: do not land.
- *alternating red and green*—warning: exercise extreme caution.
- *flashing green*—return for a landing (to be followed by a steady green at the proper time).
- *steady green*—cleared to land.

Minimum Weather Conditions

Traffic pattern operations are governed by two basic regulations:

Minimum Safe Altitudes

FAR 91.119 states that the minimum altitude, except when necessary for takeoff or landing, is:

- sufficient altitude to glide clear if an engine fails; or
- *over a congested area:* 1,000 feet above the highest obstacle within a 2,000-foot horizontal radius of the aircraft; or
- *over other than congested areas:* 500 feet above the surface.

Minimum Safe Altitudes are found in FAR 91.119.

With this in mind, the traffic pattern would have a minimum altitude above the surface of 500 feet AGL, but this is **not** recommended. Good operating practice suggests a **1,000 feet AGL** traffic pattern minimum, unless otherwise noted in the Airport/Facility Directory (A/FD).

Basic VFR Weather Minimums

FAR 91.155 states the minimum weather conditions for VFR flight in controlled and uncontrolled airspace in terms of:

- **visibility;** and
- **distance from clouds.**

Basic VFR Weather Minimums are found in FAR 91.155.

Basic VFR minimums **in controlled airspace** are:

- a flight visibility of three statute miles; and
- 500 feet below clouds (and 1,000 feet above clouds—not a consideration for traffic patterns) and 2,000 feet horizontally from clouds.

What this means is that a traffic pattern in Class C, D and E airspace has weather minimums of:

- flight visibility three statute miles; and
- cloud ceiling 1,000 feet AGL (so that at absolute minimum traffic pattern altitude of 500 feet AGL you are still 500 feet below the cloud ceiling).

Figure 13c-4. Basic VFR minimums in Classes C, D and E airspace

Control towers usually activate their airport beacon in daylight hours if weather conditions fall below the basic VFR minimums of three statute miles visibility and a cloud ceiling of 1,000 feet AGL.

Note: These are minimums, not "recommendeds". The AIM recommends a traffic pattern minimum of 1,000 feet AGL for the 500 feet-below-clouds rule to be satisfied, which means a recommended ceiling of at least 1,500 feet AGL.

Exceptions in controlled airspace are:

1. In **Class B airspace** (formerly called TCAs—Terminal Control Areas), all aircraft are under radar control, and so the distance-from-clouds rule is relaxed to: **remain clear of clouds;** this means that the bare minimum 500 feet AGL traffic pattern could be achieved with a low ceiling—but this is **not** recommended.

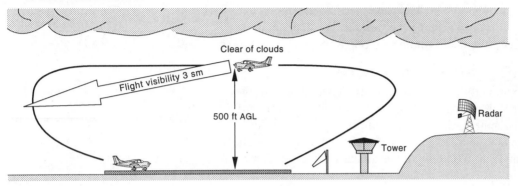

Figure 13c-5. Reduced VFR minimums in Class B airspace

2. With a **special VFR clearance** in controlled airspace, which reduces the requirements to:
   - a flight visibility of one statute mile (down from 3 sm); and
   - clear of clouds.

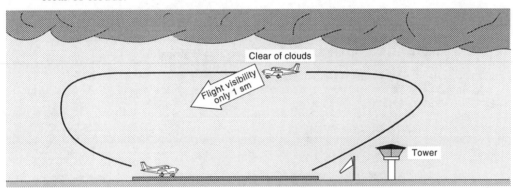

Figure 13c-6. Reduced VFR minimums with a special VFR clearance in controlled airspace (Classes B, C, D and E)

Basic VFR minimums **outside controlled airspace below 1,200 feet AGL** (that is, in Class G airspace) are:
- a flight visibility of one statute mile; and
- clear of clouds.

These are the same minimums as for a special VFR clearance in a control zone.

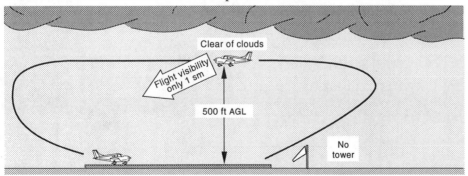

Figure 13c-7. VFR minimums in Class G airspace

Be aware that an instrument aircraft operating in Class E airspace above you could be executing an instrument approach procedure that allows it to descend to the published Minimum Descent Altitude (MDA) or Decision Height (DH) that is in the Class G airspace below. This is where you are operating, possibly in poor weather conditions.

Consequently a potential collision risk exists between your VFR aircraft and the IFR aircraft that is descending into your Class G airspace, even though both of you are operating legally. Listen on the CTAF and talk to other pilots to establish their position. If necessary, take avoiding action.

Recommended Traffic Pattern Minimums

It cannot be emphasized too strongly that the minimums shown above are the absolute legal minimums for VFR traffic patterns. We should all be careful and conservative when deciding whether or not to operate in such poor conditions.

The recommended minimums are a 1,000 feet AGL traffic pattern, with 3 sm visibility, distance from clouds as required by the airspace classification or special VFR clearance, and in sight of the surface.

In particular, **student pilots** are required by the regulations (FAR 61.89) to fly solo in minimum conditions of:
- flight or surface visibility of 3 sm or more by day; and
- with visual reference to the surface.

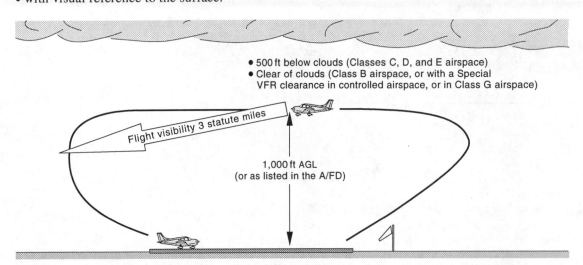

Figure 13c-8. Recommended VFR traffic pattern minimums

1. The usual traffic pattern is ___ feet AGL with (left/right) turns.

   ➤ 1,000 feet AGL, left

2. Traffic patterns that are not 1,000 feet AGL for some reason—say because of controlled airspace above, or high obstructions below—will generally lie in the range ___ feet to ___ feet AGL. Information on nonstandard traffic patterns is published in the _____ .

   ➤ 600 feet to 1,500 feet AGL, A/FD

3. Two-way radio communication (is/is not) required at tower-controlled airports.

   ➤ is

4. Two-way radio communication (is/is not) required at nontowered airports.

   ➤ is not

5. At a tower-controlled airport, you would use the (ground/tower) frequency if available when taxiing. You (must/need not) read back any instructions to "hold short of runway".

   ➤ ground, must

6. At a tower-controlled airport, you would switch from ground frequency to tower frequency (before/after) entering the active runway for takeoff.

   ➤ before

7. At an airport without an operating control tower, you should be able to obtain an airport advisory regarding wind, runway in use, and traffic from which of the following—UNICOM, MULTICOM, the local FSS, or on tower frequency?

   ➤ UNICOM and FSS (since they are manned and the others are not)

8. When departing from an airport without an operating control tower, you should make two radio calls on the ground on the C_____ T_____ A_____ F_____ . They are: (1) _____ and (2) _____ .

   ➤ Common Traffic Advisory Frequency, (1) before taxiing from the parking position, (2) before taxiing onto the runway for departure

9. Taxi and takeoff clearances (are/are not) required at an airport without an operating control tower.

   ➤ are not

10. Draw a diagram showing two methods of departing the traffic pattern at an airport without an operating control tower. Show the altitudes at which you would turn from the takeoff direction.

    ➤ *refer to our text, page 320*

11. The airport elevation is 1,230 feet MSL. The traffic pattern altitude is 1,000 feet above airport elevation, which is ___ feet MSL. What is the lowest altitude to overfly the airport and remain clear of the traffic pattern?

    ➤ 2,230 feet MSL, 2,730 feet MSL

12. There are five radio calls you are recommended to make approaching an airport without an operating control tower. Where would you make them?

    ➤ 1. 10 miles out;
    2. entering downwind;
    3. base;
    4. final; and
    5. leaving the runway

13. Approaching a tower-controlled airport, you should listen to the ATIS and monitor the tower frequency when about ___ miles out, and then contact the tower when ___ miles out.

    ➤ 25 miles, 15 miles

14. You receive a landing clearance and then land at a tower-controlled airport. Having taxied clear of the runway, you should call on the ground frequency (when directed to do so by the tower/ automatically).

    ➢ when directed to do so by the tower

15. If you are returning from a cross-country VFR flight for which you filed a flight plan with FSS, the preferred method of canceling your flight plan is to _____ _____ _____ . The tower or ground (will/will not) automatically cancel it after you have landed safely, but can relay your request to cancel your flight plan to _____ _____ _____ .

    ➢ contact FSS by phone or radio and request them to cancel your flight plan, will not, the FSS nominated on the plan

16. You appear to be catching up to an aircraft ahead of you in the traffic pattern. Which of the following are suitable solutions: slow down; make gentle S-turns; widen out; make a complete 360° turn?

    ➢ slow down, make gentle S-turns, widen out

17. The (higher/lower) aircraft on approach to land has right-of-way. It (should/should not) take advantage of this to cut in on or overtake another aircraft.

    ➢ lower, should not

18. Your radio fails totally and you are unable to re-establish two-way radio communications. You should:
    • transmit or not transmit at all;
    • listen up or not bother;
    • land immediately or first establish the traffic-pattern direction before joining and landing;
    • look for light signals at (tower-controlled/ nontowered) airports, which you could acknowledge in daylight by _____ ;
    • if under radar control, consider squawking _____ on the transponder.

    ➢ transmit blind; listen up; first establish the traffic pattern direction before joining and landing; tower-controlled; rocking the wings; 7600—*Note: This is an IFR procedure and would be appropriate for a VFR flight if, for example, operating on a VFR clearance in a radar environment.*

19. In flight, you observe a steady red light signal directed at you from the tower. This means _____ .

    ➢ give way to other aircraft and continue circling

20. In flight, you observe a flashing green light signal directed at you from the tower. This means _____ .

    ➢ return for a landing

21. In flight, you observe a steady green light signal directed at you from the tower. This means _____ .

    ➢ cleared to land

22. After landing and taxiing clear of the runway, you observe a steady red light signal directed at you from the tower. This means _____ .

    ➢ stop

23. After landing and taxiing clear of the runway, you observe a flashing green signal directed at you from the tower. This means _____ .

    ➢ cleared to taxi

24. You can acknowledge light signals from the tower in daylight when you are on the ground by _____ .

    ➢ moving the ailerons or rudder

25. The recommended traffic pattern altitude is _____ feet AGL or as published in the A_____ / F_____ Directory.

    ➢ 1,000 feet AGL, Airport/Facility Directory

26. Student pilots are only permitted to fly solo if two weather conditions are satisfied. What are they?

    ➢ flight or surface visibility three statute miles or more by day, and with visual reference to the surface at all times

27. Sketch a diagram showing the recommended VFR traffic pattern minimums.

    ➢ *see figure 13c-8 on page 330*

The Zero-Flap Approach and Landing 13d

Objective

To approach and land without the use of flaps.

Considerations

Some older model airplanes were designed without flaps. Most modern airplanes have flaps, however a zero-flaps approach will be necessary if a failure of any part of the flap system occurs (a rare event), and may be advisable in strong and gusty winds. Crosswind landings are often made in such conditions.

Compared with a normal approach and landing with flaps, **the main features of a zero-flap approach and landing** are:

- a shallower flight path, requiring an extended traffic pattern;
- a higher approach speed (because of the higher stalling speed with flaps up);
- a higher nose attitude on the approach, resulting in poorer forward vision;
- a minimal flare and a longer float (because of less drag) if the airplane is held off for a prolonged period prior to touching down;
- a greater risk of ballooning if the flare is too pronounced;
- a risk of scraping the tail on touchdown if the nose is raised too high in a prolonged float; and
- a longer landing ground roll because of the higher landing speed and lower drag.

It is most important to control the flight path and airspeed precisely on a zero-flap approach. Airspeed is controlled with elevator, and flight path with power—power and attitude control performance.

If you are too high on approach, reduce power and lower the nose slightly—if the power is already at idle, consider a **forward slip** to increase the rate of descent and steepen the approach path. Recover smoothly from the forward slip and stay aligned with the runway centerline before touching down.

A clean wing has less drag than a flapped wing, which means that excess speed takes longer to bleed off—so an airplane with no flaps extended is "slippery". This can lengthen the float considerably during the landing. To avoid using too much runway, and also to avoid the risk of scraping the tail on touchdown, approach at the corrrect speed, and do not hold the airplane off for a prolonged period, particularly on a short runway.

When the nosewheel is on the ground, brakes can be used, if required.

Note: The forward slip is approved in most training airplanes as a means of losing altitude with zero flaps, but not approved when the flaps are down, since they may disturb the airflow over the tail, or even blanket it, giving you less control.

Zero-flap approaches are shallower.

Use a forward slip to steepen the approach without gaining airspeed.

With zero flaps, the airplane is "slippery".

Airwork 13d
The Zero-Flap Approach and Landing

Objective

To approach and land without the use of the wing flaps.

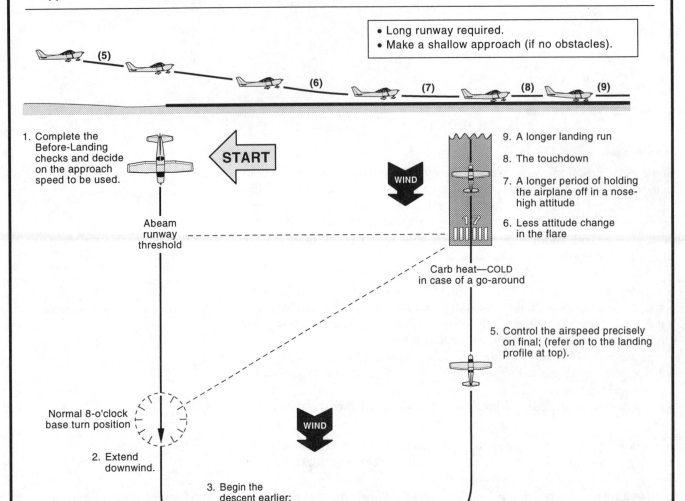

- Long runway required.
- Make a shallow approach (if no obstacles).

(5) (6) (7) (8) (9)

1. Complete the Before-Landing checks and decide on the approach speed to be used.

START

Abeam runway threshold

Normal 8-o'clock base turn position

2. Extend downwind.

3. Begin the descent earlier; carb heat—COLD, reduce power.

4. Begin the turn to final earlier.

WIND

WIND

Carb heat—COLD in case of a go-around

5. Control the airspeed precisely on final; (refer on to the landing profile at top).

6. Less attitude change in the flare

7. A longer period of holding the airplane off in a nose-high attitude

8. The touchdown

9. A longer landing run

 ## Review 13d

The Zero-Flap Approach and Landing

1. Compared with a normal full-flap approach, a zero-flap approach will require:
   - a (steeper/shallower) flight path;
   - a (faster/slower) approach speed;
   - a (higher/lower) nose attitude; and
   - a (longer/shorter) ground roll.

   ➤ shallower, faster, higher, longer

2. You can lose unwanted altitude on a zero-flap approach by using a _____ slip, which (increases/reduces) drag and so (steepens/shallows) the glide.

   ➤ forward, increases, steepens

3. A zero-flap approach is a (high/low) drag approach.

   ➤ low drag

The Power-Off Approach and Landing 13e

Objective

To carry out an approach and landing without using power.

Considerations

Why Use No Power?

The power-off approach and landing, made without the assistance of power, is good for developing your judgment, and is **good practice for emergency forced landings** following an engine failure.

The power-off approach is a glide approach. With practice, you will develop the skill of estimating the *gliding range* from various altitudes, and positioning yourself in a pattern for an accurate power-off approach and landing.

Base Leg

Your aim is to descend at a glide-path angle that clears all obstacles in the approach path so that you reach your aiming point at a safe airspeed. To achieve this, you must control both the glide path and the airspeed.

You should plan a base leg according to the estimated wind conditions: close-in if there will be a strong headwind on final approach causing a steep descent over the ground, further out from the airport boundary if the wind is light causing the descent path over the ground to be shallower.

Fly a closer base leg in strong wind conditions.

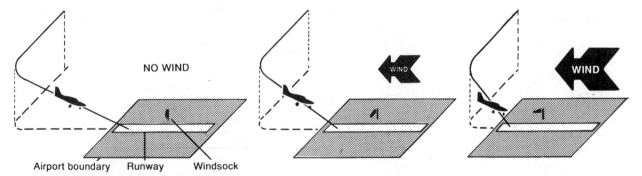

NO WIND

Airport boundary   Runway   Windsock

WIND

WIND

Figure 13e-1. The stronger the headwind on final approach, the closer your base leg should be to the airport boundary.

The Approach

During a power-off approach, the flaps may be used to steepen the glide-path angle to the runway. It is not possible to make the flight path shallower (without using power), and this is where good judgment comes in. It is best to initially have an aiming point well into the runway, then bring it closer by steepening the descent using flaps.

If flaps are not available, then a forward slip may be used to steepen the glide path without increasing the airspeed (as would happen if you simply used a dive straight ahead). Airspeed in the glide is controlled by pitch attitude (as the power is at idle).

Use the flaps to steepen the approach.

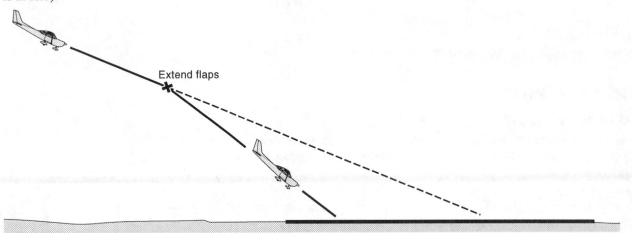

Figure 13e-2. Steepen the approach by using flaps.

The Approach Flight Path

On a normal, power-assisted approach, power is used to control the rate of descent and the flight path to the aiming point on the runway.

Without power, the descent rate is greater and the pitch attitude of the airplane must be lower to maintain the correct approach speed. The result is a steeper approach path to the runway on a glide approach, and so the airplane must be positioned higher on final than normal. The lower nose position in the glide, especially with full flaps, will mean that the change of pitch attitude in the flare will be significantly greater.

The flight path on a power-off approach is steep and the flare more pronounced.

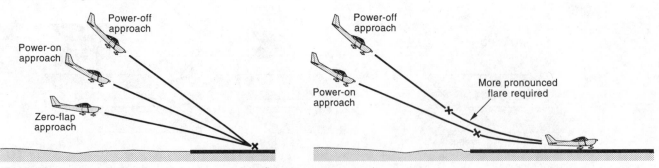

Figure 13e-3. A power-off approach is steep, and the flare more pronounced.

Developing Judgment

To develop your judgment, try making power-off approaches from various positions relative to the touchdown point.

It may be good to start with the power coming off when you are on base leg—first a 90° power-off approach, and then, when you can accomplish this consistently, try a 180° power-off approach from the downwind leg, and a 360° power-off approach from overhead the airfield.

Practice power-off approaches from various positions.

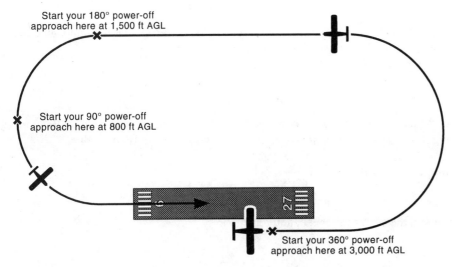

Figure 13e-4. Practice power-off approaches from various positions.

Flying the Maneuver

Base Leg Position

To achieve a steeper approach path to the aiming point on the runway, make the downwind leg shorter than normal, with base leg being flown closer to the field than in the normal power-on approach. In strong wind conditions, the base leg should be flown even closer to the field to ensure that you do not undershoot.

Fly a closer base leg for a power-off approach, especially in strong winds.

Descent Point

Descent point on base leg should be carefully chosen since the objective, when power is removed, is *not* to have to use it again. Use the amount of crab angle that is required on base to counteract wind drift as a guide to the likely wind strength on final.

Delay the descent from pattern altitude on a planned power-off approach.

Ideally, if you have judged the closer base leg correctly, a descent may be established when the runway is at 45° on a close base leg.

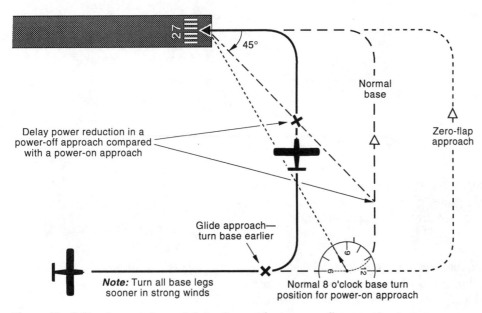

Figure 13e-5. Turn base earlier and delay descent for a power-off approach.

The Aiming Point

Initially, aim well down the runway so that the airplane is definitely higher than normal on approach, and you can be sure of reaching the runway. The approach can later be steepened with flaps, whereas it cannot be flattened without the use of power.

Use an initial aiming point well down the runway.

Controlling the Flight Path

Use the flaps in stages to steepen the glide path and progressively bring the aiming point nearer the threshold. It is preferable to be high on approach rather than low. If flaps alone do not give you sufficient flexibility, make tracking modifications so that you arrive at the aiming point at the correct speed.

Use flaps and tracking modifications to control the flight path.

If you are too high on approach:
- extend more flaps, lower the nose to maintain the correct airspeed, and retrim; or
- widen out the base leg a little; or
- fly S-turns on final—these can lead to an unstable approach and so are best avoided, except as a last resort.

If you are too low on approach:
- delay the selection of flaps; and/or
- cut in on the base leg to shorten final.

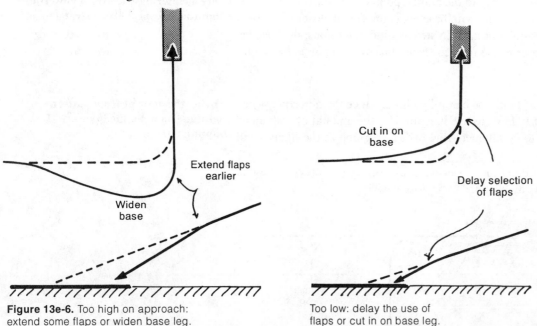

Figure 13e-6. Too high on approach: extend some flaps or widen base leg.

Too low: delay the use of flaps or cut in on base leg.

If hopelessly low, use power to reposition the airplane on the glide path or to go around and start again.

Note: During a normal powered approach, coordinated use of power and attitude is used to control airspeed and flight path. On a power-off approach, however, with no power being used, airspeed is controlled with pitch attitude only.

Turns

Avoid *steep* gliding turns, since the descent rate will increase significantly, with a corresponding increase in the stalling speed. Be prepared for an increased rate-of-descent and a steepening of the glide path during the medium turn onto final which, ideally, should not exceed a 20° bank angle.

The glide path will steepen in a turn.

The Glide

Do not allow your airspeed to get too low by raising the nose in an attempt to "stretch" the glide—it will not work! At airspeeds below the best-glide speed, the flight path will steepen even though the nose position is high.

Do not try to "stretch" the glide.

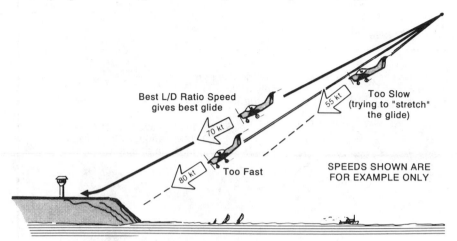

Figure 13e-7. The best-glide airspeed gives the flattest glide-path angle.

Raising the flaps in an attempt to extend the gliding distance is also not advisable, since this will initially cause the airplane to sink.

In a strong headwind, a slightly higher approach speed may give the airplane more penetration even though the descent rate is increased. Apply power and go around if the approach has been badly misjudged.

Landing Flaps

If the aiming point with partial flaps is well down the runway, further flap extension will give you a new aiming point nearer the threshold. Progressively lower the flaps as required, but delay the selection of full landing flaps until you are absolutely certain that the runway will be reached comfortably. In a power-off approach, a slight overshoot of the aiming point is preferable to an unrecoverable undershoot.

Delay the selection of landing flaps until certain of reaching the field.

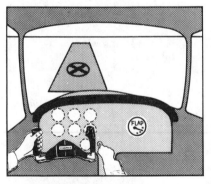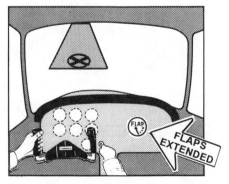

Figure 13e-8. Bring the aiming point closer by lowering additional flaps.

The Power-Off Flare

With full flaps and no power, the glide path will be steep and the nose attitude quite low to maintain the correct approach speed. The change of attitude in the roundout will be quite pronounced, and a gentle flare should be initiated a little higher than normal. Make the appropriate type of landing applicable to the conditions (crosswind, short-field, soft-field).

Begin the flare slightly higher than normal.

Airwork 13e
The Power-Off Approach and Landing

Objective

To carry out an approach and landing without the use of power.

11. A more pronounced flare.

10. Carb heat— COLD in case of a go-around.

9. Select full flaps when absolutely certain of reaching the field.

8. Medium descending turn— 20° bank angle (30° maximum); monitor the airspeed closely.

Look out

7. Adjust base leg to arrive higher than normal on final.

6. Select partial flaps as required.

5. Initially descend clean (zero flaps).

4. Descent point (P-A-T):
   - Carb heat—ON; Power—OFF.
   - Maintain altitude until the speed reduces to the best-glide speed.
   - Select the glide attitude.
   - Trim.

Look out

3. Reassess the wind effect.

1. Carry out the Before-Landing checks.

2. Turn base earlier than usual, especially in strong winds.

Normal 8-o'clock base turn position

✍ Review 13e

The Power-Off Approach and Landing

1. A power-off gliding approach will be (steeper/ shallower) than a power-on approach, and the nose attitude will be (higher/lower/the same).

   ➤ steeper, lower

2. The descent rate will (increase/decrease/remain the same) when you enter a gliding turn.

   ➤ increase

3. The descent point for a power-off gliding approach should be (closer to/further from/the same distance from) the runway compared with the descent point for a normal powered approach.

   ➤ closer to

4. If you are high on a gliding approach, you should (raise/lower/not change) the flaps.

   ➤ lower

5. The more flaps you have, the (steeper/shallower) the glide at the same airspeed.

   ➤ steeper

6. If you are a little lower on approach than you want to be you should:
   (a) delay the selection of more flaps;
   (b) immediately increase the flap setting; or
   (c) fly some S-turns on final.

   ➤ (a)

7. If you are hopelessly low on a practice glide approach you should:
   (a) raise the nose to try and stretch the glide; or
   (b) admit defeat and add power, and do better next time.

   ➤ (b)

8. When flaring the airplane after a power-off approach, the change in nose attitude is (greater than/the same as/less than) that following a normal power-on approach.

   ➤ greater than

Crosswind Operations 13f

Objective

To take off, fly a full traffic pattern and land using a runway which has a significant crosswind component.

Considerations

This exercise is divided into two parts—crosswind takeoffs and crosswind landings—but first we cover some general considerations applicable to crosswind operations in general.

Not all airports have a runway which is facing directly upwind on a given day. For this reason, takeoffs and landings on runways where there is a crosswind component are frequent events. Crosswind operations are really quite normal, with some extra considerations.

1. Allow for wind-drift in flight by applying a wind correction angle so that you can achieve the required track over the ground.

2. Prior to touchdown on landing, eliminate the wind-drift and align the wheels—in other words, align the longitudinal axis of the airplane—with the runway centerline.

3. On the takeoff and landing ground runs, keep the wings level with aileron, and keep straight with rudder.

Each airplane type—from the smallest trainers up to the MD-11 and Boeing 747—has a **maximum crosswind component** specified in the Airplane Flight Manual and Pilot's Operating Handbook. Many light aircraft do not have a crosswind limit, but rather a *maximum demonstrated crosswind* as experienced and handled adequately by a test pilot.

If the actual crosswind component on the runway exceeds the safe limit for the airplane and/or what you feel is your own personal limit, then use a different runway; this may even mean diverting to a different airport.

Crosswind Strength

It is important to estimate the strength of the crosswind for your crosswind takeoff or landing. This can be estimated from the wind strength and the angle that the wind direction makes with the runway. As a rough guide:

• a wind 30° off the runway heading has a crosswind component of one-half the wind strength;
• a wind 45° off the runway has a crosswind component of two-thirds the wind strength;
• a wind 60° off the runway has a crosswind component of nine-tenths the wind strength;
• a wind 90° off the runway is all crosswind.

Do not operate in crosswind conditions that exceed airplane or personal limits.

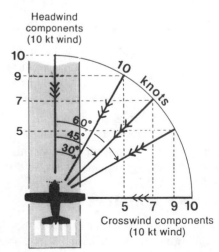

Figure 13f-1. Estimating the crosswind component.

The Crosswind Traffic Pattern

The crosswind traffic pattern is a rectangular pattern over the ground and is based on the runway used. The standard names are given to the various legs of the crosswind traffic pattern, even though the actual wind effect experienced on each of those legs may differ from what the name of the leg suggests.

Adjustments should be made to allow for the wind effect in the pattern, such as crabbing and modifying the turns. Since the wind at traffic pattern altitude may differ in direction and strength to that at ground level, make use of ground features to help you maintain the rectangular traffic pattern over the ground.

Any changes of heading around the pattern should be made with coordinated turns, and the coordination ball should be kept centered with rudder pressure.

When flying in a crosswind pattern, be aware that other aircraft may be operating in the standard into-the-wind traffic pattern that may conflict with yours. Airplanes in the standard pattern will generally have right-of-way, so the main responsibility for avoiding conflict is with the pilot flying in the crosswind pattern.

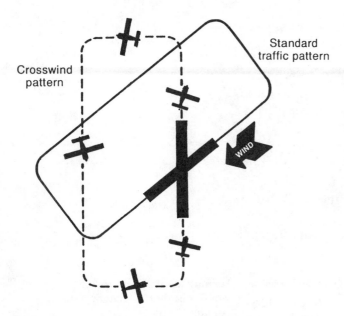

Figure 13f-2. Crabbing to maintain a rectangular traffic pattern.

Recommended Flap Settings

The Pilot's Operating Handbook might specify certain flap settings for takeoff and landing in strong crosswind conditions—often the minimum flap setting for the field length available. The lower the flap setting, the longer the ground run both for takeoff and for landing.

Low flap settings and a fairly clean wing enable quick airspeed responses to power changes in gusty conditions, because of the low drag. Also, the higher speeds with low flap settings means that you will have a smaller wind correction angle (WCA) to counteract the wind drift.

In the Flight Test

Crosswind conditions are very common, and they are a good test of your ability. If conditions are suitable, you will be able to demonstrate your crosswind skills during your practical test. If crosswind conditions do not occur, your knowledge of crosswind takeoffs, traffic patterns and landings will be tested orally.

Part (i)
The Crosswind Takeoff

Flying the Maneuver

Weathervaning

In a crosswind, an airplane will tend to weathervane (or weathercock) into the wind because of the large keel surfaces behind the main wheels.

Provided that the crosswind limit for your airplane is not exceeded, it will be possible to keep straight with rudder on the ground without too much difficulty. A crosswind from the right will require left rudder to counteract its effect—more rudder at slow speeds, and then less rudder displacement as the airflow over the rudder increases during the takeoff roll. Use whatever rudder is required to keep straight! Holding the nosewheel firmly on the ground until liftoff will assist in directional control.

Lift on the Wings

A crosswind blowing under the upwind wing will tend to lift it. Counteract this effect and keep the wings level with aileron by moving the control column into the wind. While full aileron deflection might be required early in the takeoff run, this can be progressively reduced during the takeoff run as the faster and faster airflow increases control effectiveness.

You do not have to consciously think about aileron movement; simply concentrate on keeping the wings level.

Crossed-Controls

A right crosswind, for example, requires right aileron and left rudder, therefore you will have crossed-controls. The controls should be correctly positioned prior to beginning the takeoff—a glance at the windsock as you line up will allow you to do this.

As the airspeed increases during the takeoff run, the amount of aileron and rudder required will steadily reduce—until at liftoff there will probably be some rudder still applied, but little or no aileron. There is no need to consciously think about this, just:
• keep straight with rudder; and
• keep the wings level with aileron.

Keep straight with rudder control.

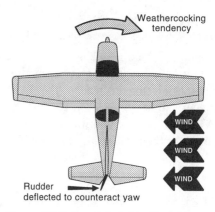

Figure 13f-3. Keep straight with rudder.

Keep the wings level with aileron control.

The controls are crossed in a crosswind takeoff.

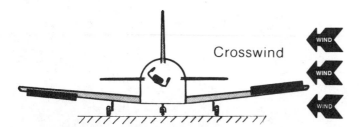

Figure 13f-4. Keep the wings level with aileron.

Drift after Takeoff

After the airplane lifts off in a crosswind, it will tend to move sideways with the air mass. Any tendency to sink back onto the ground after lifting off should be resisted, to avoid the strong sideways forces that would be exerted on the landing gear if it contacted the ground again.

For this reason it is usual, in a crosswind takeoff, to hold the airplane firmly on the ground during the ground run (with slight forward pressure on the control column), and then to **lift off cleanly and positively** with a firm backward movement of the control column.

It may be advisable to delay lifting off until five knots or so past the normal rotation speed to achieve a clean liftoff.

Hold the airplane firmly on the ground during the takeoff run.

A crosswind will cause drift after takeoff, so lift off cleanly.

Crab into the Wind

When airborne and clear of the ground, turn into the wind sufficiently to counteract the drift, using a shallow coordinated turn, and climb out normally along the extended centerline of the runway. Any remaining *crossed-control* should be removed when airborne by centralizing the coordination ball with rudder and keeping the wings level with aileron.

You can check your tracking with reference to your selected ground feature ahead, or by occasionally looking back at the runway if possible.

Complete the After-Takeoff checklist, if applicable.

After liftoff, establish coordinated flight and apply a wind correction angle.

Airmanship

An exceptionally good **lookout** is vital prior to taking off on a crosswind runway and during a crosswind pattern. Give way to airplanes using the upwind runway and standard traffic pattern, which may conflict with yours.

Exert firm, positive control during a crosswind takeoff, and ensure a clean liftoff. Depart the pattern using standard procedures, or follow the pattern correctly for a crosswind approach and landing.

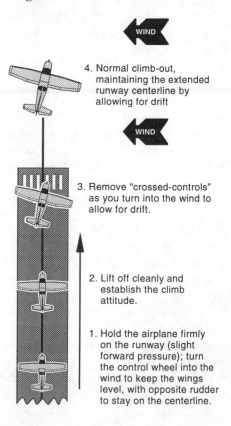

4. Normal climb-out, maintaining the extended runway centerline by allowing for drift

3. Remove "crossed-controls" as you turn into the wind to allow for drift.

2. Lift off cleanly and establish the climb attitude.

1. Hold the airplane firmly on the runway (slight forward pressure); turn the control wheel into the wind to keep the wings level, with opposite rudder to stay on the centerline.

Figure 13f-5. The crosswind takeoff

Airwork 13f, Part (i)
The Crosswind Takeoff

Objective
To take off on a runway with a crosswind component which is below limit for the airplane.

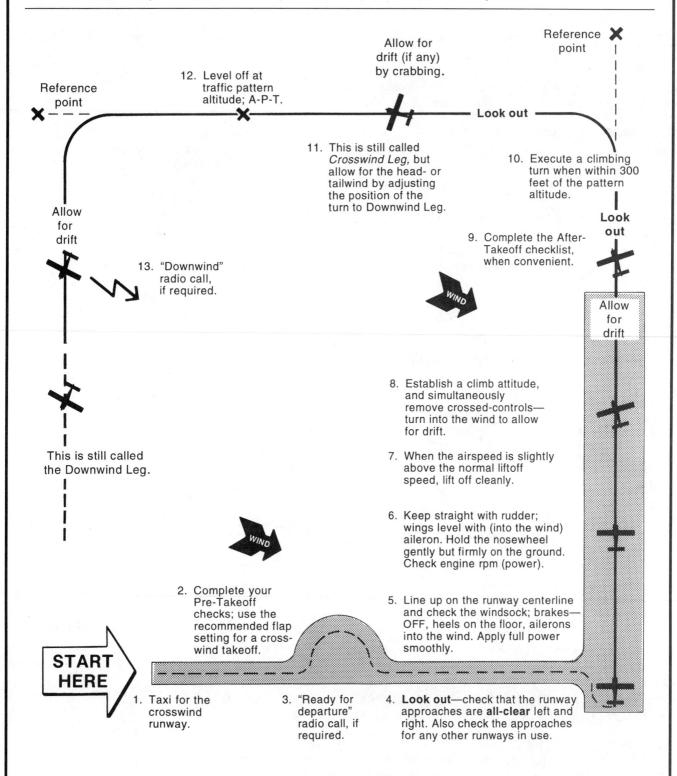

Reference point

12. Level off at traffic pattern altitude; A-P-T.

Allow for drift (if any) by crabbing.

Reference point

Look out

11. This is still called *Crosswind Leg,* but allow for the head- or tailwind by adjusting the position of the turn to Downwind Leg.

10. Execute a climbing turn when within 300 feet of the pattern altitude.

Look out

Allow for drift

13. "Downwind" radio call, if required.

9. Complete the After-Takeoff checklist, when convenient.

WIND

Allow for drift

8. Establish a climb attitude, and simultaneously remove crossed-controls— turn into the wind to allow for drift.

7. When the airspeed is slightly above the normal liftoff speed, lift off cleanly.

This is still called the Downwind Leg.

6. Keep straight with rudder; wings level with (into the wind) aileron. Hold the nosewheel gently but firmly on the ground. Check engine rpm (power).

2. Complete your Pre-Takeoff checks; use the recommended flap setting for a cross-wind takeoff.

5. Line up on the runway centerline and check the windsock; brakes— OFF, heels on the floor, ailerons into the wind. Apply full power smoothly.

WIND

START HERE

1. Taxi for the crosswind runway.

3. "Ready for departure" radio call, if required.

4. **Look out**—check that the runway approaches are **all-clear** left and right. Also check the approaches for any other runways in use.

Part (ii)
Crosswind Approach and Landing

Flying the Maneuver

Ensure that the crosswind component on the selected runway does not exceed the safe limit for the airplane (or your own personal limit).

Crosswind Pattern

Planning for the crosswind approach and landing starts early in the traffic pattern, even as you turn onto the *crosswind leg* shortly after takeoff. A tailwind on the crosswind leg will tend to carry you wide; a headwind will hold you in too close.

Fly the crosswind pattern according to the wind.

Adjust each leg of the traffic pattern to position the airplane suitably with respect to the runway. Plan on using the recommended flap setting for a landing in strong crosswind conditions, which may be the minimum flap setting required for the field length. In this case you should plan for a shallower approach than normal.

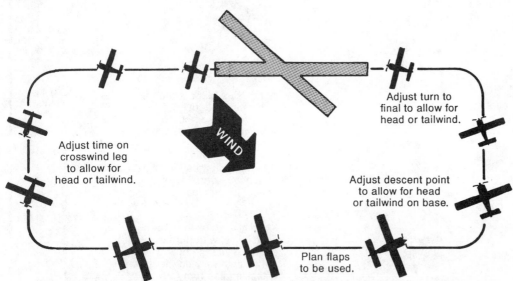

Figure 13f-6. Flying the crosswind traffic pattern.

Tailwind on Base Leg

A tailwind on base leg will increase your speed over the ground and will tend to carry you past the extended runway centerline. For this reason, you should show some anticipation and:

Anticipate the effect of a tailwind on base leg.

- begin your descent early;
- begin the turn to final early; and
- continue the turn to final beyond the runway heading, to allow for drift.

Note: If you think you are going to fly through final, then avoid any tendency to overbank in an effort to avoid or correct the overshoot—a 30° bank angle is a reasonable maximum. Simply rejoin final from the other side.

Headwind on Base Leg

A headwind on base leg will decrease your speed over the ground and so:
- delay your descent until later than usual;
- delay the turn to final until almost in line with the runway; and
- stop the turn short of runway heading to anticipate the expected drift.

- **If you turn too early** then you may not reach final, and a positive turn will have to be made into the wind to become established.
- **If you turn too late** and fly through final, simply fly the runway heading and the crosswind will most probably carry you back on to the extended centerline.

Flying into a headwind on base leg, you can afford to delay your turn to final.

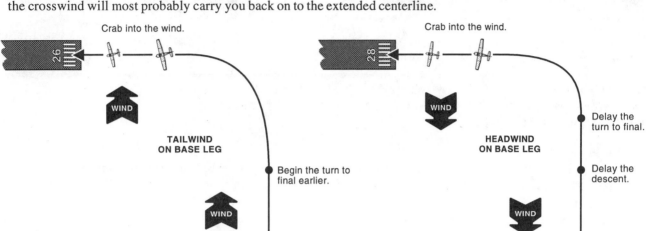

Figure 13f-7. Allow for the wind effect when turning final.

When in line with the runway, crab into the wind to track directly down final.

Tracking on Final

When using a crab angle down final approach to maintain the extended centerline in a crosswind, the runway will appear to one side of the nose, but will still look symmetrical.

Positively control tracking down final.

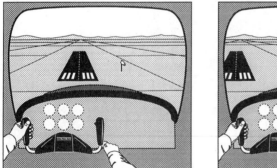

Figure 13f-8. An approach into the wind, and a crosswind approach

Position the airplane on final approach so that you have a view directly down the runway centerline. If the airplane drifts downwind, then make a definite turn into the wind and regain final without delay—do not just aim the nose of the airplane at the runway! Keep the airplane coordinated with rudder pressure.

Wind strength often decreases near the ground, so continual adjustments to heading will have to be made to maintain your track down final. This is especially the case in strong and gusty wind conditions.

Exercise 13f **Crosswind Operations**

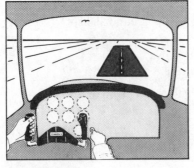
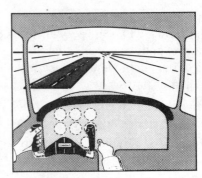

Left of Centerline   On Centerline   Right of Centerline

Figure 13f-9. Get tracking under control early on final approach.

When tracking is under control, then achieving a stabilized descent path and a good landing becomes a simpler task. It is particularly true in crosswinds that **a good landing requires a good approach.**

Align the Wheels

While an airplane is airborne, the fact that its longitudinal axis is not aligned with the runway is not significant. It would be uncomfortable to touch down in this situation, however, since the wheels are not aligned with the path of the airplane down the runway. A strong sideways force on the landing gear could do structural damage or, in an extreme case, tip the airplane over. To avoid this, use rudder to align the wheels with the runway direction prior to touchdown.

Remember that the airplane still must be flared normally to make the transition from the approach attitude into the touchdown attitude, otherwise a hard touchdown will result. The less flaps used, the less the flare you will need.

After the wheels are aligned with the runway centerline, prevent any sideways drift across the runway before the wheels actually touch down. You can do this with coordinated use of the controls (ailerons, rudder, elevator and power).

The crosswind landing is usually a little more difficult than the takeoff because the controls will become less and less effective as the airflow over them decreases—larger movements will be required to achieve the desired effect.

As your skills develop with practice, you will gain great satisfaction from consistently performing good crosswind landings.

Following a crosswind approach, align the wheels with the runway prior to touchdown.

Crosswind Landing Techniques

There are three accepted crosswind landing techniques:

(a) The crab method;

(b) The wing-down method; and

(c) The combination method (incorporating the best features of each of the above)—a crab approach followed by a wing-down landing.

Your flight instructor will teach you his or her preferred method.

General Points

Strong crosswinds are often accompanied by gusts and turbulence, and consideration should be given to using reduced landing flaps, or zero flaps, and a slightly higher approach speed than normal, to enable better controllability.

The **flare** in a crosswind landing is normal, but the airplane should not be held off the ground for a prolonged period—otherwise sideways drift could develop. Place the airplane on the ground positively and smoothly while the flight controls are still effective, with the wheels correctly aligned and with the airplane tracking along the runway centerline.

When you are on the ground, directional control is more easily achieved if the nosewheel is lowered onto the ground at an early stage in the landing run. Forward pressure on the control column may be required. Keep *flying* the airplane until the end of the landing roll, and retain firm control throughout the whole operation until the airplane is stopped.

During the landing run:

- keep straight with rudder (the crosswind will cause an upwind weathervaning tendency);
- lower the nosewheel to the ground after touchdown to assist in directional control; and
- keep the wings level with progressive use of aileron into the wind as the airspeed decreases—the crosswind will tend to lift the upwind wing. Full control wheel deflection into the wind may be required by the end of the landing run, when the reduced airflow over the ailerons will make them less effective, and the relative airflow striking the airplane will have more of a crosswind component (because of the reducing headwind component as the airplane slows down).

Airmanship

In strong crosswind conditions (more than about 10 knots of crosswind) use the flap setting recommended in the Pilot's Operating Handbook, which may be the minimum setting required considering the field length (this may mean zero flaps).

Airmanship is being positive and alert to the effects of a crosswind.

Be firm and positive in your handling of the airplane. Be decisive!

Flare the airplane normally, and touch down with the wheels aligned and with no sideways drift.

Remember that your crosswind pattern may conflict with the standard pattern, so keep a good lookout.

If at any stage you feel distinctly unhappy about the approach and landing, go around and start again.

Method (a)—The Crab Method

In the crab method, drift should be controlled by crabbing into the wind all the way down final and through the flare. This will keep the airplane tracking down the centerline, but the wheels will not be aligned with the landing direction.

Flare normally, to make the transition from the approach attitude to the touchdown attitude.

Just prior to touchdown, yaw the airplane straight with smooth and firm rudder pressure to align the longitudinal axis (and the wheels) with the centerline of the runway. Keep the wings level with ailerons.

The airplane should not be held off for a prolonged period, and the main wheels of the airplane should be lowered onto the runway before any sideways drift has a chance to develop. Do not allow the nosewheel to touch first, as this could cause a bounce as well as overstress the structure. After the main wheels have touched, however, the nosewheel should be lowered to the ground early in the landing run to aid in directional control. Center the nosewheel with rudder prior to it touching.

Judgment and Timing

The crab method requires judgment and timing. Failing to remove the crab angle prior to landing will result in the wheels touching down sideways; removing it too early will allow a sideways drift to develop and, as well as landing downwind of the centerline, the wheels will still touch down with a sideways component. In both cases the landing will feel heavy and the landing gear will be stressed unnecessarily.

A reasonable touchdown using the crab method can only be achieved with fine judgment in removing drift and contacting the ground. If, during the landing, any sideways drift looks like it is developing before touchdown, it can be counteracted by:

• applying a small amount of wing-down into the wind; and
• keeping straight with rudder.

This is really a lead-in to the next method of crosswind landing: the *sideslip* or *wing-down* method.

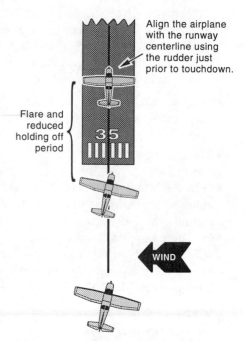

Figure 13f-10. In the crab method, align the airplane just prior to touchdown.

Airwork 13f, Part (ii)—Method (a)
Crab Method of Crosswind Landing

Objective

To carry out a crosswind approach and landing by crabbing into the wind until just prior to wheel contact on touchdown.

1. On Final Approach

- Track down the extended runway centerline by heading the airplane into the wind.
- Control airspeed with elevator, flight path with power and keep coordinated with rudder. The wings should be level except when adjusting your crab angle.

2. During the Flare

- Reduce power and raise the nose normally.
- Maintain your track above the runway centerline by crabbing into the wind.

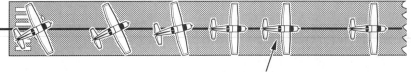

WIND   WIND

Flare and holdoff period

Align the airplane just before touchdown

Touchdown

3. Just Prior to Touchdown

- Align the airplane with the centerline with smooth and firm rudder pressure.
- Hold the wings level with aileron.

4. The Landing Run

- Keeping straight with rudder, lower the nosewheel onto the ground.
- Keep the wings level with progressive use of aileron into the wind.
- Hold the nosewheel on the ground to obtain positive steering.

Flare and holdoff period   Touchdown

Reduced holdoff compared with normal upwind landing

Method (b)—The Wing-Down Method

This method can be employed in the **latter stages of the approach**. Some instructors recommend that it be used all the way down final—others, just for the last few feet. At this stage of your training we will discuss this method as applying to the last 300 feet or so of the approach.

The airplane is made to track down the extended centerline, not by crabbing, but by slipping, with the wheels remaining aligned with the runway centerline. This is called a **sideslip.** You can change the amount of sideslip, by changing the amount of wing-down using aileron, so that the sideslip through the air matches exactly the wind drift across the runway, resulting in a flight path along the extended runway centerline. The nose of the airplane is kept heading straight down the centerline using rudder.

To initiate a sideslip:
• lower the upwind wing a few degrees; and
• apply opposite rudder pressure to stop the airplane turning and to align its longitudinal axis with the runway centerline.

In this situation, the controls are *crossed,* so the coordination ball will not be centered. The stronger the crosswind, the more wing-down and opposite rudder will be required. Airspeed control is particularly important when controls are crossed, but be aware that the unusual airflow over the pitot tube and/or static vents may cause airspeed indication errors. Discuss with your flight instructor how this may affect your particular airplane type.

Because the airplane is sideslipping through the air, the drag will be greater than normal, and so a bit more power will probably be needed —most likely you will apply this naturally as you monitor and control the flight path and airspeed.

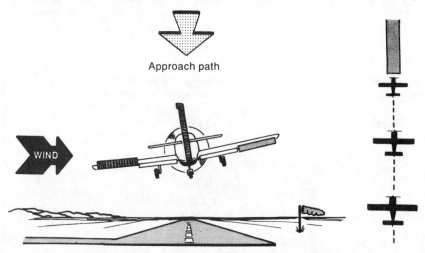

Figure 13f-11. The wing-down, or sideslip, method of crosswind landing.

In strong and gusty crosswind conditions, you may have to make continual adjustments to wing-down and rudder. It is usual for the wind strength to diminish as the ground is neared because of friction from surface objects such as trees and buildings.

Drift Control

If the airplane starts to drift **downwind** across the runway, you have applied insufficient wing-down, so increase the sideslip:
• lower the wing a few degrees further; and
• keep straight with rudder.

Control drift with wing-down, and heading with rudder.

If the airplane starts to slip **upwind** across the runway, you have applied too much wing-down, so reduce the sideslip:
• raise the wing a few degrees; and
• keep straight with rudder.

In gusty conditions especially, you will be continually varying the degree of wing-down (to control drift) and opposite rudder (to control heading).

Stay aligned by varying the amount of wing-down and rudder pressure.

The Touchdown

Flare normally to make the transition from the approach attitude to the touchdown attitude.

Touch down on the upwind main wheel.

Hold wing-down and opposite rudder on throughout the flare and touchdown, which will occur initially on the upwind main wheel. Throughout the maneuver the airplane will be tracking straight down the runway, with its longitudinal axis aligned with the centerline. No sideways drift across the runway should be allowed to develop—control this with wing-down. This will avoid side-loads on the landing gear at touchdown.

When the wing-down main wheel touches first, there may be a tendency for the airplane to yaw into the wind, but the airplane can easily be kept straight with rudder. The other main wheel will touch down naturally, after which you should lower the nosewheel onto the ground to allow more positive directional control.

Most light aircraft have the nosewheel connected to the rudder to assist in steering on the ground. If the nosewheel touches the ground in the landing while the rudder is deflected, it will not be straight and will cause a shudder—unless you are skillful enough to centralize the rudder pedals just as the nosewheel touches! This is one sign of a sensitive and talented pilot.

Figure 13f-12. Forward view from the cockpit using the wing-down method in a left crosswind

Of course, as soon as the nosewheel is on the ground, you have to move the rudder pedals to keep straight.

In the landing run:
• keep straight with rudder, holding the nosewheel on the ground; and
• keep the wings level with aileron deflection into the wind—full control-wheel deflection into the wind perhaps being required as the airplane slows down.

In the ground roll, keep straight with rudder and wings level with aileron.

Advantages of the Wing-Down Method

Less judgment and timing is required in the actual touchdown using this method, since the airplane is aligned with the runway centerline throughout the flare and touchdown. There is no crab angle to remove, no sideways drift, and the rudder and aileron controls are held in roughly the same position throughout the approach, flare, touchdown and landing roll.

Compared with the crab method, it is of little importance if the airplane touches down slightly earlier or later than expected using the wing-down method, whereas with the crab method good judgment in aligning the airplane just before touchdown is required.

Figure 13f-13. Typical airplane flare-attitude in a wing-down crosswind-landing

Airwork 13f, Part (ii)—Method (b)
The Wing-Down Crosswind Landing

Objective
To land the airplane in a crosswind following a wing-down approach.

1. On Final Approach Aligned with Runway Centerline

- Lower the upwind wing and use rudder to remain aligned with the runway centerline.
- Control airspeed with elevators, flight path with power and the track with wing-down aileron and (opposite) rudder.

2. During the Flare

- Reduce power and raise the nose normally.
- Maintain your track along the runway centerline with wing-down aileron.
- Keep the wheels aligned with opposite rudder.

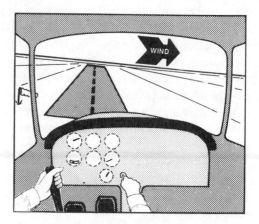

3. The Touchdown

- The touchdown will be on the upwind wheel because of that wing being lower.
- The other main wheel will follow naturally.

The wing-down crosswind landing:
- stop the wind drift with aileron; and
- keep the nose aligned with the runway centerline with rudder.

4. The Landing Run

- Keep straight with rudder.
- Lower the nosewheel to the ground.
- Maintain wings-level with aileron progressively turned into the wind.

Normal traffic pattern

WIND

Introduce wing-down.

Wing-down landing

Keep straight with rudder; keep the wings level with aileron into the wind.

Method (c)—The Combination Method:
A Crab Approach followed by a Wing-Down Landing

A distinct disadvantage of the wing-down technique being used all the way down final is that the controls are *crossed* and the airplane is not coordinated (ball not centered). This is both inefficient and uncomfortable.

A more comfortable approach can be flown if:

- the drift is controlled;
- the extended runway centerline is maintained by crabbing into the wind; and
- the airplane is flown coordinated—ball centered, pilot and passengers comfortable.

Crab into the wind on approach.

An easier crosswind landing can be made if, prior to touchdown, the wing-down method is employed by lowering the upwind wing, simultaneously applying opposite rudder to align the airplane. This aligns the wheels with the track of the airplane along the runway—the amount of wing-down and opposite rudder required being determined by the strength of the crosswind.

Before touchdown, yaw the nose straight with rudder and prevent sideways drift with wing-down.

At just what point you transfer from the crab to the wing-down depends upon your experience and the wind conditions. Initially, it may be better to introduce the wing-down at about 100 feet AGL but, as you become more experienced, this can be delayed until in the flare, below about 20 feet. **In strong and gusty crosswinds,** it is better to introduce the wing-down earlier than in steady or calm conditions.

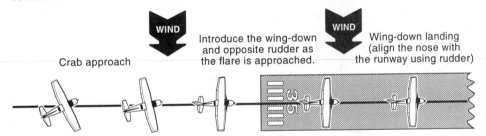

Figure 13f-14. The combination method of crosswind landing

As in every landing, in crosswind landings **you need to flare** to make the transition from the approach attitude to the touchdown attitude. Sometimes in a busy crosswind landing, some pilots tend to delay the flare (or even forget it!), making the chance of a smooth touchdown unlikely.

Remember to flare!

Even in strong and gusty crosswind conditions, you should try to fly the approach speed you have chosen to an accuracy of within 5 KIAS, and to touch down at the specified point, or within 500 feet beyond it—200 feet for a commercial pilot—with no appreciable drift. For a maximum performance landing on a short field, this tolerance is reduced to 200 feet for a private pilot and 100 feet for a commercial pilot. Right from day one, you should try to touch down right at, or only slightly past, the touchdown point that you have selected.

After touchdown, keep aligned with the runway centerline during the ground roll using your feet on the rudder pedals, and keep the wings level using the control column to position the ailerons. As the speed reduces during the landing roll, you may need to progressively increase the aileron deflection into the wind to assist in keeping the wings level. Differential aileron drag will also assist in maintaining directional control.

During the ground run, keep straight with rudder and wings level with aileron.

Because crosswind conditions are often gusty and unpredictable, be prepared for a go-around, even at a late stage, if you feel uncomfortable.

Be prepared for a go-around.

Airwork 13f, Part (ii)—Method (c)
The Combined Crab Approach and Wing-Down Crosswind Landing

Objective

To land the airplane in a crosswind using a crab approach followed by a wing-down landing.

1. On Final Approach

- Adjust the heading to track (crab) down final along the extended runway centerline.
- Keep the wings level, and coordinate with rudder pressure.

2. At or Approaching the Flare

(about 20 feet above the runway)

- Use smooth rudder pressure to align the airplane with the runway centerline—and stay aligned.
- Lower the upwind wing to prevent sideways drift.

3. During the Flare

- Reduce power and raise the nose normally.
- Maintain a track along the centerline with wing-down, and keep the nose aligned with opposite rudder.

4. The Touchdown

- Touch down on the upwind main wheel and allow the other main wheel to follow.
- Maintain directional control with rudder.

5. The Landing Run

- Keep straight with rudder.
- Lower the nosewheel to the runway.
- Keep the wings level with progressive aileron into the wind—full control-wheel movement may eventually be required.

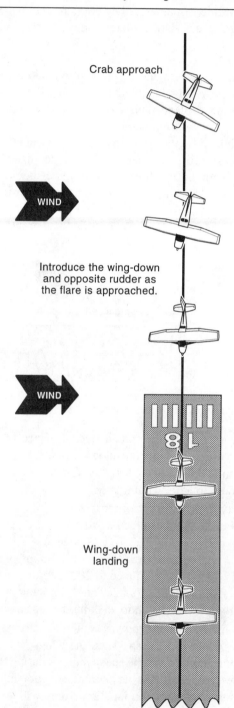

Crab approach

WIND

Introduce the wing-down and opposite rudder as the flare is approached.

WIND

8L

Wing-down landing

✍ Review 13f

Crosswind Operations

1. A 10-knot wind at 90° to the runway direction will cause a crosswind component of ____ knots.
   ➤ 10 knots

2. A 10-knot wind at 60° to the runway direction will cause a crosswind component of ____ knots.
   ➤ 9 knots

3. A 10-knot wind at 45° to the runway direction will cause a crosswind component of ____ knots.
   ➤ 7 knots

4. A 10-knot wind at 30° to the runway direction will cause a crosswind component of ____ knots.
   ➤ 5 knots

5. A 20-knot wind at 45° to the runway direction will cause a crosswind component of ____ knots.
   ➤ 14 knots

6. A 20-knot wind at 60° to the runway direction will cause a crosswind component of ____ knots.
   ➤ 18 knots

7. A 20-knot wind at 30° to the runway direction will cause a crosswind component of ____ knots.
   ➤ 10 knots

8. A 20-knot wind at 90° to the runway direction will cause a crosswind component of ____ knots.
   ➤ 20 knots

9. A crosswind limitation will be found in the Pilot's Operating Handbook, Section ____ on Limitations, whereas a maximum demonstrated crosswind will be found in Section ____ on Normal Operations.
   ➤ Section 1—Limitations, Section 4—Normal Operations

10. The recommended flap setting for takeoff is usually the (smallest/greatest) flap setting, taking into account field length.
    ➤ smallest

11. A crosswind will cause an airplane on the ground to weathercock (into/out of) the wind.
    ➤ into the wind

12. In crosswind conditions, you will keep the airplane aligned with the runway centerline on the ground using your (feet/hands).
    ➤ feet (rudder control)

13. In crosswind conditions on the ground, you will keep the wings level using your (hands/feet).
    ➤ hands (aileron control)

14. At the start of the takeoff ground roll during a crosswind takeoff, you will need (more/less) rudder and aileron deflection than just before liftoff, when the airspeed is higher.
    ➤ more

15. During the takeoff run in strong crosswind conditions, you should (hold the airplane on the ground/lift off early).
    ➤ hold the airplane on the ground

16. In crosswind conditions, you should aim to lift the airplane off the ground (cleanly and positively/slower than normal).
    ➤ cleanly and positively

17. Immediately after liftoff in crosswind conditions, the controls (will/will not) be crossed.
    ➤ will

18. When clear of the ground in a crosswind takeoff, you should (maintain/remove) crossed-controls so that the coordination ball is (centered/out to one side).
    ➤ remove, centered

19. When clear of the ground in a crosswind takeoff, you (should/should not) apply a wind correction angle, so that your flight path is along the extended runway centerline.
    ➤ should

20. In strong and gusty crosswind conditions, the airplane is easier to control on approach with (a small/full) flap setting, because of the (increased/reduced) drag.
    ➤ a small, reduced drag

21. The airplane will respond more quickly to power changes if the wing has a (high/low) flap setting, because of the (increased/reduced) drag.
    ➤ low, reduced

22. Name the three methods of handling a crosswind landing.

   ➤ the crab method; the wing-down method; the combination method (a crab approach followed by a wing-down landing)

23. To counteract the wind drift on long final in crosswind conditions, you should apply a w_____ c_____ angle, also known as a c____ angle.

   ➤ wind correction angle, crab angle

24. A good landing requires a good _____.

   ➤ approach

25. When making a crosswind landing you must still remember to _____.

   ➤ flare

26. When making a crosswind landing you should touch down with the airplane (aligned/not aligned) with the runway centerline.

   ➤ aligned

27. When making a crosswind landing, you should touch down (with/without) sideways drift across the runway.

   ➤ without

28. When using the wing-down method in a crosswind landing, you should lower the (upwind/downwind) wing and keep aligned with the runway centerline using (rudder/aileron/elevator).

   ➤ upwind wing, rudder

29. When using the wing-down method in a crosswind landing, if the crosswind is from the right you should touch down first on the (left/right) main wheel, and if the crosswind is from the left you should touch down first on the (left/right) main wheel.

   ➤ right, left

30. During the landing ground run, you should keep straight with (rudder/aileron/elevator) and keep the wings level with (rudder/aileron/elevator).

   ➤ rudder, aileron

31. Directional control will be easier in the ground roll (before/after) you have lowered the nosewheel onto the ground.

   ➤ after

32. During the landing run in crosswind conditions, you can expect to use (more/less/the same) aileron deflection to keep the wings level as you slow down.

   ➤ more

Maximum Performance Short-Field Operations

13g

Objective

To operate safely and efficiently out of and into a short field.

Considerations

Prior to using any airport or landing area, you must evaluate:
- wind direction;
- the takeoff and landing surface (length and condition); and
- obstructions and other hazards in the takeoff and approach paths.

What is a Short Field?

A short field is one in which the **runway length available** and/or the **obstacle-clearance gradients** are only just sufficient to satisfy takeoff and landing requirements.

Even if a runway is long, obstacles in the approach sector may reduce the distance available for landing, and obstacles in the takeoff sector may reduce the distance available for takeoff.

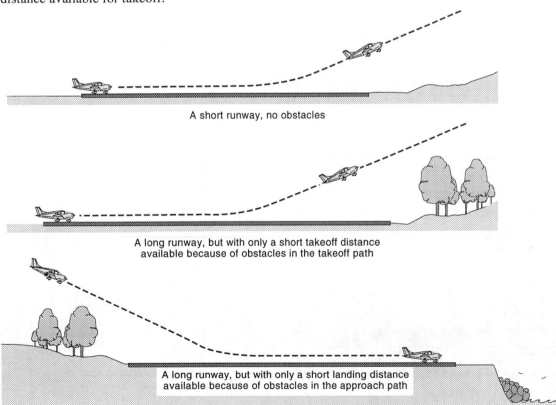

A short runway, no obstacles

A long runway, but with only a short takeoff distance available because of obstacles in the takeoff path

A long runway, but with only a short landing distance available because of obstacles in the approach path

Figure 13g-1. Short fields

Maximum performance is required when taking off or landing on a short field—and this means maximum performance from both the airplane and the pilot. In a two-pilot cockpit, you should brief the other pilot on your intentions.

Short fields require maximum performance from the pilot to achieve maximum performance from the airplane.

For takeoff, "maximum performance" means using the recommended short-field flap settings and maximum power to minimize your ground roll. For a climb-out over obstacles, you must hold the pitch attitude to achieve the steepest climb path:

- obstacle-clearance airspeed for that flap setting; or
- best-angle climb airspeed for zero flaps (V_X).

A typical situation could be: recommended 10° flaps for takeoff, with the liftoff at 50 KIAS, achieve obstacle-clearance airspeed 54 KIAS by 50 feet above the runway level, and maintain this speed until clear of obstacles. If it was a zero-flap takeoff, the steepest climb to clear obstacles is achieved at V_X, which is 60 KIAS. Because these speeds are quite near the stalling speed (perhaps only 20% greater), there is not much tolerance allowed. You should not fly slower than these speeds, because you risk a stall, and you should not fly faster than 5 KIAS above them as this will flatten the climb-out path; the tolerance is plus 5/minus 0 KIAS.

When clear of obstacles, you can lower the nose and accelerate to the best rate-of-climb airspeed, V_Y, which could be 76 KIAS. If you used flaps for the takeoff, you will raise them now. Because V_Y is well away from the stall, the tolerances are a little greater, plus or minus 5 KIAS.

For landing, *maximum performance* means a steep approach if there are obstacles to be cleared in the approach path, followed by an immediate touchdown at minimum speed, and braking to minimize the after-landing ground roll. This short-field performance can best be achieved using a full-flaps power-on approach.

Performance Charts

The **Takeoff and Landing Performance charts** for your airplane should be consulted to ensure that a short field in a confined area is indeed adequate for the planned operations under the existing conditions. **An inspection** on foot of the proposed takeoff and landing surface and the surrounding area may be necessary. During the inspection, remember that the takeoff is not complete until all obstacles are cleared, so not only the takeoff surface but also the surrounding area need to be considered.

Refer to the appropriate Performance Charts for your airplane.

CONDITIONS:
Flaps 10°
Full Throttle Prior to Brake Release
Paved, Level, Dry Runway
Zero Wind

TAKEOFF DISTANCE

[SHORT FIELD]

SAMPLE ONLY
not to be used
in conjunction
with flight operations
or flight planning

NOTES:
1. Short field technique as specified in Section 4.
2. Prior to takeoff from fields above 3000 feet elevation, the mixture should be leaned to give maximum RPM in a full throttle, static runup.
3. Decrease distances 10% for each 9 knots headwind. For operation with tailwinds up to 10 knots, increase distances by 10% for each 2 knots.
4. For operation on a dry, grass runway, increase distances by 15% of the "ground roll" figure.

WEIGHT LBS	TAKEOFF SPEED KIAS		PRESS ALT FT	0°C		10°C		20°C		30°C		40°C	
	LIFT OFF	AT 50 FT		GRND ROLL	TOTAL TO CLEAR 50 FT OBS	GRND ROLL	TOTAL TO CLEAR 50 FT OBS	GRND ROLL	TOTAL TO CLEAR 50 FT OBS	GRND ROLL	TOTAL TO CLEAR 50 FT OBS	GRND ROLL	TOTAL TO CLEAR 50 FT OBS
1670	50	54	S.L.	640	1190	695	1290	755	1390	810	1495	875	1605
			1000	705	1310	765	1420	825	1530	890	1645	960	1770
			2000	775	1445	840	1565	910	1690	980	1820	1055	1960

Figure 13g-2. Consult the Performance charts.

Flying the Maneuver

The Short-Field Takeoff

There are generally two considerations in the short-field takeoff:

1. Use of only a short ground run.
2. Avoidance of obstacles in the takeoff and climb-out flight path.

A short-field takeoff is a normal takeoff, except that you should pay special attention to the following points to achieve the shortest ground run and steepest climb-out.

- Check the performance charts, if necessary.
- Take off as much upwind as possible.

Take advantage of a headwind.

- Use the recommended best flap setting for takeoff.
- Adjust the mixture control as recommended in the Pilot's Operating Handbook for the existing condition—usually FULL RICH, except when at airport elevations above 3,000 feet, when some leaning to achieve maximum rpm might be recommended.
- Position the airplane at the end of the runway, aligned with the runway centerline to ensure that you have maximum runway available.

Start the takeoff roll right at the start of the runway.

- Apply maximum power smoothly and positively, with the toe brakes ON to stop the airplane moving forward, and holding the control column back to avoid damage to the propeller; check the engine instruments to ensure that maximum power is being delivered.
- Release the brakes as full power is reached—although, if loose stones could damage the propeller, a rolling start is preferred.
- Use your feet positively to track down the runway centerline during the takeoff ground roll, keeping the wings level with the ailerons.
- Lift off at the minimum recommended flying speed with elevator.
- Set the nose attitude for the airspeed that will give you the steepest climb over any obstacles—*with flaps:* use the obstacle-clearance airspeed; *without flaps:* use the best angle-of-climb airspeed, V_X; tolerance is plus 5/minus 0 KIAS.

Climb out well clear of obstacles.

- At a safe altitude, and when clear of obstacles, retract the flaps, and lower the nose to the pitch attitude required for the best rate-of-climb airspeed, V_Y; tolerance: plus or minus 5 KIAS.
- Remain aligned with the extended runway centerline in the climb-out, unless other obstacles preclude this.
- Finally, complete the After-Takeoff checklist, when convenient.

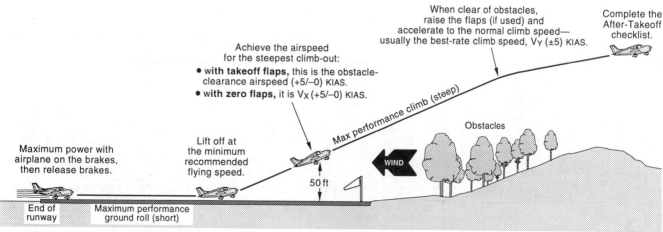

Figure 13g-3. The maximum performance short-field takeoff

The Short-Field Landing

The short-field landing is useful when the chosen landing area:
- has marginal landing distance available; or
- has a surface of which the pilot is unsure.

Land as much upwind as possible for a steeper approach and a shorter landing run. Position the airplane as for a normal approach—the preferred technique being a power-on approach at a low speed with an aiming point as close to the threshold as practicable. The airplane should touch down without much float as soon as the throttle is closed.

Land as much upwind as possible.

Full flaps is the preferred configuration if the wind conditions are suitable, since this allows a lower approach speed and there will be less float prior to touchdown due to the extra drag. A shorter landing distance will result. In gusty conditions, you might add a few knots as an aid to flying a stabilized approach, a typical gust correction being one-half of the gust value—for instance, with gusts of 10 knots, add 5 KIAS. The recommended approach speed for a short-field landing may be less than for the normal approach—check your Pilot's Operating Handbook. Fly a stabilized approach along the extended runway centerline at the selected airspeed (tolerance plus or minus 5 KIAS), down to the selected aiming point.

Fly as slow an approach speed as is safe.

If you are on the *back side of the power curve* (also known as the *back side of the drag curve*), then frequent and positive adjustments to power and attitude will be required to maintain the desired flight path and airspeed. Correct the approach path as early as possible to arrive at the flare with power on.

Use power to control the flight path and elevator to maintain airspeed.

Obstacles in the approach path may require use of an aiming point further into the short field, or an approach a little steeper than usual. Having cleared the obstacles, do not reduce power unduly, otherwise a high sink rate and a heavy touchdown may result—since at a low speed the airplane has less-effective controls and a reduced flaring capability.

Fly the approach so as to clear all obstacles.

Given a choice, you should select an approach path that does not have obstacles, in preference to one with significant obstacles. This shows good airmanship.

If there are no obstacles in the approach path, then slightly undershooting on the approach may be considered, with power being used to ensure that you clear the airport boundary safely.

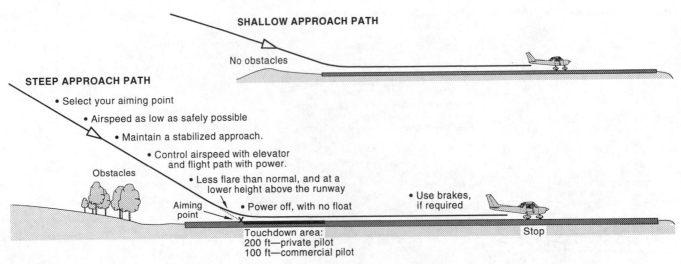

Figure 13g-4. Ensure that you clear all obstacles in the approach path.

Aim to cross the airfield boundary with power on at the selected speed, and at the minimum altitude consistent with adequate obstacle clearance. If airspeed is too high in the landing, the float may be significant, and unnecessary runway distance wasted.

Touch down with no sideways drift and with the longitudinal axis of the airplane aligned with the runway centerline. Whereas the tolerance for touch-down on a long runway is in the area from the aiming point to 500 feet beyond it, for the maximum performance landing it is:

- not before the specified aiming point; and
- at or within 200 feet beyond the specified point, for private pilots; within 100 feet beyond the specified point, for commercial pilots.

Since the nose will be higher than in a normal landing—because of the lower speed and higher power—hardly any flare is needed. The flare should be started closer to the ground than normal. Some power should be left on at the commencement of the flare if the speed is low—the airplane will touch down as soon as the throttle is closed.

Do not hold the airplane off for a prolonged period; then, after touchdown, use brakes as required.

- **If a high sink rate develops,** add power to prevent a heavy landing. Power may be required all the way to the ground—if so, close the throttle as soon as the wheels touch.

- **If an especially short landing run is required,** brakes may be used when all the wheels are firmly on the ground. Apply brakes smoothly and positively to stop in the shortest distance consistent with safety. Maintain positive directional control along the centerline in the after-landing ground roll. Early in the landing run, the wings will still be producing some lift and so all of the weight will not be on the wheels. Excessive braking at this time may cause skidding.

When clear of the runway, complete the **After-Landing checklist.**

Note: If a crosswind exists, apply crosswind, as well as short-field, techniques.

✍️ Review 13g

1. A maximum performance takeoff may be required if the available runway distance is _____ and/or if there are significant _____ in the takeoff or landing paths.

   ➤ short, obstacles

2. For a maximum performance takeoff from a short field with obstacles in the climb-out path, you should use the ____ length of the runway, _____ power with a (rolling start/standing start), and climb away at the airspeed that provides the (steepest climb gradient/fastest rate of climb in fpm).

   ➤ full, maximum, standing start, steepest climb gradient

3. For a takeoff with flaps, the steepest climb gradient can be achieved at (the published obstacle-clearance speed for that flap setting/V_X/V_Y), and the accuracy required is plus ____ and minus ____ KIAS.

   ➤ the published obstacle-clearance speed for that flap setting, plus 5/minus 0 KIAS

4. V_X is defined as the best (angle/rate) of climb airspeed, and it is used to achieve the steepest climb gradient when (some/zero) flaps are used on the takeoff. The required accuracy is plus ____ and minus ____ KIAS. If the published V_X is 56 KIAS, the required accuracy is between a minimum of ____ KIAS and a maximum of ____ KIAS.

   ➤ angle, zero, plus 5 and minus 0 KIAS, 56 to 61 KIAS

5. V_Y is defined as the best (angle/rate) of climb airspeed, and it is used to achieve the (steepest/quickest) climb to altitude. The nose attitude for V_Y is (higher/lower) than for V_X, because the airspeed is (faster/slower). The required accuracy is plus or minus ____ KIAS. If the published V_Y is 70 KIAS, the required accuracy is to fly between a minimum of ____ KIAS and a maximum of ____ KIAS.

   ➤ rate, quickest, lower, faster, plus or minus 5 KIAS, 65 to 75 KIAS

6. If you lost power at 200 feet after a maximum performance takeoff, what would your initial actions be?

   ➤ adopt the gliding attitude to maintain flying speed and try to land approximately straight ahead

Maximum Performance Short-Field Operations

7. A maximum performance landing is required if the available runway distance is _____ and/or if there are significant _____ in the approach path.

   ➤ short, obstacles

8. If the landing distance available is short because of obstacles in the approach sector, you would plan to fly a (steep/normal/shallow) approach, which is best achieved with (full/takeoff/zero) flaps and a (high/low) airspeed.

   ➤ steep, full, low

9. If the landing distance is short, and there are no obstacles in the approach sector, there (is/is not) a need to fly a steep approach.

   ➤ is not

10. For a maximum performance landing, the airspeed should be (high/low), the flare and float should be (short/prolonged), and brakes (should/should not) be used.

   ➤ low, short, should

11. On a maximum performance approach, the recommended airspeed should be maintained to an accuracy of plus or minus ____ KIAS, with the flight path and airspeed positively controlled using p_____ and a _____.

   ➤ plus or minus 5 KIAS, power and attitude

12. For a maximum performance landing, the touchdown (may/must not) be before the aiming point you have specified during the approach. It may be up to ____ feet beyond the specified point.

   ➤ must not, 200 feet (private pilots) and 100 feet (commercial pilots)

13. You have more control over the approach and the touchdown point if you fly a (power-on/power-off) approach.

   ➤ power-on

14. Reducing power in the flare, which is (higher/lower) than for a normal approach, will (hasten/delay) the touchdown.

   ➤ lower, hasten

Soft-Field Operations

Objective

To operate safely and efficiently from a soft field.

Considerations

As with any airport, before using a soft field you must evaluate:
- the wind direction;
- the takeoff and landing surface (condition and length); and
- obstructions or other hazards in the takeoff and approach paths.

What is a Soft Field?

A soft field could be an area which has a soft surface such as sand or snow, a wet grassy surface or a rough surface. A soft field may be quite long and without obstacle-clearance problems in the climb-out or approach paths. It may also be short, which means the short-field consideration of obstacle clearance also becomes important. For this exercise, however, we assume a long takeoff surface and no obstacle-clearance problems.

When operating from a soft surface, you want the wings to support the weight for as long as possible, keeping the airplane's weight off the wheels since the wheels may have a tendency to dig in. Your aim should be to achieve the shortest ground run possible on a soft surface, both in the takeoff and the landing. Only use a soft field if you are totally satisfied that a safe takeoff and/or landing can be made.

Soft surfaces create extra frictional drag and stress on the wheels, degrading the acceleration in the takeoff run, and increasing the deceleration in the landing run. Takeoffs will require more distance than usual, and landings less. Consult the Performance charts for the exact requirements for your airplane.

Flying the Maneuver

Planning the Takeoff

The main concern in a soft-field takeoff is to transfer the weight from the wheels to the wings as soon as possible, and to achieve a short ground run. Consequently the **optimum flap setting** and **maximum power** should be used.

At high-altitude airports, especially in hot conditions, adjust the mixture control as recommended by the manufacturer.

Taxiing Out

Try to avoid stopping on the soft surface; complete your engine run-up and Before-Takeoff checklist before taxiing, as the wheels may tend to sink in on the soft surface.

Keep rolling on a soft surface.

Taxi onto the takeoff surface at a speed consistent with safety and, when aligned with the takeoff path, smoothly apply full power.

The Soft-Field Takeoff

While still rolling, smoothly apply maximum power and check the engine instruments to ensure that maximum power is being delivered.

Transfer the weight from the wheels to the wings early in the takeoff run.

During the takeoff ground run, **keep the weight off the nosewheel** with the control column held back. Maintain positive directional control along the center of the takeoff path using your feet. Lift the airplane off the ground as soon as possible—at a lower speed than in a normal takeoff—and accelerate to the appropriate climb speed close to the surface and in ground effect. Because the airplane can fly in ground effect at a lower speed than when it is well away from the ground, do not climb more than about 10 feet above the ground until a safe flying speed is attained, at which time a normal climb-out can proceed.

Accelerate in ground effect.

If flaps were used for takeoff, hold the recommended obstacle-clearance airspeed until all obstacles have been cleared. If no flaps were used, hold V_X, the best-angle climb airspeed, until all obstacles are cleared. Because of the proximity of these low speeds to the stall, do not fly any slower—the speed tolerance is plus 5/minus 0 KIAS.

When any obstacles have been cleared, the airplane can be accelerated and the flaps raised at a safe altitude. The normal climb speed will be V_Y, the best-rate climb airspeed, with a tolerance of plus or minus 5 KIAS.

Apply elevator back pressure to raise the nosewheel off the ground as soon as possible.

Lift off at an early stage.

Accelerate in ground effect.

Initiate a climb-out.

Figure 13h-1. The soft-field takeoff

Apply crosswind techniques if necessary.

Maintain a straight track along the extended takeoff path, until a turn is necessary, by using a reference point ahead, or by an occasional quick glance over your shoulder at the takeoff area.

Complete the After-Takeoff checklist.

The Soft-Field Landing

Since the tendency on a soft field is for the nosewheel (and, to a lesser extent, the main wheels) to dig in, the aim should be to:
• land as slowly as possible; with
• the nose held up as long as possible during the landing roll.

The Approach

Extending full flaps reduces the stall speed, so the touchdown can be made at a very low speed. If field length is not a problem, a normal approach can be flown, with a slightly modified flare at the selected aiming point. Fly a stabilized approach along the extended landing path at the recommended airspeed right through to the touchdown zone (tolerance plus or minus 5 KIAS). Promptly correct any deviations from the desired flight path and airspeed.

Approach with full flaps, if conditions permit.

Figure 13h-2. The soft-field landing

Touchdown

Some power can be left on in the flare, as the nose is raised higher than normal in a prolonged float. Try to touch down smoothly, with a minimum descent rate, with the airspeed as slow as possible, with no drift and the wheels aligned with the landing direction. The higher the nose attitude and the lower the speed on touchdown, the better.

Touch down gently as slowly as possible.

After the main wheels touch, hold back-elevator to keep the nosewheel off the soft surface for as long as possible, and then gently lower it. Use rudder to achieve and maintain good directional control in the ground run.

Hold the nosewheel off and avoid using the brakes.

Brakes are usually not required in soft-field landings, because the soft surface will tend to slow the airplane down. Using the brakes will put additional stress on the landing gear, and may cause the nosewheel to dig in.

On occasions, power may be required toward the end of the landing run on a soft surface to keep the airplane moving, so that you can taxi to the parking area and not get stuck in the soft surface.

Keep rolling on a soft surface.

Parking

If possible, park the airplane on a hard surface to make it easier to taxi away on the next flight.

Complete the normal Shutdown checklist and secure the airplane.

Ensure that you park on a hard surface.

✍ Review 13h

1. What three items regarding a runway would you evaluate before using it?

   ➤ the wind direction;
   takeoff and landing surface (condition and length);
   obstructions or other hazards in the takeoff and approach paths

2. The risk when operating on a soft surface is that the wheels might (skid/dig in).

   ➤ dig in

3. The ground run during takeoff will be shorter if you use (takeoff flaps/zero flaps).

   ➤ takeoff flaps

4. To reduce the risk of the wheels digging in at the start of the takeoff run on a soft field, you should taxi out and align the airplane and (keep rolling/stop).

   ➤ keep rolling

5. To reduce the risk of the wheels digging in during the takeoff run on a soft-field, you should keep the weight (off/on) the nosewheel by holding the control column (back/forward).

   ➤ off, back

6. You should lift off at a slightly (faster/slower) speed than normal, and (accelerate/not accelerate) a few feet above the soft surface in ground effect.

   ➤ slower, accelerate

7. To clear obstacles in the takeoff path, if flaps are used you should initially climb at the _____ - _____ airspeed, or, if the takeoff is clean, at the best angle-of-climb airspeed, ____ . The tolerance for both these speeds is plus ____ and minus ____ KIAS.

   ➤ obstacle-clearance airspeed, V_X, plus 5/minus 0 KIAS

Soft-Field Operations

8. When clear of obstacles you can raise the flaps at a safe altitude and accelerate to the best rate-of-climb airspeed, ____ , which has a tolerance of plus or minus ____ KIAS.

   ➤ V_Y, plus or minus 5 KIAS

9. When settled in the climb, you should complete the _____ checklist.

   ➤ After-Takeoff

10. When landing on a soft field, you should try to land as (fast/slowly) as possible, with the nose held (down/up) to reduce the risk of the wheels digging in.

    ➤ slowly, up

11. To achieve the slowest touchdown speed on a soft field, you should plan on landing (downwind/upwind) with (zero/full) flaps.

    ➤ upwind, full

12. You should fly your selected approach speed to an accuracy of plus or minus ____ KIAS.

    ➤ plus or minus 5 KIAS

13. At the end of the landing roll on a soft surface you should (stop/taxi clear).

    ➤ taxi clear

14. You will need (more/less) power to taxi on a soft surface than on a hard surface.

    ➤ more

15. It is better to park the airplane on a (soft/hard) surface.

    ➤ hard

First Solo 14

Objective

To fly solo and be the pilot-in-command of an airplane for the first time.

Flying the Maneuver

When your instructor steps out of the airplane and leaves you to your first solo flight you are being paid a big compliment. You may feel a little apprehensive, but remember that he or she is trained to judge the right moment to send you solo. Your flight instructor will have a better appreciation of your flying ability than anyone (including you).

Fly your first solo traffic pattern in the same manner as you flew those patterns before your instructor stepped out. The usual standards apply to your takeoff, pattern and landing. Maintain a good lookout, fly a neat traffic pattern, establish a stabilized approach, and carry out your normal landing.

Be prepared for better airplane performance because of the lighter weight without an instructor on board. If at any stage you feel uncomfortable, go around.

If an emergency, such as engine failure, occurs—and this is an extremely unlikely event—carry out the appropriate emergency procedure. Your flight instructor considers you competent to fly a traffic pattern with a normal takeoff and landing, and also considers you competent to handle an emergency.

One takeoff, traffic pattern and landing will admit you to the **family of pilots!**

First solo is a great experience!

Post-Solo Flying

In the lessons that follow your first solo, you will further refine and consolidate your basic flying skills. You will fly solo, but you will also continue with dual flights. In the solo periods you will develop the skills of a captain—making your own decisions and acting upon them.

Your initial solo flights will be in the traffic pattern area practicing takeoffs and landings, but quite soon you will be proceeding solo to the local training area to practice other maneuvers.

Pre-Solo Written Exam

Before going solo, you must have passed a written examination administered and graded by the flight instructor who endorses your pilot certificate for solo flight. The written examination will include questions on the applicable Federal Aviation Regulations (FARs), and the flight characteristics and operational limits of your airplane.

By answering the review questions of each exercise during your training, and by gradually completing the Specific Airplane Type questions in the Appendix, you will be well prepared for the questions on the flight characteristics and operational limits of your airplane.

These next review questions prepare you for the FAR questions. They direct you into your current copy of the FARs to indicate the level of knowledge you require prior to going solo. Since FAR numbering changes from time to time, the FAR part has been identified—for example, FAR Part 91 and FAR Part 61—but not the individual FAR, which you can easily find using the Table of Contents page in your book of FARs.

Review 14

Refer to your personal copy of the FARs and AIM when completing these questions. Use the table of contents or the index to find each particular topic covered.

Federal Aviation Regulations—Part 91: General Operating and Flight Rules

Responsibility and Authority of Pilot-in-Command

1. (The pilot-in-command/Air Traffic Control) is directly responsible for, and is the final authority as to, the operation of that aircraft.

    ➤ the pilot-in-command

2. In an in-flight emergency requiring emergency action, the pilot-in-command:
    *   may deviate from any rule of this part—FAR Part 91—to the extent required to meet that emergency.
    *   must not deviate from any rule of this part—FAR Part 91.
    *   may deviate from any rule of this part—FAR Part 91—but only after receiving prior permission of ATC.

    ➤ may deviate from any rule of this part—FAR Part 91—to the extent required to meet that emergency

3. Each pilot-in-command who deviates from any rule of this part—FAR Part 91—in an in-flight emergency shall send a written report of that deviation to the administrator (immediately/within 24 hours/upon the request of the administrator).

    ➤ upon the request of the administrator

Civil Aircraft Airworthiness

1. The (mechanic/pilot-in-command/owner and operator) is responsible for determining whether the aircraft is in a condition for safe flight.

    ➤ the pilot-in-command

2. The pilot-in-command (shall/need not) discontinue the flight when unairworthy mechanical, electrical, or structural conditions occur.

    ➤ shall

First Solo

Preflight Action

1. Each pilot-in-command, before beginning a flight, (shall/need not) become familiar with all available information concerning that flight.

    ➤ shall

Use of Safety Belts

1. The pilot-in-command must ensure that all persons on board have been notified to fasten their safety belt and shoulder harness, if installed, (at all times in flight/before takeoff or landing).

    ➤ before takeoff or landing

Operating Near Other Aircraft

1. No person may operate an aircraft so close to another aircraft as to create a collision hazard. (True/False)

    ➤ True

Right-of-Way Rules

1. An airplane at 2 o'clock—that is, out to your right—at the same altitude is converging on your flight path. It (has/does not have) right-of-way.

    ➤ has

2. Each pilot (has/does not have) the responsibility to see and avoid other aircraft, irrespective of who has right-of-way.

    ➤ has

3. Which aircraft has right-of-way: (glider/balloon/ an aircraft in distress/a landing aircraft)?

    ➤ an aircraft in distress

4. Which aircraft has right-of-way: (glider/balloon/ a landing aircraft)?

    ➤ balloon

5. Which aircraft has right-of-way: (a landing aircraft/an aircraft about to taxi onto the runway for takeoff)?

    ➤ a landing aircraft

6. When two aircraft are approaching to land, the one at the (higher/lower) altitude has right-of-way. It (may/shall not) take advantage of this rule to cut in front of another or overtake it.

    ➤ lower, shall not

Minimum Safe Altitudes—General

1. Except when necessary for takeoff or landing, no person may operate an aircraft below which of the following altitudes:
(3,000 feet AGL/1,000 feet AGL/an altitude allowing, if a power unit fails, an emergency landing without undue hazard to persons or property on the surface)?

    ≫ an altitude allowing, if a power unit fails, an emergency landing without undue hazard to persons or property on the surface

2. Except when necessary for takeoff or landing, no person may operate an aircraft over congested areas below ____ feet above the highest obstacle within a horizontal radius of ____ feet of the aircraft.

    ≫ 1,000 feet, 2,000 feet

3. Except when necessary for takeoff or landing, no person may operate an aircraft below ____ feet AGL over a non-congested area, except over open water or sparsely populated areas, in which case the aircraft may not be operated closer than ____ feet to any person, vessel, vehicle or structure.

    ≫ 500 feet AGL, 500 feet

Altimeter Settings

1. For operations at an airport, the pressure window of the altimeter should be set to (the current altimeter setting for that airport/29.92).

    ≫ the current altimeter setting for that airport

2. If you are about to take off at an airport where there is no reported altimeter setting, you may (not take off/set the airport elevation in the altimeter).

    ≫ set the airport elevation in the altimeter

Operation at Airports with Operating Control Towers

1. Two-way radio communications (are/are not) required at airports with operating control towers.

    ≫ are

2. Clearances are required from ATC for you to (taxi/take off and land/taxi, take off and land) at an airport with an operating control tower.

    ≫ taxi, take off and land

3. When approaching to land at an airport with an operating control tower, you (should/need not) remain at or above the glide slope of a visual approach slope indicator (VASI) until a lower altitude is necessary for a safe landing.

    ≫ should

Compliance with Clearances and Instructions

1. You should follow any ATC clearance or instruction (at all times/at all times, except in an emergency when you, as pilot-in-command, think an alternative course of action is necessary).

    ≫ at all times, except in an emergency when you, as pilot-in-command, think an alternative course of action is necessary

2. If you deviate from an ATC clearance in an emergency you should advise ATC of that deviation (as soon as possible, for instance by radio/only after you have landed).

    ≫ as soon as possible, for instance by radio

3. If you do not deviate from the FARs, but are given priority by ATC in an emergency, you shall submit a report of that emergency to the manager of that ATC facility (immediately/after landing/within 48 hours/within 48 hours if requested by ATC).

    ≫ within 48 hours if requested by ATC

ATC Light Signals

1. Following a radio failure in flight at a tower-controlled airport, the tower directs the following light signals toward you. What do they mean?
Steady red, followed by *flashing green*, followed by *steady green* when you are on final, and, on short final, a *flashing red* (as another aircraft, unauthorized, taxis onto the runway).

    ≫ *steady red*—give way to other aircraft and continue circling,
    flashing green—return for a landing,
    steady green—cleared to land,
    flashing red—airport unsafe, do not land

Operating on or in the Vicinity of an Airport—General Rules

1. When approaching to land at an airport without an operating control tower, all turns should be made to the (left/right) unless the airport displays approved markings indicating otherwise.

    ≫ left

2. When departing from an airport without an operating control tower, you (must/need not) comply with any traffic pattern established for that airport.

➤ must

Basic VFR Weather Minimums

1. The basic VFR weather minimums inside controlled airspace (Classes C, D and E) by day are: flight visibility ____ statute miles, ____ feet below clouds, ____ feet above clouds, ____ feet horizontally from clouds.

➤ three statute miles, 500 feet, 1,000 feet, 2,000 feet

2. The basic VFR weather minimums for operating an aircraft within a control zone are visibility ____ statute miles and cloud ceiling ____ feet (AGL/MSL).

➤ three statute miles, 1,000 feet AGL

Federal Aviation Regulations—Part 61: Certification—Pilots and Flight Instructors

Requirement for Certificates, Ratings & Authorizations

1. As pilot-in-command, *which you are when you fly solo,* you (are/are not) required to have your pilot certificate and medical certificate in your personal possession.

➤ are

Duration of Medical Certificate

1. A third class medical certificate, which is what a student pilot requires, expires at the end of the ____ month after the month of the date of examination shown on the certificate. For instance, if the examination was on October 12, 1993, the certificate would expire on which date?

➤ 24th, October 31 1995

Solo Flight Requirements for Student Pilots

1. Before going solo, you (must/need not) have passed a written examination administered and graded by the flight instructor who endorses your pilot certificate for solo flight. The written examination (will/will not) include questions on the applicable FARs and the flight characteristics and operational limits of your airplane.

➤ must, will

2. Must you have received instruction in emergency procedures and equipment malfunctions prior to going solo?

➤ yes

3. To fly solo, your logbook must have been endorsed for solo flight in that specific make and model of aircraft by an authorized flight instructor within the ____ days prior to the solo flight.

➤ 90 days

General Limitations

1. A student pilot (may/may not) act as pilot-in-command of an aircraft that is carrying a passenger.

➤ may not

2. A student pilot may not act as pilot-in-command of an aircraft with a flight or surface visibility of less than ____ statute miles during daylight hours.

➤ three statute miles

3. A student pilot (may/may not) act as pilot-in-command of an aircraft when the flight cannot be made with visual reference to the surface.

➤ may not

Operations at Airports Located in Class B Airspace (formerly Terminal Control Area)

1. A student pilot (requires/does not require) special instruction and a logbook endorsement before going solo at a specific airport in Class B airspace.

➤ requires

Sharpening Your Phase Three
Flying Skills

Phase Three Completion Standards

In Phase Three, you will be consolidating what you have learned in Phases One and Two, and will be expanding and refining your flying skills with advanced maneuvers, including:

Phase Three expands and refines your flying skills with advanced maneuvers.

- Maximum performance maneuvers:
    Steep turns, and recovery from potentially hazardous attitudes.
    (*For commercial pilots:* chandelles and lazy eights).

- Flight by reference to ground objects:
    Low-level flying.
    Rectangular patterns.
    Turns around a point.
    S-turns across a road.
    (*For commercial pilots:* steep spirals, eights around pylons, and eights-on-pylons.)

- Forced landings:
    Without power.
    With power
    Ditching (theory only).

Steep Constant-Altitude Turns 15a

Objective

To perform a steep turn, using power, at a constant altitude and airspeed.

Note: This maneuver is also called a *Steep Power Turn.*

Considerations

A steep turn is a turn in which the bank angle exceeds 45°. It is a high-performance maneuver which requires good coordination and positive control.

Increased Lift

In straight-and-level flight, the lift produced by the wings acts directly upward and balances the weight of the airplane. In turns, however, the lift force is tilted to provide a horizontal component (known as the *centripetal force)* to pull the airplane into the turn.

A steep turn requires increased lift, and this requires back pressure on the control column.

To retain a vertical component equal to the weight in order not to lose altitude, the size of the lift force generated by the wings must be increased. In a 60° banked turn, for instance, the lift produced by the wings must be **double** the weight of the airplane if altitude is to be maintained.

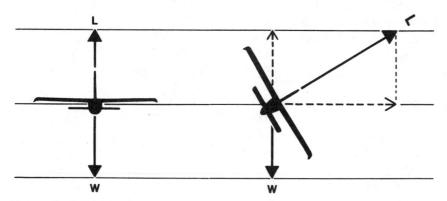

Figure 15a-1. A steep constant-altitude turn requires increased lift.

The increased lift **in a turn** is generated by back pressure on the control column, which increases the angle-of-attack. The back pressure required to maintain altitude is quite significant in a steep turn.

Increased lift in a turn is generated by an increased angle-of-attack.

Increased Load Factor

The increased g-loading that you feel during a steep turn is simply a consequence of the increased load factor (which is the ratio *lift/weight*). The normal load factor is one (1), when the airplane is either stationary on the ground or in steady straight-and-level flight. You experience this as 1g, or your normal weight.

In a 60° banked turn, the load factor is 2, and you will feel *twice* your normal weight because the lift generated by the wings is now double the airplane's weight. The human body soon becomes accustomed to these g-forces.

The need for an increased g-loading to maintain altitude as the bank angle increases is shown in figure 15a-2. The need for increased lift is proportional to this g-loading, so do not be surprised with how much **back pressure** is required to hold the altitude constant in a steep power turn.

Practice steep turns at speeds less than V_A—the airplane's design maneuvering airspeed specified in the Pilot's Operating Handbook—to protect it from overstressing if an excessively high g-loading is pulled.

Remember: The steeper the bank angle, the greater the back pressure required to maintain altitude.

The load factor increases significantly in a steep turn.

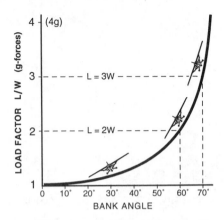

Figure 15a-2. Load Factor versus Bank Angle

Increased Stall Speed

The steeper the turn, the greater the angle-of-attack required to generate sufficient lift and, consequently, the stalling angle-of-attack will be reached at a higher airspeed than when the wings are level. In a 60° banked turn, for example, the stalling speed is some 40% greater—an airplane which stalls at 62 KIAS straight-and-level will stall at 87 KIAS when pulling 2g.

Steep turns can put you at critically slow airspeeds unexpectedly if you are not careful—for instance, you can fly the above airplane comfortably at 75 KIAS straight-and-level, but if you put it into a 60° banked turn, it will stall! An airspeed of 75 KIAS is not critically slow when flying straight-and-level, but it is in a steep bank.

Feeling a g-force is a signal that the airplane structure is under additional stress and that stalling speed has increased. At any hint of stalling in a steep turn, some of the back pressure on the control column should be released. This will reduce the angle-of-attack and move the wings away from the stalling angle. Reducing the bank angle or adding power (if there is any in reserve) will also assist in avoiding a stall in this situation.

The greater the load factor, the higher the stall speed.

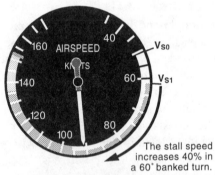

Maintain airspeed with added power.

Figure 15a-3. Be alert to the stall-speed increase in a steep turn.

Increased Drag

The greater angle-of-attack used to generate the increased lift required in a steep turn also creates additional induced drag. This must be balanced by **increased thrust** if the airplane is to maintain speed. Because there will be a significant power increase required to hold airspeed in a steep level turn, this maneuver is also known as a *steep power turn*.

Whereas it was acceptable to lose a few knots in medium turns, it is important to maintain airspeed in steep turns because of the higher stall speed. As well as coordinating the use of ailerons, rudder and elevator (as in medium turns), power now becomes an added ingredient because the **maximum achievable bank angle** in a steady steep turn is determined by the amount of power available.

Drag increases in steep turns, and so additional thrust is required to maintain speed.

Overbanking Tendency

In a steep turn the outer wing will be traveling faster through the air than the inner wing, and so will create slightly more lift. This will tend to increase the bank angle unless you "hold off bank" with the ailerons—which you will do naturally as you maintain the target bank angle.

Flying the Maneuver

Practice this maneuver at 1,500 feet AGL or higher, and use speeds less than the maneuvering speed, V_A, to avoid any risk of overstressing the airframe.

The g-forces in a 45° steep power turn are nowhere near as great as in a 60° banked turn. For this reason, you may find it easier to practice steep turns at a 45° bank angle initially, progressing to 60° bank angle turns later on in your training if your flight instructor really wants to test you.

You should be aiming to maintain the bank angle to within 5° of the target bank angle, which is 45° for a private pilot, and 50° for a commerical pilot.

Prior to practicing steep turns, your flight instructor may require you to carry out the pre-aerobatic HASELL check (as detailed in Exercise 10a).

Rolling into the Steep Turn

Trim the airplane for straight-and-level flight at the desired airspeed and altitude, and be comfortable before you roll into the steep power turn.

Be on-speed, on-altitude, and in-trim before rolling into a steep turn.

Clear the area and **look out** for other airplanes, and select a reference point on the horizon for the roll-out. Normally practice 360° steep power turns (once around), or 720° steep power turns (twice around).

Roll into the turn as you would into a normal medium turn except that as the bank angle increases through 30°:
- smoothly add power;
- progressively increase the back pressure on the control column, coordinating with rudder; and
- adjust the bank angle and back pressure to place the nose in the correct position relative to the horizon.

Do not apply too much back pressure entering the turn or the airplane will climb—just gradually increase it as you steepen the bank. The back pressure required in a steep turn will probably be much greater than you had anticipated! Do not trim, as the turn is only a transient maneuver.

Maintaining the Steep Turn

The secret of flying an accurate steep level turn is to hold the nose in the correct position relative to the horizon (even if it takes a lot of back pressure), ensuring the airspeed is maintained by adding sufficient power. Hold the chosen bank angle as accurately as possible with aileron control—there may be a tendency for the airplane to **overbank** from the higher speed of the outer wing.

Add power to maintain airspeed.

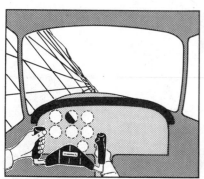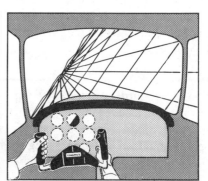

Figure 15a-4. Typical nose attitudes while flying the maneuver

---

Keep a good **lookout** during the steep turn to monitor the nose position and the approach of your roll-out reference point, as well as to look for other aircraft, especially in the direction of your turn.

An occasional glance at the instruments will confirm that the turn is proceeding satisfactorily, but do not sacrifice your outside reference by concentrating only on the instruments. In just a second or two you can quickly check:
- **altitude** on the altimeter and vertical speed indicator;
- **airspeed** on the airspeed indicator;
- **bank angle** on the attitude indicator;
- **coordination** with the ball (centered).

Adjusting the bank angle and nose position is a *continuing* requirement throughout the steep turn and keeps the pilot quite busy. That is why it is such a good training maneuver! The sooner the corrections are made, the smaller and smoother they can be, the easier it is to keep the coordination ball centered, and the better the steep turn.

Throughout the maneuver divide your attention between smooth, coordinated airplane control and orientation. Count the turns as you pass your reference point.

- **If altitude is being gained** in the steep turn, it means that the vertical component of the lift force is too great, and so you must
   steepen the bank angle, and/or
   relax some of the back pressure.

- **If altitude is being lost** in the steep turn, then the vertical component of the lift force is insufficient. To regain altitude
   reduce the bank angle slightly
   raise the nose with back pressure and
   when back on altitude, reapply the chosen bank angle and back pressure.

- **If the nose drops below the horizon during a steep turn**, trying to raise it with back pressure will only tighten the turn rather than raise the nose. Should the altitude loss rapidly increase, roll out to straight-and-level, climb back to your chosen altitude and start again. Do not allow the airspeed to exceed the design maneuver speed, and do not exceeed any structural limits.

Stall Buffet

If the airplane turns through more than 360°, you may in fact strike your own slipstream and feel some turbulence. This is not the stall buffet, but the sign of a well-executed steep turn.

If, however, the stall buffet is felt, then **release some of the back pressure** to reduce the angle-of-attack before the stall actually occurs. To avoid losing altitude, you will have to decrease the bank angle slightly as you release control column back pressure.

Accuracy

When practicing steep turns, aim to achieve an accuracy of within 100 feet of altitude and 10 KIAS of airspeed initially, bank angle within 5° of the target bank angle (45° plus or minus 5° for private pilots, 50° plus or minus 5° for commercial pilots) and then, as your training progresses, accept no variations at all.

Rolling out of the Steep Turn

This is the same as rolling out of a medium turn, except that:

- greater anticipation is required to roll out on your reference point;
- there is a great deal more back pressure to be released, otherwise altitude will be gained; and
- after the chosen airspeed has been reached, the power must be reduced to the cruise setting.

Remember to keep the airplane coordinated with rudder—any time you deflect the ailerons you will need rudder pressure to remain coordinated.

Concentrate on elevator back pressure in the roll-out, especially to avoid gaining altitude, since you may be a little reluctant to relax all the back pressure.

- When rolling out of a 45° banked turn, relaxing back pressure is usually sufficient.
- When rolling out of a 60° banked turn, the release of back pressure is so great that it may feel as though you have to push the control column forward.

Anticipate rolling out when within one-half your bank angle of the roll-out heading—for example, start rolling out 23° before the target roll-out heading if your bank angle is 45°. When you are well practiced, you can reduce this to one-third your bank angle.

Do not forget to reduce the power as you roll out, otherwise airspeed will rapidly increase. After the roll-out, immediately adjust heading, altitude and airspeed so that you are not just within limits, but *exactly* on target.

After some practice of constant altitude turns both to the left and to the right, your flight instructor may suggest that you roll from a steep turn one way immediately into a steep turn the other way.

Airmanship

Practice the maneuver in an appropriate area, and no lower than 1,500 feet AGL, and keep a good **lookout** for other traffic. Note various landmarks that will assist in orientation during and after the turn. It is easy for an inexperienced pilot to become disoriented in steep turns which involve large changes of heading.

Do not practice steep turns at speeds greater than V_A, which for your airplane is ____ KIAS. Handle the power smoothly, and monitor the gauges to ensure engine limitations are not exceeded.

Exert smooth, but firm, control over the airplane. Use rudder and ailerons together when rolling. Avoid any tendency to stall, or to exceed the structural limits of the airplane.

Divide your attention appropriately between airplane control and orientation.

Airmanship is keeping a good lookout, and flying the airplane positively.

Airwork 15a
Steep Constant-Altitude Turns

Objective
To perform a steep turn, maintaining constant altitude and airspeed.
Note: This maneuver is also known as a steep power turn.

- Complete the HASELL check.
- **Clear the area** and **look out**.
- Select a reference point on the horizon.
- Nominate the number of turns and the roll-out reference point or heading.
- Nominate bank angle, airspeed and altitude, and then stick to them.
- Roll into the turn with ailerons.
- Coordinate with rudder to keep ball centered.
- Apply sufficient back-pressure on the control column to maintain altitude.
- Add power progressively to maintain airspeed.

> **Required Accuracy:**
> - Altitude ±100 feet
> - Bank angle 45° ±5° for private pilots, and 50° ±5° for commercial pilots
> - Airspeed ±10 KIAS
> - Nominated roll-out heading ±10°
> - no tendency to stall or to reach excessive speeds

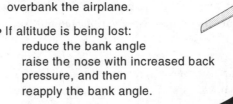

2. Maintaining the Turn

- **Clear the area** and **look out**.
- Maintain the bank angle with aileron.
- Maintain coordination with rudder.
- Maintain altitude with elevator.
- Maintain airspeed with power.
- Divide your attention between airplane control and orientation, and count turns.
- Notice the increased downward view.
- Notice the increased g-loading.

- If altitude is being gained— reduce elevator back pressure and consider steepening the bank angle temporarily—but do not overbank the airplane.

- If altitude is being lost:
  reduce the bank angle
  raise the nose with increased back pressure, and then
  reapply the bank angle.

Note: In a perfect steep power turn at a constant altitude you may meet your own slipstream, which will cause some buffeting.

3. Roll-Out

- **Clear the area** and **look out.**
- Locate roll-out reference point (anticipate by one-half the bank angle).
- Roll out of the turn with aileron.
- Maintain coordination with rudder.
- Release the elevator back pressure to maintain altitude.
- Progressively reduce power to maintain the desired cruise airspeed.
- Immediately make fine adjustments to be precisely on heading, altitude and airspeed.

> Practice this maneuver above 1,500 feet above ground level.

Note: Try 720° turns (twice around) both left and then right, rolling straight from one to the other— you must reduce power and lower the nose a little as you pass through wings level, before reapplying bank angle, back pressure and power.

Further Points

Maximum-Performance Turns

A maximum-performance steep constant-altitude turn at a particular airspeed is flown like a normal steep turn except that power is progressively applied as the bank angle is increased, until **maximum power** is reached.

The ability to maintain altitude and airspeed in this maneuver depends upon the power available. For most training airplanes, the performance limit is reached at about 65° bank.

Turning performance is measured in terms of:
- the rate of turn (the greater, the better); and
- the radius of turn (the tighter, the better).

At a constant airspeed, turning performance increases with bank angle.

At a constant bank angle, turning performance is better at low airspeeds. Therefore, the best turning performance can be achieved at a relatively low airspeed and a high bank angle (provided that the airplane is not stalled or the airframe overstressed).

Note: Steep climbing turns are possible only in very high-powered airplanes (such as military fighters); most airplanes in a steep power turn have no excess power available for a climb.

Overstressing

The lift that can be generated by the wings with full rearward movement of the control column is far greater at high airspeeds than at low airspeeds, and results in greater load factors occurring. For example, pulling the control column fully back at 150 KIAS will increase the g-loading considerably more than at 50 KIAS.

At high airspeeds, therefore, there is a danger of overstressing the airframe by exceeding the maximum allowable load factor (+3.8g for most training airplanes).

Do not overstress the airframe in a steep turn.

Maneuvering Speed (V_A)

A large elevator deflection at high airspeed can cause the wings to generate so much lift that the airplane's **limit-load-factor** is exceeded without the wings reaching their stalling angle-of-attack. At low airspeeds, the airplane will stall *before* the limit-load-factor is reached, so the airframe is protected aerodynamically at low speeds.

The airspeed at which maximum elevator deflection causes the stall to occur just at the limit-load-factor is called the *maneuvering speed* (referred to as V_A). **The best aerodynamic turning performance** can be achieved at this speed, provided that sufficient power is available.

For most training airplanes, the engine performance is the limiting factor in maximum performance steep turns.

The maneuvering speed (V_A) for maximum gross weight is specified in the Flight Manual. At airspeeds *less* than V_A full elevator deflection will not overstress the airframe—above V_A it will.

At lower weights, with the lower stalling speed, the actual V_A will be a few knots slower than that published.

Refer to figure 15a-4 on the next page.

Absolute maximum turning performance is achieved at the maneuvering speed, V_A.

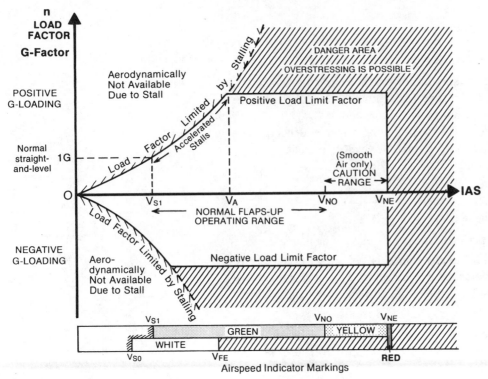

Figure 15a-4. Airspeed (V) versus allowable load factor (n)

✍ **Review 15a**

1. A steep constant-altitude turn is also known as a steep _____ turn.

   ➤ power

2. Steep turns should be practiced no lower than _____ feet AGL. If ground level is 2,200 feet MSL, you should not go below _____ feet MSL on your altimeter when practicing steep turns.

   ➤ 1,500 feet AGL, 3,700 feet MSL

3. In a steep turn, the lift is (increased/reduced) by applying back pressure on the control column. This causes (increased/reduced) drag and a need for (additional/less) power to maintain airspeed.

   ➤ increased, increased, additional

4. The wings carry (more/less/the same) load in a steep turn compared with straight-and-level flight, the stall speed (increases/reduces/stays the same), and the pilot feels (heavier/lighter/the same).

   ➤ more, increases, heavier

5. During a steep constant-altitude turn, you can expect to hold (back/forward/no) pressure on the control column, and to apply (high/low) power.

   ➤ back, high

Steep Constant-Altitude Turns

6. The load factor (increases/reduces/stays the same) in a steep turn.

   ➤ increases

7. Accuracy limits for steep constant-altitude turns are: altitude within _____ feet; bank angle *private pilots* ____ ° and within _____ °, *commercial pilots* ____ ° and within _____ °; airspeed within _____ KIAS; roll-out heading within _____ °;

   ➤ altitude within 100 feet; bank angle: private, 45°to within 5°, commercial 50° to within 5°; airspeed within 10 KIAS; roll-out heading within 10°

8. The steeper the bank angle at a constant airspeed, the (tighter/wider) the turn.

   ➤ tighter

9. The lower the airspeed at a constant bank angle, the (tighter/wider) the turn.

   ➤ tighter

10. There will be an (over-/under-) banking tendency in a steep constant-altitude turn caused by the outer wing traveling (faster/slower) than the inner wing.

   ➤ overbanking, faster

Recovery from Unusual Flight Attitudes 15b

Objective

To recognize and recover from an unusual airplane attitude that may develop into a potentially hazardous situation.

Considerations

While a steep turn should be a straightforward maneuver, it is possible that early in your steep turn training some unusual attitudes may develop.

It would be useful for you to re-read Exercises 10a & b and 11a & b at this stage.

Unusual Airplane Attitudes

The two fundamental unusual flight attitudes are:
- nose-high with a decreasing airspeed; or
- nose-low with an increasing airspeed.

Potentially hazardous attitudes are nose-high/decreasing airspeed and nose-low/increasing airspeed.

These attitudes usually result from some form of mishandling by the pilot. For example, the relatively low power available in most training airplanes will not allow a steady climb to be maintained in a steep turn—if the nose is raised in an attempt to achieve the almost-impossible steady steep climbing turn, a **nose-high/low-speed** unusual attitude can result, eventually leading to a stall or a spin if not corrected.

These attitudes are not hazardous if you have plenty of altitude to recover, but they can be hazardous near the ground!

Flying the Maneuver

Nose-High and Decreasing Airspeed

If the nose is high above the horizon and the speed is low and/or decreasing, you may stall.

Nose-high and decreasing airspeed—beware of a stall or spin.

To recover from a **nose-high/low-airspeed** unusual attitude following a stall, simultaneously:
- ease the control wheel forward;
- apply sufficient rudder to prevent further yaw;
- apply maximum power; and
- when the airspeed increases as the wings become unstalled, level the wings with coordinated use of rudder and ailerons, ease out of any descent, and resume the desired flight path.

If a full spin develops from a mishandled steep turn, probably as a result of the nose being raised too high and the speed allowed to drop too low, then recover using the recommended **spin recovery**.

The spin-recovery technique is:
- throttle closed, flaps up and ailerons neutral;
- verify the spin direction on the turn coordinator;
- apply full opposite rudder;
- **pause;**
- progressively ease the control column forward (to unstall the wings) until the rotation stops;
- center the rudder when the rotation has stopped;
- level the wings and gently ease out of the ensuing dive; and
- as the nose rises through the horizon, add power and climb away.

Nose-Low and Increasing Airspeed

If the nose is low, then you could exceed the **maximum allowable airspeed** (V_{NE}—shown on the ASI as a red line), especially if power is applied; this could overstress the airplane. A steep bank angle and a low nose attitude may develop into a spiral dive.

Nose-low and a high airspeed— beware of an overspeed or a spiral dive.

To recover from a **nose-low/high-airspeed** unusual attitude:
- reduce power;
- roll the wings level with ailerons and rudder;
- ease out of the ensuing dive; and
- as the nose passes through the horizon, reapply power and climb away.

A **nose-low/increasing-speed** unusual attitude, if not corrected, can develop into a **spiral dive.** This can be recognized by:
- a high g-loading;
- a rapidly increasing airspeed (that distinguishes it from a spin); and
- a rapid loss of altitude—probably with the rate of descent increasing.

The recovery from the spiral dive is the same as that for a nose-low/high-speed situation, but it is especially important to avoid excessive elevator deflection when easing out of the dive, otherwise the limit load factor for the airplane could be exceeded, overstressing the airframe. It is permissible to use the ailerons as firmly as needed to roll the wings level.

Airwork 15b
Recovery from Unusual Flight Attitudes

Objective

To recognize and recover from a potentially hazardous unusual airplane attitude that has developed.

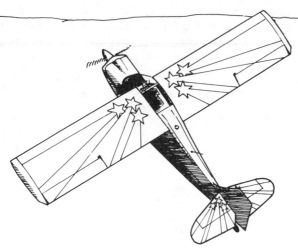

1. Nose-High/Low Airspeed

This is recognized primarily from the airspeed indicator.

Recovery:

- Simultaneously ease the control column forward and roll the wings level.
- Add power.

Note: If close to the stall, do not use the ailerons until you are certain that the wings are unstalled.

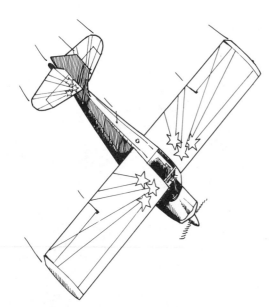

2. Nose-Low/High Airspeed

This is recognized primarily from the airspeed indicator and vertical speed indicator.

Recovery:

- Reduce power.
- Roll the wings level with aileron and coordinate with rudder.
- Ease out of the dive.
- Add power as the nose passes through the horizon.

✍ Review 15b

Recovery from Unusual Flight Attitudes

1. If a high-nose and low-speed situation occurs, there is a risk of a _____ or _____ .

   ➤ stall, spin

2. Describe how you would recover from a nose-high and low-airspeed unusual attitude.

   ➤ *refer to our text, page 387*

3. If a nose-low and high-speed situation occurs, there is a risk of an _____ which could cause structural damage, or a _____ if a steep bank occurs.

   ➤ overspeed, spiral dive

4. Describe how you would recover from a nose-low and high-airspeed unusual attitude.

   ➤ *refer to our text, page 388*

5. If the airspeed becomes too high in a steep descending turn, you should _____ .

   ➤ ease off bank angle, and raise the nose

6. When recovering from a spiral dive, it is important to avoid excessive _____ deflection when easing out of the dive; this is to prevent _____ the airframe.

   ➤ elevator, overstressing

Steep Descending Turns 15c

Objective

To perform a steep turn while descending.

Considerations

A steep descending turn can be made in:
• a glide; or
• a powered descent.

Fly Faster

It is usual to increase your airspeed as a steep descending turn is begun to retain an adequate safety margin over the stalling speed (which increases if back pressure is applied during a turn). Typical speed increases are:
• 10 KIAS for a 45° steep descending turn; and
• 20 KIAS for a 60° steep descending turn.

Fly faster in a steep descending turn because of the increased stalling speed.

In a steep gliding turn, the rate of descent will increase markedly. It can be controlled by reducing the bank angle or by adding power.

The Maneuver

The steep descending turn is usually flown at a constant airspeed and constant bank angle, without reference to any ground object. In still air, you will descend more or less straight down; in a strong wind you will be carried downwind.

The steep descending turn is an *air* maneuver.

Flying the Maneuver

A steep descending turn is flown like a steep level turn, except that the **increased airspeed** is maintained with the elevator.

The nose will tend to drop in a descending turn and so, even though the nose position is lower to achieve a higher airspeed, some back pressure on the control column will be needed to stop it from dropping too far.

If airspeed becomes excessive in a steep descending turn:
• ease off the bank angle with ailerons;
• raise the nose with elevator; and
• re-establish the desired steep turn.

Reducing the bank angle is vital, since simply exerting increased back pressure on the control column in an attempt to reduce airspeed may **tighten** the steep descending turn, and increase the g-loading beyond acceptable limits. A spiral dive may also result if attitude and airspeed are not monitored.

The lack of slipstream in a glide will mean that more rudder is required when rolling in one direction than when rolling in the other.

Keep a good lookout, especially below. The steep descending turn described here is without reference to any ground object—the aim is to hold a steady bank angle, which means you will descend through a "cylinder" of air. In zero-wind conditions, you will remain over the same patch of ground, but in a wind you will be carried along with it.

The airplane in a steep descending turn will be carried along by the wind.

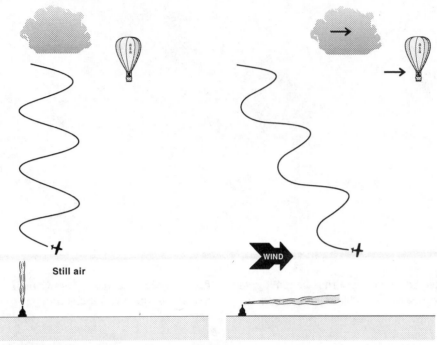

Figure 15c-1. The wind will carry you along.

Airmanship

Be aware of your proximity to the ground, since the rate of descent will be quite high in a gliding steep turn.

Allow the airspeed to increase, and maintain a safe margin over the stall, but do not let a spiral dive develop.

Keep a good lookout, especially below.

Airmanship is remaining aware of your altitude and ground clearance.

Airwork 15c
Steep Descending Turns

Objective
To perform a steep turn while descending.

---

1. Entry to the Turn

- Complete the HASELL check.
- **Clear the area** and **look out.**
- Select horizon reference point.
- Roll in bank with aileron.
- Coordinate with rudder.
- Hold the nose in a slightly lower attitude to maintain an increased airspeed—necessary due to the higher stall speed.

2. Maintaining the Steep Descending Turn

- **Clear the area.**
- Maintain the bank angle with aileron.
- Coordinate with rudder.
- Maintain the desired airspeed with elevator back pressure.

If the airspeed increases:
- Reduce the bank angle.
- Raise the nose with elevator.
- Reapply the bank angle.

3. The Roll-Out

- **Clear the area.**
- Roll out of the bank with ailerons.
- Coordinate with rudder.
- Select your desired pitch attitude with elevator.

> Maintain airspeed with elevator.
> If desired, control the rate of descent with power

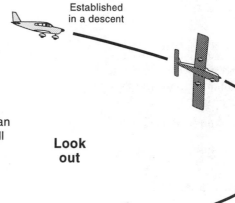

Established in a descent

Look out

Look out

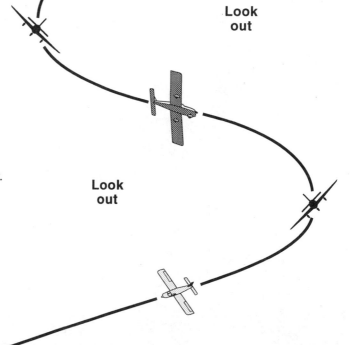

Look out

✍ Review 15c

1. Stall speed (increases/decreases) in a turn.
   ⟫ increases

2. In a steep descending turn it is usual to (increase/decrease) the airspeed to allow an adequate safety margin above the stalling speed
   ⟫ increase

3. In a steep descending turn, the nose will tend to (rise/drop) and some (back/forward) pressure on the control column will be necessary to keep it from (dropping/rising) too far.
   ⟫ drop, back pressure, dropping

4. In steep gliding turn, what will happen to the rate of descent?
   ⟫ it will increase markedly

5. If the airspeed becomes excessive in a steep descending turn, you should first (increase/reduce) the bank angle and (raise/lower) the nose, before re-establishing the desired steep turn.
   ⟫ reduce, raise

Steep Descending Turns

6. Increasing control back pressure to reduce the airspeed in a descending turn may (increase/decrease) the g-loading beyond acceptable limits.
   ⟫ increase

7. In a steep descending turn, the rate of descent is (high/low).
   ⟫ high

8. You (must/need not) remain very aware of your altitude above the ground in a steep descending turn.
   ⟫ must

9. A good lookout is essential (at all times/only occasionally) during visual flight.
   ⟫ at all times

Commercial Pilot Maximum Performance Maneuvers

15d

Maneuvers Covered

The Commercial Pilot maximum performance maneuvers comprise Steep Power Turns, Chandelles, and Lazy Eights.

Part (i)
Steep Power Turns

Steep Power Turns are the same as *steep turns at a constant altitude,* which were covered in Exercise 15a.

You should review this exercise to achieve Commercial Pilot proficiency in this maneuver, as part of your training in Maximum Performance Maneuvers.

The required accuracy in steep power turns is: bank angle 50° plus or minus 5°, within 100 feet of the specified altitude, and within 10 knots of the specified airspeed (providing the airplane is capable of maintaining a constant airspeed).

The roll-out should be accomplished within 10° of the entry heading.

The maneuver must be performed in both left-hand and right-hand directions, and the airplane should remain clear of the stall and with no tendency to exceed the structural limits of the airplane.

Select an altitude that will allow the maneuver to be performed at 1,500 feet above ground level, or higher.

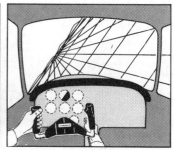

Figure 15d-1. Typical nose attitudes in steep power turns to the left and right

Part (ii)
Chandelles

Objective

To perform a chandelle—a maximum performance climbing turn with a heading change of 180°—gaining as much altitude as possible and rolling out just above stall speed.

Considerations

A chandelle requires good planning, positive control and good coordination.

Power, Momentum and Altitude

The airplane enters the chandelle at a high speed with lots of momentum, and high power. When the turn is commenced, the airplane is pulled into a climbing turn to convert this energy into altitude.

As altitude is gained, the airspeed dissipates. The purpose is to achieve the 180° turn with as much altitude gain as possible, and roll out wings-level just above the stall speed. Maintain that airspeed momentarily, avoiding the stall, then resume straight-and-level flight with a minimum loss of altitude.

The chandelle is a 180° climbing turn that converts power and momentum into altitude.

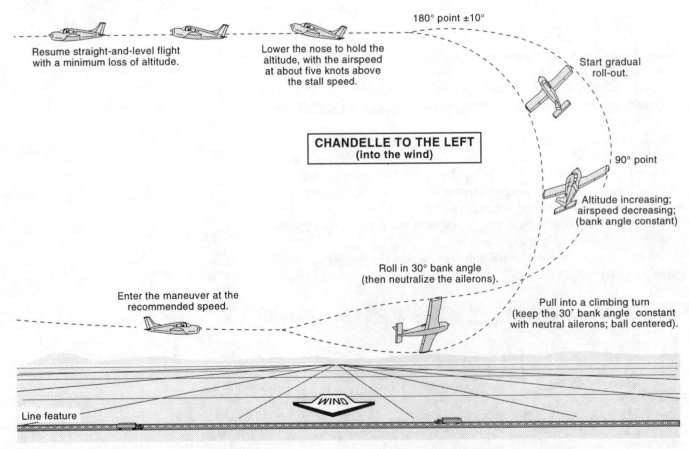

Resume straight-and-level flight with a minimum loss of altitude.

Lower the nose to hold the altitude, with the airspeed at about five knots above the stall speed.

180° point ±10°

Start gradual roll-out.

**CHANDELLE TO THE LEFT
(into the wind)**

90° point

Altitude increasing; airspeed decreasing; (bank angle constant)

Roll in 30° bank angle (then neutralize the ailerons).

Enter the maneuver at the recommended speed.

Pull into a climbing turn (keep the 30° bank angle constant with neutral ailerons; ball centered).

WIND

Line feature

Figure 15d-2. The chandelle

The high power and falling airspeed will probably mean some right rudder pressure is required to keep the coordination ball centered.

The first half of the chandelle turn, from 0° to 90°, is flown with a constant bank angle and steadily increasing pitch attitude. A lot of the airplane's power and momentum is converted to altitude—the consequence being that the airspeed drops at about 1 to 2 KIAS per second.

Flying the Maneuver

Practice this maneuver at least 1,500 feet above ground level and use speeds less than maneuvering speed V_A to avoid any risk of overstressing the airframe, even with full control deflection. V_A is found in the Pilot's Operating Handbook, under *Limitations,* and is a lower airspeed at lower weights.

Entering a Chandelle

The chandelle is entered at a recommended speed, which must not exceed V_A. If the recommended airspeed cannot be attained in straight-and-level flight with cruise power (as may be the case with some low-powered training aircraft), you may enter a straight shallow dive to accelerate. The greater airflow over the typical off-set rudder may require you to exert a little left rudder pressure to keep the coordination ball centered as speed builds up.

Roll into a turn then climb into a chandelle.

Roll into about a 30° bank angle—certainly no more and maybe a little less otherwise the airplane may not climb too well—and hold it steady by neutralizing the ailerons. This should only take a few seconds, and the airplane will start to turn away from its original heading.

Simultaneously raise the pitch attitude with back pressure on the control column, and smoothly apply the recommended power (usually full power for airplanes with fixed-pitch propellers, and cruise power for constant-speed propellers). Hold the bank angle constant at about 30° with neutral ailerons.

Exiting the Chandelle

After the 90° point, with half of the turn completed, the momentum of the airplane is diminishing with falling airspeed, and the climb performance is deteriorating. It is time to start gradually rolling out of the bank, aiming to roll out right on the 180° reference point (plus or minus 10°) traveling in the opposite direction to your entry direction, and to gradually lower the nose just above the stall speed.

To exit the maneuver, smoothly roll out of the chandelle and level off.

Momentarily maintain that airspeed, avoiding a stall, then resume straight-and-level flight with a minimum loss of altitude. Keep the coordination ball centered throughout the maneuver.

Airmanship

Do not descend below 1,500 feet above ground level at any point in the chandelle maneuver.

Airmanship is flying coordinated.

Start the maneuver flying crosswind and make the 180° chandelle turn into the wind, minimizing the horizontal distance between the entry path and the exit path, which will keep you approximately in the same area.

Handle the power smoothly, and keep the coordination ball centered at all times through the power, airspeed, and bank angle changes.

Divide your attention between smooth, coordinated airplane control, and keeping a good lookout.

Objective

To fly a chandelle, which is a maximum-performance-climb turn with a heading change of 180°, gaining as much altitude as possible and rolling out just above stall speed.

---

1. Entry

Page 221

- Complete the HASELL check.
- **Clear the area** and **look out.**
- Start the maneuver tracking crosswind and perform the chandelle climbing turn into the wind to minimize wind drift and stay in the same area.
- Establish the recommended entry speed—which must not exceed the maneuvering speed V$_A$—by adding power in straight-and-level flight, or by lowering the nose into a straight-ahead shallow dive to accelerate;

- slight left rudder pressure may be needed to keep the coordination ball centered.
- At the entry speed, fly straight-and-level, roll in approximately 30° bank (certainly no more, and maybe a little less). The airplane will start to turn.
- Establish the 30° bank angle, hold it by neutralizing the ailerons, and then simultaneously raise the pitch attitude gradually with elevator and smoothly apply recommended power, keeping the coordination ball centered with rudder.

2. The First 90° Turn

- Keep the bank angle constant at 30° with neutral ailerons.
- Continue raising the nose attitude with elevator (airspeed will be reducing at about 1 to 2 KIAS per second).

- Keep the coordination ball centered with rudder (probably some right rudder pressure will be required).
- Monitor reference points and the progress of turn.
- **Look out.**
- Keep the bank angle constant at 30° to the 90° point.

3. The Chandelle from 90° to 180° (the second 90° of the turn)

- Maintain power and maintain pitch attitude.
- Airspeed will continue to fall (as power and momentum of airplane is converted to altitude).
- Start a very gradual roll out by reducing bank with ailerons, aiming to roll out wings level at the 180° point.

- Keep coordination ball centered with rudder pressure (probably right rudder with high power and low airspeed).
- Monitor reference points and the progress of the turn.
- **Look out.**
- Monitor the airspeed as it approaches the stall speed.

4. The Roll-Out at 180°

- **Look out.**
- Aim to roll out with wings level 180° from the entry direction (±10°) at an airspeed about 5 KIAS above the stall speed.
- Momentarily maintain that airspeed without stalling.

- Resume straight-and-level flight with a minimum loss of altitude.
- Keep the coordination ball centered throughout the maneuver.

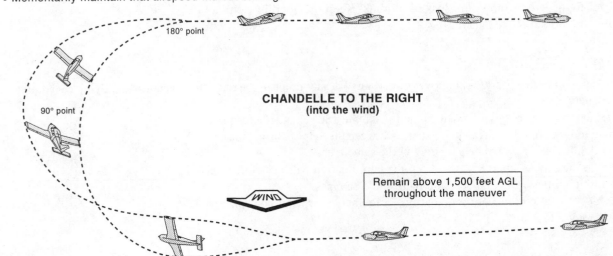

180° point

90° point

CHANDELLE TO THE RIGHT
(into the wind)

WIND

Remain above 1,500 feet AGL
throughout the maneuver

Objective

To fly a series of lazy eights, each consisting of two gentle wing-overs in opposite directions.

Considerations

The *lazy eight* is a series of S-patterns across a line feature, but *not* at constant altitude—the high *speed* at entry is traded for a higher *altitude* at the top of a climbing turn, which should occur halfway through each loop of the S-pattern. The airspeed will be lowest at this point, but must be above the stall.

Speed is traded for altitude (and vice versa) in a lazy eight.

The higher altitude is then traded for speed in a descending turn, planned to finish at the 180° point at the original entry speed and altitude, with the wings level as you roll into a climbing turn in the opposite direction.

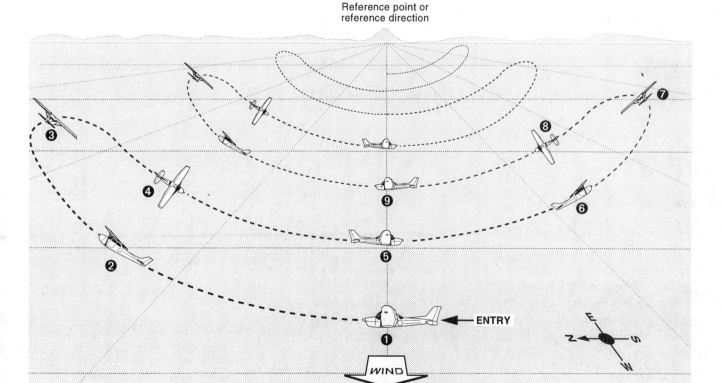

Figure 15d-3. The lazy eight

The Name

The **lazy eight** is so-named because the nose of the airplane slowly makes a figure-eight shape along half of the horizon, as illustrated. Compare figure 15d-4 below—"what the pilot sees"—with figure 15d-3, which shows the flight path of the airplane in a lazy eight.

The nose traces a lazy eight along half the horizon.

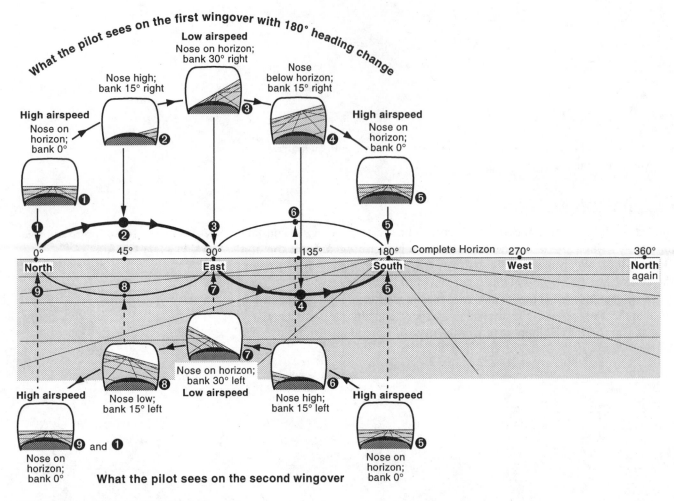

Figure 15d-4. What the pilot sees in a lazy eight

Flying the Maneuver

Starting a Lazy Eight

Like the chandelle, it is good airmanship to start the maneuver flying crosswind, and pick a distant reference point or take a reference heading on the direction indicator that lies on your upwind wingtip. By making the turns into the wind you will cover less ground than if you made the turns downwind, in which case you would be carried much further away by the wind.

Practice lazy eights at least 1,500 feet above ground level, and use an entry speed of cruise speed, or the maneuvering speed (V_A), whichever is less, to avoid any risk of overstressing the airplane. Aim to leave constant power on throughout the maneuver.

You should carry out the pre-aerobatic HASELL check prior to practicing lazy eights.

Enter the lazy eight crosswind and turn into the wind.

First Climbing Turn

Trim the airplane for straight-and-level flight at the recommended entry airspeed, and fly crosswind at your entry altitude. Select a distant reference point on your upwind wingtip, or note the heading on your heading indicator (or both).

Raise the nose into the climbing attitude, and then gently roll in bank, keeping the coordination ball centered with rudder pressure.

Pass the 45° reference point with maximum pitch-up for the maneuver—bank angle slowly increasing through 15°. The airspeed will be decreasing.

After the 45° reference point, keep the bank angle slowly increasing to a maximum of 30° bank at the top of the turn, but start lowering the nose so that it is on the horizon at the 90° point—looking at the distant reference point.

The airspeed will be at its lowest value, but still some knots above the stall. Take note of your altitude and airspeed. (To keep the coordination ball centered at this point, you may need some bottom rudder and opposite aileron.)

Make a climbing turn from zero through a 90° heading change.

Descending Turn

Continue the coordinated turn with the bank angle momentarily at its maximum value of 30°. Lower the nose into a descending turn, slowly rolling the bank out to pass through the 135° reference point with bank angle reducing through 15° and the lowest nose attitude in the whole maneuver—well below the horizon.

Continue the coordinated turn from the 135° reference point to the 180° reference point, raising the nose and rolling out the bank so as to be in level flight passing through the 180° reference point, and (ideally) at the original entry airspeed and altitude.

Next commence a descending turn from 90° through 180° of heading change.

Second Climbing Turn

Raise the nose, and roll in bank in the opposite direction to commence the climbing turn for the second wing-over—to complete the second half of the S-pattern, and keep the maneuver going.

Continue into a climbing turn in the opposite direction.

Accuracy

The nose attitude and bank angle should be constantly changing throughout the lazy-eight maneuver.

You should aim to cross the *low* points of the lazy eight within 100 feet of the entry altitude, within 10 KIAS of the chosen entry airspeed, and with a heading tolerance at the 180° and 360° points of plus or minus 10°.

You should also aim to reach the *high* points of the maneuver within 100 feet of the same high altitude, and within 10 KIAS of the same low airspeed.

If you find yourself gradually losing altitude in consecutive lazy eights, add some power (and vice versa). Try and keep everything as smooth and symmetrical as possible.

Airmanship

Practice in an appropriate area, and no lower than 1,500 feet AGL. Divide your attention between coordinated airplane control, orientation, and keeping a good lookout.

Airmanship is smooth and coordinated flying, and keeping a good lookout.

The Lazy Eight

(Commercial Pilots only)

Objective

To fly a series of lazy eights, each consisting of two gentle wing-overs in opposite directions.

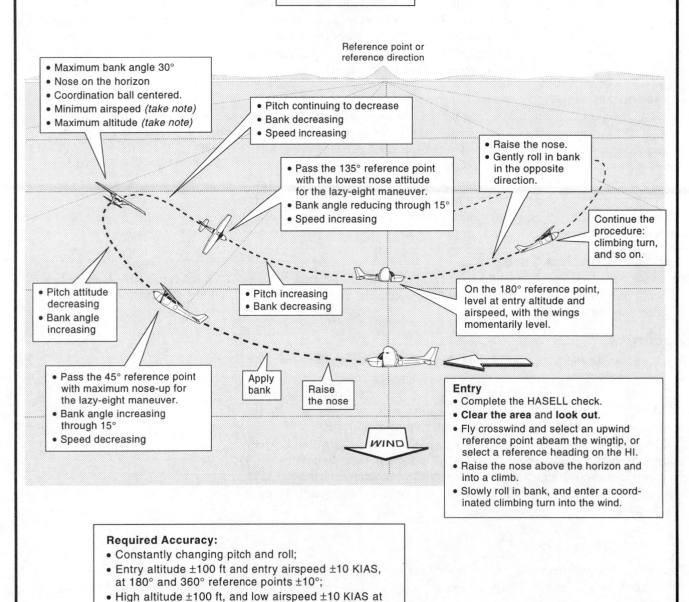

Practice this maneuver above 1,500 feet AGL.

Reference point or reference direction

- Maximum bank angle 30°
- Nose on the horizon
- Coordination ball centered.
- Minimum airspeed *(take note)*
- Maximum altitude *(take note)*

- Pitch continuing to decrease
- Bank decreasing
- Speed increasing

- Raise the nose.
- Gently roll in bank in the opposite direction.

- Pass the 135° reference point with the lowest nose attitude for the lazy-eight maneuver.
- Bank angle reducing through 15°
- Speed increasing

Continue the procedure: climbing turn, and so on.

- Pitch attitude decreasing
- Bank angle increasing

- Pitch increasing
- Bank decreasing

On the 180° reference point, level at entry altitude and airspeed, with the wings momentarily level.

- Pass the 45° reference point with maximum nose-up for the lazy-eight maneuver.
- Bank angle increasing through 15°
- Speed decreasing

Apply bank

Raise the nose

WIND

Entry
- Complete the HASELL check.
- **Clear the area** and **look out**.
- Fly crosswind and select an upwind reference point abeam the wingtip, or select a reference heading on the HI.
- Raise the nose above the horizon and into a climb.
- Slowly roll in bank, and enter a coord-inated climbing turn into the wind.

Required Accuracy:
- Constantly changing pitch and roll;
- Entry altitude ±100 ft and entry airspeed ±10 KIAS, at 180° and 360° reference points ±10°;
- High altitude ±100 ft, and low airspeed ±10 KIAS at top of wing-overs (at 90° reference point), and so on.

Review 15d

Part (i)—Steep Power Turns

Rework the review questions for this maneuver as covered in Exercise 15a: Steep Constant-Altitude Turns.

Part (ii)—Chandelles

1. The aim of the chandelle is to (gain/lose) altitude with a (climbing/level/descending) turn of ____ ° heading change.

   ➤ gain, climbing, 180°

2. The speed at the bottom of a chandelle will be (higher than/lower than/the same as) the speed at the top.

   ➤ higher than

3. The altitude during a chandelle must be ____ feet AGL or higher.

   ➤ 1,500 feet AGL

4. If the ground in the vicinity of where you are practicing chandelles is 1,800 feet MSL, your minimum altitude should be ____ feet MSL, which is ____ feet AGL.

   ➤ 3,300 feet MSL, 1,500 feet AGL

5. Maximum speed of entry to a chandelle is (V_X/V_Y/V_A) which is known as the _____ speed.

   ➤ V_A, maneuvering speed

6. The bank angle during the chandelle should be ____ ° or less, otherwise the airplane will hardly (climb/descend/stall).

   ➤ 30°, climb

7. In a correctly flown chandelle you (add/do not add) power.

   ➤ add

8. The coordination ball should (stay centered/fluctuate wildly) during a chandelle.

   ➤ stay centered

9. In a well-flown chandelle, you should roll the wings level ____ ° from the entry heading, with a speed about ____ KIAS (above/below) the stall speed, and then (accelerate/decelerate) to the normal cruise speed.

   ➤ 180°, 5 KIAS above stall speed, accelerate

10. You should start the chandelle (crosswind/downwind/upwind) and make your turn (crosswind/downwind/upwind) to minimize the ground coverage.

    ➤ crosswind, upwind

11. A good lookout (is/is not) essential during a chandelle.

    ➤ is

Part (iii)—Lazy Eights

1. During the lazy eight, the nose should pass across (90°/180°/270°/360°) of the full horizon.

   ➤ 180°

2. You should enter the lazy eight (crosswind/downwind/into the wind) and make your first turn (crosswind/downwind/into the wind) to minimize ground coverage.

   ➤ crosswind, into the wind

3. The highest pitch attitude should occur at the ____ ° reference point, when the bank angle should be about ____ ° and (increasing/decreasing).

   ➤ 45°, 15°, increasing

4. At the 90° reference point, bank angle should be about ____ °, and the nose should be (above/on/below) the horizon. Airspeed will be at its (highest/lowest) value. Altitude will be at its (highest/lowest) value.

   ➤ 30°, on, lowest, highest

5. The lowest pitch attitude should occur at the ____ ° reference point, when the bank angle should be about ____ ° and (increasing/decreasing).

   ➤ 135°, 15°, decreasing

6. The lazy eight (is/is not) a coordinated maneuver, so the ball (should/need not) be kept in the center at all times.

   ➤ is, should

7. The objective in a lazy eight is to fly the maneuver with (constant power set/power continually changing).

   ➤ constant power set

Continued

8. The required lazy-eight accuracy is to pass through the 180° reference point within ____ feet of the entry altitude, within ____ KIAS of the entry airspeed, within ____ ° of the specified bank angle, and with a heading tolerance of 180° plus or minus ____ °.

➤ 100 feet, 10 KIAS, 0°, 10°

9. Passing through the 180° reference point, you should raise the nose and gently roll into a climbing turn in the (same/opposite) direction.

➤ opposite

10. The highest pitch attitude in this climbing turn should occur (at/before/after) the top of the turn.

➤ before

11. At the top of the second turn of the lazy eight, you should aim for being within ____ feet of the previous high altitude, and within ____ KIAS of the previous low airspeed.

➤ 100 feet, 10 KIAS

12. If you find yourself becoming higher and faster at the low points of consecutive lazy eights, you could _____ .

➤ reduce power

13. A vital aspect of airmanship is to maintain a good _____ .

➤ lookout

Objective

1. To fly the airplane safely at a low level.
2. To develop **wind awareness** by observing the misleading visual effects caused by a strong wind when flying at low levels.
3. To fly various patterns by reference to ground objects.

Considerations

Wind Effects in Straight Flight

Zero Wind

An airplane flying with its wings level and the coordination ball centered will fly through an airmass in the direction it is headed. This is illustrated by an airplane flying through a particular airmass and shown at three separate times.

Figure 16a-1. An airmass at "Time 2" in zero-wind conditions

If the airmass is stationary—**no wind**—the track over the ground will be the same as the path of the airplane through the air, and the groundspeed—the speed at which the airplane passes over the ground—will be the same as the airspeed.

Figure 16a-2. Flight in zero-wind conditions

Flying into a Headwind

In a headwind, the airmass will carry the airplane back with it, causing the groundspeed to be **less** even though the airspeed remains unchanged. The effect on groundspeed is most apparent visually when you are flying fairly low, which for purposes of practicing will be in the range of 600 feet to 1,000 feet AGL.

The wind carries an airplane with it.

Figure 16a-3. Flying in a headwind

Flying with a Tailwind

In a tailwind, the airmass will carry the airplane forward with it, causing the groundspeed to be greater even though the airspeed remains unchanged.

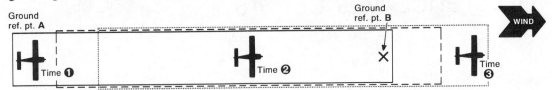

Figure 16a-4. Flight with a tailwind

There is a danger of a visual illusion in the tailwind situation. An airplane flying with an airspeed of 80 KIAS in a 35-knot tailwind, for instance, will have a groundspeed of 115 knots. The proximity of the ground will give an *illusion* of speed much greater than 80 knots, but you must resist any temptation to slow down. Reducing the groundspeed to what feels like 80 knots would require an airspeed of 45 KIAS, which may be below the stalling speed.

A tailwind causes a false impression of high speed—check the ASI regularly.

This temptation to slow down may exist if you are flying a rectangular pattern around a small field—the downwind leg at the high groundspeed will not take long, and you may feel a little rushed and tempted to slow things down—don't! Increase the speed of your thinking instead.

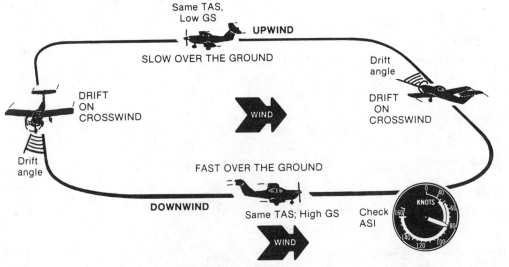

Figure 16a-5. Monitor the airspeed carefully when flying downwind close to the ground.

In a headwind, the reverse is the case. The groundspeed is lower than the airspeed, giving an **impression** of slow speed. Since there is no temptation to slow down when flying into a headwind, this situation is not as dangerous as when flying downwind.

Flying in a Crosswind

If you fly a straight path through an airmass that is moving sideways, your path over the ground will be in a different direction to the airplane's heading. This is known as *drift,* or *wind drift,* and is illustrated in figure 16a-7.

If you want to track between two ground reference points, and initially steer the desired course as heading, you will be carried downwind. You could continually turn to head directly at your target, but this will result in a curved path to the target point—an inefficient procedure called **homing** to a point, and best avoided.

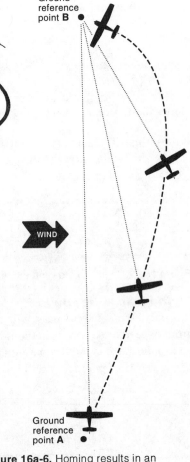

Figure 16a-6. Homing results in an inefficient curved track over the ground.

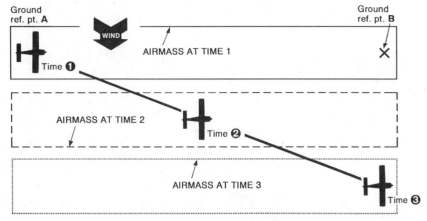

Figure 16a-7. The airplane in a crosswind is carried downwind over the ground.

It is much more efficient to fly a path through the air that is directed somewhat into the crosswind, and allow the crosswind effect to keep you on the desired ground track. The difference between the ground track and the airplane heading is called the **wind correction angle** (WCA) or **crab angle.** The slower your airspeed, or the stronger the crosswind, the more crab angle that will be required.

Apply a wind correction angle (WCA) into a crosswind.

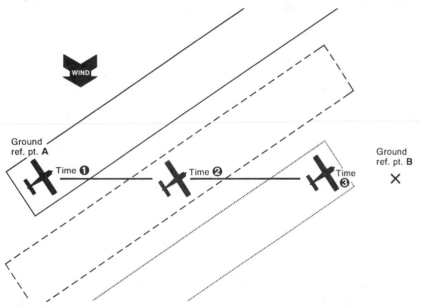

Figure 16a-8. Apply a wind correction angle, or crab angle, in a crosswind.

Sideways drift over the ground from a crosswind causes false impressions of coordination. In strong crosswinds, especially if the airspeed is low, the airplane will experience a large drift angle over the ground. This will give an **illusion** of slip or skid, even though the coordination ball is centered.

The false sensation of slip or skid, especially when turning, can tempt an inexperienced pilot to use rudder to counteract it, which would make the airplane uncoordinated, and degrade its performance. **Confirm coordination with the ball.** Since airspeed tends to reduce in a turn, it is also good airmanship when flying low to have your hand on the throttle to adjust power to maintain the airspeed if necessary.

If you want to inspect a line feature (such as a road, railroad, pipeline, fence or river), it is best to fly to one side of it—usually to the right of it, since this gives the pilot in the left seat the best view. One quarter-mile is usually sufficient. Selecting a distant ground reference point can assist in tracking and orientation.

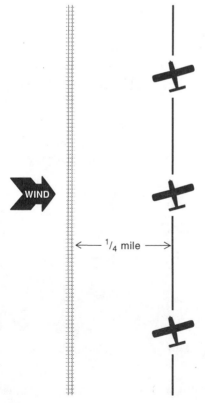

Figure 16a-9. Inspecting a line feature

Wind Effects in Turning Flight

Turning When There Is No Wind

If you fly at a **constant bank angle** at a steady speed in zero-wind conditions, your path over the ground will be the same as your circular path through the air. The maneuver illustrated below is centered above a road intersection.

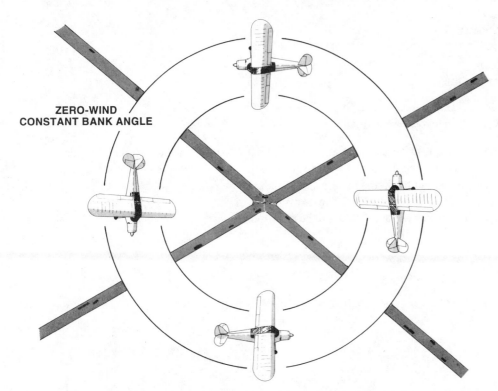

Figure 16a-10. In still air, a constant bank angle provides a circular ground path.

The turning performance of the airplane will depend on two factors:
- **bank angle**—the greater the bank angle, the tighter the turn; and
- **speed**—the lower the speed, the tighter the turn.

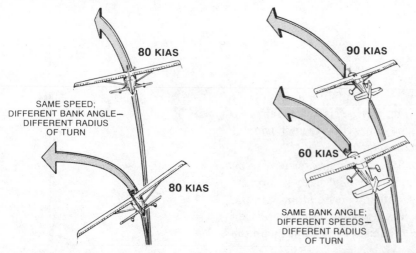

Figure 16a-11. Increase the bank angle to tighten the turn.

Decrease the speed to tighten the turn (if necessary).

So, if you want a turn of smaller radius, you can either increase the bank angle or decrease the speed (but don't forget that stall speed increases in a turn).

Turning in a Wind

If you hold a constant bank angle and a constant airspeed, the wind will carry the airplane downwind, and the result will be a circular path *through the air* but a distorted looping pattern *over the ground*.

The wind carries the airplane with it.

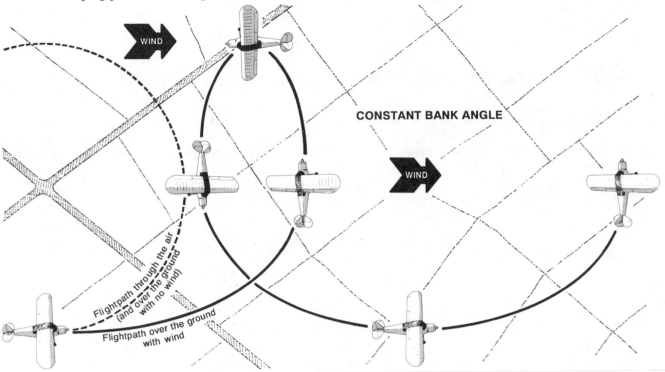

Figure 16a-12. Distorted ground track for a constant bank angle turn in a wind

The **ground radius** of the turn will be greatest when the groundspeed is greatest, which is when the airplane is headed directly downwind, and least when the groundspeed is least, which is when the airplane is headed directly into the wind.

The ground radius increases with higher groundspeeds.

To achieve a constant **ground radius,** and fly a circular path around a ground reference point, you will have to **vary the bank angle.** The lower the speed over the ground, the shallower the bank angle. The higher the speed over the ground, the steeper the bank angle. Therefore you will need to have:

As the groundspeed increases, hold the ground radius constant by increasing the bank angle.

- the **steepest** bank angle when headed directly downwind; and
- the **shallowest** bank angle when headed directly upwind.

This maneuver is illustrated in figure 16a-13.

It is a good technique, when flying turns about a ground reference object, to **enter flying downwind** at a suitable distance (one-quarter to one-half mile) so that the steepest turn required, which will be directly downwind on your entry track, does not exceed 45° bank angle. You will then start the maneuver with the steepest bank angle, gradually reducing the bank angle as you turn crosswind and then upwind, where the bank angle is shallowest.

When past the directly upwind point, you will have to gradually steepen the bank angle until it reaches its maximum value again directly downwind.

In these flight maneuvers (by reference to ground based objects), you should monitor the airspeed carefully and share your time between airplane control and ground tracking. Keep the airspeed within 10 KIAS of that chosen, the altitude to within 100 feet, and the coordination ball centered. Keep a good lookout.

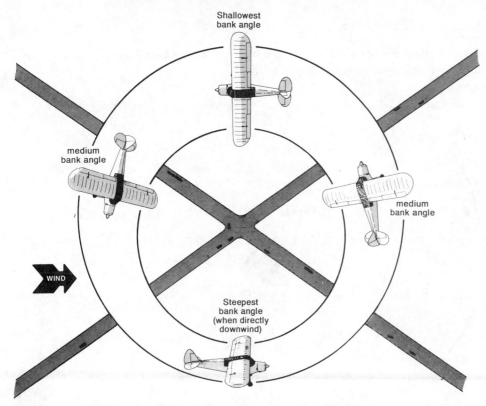

Figure 16a-13. Turns around a point—a circular ground path

Note: If you want to practice this maneuver, but there is no wind, you could perhaps generate your own "wind" by making your turns about a ground object that is moving, for instance a car or tractor moving slowly along a straight country road.

S-Turns across a Road

Making S-turns across a road uses the same principles as turning in a wind, except that, after each 180° of turn, the direction of turn is changed. The object is to fly a series of equi-size semicircles either side of a road that lies perpendicular to the wind.

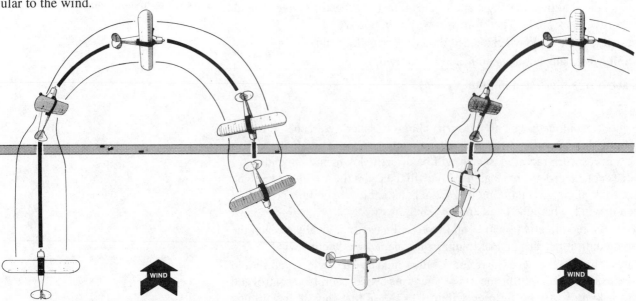

Figure 16a-14. S-turns across a road

The ground radius of each semicircle is adjusted by changing the bank angle, which will be *steepest* when flying downwind. You will briefly level the wings passing overhead the road as you reverse the direction of the turn.

The bank angle will be *shallowest* when heading upwind, with the wings being leveled again as you cross the road and reverse the direction of turn.

Low Flying

A low level is generally considered to be 500 feet above ground level (AGL) or lower. Low-level flying may be necessary:

Low level flying is 500 feet AGL or below.

- **in poor weather conditions** such as low cloud and/or poor visibility; or
- **to inspect a field** in preparation for a forced landing with power available (known as a *precautionary landing*).

Pilot Responsibilities

Do not fly below 500 feet AGL, except when taking off or landing. There are other restrictions regarding flight over built-up areas (1,000 feet above the highest obstacle within a horizontal radius of 2,000 feet from the aircraft), and so on. For the purpose of training, it is usual to select an altitude 600 feet to 1,000 feet AGL in a suitable area.

Remain aware of your pilot responsibilities when low flying.

Low clouds, or some other unforeseen situation, may force you below the minimum legal levels. As a visual pilot, you are not qualified to enter clouds and this should be avoided at all costs. If low clouds are encountered, it is better to fly slowly beneath them closer to the ground and turn back as soon as possible, rather than to enter clouds. This is because, in clouds, all visual contact with the ground and the horizon will be lost, and the consequences for an untrained pilot are usually fatal!

Be aware that **radio communication,** which depends on line-of-sight transmission, may be poor at low levels.

Watch out for radio towers, and elevated cables when low flying, especially in valleys.

Around the country there are some areas that have been set aside for local low-level training. Other aircraft may be operating there at the same time as you, so maintain a good **lookout** for them (and for obstructions such as TV towers and transmission lines). Do not forget that balloons, helicopters, sailplanes, hang-gliders and ultralight aircraft may also be operating at low levels.

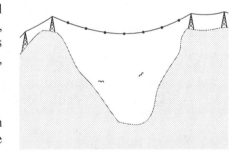

Obstacle Clearance

A close study of maps of the area is advisable prior to flight—special attention should be given to the elevation of the ground above sea level, the nature of the terrain, and the position of obstacles.

You have a limited field of vision when flying low, and ground features move rapidly through it. You need to **anticipate any ground features and recognize them quickly.** Obstacles such as overhead cables, radio and TV towers, chimneys and rising ground deserve particular attention—especially when flying in valleys where power transmission lines could be suspended up to 2,000 feet above the valley floor. Transmission towers are sometimes 1,000 feet high, with almost invisible supporting guy-wires.

Ground obstructions can be noted prior to starting to fly at low level.

Aeronautical charts may show only obstacles higher than 300 feet above ground level. If you fly 500 feet higher than the highest elevation shown on the chart for the area, your obstacle clearance may in fact be only 200 feet. Flying at 300 feet AGL you may have no obstacle clearance at all, especially if significant altimeter errors are present. Charts specify terrain and obstacles in terms of altitude above mean sea level (MSL). If you are using a chart to determine vertical clearance from obstacles, then the current *altimeter setting* should be set in the pressure window so that the altimeter reads altitude *MSL*.

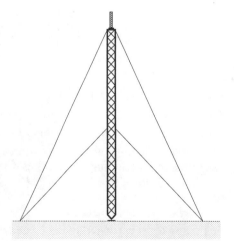

Figure 16a-15. Elevated cables and radio towers are a hazard to low-flying aircraft.

If there are air currents running down a slope, then be certain that your airplane has the performance to outclimb them. For instance, if your airplane climbs at 700 feet per minute (fpm), and the downdraft is at 600 fpm, then your climb over the ground is quite shallow, in fact only 100 fpm. If the ground is rising, you may not clear it. Raising the nose will not help—it will lead to a loss of airspeed, and a poorer climb performance if you are already at the best climb speed.

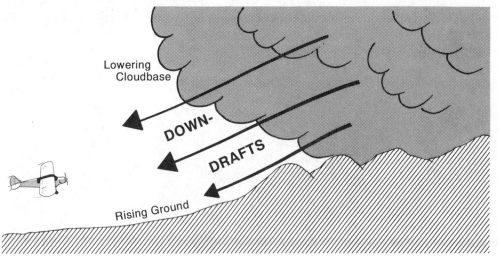

Figure 16a-16. Avoid a lowering cloud base, rising ground and downdrafts.

Some common sense rules for obstacle-clearance are:
- anticipate rising ground and climb early to remain at the desired altitude above it;
- ensure that the airplane can actually out-climb the rising ground, especially if a wind is blowing down its slope;
- avoid areas of rising ground associated with a lowering cloud base;
- always be prepared to turn back.

Ground Features
Features with significant vertical dimensions are good landmarks for low level navigation. Isolated hills and peaks, high monuments, factory chimneys and radio or television towers fall into this category.

Select ground features suitable for low flying.

Figure 16a-17. Choose landmarks suitable for low-level flying.

Misleading Visual Effects
The dangers when low flying are:
- the illusion of a high speed when flying downwind—do not be tricked into reducing power and slowing down— monitor your airspeed indicator;
- the illusion of slipping or skidding when flying crosswind—keep the coordination ball centered.

Be careful of the visual illusions caused by wind when low flying.

Obstacle Avoidance
Begin any turns early enough to be certain of remaining **downwind** of them. If you try to turn upwind of them, there is a risk that the wind will carry you back into the obstacles.

Remain downwind of obstacles.

Turbulence and Windshear

The air is often more turbulent near the ground than at higher altitudes for various reasons, the main ones being:

- surface friction slowing down strong winds;
- changes in wind speed and/or direction—windshear; and
- uneven heating of the earth's surface creating convection currents.

Expect increased turbulence and windshear at low levels.

The possibility of turbulence at low level is another reason why it is good airmanship to **keep your hand on the throttle** most of the time when low flying, to enable an immediate response to airspeed variations if they occur.

Airplane Configuration

In good visibility and over open country, the normal cruise configuration of *clean* wings may be suitable for low-level flying.

Consider the precautionary configuration for low flying.

In poor visibility, or in confined areas where good maneuverability is required, however, a *precautionary configuration* of some flaps extended may be preferable.

Using the **precautionary configuration** allows:

- *better vision* because of the lower nose attitude with flaps extended;
- *a lower cruise speed* because of the reduced stalling speed;
- *better maneuverability* and smaller radius turns because of the lower airspeed; and
- *better response* to elevator and rudder, because the extra power required causes a greater slipstream effect.

A *disadvantage* of having flaps extended for long periods, however, is the increased fuel consumption and consequent reduced range capability of your airplane.

Flying the Maneuvers

Flight maneuvering by reference to ground objects, for the private pilot, involves flying a rectangular course, S-turns across a road, and turns around a point. These maneuvers are described in the four **Airwork** diagrams that follow.

Preparation for Low Flying

Since it is important that the pilot maintains a good lookout when flying at a low level, a **low flying check** of items in the cockpit should be completed prior to descending. The **FREHA** check, outlined previously, may be adequate:

Be well prepared before descending to a low level.

F—Fuel: on and sufficient;

    Fuel tank usage: monitored;

    (Fuel) Mixture: RICH;

    Fuel pump (if fitted): ON and fuel pressure checked;

R—Radio frequency: correctly selected, volume and squelch satisfactory; make any necessary radio calls (reception will decrease at low levels);

E—Engine: oil temperature and pressure, carburetor heat if required, check other systems (ammeter for electrical system, suction gauge for air-driven gyroscopic instruments if installed);

H—Heading indicator: aligned with magnetic compass, and your position on the chart checked;

A—Altitude checked and altimeter setting correct.

Additional check items prior to low-level flight should include:

- the security of the airplane (doors and harnesses), and take steps to make the airplane more visible (landing lights, rotating beacon and strobe lights *ON,* if appropriate);
- check the surface wind direction (use smoke, dust, wind lines on lakes, and so on);
- adopt the chosen configuration (clean, or with some flaps extended in the precautionary configuration);
- trim.

A good **lookout** is essential! Study the ground even before you begin the descent to a low level, to ensure that adequate clearance above obstacles can be maintained and also look out for other aircraft. **Beware of rising ground,** especially if a wind is blowing down its slopes!

Allow for Airplane Inertia

The airplane will take time to respond to any control movements because of its inertia, which is a resistance to change. Begin climbs and turns early to avoid obstacles. Turn downwind of obstacles, rather than upwind of them, to avoid being blown back onto them. Avoid harsh maneuvers (such as steep turns or high-g pull-ups) which may lead to accelerated or "high-speed" stalls.

Trim

An airplane that is correctly trimmed is easier to fly and more likely to maintain altitude. Since your attention is directed out of the cockpit for most of the time in low-level flying, a well trimmed airplane is essential.

A slight nose-up trim will help ensure that an unintentional descent does not occur.

Figure 16a-18. Monitor the airspeed and coordination ball when flying at low level.

Keep in trim when low flying.

Airmanship

Maintain a high visual awareness. Keep a good lookout for other aircraft and also for birds. Avoid **congested areas** and maintain a suitable altitude (at least 500 feet AGL). Also, avoid annoying people or farm animals. Select a suitable area with good ground references.

Beware of false impressions caused by the wind effect, best counteracted by reference to the airspeed indicator and the coordination ball. Be aware of false horizons.

Share your time appropriately between:

- airplane control;
- maintaining and adjusting the path over the ground, keeping coordinated with rudder pressure; and
- maintaining a visual scan so that you can see-and-avoid other aircraft or obstacles, if necessary.

Apply the necessary wind drift corrections in straight flight by adjusting heading, and in constant ground radius turns by adjusting bank angle (but not to exceed 45°). Entering a maneuver with the wind behind you will mean that the first turn will be the steepest.

Turbulence may be greater at low levels, so ensure that you are strapped in securely.

Hold the chosen speed to within 10 KIAS and altitude to within 100 feet. Avoid bank angles in excess of 45°.

Vital points when flying low are to:
- **keep a good lookout for other aircraft and for obstacles;**
- **monitor the airspeed (resist any temptation to slow down in a tailwind);**
- **keep coordinated and in trim;**
- **stay well clear and turn downwind of obstacles.**

Airwork 16a, Part (i)
Low-Level Flying and Wind Awareness

Objectives
1. To fly the airplane safely at a low level.
2. To observe the misleading visual effects caused by a strong wind at low levels.

---

1. Prior to Descending

- Complete FREHA check *(refer to full version earlier in the text)*
- Additional considerations:
    Security of the airplane (doors and harnesses, and so on) and its visibility (landing lights, beacon, strobes ON)
    Note the surface wind speed and direction
    Select a suitable area with good ground references and no obstructions or other hazards
    Airplane configuration (clean or with some flaps extended)
    Trim
    Decide on a suitable IAS for the operation
    Low flying regulations

> **F**—Fuel system checks.
> **R**—Radio correctly set.
> **E**—Engine and systems for normal operation.
> **H**—Heading indicator aligned correctly and position on the chart checked.
> **A**—Altitude and altimeter pressure setting checked.

2. Descent to Low Level

- Begin the descent, hand on the throttle, and **keep a good lookout.**
- Fly no lower than 500 feet AGL *(or as advised by your flight instructor).*
- Estimate terrain clearance visually, with back-up from the altimeter and know the elevation MSL of the terrain.

> **Clear the area** and **look out** for obstacles and other aircraft—including balloons, ultralight airplanes, gliders and sailplanes, parachutists, airships, towers, masts, hang-gliders, large birds and flocks of birds.

3. Establish Cruise Flight at the Desired Level

- Establish the airplane at your chosen airspeed and altitude.
- Trim.
- Consider increasing power in any medium turns to maintain airspeed.

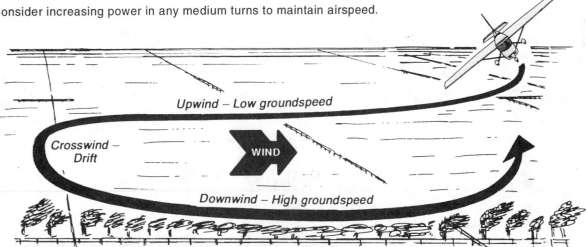

Upwind – Low groundspeed

Crosswind – Drift

WIND

Downwind – High groundspeed

4. Observe the Various Effects of Wind—Look Out

These are more noticeable as you near the ground.

- For the same IAS, there is a low groundspeed **upwind**—check the ASI, and a high groundspeed **downwind,** so do not remove power without first checking the ASI when flying downwind.
- Noticeable drift on crosswind legs—check **coordination ball centered**
- Significant downwind drift in turns—again check the coordination ball—and do not fly close to obstacles.

Airwork 16a, Part (ii)
Rectangular Pattern

Objective
To fly a rectangular pattern at constant altitude and constant airspeed around the edges of a field, allowing for wind effects.

Practice at 600 to 1,000 feet AGL. Select a suitable field or road pattern with sides about one mile long, and fly about one-half to one-quarter mile from the boundary for good vision and to keep the bank angle in the turns to less than 45°.

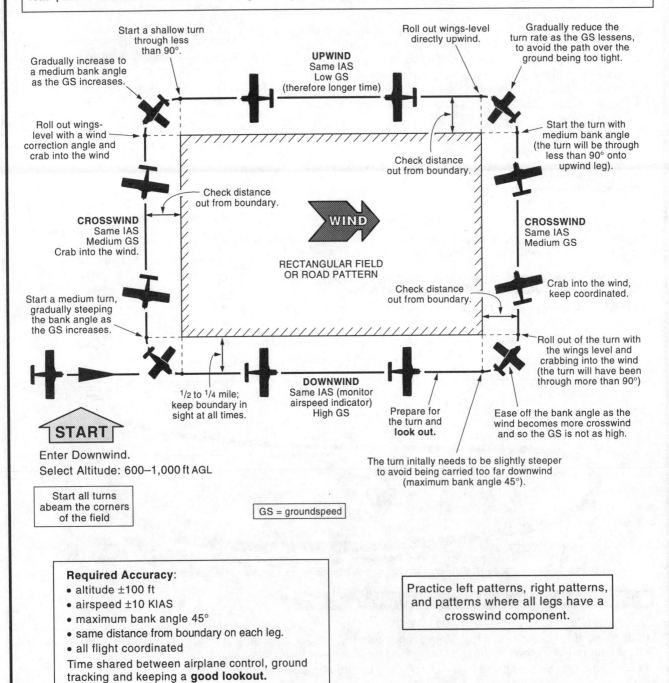

Start a shallow turn through less than 90°.

Gradually increase to a medium bank angle as the GS increases.

Roll out wings-level with a wind correction angle and crab into the wind

Check distance out from boundary.

CROSSWIND
Same IAS
Medium GS
Crab into the wind.

Start a medium turn, gradually steeping the bank angle as the GS increases.

UPWIND
Same IAS
Low GS
(therefore longer time)

Roll out wings-level directly upwind.

Gradually reduce the turn rate as the GS lessens, to avoid the path over the ground being too tight.

Start the turn with medium bank angle (the turn will be through less than 90° onto upwind leg).

Check distance out from boundary.

WIND

RECTANGULAR FIELD OR ROAD PATTERN

CROSSWIND
Same IAS
Medium GS

Crab into the wind, keep coordinated.

Check distance out from boundary.

Roll out of the turn with the wings level and crabbing into the wind (the turn will have been through more than 90°)

½ to ¼ mile; keep boundary in sight at all times.

DOWNWIND
Same IAS (monitor airspeed indicator)
High GS

Prepare for the turn and **look out.**

Ease off the bank angle as the wind becomes more crosswind and so the GS is not as high.

START

Enter Downwind.
Select Altitude: 600–1,000 ft AGL

The turn initally needs to be slightly steeper to avoid being carried too far downwind (maximum bank angle 45°).

Start all turns abeam the corners of the field

GS = groundspeed

Required Accuracy:
- altitude ±100 ft
- airspeed ±10 KIAS
- maximum bank angle 45°
- same distance from boundary on each leg.
- all flight coordinated

Time shared between airplane control, ground tracking and keeping a **good lookout.**

Practice left patterns, right patterns, and patterns where all legs have a crosswind component.

Airwork 16a, Part (iii)
Turns Around a Point

Objective

To fly a constant ground-radius turn about a ground reference point, and to maintain a constant altitude and constant airspeed.

> Practice this maneuver no lower than 500 feet AGL (typically 600 to 1,000 feet AGL).
> Practice in both directions, for at least 2 turns.

- Select a suitable ground reference point (house, crossroads, and so on).
- Clear the area and **keep a good lookout**.
- Select a roll-out point, or choose a roll-out heading.
- Choose an altitude and airspeed.
- Enter downwind and commence turn (maximum bank angle 45°).
- Gradually reduce bank angle as you turn from downwind to upwind.
- Monitor ground track, and alter bank angle to maintain it.
- Gradually increase bank angle as you turn from upwind to downwind.
- Fly at least two turns and roll out on desired heading.

Required Accuracy:
- altitude ±100 ft
- airspeed ±10 KIAS
- coordination ball centered

Do not exceed 45° bank angle.

Divide attention between coordinated airplane control, ground tracking, and keeping a **good lookout.** Also, practice entering at points other than direct downwind.

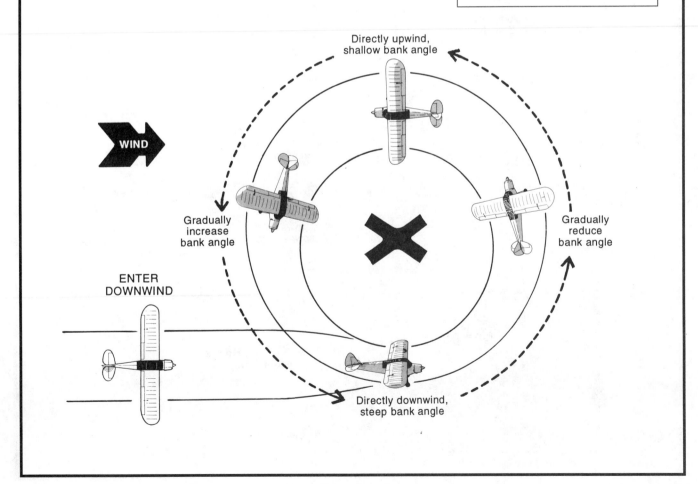

Airwork 16a, Part (iv)
S-Turns Across a Road

Objective

To fly a series of S-turns across a line feature, with semicircles of equal ground-size, and to maintain a constant altitude and a constant airspeed.

> Practice this maneuver no lower than 500 feet AGL—typically 600 to 1,000 feet AGL.

- Select a suitable road, highway, railroad or other line feature that lies crosswind.
- Clear the area and **keep a good lookout**.
- Choose an altitude and airspeed.
- Approach the line feature from the upwind side, so that the initial turn will be the steepest bank angle (do not exceed 45°).
- Crossing the reference feature, apply the steeper bank angle, gradually decreasing it as you turn upwind.
- Level the wings crossing the feature upwind, and apply a shallow bank angle in the opposite direction.
- Gradually increase the bank angle as you turn downwind.
- Level the wings as you cross the feature downwind, and then apply a steep bank angle in the opposite direction.

> **Required Accuracy**:
> - altitude ±100 ft
> - airspeed ±10 KIAS
> - coordination ball centered
>
> Do not exceed 45° bank angle.
>
> Time share between coordinated airplane control, ground tracking, and keeping a **good lookout**.

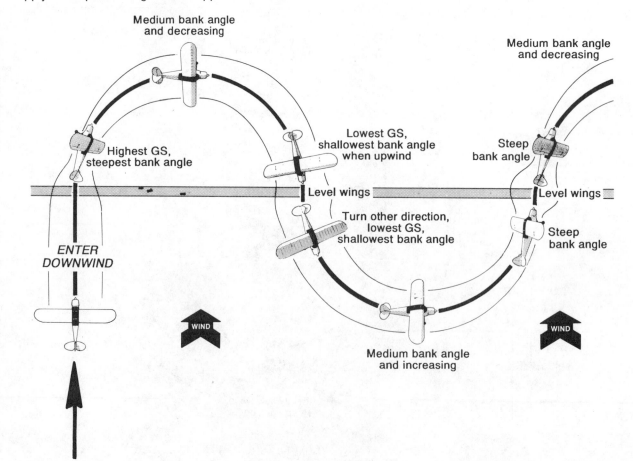

Further Points

Low Flying in Bad Weather

Poor visibility, a descending cloud base or rising ground may require some unplanned low flying. You are obliged to remain in visual meteorological conditions, but if you are caught out in really marginal conditions, maintain as much separation from the ground as possible, but **avoid entering clouds.**

Do not enter clouds.

In reality, you should never find yourself in this situation! Always plan carefully, and exert strong operational control over your flight to avoid this sort of situation.

If you are caught out in bad weather, however, use any aircraft systems that can assist you in coping with it, such as carburetor heat (if appropriate), pitot heaters, and so on. Make your airplane more visible by switching on the rotating beacon, strobe, and landing lights.

If the legal requirements of minimum visibility and distance from clouds cannot be satisfied, then consideration should be given to:
- diverting to an area where better weather exists;
- landing at a nearby airport;
- requesting radar guidance if navigation is a problem; or
- making a precautionary landing in a field (this procedure is discussed in Exercise 17b).

The Bad-Weather Traffic Pattern

At a tower-controlled airport in bad weather, the controllers may pick the traffic pattern they wish you to fly. ATC may switch on the airport beacon in daylight if conditions are less than VFR (visibility less than three miles and/or cloud ceiling less than 1,000 feet). **At nontowered airports** in bad weather, while ideally you would fly the standard traffic pattern, this may not be possible. You will have to devise your own safe pattern in terms of track, altitude, airplane configuration and airspeed.

A traffic pattern in bad weather—poor visibility and/or a low cloud base—should be organized so that **visual contact with the field** is not lost. This may require a tight pattern flown at low level in the precautionary configuration. Aim for a traffic pattern altitude of **at least 500 feet** AGL, if possible, but **do not enter clouds!** Maintain a clearance of at least 300 feet vertically from obstacles.

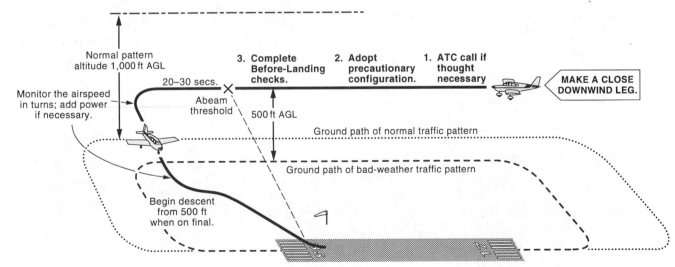

Figure 16a-19. The bad-weather traffic pattern at an uncontrolled airport

---

Exercise 16a **Private Pilot Ground Reference Maneuvers**

✍️ Review 16a

1. The speed of an airplane through the air is called its _____ speed.

   ➤ air

2. The speed of an airplane over the ground is called its _____ speed.

   ➤ groundspeed

3. In headwind conditions, the groundspeed will (exceed/be less than/be the same as) the airspeed.

   ➤ be less than

4. In tailwind conditions, a tailwind could give a false impression of (high/low) speed, so check the a_____ i_____ , and do not fall into the trap of (reducing/increasing) airspeed.

   ➤ high, airspeed indicator, reducing

5. To maintain a desired track over the ground, apply a w_____ c_____ a_____ , also known as a c_____ a_____ , (into/out of) the wind.

   ➤ wind correction angle, crab angle, into

6. The flying characteristics of an airplane, such as the stall, are determined by its (airspeed/ groundspeed).

   ➤ airspeed

7. When maintaining a straight track in a crosswind by applying a wind correction angle, the coordination ball should be (kept centered/out to one side).

   ➤ kept centered

8. Check airspeed on the _____ _____ , and check that flight is coordinated on the _____ _____ .

   ➤ airspeed indicator, coordination ball

9. For a given speed, the steeper the bank angle, the (tighter/wider) the turn.

   ➤ tighter

10. For a given bank angle, the higher the speed, the (tighter/wider) the turn.

    ➤ wider

Private Pilot
Ground Reference Maneuvers

11. To maintain a constant ground radius about a reference ground object in a turn in a strong wind, you need to (vary bank angle/maintain bank angle constant).

    ➤ vary bank angle

12. When downwind in a turn, the groundspeed will be (greatest/least), and so the bank angle will have to be (greatest/least) to maintain a constant ground radius.

    ➤ greatest, greatest

13. When upwind in a turn, the groundspeed will be (greatest/least), and so the bank angle will have to be (greatest/least) to maintain a constant ground radius.

    ➤ least, least

14. A low level is considered to be _____ feet AGL or below.

    ➤ 500 feet AGL

15. Most low-level maneuvers are carried out at _____ to _____ feet AGL.

    ➤ 600 to 1,000 feet AGL

16. Aeronautical charts (will always/may not) show transmission towers and other obstacles less than 300 feet high.

    ➤ may not

17. Required accuracy in ground reference maneuvers for private pilots is:
    - nominated altitude plus or minus _____ feet;
    - nominated airspeed plus or minus _____ KIAS;
    - maximum bank angle _____ °; and
    - coordination ball (centered/not centered).

    ➤ plus or minus 100 feet, plus or minus 10 KIAS, 45°, centered

18. In poor weather conditions, you notice that an airport beacon is operating even though it is daylight. This indicates that VFR conditions of at least visibility _____ miles and/or a cloud ceiling of _____ feet above the airport elevation (do/do not) exist, and that a 1,000 feet AGL traffic pattern (will/may not) be possible.

    ➤ 3 miles, 1,000 feet, do not, may not

Commercial Pilot Ground Reference Maneuvers 16b

Maneuvers Covered

Steep Spirals, Eights Around Pylons and Eights-On-Pylons are covered in these commercial pilot flight maneuvers by reference to ground objects.

Part (i)
Steep Spirals

The Steep Spiral is a combination of:
- a steep descending turn (to lose altitude quickly); and
- turns around a point (to remain over a ground reference point).

The practical purpose of a steep spiral over a ground reference object could be to lose altitude rapidly over a selected emergency landing field.

To maintain a constant ground radius around a ground reference object, you need to **vary the bank angle.** It will be steepest when the wind is from behind you, and shallowest when you are heading into the wind.

The steep descending turn, as an air maneuver with a constant bank angle, will allow the wind to carry the airplane with it. The steep spiral, based on a ground reference point, uses a varying bank angle to counteract this wind drift.

You should re-read *Steep Descending Turns* and *Turns Around a Point,* and apply the techniques discussed there to this exercise. Since the stalling speed increases in a turn, it is usual to fly at a greater airspeed than the best-glide airspeed when performing a steep spiral.

Altitude loss is quite rapid in the steep-spiral maneuver. Depending on the airplane used, it could be as much as 1,000 feet per 360° turn—so in three complete turns you may lose 3,000 feet. The object is to roll out toward a distant reference point or on a specified heading after three or more 360° turns, no lower than 1,500 feet AGL.

In a prolonged spiral, you may decide to warm the engine by opening the throttle. This is best done as you turn through the upwind direction where the bank angle is shallowest. Throughout the maneuver, divide your attention between airplane control, flight path over the ground and orientation. **Keep a good lookout** for other airplanes, especially below.

If you are using this maneuver to position yourself for either a practice or a real power-off forced landing, then a suitable roll-out point could be 1,500 feet AGL or higher, in a position from where you can successfully complete a traffic pattern to a simulated or actual forced landing—discussed later in Exercise 17a.

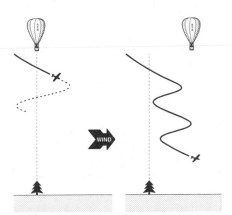

Figure 16b-1a. The steep descending turn moves with the wind.

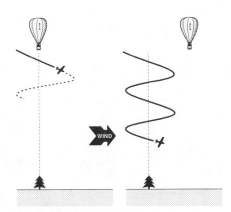

Figure 16b-1b. The steep spiral remains centered on a ground object.

Airwork 16b, Part (i)
Steep Spirals

(Commercial Pilots only)

Objective
To descend in a steep spiral, maintaining a constant-ground-radius turn over a ground reference point.

> Practice this maneuver by starting at an altitude that enables you to roll out in level flight no lower than a minimum safe altitude to maneuver for a traffic pattern (recommended roll-out at or above 1,500 feet AGL). You will need to complete at least three 360° turns.

1. Entering a Steep Spiral

- Climb to a suitable starting altitude.
- Select a suitable ground reference point that is prominent (tree, road intersection).
- Complete the HASELL pre-aerobatic check.
- **Clear the area** and **look out.**
- Select a roll-out point or roll-out heading, specifying the number of 360° descending turns you will make.
- Enter the Steep Spiral downwind so that the first turn will be steepest (maximum 55° bank angle).
- Reduce power (carb heat—ON, throttle—CLOSED, mixture RICH) and enter straight glide.

- Add some speed to the best wings-level gliding speed to retain an adequate margin over the increased stalling speed in a turn (it is +20 knots for a 60° steep descending turn). Hold this speed throughout the maneuver.
- Roll into a bank with aileron and coordinated rudder (maximum 50° to 55°), adjusting the bank angle as necessary to maintain the specified ground radius.
- Hold the nose in a slightly lower pitch attitude to maintain an increased airspeed.

2. Maintaining the Steep Spiral

- **Clear the area**.
- Monitor the ground reference point and your ground track around it (maintain a constant ground radius).
- Expect to reduce the bank angle as you turn from downwind to upwind, and then increase the bank angle again as you turn downwind once again.
- Keep coordinated with rudder.
- Maintain the target airspeed (±10 KIAS)—if the airspeed increases, reduce the bank angle, raise the nose with elevator control and reapply the desired bank angle.

- Periodically clear the engine by briefly advancing the throttle to normal cruise power (upwind is best, where the bank angle is shallowest).
- Divide your attention between airplane control, flight path over the ground, and orientation (note the roll-out reference point or heading on each turn, and count the turns).
- Check your altitude (and roll out early, if necessary, to avoid going below the minimum safe altitude—recommended minimum 1,500 feet AGL).
- Be prepared for the wind to decrease and change in direction as you descend, but maintain a constant ground radius by varying the bank angle.

3. The Roll-Out

- **Clear the area**.
- Roll out of the bank using aileron and coordinated rudder, starting about 30° before the selected reference point or heading.

- Select the desired pitch attitude with elevator (for a straight glide, straight-and-level, or climb), and apply power as required (mixture—RICH, carb heat—OFF, throttle—INCREASE).

> Maintain airspeed with elevator.
> Maintain a constant ground radius with bank angle.
> If desired, control the rate of descent with power.

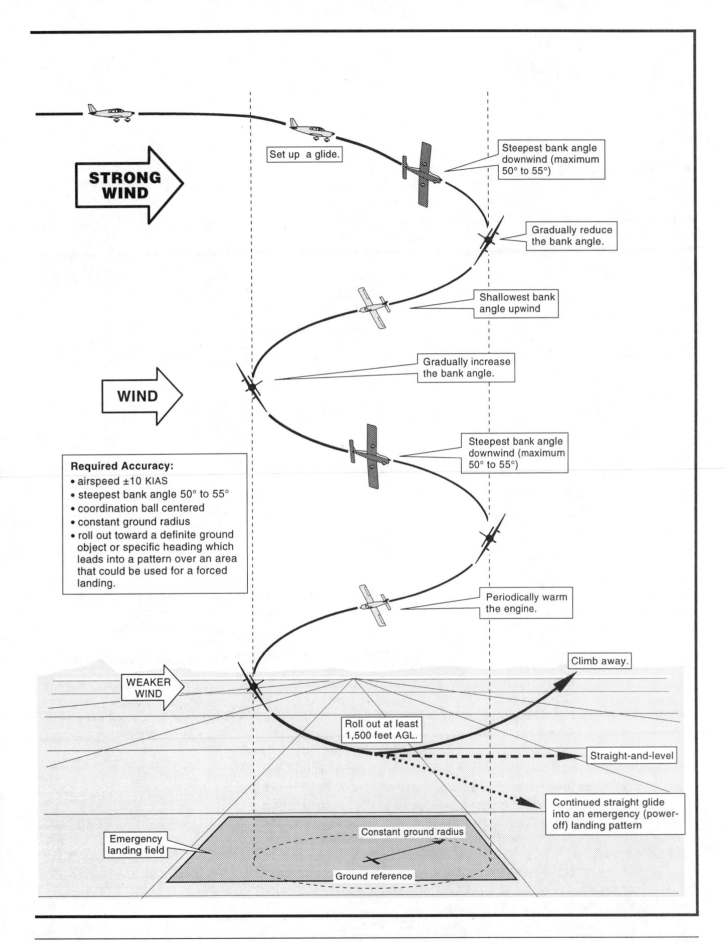

STRONG WIND

Set up a glide.

Steepest bank angle downwind (maximum 50° to 55°)

Gradually reduce the bank angle.

Shallowest bank angle upwind

Gradually increase the bank angle.

WIND

Steepest bank angle downwind (maximum 50° to 55°)

Required Accuracy:
- airspeed ±10 KIAS
- steepest bank angle 50° to 55°
- coordination ball centered
- constant ground radius
- roll out toward a definite ground object or specific heading which leads into a pattern over an area that could be used for a forced landing.

Periodically warm the engine.

Climb away.

WEAKER WIND

Roll out at least 1,500 feet AGL.

Straight-and-level

Continued straight glide into an emergency (power-off) landing pattern

Emergency landing field

Constant ground radius

Ground reference

Part (ii)
Eights Around Pylons

Eights around pylons is a constant-altitude maneuver in which you fly a symmetrical figure-eight pattern around two ground features, known as *pylons*.

To fly a symmetrical pattern over the ground, you have to counteract the wind drift, which you can do by varying the bank angle while you maintain a constant altitude—the steepest bank angle being needed when the groundspeed is highest (when the wind is behind you), and the shallowest angle when you are flying upwind and the groundspeed is least. Eights around pylons is really *turns around a point* multiplied by two.

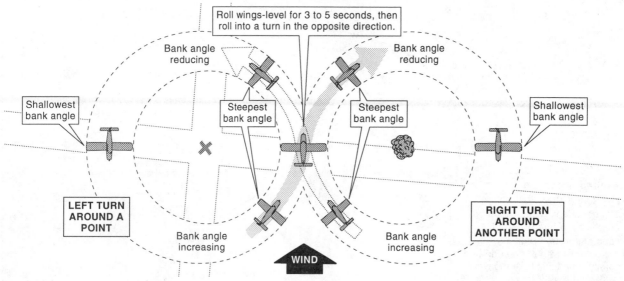

Figure 16b-2. Constant-altitude eights around pylons

The closer the two selected pylons are to each other, the tighter the ground radius will have to be, and the steeper the bank angle. Also, the higher the speed of the airplane, the steeper the bank required.

The recommended maximum bank angle for this maneuver is 30° to 40° at the steepest point, which will be downwind. At typical cruise speeds, this will mean a ground radius of one-quarter to one-half mile, so choose two pylons about one mile apart and perpendicular to the wind. This will enable you to enter the eight pattern at the midpoint, with the wind behind you, and roll into the steepest bank angle required.

As you fly around the first circle, you will reduce the bank angle gradually to its lowest value, which should occur as you fly directly upwind on the outer sides of the eight, and then steepen the bank angle as you approach the midpoint.

You then roll the wings level for three to five seconds and fly a straight path across the midpoint before rolling into a steep bank in the other direction. The figure-eight pattern will then look like two circles, with a short, straight transition where you roll out of the turn one way, wings-level for three to five seconds, and then turn the other way. Throughout the maneuver divide your attention between coordinated airplane control, checking your ground track, and looking out for other aircraft.

The turn is tightened by:
- **a steeper bank angle; or**
- **a slower groundspeed.**

The turn radius is kept constant by using:
- **a steeper bank angle when you have a higher groundspeed; and**
- **a shallower bank angle when you have a lower groundspeed.**

The further the pylons are apart, the shallower the turns required to follow two circles over the ground. You can tighten the turns, if you wish, by crossing the midpoint at an angle, flying a straight leg for more than three to five seconds and applying a wind correction angle into the wind on these straight legs to keep the ground paths symmetrical. Then, passing abeam the pylon, roll into the turn. You could also tighten the turns by selecting two pylons closer to each other.

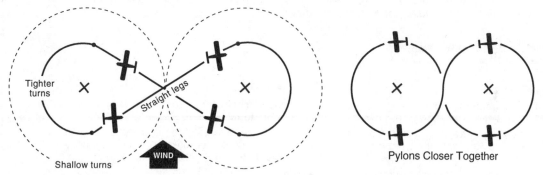

Figure 16b-3. Tightening the turns-required by flying straight legs, or selecting pylons closer to each other

How to Select Two Pylons

The better your choice of pylons, the easier the maneuver will be to fly. The **ideal** pair of pylons will satisfy the following requirements:
* The line joining them will be perpendicular to the wind (to make a straight downwind entry easy, and so that the initial bank angle will be the steepest).
* They will be situated about one mile apart (so that the ground radius of each circle will be one-quarter to one-half mile).
* They will be located on a line feature such as a straight road, which is not likely to be confused with other ground objects.

Suitable ground objects to choose as pylons include a large isolated tree or clump of trees, an isolated barn, a crossroad junction, or a railroad bridge.

A good technique when selecting pylons is to fly crosswind between two line features (roads, railroads, fence lines, and so on), and to search both left and right. Having found two pylons, you can then position to fly downwind at the midpoint between them and roll into the steepest turn of the *eights around pylons* maneuver (recommended bank angle 30° to 40° at the steepest point).

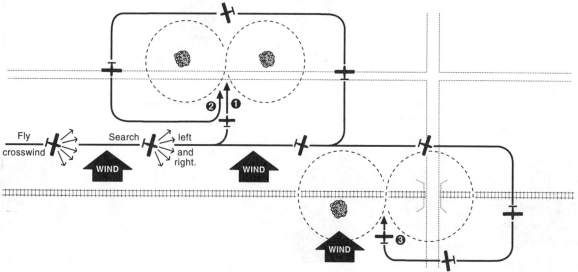

Figure 16b-4. Selecting a pair of pylons and positioning for a downwind entry

Airwork 16b, Part (ii)
Eights Around Pylons

(Commercial Pilots only)

Objective

To fly a figure-eight pattern over the ground consisting of alternating left and right circles of equal ground radius, centered on two pylons, maintaining a constant altitude and airspeed.

Entering and Maintaining the Eight

- Fly crosswind and select two pylons about one mile apart that are perpendicular to the wind.
- **Look out** for hazards and other aircraft.
- Position the airplane so that you can enter the eight-pattern at normal cruise airspeed flying across the midpoint between the pylons with the wind from behind (so the groundspeed will be highest).
- Look for a distant reference point to assist in rolling wings-level as you transition from one circle to the other.
- Select your airspeed and altitude (and then **keep** them!).
- Crossing the midpoint, roll into a turn (the recommended maximum bank angle is 30° to 40°), gradually decreasing it to its shallowest value as you turn upwind on the outer sides of the eight. Be prepared to apply slight back pressure in the turn to maintain a constant altitude.

- Turning in toward the midpoint again, gradually steepen the bank angle.
- Continually monitor the ground track, and alter the bank angle to maintain it.
- Shortly before reaching the midpoint, and using the distant reference point to assist in orientation, roll wings-level for 3 to 5 seconds. Relax the back pressure as you roll the wings level to avoid gaining altitude.
- Immediately after crossing the midpoint, roll in to a steep bank in the other direction to commence the second half of the eight. Gradually reduce the bank angle as you turn upwind ....
- Throughout the maneuver, divide your attention between coordinated airplane control, maintaining the desired ground track, and looking out for hazards and other aircraft.
- Fly at least three patterns—each one getting better!

Practice this maneuver at a constant altitude between 600 and 1,000 feet AGL.

Accuracy:
- constant altitude ±100 ft
- airspeed ±10 KIAS
- coordination ball centered

Recommended maximum bank angle 30° to 40° at the steepest point

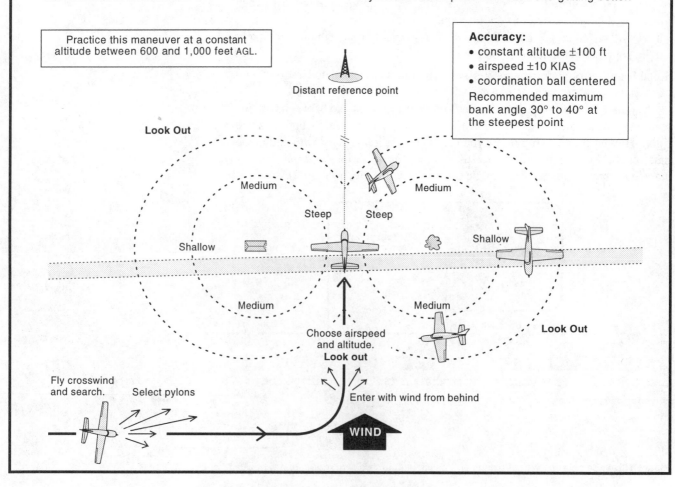

Part (iii)
Eights-On-Pylons

Eights-on-pylons is an approximate figure-eight flown around two pylons, with the wingtip pivoting on the pylons.

The aim is **not** to fly a perfect figure-eight pattern over the ground (as in the eights *around* pylons ground reference maneuver), but to keep the wingtip pinned on the pylon.

Eights-on-pylons is a three-dimensional maneuver, with altitude, airspeed and bank angle varying gradually throughout the maneuver (especially in strong winds).

Using two pylons, you will fly alternating left and right 360° turns, making an approximate figure-eight pattern about the pylons.

Figure 16b-5. What you want to see out of the side window—the wingtip "pinned" on the pylon

Bank Angle

The eights-on-pylons maneuver is easier to understand if we consider the turn pivoted on one of the pylons first—that is, only one-half of the complete eight. The closer you are to the pylon, the steeper the bank angle needed to put the wingtip on the pylon, as shown in figure 16b-6a below.

- At a given altitude, the closer you are to a point above the pylon, the steeper the bank angle has to be to place the wingtip on the pylon.

- At a given speed, the radius of turn will depend upon the bank angle—the steeper the bank angle, the tighter the turn. We can see this effect in the figure below, where, at 100 knots, the shallower bank angle results in a wider turn and the steeper bank angle results in a tighter turn—with all of the turns being centered on a point above the pylon.

Bank and put the wingtip on the pylon.

Near the pylon, the bank angle has to be steeper to put the wingtip on the pylon.

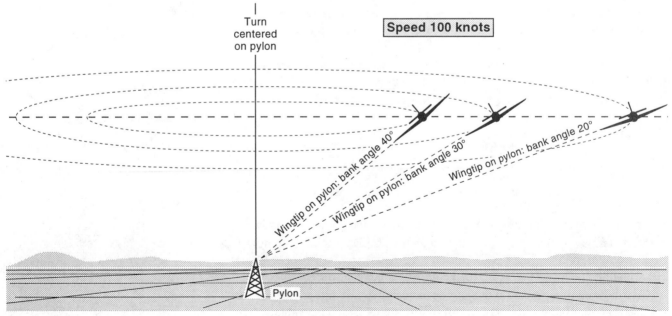

Figure 16b-6a. Near the pylon the bank angle has to be steeper to put the wingtip on the pylon.

Speed

The radius of turn depends not only upon bank angle, but also upon speed—the higher the speed, the wider the turn at a given bank angle.

If the airplane in the previous illustration was flying at the same altitude, but faster, say 120 knots instead of 100 knots, the turns would all be wider and so would no longer be centered on a point above the pylon. The airplane would fly away from the pylon—in other words, the pylon would appear to drift gradually behind the wingtip.

You could steepen the bank angle to reduce the turn radius, but the wingtip would then no longer be pinned on the pylon.

The radius of turn depends on bank angle and speed.

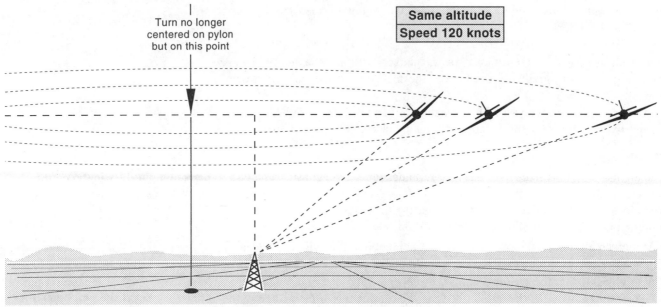

Turn no longer centered on pylon but on this point

| Same altitude |
| Speed 120 knots |

Figure 16b-6b. The higher the speed, the wider the turn (compare with previous figure)

Speed and Altitude

At the higher speed, you can still (1) place the wingtip on the pylon, and (2) center the turn on a point above the pylon, if you fly at a **higher** altitude and **steepen** the bank angle. Conversely, at a lower speed, you should fly at a lower altitude and a shallower bank angle.

The particular altitude for each speed is known as the **pivotal altitude.** It is only at this vertical distance above the pylon that you can place the wingtip on the pylon and pivot about it as the turn proceeds. See figure 16b-8.

At higher speeds, fly at a higher altitude.

Altitude Terminology

To make clear the important distinction between vertical distance above ground level (AGL) and above mean sea level (MSL), you could use the term *pivotal height* for the vertical distance of the airplane above ground level, and *pivotal altitude* for the vertical distance above mean sea level; this latter value is what you fly on the altimeter (with sea level pressure set in the pressure window).

Some terms you will encounter later, in your instrument rating training, use *height* to refer to the vertical distance above a ground reference—for example, HAA, height above airport, and HAT, height above touchdown.

To follow common usage in this maneuver, however, we refer to the vertical distance above ground level as the **pivotal altitude AGL,** and the value you fly on your altimeter, set on sea level pressure, as the **pivotal altitude MSL.** Be sure that you use the MSL pivotal altitude on your altimeter.

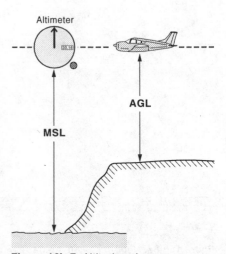

Figure 16b-7. Altitudes above mean sea level and above ground level

Calculating Pivotal Altitude AGL

If you fly at the pivotal altitude for your speed, then you only need to place the wingtip on the pylon and you will pivot about it (irrespective of the bank angle needed to place the wingtip on the pylon).

You can determine the pivotal altitude above the level of the pylon—that is, above ground level—using the (fairly simple) formula:

$$\text{Pivotal altitude AGL} = \frac{(\text{groundspeed in knots})^2}{11.3} \text{ feet AGL}$$

For example, at a groundspeed of **100 knots:**

$$\text{pivotal altitude AGL} = \frac{100^2}{11.3} = \frac{10,000}{11.3} = 885, \text{ (890 feet AGL to nearest 10 ft)}$$

At a groundspeed of **120 knots:**

$$\text{pivotal altitude AGL} = \frac{120^2}{11.3} = 1,274, \text{ (or 1,280 feet)}$$

At a groundspeed of **80 knots:**

$$\text{pivotal altitude AGL} = \frac{80^2}{11.3} = 566, \text{ (or 570 feet)}$$

Note: For those who are interested, a simple mathematical proof of this formula follows in the **Further Points** toward the end of this chapter.

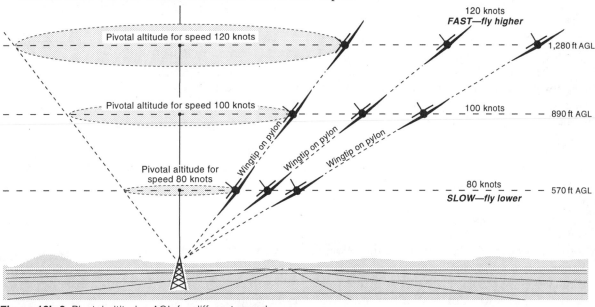

Figure 16b-8. Pivotal altitudes AGL for different speeds

What is interesting to note, and the crucial point to understand for this maneuver, is that each speed has its own pivotal altitude AGL. It does not depend on the bank angle at all, but only groundspeed.

Each groundspeed has its own pivotal altitude above the pylon.

If you are at the correct pivotal altitude for that speed, you simply place the wingtip on the pylon, using whatever bank angle is necessary, and the wingtip will pivot on the pylon as the turn progresses. The distance from the pylon is *not* important. The greater the distance, the shallower the bank angle required to place the wingtip on the pylon. If you are at the correct pivotal altitude for the speed, the turn will automatically center on the pylon.

Important: To use your altimeter when it is set on mean sea level pressure (as it usually is), add the calculated pivotal altitude AGL to your estimation of the ground elevation above mean sea level—for example, a calculated pivotal altitude of 890 feet AGL, plus a ground elevation of 1,200 feet MSL, equals **2,090 feet MSL,** which you would fly on the altimeter.

Flying the Maneuver in Zero-Wind

Flying at a constant airspeed in a zero-wind situation, the groundspeed of the airplane around a ground object (the pylon) will remain constant. Groundspeed will equal airspeed all the way around the turn.

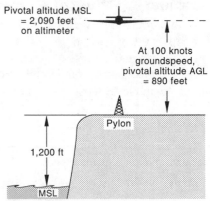

Pivotal altitude MSL = 2,090 feet on altimeter

At 100 knots groundspeed, pivotal altitude AGL = 890 feet

1,200 ft

Pylon

MSL

Figure 16b-9. Calculating the pivotal altitude MSL

Calculate the Pivotal Altitude MSL

First, calculate the **pivotal altitude** AGL for your groundspeed using the formula (or read it off a card that you have prepared earlier, to simplify the task in the air); add this figure to your estimate of the elevation of the pylon above sea level to obtain the **pivotal altitude MSL,** to use on your altimeter.

Plan on using the normal cruise speed.

Entering the Maneuver

Position yourself to fly abeam the pylon at a distance where you can place the wingtip on the pylon without having to exceed 40° bank angle. The recommended maximum bank angle is 30° to 40° at the steepest point, which is downwind.

Fly abeam pylon at, or slightly above, pivotal altitude.

Bank Angle

Passing abeam the pylon, roll into the turn and place the wingtip on the pylon. If you are close to the pylon, the bank angle will be steep; if you are further away, the bank angle will be shallow. This will not affect the maneuver since, if you are at the correct pivotal altitude for that speed, the turn will be centered above the pylon, provided you keep the wingtip on the pylon. The turns will be of different radii, but you will pivot about the pylon.

Roll into the turn and place the wingtip on the pylon.

Accuracy of the Maneuver

It is likely that your estimation of pivotal altitude is not exact, since it involves an estimation of the pylon's elevation above sea level if you want to use your altimeter, or it involves an estimation of your vertical distance above the pylon if you want to "eyeball" it. This does not create a problem—you simply begin the maneuver, then adjust your altitude if necessary.

If you are too high, you will tend to turn inside the pylon. From the cockpit, the pylon will appear to move gradually forward of the wingtip. Do not try to chase it using rudder; this will put the ball out of the center. Correct it by dropping down to a slightly lower altitude (use forward pressure on the control column).

Conversely, if you are too low, your turn will gradually take you wide of the pylon, which will appear to gradually slip back behind the wingtip. The solution is to climb to a slighly higher altitude (using back pressure on the control column). See figure 16b-10.

If calculated pivotal altitude is not correct, climb or descend as appropriate.

The Eights-On-Pylons Technique
1. Enter the maneuver at the estimated pivotal altitude MSL.
2. Abeam the pylon, place the wingtip on the pylon using the ailerons; keep coordinated with rudder—coordination ball centered.
3. Adjust the altitude if necessary.
   - *If the pylon moves forward:* apply forward pressure to descend.
   - *If pylon moves back:* apply back pressure to climb.

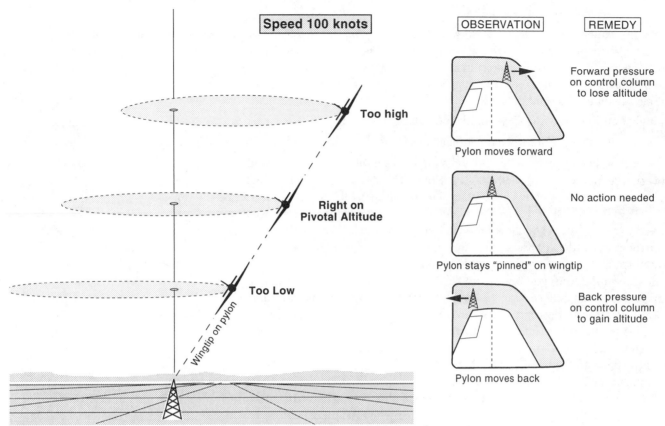

Figure 16b-10. Adjusting the altitude—apply elevator in the direction in which the pylon is moving, to move wingtip toward the pylon.

Control in the Maneuver

It was suggested earlier to enter the maneuver at, or slightly above, your estimated pivotal altitude MSL. This is because it is easier to lose a little altitude without having to change power than it is to gain it.

A benefit of this technique is that, in descending without reducing power, you will gain a little airspeed, which will mean a slightly higher pivotal altitude than earlier, and so you will not have to descend quite as far.

Conversely, in climbing without adding power, you will lose a little speed, so the pivotal altitude will be slightly lower than before, and hence you will not have to climb quite as far.

This does not require any calculation—you simply observe the movement of the pylon relative to the wingtip, and "pin" it with movements of the control column:

• aileron to keep it level with the wingtip;

• elevator to stop it moving fore or aft.

Note: Theoretically there is a second technique, but one that is **not recommended.** If you are not right at the pivotal altitude for your current speed, then alter the speed (rather than the altitude). This will require power changes and trim changes, making it more difficult to fly accurately. If you are flying in strong wind conditions, large power changes will be required to alter the airspeed in an attempt to keep the groundspeed constant. To keep it constant in a 20-knot wind, for instance, will require a 40-knot airspeed increase as you turn from flying downwind to flying upwind—the power demand may exceed the capability of the airplane.

Follow the pylon with the control column.

Exercise 16b **Commercial Pilot Ground Reference Maneuvers**

431

Flying the Maneuver in a Wind

To fly a complete 360° turn in a 20-knot wind at a constant airspeed, say 100 KIAS, your groundspeed will vary between 120 knots downwind and 80 knots upwind. The eights-on-pylons maneuver depends on groundspeed (since you are placing the wingtip on a ground object), so you will have to vary the altitude as you turn around the pylon.

- A higher altitude downwind, when the groundspeed is higher.
- A lower altitude upwind, when the groundspeed is lower.

The accepted entry technique is to fly diagonally crosswind (and downwind) between the pylons. The wind coming from behind will give you a high groundspeed, and consequently a higher pivotal altitude AGL. At 120 knots, it will be 1,280 feet AGL. Fly over the midpoint between the pylons, using a wind correction angle (WCA) to allow for drift. Wait until your wingtip is abeam the pylon (or even a little past it), and then roll into the turn using coordinated aileron and rudder, and place the wingtip on the pylon.

In your initial turn, you can expect the pylon to move forward gradually as your groundspeed reduces (and your pivotal altitude AGL reduces). Apply forward pressure to descend. Flying into the wind with a groundspeed of 80 knots, the pivotal altitude AGL is 570 feet, but you will have picked up a little airspeed in the descent, so the pivotal altitude will not be quite so low. Keep the wingtip pinned on the pylon as you descend.

In the second half of the turn, as you go from upwind to downwind again, the higher groundspeed will mean a higher pivotal altitude and you will have to gradually climb to keep the wingtip pinned on the pylon. The pylon will start to move back, so apply back pressure to climb.

Change the altitude as wind causes the groundspeed to change.

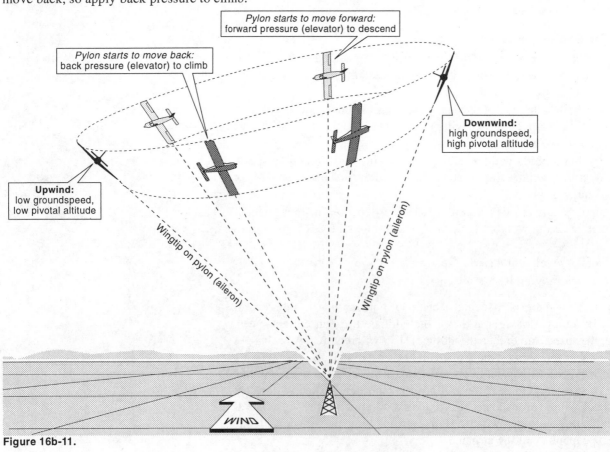

Figure 16b-11.

Airwork 16b, Part (iii)
Eights-On-Pylons

(Commercial Pilots only)

Objective

To pivot the wingtips on two pylons as you fly a figure-eight based on them. (Altitude, bank angle, and airspeed will vary throughout this maneuver, but the wingtip should stay fixed on the pylon in each turn.)

- Estimate the wind strength and direction, and calculate the pivotal altitude MSL for your entry downwind (highest groundspeed), adding the estimated pylon elevation to the pivotal altitude AGL obtained from the formula.

Pivotal altitude AGL = $\dfrac{\text{(groundspeed in knots)}^2}{11.3}$ feet AGL

Groundspeed	Pivotal Altitude AGL
120 knots	.... feet AGL
110 knots	.... feet AGL
100 knots	.... feet AGL
90 knots	.... feet AGL
80 knots	.... feet AGL

- Fly crosswind and select two suitable pylons perpendicular to the wind. Since the maneuver depends upon the pivotal altitude AGL, it is made easier if you select two pylons at approximately the same elevation.
- **Look out** for hazards and other aircraft.
- Position the airplane to enter the eight at normal cruise speed, flying diagonally across the midpoint, with the wind from the side and behind (so the GS will be high) at, or just above, your calculated pivotal altitude MSL.

- Wait until you are just past the right pylon and roll into a right turn (recommended bank angle 30° to 40° at the steepest point) to position the wingtip on the pylon.
- If too high (as expected) the pylon will move **forward** of your line-of-sight along the wingtip—apply **forward** pressure to descend. Expect the lowest altitude upwind. Prevent up–down movement of the pylon using aileron; prevent fore–aft movement of the pylon using elevator. Follow the pylon with the control column.
- In the second half of the turn around the pylon, the groundspeed will gradually increase. As the pylon starts to move **back**, apply **back** pressure to climb, to keep the wingtip pinned on the pylon.
- Approaching the midpoint between the two pylons, roll the wings level for 3 to 5 seconds, then roll in the other direction and place the wingtip on the second pylon. Keep coordinated with rudder.
- Prevent the pylon moving forward by using forward pressure on the elevator; prevent the pylon moving back by using back pressure on the elevator. Follow the pylon with the control column.
- Throughout the maneuver, divide your attention between coordinated airplane control, keeping the wingtip pivoting on the pylon, and looking out for hazards & other aircraft.
- Fly at least three patterns (with each one getting better).

FOLLOW THE PYLON WITH THE CONTROL COLUMN

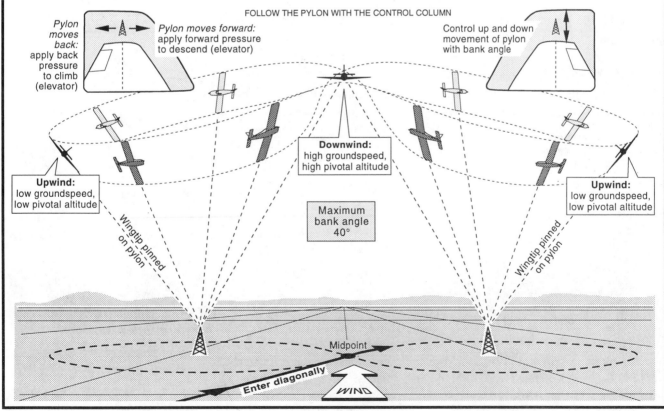

Pylon moves back: apply back pressure to climb (elevator)

Pylon moves forward: apply forward pressure to descend (elevator)

Control up and down movement of pylon with bank angle

Downwind: high groundspeed, high pivotal altitude

Upwind: low groundspeed, low pivotal altitude

Upwind: low groundspeed, low pivotal altitude

Maximum bank angle 40°

Wingtip pinned on pylon

Wingtip pinned on pylon

Midpoint

Enter diagonally

WIND

Further Points

The Formula for Pivotal Altitude AGL

The following discussion is for those who are mathematically inclined.

1. Consider the airplane is at the pivotal altitude AGL (H) and turning with bank angle θ (theta).

> (a) The wingtip as seen by the pilot lies **on** the pylon.

> (b) The turn of radius (R) is centered directly above the pylon.

From this large triangle: $\boxed{\tan \theta = \dfrac{H}{R}}$

2. The forces acting on the airplane are:

> (a) The **vertical component** of the lift force which counteracts the weight W (where W = mg, *m* being the mass in pounds, and *g* being the acceleration due to gravity: 32.2 feet-per-second^2).

> (b) The **horizontal component** of the lift force, also known as the *centripetal force* (C), which pulls the airplane into the turn of radius R. From physics, we know that $C = \dfrac{mV^2}{R}$, where V is velocity in feet per second, in this case **groundspeed**. From this small triangle: $\boxed{\tan \theta = \dfrac{C}{W}}$

3. These two relationships for tan θ must be equal, therefore:

$$\frac{H}{R} = \frac{C}{W} \qquad : \text{where } C = \frac{mV^2}{R} \text{ and } W = mg$$

$$\therefore \frac{H}{R} = \frac{mV^2}{R} \times \frac{1}{mg} \qquad : \text{cancel m's, cancel R's}$$

$$\therefore H = \frac{V^2}{g} \qquad : \text{where V is velocity in feet per second}$$

Result. H, the pivotal altitude AGL, depends **only** on speed V (in fact V-squared), since *g* is a constant. There is no mention of bank angle θ.

- If the speed (V) increases, the pivotal altitude AGL (H) must therefore be greater for the wingtip to pivot on the pylon.

- Conversely, if the speed (V) decreases, the pivotal altitude AGL (H) must be lower for the wingtip to pivot on the pylon.

Then, for a speed in knots (rather than in feet per second):

$$
\begin{aligned}
1 \text{ knot} &= 1 \text{ nautical mile per hour} \\
&= 6{,}080 \text{ feet per hour} \\
&= {}^{6{,}080}/_{60} \text{ feet per minute} \\
&= {}^{6{,}080}/_{60 \times 60} \text{ feet per second} \\
&= 1.69 \text{ feet per second}
\end{aligned}
$$

$$
\begin{aligned}
\therefore H &= \frac{V^2}{g} & : \text{where V is in feet per second} \\
&= \frac{(\text{groundspeed in knots} \times 1.69)^2}{32.2} \\
&= \frac{(\text{groundspeed in knots})^2 \times 2.86}{32.2} \\
\mathbf{H} &= \mathbf{\frac{(\text{groundspeed in knots})^2}{11.3}} & : \textbf{which is the formula we use.}
\end{aligned}
$$

Then, to obtain the **pivotal altitude MSL,** which we can use on our altimeter, simply add the calculated pivotal altitude AGL (that is, H) to the estimated **elevation MSL of the pylon.**

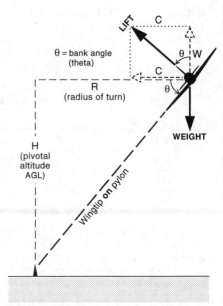

Figure 16b-12. Pivotal altitude AGL

The pivotal altitude AGL depends only on the airplane's groundspeed.

✍ Review 16b

Part (i)—Steep Spirals

1. A steep descending turn with a constant bank angle (moves with the wind/stays centered on a ground object).

   ➤ moves with the wind

2. A steep spiral is flown so that the turn (is at a constant bank angle/stays centered on a ground object).

   ➤ stays centered on a ground object

3. In a strong wind, to descend on a ground reference point in a steep spiral, you need to (vary the bank angle/hold the bank angle constant).

   ➤ vary the bank angle

4. The steepest bank angle will be when you are flying (downwind/upwind).

   ➤ downwind

5. Accuracy required in a steep spiral is:
   • airspeed plus or minus ____ KIAS;
   • bank angle maximum ____ ° to ____ °;
   • coordination ball (centered/not centered).

   ➤ 10 KIAS, 50° to 55°, centered

6. You should commence the steep spiral at an altitude that allows you to roll out at least ____ feet AGL.

   ➤ 1,500 feet AGL

7. If the terrain in the vicinity is 2,100 feet MSL, you should roll out of a steep spiral when the altimeter indicates at least ____ feet MSL, which is ____ feet AGL.

   ➤ 3,600 feet MSL, 1,500 feet AGL

8. It (is/is not) a vital point of airmanship that you always retain an awareness of your height above the ground.

   ➤ is

Part (ii)—Eights Around Pylons

1. Eights around pylons (is/is not) a ground reference maneuver.

   ➤ is

Commercial Pilot
Ground Reference Maneuvers

2. Eights around pylons (is/is not) a constant-altitude maneuver, and (is/is not) a constant-airspeed maneuver.

   ➤ is, is

3. The constant altitude you choose for this maneuver should lie between ____ feet AGL and ____ feet AGL.

   ➤ 600 feet AGL and 1,000 feet AGL

4. If the local terrain is 800 feet MSL, you would select a constant altitude somewhere between ____ feet MSL and ____ feet MSL for this maneuver.

   ➤ 1,400 feet MSL, 1,800 feet MSL

5. Eights around pylons is the turns-around-a-point maneuver multiplied by ____ .

   ➤ two

6. Pylons that you select should be about (one/two/three) miles apart and the line joining them should be (perpendicular/parallel) to the wind so that it easy to enter the pattern over the midpoint with the wind from (ahead/behind/the side).

   ➤ one mile apart, perpendicular, behind

7. The closer the two pylons are to each other, the (steeper/shallower) the turns required.

   ➤ steeper

8. To maintain a constant ground radius in a turn, the bank angle will have to be (steeper/shallower/the same) at a higher groundspeed.

   ➤ steeper

9. With the wind from behind, the bank angle will have to be the (steepest/shallowest) to maintain the constant ground radius.

   ➤ steepest

10. The recommended maximum bank angle for this maneuver is between ____ ° and ____ °, which will occur on the (inner/outer) parts of the eight which should be flown with the wind from (ahead/behind/the side).

    ➤ 30 to 40°, inner, behind

Continued

11. The outer parts of the eight will be (upwind/
downwind), and so the bank angle required to
hold the desired ground radius will be (steepest/
shallowest).

> upwind, shallowest

12. For eights around pylons you (should/need not)
maintain your selected altitude and airspeed.

> should

13. Tolerances for the eights around pylons maneuver
are: selected altitude plus or minus ____ feet,
selected airspeed plus or minus ____ KIAS, and
recommended maximum bank angle ____ ° to
____ °. The coordination ball (should/need not) be
centered.

> plus or minus 100 feet, plus or minus 10 KIAS,
30° to 40°, should

Part (iii)—Eights-On-Pylons

1. The eights-on-pylons maneuver is to (pivot the
wingtip on a pylon/fly a circular ground pattern).

> pivot the wingtip on a pylon

2. Eights-on-pylons (is/is not) a constant-altitude
maneuver.

> is not

3. Eights-on-pylons (is/is not) a constant-airspeed
maneuver.

> is not

4. The bank angle is controlled with (aileron/
elevator).

> aileron

5. The altitude at which the turn is centered above a
pylon when the airplane is banked to place the
wingtip on the pylon is called the _____ altitude.

> pivotal

6. AGL stands for _____ _____ _____ , and MSL
stands for _____ _____ _____ .

> above ground level, (above) mean sea level

7. The pivotal altitude AGL above the pylon depends
on (speed only/bank angle only/both speed and
bank angle).

> speed only

8. The simple formula for calculating the pivotal
altitude AGL is
_____ .

> pivotal altitude AGL = $\dfrac{\text{groundspeed}^2}{11.3}$ feet

9. If the airspeed is 90 KIAS, what is the pivotal
altitude AGL, to the nearest 10 feet, in a
zero-wind situation?

> 720 feet AGL

10. If the airspeed is 100 KIAS, what is the highest
pivotal altitude AGL, and the lowest, in a 10-knot
wind? What pivotal altitudes MSL would you
expect to use on your altimeter if the pylons are at
approximately 800 feet MSL?

> 1,070 feet AGL or 1,870 feet MSL, 720 feet AGL
or 1,520 feet MSL.

11. The recommended steepest bank angle acceptable
for this maneuver is ____ ° to ____ °.

> 30° to 40°

12. The pylon is gradually moving back from your
line-of-sight down the wingtip. You should apply
(forward/back) pressure to the elevator and
(climb/descend).

> back, climb

13. The pylon is gradually moving forward from your
line-of-sight along the wing. You should apply
(forward/back) pressure to the elevator and
(climb/descend).

> forward, descend

14. The pivotal altitude AGL depends only on the
(airspeed/groundspeed).

> groundspeed

15. The pivotal altitude AGL is higher when the
groundspeed is (higher/lower).

> higher

16. A higher groundspeed means a (higher/lower)
pivotal altitude AGL.

> higher

17. A lower groundspeed means a (higher/lower)
pivotal altitude AGL.

> lower

18. It (is/is not) vital to maintain a good lookout
during the maneuver.

> is

Emergency Forced Landing without Power 17a

Objective

To carry out a safe approach and landing following engine failure.

Considerations

Why Would an Engine Fail?

A forced landing resulting from a mechanical malfunction or a structural problem is a rare event with modern airplanes. However, it **does** happen occasionally, so a pilot should be prepared.

Fuel starvation is often the cause of an engine stopping in flight. Fuel gauges can be inaccurate, and fuelers have on rare occasions loaded contaminated fuel or the incorrect grade or type of fuel. A visual inspection of the fuel tanks, and of the fuel itself, during your preflight inspection and during fueling should prevent insufficient or incorrect fuel causing a forced landing.

Always check the fuel prior to flying.

Pilot error or misjudgment in flight can also lead to an engine stoppage. Forgetting to switch from a near-empty fuel tank in flight to an alternative tank, incorrect use of the mixture control, or failure to use carburetor heat in conditions where carburetor ice could form, may all lead to an engine stoppage through fuel starvation.

Always check your fuel selection and be aware of the actual fuel situation; use the mixture and carburetor heat controls correctly.

Airplane performance data published in Flight Manuals is obtained from test results achieved by experienced test pilots flying new airplanes under ideal conditions. Similar results will be difficult for an average pilot in a well used airplane to achieve. The published fuel consumption and range capability figures assume **correct leaning** of the mixture. If this is **not** done by the pilot when cruising at 75% maximum continuous power or less, the manufacturer's range figures will **not** be attained. A careless pilot could run out of fuel.

As the captain of an airplane, you must show good airmanship and always be aware of the actual **fuel situation.** Never allow fuel starvation to force you into an unwanted landing!

Other possible causes of engine stoppage include faults in the magneto system, in ancillary equipment (such as, a carburetor malfunction or a broken fuel line), mechanical failure, or an engine fire. Bad luck sometimes plays a role—for instance, a bird-strike damaging the propeller.

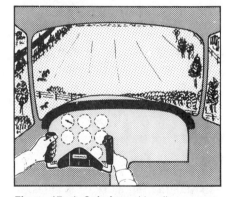

Figure 17a-1. Safe forced landings can be made in small fields.

Rectification of an engine stoppage by a pilot is generally limited to seeing that:
- the engine controls are providing the correct amount of fuel and air to the engine—fuel selector, mixture control, throttle and carburetor heat; or
- the ignition system is functioning satisfactorily (for instance, eliminating a faulty magneto).

This is not to say that you will have to cope with an engine stoppage each and every time you go flying—it is not unusual to go through a whole career without a real engine failure, although simulated engine failures will have been practiced many times. However, a well-trained pilot is prepared for an engine failure **at any time** in flight or on the ground.

A good time for a flight instructor to test your reflexes and preparedness is to simulate an engine failure when you are busy with some task, such as low flying or a ground reference maneuver. Now that you are nearing the end of your flight training, keep on your toes.

A **disciplined approach** to checklists and the sequence of events during training is important, as the recall of procedures can be difficult when faced with a real emergency. Maintain positive control of the airplane and of the situation at all times.

Forced Landings without Power

All pilots must be able to cope with an emergency landing without the use of engine power, possibly on an unprepared surface. This can be done quite successfully. The low landing speed of a modern training aircraft, and its robust construction, allow it to be landed safely in quite small fields, provided that the airplane is positioned accurately.

Forced landings without power can be made quite safely.

No new flying skills are introduced with this exercise; it is simply a matter of applying what you already know, making sound decisions quickly, and then acting positively on them.

The **altitude** of an airplane above the ground converts to *time available* in the event of an engine failure. An airplane that glides at 700 fpm rate of descent will give you only three minutes from 2,000 feet AGL.

- Flying the airplane is number one priority—maintain a safe gliding airspeed (usually the best-glide airspeed recommended in the Pilot's Operating Handbook, plus or minus 5 KIAS), and keep the airplane in trim.
- Planning and executing the approach comes next, with an attempt (if you think it advisable) to restart the engine.

Partial power from an engine that has not completely failed may give you extra time and the possibility of gaining some extra distance, but do not rely upon it. The engine may fail completely at a most inopportune moment, so plan your approach and landing as if no power is available.

Engine Failure at Altitude

Altitude means time to a pilot, and the amount of time that you have available determines what options you have. If the engine fails, convert any excess speed into altitude by making a gentle climb, or into useful distance by maintaining altitude until the airspeed decays to gliding speed, and then **establish a glide** with the airplane in trim.

When the airplane is comfortably under control, perform some **simple emergency actions** and attempt an engine restart—provided that you think restarting the engine is a good idea. It is possible that a restart is *not* advisable, for instance following an engine fire or mechanical damage. This is a command decision that only the pilot-in-command can make.

An engine fire may not be immediately obvious, but can be checked for by yawing the nose left, and then looking left and rearward for trailing smoke.

Engine Restart

An experienced pilot may decide quickly to attempt an immediate restart, and will perform the required actions during the time the airplane is slowing down to gliding speed.

An immediate engine restart may be possible.

A less experienced pilot may be well-advised to concentrate just on flying the airplane, first establishing it in the glide and trimming it **before** performing any restart actions. Your flight instructor will advise you on this point.

If the propeller is still turning, then rectification of the fuel or ignition problem—if that is the cause—may see the engine fire-up again without any need to use the starter.

Rectify the problem if possible.

There are some obvious items to be considered in an attempted restart of the engine.

- **A Fuel Problem:**
  Change fuel tanks.
  Fuel pump—ON (if fitted).
  Mixture—RICH.
  Primer—LOCKED.

- **An Ignition Problem:**
  Check the magneto switches individually (BOTH–LEFT–RIGHT). If the engine operates on one magneto as a result of a fault in the other magneto system, then leave it there, otherwise return to BOTH.

- **An Icing Problem:**
  Carburetor heat—FULL HOT.

Note: Following a **mechanical failure** or **fire,** the engine should be stopped immediately. If the failure is **partial,** resulting in reduced or intermittent running, then use the available engine power at your discretion. There is a likelihood that the engine may fail completely at a critical stage, so it may be best not to rely on it, and simply assume a total failure right at the beginning.

Following a failure caused by **faulty operation** on the part of the pilot, restart the engine in the glide.

The Legal Situation

The Federal Aviation Regulations permit a pilot to deviate from the rules to the extent required to meet an in-flight emergency requiring immediate action. The pilot is directly responsible for, and is the final authority as to, the operation of the aircraft, but *may* be asked to send a written report of any deviation to the FAA (FAR 91.3).

The pilot has final authority when operating an aircraft.

This means that in an emergency situation you should take whatever action you consider necessary for the safety of your airplane and its occupants. Paperwork, if any, can always follow.

Flying the Maneuver

Forced Landing Scenario

Many scenarios are possible, and your actions will depend upon the situation at the time, the altitude above the terrain at which the failure occurs, the surface wind, and the availability of good fields—possibly even an airfield. **Altitude is time.**

We will consider a general procedure which is capable of being modified to suit your precise set of circumstances.

If the engine fails at a reasonable altitude (say 3,000 feet or more above ground level), a basic order of actions that may be followed is:
- Convert excess speed to altitude or to useful distance.
- Set up a safe glide at the recommended best-glide airspeed.
- Attempt a restart.
- Select a suitable landing area within gliding distance and plan an approach to it.
- Make a distress (MAYDAY) radio call, and squawk 7700 on your transponder.
- Attempt to resolve the emergency (while maintaining a safe glide).
- Complete the appropriate **emergency checklist.**
- Carry out a safe approach and landing (in the case of training, a go-around rather than a landing will usually be performed).

Know the Ground Wind

While flying along with the flight proceeding normally, it is good airmanship to keep an eye on the surface wind. A forced landing, if required, is generally safer into the wind because of the lower groundspeed on touchdown and the shorter landing run.

Good indicators of surface wind include:
- smoke;
- a windsock;
- cloud shadows on the ground, especially if the clouds are low;
- the drift angle of the airplane over the ground; and
- wind lines on water surfaces.

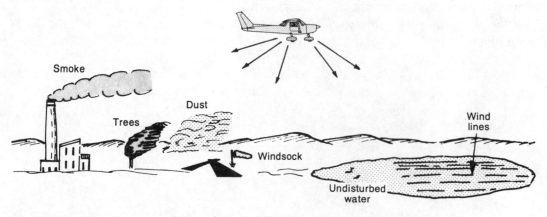

Figure 17a-2. Always be aware of the surface wind direction.

Estimate the Gliding Range

A typical training aircraft has a *best lift/drag ratio* of approximately 9:1, which means that, when flown at the correct gliding speed, 9,000 feet (or 1.5 nm) can be covered horizontally for each 1,000 feet loss of altitude. Losing 1,000 feet vertically in 9,000 feet horizontally is an angle of depression (down from the horizontal) of about 7°.

In the cockpit, to estimate your approximate gliding range in still air conservatively, lower your arm about 10° from the horizontal. You should be pointing at a position on the ground to which a glide in still air is possible. Of course, the closer the chosen field is, the more certain you are of reaching it comfortably. Fly at the recommended best-glide speed to achieve the best gliding range.

Fly at the recommended gliding speed to achieve the best gliding range.

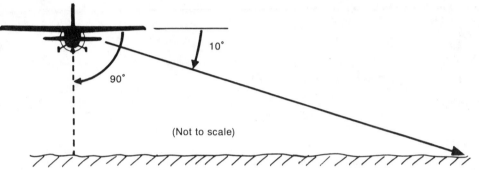

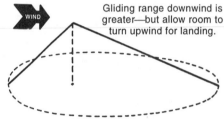

Figure 17a-3. An approximate estimate of gliding range in zero-wind conditions

A **headwind** will reduce the gliding range; **a tailwind** will increase it. A windmilling or stopped propeller causes a large increase in drag, and will decrease the gliding range. In your training so far, you have become familiar with the glide path achievable with the engine idling and the propeller turning over but, if the engine has failed, the propeller—either stopped or windmilling—will cause a significant increase in drag.

The nose of the airplane will have to be lowered to maintain airspeed and the rate of descent will increase. The increased drag will mean a poorer lift/drag ratio, a steeper glide path, and a reduced gliding range.

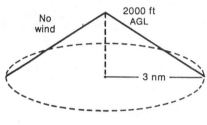

Figure 17a-4. Wind affects gliding range over the ground.

Select a Suitable Field

When **settled into the glide**, select a suitable field for a forced landing. It is safest to select a field well within your gliding range and to fly a pattern around it, rather than to try a long straight glide to a distant field. Choosing a nearby field makes correct judgment of the glide path easier, and gives you more flexibility and room to correct if your original estimates are not precise.

The easiest place to look for a field is out of the left window, since you, as the pilot-in-command, sit in the left seat; but do not fail to look out to the right, just in case a perfectly suitable field is available there. Maneuver the airplane if necessary, and look beneath it. Ideally, select a field downwind of your present position, because that direction is where the gliding range of the airplane will be greatest.

Make all turns toward the field so that you do not turn your back on it—it is possible to lose sight of the field and waste time re-identifying it.

Choose a forced-landing field well within your gliding range.

Make all turns toward the field.

The forced landing field should:
- be well within gliding range;
- be large and preferably surrounded by other suitable fields;
- have no obstacles on the approach and overshoot areas;
- be level or slightly uphill;
- have a suitable surface—ideally an airport, but pasture may be satisfactory; wetness, often indicated by dark green areas, may be a disadvantage; crops and beaches in general should be avoided—the preferred order being pasture, ploughed fields, beaches, standing crops. Avoid roads if possible, because of the danger of vehicular traffic, power lines and roadside posts or signs, although, especially after heavy rain, a quiet straight country road might be the best option;
- be close to civilization (communication and assistance may be valuable).

Apply **"W O S S S S S"**:

W—Wind.

O—Obstacles (on the surface: trees, rocks, buildings, power cables, and so on).

S—Size and Shape (considering the wind velocity).

S—Surface and Slope.

S—"Shoots" (undershoot and overshoot areas).

S—Sun (position relative to final approach).

S—S(c)ivilization.

Planning the Approach

The basic plan that you formulate depends mainly upon the altitude above the ground. Various patterns and **key points** around a field can assist you in flying a suitable glide descent. Estimate the elevation of the field and calculate your approximate altitude above it.

Use key points in planning the approach.

Each flight instructor will have a preferred technique, but the aim is the same in every case—consistently good positioning for a power-off approach and landing. We discuss different planning techniques here. Your flight instructor will give you sound advice on which to use.

If you wish, you can spiral down from high overhead a suitable field to a position and altitude from which a safe approach and landing can be made. A steep spiraling turn will allow you to lose altitude quickly, for instance in the event of a fire, when you want to land as soon as is safely possible. In general, however, if there is no rush to land then you should not rush the descent.

Method (a):
The 1,000 feet "Close Base Leg" Technique

The basic objective using this technique is to arrive at 1,000 feet AGL on a close base leg, from which a comfortable glide well into the field can be made. If the engine is stopped, the drag from the propeller will steepen the glide path compared with the glide angle when the engine is idling—as in the practice maneuver—so allow for this possibility.

A wide base leg allows little room for error, but a close base leg gives flexibility in the case of over- or under-shooting the field, allowing adjustments to be made quite easily. According to your position when the engine fails, choose either a left or right 1,000-foot base area, with a long base leg and a short final. Left turns provide you with a better view of the field.

A close base leg gives flexibility.

Noting a ground reference point near the 1,000-foot position will assist in re-identifying the turning-base point if you are distracted.

A suitable distance for the downwind leg is approximately one-third mile from the selected landing path. In flying a square pattern around the chosen field, approximately 1,000 feet per leg will be lost, and this must be considered in your planning.

Stay close to the field and make all turns toward it.

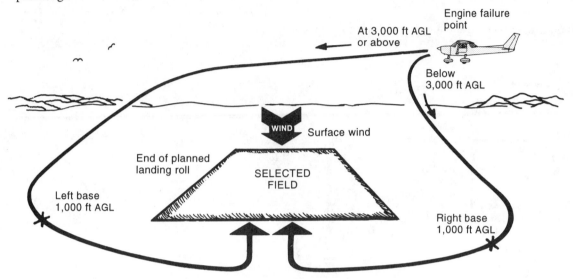

Figure 17a-5. A very basic traffic pattern plan for a forced landing

Method (b):
The "High Key and Low Key" Technique

The advantage of using the *High Key* and the *Low Key* is that they are closely related to the selected landing strip and therefore are easily re-identified:

- **the Low Key**—1,500 feet AGL, about one-third mile abeam the landing threshold—this is a similar position to where the airplane would be if using Method (a);
- **the High Key**—2,500 feet AGL, in line with, and about three-quarters to one mile upwind of, the far end of the selected landing strip.

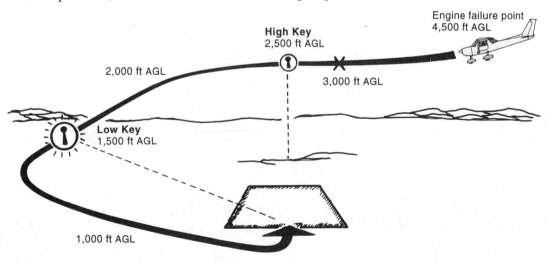

Figure 17a-6. The High Key and the Low Key

The first aim in the descent is to glide to the high key, keeping the field in sight. The purpose of the High Key is simply to assist your judgment in reaching the Low Key, which is of course the more important key point. After some practice in making glide descents, you may find that you can glide direct to the Low Key without any definite consideration of the High Key.

Engine failure at a low altitude (say 2,000 feet AGL) will also mean flying direct to the Low Key.

On approach, plan on a long base leg and a short final. If too high, widen out; if too low, cut in.

Monitor the descent to the key points, and plan on a long base and a short final.

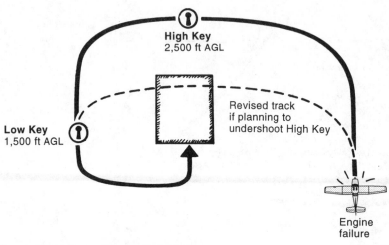

Figure 17a-7. Descent to the key points.

Estimates of familiar positions above ground level (such as the 1,000 feet AGL traffic pattern altitude) will generally be reasonably accurate. You should develop the same skill with other altitudes.

Assess the wind during the descent to assist in choosing a suitable base point. A reasonably long base leg allows:

Assess the wind during the descent.

- more time to judge the wind strength (using the drift angle on base);
- better judgment of altitude above the ground (since it is easier to judge this out to one side of the airplane rather than straight ahead);
- flexibility in adjusting the descent path:
    cutting in, if too low;
    widening out, lengthening the base leg, or extending flaps, if too high.

A short final allows you to cope with a glide path that is steeper than expected.

Rectifying the Problem

When established in the glide, there may be time to look for the cause of the failure and to remedy it (unless the engine is on fire or has obviously suffered severe damage). The Pilot's Operating Handbook will contain a list of the appropriate items to check. It will include:

Attempt to rectify the engine problem if there is time.

- fuel;
- mixture;
- carburetor heat;
- throttle linkage;
- fuel pump (if fitted)—ON;
- primer (check locked); and
- magneto switches.

If the propeller is rotating, then having the fuel and ignition ON should be enough to restart the engine, otherwise the starter may be required. While attempting to rectify the problem, the continuing descent toward the key points should be monitored and the suitability of the field confirmed. If you decide that your chosen field is unsuitable, select another as early as possible.

Control the flight path.

Radio Calls and Passenger Briefing

Make a MAYDAY distress call (in a real forced landing, but *not* when practicing). VHF radio signals may not be effective from low levels, so the sooner a MAYDAY call is made in the glide, the better. The call should be made on the frequency that you are currently using or on the emergency frequency 121.5 MHz.

Advise others of your planned forced landing.

Keep radio conversations brief and do not be distracted from your main duty, which is to fly the airplane. Squawk transponder code 7700, which helps ATC radar controllers to identify an airplane experiencing an emergency.

Advise your passengers of your intentions. Request them to remain calm, to remove sharp objects from their pockets, to remove glasses and dentures and ensure that their seat belts are fastened. Use any soft clothing or pillows to protect them from a sudden deceleration or impact. Harnesses should remain fastened until the airplane stops. Be firm and brook no interference. Request complete silence.

Do not be distracted from your main duty, which is to fly the airplane.

Approaching the Low-Key Point 1,500 feet AGL

As the normal traffic-pattern altitude is approached, all of your attention needs to be focused on positioning for the approach and landing. Further attempts to restart the engine would only distract you from this. **Secure the airplane,** placing it in a safer condition for a landing on an unprepared field by carrying out the required **security check** (also known as the *Crash* or *Impact check*):

Secure the airplane for touchdown on a rough surface.

- mixture—IDLE CUTOFF;
- fuel—OFF;
- ignition—OFF;
- radio—OFF;
- master switch—OFF (unless the wing flaps are electrically operated);
- cabin heater—OFF;
- brakes—OFF;
- harnesses—SECURE;
- doors unlatched (if appropriate to your airplane type);
- all loose items secured and the position of safety items noted (for example, the fire extinguisher and first-aid kit).

Where to Turn onto Base Leg

From the low key, 1,500 feet AGL abeam the touchdown point, extend your downwind according to the wind. The stronger the wind, the shorter the extension of the downwind leg, bearing in mind that it is preferable to be a little high on final approach than too low. If the surface wind is:

Extend downwind according to the wind.

- greater than 20 knots, commence the base turn at the low-key point abeam the aiming point for landing—that is, at about 1,500 feet AGL;
- between 10 to 20 knots, commence the base turn when the aiming point for landing appears about one-half chord length behind the trailing edge (for a low-wing airplane), which will occur at about 1,300 feet AGL;
- less than 10 knots, commence the base turn when the aiming point for landing appears about one chord length behind the trailing edge (for a low-wing airplane), which will occur at about 1,100 feet AGL.

When to Use Flaps

A typical technique is to lower:
- the first stage of flaps at the low key on downwind leg;
- the second stage when turning base leg;
- full flaps on final and when assured of making the field.

If the airplane appears to be **high on base leg,** then you can:
- lengthen the base leg;
- widen the base leg;
- extend some flaps;
- forward slip (if permitted—refer to the Pilot's Operating Handbook); or
- carry out some S-turns (but try and avoid this).

If the airplane appears to be **low on base leg,** then:
- shorten the base leg;
- cut in toward the field for a shorter final;
- delay the use of flaps.

A long base leg and a short final give you the greatest flexibility.

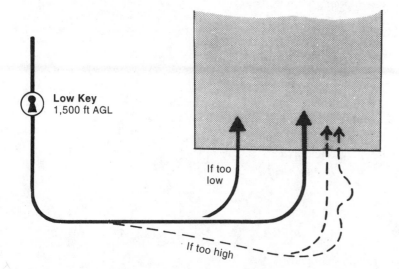

Low Key
1,500 ft AGL

If too
low

If too high

Figure 17a-8. Maneuver for a long base and a short final.

Monitor Airspeed and Bank Angle

It is most important that you maintain the correct gliding speed, especially when turning. A **gliding turn near the ground should not be steep** because:
- stalling speed increases with increasing bank angle and wing loading; and
- rate of descent in a glide increases with bank angle.

Monitor airspeed and bank angle closely in the gliding turn to final.

Be conscious of your airspeed during the turn onto final, and limit the bank angle to 20° (30° maximum). Do not stall or even allow the airplane to approach the stall!

Make your turn to final so that the aiming point is well into your chosen field, say one-half to one-third into the field, to ensure that you make it.

Final Approach

Keep an eye out for obstructions such as overhead cables that may not have been seen at altitude. When certain that you can glide well into the field, continue extending flaps in stages to steepen your approach and to bring the aiming point closer to you.

Keep the aiming point comfortably past the near boundary so that, even if an undershoot occurs, a safe landing in the field can be made.

It is safer to hit an obstacle at the far end at slow speed than to hit the fence before landing. It is safest of course to judge your aiming point so that neither occurs, and so that you land comfortably into the field and stop before the far boundary without any drama.

Ensure that the master switch is OFF after electrically operated flaps (if applicable to your airplane) have been extended to the landing position.

If you are **too high** on final approach:
• extend flaps;
• use a forward slip if permitted, or if flaps are not working;
• make shallow S-turns (but avoid this, if possible);
• dive off excess altitude (avoid this also, if possible).

If you are **too low** on final approach, delay extending flaps. Do not fall into the trap of trying to stretch the glide by raising the nose—your airspeed will fall and the flight path will in fact be steeper. In an extreme case you may have to land in a closer field.

If flaps are not available, you can use the **forward slip** technique to steepen the descent and lose excess altitude (see Exercise 8d). Be prepared in a zero-flap landing for a high nose attitude in the approach and touchdown, and a long ground run.

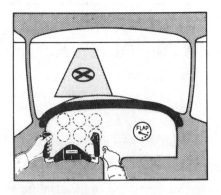

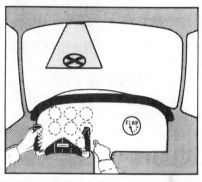

Figure 17a-9. Use of more flaps brings the aiming point closer.

The Actual Landing

A forced landing with **full flaps** is generally safest because:
• the touchdown speed is low (because of the lower stalling speed);
• the landing roll is shorter; and
• if the field is rough, there will be less stress on the airframe.

Touch down on the main wheels, holding the nosewheel off to avoid unnecessary stress. Be prepared for rough and/or sloping ground. Brakes can be used as necessary to shorten the ground run.

Hold the nosewheel off during the landing.

Unseen obstacles and ditches could be a problem. If collision with an obstacle is imminent (say the far fence), apply rudder, and brake on one side only to initiate a controlled ground loop if possible.

Airplane at Rest

A forced landing is not complete until the airplane is stopped, the passengers evacuated, the airplane made secure and assistance obtained. So, as soon as the airplane stops:
• set the parking brake;
• secure the airplane (check all switches—OFF, fuel—OFF, control locks—IN);
• evacuate, taking the fire extinguisher with you (if appropriate);
• chock the airplane;
• remove any items thought necessary;
• protect the airplane—for example, keep animals away;
• seek assistance, and telephone the chief flight instructor and the appropriate authorities. If possible, leave someone in charge of the airplane.

Secure the airplane and evacuate.

Do not attempt to take off!

Note: NTSB 830 refers to removal of or interference with an aircraft that has suffered an accident.

Part (ii)
A Simulated Forced Landing

Flying the Maneuver

Engine Operation

So far we have covered the **genuine** engine-failure situation. In practice, however, we only **simulate an engine failure** and, having demonstrated that we could have made a safe landing, go around off the approach from a safe altitude. Go-around actions should normally be completed above 500 feet AGL, unless a lower altitude is approved.

To ensure that the engine will respond at the time of go-around:

- ensure that the mixture is RICH and move the carburetor heat control to HOT to avoid carburetor icing—prior to reducing power in the simulated engine-failure. If a fuel pump is fitted, switch it ON;
- clear the engine and keep it warm by increasing rpm for 10 to 15 seconds every 500 feet or 1,000 feet on descent;
- when applying power for the go-around, check that the mixture is RICH and the carburetor heat is FULL COLD—most engine manufacturers recommend that you apply power first, then move the carburetor heat control to COLD.

Simulate the Trouble check, MAYDAY call, transponder squawk 7700, and Security check that you would carry out in a real forced landing—call them out at the appropriate time in your glide descent, but **do not action them.** For example, call out the actions: *"fuel—OFF, magneto switches—OFF"*, and so on, but do not carry them out.

Keep a good **look out**. Other aircraft may be practicing glide approaches to the same field in the training area, possibly from the other direction in calm wind conditions. Ensure that the climb-out area following the go-around is clear of obstacles. Check this well before you descend to a point where the go-around could become marginal.

Practicing forced landings requires steady concentration. It is practicing for an emergency, and the practice itself has its own peculiar risks. You are calling out items associated with a real forced landing, yet operating the airplane so that it will function normally when you carry out a go-around from a safe altitude. Be extremely careful not to take any action that would endanger the airplane.

Practicing forced landings **without** the use of engine power is good training in developing the skills of command. One of these skills is to manage your resources effectively and efficiently in an **emergency** situation.

Airmanship

When **practicing forced landings** without the use of engine power:

- look out, especially in the latter stages of the power-off approach—other aircraft may be practicing forced landings into the same or a nearby field;
- clear the engine by increasing rpm at least every 10 to 15 seconds on descent;
- do not descend below the authorized **break-off altitude;**
- know your checks thoroughly and execute them in the correct sequence;
- do not turn your back on the field—keep it in sight at all times;

Ensure correct engine operation (and a few other things).

Airmanship is flying well and making sound decisions.

- do not make any unnecessary changes in the field you select;
- make command decisions in a calm but firm manner;
- be prepared for a *real* engine failure at any time.

An Actual Forced Landing

When carrying out an actual forced landing without the use of engine power, most of the points above related to **practicing** also apply in the real forced landing situation.

- Do not rely on a partially failed engine.
- Ensure that the Trouble check, MAYDAY call, transponder squawk on 7700, and Security check are all done, and not just called out (as they were in the practice forced landing):

   The MAYDAY call, to be effective, must be made at a reasonable altitude. It may be made earlier in the sequence, according to actual circumstances. For instance, if the engine fails at a low altitude, the MAYDAY call could be made as the last item of No. 1 in the following Airwork diagram. If the engine fails at altitude, then the MAYDAY call can be made at position (5) shown on the diagram.

- Be certain to know the recommended door position for a forced landing—either open or closed—as specified in your Pilot's Operating Handbook.
- Brief the passengers to brace for the landing, and not to leave the airplane until it has stopped.
- Ensure the safety of your airplane and passengers after landing, stopping and securing the airplane.
- Notify the authorities as soon as possible.

In both *actual* or *practice* forced landings, divide your attention appropriately between aircraft control, maintaining the proper flight path, and accomplishing the Emergency checklist.

Airwork 17a
Practicing the Forced Landing

Objective
To carry out a safe approach and landing following engine failure.

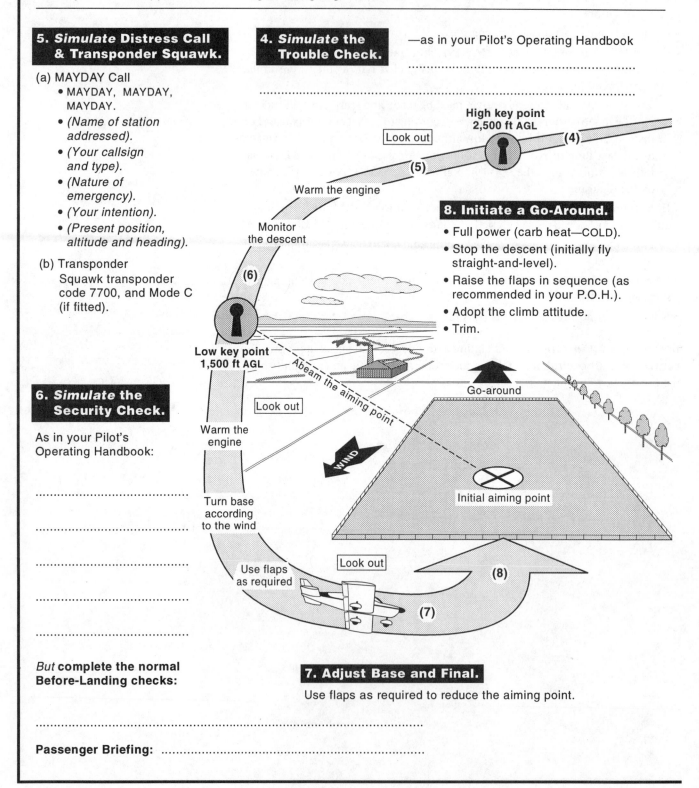

5. *Simulate* Distress Call & Transponder Squawk.

(a) MAYDAY Call
- MAYDAY, MAYDAY, MAYDAY.
- *(Name of station addressed).*
- *(Your callsign and type).*
- *(Nature of emergency).*
- *(Your intention).*
- *(Present position, altitude and heading).*

(b) Transponder
Squawk transponder code 7700, and Mode C (if fitted).

6. *Simulate* the Security Check.

As in your Pilot's Operating Handbook:

....

....

....

....

....

But **complete the normal Before-Landing checks:**

....

Passenger Briefing: ....

4. *Simulate* the Trouble Check.   —as in your Pilot's Operating Handbook

....

....

Look out

High key point 2,500 ft AGL

(4)

(5)

Warm the engine

Monitor the descent

(6)

Low key point **1,500 ft AGL**

Abeam the aiming point

Look out

Warm the engine

Turn base according to the wind

Use flaps as required

Look out

(7)

(8)

8. Initiate a Go-Around.
- Full power (carb heat—COLD).
- Stop the descent (initially fly straight-and-level).
- Raise the flaps in sequence (as recommended in your P.O.H.).
- Adopt the climb attitude.
- Trim.

Go-around

WIND

Initial aiming point

7. Adjust Base and Final.
Use flaps as required to reduce the aiming point.

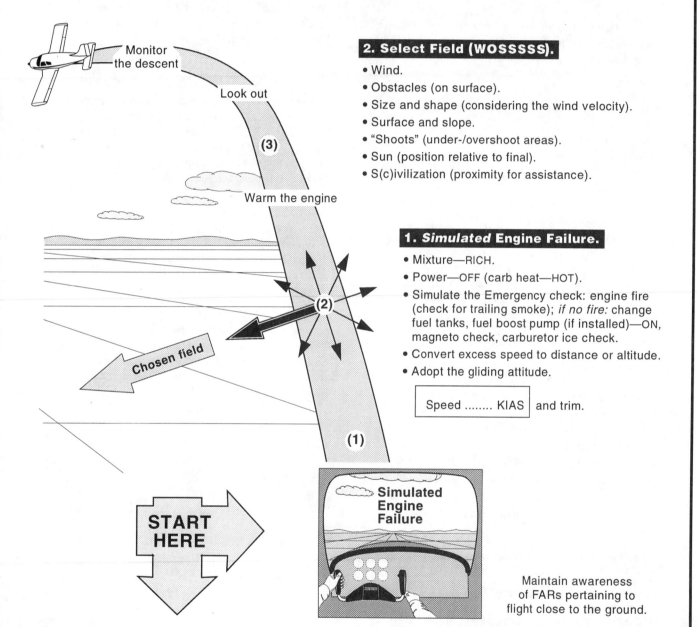

3. Plan the Approach.

- Select key positions.
- Keep all turns toward the selected field.

Monitor the descent

Look out

(3)

Warm the engine

2. Select Field (WOSSSSS).

- Wind.
- Obstacles (on surface).
- Size and shape (considering the wind velocity).
- Surface and slope.
- "Shoots" (under-/overshoot areas).
- Sun (position relative to final).
- S(c)ivilization (proximity for assistance).

1. *Simulated* Engine Failure.

- Mixture—RICH.
- Power—OFF (carb heat—HOT).
- Simulate the Emergency check: engine fire (check for trailing smoke); *if no fire:* change fuel tanks, fuel boost pump (if installed)—ON, magneto check, carburetor ice check.
- Convert excess speed to distance or altitude.
- Adopt the gliding attitude.

  Speed .... KIAS and trim.

(2)

Chosen field

(1)

START HERE

Simulated Engine Failure

Maintain awareness of FARs pertaining to flight close to the ground.

Prior to Practicing a Forced Landing

Check:
- Correct local flight training area. • At a suitable altitude AGL. • **Look out** for other aircraft.

Emergency Forced Landing without Power

1. Following a sudden engine failure in flight, your first action should be to (adopt the gliding attitude/make a radio call to ATC).

   ➤ adopt the gliding attitude

2. When maneuvering for a forced landing after engine failure, you should alter the pitch attitude to maintain (minimum/best glide/maximum) airspeed as closely as possible.

   ➤ best glide

3. You should be aware of the wind direction and have a suitable emergency landing area picked out (at all times/only after an emergency has occurred).

   ➤ at all times

4. You will travel further through the air in the glide if you fly (at/faster than/slower than) the best-glide airspeed.

   ➤ at

5. You should make an emergency call on the frequency you are currently using or on the emergency frequency, which is ____ MHz.

   ➤ 121.5

6. In a radar environment, you can alert a radar controller to your emergency situation by squawking code ____ on your transponder.

   ➤ 7700

7. There are three possible problems that could cause an engine to fail in flight which you could check. They are a ____ ____ , an ____ ____ , and ____ ____ .

   ➤ a fuel problem, an ignition problem, carburetor icing

8. Recall the items in your emergency forced landing checklist.

   ➤ *refer to your Pilot's Operating Handbook*

9. If the flaps are not available and you find yourself too high on final approach to the forced landing area, you could steepen the descent and lose excess altitude by using the ____ ____ technique.

   ➤ forward slip

10. During a simulated forced landing you (should/ need not) clear the engine periodically and keep it warm during the prolonged descent.

    ➤ should

11. While practicing forced landings after simulated engine failure, it (is/is not) possible that you could still suffer a genuine engine failure.

    ➤ is

12. You have suffered an engine failure in Mooney 8536C, five miles south of Eltville at an altitude of 7,000 feet MSL. You are descending through 6,000 feet MSL on a heading of south and plan to land in a farmer's grass-covered field. You have been using the Chicago FSS frequency. How would you construct your MAYDAY call?

    ➤ MAYDAY MAYDAY MAYDAY
    Chicago radio
    Mooney eight five three six Charlie
    Engine failure
    Forced landing five miles south of Eltville
    Passing six thousand feet
    Heading one eight zero

13. Sketch your "plans of attack" if you suffered engine failure in the three positions: A, B and C. Mark your planned tracks and key points. Suitable fields to land in are shown as shaded areas.

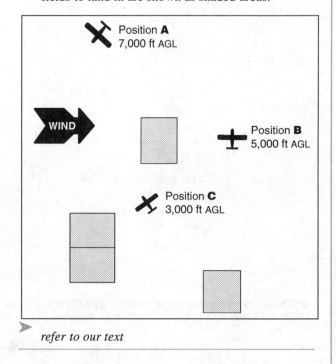

    ➤ *refer to our text*

The Precautionary Landing 17b

Objective

To carry out a safe powered-assisted approach and landing at an unfamiliar field.

Considerations

Landing at an Unfamiliar Field

A pilot may be faced with the decision to land away from an airport for a number of reasons. These include:

- suspected engine or airframe problems;
- a sudden deterioration in the weather, with low clouds and decreasing visibility making further flight unsafe; or
- deficient flight planning or navigation.

Being totally lost, or having insufficient fuel or insufficient daylight remaining, are good enough reasons to consider making a precautionary landing away from an airfield.

Occasionally an unscheduled landing is necessary.

Another reason could be impending incapacitation of the pilot, say from food poisoning, which is best coped with on the ground. Land sooner rather than later, but ensure that the field chosen for landing is suitable.

If you are about to land at an unfamiliar nontowered airport, then you should consider a **precautionary inspection** before landing, especially if there is no other activity at the field. This is known as *dragging the area*.

Decision to Land

If any doubt exists as to the advisability of continuing the flight, you should make the decision to land while there is still time to do so with the airplane under full control, and before conditions deteriorate to a dangerous level. It is better to land *before* you run out of fuel, daylight or visibility, even if the landing is in a field rather than at an airport.

Make an early decision to land.

Estimate the time you have available and act accordingly.

Slowing the airplane down and lowering some flaps may assist you greatly. Slow flight gives you more time to observe the ground and to formulate a plan, as well as making the airplane more maneuverable. Also, the turning performance is better at slow speeds, and forward vision from the cockpit is improved. Slow flight may reduce the problems facing you, and even eliminate them.

Estimate what time you have available and act accordingly.

Flying the Maneuver

Search for a Suitable Landing Area

When the decision to land has been taken, immediately search for a suitable landing area. Ideally, choose an active airport; otherwise select the most suitable landing field, as outlined in the previous exercise.

Consider advising FSS or ATC of your intentions by radio on the normal frequency and, if not satisfactory, on the emergency frequency 121.5 MHz.

Items to consider when selecting a suitable field include:

W—Wind (alignment of field).

O—Obstacles (on surface: trees, rocks, power cables, buildings, and so on).

S—Size and Shape (considering the wind velocity).

S—Surface and Slope.

S—"Shoots" (undershoot and overshoot areas).

S—Sun (position relative to final approach).

S—S(c)ivilization.

If no suitable field is obvious, then searching *downwind* will allow you to have a higher groundspeed and so cover more area.

Airplane Configuration

If a low cloud ceiling, poor visibility or a restricted maneuvering area are involved, then adopt the *precautionary* (or *bad weather) configuration.* Use the optimum stage of flaps, which may be just the first 10° to 15°. Extending the flaps enables:

Consider adopting the slower precautionary configuration.

- slower speeds;
- a smaller turn radius and a higher rate of turn;
- better visibility from the cockpit; and
- improved elevator and rudder response.

Staying in the one configuration allows you to fly the whole sequence—descents, straight-and-level, and climbs—at a constant airspeed, thereby removing one variable. Fly the attitude for the selected airspeed, and control the descent, level flight and climb-out with the use of power.

Field Inspection

The low-flying check should be completed before descending to a low level. It is good airmanship to keep your workload to a minimum in low-level flight. Flying low to inspect a surface means accurate flying and a good **lookout**. Keep the airplane in trim or, if anything, trim slightly nose-up so that the airplane will have no tendency to descend while your attention is directed outside.

Inspect the selected landing area.

Several inspection runs of the field should be made in the precautionary configuration, and a traffic pattern and altitude established. With no restrictions, a normal traffic pattern should be suitable.

In bad weather, a low and tight pattern (for example, at 500 feet AGL) may be advisable. The altitudes at which the patterns are flown, and the number of inspection runs carried out, depend upon the situation. Command decisions must be made by the pilot.

If three inspection patterns are thought necessary, a suitable plan might be:
- **Pattern A.** At 1,000 feet above ground level, to establish the pattern and note landmarks and magnetic headings. Low clouds might make a lower altitude necessary. Some flight instructors may consider this preliminary pattern unnecessary. Complete low-flying checks before you descend.
- **Pattern B.** To select and make a preliminary evaluation of the optimum landing path. Descend on final and make a run at 500 feet AGL (or 300 feet AGL or 200 feet AGL—refer to your flight instructor) slightly right of the landing path to give you a good view of the approach path and landing surface out of your left cockpit window. Search for large obstacles and obstructions, ditches, animals, wires, fences, and so on. Climb back to the pattern altitude as you near the end of the field.
- **Pattern C.** Descend on final and make a run to the right of and along the selected landing path at a lower, but still safe, level (say 100 or 50 feet AGL) for a closer inspection of the landing surface itself. Return to pattern altitude.
- **Pattern D.** A normal pattern, followed by a landing appropriate to the type of field, using soft-field and/or short-field techniques.

Make each inspection run alongside the selected landing path at a constant altitude, and not as a slow descent that necessitates a frantic climb at the far boundary of the field to avoid obstacles. If there are time, fuel, daylight or weather restrictions, you might have to reduce the number of patterns flown.

Even though three preliminary patterns are used in the *Airwork* example (which follows), adapt the procedure according to your requirements.

Adapt your plan to suit the conditions—for example, low clouds, imminent darkness, low fuel. A close-in pattern at 500 feet AGL, with only one inspection run, might be called for, with no delay in making a landing. Your flight instructor will give you plenty of practice at this procedure in many different situations. Adapt to each situation as you see fit.

Be alert to the visual illusions associated with low flying resulting from the wind effect. Keep your turns accurate and coordinated in spite of the deceptive appearance of the ground if there is a strong wind. Add power to maintain airspeed in the turn if necessary, and monitor the airspeed indicator closely.

Learn to make command decisions quickly and efficiently.

Final Approach and Landing

Position the airplane for a normal engine-assisted approach. Consider making a soft-field landing to minimize stress on the landing gear and airframe during the touchdown and landing run, if the field is rough. If the field is also short, then apply short-field techniques as well. Complete the appropriate Before-Landing checklist. If time is not a consideration, be prepared to go around if you are not totally satisfied with the approach.

Airmanship

When practicing the precautionary landing:
- ensure that you are in the correct local flying area and keep a good **lookout** for other aircraft;
- consider any regulations or local rules (such as no descents below 500 feet AGL, do not frighten farm animals) and obey the rules;
- align the heading indicator with the landing direction (either on 360° or 180°) to help with orientation;
- select physical landmarks on the ground as turning points in the pattern if possible.

Airwork 17b
The Precautionary Search and Landing

Objective

To carry out a safe approach and landing at an unfamiliar field, or on an unprepared surface, with engine power available.

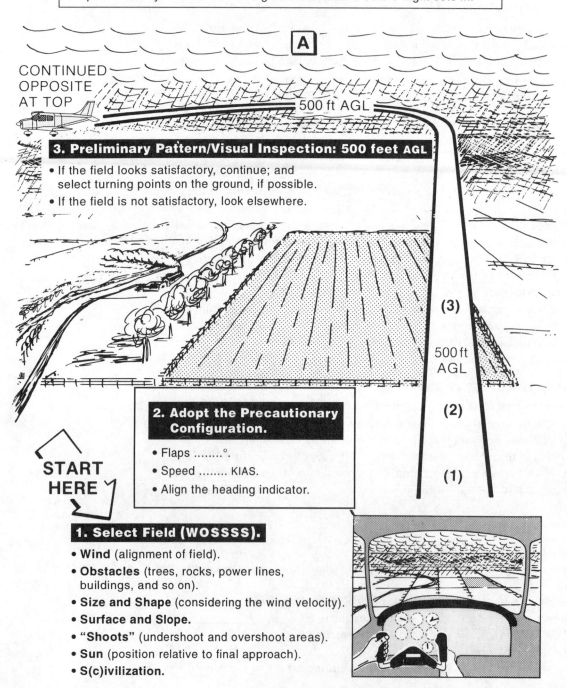

For the purpose of this exercise, the scenario is a cloud base of 600 feet AGL, poor visibility and 20 minutes flight time available before night sets in.

A

CONTINUED
OPPOSITE
AT TOP

500 ft AGL

3. Preliminary Pattern/Visual Inspection: 500 feet AGL

- If the field looks satisfactory, continue; and select turning points on the ground, if possible.
- If the field is not satisfactory, look elsewhere.

(3)

500 ft AGL

(2)

(1)

2. Adopt the Precautionary Configuration.

- Flaps ....°.
- Speed .... KIAS.
- Align the heading indicator.

START
HERE

1. Select Field (WOSSSS).

- **Wind** (alignment of field).
- **Obstacles** (trees, rocks, power lines, buildings, and so on).
- **Size and Shape** (considering the wind velocity).
- **Surface and Slope.**
- **"Shoots"** (undershoot and overshoot areas).
- **Sun** (position relative to final approach).
- **S(c)ivilization.**

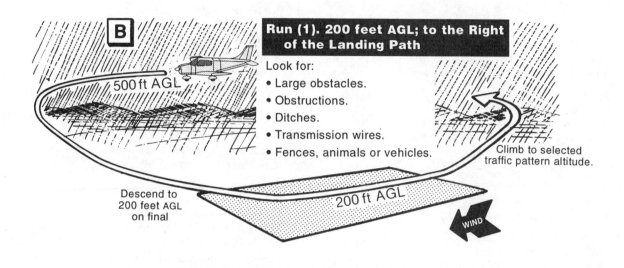

Run (1). 200 feet AGL; to the Right of the Landing Path

500 ft AGL

Look for:
- Large obstacles.
- Obstructions.
- Ditches.
- Transmission wires.
- Fences, animals or vehicles.

Climb to selected traffic pattern altitude.

Descend to 200 feet AGL on final

200 ft AGL

WIND

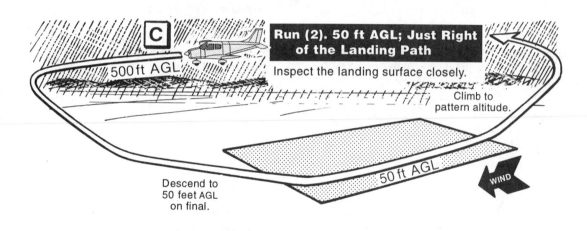

Run (2). 50 ft AGL; Just Right of the Landing Path

500 ft AGL

Inspect the landing surface closely.

Climb to pattern altitude.

Descend to 50 feet AGL on final.

50 ft AGL

WIND

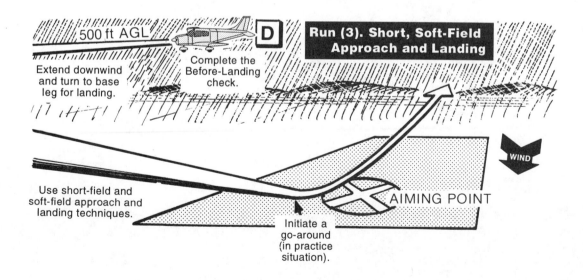

500 ft AGL

Complete the Before-Landing check.

Run (3). Short, Soft-Field Approach and Landing

Extend downwind and turn to base leg for landing.

WIND

Use short-field and soft-field approach and landing techniques.

AIMING POINT

Initiate a go-around (in practice situation).

✍ Review 17b

The Precautionary Landing

1. Carrying out a precautionary inspection of an unfamiliar airfield before deciding whether or not to land on it, is called "_____ the area".

   ➤ dragging

2. In the space below, sketch the patterns you would fly to inspect an unfamiliar field before deciding whether or not to land on it.

   ➤ *refer to our text and your Pilot's Operating Handbook*

3. What items would you consider when selecting a field for a precautionary landing.

   ➤ WOSSSS:
   - Wind (alignment of field).
   - Obstacles (on the field —trees, rocks, transmission lines, buildings, and so on).
   - Size and Shape (in relation to wind).
   - Surface and Slope.
   - "Shoots" (undershoot/approach and overshoot/go-around areas).
   - Sun (position relative to final approach).
   - S(c)ivilization.

4. If it is difficult to determine just how rough the surface of the proposed landing area is, you should make a (normal/soft-field) landing.

   ➤ soft-field

5. In conditions of low clouds and poor visibility that cause you to adopt a precautionary landing procedure, there (may/will not) be visual illusions to be careful of, caused by _____ .

   ➤ may, wind

6. Flying downwind, the groundspeed will be (higher/lower) than the airspeed; the (high/low) groundspeed can cause a visual illusion of (high/low) airspeed and trap an unwary pilot into (reducing/increasing) power.

   ➤ higher, high, high, reducing

7. When flying crosswind at a low level, the drift caused by the crosswind (can/will not) give a visual illusion of slipping or skidding, and (may/will not) lead an unwary pilot into applying unnecessary rudder.

   ➤ can, may

Space to sketch your answer to question 2

Ditching in Water **17c**

Objective

To touch down on water as successfully as possible, if ditching is the best available option.

Considerations

Being forced to ditch in the ocean is a remote possibility, however it is worthwhile having a suitable procedure in the back of your mind.

Try to touch down near a ship or in a shipping lane if possible, and make a MAYDAY radio call on the frequency in use or on the emergency frequency 121.5 MHz. Squawk 7700 on the transponder before too much altitude is lost to ensure the best chance of signal reception by ground stations.

Make emergency calls before ditching.

Landing Direction

Determine the direction of the swells before you depart from over land. Around 2,000 feet is the best altitude from which to visually assess the swell pattern.

If the water is smooth, or smooth with a long swell, then land into the wind.

If there is a large swell or a rough sea, then land along the swell, even if you have to accept a crosswind. This avoids the danger of nosing into a big wave.

Waves generally move downwind, except near a shoreline or in fast moving estuaries, however **swells** may not bear any relationship at all to the surface wind direction.

Clues to wind direction include:
- wave direction (with white-caps being blown back in strong winds);
- wind lines (the streaked effect being more apparent when viewed from upwind);
- gust ripples on the water surface;
- airplane drift.

If planning to land along a swell, it is recommended that you touch down on top of the swell or just on the back side of it. Avoid landing on its advancing face.

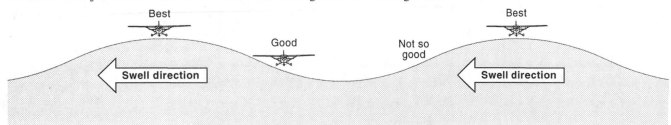

Figure 17c-1. Touch down on top of a swell, or just after it.

Flying the Maneuver

The Approach

If your engine is running, use a powered approach for ditching. From altitude, water generally appears to be calmer than is actually the case. Fly low and study the water surface before ditching. Consider jettisoning any heavy or sharp objects to lighten the aircraft and remove potentially dangerous objects.

Generally the airplane should ditch with some flaps extended, at a low speed, in a high nose attitude (tail-down) and at a low rate of descent controlled by power (if available). Power gives you a lot more control over the touchdown point, so avoid running out of fuel prior to ditching.

Touch down with as low a flying speed as possible, but **do not stall in.**

Alert the Passengers

Warn the passengers. Buckle up and don life jackets, if available, but do not inflate them until in the water, as they may inhibit the evacuation. Remove headsets and anything else that may get in the way during the evacuation.

Be prepared for a double impact—the first when the tail strikes the water, the second (and greater) when the nose hits the water. The aircraft may also slew to one side and nose over.

Evacuation should be carried out as calmly as possible, life jackets being inflated *outside* the cabin. You may have to open a window and flood the lower half of the cabin to equalize pressures so that the doors can be opened. The pilot-in-command should supervise.

Wear your flotation gear if your flight is over water, and out of gliding distance from land. If you have to ditch, the aircraft will possibly nose over upside down and you may get out with only the equipment attached to your body.

Use a powered approach, if possible, for ditching.

 ## Review 17c

1. If the wind is light and there is a large swell running, then you should plan to ditch (along the swell/into the swell/into the wind).

   ➤ along the swell

2. The area of a swell to avoid when ditching is (the top of the swell/the bottom of the swell/the advancing face of the swell).

   ➤ the advancing face of the swell

Ditching in Water

3. When ditching, you (should/should not) use power to minimize the rate of descent.

   ➤ should

4. When ditching, touch down (at as low a flying speed as possible/by stalling in).

   ➤ at as low a flying speed as possible

Expanding Your Horizons Phase Four

Phase Four Completion Standards

In Phase Four, you will be consolidating what you have learned in Phases One, Two and Three, and will be expanding your horizons with:

Phase Four consolidates all that you have learned, and completes your basic flight training.

- Cross-country flying, with an emphasis on:

    Good preparation, and analysis of weather information and NOTAMs.

    A competent go/no-go decision.

    Check of maintenance documents.

    Correct performance calculations.

    Correct weight-and-balance calculations.

    An accurate flight plan filed with FSS.

    Preflight inspection and fueling of the airplane without error.

    Good cockpit management.

    Good in-flight knowledge (the Visual Flight Rules, cruising altitudes, radio communication).

    Good navigation by pilotage, dead-reckoning and radio navigation aids.

    An in-flight log of headings, fixes, groundspeeds, ETAs (updated with FSS), and fuel remaining.

    Checks and checklists performed without error.

    Weather advisories obtained en route from Flight Watch.

    A diversion to a suitable alternate airport, promptly executed, with accurate ETA and fuel-required calculations, and FSS advised.

    A knowledge of what to do if uncertain of position, or if lost.

    Correct traffic pattern entry, with competent landings.

    Correct closing of flight plan with FSS.

    Accident reporting procedures.

- Instrument flying, performing the basic maneuvers—straight-and-level, climbing, descending and turning—with reference only to the flight instrument, and en route navigation using radio navigation aids and/or radar directives, with an emphasis on:

    Instrument crosscheck (scan).

    Instrument interpretation.

    Airplane control.

- Night flying:

    Airport lighting.

    Night vision.

    Takeoffs, traffic patterns and landings at night.

    Night VFR navigation.

At the completion of this phase, your flying will be positive and sound, you will have satisfied the aeronautical knowledge requirement by having passed the FAA written test, and you will be prepared to take your practical flight test.

Cross-Country Flying 18

Objective

To plan and fly cross-country under the Visual Flight Rules (VFR).

Considerations

Cross-country flying is a significant step forward in your training which, so far, has been restricted to the local training area and has concentrated on:

- **basic flying skills** (climbing, turning, straight-and-level, landing, and so on); and
- **basic procedures** (traffic patterns, forced landings, flight maneuvers by reference to ground objects, and so on).

Flying to another airport, perhaps quite distant, requires the additional skills and knowledge which are summarized here in this chapter.

Flight Management

As the pilot-in-command of a cross-country flight, you have certain duties to perform, both on the ground and in flight. The main flight management tasks are:

- **to fly the airplane;** and
- **to navigate it to the destination,** which involves:
    careful flight planning; and
    accurate en route navigation.

Control the progress of your flight from the planning stage to closing the flight plan.

Flight management applies to the planning stage on the ground as well as to the actual flight. You should train yourself to plan a long VFR cross-country flight within **30 minutes.** This includes completing a flight log, preparing a fuel log, calculating weight-and-balance—taking into account the expected loading— and filing a flight plan. Doing all this inside 30 minutes takes practice!

Get organized and plan within 30 minutes.

You have limited resources in the cockpit that need to be managed efficiently. For example, it is difficult to measure course directions and distances on a chart in flight while trying to fly in rough air—it shows better management to do the chart work on the ground prior to flight. The better the flight planning prior to flight, the easier the en route navigation!

Personal Navigation Equipment

Organize your personal equipment.

The two most vital instruments for visual navigation are the **magnetic compass** and the **clock,** so always carry a serviceable wristwatch. Provided that the airplane's position has been positively fixed within the previous twenty minutes or so, and its speed is known (at least approximately), its position during the flight can be deduced from the direction it has traveled and the time taken from the last fix—hence the name *dead reckoning.*

A **flight case,** satchel or nav bag that fits comfortably within reach in the cockpit should be used to hold your navigation equipment. A typical flight case should contain:

- relevant charts covering at least 50 nm either side of your planned course;
- Airport/Facility Directory (A/FD) and current AIM;
- a navigation computer;
- a plotter;
- pens and pencils;
- spare flight log forms;
- a flashlight; and
- sunglasses.

The Flight Log

The flight log is designed to keep the necessary data and calculations orderly. It has a **preflight** section for your planning calculations and weather forecasts, and an **en route** section where you can keep a record of your flight progress.

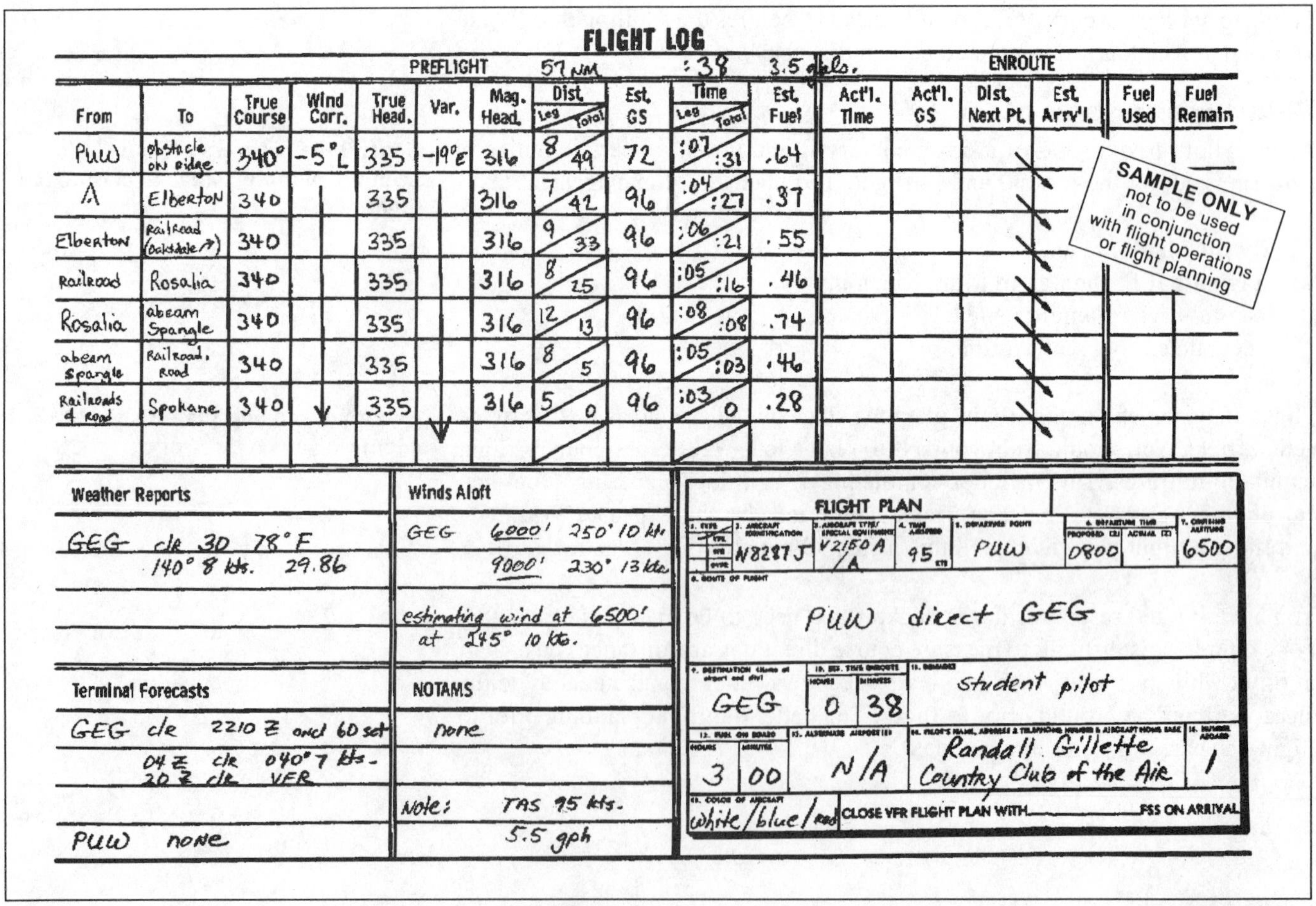

FLIGHT LOG

PREFLIGHT 57 NM :38 3.5 gals. | ENROUTE

From	To	True Course	Wind Corr.	True Head.	Var.	Mag. Head.	Dist. Leg	Dist. Total	Est. GS	Time Leg	Time Total	Est. Fuel	Act'l. Time	Act'l. GS	Dist. Next Pt.	Est. Arrv'l.	Fuel Used	Fuel Remain
PUW	obstacle on ridge	340°	-5°L	335	-19°E	316	8	49	72	:07	:31	.64						
A	Elberton	340	↓	335	↓	316	7	42	96	:04	:27	.37						
Elberton	Railroad (Oakesdale ↗)	340		335		316	9	33	96	:06	:21	.55						
Railroad	Rosalia	340		335		316	8	25	96	:05	:16	.46						
Rosalia	abeam Spangle	340		335		316	12	13	96	:08	:08	.74						
abeam Spangle	Railroad, Road	340		335		316	8	5	96	:05	:03	.46						
Railroads & Road	Spokane	340		335		316	5	0	96	:03	0	.28						

SAMPLE ONLY not to be used in conjunction with flight operations or flight planning

Weather Reports
GEG clr 30 78°F 140° 8 kts. 29.86

Winds Aloft
GEG 6000' 250° 10 kts
9000' 230° 13 kts
estimating wind at 6500' at 245° 10 kts.

Terminal Forecasts
GEG clr 2210 Z and 60 sct
04 Z clr 040° 7 kts.
20 Z clr VFR
PUW none

NOTAMS
none
Note: TAS 95 kts. 5.5 gph

FLIGHT PLAN
1. Type: VFR — 2. Aircraft identification: N8287J — 3. Aircraft type/special equipment: V2150A /A — 4. True airspeed: 95 kts — 5. Departure point: PUW — 6. Departure time: Proposed (Z) 0800 — 7. Cruising altitude: 6500
8. Route of flight: PUW direct GEG
9. Destination (name of airport and city): GEG — 10. Est. time enroute: Hours 0, Minutes 38 — 11. Remarks: student pilot
12. Fuel on board: Hours 3, Minutes 00 — 13. Alternate airport(s): N/A — 14. Pilot's name, address & telephone number & aircraft home base: Randall Gillette, Country Club of the Air — 15. Number aboard: 1
16. Color of aircraft: white/blue/red — CLOSE VFR FLIGHT PLAN WITH ______ FSS ON ARRIVAL

Figure 18-1. A typical flight log prepared prior to flight: Pullman-Moscow Regional Airport (PUW) to Spokane Int'l Airport (GEG)

Flight Planning

Weather and Operational Considerations

You should obtain **weather information** and **Notices to Airmen (NOTAMs)** by the most convenient means available to you. This may be via a computer print out, a briefing office or by telephone. When requesting a preflight briefing by telephone from a Flight Service Station (FSS), you should identify yourself as a pilot and provide the following information:

Obtain a thorough briefing.

- VFR (or IFR).
- Aircraft's N-number or pilot's name.
- Aircraft type.
- Departure airport.
- Route of the flight.
- Destination.
- Flight altitudes.
- Estimated Time of Departure (ETD) and Estimated Time En route (ETE).

```
********  Surface Observations  ********
MWH SA 0245 80 SCT 200 SCT 30 85/49/1206/979      ←
GEG SA 0250 CLR 30 098/78/55/1408/986/ 707        ←
SKA SA 0255 CLR 25 109/74/56/1402/988/ 607=
SFF SA 0250 CLR 20 80/56/1509/985
EPH SA 0258 80 SCT E200 BKN 40 076/84/53/1808/979/ 607
PSC SA 0245 160 SCT 35 90/53/0607/973
ALW SA 0255 CLR 20 083/86/53/0806/979/ 710        ←
LWS SA 0250 AMOS 84/57/0504/M PK WND 08 000
LWS SP 0329 AMOS 82/55/0903/M PK WND 05 000
current hourly report not available for PUW
PUW SA 0148 CLR 30 80/52/0000/989                 ←

********  Terminal Forecasts  ********
MWH FT 240202  80 SCT 200 SCT.  05Z CLR.  20Z VFR NO CIG.   ←
    NO AMDTS AVBL AFT 06Z..
GEG FT 240202  CLR 2210 OCNL 60 SCT.  04Z CLR 0407.  20Z VFR  ←
    NO CIG..
SKA 0024 20008KT 9999 2CU040 2CI250
QNH2984INS=
```

SAMPLE ONLY not to be used in conjunction with flight operations or flight planning

Figure 18-2. Some typical weather information

```
-->NOSUM18   0604
-->SLC   06/001   LGU RWY 07/25 CLSD
-->SLC   06/002   PVU CTZL 05-2200 LOCAL EXCP HOL
```

Figure 18-3. A typical NOTAM

Flight Service Stations (FSS) can provide three basic types of preflight briefing:

- a **standard briefing**—a *full* briefing including adverse conditions, VFR flight recommended or not, weather synopsis, current conditions, en route forecast, destination forecast, winds aloft, relevant NOTAMs, known ATC delays; or

- an **abbreviated briefing**—to supplement information you already have; or

- an **outlook briefing**—for advanced planning purposes (for a flight six or more hours from the time of briefing).

You should read and analyze the weather information so that you can make well-based judgments regarding your proposed flight, especially the *go/no-go* decision. **Analyze the weather reports and forecasts,** weather charts, SIGMETs, AIRMETs and pilot weather reports (PIREPs). Don't forget to walk outside and look at the sky yourself.

Make an informed *go/no-go* decision.

Significant weather prognostic charts and constant pressure prognostic charts are useful for high-altitude flights. Remember that the minimum conditions in most airspace for VFR flight are:

- flight visibility at least three statute miles;
- distances from clouds: at least 500 feet below, 1,000 feet above and 2,000 feet horizontally from clouds.

You should also **check any NOTAMs** (Notices to Airmen) relevant to your flight, and whatever other relevant information is available.

This all sounds like a lot, but the information will be presented to you in a logical manner—and the more practiced you become in planning a flight, the easier it will seem.

From this information, and from your knowledge of your own experience and capabilities, you can now make a firm, positive and confident go/no-go decision. This is a **command decision**—possibly the most important decision of the whole flight.

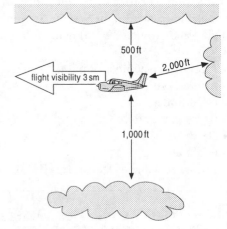

Figure 18-4. Basic VFR minimum weather conditions

Compiling a Flight Log

While your first few cross-country flights will take a long time to plan, you should aim, by practice, to speed up the process so that you can do this within 30 minutes from start to finish.

Select a suitable route.

Select and use **current and appropriate aeronautical charts** which, for most VFR flights will be a **sectional chart,** together with **terminal charts** for any nearby Class B airspace.

Select the route over which you want to fly. Note the nature of the terrain and the type of airspace along this route and to either side of it:

- **Terrain:** check the elevation of any obstacles within 10 miles either side of your proposed course.

- **Airspace:** check the route for:
    class of controlled airspace;
    prohibited areas, restricted areas or warning areas; and
    other airports.

- **Expanses of water:** if you will be flying over water for an extended period, you should ensure that there are life preservers or other approved flotation means on board for each occupant.

It may be best to avoid particularly high or rugged terrain (especially if you are flying a single-engine airplane) and areas of dense air traffic.

Choose turning points and prominent checkpoints that will be easily identified in flight, and which cannot be confused with other nearby ground features. Select appropriate en route radio navigation aids, and note the communications facilities at the departure, destination, and alternate airports, as listed on your charts and in the A/FD.

Allow for necessary **fuel stops.** Mark the route on your sectional chart, and enter the checkpoints on the flight log. Note any suitable **alternate airports** available on or adjacent to the route, in case an unscheduled landing becomes necessary. It shows good airmanship to be thinking of en route problems (such as bad weather or a sick passenger) even on the ground.

Look for suitable en route alternate airports.

Safe Altitudes and Cruising Altitudes

For each leg of the flight, it is advisable to calculate a **safe altitude** that is 1,000 feet higher than any obstacle within 10 miles either side of the planned course, and enter the altitude on the flight log. This is not a requirement, but it provides a safe minimum altitude to use if, for instance, clouds force you down. Also check the meteorological information to confirm that the forecast clouds are above this minimum altitude. Remember that you should remain at least 2,000 feet above mountainous terrain.

Select a **suitable cruising altitude for each leg** and enter it in the flight log. Considerations should include:
- terrain;
- overlying airspace restrictions;
- the cloud base;
- favorable (or unfavorable) winds aloft at various altitudes;
- line-of-sight VHF radio reception (higher altitudes are better in mountains); and
- VFR cruising altitudes.

The VFR cruising altitudes, when more than 3,000 feet above the surface, are:
- on a magnetic course 000°M to 179°M: *odd* thousands plus 500 feet—for example, 3,500 feet MSL, 5,500 feet MSL, 7,500 feet MSL and 9,500 feet MSL;
- on a magnetic course 180°M to 359°M: *even* thousands plus 500 feet—for example, 4,500 feet MSL, 6,500 feet MSL, 8,500 feet MSL and 10,500 feet MSL.

Select a safe cruising altitude.

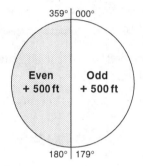

Figure 18-5. VFR cruising altitudes above 3,000 feet AGL

Courses and Distances

For each leg of the flight, mentally estimate the course direction (in degrees) and distance (in nautical miles) before measuring them accurately (ensuring that you are using the correct scale).

Add the accurately measured figures to the flight log. Be sure to apply **magnetic variation** to the measured true course to find the magnetic course:
- **variation east, magnetic least;**
- **variation west, magnetic best.**

Note: If you are tracking between VOR or VORTAC stations, remember that the VOR compass roses on your chart are aligned with *magnetic* north.

Estimating course and distance prior to actual measurement will avoid gross errors.

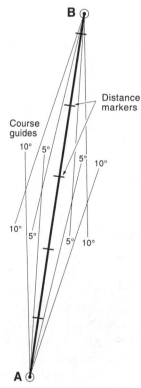

Figure 18-6. Course guides and distance markers

Distance Markers or Time Markers

To assist you in flight, you can subdivide each leg using small marks placed at regular intervals along the course lines drawn on the chart. These may be:
- distance markers each 10 nm; or
- distance markers at the one-quarter, one-half and three-quarter points; or
- time markers each 10 minutes; or
- time markers at the one-quarter, one-half and three-quarter points.

Note: Time markers will, of course, have to wait until you have calculated groundspeeds and time intervals. When in flight, you may find that these vary from the flight planned values, unlike the distance markers.

Course Guides

To allow easier in-flight estimation of any deviation from the planned course, it is useful to draw in 5° and 10° guides either side of course emanating from each turning point. This avoids having to use a plotter in flight.

Groundspeeds and Time Intervals

Calculate the required headings, expected groundspeeds and time intervals using your flight computer.

Add the forecast winds (using magnetic variation to convert the forecast true winds into magnetic), the selected cruising altitude, and the true airspeed (TAS) for each leg onto the flight log in their columns.

The appropriate TAS and fuel flow for your selected cruise power setting (typically 55% to 75% brake horsepower) can be found from the cruise performance tables in the Pilot's Operating Handbook—or convert your known indicated airspeed (IAS) to a TAS using your flight computer (see figure 18-7).

For a given indicated airspeed, the true airspeed will be greater at higher altitudes and temperatures because of the decreased air density.

On the **wind side** of the computer, use the forecast wind to set up the *triangle of velocities* and calculate the **wind correction angle** (WCA), **heading** in degrees magnetic [HDG(M)] and **groundspeed** (GS) for each leg (figure 18-8). Having obtained the values for GS and HDG(M), add them to the flight log.

Note: It is important when using the flight computer to work in degrees magnetic.

Calculate expected headings, groundspeeds and time intervals.

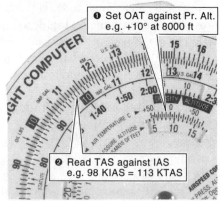

Figure 18-7. If necessary, convert IAS to TAS (using the pressure altitude and the air temperature).

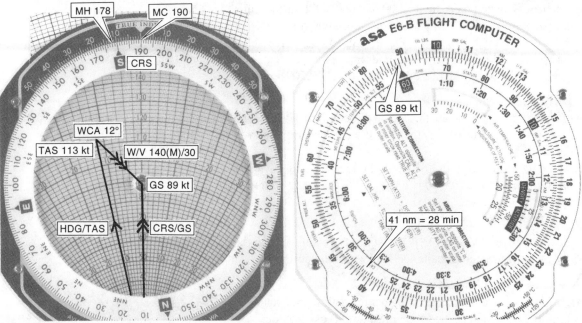

Figure 18-8. Calculate heading and groundspeed, and the estimated time intervals.

Using the measured distance of each leg and the expected groundspeed, determine the *estimated time interval* and add it to the flight log (figure 18-8). Then, add all of the individual time intervals together and obtain the **total** time interval for the whole flight.

It is good airmanship at this point to compare this result with the total distance for the flight and verify that it is a reasonable result, considering the average groundspeed (GS) expected to be achieved.

Also, confirm that you will arrive with adequate daylight remaining; allow at least 30 minutes, but a prudent pilot will plan for significantly more than this, say one hour—your flight instructor will offer guidance on this.

If planning to land at other airports en route, allow at least 10 minutes maneuvering time for landing and taxiing, then at least 30 minutes on the ground for fueling, and so on, followed by another 10 minutes for taxiing, takeoff and departure—in other words, about one hour extra compared with overflying it.

Allow realistic times for ground stops.

Fuel Calculations

The fuel consumption for various power settings is published in the Pilot's Operating Handbook. These figures assume correct leaning of the fuel/air mixture when cruising at 75% maximum continuous power or less. Leaning the mixture can decrease fuel consumption by up to 20%. From the estimated time interval for the whole flight and the published fuel consumption rate, **calculate the expected flight fuel.** Remember to allow for the additional fuel required for the taxi out, takeoff and climb.

Reserve fuel of 30 minutes by day and 45 minutes by night should also be carried to allow for in-flight contingencies including diversions, fuel consumption poorer than that published, unexpected headwinds en route, and so on. This fixed reserve is only intended to be used in an emergency—in other words, we plan to land with at least this fixed reserve still in the tanks. Any fuel over and above the minimum fuel required is known as **margin fuel.**

Some aircraft are unable to carry both a full payload (passengers and baggage) *and* full fuel tanks, in which case you have to make a decision whether to restrict payload or fuel. You must carry **at least flight fuel plus a fixed reserve.** You can then carry payload up to the weight-and-balance limitations.

Add the fuel calculations to the flight log.

A fixed fuel reserve of 30 minutes by day and 45 minutes by night is required for VFR operations.

The Flight Plan Form

Fill out the flight plan form, and be sure to insert the relevant **emergency equipment** carried in the *REMARKS* section.

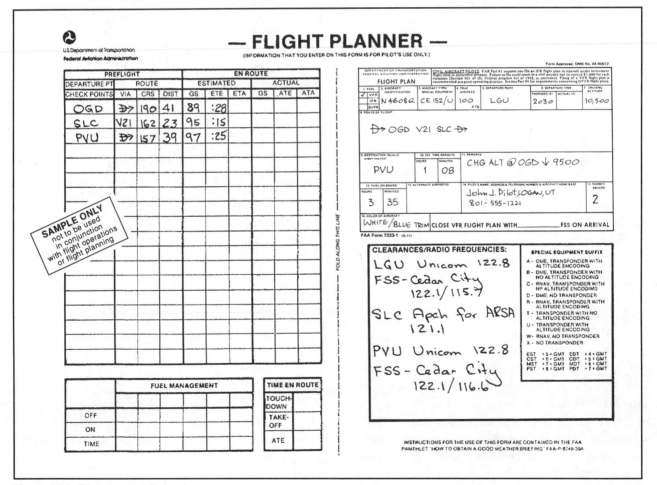

Figure 18-9. Flight log and flight plan

Weight-and-Balance

At this stage of flight planning, when the fuel required and the passenger and baggage load is known, it is appropriate to consider weight-and-balance. For a flight to be **legal**, the airplane must not exceed any weight limitation, and must be loaded so that the center of gravity (CG) lies within the approved range throughout the flight. Complete a load sheet (if necessary) to verify that the requirements are met.

The airplane must be loaded within its weight-and-balance limits.

An **overweight** airplane will perform poorly, possibly be difficult to control, and may suffer structural damage, especially when the load factor increases in maneuvers and turbulence. An **out-of-balance** airplane may be difficult (or impossible) to control. Remove or shift weight to keep the CG within limits.

Some aircraft that operate in the normal category are also permitted to operate in the utility category (some aerobatics permitted), provided that:
- the weight is limited (so as not to exceed wing-loading limits in maneuvers); and
- the center of gravity is well forward (to make spin recovery easier).

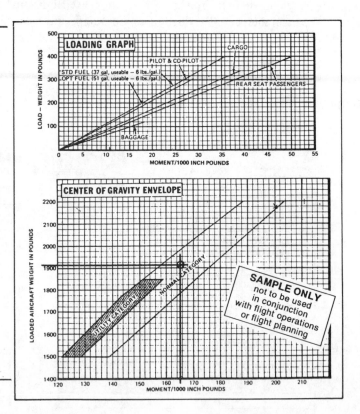

SAMPLE LOADING PROBLEM	SAMPLE AIRPLANE			YOUR AIRPLANE		
	WEIGHT (LBS.)	ARM (IN.)	MOMENT (LB.-IN. /1000)	WEIGHT (LBS.)	ARM (IN.)	MOMENT (LB.-IN. /1000)
*1. Licensed Empty Weight (Typical)	1262	83.4	105.25	1267		105.05
2. Oil (8 qts.) 1 qt. = 1.875 lbs.	15	32.0	.48	15	32.0	.48
3. Fuel (in excess of unuseable) Standard Tanks (37 gal.)	222	90.9	20.18	222	90.9	20.18
Long Range Tanks (51 gal.)		94.81			94.81	
4. Pilot and Co-Pilot	340	90.6	30.80	340	90.6	30.80
5. Rear Seat Passengers	340	126.0	42.84	—	126.0	—
*6. Baggage (in baggage compartment) Max. allowable 120 lbs.	21	151.0	3.17	45	151.0	6.80
7. Cargo Area Max. allowable 340 lbs.		116.4		20	116.4	2.32
8. Total Airplane Weight (loaded)	2200	92.17	202.72	1909		165.63

NOTE: Change in moment from upright to fold-down position of rear seat is negligible.

*Maximum allowable is 120 pounds if C.G. is within Center of Gravity Envelope. Refer to Cargo Loading and Weight and Balance Section for cargo loading instructions.

Figure 18-10. A typical load sheet

Takeoff and Landing Performance

Having considered weight-and-balance, you will know the expected takeoff weight and landing weight of the airplane. If any doubt exists regarding the suitability of the departure, destination and alternate airports, then reference should be made to the Takeoff and Landing **Performance charts** in the Pilot's Operating Handbook.

Check runways are adequate.

The official source of **airport data** is the Airport/Facility Directory (A/FD). **Meteorological data** affecting the performance (wind and temperature) can be obtained from the forecast. Check NOTAMs to ensure that the full length of the runway is available. Sometimes it can be reduced by works-in-progress, or by temporary obstructions in the takeoff and approach paths.

TAKEOFF DISTANCE

SHORT FIELD

CONDITIONS:
Flaps 10°
Full Throttle Prior to Brake Release
Paved, Level, Dry Runway
Zero Wind

NOTES:
1. Short field technique as specified in Section 4.
2. Prior to takeoff from fields above 3000 feet elevation, the mixture should be leaned to give maximum RPM in a full throttle, static runup.
3. Decrease distances 10% for each 9 knots headwind. For operation with tailwinds up to 10 knots, increase distances by 10% for each 2 knots.
4. For operation on a dry, grass runway, increase distances by 15% of the "ground roll" figure.

WEIGHT LBS	TAKEOFF SPEED KIAS		PRESS ALT FT	0°C		10°C		20°C		30°C		40°C	
	LIFT OFF	AT 50 FT		GRND ROLL FT	TOTAL FT TO CLEAR 50 FT OBS	GRND ROLL FT	TOTAL FT TO CLEAR 50 FT OBS	GRND ROLL FT	TOTAL FT TO CLEAR 50 FT OBS	GRND ROLL FT	TOTAL FT TO CLEAR 50 FT OBS	GRND ROLL FT	TOTAL FT TO CLEAR 50 FT OBS
1670	50	54	S.L.	640	1190	695	1290	755	1390	810	1495	875	1605
			1000	705	1310	765	1420	825	1530	890	1645	960	1770
			2000	775	1445	840	1565	910	1690	980	1820	1055	1960
			3000	855	1600	925	1730	1000	1870	1080	2020	1165	2185

Figure 18-11. Excerpt from a Cessna 152 Takeoff Performance chart

LANDING DISTANCE

SHORT FIELD

CONDITIONS:
Flaps 30°
Power Off
Maximum Braking
Paved, Level, Dry Runway
Zero Wind

NOTES:
1. Short field technique as specified in Section 4.
2. Decrease distances 10% for each 9 knots headwind. For operation with tailwinds up to 10 knots, increase distances by 10% for each 2 knots.
3. For operation on a dry, grass runway, increase distances by 45% of the "ground roll" figure.
4. If a landing with flaps up is necessary, increase the approach speed by 7 KIAS and allow for 35% longer distances.

WEIGHT LBS	SPEED AT 50 FT KIAS	PRESS ALT FT	0°C		10°C		20°C		30°C		40°C	
			GRND ROLL FT	TOTAL FT TO CLEAR 50 FT OBS	GRND ROLL FT	TOTAL FT TO CLEAR 50 FT OBS	GRND ROLL FT	TOTAL FT TO CLEAR 50 FT OBS	GRND ROLL FT	TOTAL FT TO CLEAR 50 FT OBS	GRND ROLL FT	TOTAL FT TO CLEAR 50 FT OBS
1670	54	S.L.	450	1160	465	1185	485	1215	500	1240	515	1265
		1000	465	1185	485	1215	500	1240	520	1270	535	1295
		2000	485	1215	500	1240	520	1270	535	1300	555	1330
		3000	500	1240	520	1275	540	1305	560	1335	575	1360

Figure 18-12. Excerpt from a Cessna 152 Landing Performance chart

Flight Notification

Prior to flight, contact the Flight Service Station (FSS) and file the flight plan, in person or by telephone. Use radio only as a last resort for filing a flight plan as it takes some minutes (whereas canceling a flight plan with FSS by radio is usual, since it only takes a few seconds).

Filing a flight plan with FSS is recommended.

It is not mandatory to file a flight plan for VFR flights (except when penetrating defense identification zones), but it is highly recommended, so that you will receive VFR Search and Rescue protection.

If you plan to break your journey at an en route airport for an hour or more, it is usual to file a separate flight plan for each flight. Having filed a flight plan, you must remember to cancel it with FSS after the flight to avoid unnecessary search and rescue procedures.

Close the flight plan with FSS at the end of the flight.

Airplane Documentation

You should check that the required documents are carried:
- ARROW—for the airplane; and
- pilot certificate and medical certificate—for yourself, as pilot-in-command.

You must be familiar with these airplane documents, any equipment list, weight-and-balance data, maintenance requirements and appropriate records. (For your *practical flight test,* you should also bring along the maintenance records for the examiner to inspect: the airframe and engine logbooks, with a current 24-month transponder test, and a current 24-month ELT battery logbook entry.)

An easy way to remember the required documents is with the mnemonic **ARROW**:

A—Airworthiness Certificate
R—Registration Certificate
R—Radio Station License
O—Operating Limitations (in Pilot's Operating Handbook, color-coding on instruments, and speed decals in the cockpit).
W—Weight-and-Balance (included in the POH or FAA-approved AFM, and sometimes found folded and stapled in the map box or a seat pocket; weight-and-balance paperwork needs to be available on board the aircraft, but on many flights need not be filled in).

An **equipment list** should always be on board; this is often found with the weight-and-balance information in the POH.

Figure 18-13. Examples of Airworthiness and Registration Certificates

Preparing the Airplane

Ensure that there is **adequate fuel on board** and complete your normal preflight duties, such as the external (walk-around) inspection and internal inspection. Never hurry this aspect of the flight. It is most important that the preflight preparation is thorough and, even if you are running behind schedule because your flight planning took longer than expected, **do not rush your normal preflight duties.**

Settle into the cockpit and place your navigation equipment and charts where they are readily accessible. Ensure that the charts are folded so that at least 20 nm either side of your course is visible. Ensure that no metallic or magnetic objects are placed near the magnetic compass. Check on the comfort of your passengers (at this stage your flight instructor), and carry out any necessary briefing.

These final checks are worthwhile since, after the engine starts, the noise level will be higher, communication will be slightly more difficult, and you will be busier with the normal workload of manipulating the airplane.

Prepare the airplane in an orderly manner.

The Flight

Start-Up and Taxi

Obtain the airport information from the ATIS or by radio, if available. If in any doubt about the exact time, confirm it with ATC and **ensure that your clock is set correctly.** Ensure that your navigation equipment is accessible, but will not restrict the controls in any way. Have your charts prefolded.

Following normal procedures, start the engine, switch on the radio and make the appropriate radio calls if required. At tower-controlled airports, you will require a taxi clearance from the tower, perhaps on a separate ground frequency. At airports without an operating tower, you should announce your intentions on the CTAF frequency—the Common Traffic Advisory Frequency (which may be FSS, UNICOM, MULTICOM or tower frequency).

Taxi to the takeoff position. At tower-controlled airports, read back any instructions to hold short of a runway. Complete all of the normal preflight checks.

Takeoff and Set Heading

At tower-controlled airports, you require a clearance to line up on the runway and take off. At airports without an operating control tower, you are totally responsible, but you should announce your intentions on the CTAF and have a good look around (especially in the approach paths from either direction) before taxiing onto the runway for departure.

When aligned on the runway, but not accelerating, check that the magnetic compass is reading correctly and that the heading indicator is aligned with it.

Following takeoff, the easiest method of **setting heading** is from directly overhead the airport, at which time you would mentally note your **actual time of departure**.

You can also set your heading en route, by climbing out straight ahead before turning to intercept the course at some short distance en route. A radar controller (possibly on a **departures** frequency) may give you **radar vectors** as headings to steer to get you on course. Ensure that you do not violate any FARs (such as entering clouds as a VFR pilot). In the case of radar vectors—keep clear of the clouds and request a revised clearance or instructions. When on course, you should estimate what the actual time of departure from overhead the airport would have been.

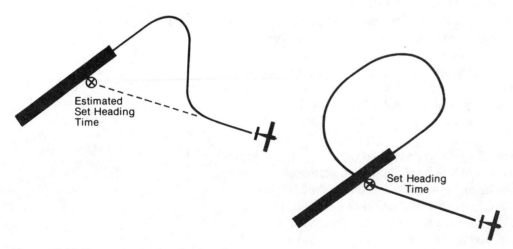

Estimated
Set Heading
Time

Set Heading
Time

Figure 18-14. Two methods of setting heading

To use the magnetic compass precisely, you should refer to the **compass deviation card** in the cockpit so that the magnetic heading can be modified if necessary to the slightly more accurate compass heading. (Deviation is usually less than 3° and so is not really operationally significant.) Figure 18-15.

When well clear of the traffic pattern, enter the ATD (actual time of departure) on the flight log, and estimate the arrival time at the destination and at selected points en route. **Advise FSS of your departure time.** The current **altimeter setting** (obtainable by radio) should be set in the pressure window of the altimeter so that altitude **above mean sea level** is indicated. Look well ahead to ensure that visual flight and the required separation from clouds can be maintained and, if not, consider making a diversion.

When established outbound from the airport:

- arrange the chart so that your planned course runs up the page, making it easier for you to read **chart to ground;**
- confirm that the heading indicator is aligned with the magnetic compass; and
- positively check a definite ground feature or group of features within the first 10 miles to ensure that you are indeed on course, and that no gross error has been made—misreading the compass or misaligning the heading indicator is always a possibility.

Set course and advise FSS of your departure time.

DEVIATION CARD	
FOR	STEER
N (360)	002
E (090)	092
S (180)	179
W (270)	268

Figure 18-15. A deviation card

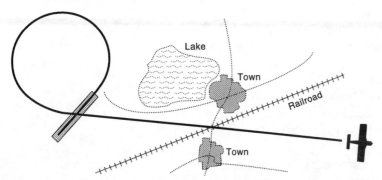

Figure 18-16. Check that tracking is correct soon after you set your heading.

En Route Navigation

Pilotage is flying with visual reference to ground features, such as following a highway or river between two towns, and requires constant sighting of the ground. **Dead reckoning** is deducing the current position of the airplane by calculations of speed, course, time, wind effect and previous known position, and requires only periodic identification of ground features.

En route visual navigation involves pilotage and dead reckoning.

It is important to **maintain steady headings for known times** when flying cross-country to simplify your dead reckoning. You should navigate by means of precomputed headings, groundspeeds and elapsed times (adjusted as necessary in flight). You should aim to hold altitude and heading as accurately as possible, but certainly within the limits of cruise altitude plus or minus 200 feet, and within 10° of the selected heading. The 200-foot tolerance on altitude is a little more lenient than usual, since you have navigational tasks to perform as well as manipulate the airplane.

Holding heading is vital.

There is no need to refer to the chart all the time, but be sure to keep it handy (and usually on your lap). It is best to select certain ground features that will occur at intervals of 10 minutes or so (which, at a groundspeed of 100 knots, puts them about 17 nm apart) to verify that you are on or near your planned course. Selecting checkpoints this far apart allows you to divide your time for the other duties, which include flying the airplane, making radio calls and carrying out periodic checks of the airplane systems.

Ensure that you use the appropriate **checklists** throughout the flight—the Climb, Cruise and Descent checklists—and use recommended cruise procedures.

At the appropriate time, look ahead for the next checkpoint that should be coming into view—in other words, look at the chart, note the features that should shortly come into view and then look outside with the expectation of seeing them.

Read from chart to ground—then use features to either side of course and well ahead to confirm your position. You must identify landmarks by relating the surface features to chart symbols. Aim to stay within 3 nm of the flight-planned route at all times, and to arrive at en route checkpoints and the destination within five minutes of the initial or revised ETA.

> **Know from the chart which features to expect ahead.**

Groundspeed Checks

The actual groundspeed is easily calculated from distance/time, using the time and distance between two fixes or crossing two position lines.

> **Make regular checks of the groundspeed and revise your ETAs.**

For example, if you cover 5 nm in 3 minutes, then the GS is 100 knots (3 minutes = $1/20$ th of an hour, therefore the GS = $20 \times 5 = 100$ knots). These calculations can be done mentally or on your flight computer. Mentally is better, if you can manage it. In the same way, 8 nm covered in 5 minutes ($1/12$ th hour) gives a groundspeed of 96 knots.

When you know the groundspeed, you can revise your ETA for the next checkpoint (and others further on). Again, this can be done mentally or by flight computer. For example, if it is 40 nm to the next checkpoint, this will take 5 times as long as the 8 nm, 25 minutes. If the time now is 0345 UTC, your ETA at the checkpoint is 0410 UTC.

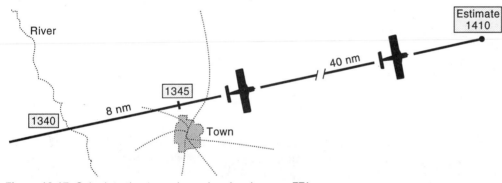

Figure 18-17. Calculate the groundspeed and revise your ETAs.

Checking the actual time at the one-quarter, one-half and three-quarter points makes the mental calculation of the next ETA easy. Also, it is good airmanship to log the times at fixes (or mark them on the chart), so that you have some record of what positions the airplane passed over, and when. Your aim should be to arrive at en route checkpoints and at the destination right at the initial or revised ETA, but certainly within five minutes of it. If this does not look possible, then advise FSS of a further revised ETA.

Off-Course Corrections

It is usual to find that the actual **ground track** differs from the planned course plotted on the chart, possibly because the winds aloft are different to those forecast. Whatever the cause, it is a simple calculation to revise the heading to rejoin the planned course.

> **Adjust heading as necessary.**

There are various means of doing this and your flight instructor will inform you of the preferred method. It can be done by flight computer, or it can be done mentally (which leaves your hands free for other duties and avoids having your head in the cockpit for too long).

It is good airmanship to log the heading changes and the times at which they were made.

In each of the three methods shown in the next figure, the same result from a known tracking error (TE) and a calculated closing angle (CA) is obtained—a turn of 12° to the right. Having regained course, turn 4° left to maintain it. Your aim should be to stay within 3 nm of the flight-planned course at all times.

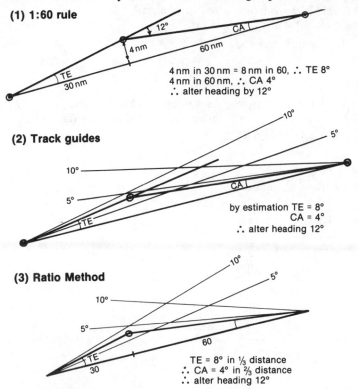

(1) 1:60 rule

4 nm in 30 nm = 8 nm in 60, ∴ TE 8°
4 nm in 60 nm, ∴ CA 4°
∴ alter heading by 12°

(2) Track guides

by estimation TE = 8°
CA = 4°
∴ alter heading 12°

(3) Ratio Method

TE = 8° in ⅓ distance
∴ CA = 4° in ⅔ distance
∴ alter heading 12°

Figure 18-18. Various methods of revising heading

Regular Airplane Checks

The correct operation of the airplane and its systems should be checked on a regular basis (say each 15 minutes, or just prior to arrival overhead a check-point). A suitable periodic check is the FREHA check detailed in Exercise 13c. Also, leaning the mixture correctly is vital for fuel efficiency and obtaining the range you have planned for.

Periodically check the airplane systems (fuel, and so on).

Turning Points

Just prior to reaching a turning point, check that the heading indicator is aligned with the magnetic compass (part of the FREHA check). Take up the new heading over the turning point, log the time and calculate the ETA for the next check-point. Then, within 10 nm of passing the turning point, confirm from ground features that you are on the planned course, and that no gross error has been made. Monitor fuel usage at each turning point.

Use of the Radio

The radio is a very useful aid to a pilot. En route and outside controlled airspace, you will normally select the local FSS frequency to enable immediate contact with the nearest FSS (Flight Service Station). It is good airmanship to pass accurate and frequent position reports to FSS, update ETAs, and to advise any change in plans, such as a diversion or if you will arrive more than 30 minutes after planned ETA (to prevent unnecessary search-and-rescue procedures from commencing).

Use the radio.

A position report should include your:
- aircraft identification;
- position and time;
- altitude or flight level, and type of flight plan—for example, VFR;
- next reporting point and ETA;
- next succeeding reporting point (name only);
- pertinent remarks, such as weather conditions.

Example 1

Pilot: *Sacramento, Cessna 1238 Sierra,*
    Sacramento at zero two two eight,
    Niner thousand five hundred, VFR,
    Estimate Manteca at zero two four seven Zulu, Panoche next,
    Light turbulence, high cirrus above.

Make use of the radio to obtain **in-flight weather advisories** from the En Route Flight Advisory Service (EFAS)—radio callsign "...*(FSS name)*... Flight Watch" —on frequency 122.0 MHz. Give your aircraft identification and the name of the nearest VOR so that only appropriate information will be given. You are encouraged to report your current weather (bad or good) to Flight Watch, since this may be of assistance to other pilots.

> Use the EFAS by calling *Flight Watch* on 122.0 MHz.

You can also tune to a **hazardous in-flight weather advisory service** (HIWAS) broadcast or a **transcribed weather broadcast** (TWEB) by selecting the VOR or ADF receiver to the appropriate station; shown on sectional charts.

> Make use of HIWAS and TWEB broadcasts.

En Route Radio Navigation

Radio navigation aids can be useful on a cross-country VFR flight, provided you **select**, **identify** and **check the operation** of each aid before using it. The main radio navigation aids for en route use are the VOR and DME (VORTAC), LORAN C, and the NDB.

> Use radio navigation aids for tracking and for groundspeed checks.

You should be able to locate your position relative to the radio navigation facility, intercept and track along the selected radial or bearing, locate your position using cross-radials or cross-bearings, recognize station passage, and recognize a signal loss and take appropriate action.

Illustrated in figure 18-20 on the next page is how you could intercept a magnetic course (MC) of 030° to a particular VORTAC—that is, inbound on the 210 radial—by setting 030 with the omni bearing selector (OBS) and initially steering a magnetic heading of 050° until the course deviation indicator (CDI) centers. You then determine a heading that will keep the CDI centered, which may take a little trial and error. Passing overhead the VOR station, the CDI will flicker, and the flag will change from *TO* to *FROM*, at which time the new course—outbound from the VOR station—should be set with the OBS.

Groundspeed checks are also made easy by using DME distances when some distance away from the VORTAC and tracking directly to or away from it.

The ADF can also be tuned into en route NDBs and used for tracking or orientation purposes, as shown below.

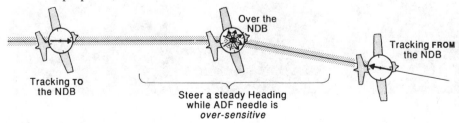

Figure 18-19. Do not overcorrect when close to the NDB.

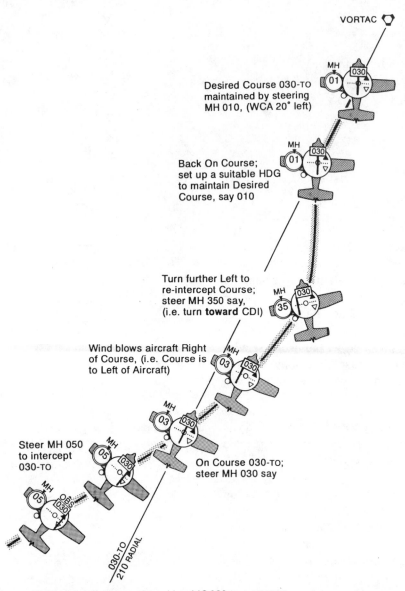

VORTAC ⬡

MH
030
01

Desired Course 030-TO
maintained by steering
MH 010, (WCA 20° left)

MH
030
01

Back On Course;
set up a suitable HDG
to maintain Desired
Course, say 010

MH
030
35

Turn further Left to
re-intercept Course;
steer MH 350 say,
(i.e. turn **toward** CDI)

MH
030
03

Wind blows aircraft Right
of Course, (i.e. Course is
to Left of Aircraft)

MH
030
03

On Course 030-TO;
steer MH 030 say

MH
030
05

Steer MH 050
to intercept
030-TO

MH
OBS
030
05

030-TO
210 RADIAL

Figure 18-20. Intercepting and tracking MC 030 to a VORTAC

Many aircraft now have a **LORAN C** set installed, which, like other **area
navigation (RNAV)** systems, allows a pilot to navigate between preset
waypoints that can be determined. (See figure 18-22.)

Global Positioning Systems (GPS) are also becoming commonly used.

Ensure that you know how to operate your particular equipment, and know
its limitations, before you rely on it to support your visual navigation.

Figure 18-21. Typical RNAV and LORAN displays

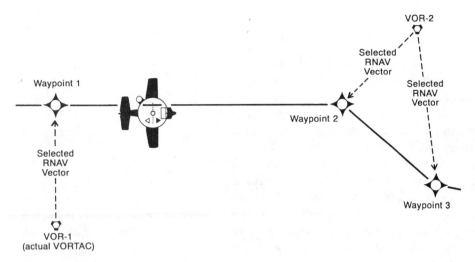

Figure 18-22. Tracking between waypoints

Occasionally electronics and electrical systems fail, and you have to rely on basic VFR navigation, which is pilotage and dead-reckoning. Do not neglect these just because your current aircraft has sophisticated radio navigation equipment!

Always be prepared for basic navigation, even with sophisticated electronic equipment on board.

Arrival at the Destination

If flying high, plan to commence descent some distance from the airport so that you arrive at a suitable altitude to join the traffic pattern. Do not forget to move the mixture control to RICH in the descent.

Plan an efficient descent.

Listen to the ATIS (if provided) or the recorded weather information (Automated Surface Observing System—ASOS or Automated Weather Observing System—AWOS) well before arriving in the traffic pattern. Follow the procedures for pattern entry appropriate to that airport. When approaching an airport without an operating control tower, you should announce your intentions on the CTAF when 10 miles out, entering downwind, base and final, and when leaving the runway. Approaching a tower-controlled airport, it is usual to be in contact with the tower by 15 miles out.

Note down the ATIS or recorded weather information, and plan your traffic pattern entry.

Normal procedures at a nontowered airport are to join downwind at 45° to the traffic pattern. After landing, make the appropriate radio calls, taxi in, shut down, complete appropriate **checklists,** and make sure that you secure the airplane before leaving it.

Unless hangared or about to be flown again, tie the airplane down, with chocks in position, but release the parking brakes so that the airplane can be moved easily by hand if necessary without having to unlock the doors.

Fueling may be a consideration, especially if you are leaving the airplane overnight. Full tanks minimize condensation of water in the tanks, as well as saving you having to call the fueler out early the next morning.

Close the flight plan directly with FSS (the preferred method) or ask an ATC facility to relay your cancelation to the FSS designated on your flight plan. A control tower will not automatically close your flight plan, since not all VFR flights file flight plans—you need to request it.

Ensure that you have closed your flight plan with FSS.

Further Points

Diversions

A successful cross-country flight does not necessarily mean arriving at the destination. Sometimes conditions are such that continuing to the destination would expose your flight to unnecessary risk.

Weather forecasters are not infallible. If the **actual weather conditions** ahead deteriorate to such a degree that onward visual flight would be unsafe (or less safe than you wish it to be), then to divert is good airmanship. You should learn to recognize adverse weather conditions, and to divert promptly to an appropriate airfield using a suitable route. Other reasons for diverting could be an airplane malfunction, pilot fatigue, a sick passenger, or impending darkness.

There will always be pressures to press on from, for example, passengers wanting to get home, a sense of failure if you do not make it to the planned destination, or the inconvenience of having to overnight away from home unexpectedly.

When faced with an operational decision of what-to-do, forget all of these secondary problems! They are irrelevant to your decision of whether to divert or not, which should be made purely on **flight safety** and nothing else.

Having decided to divert, perhaps in difficult conditions such as turbulence, there is a **basic diversion procedure** that you should follow.

- Maintain positive and authoritative control of the airplane at all times—altitude within 200 feet, heading within 10° and airspeed within 10 KIAS.
- Make your decision to divert earlier rather than later.
- Select an appropriate airport within range—request weather and other information from Flight Watch on 122.0 MHz.
- If possible, plan to divert from a prominent ground feature ahead, so that the diversion is started from a known point; if time does not permit, divert immediately and look for good checkpoints—make use of radio navigation aids.
- Mark the diversion course on the chart and **estimate course direction and distance**—estimate the direction in degrees true with reference to the latitude–longitude grid and estimate the distance with your thumb (from the top joint of your thumb to the tip is typically about 10 nm at a chart-scale of 1:500,000).
- At the prominent feature, take up the estimated diversion **heading,** which you have calculated from the estimated course, allowing for magnetic variation and wind drift. **Your heading is extremely important** at this stage—even more important than distance (within reason).
- Log the time at the diversion point and log your new heading.
- Refer to the chart and look for a positive ground feature soon after altering heading to ensure that no gross error has been made.
- When time permits, measure the course direction and distance accurately— ideally this would be done prior to the actual diversion.
- Estimate the groundspeed, time interval and the ETA at the diversion airfield or next turning point.
- Estimate the fuel consumption to the diversion airfield (plan to arrive with at least 30 minutes reserve by day and 45 minutes by night, at cruise rate).
- Inform the nearest FSS or ATC Center by radio of your actions (new destination, cruising altitude and ETA).
- Continue with normal navigation until you reach the diversion airfield.
- Obtain the ATIS, join the traffic pattern normally, land, close your flight plan —consider if the original destination airfield should be advised—and then advise your home base of the situation.

Never be afraid to divert if you feel it is the appropriate thing to do.

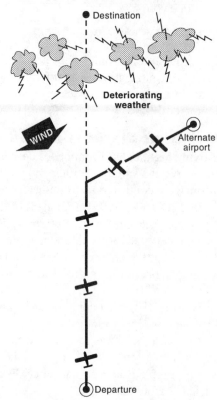

Figure 18-23. Divert earlier than later.

Inform FSS of your revised intentions.

Always remember to close your flight plan with FSS.

Low-Level Navigation

If a diversion is necessary because of a lowering cloud base, you may find yourself involved in low-level navigation. Low-level flying itself has been covered in a previous exercise, but navigational aspects worth noting are:

- If possible, perform any required checks before descent to a low level.
- Consider using the precautionary configuration (which allows slower flight, a better forward view, better maneuverability, but poorer fuel consumption).
- Your field of vision at low level is small and the speed that ground features pass through it is greater.
- Check-features need to be close to your course to fall within this field of vision and must be prominent in profile (when seen from the side).
- Anticipate reaching the ground features, because they may not be in your field of vision for long.
- Keep your eyes out of the cockpit as much as possible.

Uncertain of Position

You can prevent becoming uncertain of your position by *always* knowing (at least approximately) where you are—by flying accurate headings, looking out for prominent landmarks, and making use of available radio navigation aids.

Being temporarily uncertain of your position is not the same as being lost.

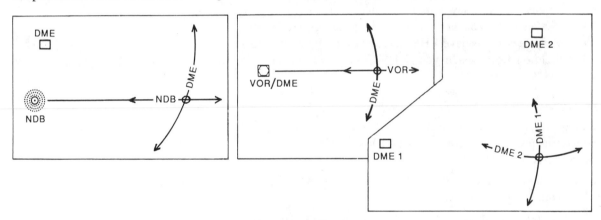

Figure 18-24. Three examples of using two radio navigation aids to fix your position

One position line is useful, but two position lines that cut at a good angle enables you to immediately fix your position accurately. With a VOR, you would select what you think is a nearby station, identify it, and turn the OBS until the CDI centers, then note whether the bearing is *TO* or *FROM* the VOR.

A simultaneous DME reading from a VORTAC is all you need to fix your position. Without DME, you could select your VOR receiver to another VORTAC and obtain a bearing of it by centering the CDI. Nearby NDBs may also be useful.

A DR (dead reckoning) position can be calculated which, hopefully, can shortly be backed up with a positive fix over or abeam a ground feature. If, at any time, you feel **uncertain** of your position:

1. Log your heading—compass and heading indicator (HI)—and the time.

2. If the HI is **incorrectly** set, then you have the information needed to make a reasonable estimate of your actual position. Realign the HI with the compass, and calculate a heading and time interval to regain the planned course.

3. If the HI *is* aligned correctly with the compass, then the nonappearance of a landmark, while it will perhaps cause you some concern, need not indicate

that you are grossly off course. You may not have seen the landmark for some perfectly legitimate reason (bright sunlight, poor visibility, a change in features not reflected on the chart, or clouds).

4. Consider a precautionary landing if the onset of bad weather, fuel exhaustion, or darkness is imminent.

5. Request assistance from FSS or ATC. In a radar environment, it may be quite easy to be identified using your transponder. Also, some airports have **VHF direction finding** antennas which can determine the direction your voice transmissions are coming from. If you feel it is appropriate, make an **urgency call** *(PAN-PAN PAN-PAN PAN-PAN)* on the frequency in use or on the emergency frequency 121.5 MHz.

6. If still unable to fix your position, follow the procedure below.

Lost

Becoming lost is usually the result of some human error. Careful preflight planning followed by in-flight attention to the simple navigational tasks will ensure that you never become lost. You may become temporarily uncertain of your exact position, but this is not being lost because you can calculate an approximate dead-reckoning position.

If you are in a radar environment, say within 100 nm of a major city airport, ATC may be able to locate you on radar and provide radar headings to a suitable airport. Some Flight Service Stations have VHF direction-finding facilities that can determine the direction from which your VHF-COM transmissions are coming.

If you ever become lost, then formulate a plan of action and do not fly around aimlessly.

Procedure to Follow

1. It is important that you initially maintain the heading (if terrain, visibility and what you know of the proximity of controlled airspace permit) and carry out a **sequence of positive actions**.

2. If a vital checkpoint is not in view at your ETA, then continue to fly for 10% of the time since your last positive fix.

3. Start from the chart position of your last known fix, **check the headings flown since that last fix,** and ensure that:
    • the magnetic compass is not being affected by outside influences such as a camera, portable radio, or other metal objects placed near it;
    • the gyroscopic heading indicator is aligned with the magnetic compass;
    • magnetic variation and the wind correction angle have been correctly applied to obtain your headings flown;
    • an estimate of the course direction on the chart against that shown on the flight plan is correct.

4. **When lost, read from ground to chart**—that is, look for significant ground features or combinations of features and try to determine their position on the chart.

5. Establish a **most probable area** in which you think you are. There are several ways in which this can be done, and we recommend you consult your flight instructor for his or her preferred method. Two suggested methods follow.

Establishing your Most Probable Area

Method 1. **Estimate the distance flown** since the last fix and apply this distance, plus or minus 10%, to an arc 30 degrees either side of what you estimate is the **probable ground track.**

Choose either of these two suggested methods of establishing a *most probable area.*

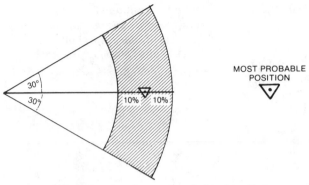

Figure 18-25. Estimating the most probable area that you are in

Method 2. Estimate your **most probable position** and draw a circle around it of radius equal to 10% the distance flown since the last fix.

Figure 18-26. Another means of estimating the most probable position

Establish a safety altitude to ensure there is adequate clearance above all obstacles in what you consider the general area to be—being especially careful in conditions of poor visibility or low clouds, or when near or over mountains.

Check large features within this area of the chart with what can be seen on the ground. Try and relate features seen on the ground with those shown on the chart—that is, read from ground to chart. Confirm the identification of any feature by closely observing secondary details around the feature.

When you do positively establish a fix, recheck your heading indicator and recommence normal navigational activity. Calculate the heading, groundspeed, and time interval for the next check feature, and set course for it.

If you are still unable to fix your position, you should consider taking one of the following actions:
- increase your **most probable area** by from 10% to 15% or even 20% of the distance flown from the last fix.
- climb to a higher altitude to increase your range of vision, and for better line-of-sight VHF radio reception.
- turn toward a prominent **line-feature** known to be in the area, such as a coastline, large river, railroad or highway, and then follow it to the next town, where you should be able to obtain a fix.
- steer a reciprocal heading, and attempt to return to your last fix.
- seek navigational assistance from the FSS or ATC Center with which you are in radio contact. It is wise to take this step prior to reaching the desperation stage.

A **radar advisory service** may be available. If not, information that may be requested to establish your position is the time and position of your last fix, with headings and times flown since then.

Important Points

- If you want to cover as much ground as possible with the fuel available, you should fly the airplane for **best range.**
- Keep a **navigation log.**
- Remain positively **aware of time.** Keep your eye on the fuel and on the amount of time remaining until last light. If last light is approaching, remember that it will be darker at ground level than at altitude and, if you are flying in the tropics, that it will become dark quickly following sunset.
- If you decide to carry out a precautionary search and landing, allow sufficient time and fuel to accomplish this because two or three inspections might have to be made before finding a suitable landing area.

At all times continue to fly the aircraft safely, maintaining an awareness of time, especially with respect to *last light* and your fuel state.

Why Did You Become Lost?

If at any stage you became lost, try to determine the reason systematically (either in flight or post flight) so that you can learn from the experience. Common reasons for becoming lost include:

- incorrectly calculated headings, groundspeeds and time intervals—hence the need to make mental estimates of approximate answers to these items;
- an incorrectly synchronized heading indicator—that is, the gyroscopic HI was not aligned correctly with the magnetic compass (the HI should be aligned every 10 or 15 minutes against the compass);
- a faulty compass reading (caused by transistor radios, cameras and other metallic objects placed near the compass);
- incorrectly applied magnetic variation;
- incorrectly applied wind drift ;
- an actual wind velocity significantly different to the forecast, and not allowed for in flight by the pilot;
- a deterioration in weather, a reduced visibility, or an increased cockpit work-load;
- an incorrect fix or mis-identification of a check feature;
- a poorly planned diversion from the original planned course;
- not paying attention to carrying out normal navigational tasks en route.

With regular checks of the HI alignment with the compass, reasonably accurate flying of heading, and with position fixes every 10 or 15 minutes, none of the above errors should put you far off course. It is only when you are slack and let things go a bit too far that you becomes lost.

System and Equipment Malfunctions

Prior to setting out on a cross-country flight, you should be prepared to handle certain system and equipment malfunctions. These may be simulated on your training exercises by your flight instructor.

Consider these possible malfunctions, read your POH, discuss them with your flight instructor and make your own notes. A discussion of such items will occur on your *practical flight test* at the preflight stage and/or in flight. **In a real situation** where you feel apprehensive, you could declare an emergency (by radio on the frequency in use or on the emergency frequency 121.5 MHz), and squawk the emergency code 7700 on your transponder.

Emergencies are thought of as:

- **distress situations:** fire, mechanical failure, structural damage, immediate assistance required (a MAYDAY call is appropriate); and
- **urgency situations:** lost or doubtful of position, problems with fuel endurance or weather, another aircraft in trouble (a PAN-PAN call is appropriate).

Fill in the blank lines below with answers applicable to your airplane type.

Carburetor or Induction Icing
Cause: *ice forming in the carburetor.*
Indications: *rpm decrease (fixed-pitch prop), rough running, engine stoppage.*
Action: *apply full carburetor heat.*

Partial Power Loss
Cause: ....
Indications: ....
Action: ....

Rough-Running or Overheating Engine
Cause: ....
Indications: ....
Action: ....

Loss of Oil Pressure
Cause: ....
Indications: ....
Action: ....

Fuel Starvation
Cause: ....
Indications: ....
Action: ....

Engine Compartment Fire
Cause: ....
Indications: ....
Action: ....

Smoke or Fumes in Cockpit
Cause: ....
Indications: ....
Action: ....

Electrical System Malfunction
Cause: ....
Indications: ....
Action: ....

Electrical Fire
Cause: ....
Indications: ....
Action: ....

Wing Flaps Malfunction
Cause: ....
Indications: ....
Action: ....

Landing Gear Malfunction

Cause: . . . .

Indications: . . . .

Action: . . . .

Door Opening In Flight

(*Note:* Noise level may be very high—do not let this distract you from controlling the airplane.)

Cause: . . . .

Indications: . . . .

Action: . . . .

Trim Inoperative

Cause: . . . .

Indications: . . . .

Action: . . . .

Airframe and Pitot-Static Icing

Cause: . . . .

Indications: . . . .

Actions: . . . .

Vacuum System Malfunction (and Associated Instruments)

Cause: . . . .

Indications: . . . .

Action: . . . .

Loss of Pressurization

Cause: . . . .

Indications: . . . .

Action: . . . .

Emergency Descent

Action: . . . .

Landing with a Flat Tire

Action: . . . .

Use of Emergency Exits

Action: . . . .

Windshield Damage

Action: . . . .

Other Malfunctions

. . . .

. . . .

. . . .

. . . .

. . . .

. . . .

. . . .

. . . .

. . . .

. . . .

✍ Review 18

Cross-Country Flying

1. When planning a cross-country flight when you have no recent weather information, you should contact FSS for a _____ briefing.

   ➤ standard

2. If you are doing advance planning for a flight which will not commence until six hours or more later, you can request an _____ briefing.

   ➤ outlook

3. If you have current weather information, and just require an update, you can request an _____ briefing.

   ➤ abbreviated

4. Operational information important for a flight may be contained in NOTAMs, which are N____ to A____ .

   ➤ Notices to Airmen

5. The main chart for VFR navigation is the s____ chart. You should also carry the t____ chart for any nearby Class B airspace.

   ➤ sectional, terminal

6. You should also carry the A____ /F____ D____ and the A____ I____ M____ .

   ➤ Airport/Facility Directory, Airman's Information Manual

7. What is the next suitable VFR cruising altitude at or above 4,000 feet MSL on a course of: 030°M; 150°M; 200°M; and 330°M?

   ➤ 5,500 feet MSL, 5,500 feet MSL, 4,500 feet MSL and 4,500 feet MSL

8. When planning a flight you (must/need not) allow additional fuel for start-up, taxi, takeoff and climb.

   ➤ must

9. Reserve fuel, over and above the actual flight fuel, must be at least ____ minutes by day, and ____ minutes by night.

   ➤ 30 minutes, 45 minutes

10. Fuel over and above the required flight and reserve fuel is known as _____ fuel.

    ➤ margin

11. Weight-and-balance, and takeoff and landing performance, (must/need not) be considered.

    ➤ must

12. Takeoff and landing performance will be worse on (hot/cold) days, at (high/low) elevation airports, in (head/tail) wind conditions when it is (humid/dry).

    ➤ hot, high, tailwind, humid

13. What aircraft and personal documents are required to be on board?

    ➤ *refer to the ARROW list on page 472.*

14. What personal documents must you carry?

    ➤ your pilot certificate and current medical

15. You (must/need not) file a flight plan for VFR flight, but it is good airmanship to file a flight plan for a VFR cross-country flight (at all times/only in bad weather).

    ➤ need not, at all times

16. It (is/is not) good airmanship to brief passengers on safety matters and the route to be flown before starting the engine.

    ➤ is

17. When operating at or within ____ miles of a non-towered airport, it is usual to listen and advise intentions on the C____ T____ A____ F____ .

    ➤ 10 miles, Common Traffic Advisory Frequency

18. Flying along ground features such as roads or rivers is known as _____ .

    ➤ pilotage

19. Maintaining calculated headings for known times, with a periodic check against prominent ground features, is known as _____ _____ .

    ➤ dead reckoning

20. For accurate navigation it is (very/not very) important to fly accurate headings.

    ➤ very

Continued

21. The tolerances expected in cross-country flying are: *altitude* plus or minus ____ feet, *heading* plus or minus ____ °, *airspeed* plus or minus ____ KIAS, and *arrival at your ETA,* as revised in position reports, within plus or minus ____ minutes.

    ≫ 200 feet, 10°, 10 KIAS, 5 minutes

22. Making regular and accurate position reports en route, and advising FSS or ATC of revised ETAs or changes of plan, is (good airmanship/totally unnecessary).

    ≫ good airmanship

23. Available radio navigation aids to back up your visual navigation (may/should) be used.

    ≫ should

24. It is good airmanship to use the radio to obtain in-flight weather advisories from the E____ F____ A____ S____ , callsign "____ ____" on frequency ____ MHz.

    ≫ En route Flight Advisory Service (EFAS), "(FSS) Flight Watch", 122.0 MHz

25. When requesting an in-flight weather advisory on the EFAS, you should specify the nearest ____ so that only appropriate weather information will be given.

    ≫ VOR

26. The H____ I____ W____ A____ S____ , or the T____ W____ E____ B____ service, are available on many VORs and NDBs. These (are/are not) detailed on sectional charts.

    ≫ Hazardous In-flight Weather Advisory Service (HIWAS), Transcribed Weather Broadcast (TWEB), are

27. It is good airmanship to occasionally report your current weather, bad or good, to Flight Service Stations of the ____ ____ ____ ____ for the benefit of other pilots. This is called making a pilot report or P____ .

    ≫ En route Flight Advisory Service (EFAS) (callsign "........ Flight Watch"), PIREP

28. Weather and other information at some airports is available on an A____ T____ I____ S____ or other recorded systems: ____ ____ ____ ____ .

    ≫ Automatic Terminal Information Service, Automated Weather Observing System (AWOS) and Automated Surface Observing System (ASOS)

29. It is (good/poor) airmanship to plan an efficient descent to arrive overhead the destination airport near to, but at least 500 feet above, the traffic pattern altitude.

    ≫ good

30. If bad weather ahead forces you to divert to an alternate airport, you (should/need not) advise FSS of your change in plans.

    ≫ should

31. It (is/is not) important for navigational purposes to keep a record of any major heading changes and the time and position where they were made.

    ≫ is

32. You should close your flight plan with FSS within ____ minutes of your ETA to prevent unnecessary ____ and ____ procedures from commencing.

    ≫ 30 minutes, search and rescue

33. At a tower-controlled airport, the tower (will/will not) automatically close a VFR flight plan after the aircraft has landed safely.

    ≫ will not

34. You should practice planning for cross-country flights until you can complete it all within a period of ____ minutes.

    ≫ 30 minutes

Instrument Flying 19

Introduction to Attitude Flying

We normally use our **vision** to orient ourselves with the surroundings, supported by other bodily senses which can sense gravity, such as *feel* and *balance*. Even with our eyes closed, however, we can usually manage to sit, stand and walk on steady ground without losing control. This becomes much more difficult standing on the bed of an accelerating or turning truck, or even in an accelerating elevator.

As an instrument pilot, you must learn to trust what you see on the instruments.

Figure 19-1. Flying on instruments

In an airplane, which can accelerate in three dimensions, the task of orienting ourselves becomes almost impossible without using our eyes. The eyes must gather information from the external ground features, including the horizon, or, in poor visibility, gather **substitute information** from the instruments.

A pilot's eyes are very important, and the starting point in your instrument training will be learning to use your eyes to derive information from the flight instruments.

The flight instruments provide substitute information to that obtained from the real world in visual flight.

Lowest Safe Altitude

One thing that your eyes cannot do in clouds or on a dark night is see the ground. You should therefore calculate a lowest safe altitude at all times to ensure that you remain well above any obstructions—normally plan to remain at least 1,000 feet above the highest obstacle within four nautical miles of your planned course (2,000 feet in mountainous areas). It is good airmanship for you to calclute this, even with a flight instructor on board.

Stay above a lowest safe altitude when flying on instruments.

Fundamental Skills

The three fundamental skills in instrument flying are:
• instrument cross-check—also known as *scanning* the instruments;
• instrument interpretation—understanding their message; and
• airplane control—directing the airplane along the required flight path at the selected airspeed, using attitude flying.

Cockpit

Instrument flying is much easier if you are comfortable in the cockpit and know your airplane well. Adjust the seat position prior to flight to ensure that you can reach all of the controls easily, and so that you have the correct **eye position.** Ensure that your seat is locked into position.

Make yourself comfortable in the cockpit.

Attitude Flying

Attitude flying is the name given to the technique of using a selected **power** and a selected **attitude** to achieve the required **performance** of the airplane in terms of **flight path and airspeed**.

Power + attitude = performance.

For a given airplane weight and configuration, a particular attitude combined with a particular power setting will always result in a specific path through the air, be it a straight-and-level flight path, a climb, a descent or a turn. Any change of power and/or attitude will result in a change of flight path and/or airspeed.

Airplane attitude has two aspects: pitch and bank. **Pitch attitude** is the angle between the longitudinal axis of the aircraft and the horizontal. **Bank angle** is the angle between the lateral axis of the airplane and the horizontal.

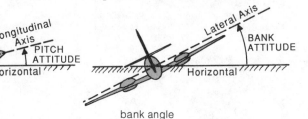

Figure 19-2. Pitch attitude;   bank angle

Pitch Attitude

The pitch attitude is the geometric relationship between the longitudinal axis of the airplane and horizontal. Pitch attitude refers to the airplane's inclination to the horizontal, and not to where the airplane is actually going. The angle-of-attack, however, is the angle between the wing chord and the relative airflow. The angle-of-attack, therefore, is closely related to the airplane's flight path.

Pitch attitude is not angle-of-attack.

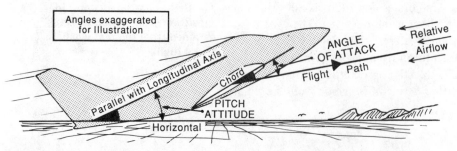

Figure 19-3. Pitch attitude and angle-of-attack are not the same.

Note: Although pitch attitude and angle-of-attack are different, they are related in the sense that if the pitch attitude is raised, then the angle-of-attack is increased. Conversely, if the pitch attitude is lowered, then the angle-of-attack is decreased.

Attitude Flying on Instruments

Attitude flying on instruments is an extension of visual flying, with your attention gradually shifting from external visual cues to the instrument indications in the cockpit, until you are able to fly accurately on instruments alone.

The pitch attitude is selected using the elevator. In visual conditions, you select the required pitch attitude by relating the nose position to the external natural horizon. In instrument flight, **pitch attitude** is selected with reference to the attitude indicator (AI), using the position of the center dot of the wing bars relative to the horizon bar. The center dot represents the nose of the airplane.

Bank is controlled by the ailerons. In visual conditions, you refer to the angle made by the external natural horizon and the top of the instrument panel at the base of the windshield. On instruments, you **select bank angle on the attitude indicator,** either by estimating the angle between the wing bars of the miniature airplane and the horizon bar, or from the sky pointer (or bank pointer) position on a graduated scale at the top of the AI.

Most of your attention during flight, both visual and on instruments, is concerned with achieving and holding a suitable attitude. An important skill to develop when flying on instruments, therefore, is to **check the attitude indicator every few seconds.** There are other tasks, of course, to be performed, and there are other instruments to look at as well, but the eyes should always return fairly quickly to the AI.

To achieve the required **performance** (in terms of flight path and airspeed), you must not only place the airplane in a suitable **attitude** with the flight controls, you must also apply suitable **power** with the throttle. Just because the airplane has a high pitch attitude does **not** mean that it will climb—it requires climb power as well as climb attitude to do this. With less power, it may not climb at all.

Attitude flying is the name given to this skill of controlling the airplane's flight path and airspeed with changes in attitude and power. The techniques used in attitude flying are the same visually or on instruments.

Scanning the Instruments

Scanning the instruments with your eyes, interpreting their indications, and applying this information is a **vital skill** to develop if you are to become a good instrument pilot.

Power is selected with the throttle, and can be checked on the power indicator. Pitch attitude and bank angle are selected using the control column, with **frequent** reference to the attitude indicator. With both correct power and attitude set, the airplane will perform as expected. The attitude indicator and the power indicator, because they are used when controlling the airplane, are known as the *control instruments*.

The actual **performance** of the airplane, when its power and attitude have been set, can be cross-checked on what are known as the *performance instruments*—the altimeter for altitude, the airspeed indicator for airspeed, the heading indicator for direction, and so on.

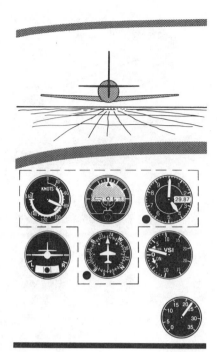

Figure 19-4. The full panel

Figure 19-5a. Low pitch attitude and wings level.

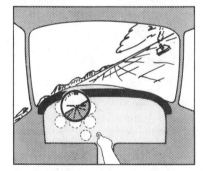

Figure 19-5b. High pitch attitude and right bank

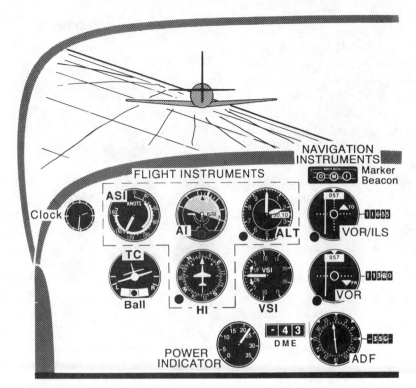

Figure 19-6. Layout of a typical instrument panel

Scanning is an art that will develop naturally during your training, especially when you know what to look for. The main scan to develop initially is that of the six basic flight instruments, concentrating on the AI and radiating out to the others as required. Having scanned the instruments, interpreted the message that they contain, built up a picture of where the airplane is and where it is going, you can now control it in a meaningful way.

Controlling the Airplane

During instrument flight, the airplane is flown using the normal controls according to the picture displayed on the instrument panel. From this picture, you will, with practice, know what control movements (elevator, aileron, rudder and throttle) are required to either maintain the picture as it is, or to change it.

When maneuvering the airplane, a suitable **control sequence** to follow (the same as in visual flight) is:

1. **Visualize** the new flight path and airspeed.
2. **Select the attitude and power required** to achieve the required performance by moving the controls, and then **check** when the airplane has achieved the estimated attitude on the AI.
3. **Hold the attitude** on the AI, allowing the airplane to settle down into its new performance, and allowing the pressure instruments that experience some lag to catch up.
4. **Make small adjustments** to attitude and power until the actual performance equals the desired performance.
5. **Trim** (which is vital, if you are to achieve accurate and comfortable instrument flight). Heavy loads can be trimmed off earlier in the sequence to assist in control, if you want, but remember that the function of trim is to relieve control loads on the pilot, and *not* to change aircraft attitude.

Your main scan is across six basic instruments:
- ASI
- AI
- ALT
- TC
- HI
- VSI

Figure 19-7. Control sequence

Some helpful hints to follow:

- **Derive the required information** from the relevant instrument, such as the direction from the heading indicator or altitude from the altimeter.

- **Respond to deviations** from the required flight path and/or airspeed. Use the AI as a control instrument, with power as required. For instance, if you are 50 feet low on altitude, raise the pitch attitude on the AI slightly and climb back up to altitude. Do **not** just accept steady deviations—it is just as easy to fly at 3,000 feet as it is to fly at 2,950 feet. A lot of instrument flying is in the mind and, in a sense, instrument flying is a test of character as well as of flying ability. Be as accurate as you can!

- **Do not over-control**. Avoid large, fast or jerky control movements, which will probably result in continuous corrections, over-corrections and then re-corrections. This can occur if attitude is changed without reference to the AI, or if the airplane is out-of-trim, or possibly by a pilot who is fatigued or tense.

- **Do not be distracted** from a scan of the flight instruments for more than a few seconds at a time, even though other duties must be attended to, such as checklists, radio calls and navigational tasks.

- **Be relaxed**—easier said than done at the start, but it will come with experience.

Sensory Illusions

Most people live in a "1g" situation most of the time, with their feet on the ground. The force of gravity is 1g. Some variations to 1g, however, do occur in everyday life—for instance, when driving a car. Accelerating a car, hard braking, or turning on a flat bend will all produce g-forces on the body that are different to the 1g force of gravity alone. A passenger with eyes closed could perhaps detect this by bodily feel or with the sense of balance.

A right turn on a flat road, for instance, could be detected by the feeling of being thrown to the left—but it might be more difficult to detect if the curve was perfectly banked for the particular speed. A straight road sloping to the left (and causing the occupants to lean to the left) might give the passenger with eyes closed the **false impression** that the car is turning right, even though it is in fact not turning at all.

The position-sensing systems of the body, using nerves all over the body to transmit messages of feel and pressure to the brain, can be fooled in this and other ways.

The **organs within the inner ear**—used for balance and to detect accelerations—can also be deceived. For instance, if you are sitting in a car traveling around a suitably banked curve, the sensing system in your ears falsely interprets the g-force holding you firmly and comfortably in the seats as a vertical force, as if you were moving straight ahead rather than in a banked turn.

The inner ear organs also have other limitations, one being that a constant velocity is not detected, nor is a gradual change in velocity. If you are sitting in a railroad car, for instance, and there is another train slowly moving relative to you on an adjacent track, it is sometimes difficult to determine which train is moving, or if indeed both are moving.

Sensory illusions can lead you astray.

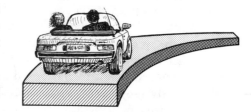

Figure 19-8. Turning right—or simply leaning?

False impressions of motion can also be caused by unusual g-forces—for instance, by rapid head motion, or by lowering the head. If you happen to drop your pencil while instrument flying, don't just lower your eyes and lean down to look for it in one motion; take it carefully step by step to avoid any feeling of vertigo.

Because an airplane moves in three dimensions, there is the possibility to accelerate and decelerate in three normal dimensions, and this can lead to more complicated illusions. Pulling up into a steep climb, for instance, holds you tightly in your seat, which is exactly the same feeling as in a steep turn. With your eyes closed, it is sometimes difficult to tell which maneuver it is.

Decelerating while in a turn to the left may give a false impression of a turn to the right. Be aware that your senses of balance and bodily feel can lead you astray in an airplane, especially with rapidly changing g-forces. The one sense that can resolve most of these illusions is **sight.** If the car passenger could see out, or if the pilot had reference to the natural horizon and landmarks, then the confusion would be easily dispelled.

The senses of balance and bodily feel can be misleading; trust your eyes and what the instruments tell you.

Unfortunately, in instrument flight you do *not* have reference to ground features, but you can still use your vital sense of sight to **scan the instruments,** and obtain substitute information. Therefore, an important instruction to the budding instrument pilot is: *believe your eyes and what the instruments tell you.*

An instrument pilot must learn to believe the instruments.

While sight is the most important sense, and must be protected at all costs, also make sure that you avoid anything that will affect your balance or position-sensing systems.

Avoid alcohol, drugs (including smoking in the cockpit) and medication. Do not fly when ill or suffering from an upper respiratory infection. Do not fly when tired or fatigued. Do not fly with a cabin altitude higher than 10,000 feet MSL without using oxygen. Avoid sudden head movements, and avoid lowering your head or turning around in the cockpit.

Despite all these *don'ts,* there is one very important *do*—**do trust what your eyes tell you from the instruments.**

Developing a Scan Pattern

The performance of an airplane is, as always, determined by the power setting and the selected attitude.

In **visual** flying conditions, the external natural horizon is used as a reference when selecting pitch attitude and bank angle. The power indicator (rpm gauge) in the cockpit is only referred to occasionally—for instance, when setting a particular power for cruise or for climb.

In **instrument conditions**, when the natural horizon cannot be seen, pitch attitude and bank angle information is still available to the pilot in the cockpit from the **attitude indicator.** Relatively large pitch attitude changes against the natural horizon are reproduced in miniature on the attitude indicator.

In straight-and-level flight, for instance, the wings of the miniature airplane should appear against the horizon line, while in a climb they should appear one or two bar widths above it.

In a turn, the wing bars of the miniature airplane will bank along with the real airplane, while the horizon line remains horizontal. The center dot of the miniature airplane represents the airplane's nose position relative to the horizon.

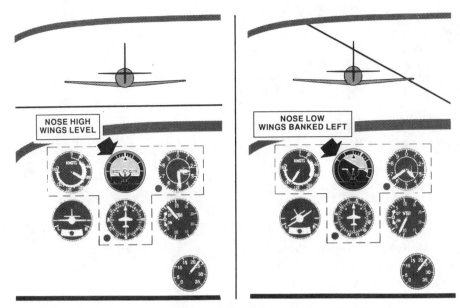

Figure 19-9. The AI is the master instrument for pitch attitude and bank angle

Simple Scans

Coordination. The AI, while it shows pitch attitude and bank angle directly, does not indicate coordination or yaw. Coordination information can be obtained simply by moving the eyes from the attitude indicator diagonally down to the left to check that the **coordination ball** is indeed being centered with rudder pressure. The eyes should then return to the AI (figure 19-10).

Heading. Directional information can be obtained from the **heading indicator** (HI) or from the magnetic compass. From the AI, the eyes can be moved straight down to the HI to absorb heading information, before returning to the AI.

Each eye movement to obtain particular information is simple, starting at the attitude indicator and radiating out to the relevant instrument, before returning again to the AI (figure 19-11).

Figure 19-10. A simple scan for coordination

Figure 19-11. A simple scan for heading

Airspeed. Airspeed information is also important, and this is easily checked by moving the eyes left from the AI to the **airspeed indicator (ASI),** before returning them to the AI (figure 19-12).

Altitude. The **altimeter** is the only means of determining the precise altitude of the airplane in visual as well as in instrument conditions. To obtain altitude information, the eyes can move from the AI to the right, where the altimeter is located, before moving back to the AI (figure 19-13).

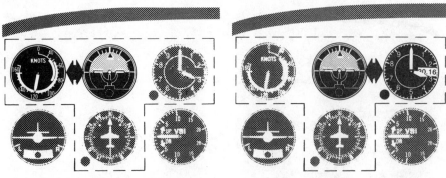

Figure 19-12. A simple scan for airspeed

Figure 19-13. A simple scan for altitude

Vertical Speed. Rate of change of altitude, either as a rate of climb or a rate of descent in feet per minute (fpm), can be monitored on the **vertical speed indicator** (VSI) by moving the eyes from the AI diagonally down to the right to the VSI, before returning to the AI. Since it is often used in conjunction with the altimeter, the VSI is located directly beneath it on most instrument panels (figure 19-14).

Turning. A turn is entered using the AI to establish the bank angle and the ball to confirm coordination. Additional information on the turning rate is available from the **turn coordinator** when the bank angle is established (figure 19-15).

Figure 19-14. A simple scan for vertical speed

Figure 19-15. A simple scan for turn rate

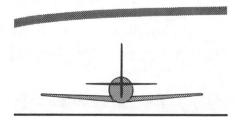

The normal rate of turn in instrument flying is 3° per second. This is known as *standard-rate* or *rate one,* and is clearly marked on the turn coordinator (or older turn-and-slip indicator).

With these **six basic flight instruments, plus the power indicator,** it is possible to fly the airplane accurately and comfortably without any external visual reference, provided the instruments are scanned efficiently, and the pilot controls the airplane adequately in response to the information derived from them.

The attitude selected on the **AI** and the power setting on the **power indicator** determine the performance of the airplane, hence these two instruments are known as the **control instruments**.

Control and Performance

The attitude indicator is located centrally on the instrument panel directly in front of the pilot, so that any changes in attitude can be readily seen. Because continual reference to the power indicator is not required, it is situated slightly away from the main group of flight instruments, easy to scan occasionally, but not in the main field of view (figure 19-16).

Figure 19-16. The control instruments are used to select attitude and power.

The other flight instruments are **performance instruments** that display how the airplane is performing (as a result of the power and attitude selected) in terms of:

- *altitude*—on the altimeter and VSI;
- *direction*—on the HI and turn coordinator; and
- *airspeed*—on the ASI.

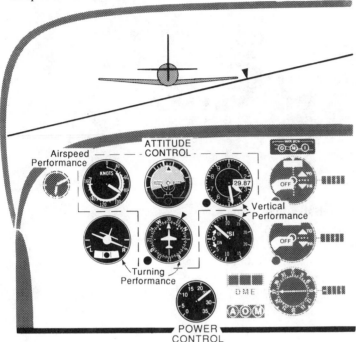

Figure 19-17. Performance is displayed on the performance instruments.

Changes in **pitch attitude** are shown directly on the AI, and are reflected on the altimeter, VSI and ASI. Changes in **bank angle** are shown directly on the AI, and are reflected on the turn coordinator and the heading indicator. The quality of flight is shown by the coordination ball (figures 19-18 and 19-19).

The Selective Radial Scan

Of the six main flight instruments, the **attitude indicator** is the master instrument. It gives you a direct and immediate picture of pitch attitude and bank angle. It will be the one most frequently referred to (at least once every few seconds in most stages of flight).

The eyes can be directed selectively to the other instruments to derive relevant information from them as required, before being returned to the AI. This eye movement radiating out and back to selected instruments is commonly known as the *selective radial scan*.

For instance, when **climbing** with full power selected, the estimated climb pitch attitude is held on the attitude indicator, with subsequent reference to the airspeed indicator to confirm that the selected pitch attitude is indeed correct. If the ASI indicates an airspeed that is too low, then lower the pitch attitude on the AI (say by a half bar width or by one bar width); allow a few seconds for the airspeed to settle, and then check the ASI again.

The key instrument in confirming that the correct attitude has been selected on the AI during the climb is the airspeed indicator. Because it determines what pitch attitude changes should be made on the AI during the climb, the **ASI** is the **primary performance guide** for pitch attitude in the climb. It is supported by the AI and the VSI.

Figure 19-18. The pitch instruments

Figure 19-19. The bank instruments

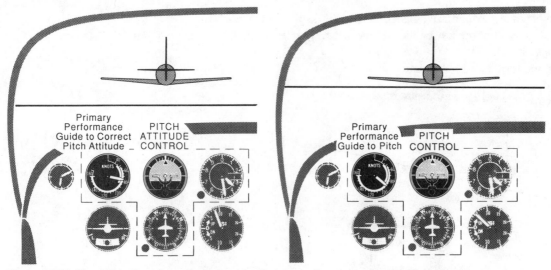

Figure 19-20. The ASI is the primary instrument in climb to confirm correct pitch attitude.

Approaching the chosen cruise altitude, however, more attention should be paid to the altimeter to ensure that, as the pitch attitude is lowered on the AI, the airplane levels off right on the selected altitude. When cruising, any minor deviations from altitude detected on the altimeter can be corrected with small changes in the pitch attitude. Because the altimeter is now the instrument that determines if pitch attitude changes on the AI are required to maintain level flight, the **altimeter** is the primary performance guide for pitch attitude in cruise. It is supported by the AI and the VSI.

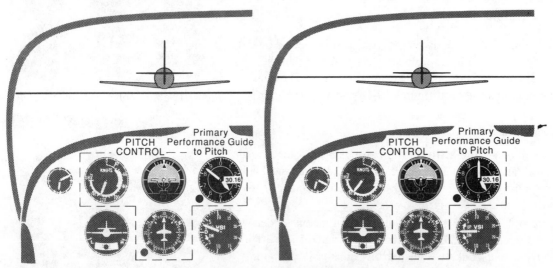

Figure 19-21. The altimeter is the primary instrument in cruise to confirm correct pitch attitude.

If climb power is retained after the airplane has been leveled off at the cruise altitude, the airplane will accelerate—shown by an increasing airspeed on the ASI. When the selected speed is reached, the power should be reduced to a suitable cruise setting.

While it is simple to set cruise power and then accept the resulting airspeed, it is possible to achieve a precise airspeed by adjusting the power. Because the ASI indications will then determine what power changes should be made during level flight, the **airspeed indicator** is the primary performance guide to power requirements in cruise.

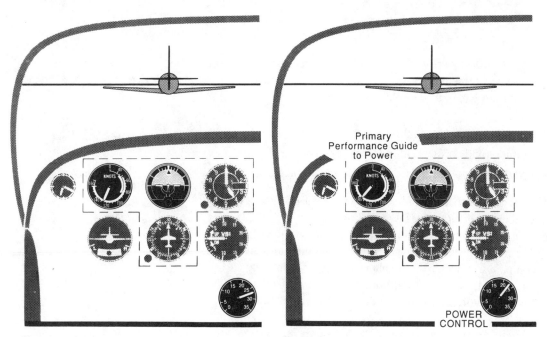

Figure 19-22. The ASI is the primary instrument in cruise to confirm correct power.

The heading is maintained with reference to the HI—any deviations being corrected with gentle coordinated turns. Because the indications on the HI will determine what minor corrections to the bank angle should be made on the attitude indicator during straight flight, the HI is the primary performance guide to zero bank angle to maintain a constant heading for straight flight. It is supported by the turn coordinator and the AI.

The ball should be centered to keep the airplane coordinated, avoiding any slip or skid, and to provide **coordinated** straight flight.

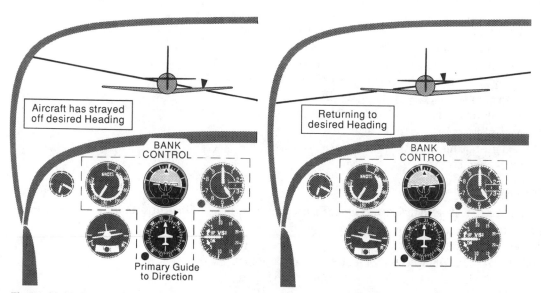

Figure 19-23. The heading indicator is the primary instrument in straight flight to confirm wings-level.

The Basic-T Scan

A basic scan suitable for **straight-and-level** flight (where altitude, direction and airspeed need to be monitored) is centered on the AI, and radiates out and back, following the basic-T pattern on the panel, to the relevant performance instrument.

- The HI to confirm heading (and correct with shallow turns on the AI).
- The altimeter to confirm altitude (and correct with pitch changes on the AI).
- The ASI to confirm airspeed (and, if you want, correct with power changes).

If cruise power is set and left alone, then scanning the ASI need not be as frequent, and the scan can concentrate on the AI, HI and altimeter.

Figure 19-24. The basic-T scan in cruise

Also, when established and well trimmed in cruise, the airplane will tend to hold altitude because of its longitudinal stability, making it less essential to scan the altimeter continually compared to when the airplane is out of trim. The airplane may not be as stable laterally as it is longitudinally, however, and so **the HI should be scanned quite frequently** to ensure that the chosen heading is maintained.

Visual pilots are already well-practiced at scanning the altimeter regularly, since it is the only means of accurately holding the chosen altitude, but they may not be accustomed to scanning the HI quite so frequently, as is necessary in instrument conditions. This skill will have to be developed.

What About the Other Flight Instruments?

In smooth air, the **VSI** will show a trend away from cruise altitude often before it is apparent on the altimeter, and can be used to indicate that a minor pitch attitude correction is required to maintain altitude. The VSI provides *supporting* pitch information to that provided by the altimeter, although it is of less value in turbulence because the VSI needle fluctuates.

If the wings are held level on the AI, and the heading is being maintained on the HI, then it is almost certain that the airplane is coordinated, with the **ball centered.** Normally, the coordination ball does not have to be scanned as frequently as some of the other instruments, but it should be referred to occasionally, especially if the heading is changing while the wings are level, or if the "seat of your pants" tells you that the airplane is skidding or slipping.

The **turn coordinator** will show a wings-level indication during straight flight, and provides supporting information regarding bank to that provided by the heading indicator. In a standard-rate turn, it is the primary performance guide to confirm that the bank angle is correct.

Choice of Scan Pattern

Starting with your eyes focused on the AI, scan the performance instruments that provide the information required. Relevant information can be obtained from different instruments, depending on the maneuver.

Use a logical scan for each maneuver.

Primary pitch information—to confirm whether or not the pitch attitude selected on the AI is correct—is obtained from the altimeter during cruise flight, but from the ASI during climb and descent.

There is no need to memorize particular scan patterns, since they will develop naturally as your training progresses.

Do not allow the radial scan to break down. Avoid fixation on any one instrument, since this will certainly cause a breakdown in the radial scan, and result in delayed recognition of deviations from the intended flight path and/or airspeed. If you fixate on the HI, for instance, you may hold heading perfectly, but in the meantime the altitude and airspeed may change—tendencies which would have been detected (and corrected for) if the altimeter, VSI and ASI had been correctly scanned.

Occasionally, the eyes will have to be directed away from the main flight instruments for a short period—for instance, when checking the power indicator during or following a power change, or when periodically checking the oil temperature and pressure instruments, the ammeter, or the suction (vacuum) gauge, or when realigning the heading indicator with the magnetic compass. Do not neglect the radial scan for more than a few seconds at a time, even though other necessary tasks have to be performed.

Avoid missing any relevant instrument. For instance, after rolling out of a turn, check the HI to ensure that the selected heading is being achieved and maintained. The wings might be level and the airplane flying straight, but on the wrong heading.

Use all available resources. For instance, with correct power set and the correct attitude selected on the AI, it is possible to hold altitude at least approximately using only the AI and the power indicator but, if precision is required, then the altimeter must be included in the scan as the primary reference for altitude. Furthermore, do not forget that supporting instruments can provide additional information to back-up primary instruments. (Refer to figure 19-25.)

For instance, altitude is indicated directly on the altimeter, but any *tendency* to depart from that altitude may first be indicated on the VSI (especially in smooth air), which makes it a valuable supporting instrument to the altimeter.

Other Scans

It is necessary on some occasions to have a fast scan, such as on final for an instrument approach. On other occasions, however, the scan can be more relaxed—for instance, when cruising with the autopilot engaged. It may then be suitable just to have a fairly relaxed **circular scan.**

If you are performing other tasks while flying a constant heading, such as map reading, then a simple scan to make sure things do not get out of hand is a **vertical scan** from the AI down to the heading indicator and back again.

If at any time, you suspect an **instrument failure,** then an efficient means of establishing what instrument or system has failed is to commence with an **inverted-V scan,** centered on the AI and radiating to the turn coordinator and the VSI.

Each of these instruments normally has a different power source—the *vacuum system* for the AI, the *electrical system* for the turn coordinator, and the *static system* for the VSI—so a false indication on one should not be reflected on the others. Confirmation of attitude and flight path can then be achieved using the other instruments.

With practice, you will develop scans suitable to every situation.

Keep the eyes moving, and continually return to the AI.

Figure 19-25. A suitable scan during straight-and-level flight

Figure 19-26. A circular scan

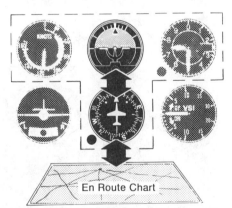

Figure 19-27. The vertical scan

Figure 19-28. The inverted-V scan

Performance Table

To help you adjust to a new airplane type, we have included a **Type Performance Table** (shown opposite). You can fill this table in as you become familiar with the power settings and attitudes required to achieve the required performance in the various phases of flight.

Attitude can be shown on the AI by inserting a horizon line. The table allows for aircraft with rectractable landing gear—if yours has a fixed landing gear, then just pencil the wheels in on the chart, and only fill in the powers and attitudes that you need.

Knowing the numbers simplifies the game!

Airmanship

Never proceed into instrument conditions without a flight instructor unless you are properly qualified (with a valid instrument rating) in a suitably equipped airplane, and within the limitations of your ability and certificate rating privileges.

Always calculate a lowest safe altitude *before* entering instrument conditions.

Keep in practice! Use smooth and coordinated control movements.

Airmanship is never proceeding into instrument conditions unless you and the airplane are properly equipped to handle them.

Airwork

The basic manuevers will be practiced initially while you have visual reference to the outside world, and then solely by reference to the cockpit instruments.

This **introduction to instrument flying** may best be handled in the following four separate parts:

- **Part (i)—Straight-and-Level;**
- **Part (ii)—Climb, Cruise and Descent;**
- **Part (iii)—Turning; and**
- **Part (iv)—Recovery from Unusual Flight Attitudes.**

Figure 19-25. Typical installation of flight instruments in a light airplane (Cessna 172)

PERFORMANCE TABLE

	Configuration Flaps Gear	Power MP rpm	Attitude	Performance Airspeed VSI	V-Speeds
TAKEOFF	.....° DN				Obstacle-clearance speed = ... KIAS
	.....° UP				
CLIMB	0° UP				V_{S1} = ... KIAS (stall speed, clean) V_X = ... KIAS (best angle) V_Y = ... KIAS (best rate)
CRUISE					V_A = ... KIAS (maneuvering speed) V_{NO} = ... KIAS (normal maximum) V_{NE} = ... KIAS (never-exceed speed)
CRUISE DESCENT (500 fpm)					
SLOW-SPEED CRUISE **1.** **Clean**					
2. **Flaps Extended**	.....° UP				V_{FE} = ... KIAS (flaps extended)
3. **Flaps and Gear Extended**	.....° DN				V_{LO} = ... KIAS (gear operation) V_{SO} = ... KIAS (landing flaps and landing gear extended)

Airwork 19, Part (i)
Flying Straight-and-Level on Instruments

Objective
To maintain a steady cruise straight-and-level with reference to the flight instruments only.

1. To Establish Straight-and-Level Flight

- Select the power setting for level flight.
- Set the pitch attitude for level flight by positioning the miniature airplane against the horizon line of the attitude indicator.
- Hold the attitude and allow the airplane to stabilize.
- Monitor: AI–ALT–AI–HI–AI–ASI–AI–VSI–AI–TC–AI–ALT, and so on.
- Trim the airplane carefully so it will fly hands-off.

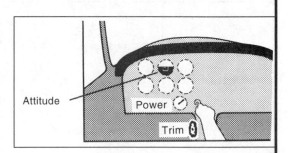

2. Raising the Nose at Constant Power

- Place the miniature airplane a little above the horizon line on the AI (say one-half or one bar width) and hold.
- The ASI will show a gradual decrease and finally settle on a lower indicated airspeed (IAS).
- The altimeter, after some lag, will start showing an increase in altitude.
- The VSI, after some initial fluctuations, will settle on a steady rate of climb.

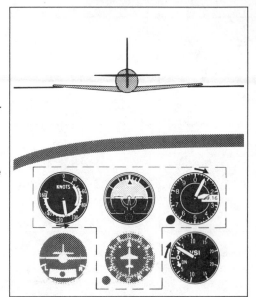

3. Lowering the Nose at Constant Power

- Place the miniature airplane a little below the horizon line on the AI and hold this attitude.
- The ASI will show a gradual increase and finally stabilize at a higher IAS. Note that a relatively large airspeed change will occur after a small change in attitude.
- The altimeter, after some lag, will start showing a gradual decrease in altitude.
- The VSI will eventually stabilize on a steady rate of descent.

Continued

4. Maintaining Straight-and-Level at Constant Power

Monitoring straight-and-level flight

Required accuracy:
- airspeed ±10 KIAS
- heading ±10°
- altitude ±100 ft

- Correct variations in:

Altitude:
by making very small changes in the postion of the miniature airplane relative to the horizon line on the AI.

Within ±100 feet is acceptable.*

Heading:
by using small bank angles and checking that the airplane is coordinated.

Within ±10° is acceptable.*

Airspeed:
by adjustments in power, followed by, as a consequence, a small change in attitude.

Within ±10 KIAS is acceptable.*

- Keep in trim.

*Aim to have airspeed, altitude and heading precisely on the desired numbers. If they are not, take corrective action immediately.

5. Changing Airspeed, Straight-and-Level

(a) To increase airspeed at a constant altitude:
- Add power with the throttle—coordinate with rudder and forward pressure on the control column.
- Gradually lower the pitch attitude to avoid climbing, and allow the airspeed to increase to the desired value.
- Adjust power to maintain the desired airspeed, and hold the pitch attitude.
- Trim.

(b) To decrease airspeed at a constant altitude:
- Reduce power with the throttle—coordinate with rudder and hold the nose up with elevator back pressure.
- Gradually raise the pitch attitude to avoid descending and allow the airspeed to reduce to the desired value.
- As the desired airspeed is approached, adjust the power to maintain it, and hold the pitch attitude.
- Trim.

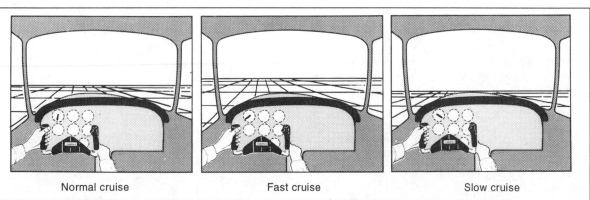

Normal cruise　　　Fast cruise　　　Slow cruise

Different pitch attitudes for different airspeeds

End of Part (i)

Airwork 19, Part (ii)
Climbing, Cruising and Descending on Instruments

Objective
To climb, cruise and descend, and to change from one to another, with reference only to the flight instruments.

1. Climb, Cruise and Descent at a Constant Airspeed

Climb, cruise and descent speeds are usually different. However, by using a constant airspeed in these initial maneuvers, we simplify the task by removing one of the variables.

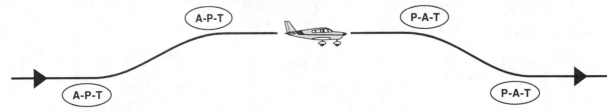

(a) From straight-and-level, enter a climb at a constant airspeed:
- Settle into straight-and-level cruise flight and note the airspeed.
- Smoothly open the throttle to full power—coordinate with rudder.
- Simultaneously raise the nose slightly to maintain airspeed, and hold the pitch attitude.
- Note that the VSI shows a rate of climb, and the altimeter shows a gain in altitude.
- Trim.

(b) From a climb, level off and maintain a constant airspeed:
- Lower the nose to maintain a constant airspeed.
- Reduce to the normal cruise power setting (as before)—coordinate with rudder.
- Note that the VSI shows zero and the altimeter a constant altitude.
- Trim.

(c) From straight-and-level, commence a descent:
- Reduce power (by 600 rpm or so)—coordinate with rudder.
- Lower the nose to maintain a constant airspeed.
- Note the VSI shows a rate of descent and the altimeter shows a decrease in altitude.
- Trim.

(d) From a descent, enter a climb:
- Smoothly open the throttle to full power—coordinate with rudder—and simultaneously allow the nose to rise to the climb attitude.
- Hold the attitude to maintain the desired airspeed.
- Note that the VSI shows a rate of climb and the altimeter a change in altitude.
- Trim.

> **Required accuracy:**
> - airspeed ±10 KIAS
> - heading ±10°
> - level off at desired altitude ±100 ft

Continued

2. Initiating a Climb at Normal Climb Speed

Usually the normal climb speed is less than the cruise speed. As in normal visual flight, a climb is initiated in the A-P-T sequence: attitude–power–trim.

Procedure:
- Settle in straight-and-level flight and note the airspeed.
- Raise the nose to the pitch attitude for climbing.
- Increase power to the climb figure—coordinate with rudder.
- Hold the new attitude as the airspeed decreases to the desired climbing speed; the VSI will show a rate of climb and the altimeter an increase in altitude.
- Make minor pitch attitude adjustments to achieve and maintain the correct climb airspeed.
- Trim.

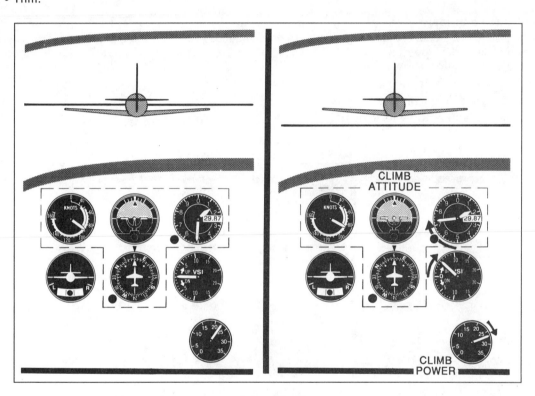

Required accuracy:
- airspeed ±10 KIAS
- heading ±10°

Note: If desired, you can trim earlier in the sequence, while holding the new attitude as the airspeed decreases, to off-load some control column pressure. However, a final trim adjustment will need to be made. Do not use trim to change the attitude; pitch attitude must only be changed with elevator. The trim is used solely to relieve sustained control pressures.

A steady climb is maintained with reference to all flight instruments, with the ASI confirming that you are indeed holding the correct attitude for climbing, as shown in the AI.

Continued

3. Leveling Off from a Climb

As in normal visual flight, leveling off from a climb follows the A-P-T sequence: attitude–power–trim. Since the cruise speed is normally greater than the climb speed, the airplane is allowed to accelerate before the power is reduced from climb to cruise power.

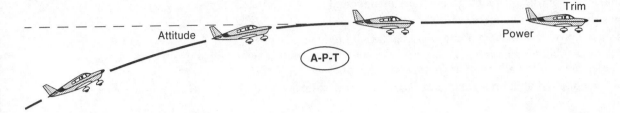

To level off at the desired altitude:

- Smoothly lower the nose to the cruise position slightly before the altitude is reached—a suitable amount of "lead" being approximately 10% of the rate of climb. (For example, at 500 fpm rate of climb, begin lowering the nose 50 feet prior to reaching the desired altitude.)
- Allow the airspeed to increase toward the cruise figure.
- Reduce power to cruise rpm as the cruise speed is reached.
- Make minor adjustments to hold altitude, heading and airspeed.
- Trim.

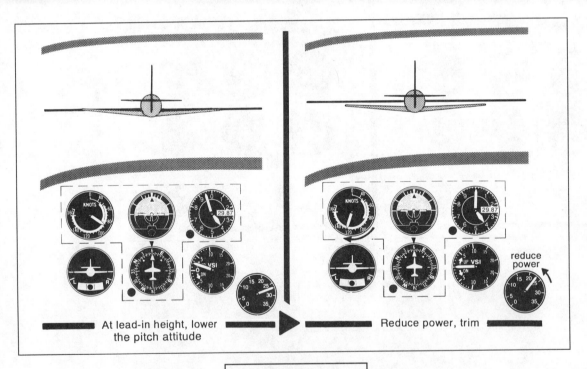

At lead-in height, lower the pitch attitude

Reduce power, trim

Required accuracy:
- altitude ±100 ft
- airspeed ±10 KIAS
- heading ±10°

Note: Steady straight-and-level flight is maintained by reference to all flight instruments, with the altimeter confirming that you are holding the correct attitude for straight-and-level, as shown on the attitude indicator.

Continued

4. Initiating a Descent on Instruments

As in normal visual flight, a descent is initiated in the order P-A-T: power–attitude–trim. Descent speed is usually less than cruise speed—decelerate to the descent airspeed at the cruise altitude before lowering the nose to descend.

The standard rate of descent in instrument flying is 500 fpm. This may be achieved by a reduction of 600 rpm or so from the cruise power setting. However, you may remove more power, and descend at a greater rate, if desired. A glide descent may also be made with the throttle fully closed.

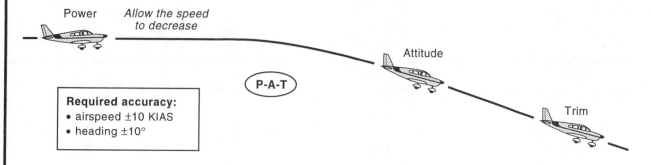

Power

Allow the speed to decrease

Attitude

Trim

P-A-T

Required accuracy:
- airspeed ±10 KIAS
- heading ±10°

Procedure:

- Reduce power—coordinate with rudder and exert back pressure on the control column as necessary to maintain altitude.
- Allow the airspeed to decrease toward the desired descent speed.
- Approaching the descent speed, smoothly lower the nose to the estimated descent attitude.
- Hold the new attitude to allow the descent speed to stabilize—the VSI will show a rate of descent and the altimeter will show an altitude decrease.
- Make minor adjustments to achieve the desired descent airspeed and rate of descent—control airspeed with pitch attitude and rate of descent with power.
- Trim.

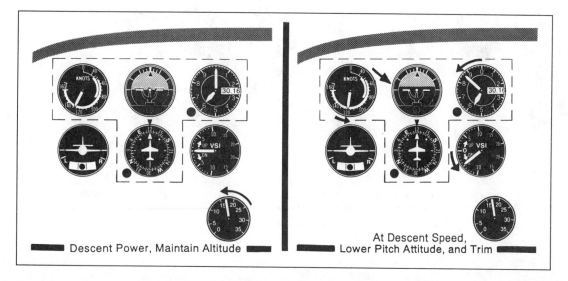

Descent Power, Maintain Altitude

At Descent Speed, Lower Pitch Attitude, and Trim

Note: A steady descent is maintained with reference to all the flight instruments, with the ASI confirming you are holding the correct attitude for descent, as shown on the AI.

Continued

5. Controlling the Rate of Descent at a Constant Airspeed

To achieve any desired rate of descent while maintaining a constant airspeed, both the power and attitude must be adjusted.

The rate of descent is indicated to the pilot by:
• the vertical speed indicator (primarily); or
• the altimeter and clock.

(a) To increase the rate of descent:
  • Reduce power.
  • Lower the pitch attitude to maintain airspeed.
  • Trim.

(b) To decrease the rate of descent:
  • Increase power.
  • Raise the pitch attitude to maintain airspeed.
  • Trim.

> **Required accuracy:**
> • airspeed ±10 KIAS
> • heading ±10°
> • desired rate of descent ±100 fpm

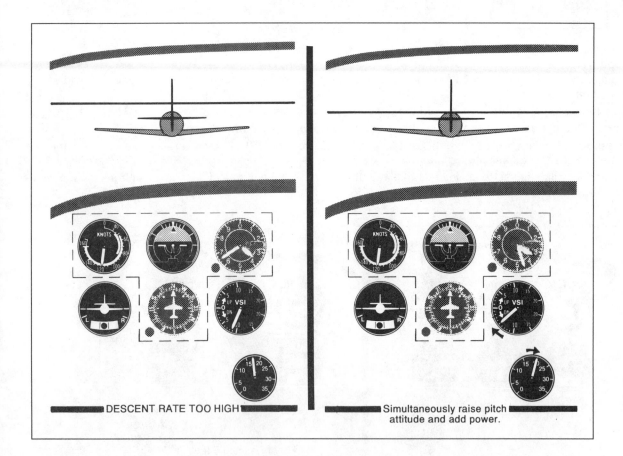

DESCENT RATE TOO HIGH

Simultaneously raise pitch attitude and add power.

Continued

6. Leveling Off from a Descent

As in normal visual flight, leveling off from a descent follows the P-A-T sequence: power–attitude–trim.

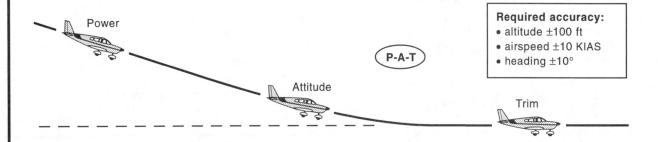

Power

Attitude

Trim

P-A-T

Required accuracy:
- altitude ±100 ft
- airspeed ±10 KIAS
- heading ±10°

To level off at a specific altitude, increase the power and gradually raise the nose toward the cruise position just before the altitude is reached—the amount of lead being approximately 10% of the rate of descent. So, at a 500 fpm rate of descent, start increasing the power and raising the nose 50 feet prior to reaching the desired altitude.

- Increase power to the cruise rpm (and coordinate with rudder pressure).
- Raise the pitch attitude to the cruise position.
- Make minor adjustments to maintain altitude.
- Trim.

Steady straight-and-level flight is maintained with reference to all flight instruments—with the altimeter confirming that you are holding the correct attitude for straight-and-level as shown on the attitude indicator.

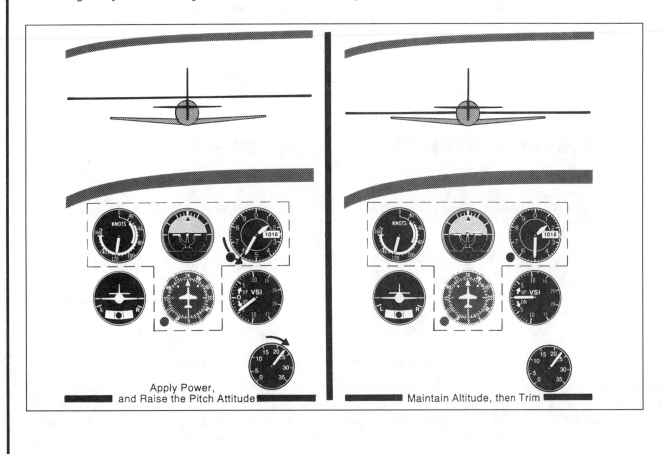

Apply Power, and Raise the Pitch Attitude

Maintain Altitude, then Trim

Continued

7. Climbing Away from a Descent

The procedure is the same as leveling off from a descent, except that climb power and climb attitude are selected instead.

Be prepared for strong nose-up and yawing tendencies as climb power is applied.

Even though the climb attitude is higher than the descent attitude, it may initially require forward pressure to stop the nose rising too far. Rudder will of course be required to coordinate the increase in slipstream effect.

Trim off any steady pressure remaining on the control column.

Procedure:
- Apply climb **power**—coordinate with rudder.
- Set the desired pitch **attitude** for the climb.
- **Trim**.

> **Required accuracy:**
> - airspeed ±10 KIAS
> - heading ±10°

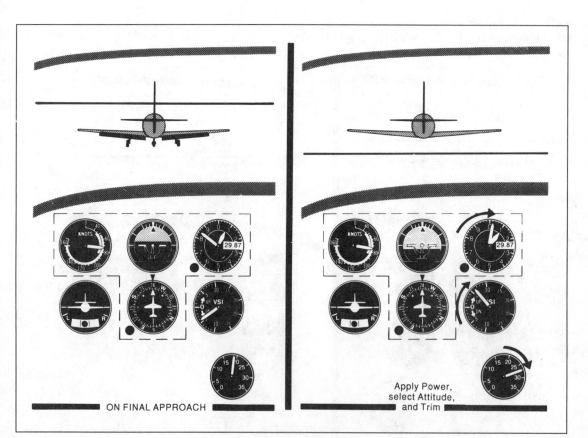

ON FINAL APPROACH

Apply Power, select Attitude, and Trim

Note: If making a go-around from an approach, you should apply maximum power—keeping the ball centered with rudder; hold a higher pitch attitude to establish a climb, and then raise the flaps in stages. If your airplane has a retractable landing gear, you would retract it when you have established a positive rate of climb.

End of Part (ii)

Airwork 19, Part (iii)
Turning Using the Flight Instruments

Objective

To turn the airplane solely by reference to the flight instruments.

1. A Standard-Rate Level Turn

The required bank angle for a standard-rate turn will equal one-tenth of the airspeed, plus half of that. For example, at 80 KIAS, the bank angle required will be (8 + 4 =) 12°.

Trim for straight-and-level flight.

To enter and maintain the turn:
- Roll into the turn using aileron, and coordinate with rudder pressure.
- Hold a constant bank angle and keep the coordination ball centered.
- Hold the correct pitch attitude to maintain altitude using elevator.
- Do not use trim in a turn, since turning is normally only a transient maneuver (although you may trim for a sustained turn).

The rate of turn is indicated to the pilot by:
- the turn coordinator (standard rate = 3° per second, or 360° in 2 minutes); or
- the heading indicator and clock.

To stop the turn on a desired heading:
- Anticipate and begin recovery from the turn about 5° prior to reaching the desired heading.
- Roll the wings level, and coordinate with rudder.
- Lower the pitch attitude to that required for straight-and-level flight.
- Trimming will not be necessary, if trim was not adjusted during the turn.

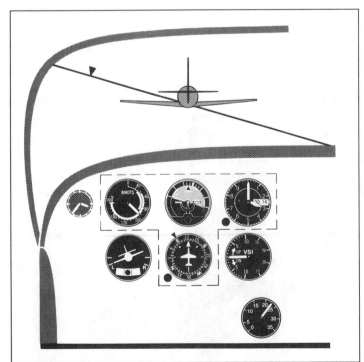

A standard-rate level turn to the left

Required accuracy:
- altitude ±100 ft
- bank angle ±5°
- heading ±10°
- airspeed ±10 KIAS

Note: A standard-rate turn may also be achieved by using the clock and the heading indicator. By holding the calculated bank angle you should achieve a turn rate of 3° per second, which will give a 45° heading change in 15 seconds, a 90° heading change in 30 seconds, a 180° heading change in one minute and a 360° heading change in two minutes—hence the **2 MIN** that is marked on many turn coordinators.

Continued

2. A 30° Banked Level Turn

At the speeds achieved by most training aircraft, a 30° banked turn is greater than standard rate. A steeper bank angle requires a greater back pressure to maintain altitude, so the airspeed will decrease a little further—by about 5 or 10 knots. If you wish to hold the airspeed constant, then a little power will be required. The pitch attitude will be slightly higher than for straight-and-level.

The rate of turn can be estimated from the turn coordinator, or by using the clock and the heading indicator (bearing in mind that the turn coordinator may be limited by stops at about twice standard rate—so that steeper bank angles will not be accompanied by an increased rate of turn indication).

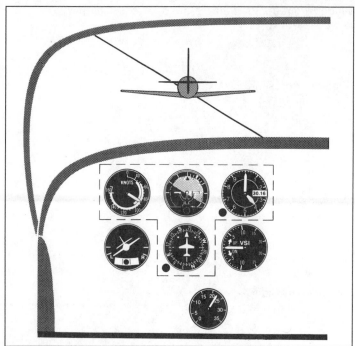

Required accuracy:
- altitude ±100 ft
- bank angle ±5°
- heading ±10°
- airspeed ±10 KIAS

A 30-degree level turn to the left

3. The Climbing Turn

The climbing turn will normally be entered from a straight climb. To ensure adequate climb performance, do not exceed a 20° bank angle in a typical training airplane.

The pitch attitude will have to be lowered slightly to maintain a constant airspeed in a climbing turn. (In climbing and descending turns, speed is maintained with the elevator, whereas in level turns it is altitude that is maintained with the elevator.)

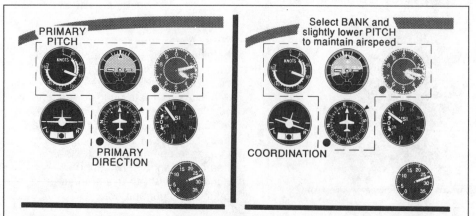

Required accuracy:
- altitude ±100 ft
- bank angle ±5°
- heading ±10°
- airspeed ±10 KIAS

Maintaining a climbing turn to the right

Continued

The descending turn will normally be entered from a straight descent.

A lower pitch attitude will be required in the turn to maintain airspeed.

The rate of descent will increase in a turn—it can be controlled with power, if you wish.

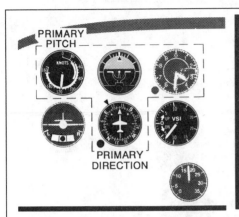

Required accuracy:
- altitude ±100 ft
- bank angle ±5°
- heading ±10°
- airspeed ±10 KIAS

Maintaining a descending turn to the left

End of Part (iii)

Airwork 19, Part (iv)
Recovery from Unusual Flight Attitudes

Objective
To recognize a potentially hazardous flight attitude from instrument indications and recover before a hazardous attitude develops.

An **unusual attitude** is considered to be a potentially hazardous attitude where either:
- the airplane's nose is unusually high with the airspeed decreasing, or
- the airplane's nose is unusually low with the airspeed increasing; the airplane may also be banked.

The **easiest recovery** from an unusual attitude is not to get into one!

In extreme attitudes, the attitude indicator (a gyroscopic instrument) may tumble, depriving you of your most important instrument. Most of its information can be derived, however, from other sources.

- Approximate **pitch attitude** can be determined from the airspeed indicator (increasing or decreasing airspeed) and the altimeter and vertical speed indicator (descent or climb). A *decreasing airspeed* indication and a decreasing rate of climb would indicate an unusually high nose-up attitude; conversely a *rapidly increasing airspeed* and rate of descent would indicate a nose-low attitude.

- **Turning** can be detected on the turn coordinator:
    The heading indicator (a gyroscopic instrument) may have tumbled and the magnetic compass will probably not be giving a steady reading if there is any significant turn occurring.
    The turn coordinator is gyroscopic but it will not topple.

Continued

Beware of a stall.

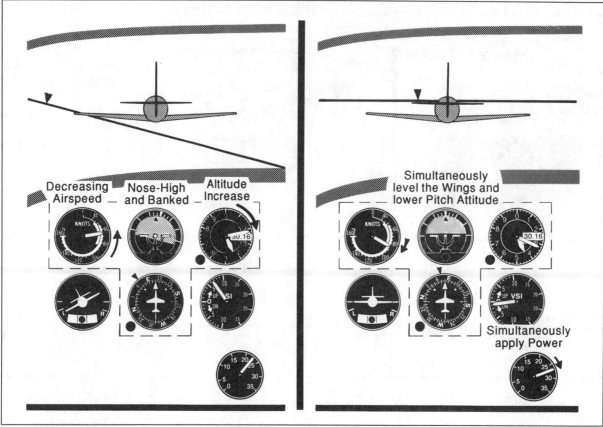

A nose-high unusual attitude

Recovery Procedure

(a) If close to the stall:
- Simultaneously lower the nose to the level pitch attitude (referring to the AI) and apply full power—coordinate with rudder.
- As speed increases, level the wings (refer to the AI).

(b) If not close to the stall:
- Select straight-and-level flight (refer to the AI):
  Control wheel forward.
  Roll wings-level with aileron—the ailerons can be used since the wings are not stalled—coordinating with rudder.
- Add power as necessary.

Note: Do not exceed 45° bank angle or 10° pitch from level flight when practicing recovery from unusual flight attitudes on instruments. Recover to a stabilized level flight attitude or climb using prompt coordinated control movements applied in the proper sequence. Avoid any excessive load factors, and do not exceed airspeed limits, or stall the airplane.

Continued

2. Nose-Low and Increasing Airspeed

Beware of an overspeed or a spiral dive.

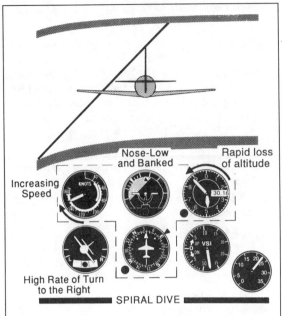

Recovery procedure:
- Reduce the power (throttle closed).
- Roll the wings level with aileron and rudder.
- Ease out of the ensuing dive into the straight-and-level attitude (AI).
- Reapply power.
- Regain altitude, if necessary.

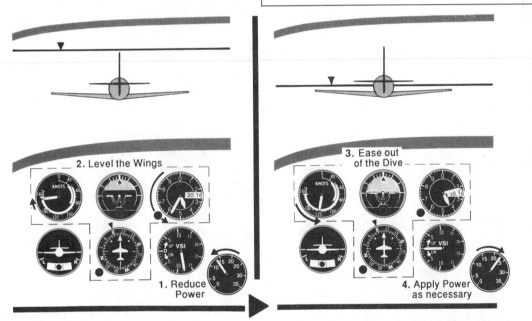

A nose-low unusual attitude

Note: Do not exceed 45° bank angle or 10° pitch from level flight when practicing recovery from unusual flight attitudes on instruments. Recover to a stabilized level-flight attitude or climb using prompt, coordinated control movements applied in the proper sequence. Avoid pulling any excessive g-loadings, and do not exceed airspeed limits, or allow the airplane to stall.

The End

✍ Review 19

Instrument Flying

1. As an instrument pilot, you must learn to (trust/doubt) what your eyes see on the instruments.

   ➤ trust

2. What are the three fundamental skills in instrument flying?

   ➤ instrument crosscheck, instrument interpretation, airplane control

3. Looking at the instruments in a systematic manner to extract the information you need, is known as an instrument _____ .

   ➤ scan

4. The two control instruments are the _____ _____ and the _____ _____ .

   ➤ attitude indicator, power indicator

5. The performance instruments for altitude are the _____ and the _____ _____ _____ .

   ➤ altimeter, vertical speed indicator

6. The performance instruments for direction are the _____ _____ and the _____ _____ .

   ➤ heading indicator, turn coordinator

7. The performance instrument for airspeed is the _____ _____ .

   ➤ airspeed indicator

8. When flying on instruments you (must always/need not) know approximately how far you are above the ground and any nearby obstructions.

   ➤ must always

9. A suitable lowest safe altitude to fly when using instruments is ____ feet above the highest obstacle within ____ nm. In designated mountainous terrain, this is raised to ____ feet.

   ➤ 1,000 feet, 4 nm, 2,000 feet

10. Required accuracy when flying on instruments is:
    • airspeed plus or minus ____ KIAS;
    • heading plus or minus ____ °; and
    • altitude plus or minus ____ feet.

    ➤ 10 KIAS, 10°, 100 feet

11. The primary guide to coordination—that is, no slip or skid—in all flying is the _____ _____ .

    ➤ coordination ball

12. During a climb, you can check that the climb attitude set on the attitude indicator is correct by checking the (altimeter/airspeed indicator/vertical speed indicator).

    ➤ airspeed indicator

13. During a descent, you can check that the descent attitude set on the attitude indicator is correct by checking the (altimeter/airspeed indicator/vertical speed indicator).

    ➤ airspeed indicator

14. During straight-and-level flight, you can check that the attitude set on the attitude indicator is correct by checking the (altimeter/airspeed indicator/vertical speed indicator).

    ➤ altimeter

15. During a standard-rate turn, you can check that the bank attitude set on the attitude indicator is correct by checking the (heading indicator/turn coordinator/magnetic compass)

    ➤ turn coordinator

16. When applying full power in a conventional training airplane, you will have to apply some (left/right) rudder to keep the coordination ball centered, and when reducing power you will have to apply some (left/right) rudder to keep the coordination ball centered.

    ➤ right, left

17. As power is added, the nose tends to (rise/fall).
    ➤ rise

18. What are two potentially hazardous attitudes?
    ➤
    1. Nose-high with airspeed decreasing
    2. Nose-low with airspeed decreasing

19. When practicing recovery from unusual flight attitudes on instruments, you should at no stage exceed a bank angle of ____ ° or ____ ° pitch up or down.

    ➤ 45° bank angle or 10° pitch

Night Flying **20**

Nighttime

Night is considered to occur between the end of evening civil twilight, which occurs some time after sunset, and the beginning of morning civil twilight, which occurs some time before sunrise. The period of twilight that occurs between the sun setting or rising and darkness can sometimes be quite lengthy, especially in areas of high latitude near the Poles, such as Alaska, Canada, Scandinavia and Russia.

Certain aspects of flight have to be considered when flying at night, such as:
- adaptation of your eyes to night vision;
- additional personal equipment;
- additional aircraft equipment and lighting;
- airport lighting; and
- navigating at night.

To have night-flying privileges, you must receive at least three hours of flight instruction at night, including at least 10 takeoffs and landings.

Personal Pilot Equipment

As well as your normal daytime equipment, you must carry a serviceable **flashlight.** A good **white** beam is essential for your external preflight checks. A fairly weak **red** light is best for use in the darkened cockpit, since it will not destroy your night vision—however, it will make red items on your charts difficult or impossible to see.

It is important that your personal equipment is well organized, since things are always more difficult to find when it is dark—especially when you have to fly the airplane with little external visual reference. Fold your charts with the course line visible, so that they are immediately available for use. Carry spare batteries and bulbs for your flashlight, or ensure it is always well charged (if a rechargeable type).

Carry your own flashlight at night.

Aircraft Equipment and Lighting

The cockpit instrumentation required for VFR daytime flight is also required for VFR night flight. This includes:
- certain flight instruments;
- certain engine gauges; and
- fuel quantity gauges.

Surprisingly, an artificial horizon is not required, although it will be very useful at night.

Aircraft with retractable landing gear must also have a landing gear position indicator, and those with a constant-speed propeller must have a manifold pressure gauge.

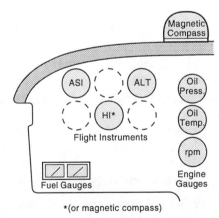

Figure 20-1. Required instruments

The **additional** equipment required for **VFR night flight** includes:
- approved position lights (red, green, and white);
- an approved anticollision light system (usually a red rotating beacon and white strobe lights);
- landing light(s)—if the aircraft is for hire;
- an adequate source of electrical power (engine-driven alternator and onboard battery);
- spare fuses stored in an accessible place.

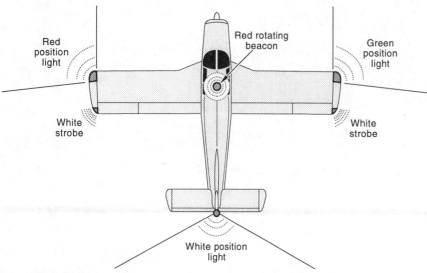

Figure 20-2. Required lights

Airport Lighting

The main aeronautical lighting provided at an airport to assist you to maneuver your airplane at night consists of:
- taxiway lighting;
- runway lighting;
- the airport beacon;
- approach lighting;
- visual approach slope indicators (VASI); and
- red warning lights on significant obstacles.

You may be night flying at an airport with fairly simple lighting, or you might be at a sophisticated international airport with advanced lighting, especially approach lighting. In this section you should read about **taxiway lighting** (blue edge or centerline green), simple **runway lighting** (white), and **airport beacons** (alternating green and white), but only take what you need from the advanced approach lighting and runway lighting descriptions. Definitely read about **pilot-controlled airport lighting.** Particulars of lighting at specific airports are shown on aeronautical charts and in the A/FD.

Airport Beacons

The airport beacon is designed to help the pilot visually locate the airport from some distance away. Some airport beacons rotate, others transmit pulses of light, the effect being the same—flashes of one or two alternating colors, which are:
- *green–white–green–white* at **civil airports;** and
- *green–white–white–green–white-white* at **military airports.**

Obstruction Lights

Many obstructions that could be hazardous to aircraft are marked at night by flashing red or white lights, and/or steady red lights.

Taxiway Lights

Taxiways are lit in one of two ways for the guidance of pilots, with either:
- two lines of taxiway **blue edge** lights; or
- one line of **centerline green** taxiway lights.

Taxiway lights are centerline green or sideline blue.

At some airports, there is a mixture of the two types, centerline green on some taxiways, and blue edge on others. Centerline green lights will be flush with the taxiway surface (or almost so) and can be taxied over. On the other hand, sideline blue taxiway lights (and the white runway edge lights) may not be flush, and are also used to indicate boundaries, so do **not** taxi across them.

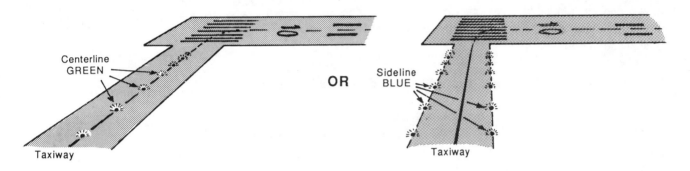

Centerline GREEN — Taxiway — OR — Sideline BLUE — Taxiway

Figure 20-3. Taxiway lighting

At certain points on the taxiway, there may be **red stop-bars** installed, to indicate the position where an airplane should hold position—for instance, before entering or crossing an active runway.

Runway Lighting

Runway lighting defines the boundaries of the actual landing area. Some advanced systems on precision instrument approach runways provide you with *distance-down-the-runway* information as well, but this is not vital for a visual pilot who can see the end of the runway and its lights.

Runway Edge Lights

Runway edge lights are white, and outline the edges of runways during periods of darkness or restricted visibility.

Runway End Lights

The runway end lights each have two colors, showing green at the near end to aircraft on approach, and red to airplanes stopping at the far end.

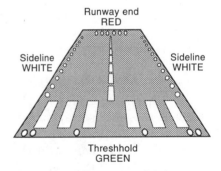

Runway end RED — Sideline WHITE — Sideline WHITE — Threshhold GREEN

Figure 20-4. Basic runway lighting at night

Note for Private Pilot applicants: This is the extent of the airport lighting at fairly basic airports. It is appropriate for you now to bypass the rest of this lighting section, except for pilot-controlled lighting systems (page 526), and move on several pages to the topic *Night Flying at an Airport*—unless you wish to know about some of the sophisticated lighting available at major airports, so that you will not be dazzled by the extent and intensity of the lighting on your first approach to a precision instrument runway at night.

Advanced Runway Edge Lights. Runway edge lights are classified according to the intensity or brightness they are capable of producing:
- HIRL: high intensity runway lights;
- MIRL: medium intensity runway lights;
- LIRL: low intensity runway lights.

Runway edge lights are white, except on instrument runways where amber replaces white for the last 2,000 feet (or last-half on runways shorter than 4,000 feet), to form a **caution zone** for landings in restricted visibility. When the pilot sees the white edge lights replaced by amber, he has some idea of how much runway is left for stopping.

Runway End Identifier Lights. Runway end identifier lights (REIL) consist of a pair of synchronized white flashing lights located each side of the runway threshold at the approach end. They serve to identify:
- a runway end surrounded by many other lights;
- a runway end which lacks contrast with the surrounding terrain; and
- a runway end in poor visibility.

In-Runway Lighting. Some precision approach runways have additional in-runway lighting embedded in the runway surface consisting of:
- **touchdown zone lights** (TDZL): bright white lights either side of the runway centerline in the touchdown zone (from 100 feet in from the landing threshold to 3,000 feet or the half-way point, which ever is the lower);
- **runway centerline light systems** (RCLS): flush centerline lighting at 50 feet intervals, starting 75 feet in from the landing threshold to within 75 feet of the stopping end; RCLS also includes **runway-remaining lighting,** where the centerline lighting seen by a stopping airplane is:
  initially all white;
  alternating red and white from 3,000 feet-to-go point to 1,000 feet-to-go;
  all red for the last 1,000 feet.
- **taxiway turn-off lights:** a series of green in-runway lights spaced at 50 feet intervals defining a curved path from the runway centerline to a point on the taxiway.

Approach Light Systems

At many airports, an approach lighting system (ALS) extends out from the approach end of the runway to well beyond the physical boundaries of the airport, possibly into forested or built-up areas.

Approach lights do *not* mark the boundaries of a suitable landing area—they simply act as a lead-in to a runway for a pilot on approach to land.

ALS lighting is a standardized arrangement of white and red lights, consisting basically of **extended centerline lighting,** with **crossbars** sited at specific intervals back along the approach path from the threshold, out to a distance of:
- 2,400 to 3,400 feet for **precision** instrument approach runways; or
- 1,400 to 1,500 feet for **nonprecision** instrument approach runways.

Approach light systems assist an instrument pilot to transition from instrument flight to visual flight for a landing.

The approach lighting provides you with a visual indication of how well the airplane is aligned with the extended runway centerline as well as helping you to estimate the distance the airplane has to fly to the touchdown point on the runway.

There are various types of approach light systems in use, the sophistication of the system depending upon the importance of the airport and the frequency and type of operations. Some typical **precision instrument runway ALSs** are shown below.

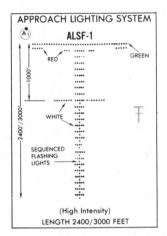
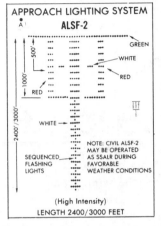

Figure 20-5. Approach lighting systems for precision instrument runways

Some approach lighting systems include **sequenced flashing lights** (SFL), or **runway alignment indicator lights** (RAIL), which appear to the pilot as a ball of white light traveling toward the runway at high speed (twice per second), along the extended centerline.

The runway threshold is marked with a row of green lights, and some runway thresholds have flashing strobes either side to act as **runway end identifier lights** (REIL).

Visual Approach Slope Indicator (VASI)

In conditions of poor visibility and at night, when the runway environment and the natural horizon may not be clearly visible, it is often difficult for a pilot to judge the correct approach slope of the airplane toward the touchdown zone of the runway. A number of very effective visual slope indicators provide visual **slope guidance** on approach. Especially at night, you should not fly a shallower approach than the typical 3° VASI slope.

Lateral guidance is provided by the runway, the runway lights or the approach light system. The slope guidance provided by a VASI is to the touchdown zone, which will probably be some 1,000 feet in from the runway threshold.

VASIs provide approach-slope guidance by day and by night.

Two-Bar Red-on-White VASI

The typical **two-bar** VASI has two pairs of wing bars alongside the runway, usually at 500 feet and 1,000 feet from the approach threshold. It is sometimes known as the *red/white system*, since these two colors are used to indicate whether you are right on slope, too high or too low. You will see:

- **if high on slope**—all bars are white;
- **if right on slope**—the far bars are red and the near bars are white; and
- **if low on slope**—all bars are red.

During the approach, the airplane should be maintained on a slope within the white sector of the near bars and the red sector of the far bars. If the airplane flies above or below the correct slope, the lights will change color, there being a pink transition stage between red and white.

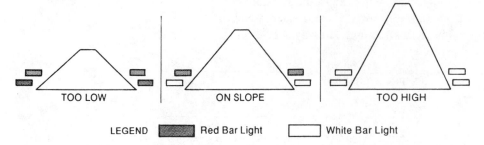

LEGEND ▨ Red Bar Light □ White Bar Light

Figure 20-6. Perspectives on approach using a two-bar red-on-white VASI

The plane of the VASI approach slope only provides guaranteed obstacle clearance in an arc 10° left or right of the extended centerline out to a distance of 4 nm from the runway threshold, even though the VASI may be visible in good conditions out to 5 nm by day and 20 nm by night. Before relying solely on the VASI for descent guidance, therefore, the airplane should be within 4 nm and inside this arc, preferably aligned with the extended runway centerline.

There are other operational considerations when using the red/white VASI. At maximum range, the white bars may become visible before the red bars, because of the nature of red and white light. In haze or smog, or in certain other conditions, the white lights may have a yellowish tinge about them.

When extremely low on slope, the two wing bars (all lights red) may appear to merge into one red bar—at close range to the threshold this would indicate a critical situation with respect to obstacle clearance, and the pilot should take urgent action to regain slope or make a missed approach.

Some VASI systems use a reduced number of lights, in which case they may be known as an *Abbreviated VASI* or *AVASI*.

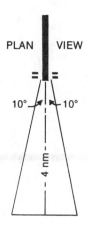

Figure 20-7. The extent of useful VASI information

Three-Bar VASI

The **three-bar VASI** has an additional wing bar at the far end, intended to assist the pilots of long-bodied airplanes such as the Boeing 747 or the McDonnell Douglas MD-11.

A VASI shows the deviation of the pilot's eyes from the approach slope, and **not** the deviation of the wheels. Since the wheels of an airplane with a very long fuselage will be much further behind and below the eyes, it is essential that the eyes follow a parallel but higher slope to ensure adequate mainwheel clearance over the runway threshold. The additional wing bar on the three-bar VASI, placed further into the runway, makes this possible.

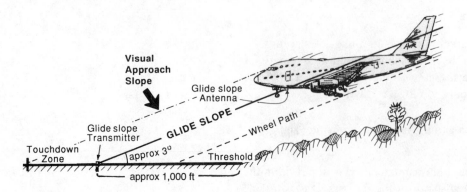

Figure 20-8. A three-bar VASI ensures adequate wheel clearance over the threshold for long-bodied aircraft.

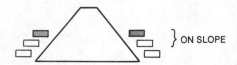

Figure 20-9. Correct view for the pilot of a long-bodied airplane using the three-bar VASI

Pilots of such airplanes should use the second and third wing bars, and ignore the first. When the pilot's eyes are positioned on the correct slope for a long-bodied airplane, they will see the top bar red, the middle bar white (and ignore the lower bar which is also white).

Pilots of smaller airplanes should refer only to the two *nearer* wing bars, and ignore the further "long-bodied" wing bar. **When on slope,** the indications will be: top bar red and ignored, middle bar red and lower bar white.

Figure 20-10. Correct view for the pilot of a smaller airplane using the three-bar VASI

Precision Approach Path Indicator (PAPI)

PAPI is a development of the VASI, and also uses red/white light signals for guidance in maintaining the correct approach angle, but the lights are arranged differently and their indications must be interpreted differently. PAPI has a single wing bar, which will consist of four light units on one or both sides of the runway adjacent to the touchdown point. There is no pink transition stage as the lights change from red to white.

If the airplane is on slope, the two outer lights of each unit are white and the two inner lights are red. Above slope, the number of white lights increase, and below slope the number of red lights increase.

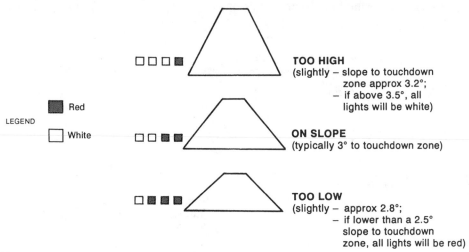

Figure 20-11. Slope guidance using PAPI

Pulsating Visual Approach Slope Indicator (PVASI)

PVASI consists of a single light unit, positioned on the left side of a runway adjacent to the touchdown point, which projects three or four different bands of light at different vertical angles, only one of which can be seen by a pilot on approach at any one time. The indications provided by a typical PVASI are:

• *fast-pulsing white*—well above the glide slope (or glide path);
• *pulsing white*—above the glide slope;
• *steady white*—on the glide slope (or alternating red/white for some systems);
• *pulsing red*—below the glide slope; and
• *fast-pulsing red*—well below the glide slope.

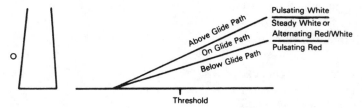

Figure 20-12. The PVASI

Tri-Color VASI

The tri-color VASI is a short-range visual slope aid (one-half mile by day, five miles by night), and consists of a single-light unit that indicates:

• *amber* if above slope;
• *green* if on slope; and
• *red* if below slope.

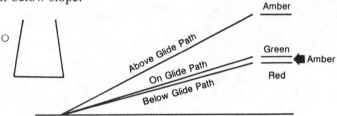

Caution: When the aircraft descends from green to red, the pilot may (or may not) see a dark amber color during the transition from green to red.

Figure 20-13. The Tri-color VASI

T-VASI

The T-VASI is a system that has a horizontal bar of white lights either side of the runway aiming point. If the airplane is right on slope, you will see the horizontal bar only.

• If you are high on slope, single lights will appear above this bar, forming an inverted-T, and indicating *fly down*.
• If you are low on slope, single lights will appear below the bar, forming a T, and indicating *fly up*.

The number of vertical lights give an indication of how far off slope you are. If you are extremely low, the lights turn red.

Pilot Control of Some Lighting Systems

The approach lights and runway lights at an airport are controlled by:

• the control tower personnel (when the tower is active);
• the FSS, at some locations where no control tower is active; or
• the pilot (at certain airports).

The pilot may request ATC or FSS to turn the lights on (or off), or to vary their intensity if required. On a hazy day, with restricted visibility but a lot of glare, maximum brightness might be necessary; on a clear dark night, a significantly lower brightness level will be required.

At selected airports, when ATC and/or FSS facilities are not manned, airborne control of the lights by the pilot is possible using the VHF-COM. The A/FD specifies the type of lighting available, and the VHF-COM frequency used to activate the system (usually the CTAF).

To use an FAA-approved pilot-controlled lighting system, simply select the appropriate VHF frequency on the VHF-COM, and depress the microphone switch a number of times. A good technique involves keying the mike seven times within five seconds, which will activate the lights at maximum intensity, and then subsequently keying it a further five or three times for medium or low intensity respectively, if desired. For more detailed information, refer to the Airman's Information Manual.

All lighting is activated for 15 minutes from the time of the most recent key transmission. If pilot-controlled lights are already on as you commence an approach, it is good airmanship to reactivate them and thereby ensure that they will stay on for the duration of the approach and landing.

"T" ON BOTH SIDES OF RWY ALL LIGHTS VARIABLE WHITE. CORRECT APPROACH SLOPE- ONLY CROSS BAR VISIBLE. UPRIGHT "T" - FLY UP INVERTED "T" - FLY DOWN RED "T" - GROSS OVERSHOOT.

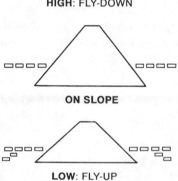

HIGH: FLY-DOWN

ON SLOPE

LOW: FLY-UP

Figure 20-14. T-VASI

Some airport lighting systems can be controlled directly by the pilot.

Night Vision

There are two aspects of vision that are important to a pilot flying in a night sky:
- dark adaptation; and
- peripheral vision.

The Structure of the Eye

Light rays pass through the pupil of the eye and are focused by the lens onto the retina, which is a light sensitive layer at the back of the eye. It sends electrical signals along the optic nerve to the brain, allowing us to *see*.

The central part of the retina contains **cone** cells which are most effective in daylight, and least effective in darkness. They allow us to see color, small details, and distant objects.

The outer band of the retina contains **rod** cells which are responsible for your peripheral—that is, off center—vision, and are effective in both daylight and darkness. They are sensitive to movement, but not to detail or color, and so only register black, white and gray.

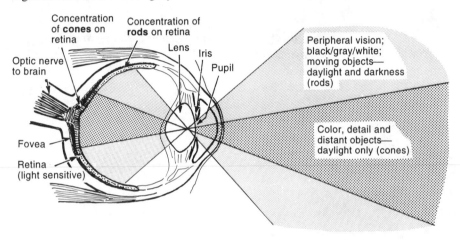

Figure 20-15. Structure of the eye

Adaptation of the Eyes to Darkness

It takes the eyes about **30 minutes** to adapt to a dark environment, as most of us have experienced when we enter a darkened cinema (late) and stumble across other patrons in an attempt to find an empty seat.

The rate at which *dark adaptation* of the eyes occurs depends to a large extent upon the contrast between the brightness of light previously experienced and the degree of darkness of the new environment.

While bright lighting within the previous few minutes has the strongest effect, bright light experienced for some period within the preceding few hours will also have an effect. Bright lighting should therefore be avoided prior to night flying.

Bright lighting should be avoided prior to night flying.

Generally, this is difficult to achieve, since flight planning in a well-lit room and preflight inspections with a strong flashlight or on a well-lit tarmac will almost always be necessary. The best that can be achieved in many cases is to **dim the cockpit lighting prior to taxiing,** and to avoid looking at bright lights during those few minutes prior to takeoff.

Night vision can also be affected by the lack of oxygen, so ensure that you use oxygen when flying above 10,000 feet MSL. On a more mundane level, avoid cigarette smoke in the cockpit at night, since it will displace oxygen in your blood to an appreciable extent, and consequently reduce your night vision by an amount comparable to an extra 5,000 feet in altitude. In the long term, a good diet containing foods with Vitamins A and C can improve your night vision.

Since bright lights will impair your outside vision at night, it is good airmanship to keep the cockpit lighting at a reasonably low level, but not so low that you cannot see your charts, or find the fuel selector.

There are some occasions, however, when bright cockpit lighting can help preserve your vision. This can occur on an instrument flight, for instance, if flying in the vicinity of electrical storms. Nearby lightning flashes can temporarily degrade your dark adaptation and your vision, particularly if it is in contrast to a dim cockpit. Bright lighting in the cockpit can minimize this effect and, although your external vision will not be as good as with dim cockpit lighting, you will avoid being temporarily blinded by the lightning flashes.

Note: Flying near electrical storms is not recommended. They should be avoided by at least 10 miles and, if you are not an instrument-rated pilot in a suitably equipped airplane, then you should probably stay on the ground at night if there are storms around.

Scanning for Other Aircraft at Night

Because only the **rod** cells in your eyes are sensitive in darkness, objects will be more readily visible in your **peripheral vision.** You will see objects better when your eyes are looking to one side of them at night, rather than straight at them as in daylight.

Use off-center scanning at night.

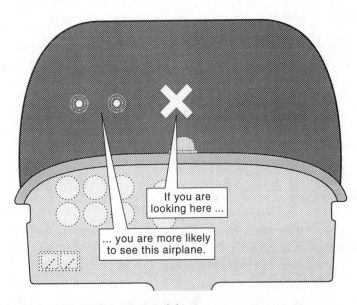

If you are looking here ...

... you are more likely to see this airplane.

Figure 20-16. Peripheral viewing at night

Night Flying at an Airport

Night flying requires a combination of visual and instrument flying skills. The takeoff run at night, for instance, is made with visual reference to the runway. Shortly after takeoff, however, outside visual reference might be very poor, and transferring your attention from outside the cockpit to the instruments in the cockpit at or before that time is essential. In contrast, flying by day and in good weather conditions, your attention can remain outside the cockpit.

Preparation for Flying at Night

Night flying requires careful attention to preflight preparation and planning. In contrast to daylight hours, weather conditions in the vicinity of the airport are difficult to assess visually at night. While stars might be clearly visible overhead one minute, the next they may be covered unexpectedly by low clouds, which could have a significant effect on flight in the area.

Study the available **weather reports and forecasts,** paying special attention to any item that could affect visibility and your ability to fly at a safe operating altitude. Some of the main items to consider are:

Study the available weather reports and forecasts.

- cloud base and amount;
- weather such as rain, snow, fog and mist;
- temperature/dewpoint relationship—the closer they are, the more likely it is that fog will form as the temperature drops further; and
- wind direction and strength, to assess the most suitable runway, the possibility of fog being blown in, and the likelihood of windshear caused by the diurnal effect (a light surface wind with a strong wind at altitude, less vertical mixing).

Check any special procedures for night flying at that airport and in the vicinity.

Minimum Weather Conditions

The Basic VFR minimums apply for night flying:
- flight visibility three statute miles; and
- distances from clouds: 500 feet below (and 1,000 feet above) and 2,000 feet horizontally from clouds.

What this means in the traffic pattern at night is:
- a flight visibility of at least three statute miles; and
- a cloud ceiling of at least 1,000 feet AGL—so that you can fly in the traffic pattern at 500 feet AGL and still have a 500-foot clearance from clouds above.

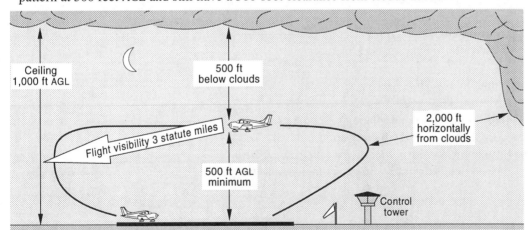

Figure 20-17. Basic VFR minimums at night are flight visibility at least 3 sm, and cloud ceiling at least 1,000 feet above the airport elevation.

Exception: See next page.

Exception: In Class G airspace at nontowered airports, the reduced day minimums (flight visibility at least 1 sm, cloud ceiling at least 500 feet AGL) do *not* apply, however the above basic VFR minimums are relaxed in terms of flight visibility only—it is reduced from 3 sm to a minimum flight visibility of 1 sm, provided you operate in the traffic pattern within $^1/_2$ sm of the runway.

Cross-Country

For a cross-country flight at night, carry the appropriate aeronautical charts, and have them suitably prepared and available for quick use in the cockpit. The better the preflight preparation of the charts, the lower the in-flight workload. Note that, if *red* light is to be used in the cockpit, then red print on the chart will not be easily seen.

All lines drawn on your charts should be in heavy **black,** since even white light in the cockpit will probably be dimmed to ensure that good external night vision is retained. If you are instrument-qualified, carry the Instrument Approach Charts for the expected airports of operation, as well as for any other suitable airports nearby just in case unexpected cloud cover rolls in and an in-flight diversion becomes necessary.

Note on the chart any **well-lit landmarks** that may be useful, including airport beacons, towns, major roads, railroad yards, and so on, as well as any **radio navigation aids** available for use. Be especially aware of significant lit or unlit **obstructions.**

Try to choose well-lit checkpoints, and use the radio navigation equipment fully.

Check your personal equipment, including the normal daylight items such as a navigation computer, a plotter (or a protractor and scale rule) and pencils. A definite requirement for night flying is a serviceable **flashlight**—essential for your external preflight checks, and very useful in the cockpit in case of electrical failure.

Personal equipment is important on a night cross-country flight.

The External Preflight Check

A strong flashlight is essential if the external preflight check is to be carried out successfully at night. Not only must the airplane be checked, but the surrounding area should also be scanned for obstructions, rough ground and other aircraft. Tie-down ropes and wheel chocks are also difficult to see (and remove) at night.

Additional items, such as the position lights, need to be checked prior to a night flight.

All normal external checks should be made, although some additional items must also be included at night. These should be incorporated into the external preflight check if any night flying at all is to occur, even though the takeoff might be made in daylight.

A check of the aircraft lights is important. A typical technique during the preflight check is to position yourself near (or in) the cockpit and:
- place the master switch on;
- check the instrument lighting and dimmers (if fitted);
- check the cabin lighting;
- check the taxi light, landing light, strobe lights and rotating beacon by switching them on, then off, so that they do not drain the battery unnecessarily; and
- switch the position lights on (also known as *navigation lights)* and leave them on for the walk-around, since it may not be possible to check them from the cockpit.

During the walk-around:
- check the surrounding area for obstructions and other hazards, and determine a clear taxi path;
- all of the lights and their covers should be clean and serviceable, and the cockpit windows should also be clean;

- the position lights should be carefully checked (*red*–left, *green*–right, *white*–tail), as **position lights are essential for night flying.** The taxi light is essential for safe taxiing, but the landing lights, while useful, are not essential for flight—good takeoffs and landings can be made without them; and
- for a neat external check, a test of any electrical stall warning device can be made at this time, before returning to the cockpit and placing the master switch back to off, to minimize electrical drain on the battery.

Take great care during the preflight check at night, focusing the torch on each specific item as it is checked, and also running its beam over the airplane as a whole. Ensure that the windshield is clean and free of dust, dew, frost or ice.

If **ice or frost** is present, check the upper leading edge of the wing (the main lift-producing part of the airplane) to ensure that it is also clean. Any ice, frost or other accretion should be removed from the airplane (especially from the lift-producing surfaces such as wings and horizontal stabilizer) prior to flight.

Do not forget to remove the pitot cover, otherwise there will be no airspeed reading on the ASI.

Internal Preflight Check

Carry out the internal preflight check. Ensure that spare fuses, if required, are available. Place all items that might be required in flight in a handy position, especially the flashlight, which should be placed where you can lay your hands on it in complete darkness. While handy, it should still be secure, otherwise it could become a dangerous missile in the cockpit during turbulence. A red lens on the flashlight is useful, as red light will not diminish your night vision as much as white light.

Cabin lighting should be set at a suitable level. Dim the cabin lights so that external vision is satisfactory, and reflection from the canopy minimized, but do not have them so dim that you cannot see the controls or fuel selector. Check and set individual instrument lighting, if fitted. It is unwise to commence night flying immediately after being in a brightly lit environment. **Allow your eyes time to adjust to natural night light.**

Complete the **Preflight checklist,** making sure that the **additional night items** are covered.

Cockpit and Cabin

Do not start up until you have the cockpit well organized:
- your equipment stowed for easy in-flight access, especially the flashlight;
- lighting set adequately; and
- passenger briefing, and so on—completed.

Make sure that you have the parking brake set before starting the engine, especially since any movement of the airplane will be more difficult to detect than during daylight hours. To avoid draining the battery, any unnecessary electrical services should be off until after start-up. Ideally, the **anti-collision beacon** should be turned on just prior to engine start, to warn any person nearby that the airplane is active.

Keep a sharp lookout before starting the engine—**a spinning propeller is deadly,** and may be difficult to see at night. With dim cabin lights, an open window and a loud warning that you are about to start the engine ("**clear**") and the flashing of the taxi lights or landings lights several times, the risk will be minimized. Complete the Prestart checklist if applicable, then start the engine normally.

- When the engine is running, check outside to make sure that the airplane is not moving.
- The alternator/generator should be checked to ensure that it is functioning correctly, with the ammeter showing a positive reading after the start-up.
- Adjust the engine rpm if necessary to achieve a suitable charging rate. If the anti-collision beacon was off for the start-up, it should now be turned on for added safety.
- Confirm that the position lights are on; they are required to be on when the aircraft moves at night, since this is how other pilots determine which way your airplane is pointed.
- Complete the After-Start checklist, if applicable.
- Adjust cockpit lighting to assist your eyes in adapting to the darkness outside.

Taxiing at Night

The responsibility for all movement of the airplane, on the ground and in the air, lies with the pilot. Take advantage of any assistance provided by a **marshaler,** but remember that **you carry the final responsibility.** Use the taxi light, but avoid blinding the marshaler or pilots of other airplanes, if possible. The taxi light not only assists you to see obstructions and avoid them, it also makes it more obvious to other people that your aircraft is moving, or about to.

Take extra care when taxiing at night. Request a taxi clearance at tower-controlled airports, and at airports without an operating control tower, advise others of your movements on the CTAF.

Taxi slowly and carefully. Taxiing at night requires additional attention because:
- distance at night is deceptive—stationary lights may appear to be closer than they really are;
- speed at night is deceptive, and there is almost always a tendency to taxi too fast, since there are fewer ground references. Consciously check taxi speed by looking at the wingtip area (where reflected light off surface objects will help you to judge speed), and slow down if necessary;
- other aircraft and any obstacles will be less visible at night; an airplane ahead on the taxiway may be showing just a single white tail-light that can be easily lost in the multitude of other lights; so, **keep a good lookout;** and
- when stopped, double check that the parking brake is set.

Follow taxi guide-lines or lights. Taxiway lighting will be either two lines of sideline blue along the taxiway edges, or one line of centerline green. Yellow taxi guide lines may be marked on hard surfaces, and will be visible in the taxi light. Stay in the center of the taxiway to preserve wingtip clearance from obstacles.

The ground reflection of the wingtip position lights, especially on a high-wing airplane, are useful in judging the clearance between the wingtips and any obstacles at the side of the taxiway.

If there is any doubt about your taxi path, slow down or stop. If you stop, set the parking brake. In an extreme situation, say on a flooded or very rough taxiway, it may be advisable to even stop the engine, seek assistance, or check the path ahead on foot. The landing lights may be used to provide a better view ahead, but they will draw additional electrical power, and their continuous use on the ground may not be advisable (refer to your Pilot's Operating Handbook).

Pay attention to the welfare of other pilots. Some taxiways run parallel to the runway, so avoid shining your bright lights into the eyes of a pilot taking off or landing, or taxiing, either by switching them off, or positioning the airplane conveniently. Avoid looking into the landing lights of other aircraft yourself, since this could seriously degrade your night vision.

Following the start-up and prior to takeoff, all of the vital radio navigation equipment should be checked—including the VHF-COM, VHF-NAV, DME, ADF, marker lights and transponder. The altimeter should be checked for the correct **altimeter setting,** and an indication close to airport elevation. During the taxiing run, the instruments should be checked.

Turning left:

- HI and magnetic compass decreasing;
- ADF tracking;
- the turn coordinator indicates a left turn, and the coordination ball indicates that the airplane is skidding right; and
- AI steady.

Turning right:

- HI and compass increasing;
- ADF tracking;
- turn coordinator shows a right turn, and ball indicates skidding left; and
- AI steady.

At the Holding Point

The holding point or holding bay may have special lights or markings. Do not enter the runway until you are ready, you have a clearance (if appropriate), and the runway and its approaches are clear of conflicting aircraft.

While completing the pretakeoff checks at the holding position, ensure that your taxi and/or landing lights do not blind other pilots. Ensure that the **parking brake** is on—an airplane can easily move during the power check, and at night there are few visual cues to alert the pilot. During the pretakeoff checks, do not have the cabin lighting so bright that it impairs your night vision. (The flashlight can be used if bright light is needed temporarily.) Check outside regularly to confirm that the aircraft is stationary.

Pay special attention to the **fuel selection,** since the fuel selector may be in a poorly lit area. Correct **trim** will ensure that you have no unusual control forces to contend with when airborne. Ensure that any item required in flight is in a handy position. Complete the **Before-Takeoff checklist** thoroughly. Checking the **heading indicator** for alignment with the magnetic compass while the airplane is stationary is especially important at night, since it will be used for heading guidance, both in the traffic pattern and on cross-country flights.

A final check of cockpit lighting should be made. Ensure that it is adjusted to a suitable minimum, bright enough to see the major controls and instruments in the cockpit, but not so bright as to seriously affect your outside vision.

A **10-second review** prior to lining up of your proposed flight path, and also proposed actions in the event of engine failure, shows good airmanship.

The Night Takeoff

When ready to line up for takeoff, make any required **radio call,** and **look carefully for other traffic on the ground and in the air.** Clear the approach path to the runway, checking both left and right.

Check the windsock for wind direction and strength. Conditions are often calm at night, making either direction on the runway suitable for operations—so ensure that the approach areas at both ends of the runway are clear.

The landing lights of an approaching airplane are generally quite visible, but sometimes a pilot will choose to practice a night landing without using them, in which case the airplane will be more difficult to see unless it has strobe lights.

Do not waste runway length when lining up for takeoff, especially on a short runway. Line up in the center of the runway, check that the HI agrees with the runway direction and, with the brakes off and your feet well away from the brakes and on the rudder pedals, smoothly apply maximum power.

Directional control during a night takeoff is best achieved with reference to the runway edge lighting, using your peripheral vision, since your eyes should be focused well ahead of the airplane toward the far end of the runway. Runway centerline markings may also assist you. Avoid over-controlling during the ground run, keeping straight with rudder, and wings level with ailerons. If a problem occurs during the takeoff ground run prior to liftoff, close the throttle and apply the brakes as necessary, keeping straight with rudder.

The takeoff is the same by night as it is by day. Fly the airplane away from the ground at the normal liftoff speed, and adopt the normal climb-out attitude. The big difference is that, at night, visual reference to the ground is quickly lost after liftoff, and any tendency to settle back onto the ground will not be as easily noticed. As soon as the airplane is airborne, therefore, **transfer your attention to the flight instruments.**

Transfer your attention to the instruments before losing the last visual references, which typically will be the last set of runway lights. The first 300 to 400 feet of the climb-out will probably have to be totally on instruments until you are high enough to regain usable visual references.

Maintain the normal takeoff pitch attitude and wings-level on the attitude indicator. Climb power and climb attitude should result in a **positive climb away from the ground,** reflected in a positive climb rate on the VSI and a gradually increasing altimeter reading.

The airspeed indicator should be checked periodically to ensure that a suitable **airspeed** is being maintained on the climb-out, with minor adjustments being made on the attitude indicator as necessary. When well away from the ground and comfortable in the climb-out, the HI can be checked for heading.

Retractable Gear. In a retractable-gear airplane, the landing gear should not be raised until a positive climb is indicated on both the altimeter and the VSI, and perhaps until insufficient runway remains ahead for a safe landing in case of engine failure (a very rare event these days with well-maintained aircraft and well-trained pilots).

Flaps. The flaps should not normally be raised until at least 200 feet above the airport, and no turns should be made until a safe altitude is reached. Normally, a steady straight climb is maintained until within 300 feet of pattern altitude before turning onto the crosswind leg.

Landing Lights. With little or no natural external horizon visible, **the instruments** become very important. If glare from the landing lights is distracting in the cockpit, turn them off when established in the climb. Mist, haze, smoke or cloud will reflect a lot of light.

Engine Failure. The actions to follow in the event of a problem during the takeoff run were covered above. If an **engine failure** occurs **during the climb-out,** follow the normal daylight procedures. Lower the nose to the gliding attitude to ensure that a stall does not occur, and use the landing lights to assist in ground recognition. Maintain control of the airplane. If sufficient altitude is available, restart the engine and climb away.

Visual reference to the ground is quickly lost after liftoff.

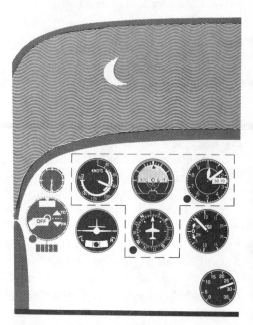

Figure 20-18. Transfer to the instruments after liftoff, and maintain a positive climb.

The Night Traffic Pattern

The traffic pattern at night is usually the same as that by day, except that it is flown mainly on instruments, with occasional reference to the airport lighting to assist in positioning the airplane suitably. The normal techniques of **attitude flying** apply. There is often a tendency to overbank at night, so special attention should be paid to bank angle.

When the airplane makes the first turn, the runway and airport lights will be easily seen and should be referred to frequently. Well-lit landmarks may also be useful for positioning in the traffic pattern.

Allow for drift on the crosswind leg, and level the airplane off using normal instrument procedures when you reach the pattern altitude. Maintain this altitude accurately, and carefully scan outside before making any turns. A good **lookout** for other aircraft must be maintained at all times, and the usual radio procedures followed. Look for the position lights of other airplanes, and respond with appropriate heading changes to avoid collisions.

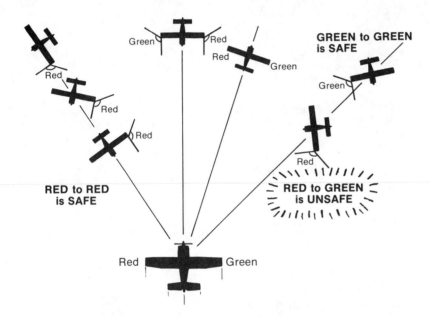

Figure 20-19. Using the observed position lights of other traffic to avoid a collision

While *green-to-red* is not safe, green-to-red will be the situation with two airplanes flying parallel on downwind. An especially careful lookout will need to be maintained. The usual right-of-way rules apply.

Listening to radio transmissions will help you maintain a picture of what else is happening in the traffic pattern.

The **turn from downwind to base leg** should be made at the normal position, with reference to the runway lights and any approach lighting, and the descent planned so that the **turn to final** commences at about 600 to 700 feet above the airport elevation—ideally with a 20° bank angle, and certainly no more than 30°.

When on final, confirm that you are in fact lined up with the runway, and **not** just a well-lit road—check that your heading agrees approximately with the runway direction, and make use of any radio navigation aids you have available.

The Night Approach

Make a powered approach at night, rather than a glide approach; in modern training aircraft, the powered approach is generally used by day also. Power gives the pilot more control, a lower rate of descent and, therefore, a less steep approach slope. The approach to the aiming point should be stable, using any available aids, such as the **runway lighting** and a **VASI** if available.

Using the **runway edge lighting** only, correct tracking and slope is achieved when the **runway perspective** is the same as in daylight. For **correct tracking,** the runway should appear symmetrical in the windshield.

Guidance on achieving the **correct approach slope** is obtained from the apparent spacing between the runway edge lights. If the airplane is getting low on slope, the runway lights will appear to be closer together. If the airplane is flying above slope, then the runway lights will appear to be further apart. Attention should also be paid to the airspeed indicator throughout the approach, to ensure that the correct **airspeed** is being maintained.

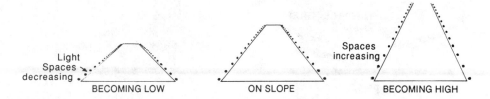

Figure 20-20. Perspectives on approach using runway edge lighting

If no VASI is available, then the **aiming point** during the approach should be a point selected somewhere between two to four runway-edge lights along the runway from the approach threshold.

If there is a VASI available, however, the **aiming point** provided by this system should be used. Because it is an approach aid and not a landing aid, the VASI should be disregarded when below about 200 feet above the airport, and attention placed on the perspective of the runway edge lighting in anticipation of the flare. Following the landing flare and holdoff period, the airplane will touch down some distance beyond the aiming point used during the approach.

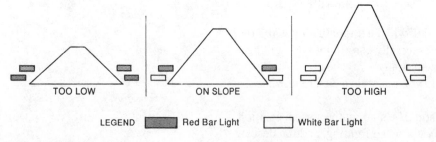

Figure 20-21. Perspectives on approach using a VASI

Tracking

Stay on centerline during the approach. Any tendency to drift off the extended centerline can be counteracted with coordinated turns, and drift can be laid off if a crosswind exists. Be prepared for wind changes as the descent progresses— the difference between the wind at 1,000 feet above the airport and at ground level is likely to be more pronounced at night than by day. It is common for the wind strength to decrease and the wind direction to *back*—change direction counterclockwise—as the airplane descends.

A powered approach is preferable at night.

Stay on centerline during the approach.

Stay on slope during the approach. Any variations in slope should be corrected with coordinated use of power and attitude. The aiming point should stay, on average, in the same position in the windshield. **Stay on airspeed** during the approach. Check your airspeed on the airspeed indicator, and do not be afraid to use power. Overcome any tendency to fly too fast (a common fault at night). Occasionally check the altitude. Use the landing light as desired (not essential).

Approaching the threshold, the runway lights near the threshold should start moving down the windshield, and certain runway features may become visible in the landing lights. The VASI guidance will become less valuable below about 200 feet and should not be used in the latter stages of the approach, and certainly not in the flare and landing. The VASI is an approach guide only—it has no value in the flare and touchdown. It is pilot judgment that counts in the landing.

> **Stay on slope and on airspeed during the approach.**

> **A VASI, if available, should be used as an approach guide.**

The Flare, Holdoff and Landing at Night

The airplane should be flown *on slope* toward the aiming point, where the landing flare will begin. The best guide to the round-out (or flare) height and holding the airplane off is the runway perspective given by the runway edge lighting. As the airplane descends toward the runway, the runway edge lighting that you see in your peripheral vision will appear to rise.

The appearance of the ground can sometimes be deceptive at night so, even with the landing light on, use the runway lighting as your main guide in the flare, both for depth perception as well as tracking guidance. For this reason, your first landings may be made *without* using the landing light. When using the landing light, however, do not stare straight down the beam, but to one side.

> **Use the runway lighting as your main guide in the flare.**

There is a common tendency to round out a little too high in the first few night landings, but this tendency can soon be modified with a little practice. The runway perspective on touchdown should resemble that on liftoff, and an appreciation of this is best achieved by looking well ahead toward the far end of the runway. Avoid trying to see the runway under the nose of the airplane—this will almost certainly induce a tendency to fly into the ground without flaring.

As you flare for the landing, the power should gradually be reduced entering the holdoff phase, and the **throttle fully closed** as the airplane settles onto the runway at touchdown. Keep straight with rudder during the landing ground run and, in any crosswind, keep the wings level with aileron. Use back elevator as necessary to keep weight off the nosewheel.

> **Gradually reduce the power to idle as you enter the holdoff phase and touch down.**

Stay on the centerline until the airplane has slowed to taxiing speed, using brakes if necessary. Speed is deceptive at night—you are usually moving faster than you think, so be careful and slow down. Taxi clear of the runway, stop the airplane, set the brakes to PARK, and complete the After-Landing check.

The Go-Around at Night

The technique is the same as by day, except that a go-around by night is performed primarily by reference to instruments, rather than external features such as the horizon (which may not be discernible).

> **A go-around by night is performed primarily by reference to instruments.**

Whereas the eyes may be concentrated on the runway lighting during the latter stages of the approach, these lights are no longer necessary during a go-around and, when full power is applied and the pitch attitude raised to the go-around attitude, it is possible that they may no longer be in view.

There will be a strong pitch/yaw tendency as go-around power is applied, and this must be controlled with reference to the flight instruments. Hold the desired pitch and bank attitudes on the AI, monitor vertical performance on the altimeter, monitor airspeed on the airspeed indicator, and hold direction on the heading indicator. Keep the coordination ball centered with rudder pressure.

> **Hold the desired pitch and bank attitudes on the AI.**

Do not change configuration (flaps/gear) until established in the go-around, with a positive rate of climb indicated on both the altimeter and the VSI.

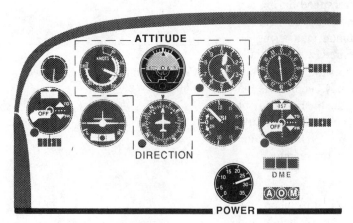

Figure 20-22. The go-around at night

Wind Variations with Altitude

The surface wind at night may differ significantly from the wind at altitude. The term *surface wind* refers to the wind measured 30 feet above open-and-level ground—the height of most windsocks. The wind well away from the influence of the surface—typically some thousands of feet above it by day, and possibly only 500 feet above it by night—is known as the gradient wind.

There will be some vertical mixing in the air mass near the earth's surface, depending upon a number of things, including **heating,** which will cause thermal eddies in the lower layers. During a typical day, the earth's surface is heated by the sun. The earth's surface, in turn, heats the air near it, causing the air to rise in thermal eddies and mix with the upper air. This vertical mixing in the lower levels of the atmosphere brings the effect of the *gradient wind* closer to the ground. With vigorous heating (such as over land on a sunny day), the friction layer is deep, and so the stronger upper winds are brought down to lower levels.

The Surface Wind at Night

If the thermal eddying is weak—such as at night—then the vertical mixing is less and the friction layer shallower. With less warming and mixing, the effect of a strong gradient wind may not reach the ground, resulting in a surface wind that is lighter at night than by day. A light daytime wind of 10 knots may become practically calm by night, even though the upper winds have not changed.

A consequence of a reduced wind speed is a reduced **coriolis effect,** hence the surface wind will *back* compared with the wind at altitude—that is, the wind direction will move counterclockwise as the airplane descends. (The effect is reversed in the southern hemisphere.) See figure 20-23.

The Climb-Out at Night

Expect stronger and sharper wind changes as you climb out by night. The difference in wind strength between the surface and at altitude will usually be more marked at night and, if there is a sudden transition from the lower winds in the shallow friction layer to the undisturbed upper winds at a particular altitude, say at about 500 feet, then **windshear** could be experienced as the airplane passes through this level.

A surface wind of 5 knots on takeoff may suddenly become 20 knots at some low altitude on a clear night—possibly with a significant change in direction as well—yet it may be only 10 knots at 1,000 feet AGL on a clear and sunny day.

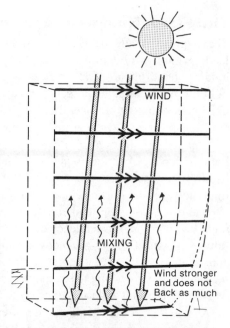

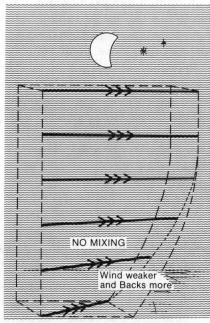

Figure 20-23. The diurnal (daily) variation of wind

Emergencies at Night

Engine Failure

A forced landing at night away from an airport is obviously a more dangerous event than by day, when better vision will allow the easier selection of a suitable field. Moonlight may help at night, but do not count on it! Normal daylight procedures should be followed if the engine fails at night, with the emphasis on **keeping the airplane at flying speed** and **restarting the engine.**

Flying the airplane at a low forward airspeed—lower than normal gliding speed but consistent with retaining full control—will help achieve a lower rate of descent and allow more time for remedial action and for carrying out a *forced landing* if necessary. A **MAYDAY call** should be made promptly on the frequency in use, or on the emergency frequency 121.5 megahertz, to alert the rescue services. **Squawk 7700** on the transponder if time permits.

Time available for action will depend upon your altitude above the ground, so reference to the altimeter is important. With the correct *altimeter setting* set in the pressure window, the altimeter will read altitude MSL. If sufficient altitude and time is available, glide the airplane (at a safe speed) back toward the airport, while you continue trouble shooting the problem.

Make a common sense estimate of your altitude above the ground and keep a good lookout.

The full procedures for rectifying the problem and restarting the engine should be carried out if time permits. **Fuel selection** is a major item to consider. If, however, a landing has to be made, then consideration should be given to landing upwind, using only a partial flap setting (rather than full flaps) to avoid a steep nose-down gliding attitude with a high descent rate, and to minimize the amount of flare required prior to touchdown.

Well-lit roads will almost certainly have light poles and overhead wires, so they may not be suitable for landing, even though they look like nice runways.

It is preferable to touch down in a fairly flat attitude. The landing light may be useful during the last few hundred feet, especially to make visual contact with the ground.

Electrical Failure

An electrical failure may cause the loss of instrument and cockpit lighting, which will necessitate the use of your **flashlight** (kept in a handy position and with good batteries). A sudden failure of lighting should only deprive you of the instruments for a few seconds but, in this time, make use of visual cues such as the natural horizon.

If discernible, the natural horizon will generally be of more value when the airplane is well above the ground. Close to the ground, shortly after takeoff for instance, there may be insufficient ground lighting to provide a horizon and, in any case, the ground lights could possibly be on a sloping hillside giving a false horizon, or there could be so few that the airplane will quickly fly over them anyway. **Scan the flight instruments!**

If the electrical failure is only partial, then alternative lighting may be available in the cockpit from another light source. If a bulb has blown, interchange it. Panic action is not required—calm and careful consideration is. Do not be distracted from controlling the attitude of the airplane.

The attitude indicator, if it is electrical, will gradually run down if electrical power is removed, but it could remain useful for a brief period. Attention should be paid to the airspeed indicator, however, to ensure that flying speed is maintained. The first step following a failure of any kind is: **fly the airplane!**

When flying the airplane is under control, try to **rectify the problem,** and follow the appropriate emergency procedures or checklists. For an electrical failure, check the switching, monitor the alternator/generator or battery discharge rate, and check circuit breakers and fuses (if convenient) without disturbing your control of the airplane. If the electrical failure is only partial, but with a high discharge rate, then off-load the alternator or battery by switching off nonessential services, such as some radios, the landing lights, and so on. A landing as soon as reasonably possible on a suitable runway should be considered.

A return to the airfield should be planned, making a radio call if possible, and keeping a good **lookout** for other aircraft. If it is only a **radio failure,** then ATC can perhaps be alerted by flying a traffic pattern, descending, and then flying above the landing runway, flashing the landing light and/or position lights ON and OFF. Without radio, light signals from the ATC personnel on the ground may be used—the main ones being:

- *continuous red*—give way to other aircraft and continue circling;
- *red flashes*—do not land (the airport is not available for landing);
- *green flashes*—return to the airport vicinity, but wait for permission to land;
- *continuous green*—you may land.

If your **position lights** have failed, then the airplane should be landed normally as soon as it is safe to do so, unless ATC authorizes the continuation of the flight. ATC should be informed of the lack of position lights as soon as possible, so that other aircraft can be warned. Loss of the position lights will not affect control of the airplane in any way—in fact, the pilot generally cannot even see these lights—however it will affect the ability of other airplanes to see you and remain clear. A normal traffic pattern and landing should be made.

If the **landing light** has failed, then this is of little importance. It is not required for a pilot to make a normal, safe landing. You should, from time to time, practice night landings without using the landing light.

Failure of Airport Lighting

Most airports have a **standby power supply** that will operate within seconds of an airport power failure. There is a possibility, although remote, that a complete power failure could occur. Airplanes in the vicinity of an airport without any runway lighting at night should hold at a safe altitude and maintain a good lookout. Radio contact should also be maintained, preferably with ATC on the ground, but if that is not possible, with other aircraft in the traffic pattern or with ATC on an alternative frequency.

If the lighting is not returned to service, then consideration should be given to **diverting** (at a safe altitude) to a nearby airport where runway lighting is available. Radar service may be available to assist in tracking. **A lowest safe altitude** of 1,000 feet above the highest obstacle—2,000 feet in mountainous terrain—within four nautical miles either side of the diversion course should be allowed for—possibly higher if conditions permit.

It is always advisable to carry sufficient fuel at night for an unexpected flight to an alternate field.

Lost

If you become temporarily uncertain of your position, follow the same procedures as you would during daylight hours. Radio navigation aids, if available in the vicinity, should always be taken advantage of if you know how to use them. If you are really lost, then do not hesitate to ask for navigational assistance from ATC, either by radar or with VHF direction finding using the VHF-COM radio. The choice of alternative airports will be more limited at night, of course, since runway lighting will be necessary.

Night Navigation

Navigating at night follows the same basic principles as navigating by day, except that ground features are more difficult to see, distances are more difficult to estimate, and the likelihood of encountering unexpected clouds or areas of restricted visibility is greater.

The best ground features to use at night are usually the light patterns of towns, and the beacons of any nearby airports. Cities like Los Angeles are generally too large for distinctive light patterns to be meaningful to a novice night flyer, but small towns, especially if they have areas of darkness around them, are generally good. Busy freeways delineated by a stream of car headlights may also be useful ground features for navigation.

On moonlit nights, reflections off the surface of lakes and other large bodies of water may make them very visible—especially when viewed against the moon—although this should not be relied upon for navigation purposes, in case clouds cover the sky unexpectedly. On clear and calm nights, the reflections of stars off mirror-like water surfaces may give the impression of surface lights.

Flying over dark unlit ground or water can be disconcerting, and can lead to disorientation. Concentrate on the flight instruments.

Airport beacons, which are installed at various civil and military airports, are good landmarks. During the airport's hours of operation, the controllers will switch the airport beacon on at night, and also by day in bad visibility (below VFR minimums). Flashing lights, especially marine beacons on dark patches of water, can sometimes cause disorientation.

The runway lights themselves may be difficult to pick out, especially if the airport is surrounded by brightly lit streets. Use the airport beacon as a guide to the airport, and monitor your HI so you can determine the orientation of the runway.

Radio navigation aids are very useful at night, if you know how to use them correctly. For instance, positive identification of a runway by using the localizer is helpful. Some aids experience errors at night—for instance, *NDB night effect,* which may be greatest during the periods around dawn and dusk. In general, you can expect major en route VORs and NDBs to be operating continuously, but some aids associated with a particular airport may not be available outside specified hours of operation. This could also apply to a radar service or an ILS. It is better to check first, and be sure.

Availability of Airports

Many airports close down at night. It is always advisable to check which airports are available at night, and which are not. Call an FSS briefing office if you are unsure. Check not only your planned departure and destination airports, but also those airports which might be useful as *alternates* in case of a diversion. You must be certain that runway lighting will be available for your landing.

Flight Planning

Good flight planning is especially important at night, since there will be **fewer visible ground features** to assist in determining navigation errors, as well as less assistance available from ATC or FSS in the form of communications or radar.

The weather takes on special importance at night. All relevant information should be studied carefully, especially the airport forecasts for your destination, as well as those for a number of alternates and your airport of departure. Remember that the temperature/dewpoint spread provides some clue as to the possibility of **mist or fog** forming when the temperature falls during the night.

A weather briefing is essential before any night flight.

Also, fewer weather observers on duty at night will mean fewer weather updates. Make use of automated weather services (HIWAS, ATIS, ASOS and/or AWOS).

Attention should be paid to the possibility of low clouds, mist or fog, and also to the wind strength and direction, at altitude as well as at the surface. The presence of clouds might be indicated by surface lights or the stars and moon disappearing. If you inadvertently enter clouds, concentrate on the flight instruments and make a medium or shallow 180° turn to the reciprocal heading—this should bring you back into the clear within a short time.

Mist or fog might be indicated by lights and stars appearing fuzzy. Remember that vertical visibility through mist and fog is much better than slant visibility. Even though you can see the airport clearly from overhead, the slant visibility on approach might make an approach and landing impossible.

A suitable route should be chosen that utilizes the best features available at night—the lights of small towns, airport beacons, operating radio navigation aids, marine beacons, freeways—even if this route is slightly longer than the direct route. Rugged and/or high terrain is best avoided, and a **safety altitude** to ensure adequate terrain clearance should be calculated. A vertical clearance of at least 1,000 feet above the highest obstacle within 4 nm of your planned course is recommended. Take along adjoining sectional charts, since you can see long distances at night, and far-distant towns might still be good landmarks.

Courses should be marked on the chart with conspicuous black lines, to ensure that they will be clearly seen in a dimly lit cockpit. The flight log should also be filled in with a dark pencil or pen, so that it is easily read in dim lighting. Red lines will not be visible in red lighting, and certain colors on the map may not be as distinguishable by night, which may lead to some difficulties.

Care should be taken in measuring courses and distances, and then in calculating **headings** and **groundspeeds.** Always recheck! *Dead reckoning* is very important at night, and a correct flight log is a much better starting point than an incorrect one.

Calculate an accurate **fuel log,** ensuring that there is sufficient fuel available for a successful diversion and landing, with adequate reserves remaining.

It is recommended that a flight plan be submitted for a night cross-country flight, since this increases your protective search-and-rescue cover.

Headings and Airspeed

Distance at night can be deceptive, since there will be **fewer ground features** visible and available for comparison in terms of size and location. The usual tendency at night is to underestimate distance. What appears to be about 5 miles may in fact be 10. Altitude and speed may also be difficult to estimate, so careful attention should be paid to the altimeter and to the airspeed indicator.

Fly accurate headings and airspeed.

The airplane should be navigated, according to a predetermined flight log, by flying planned heading and true airspeed. From time to time occasional track corrections and revised ETAs may be required, using reliable pinpoints and radio navigation aids. **Accurate heading and time-keeping is essential,** and changes should only be made when you are absolutely certain that a change is required.

If you become lost on a night cross-country flight, follow the normal daylight procedures. Use available visual features and radio navigation aids to fix your position, or request assistance from ATC or FSS—they may be able to provide a radar fix or a DF bearing. However, with good flight planning and accurate flying in terms of airspeed and heading, you will always know where you are, even at night.

✍ Review 20

1. What are the two types of light-sensitive cells on the retina of the eye?

   ➤ cones and rods

2. The central part of the retina is occupied mainly by _____ cells, which see (colors/only black-and-white and gray), and are especially (good/poor) for small detail. They are used for (central/peripheral) vision.

   ➤ cone, colors, good, central

3. The outer band of the retina is occupied mainly by _____ cells, which see (colors/only black-and-white and gray), and are especially (good/poor) for small detail. They are used for (central/peripheral) vision.

   ➤ rod, only black-and-white and gray, poor, peripheral

4. Another name for peripheral vision is _____-_____ vision.

   ➤ off-center

5. At night, your (central/peripheral) vision is better.

   ➤ peripheral

6. It takes about ____ minutes for your eyes to adapt fully to darkness.

   ➤ 30 minutes

7. Bright light can impair your dark adaptation (almost immediately/only after 30 minutes).

   ➤ almost immediately

8. Smoking in the cockpit will (improve/impair/not affect) your night vision.

   ➤ impair

9. A good diet will (improve/impair/not affect) your night vision.

   ➤ improve

10. The best light to use in a cockpit to avoid impairing your night vision is (white/green/red).

    ➤ red

11. If you use red light in a darkened cockpit, you (will/may not) be able to see red markings or features on your navigation chart.

    ➤ may not

12. You (should/need not) carry a flashlight with you at night.

    ➤ should

13. You should turn the position lights on (at all times/when the aircraft is moving or about to be moved).

    ➤ when the aircraft is moving or about to be moved

14. Sketch a diagram showing the placement in your cockpit of the instruments required for night flight.

    ➤ *refer to our text*

15. Position lights consist of a _____ light on the left wing, a _____ light on the right wing, and a rear-facing _____ light on the tail.

    ➤ red, green, white

16. An approved anti-collision light system (is/is not) required at night.

    ➤ is

17. You (must/need not) always use the landing light when landing at night.

    ➤ need not

18. For night flight, the airplane (must/need not) have spare fuses stored in an accessible place.

    ➤ must

19. Taxiway lights are centerline _____ or sideline _____ .

    ➤ green, blue

20. Runway edge lights are colored _____ . The runway threshold lights are _____ when seen from the approach side. The runway end lights at the far end of the runway are _____ .

  ➤ white, green, red

21. A civil airport beacon will flash in the following sequence: _____ .

  ➤ green–white–green–white ....

22. VASI stands for V_____ A_____ S_____ I_____ and will provide an approximately ____ ° slope to the runway.

  ➤ Visual Approach Slope Indicator, 3°

23. A two-bar VASI will show _____ on top of _____ when the airplane is on slope.

  ➤ red, white

24. A two-bar VASI showing red-on-red indicates that the aircraft is too (high/low) on slope.

  ➤ low

25. A two-bar VASI showing white-on-white indicates that the aircraft is too (high/low) on slope.

  ➤ high

26. Describe how to switch on pilot-controlled runway lights to maximum intensity. When activated, they should stay on for ____ minutes.

  ➤ select the appropriate frequency on the VHF-COM and then depress the mike key seven times within five seconds, 15 minutes

27. Because of the lack of ground references, many pilots show a tendency to taxi too (fast/slow) at night.

  ➤ fast

28. After takeoff at night, you should (keep your attention outside/shift your attention to the flight instruments).

  ➤ shift your attention to the flight instruments

29. Many pilots show a tendency to fly too (fast/slow) on final approach to land at night.

  ➤ fast

30. To assist in orientation at night, you (should/need not) keep the HI aligned with the magnetic compass.

  ➤ should

31. When flying VFR at night, you will use the flight instruments (more/the same/less) than by day.

  ➤ more

32. If you see a red position light from another aircraft out to the right, the situation is (safe/unsafe).

  ➤ unsafe

33. If you see a green position light from another aircraft out to the left, the situation is (safe/unsafe).

  ➤ unsafe

34. Red-to-green is (safe/unsafe).

  ➤ unsafe

35. The usual tendency is to (overestimate/underestimate) distance at night. A town that appears to be 10 nm distant is likely to be (20 nm/5 nm) distant.

  ➤ underestimate, 20 nm

36. Wind on the runway is usually (lighter/stronger) at night compared with during the day because of (less/more) mixing of the layers of air.

  ➤ lighter, less

37. Sharp changes in wind speed and/or direction as you climb out after takeoff are more likely by (day/night), because of (less/more) mixing of the layers of air.

  ➤ night, less

38. It (is/is not) good airmanship to carry sufficient fuel for diversion to another airport at night in case the lighting at your airport fails or if the weather deteriorates unexpectedly.

  ➤ is

Specific Airplane Type

Introduction

The basic principles of flight, of engines, of systems and of performance apply to all airplanes, but there are differences between one airplane type and another. It is a requirement that you should be thoroughly familiar with the type of airplane that you are about to fly.

For this reason, you should develop a sound knowledge of the specific airplane that you are training on and that you will be flying during the flight test.

The primary source of this specific knowledge is the FAA **Approved Flight Manual (AFM),** which is associated with the airplane's Certificate of Airworthiness, and the **Pilot's Operating Handbook (POH).** You may be using an **Information Manual** based upon the Pilot's Operating Handbook, but it must be kept amended for it to remain current.

Having learnt to fly one specific type of airplane, it is a relatively straightforward matter to be trained on another. Following an endorsement program, you must display not only an ability to fly the airplane but also a sound knowledge of it, along the same lines as described here. You should also have an understanding of what maintenance a pilot is permitted to perform on the airplane (speak with your flight instructor).

At the same time as the **flight test** for your Private or Commercial Pilot Certificate you should be prepared to answer questions similar to those asked below, specifically related to the type of airplane that you will be flying. Since each specific type of airplane may require a different answer to the questions asked, no answers are provided here. You should research them in the primary reference documents mentioned above, discuss them with your flight instructor, and gradually fill in the answers as your training progresses.

Know your airplane.

The Flight Manual

1. The Flight Manual that I am using is for a _____ _____ (manufacturer's name and model) type of airplane.

   ....

2. The Flight Manual is (required/not required) to remain with the particular airplane. It is located _____ .

   ....

The Airworthiness Certificate & Other Documents (ARROW)

1. The Airworthiness Certificate is located _____ . It (must/need not) be displayed at the cabin or cockpit entrance so that it is legible to passengers or crew.

   ....

2. The Registration Certificate is located _____ .

   ....

3. The Radio Station License is located _____ .

   ....

4. The operating limitations (Flight Manual, Pilot's Operating Handbook, placards) are located _____ .

   ....

5. Weight-and-Balance information is located _____ .

   ....

6. A list of required placards is found in the Pilot's Operating Handbook, Section _____ .

   ....

7. A copy of the checklists is located _____ .

   ....

Emergency Equipment

1. The aircraft (has/does not have) a fire extinguisher, which is located _____ . The type, and how to use it, can be found in the Pilot's Operating Handbook, Section _____ .

   ....

2. The aircraft (has/does not have) an E_____ L_____ T_____ (ELT), which is located _____ . Information on the ELT may be found in the Pilot's Operating Handbook, Section ____ . FAR 91 specifies that the ELT battery expiry date (must/need not) be marked on the ELT and entered in the aircraft maintenance record. It also specifies that a training aircraft without an ELT may not proceed more than ____ nm from the training airport.

   ....

   ....

   ....

3. The aircraft (has/does not have) a first aid kit. It is located _____ .

   ....

4. The aircraft (has/does not have) survival gear. It is located _____ .

   ....

5. The aircraft (has/does not have) flotation devices. They are (life jackets/seat cushions/other) and are located _____ .

   ....

6. The aircraft (has/does not have) a flashlight. It is located _____ .

   ....

7. The aircraft (has/does not have) a transponder. The code to squawk in an emergency situation is _____ .

   ....

8. The aircraft (is/is not) fitted with seat belts which must be worn (only during takeoff and landing/in turbulence only/takeoff, landing and turbulence/at all times while at the flight crewmember station). *See FAR 91 under "Flight Crewmembers at Station"*.

   ....

9. The aircraft (is/is not) fitted with shoulder harnesses which must be worn (only during takeoff and landing/in turbulence only/during takeoff, landing and turbulence/at all times while at the flight crewmember station). *See FAR 91 under "Flight Crewmembers at Station"*.

   ....

10. The aircraft (is/is not) fitted with supplemental oxygen which the pilots must use for extended flights above ____ feet MSL cabin altitude.

    ....

Weight-and-Balance Limitations

1. The maximum takeoff weight is ____ lb.

   ....

2. The maximum landing weight is ____ lb.

   ....

3. The maximum passenger load (excluding the pilot) is ____ passengers.

   ....

4. The maximum number of persons on board (POB), including the pilot, is ____ .

   ....

5. The maximum baggage weight that can be carried is ____ lb.

   ....

6. The empty weight of the airplane is ____ lb.

   ....

7. If you carry one adult passenger and full fuel, how much baggage can you carry?

   ....

8. In which category (or categories) is the airplane permitted to fly?

   ....

9. Do these weight limitations vary if the airplane is certificated to fly, not only in the normal category, but also in another category such as the utility category, or the acrobatic category? Why are the weight limits less, and the CG limits not as far rearward?

   ....

   ....

10. Calculate the weight-and-balance situation—the gross weight and center of gravity position—given certain requirements, such as a certain number of passengers, a given amount of fuel, a given amount of baggage, and so on, using the airplane weight information found in the Flight Manual.

    ....

    ....

Airspeed Limitations

1. The normal operating airspeed range is marked on the airspeed indicator with a _____ arc.

   ....

2. The caution airspeed range is marked on the airspeed indicator with a _____ arc.

   ....

3. The flaps-extended airspeed range is marked on the airspeed indicator with a _____ arc.

   ....

4. V_{NE} is known as the _____ airspeed. Its value is ____ KIAS. It is marked on the airspeed indicator as a _____ .

   ....

5. V_{NO} is known as the _____ airspeed and its value is ____ KIAS. It is marked on the airspeed indicator as a _____ .

   ....

6. V_A is known as the _____ airspeed and its value is ____ KIAS. It (is/is not) marked on the airspeed indicator.

   ....

7. V_B, if specified, is known as the _____ airspeed (or *rough air* airspeed) and its value is ____ KIAS. It (is/is not) marked on the airspeed indicator.

   ....

8. V_{S1} is known as the _____ speed wings level and flaps up, and its value is ____ KIAS. It (is/is not) marked on the airspeed indicator as the (high/low) speed end of the _____ arc.

   ....

9. V_{FE} is known as the _____ airspeed and its value is ____ KIAS. It (is/is not) marked on the airspeed indicator as the (high/low) speed end of the _____ arc.

   ....

10. The stall speed with full flaps extended and the wings level is ____ KIAS, known as V_{S0}.

    ....

11. The published stall speeds assume the airplane (is/is not) at maximum gross weight.

   ....

12. Stall speed (increases/decreases/does not change) if the airplane is at less than maximum weight.

   ....

13. Stall speed (increases/decreases/does not change) if significant power is applied.

   ....

14. Stall speed (increases/decreases/does not change) if the airplane is banked.

   ....

15. Stall speed (increases/decreases/does not change) if the airplane is maneuvering, for instance pulling out of a dive.

   ....

16. In a 30° banked turn, the stall speed will increase by ____ % and is ____ KIAS.

   ....

17. In a 60° banked turn, the stall speed will increase by ____ % and is ____ KIAS.

   ....

18. The maximum speed at which you may use abrupt and full elevator travel is ____ KIAS.

   ....

Aerodynamic Load Limitations

1. Maximum load factor (flaps up) is + ____ g and – ____ g.

   ....

2. Maximum load factor (flaps extended) is + ____ g and – ____ g.

   ....

3. Are there any other handling limitations if, for instance, the airplane has a full load of passengers, of maximum baggage, or a maximum fuel load?

   ....

   ....

Authorized Operations

1. The airplane (is/is not) certificated to fly during the day.

   ....

2. The airplane (is/is not) certificated to fly during the night.

   ....

3. The airplane (is/is not) certificated to fly under the Visual Flight Rules (VFR).

   ....

4. The airplane (is/is not) certified to fly under the Instrument Flight Rules (IFR).

   ....

5. The airplane (is/is not) certificated for flight into known icing conditions.

   ....

6. Forward slips with flaps extended (are/are not) prohibited. There (is/is not) a placard regarding this near the flap control.

   ....

Takeoff Performance Limitations

1. The maximum structural takeoff weight is ____ lb.

   ....

2. Be able to use the takeoff chart(s) in the Flight Manual to calculate the performance figures (performance-limited takeoff weight, or runway length required) given a specific situation.

   ....

3. The takeoff distance required, under standard MSL conditions, for a takeoff at maximum weight and a climb to clear a 50-foot obstacle is ____ feet.

   ....

4. Compared with a takeoff at a sea-level airfield, a takeoff at a high-elevation airfield will require (the same/more/less) runway length.

   ....

5. Compared with a takeoff in standard conditions, a takeoff in high humidity will require (the same/more/less) runway length.

   ....

6. Compared with a takeoff under standard conditions, a takeoff at a higher temperature will require (the same/more/less) runway length.

....

7. The obstacle-clearance speed with takeoff flaps extended is ____ KIAS. This is found in the Pilot's Operating Handbook, Section ____ .

....

8. The best angle-of-climb airspeed (V_X) and the best rate-of-climb airspeed (V_Y) are ____ and ____ KIAS. They are found in the Pilot's Operating Handbook, Section ____ .

....

Landing Performance Limitations

1. The maximum structural landing weight is ____ lb.

....

2. Be able to use the landing chart(s) in the Flight Manual to calculate the performance figures (performance-limited landing weight, or runway length required) given a specific situation.

....

3. The landing distance required, under standard MSL conditions, for a landing at maximum weight approaching over a 50-foot obstacle is ____ feet.

....

4. Compared with a landing at a sea-level airfield, a landing at a high-elevation airfield will require (the same/more/less) runway length.

....

5. Compared with a landing at standard temperature, the landing at a higher air temperature will require (the same/more/less) runway length.

....

6. The normal approach speed is ____ KIAS.

....

7. The maximum demonstrated crosswind component for landing is ____ knots.

....

Cruise Flight (Maximum Range)

1. Be able to use any tables or graphs in the Flight Manual to calculate range—that is, the **distance** that the airplane can fly under given conditions.

....

2. What is the recommended power setting (rpm) to achieve 65% power at 5,000 feet?

....

3. What fuel flow in gallons per hour can you expect at 5,000 feet using the 65% best economy setting.

....

4. What fuel flow in gallons per hour can you expect at 5,000 feet using 65% power and the best power setting.

....

5. A gliding speed of ____ KIAS will give you the best gliding range.

....

Maximum Endurance

1. Be able to use any tables or graphs in the Flight Manual to calculate endurance—that is, the **time** that the airplane can remain airborne under given conditions. At 5,000 feet MSL, the maximum endurance figures are ____ rpm and ____ KIAS, with an expected fuel consumption of ____ gph.

....

Flight Controls

1. Understand how the elevator (or stabilator) system works—for example, moving the control column back will cause the airplane's nose to (rise/drop) as a result of the elevator moving (up/down).

....

2. Understand how the aileron system works— moving the control column to the left will cause the airplane, at normal flying speeds, to roll toward the (left/right) by moving the left aileron _____ and the right aileron _____ .

....

3. Understand how the rudder system works.

   (a) Moving the left rudder pedal in will cause the right rudder pedal to move _____ .

....

(b) Moving the left rudder pedal in will cause the airplane's nose to yaw (left/right), due to the trailing edge of the rudder moving (left/right).

....

(c) The main function of the rudder in normal flight is to (yaw the airplane/prevent unwanted yaw and keep the airplane coordinated).

....

(d) There (is/is not) an interconnection between the rudder and the aileron systems on this specific airplane.

....

4. Understand how the trim system works:

(a) Is there an elevator trim?

....

(b) Is there a rudder trim?

....

(c) Is there an aileron trim?

....

(d) The elevator trim is a (servo/balance/ anti-servo) type.

....

(e) The main function of a trimming device is to (relieve steady pressures/maneuver the airplane).

....

5. Understand how the flap system works.

(a) The flap system is (mechanical/electrical/ hydraulic).

....

(b) The flaps are operated with a (switch/lever).

....

(c) The flap indicating system is (mechanical/ electrical).

....

(d) The flap range is from 0° to ____ °.

....

(e) The flap position is indicated by _____ .

....

6. The airplane (has/does not have) a stall warning device.

....

7. The stall warning device, if installed, (is/is not) interconnected with the flap system.

....

8. The aircraft (has/does not have) leading edge devices. They are operated by _____ .

....

9. The aircraft (has/does not have) spoilers. They are operated by _____ .

....

10. The aircraft (has/does not have) deicing or anti-icing capability on the wings and other aerodynamic surfaces.

....

The Propeller

1. The propeller is a (fixed-pitch/constant-speed) propeller.

....

2. Will nicks, mud, insects or other contamination affect the performance of the propeller?

....

3. Should new nicks or damage to the propeller be referred to a mechanic if possible prior to flight?

....

4. Most training airplanes used for initial instruction have a fixed-pitch propeller, but if yours has a constant-speed propeller, then you should know how it works, how to control the rpm/manifold pressure with the propeller control and the throttle, and list the recommended *rpm/map* settings and limits.

....

Landing Gear and Brakes

1. The airplane is a (tricycle landing gear/tailwheel) type.

....

2. The airplane (has/does not have) nosewheel steering.

....

3. The rudder and the nosewheel steering (are/are not) interconnected.

....

4. The rudder pedals (can/cannot) be used to provide directional control when taxiing.

....

5. The landing gear (is/is not) retractable; if retractable, it is operated by _____ power. It (does/does not) have an emergency means of extension.

....

6. Shocks on the nosewheel during taxiing, takeoff and landing are absorbed by a (leaf spring/ bungee/oleo-pneumatic strut).

....

7. Shocks on the main wheels during taxiing, takeoff and landing are absorbed by a (leaf spring/ bungee/oleo-pneumatic strut).

....

8. Brakes are fitted to the (main wheels/ nosewheel/mainwheels and nosewheel).

....

9. The brakes are operated from the cockpit using _____ .

....

10. The wheel brakes are operated (mechanically/ hydraulically).

....

11. The wheel brakes are (disc/drum) type.

....

12. Normal tire pressure is ____ main wheels, ____ nosewheel.

....

13. Know what defects in the tires are acceptable or unacceptable for flight, such as cuts, wear or bald spots.

....

The Electrical System

1. The DC electrical system operates at (12/24) volts.

....

2. The battery is located _____ .

....

3. The battery (does/does not) supply electrical power to the engine starter motor.

....

4. When the engine is running, electrical power is supplied by (an alternator/a generator).

....

5. A serviceable battery (is/is not) required for the alternator to come on-line.

....

6. When on-line, the alternator (will/will not) recharge the battery.

....

7. Understand how to manage the electrical system, for instance the indications and actions to be taken if the alternator (or generator) system fails or malfunctions.

....

8. If the alternator (or generator) fails in flight, then as much electrical load as possible (should/need not) be shed by switching nonessential services off. Which services would you switch off?

....

9. A fully charged battery should supply emergency power for a period of approximately _____ if required.

....

10. Know the function and location of circuit breakers and fuses, and what to do if they *pop* or fail. How many times should you reset a popped circuit breaker?

....

11. Is it possible to use external power when parked and, if so, what are the procedures? They can be found in the Pilot's Operating Handbook, Section ____ .

....

12. Which of the following lights does the airplane have: rotating beacon, position lights, strobe, taxi light, landing light, cockpit lights, internal instrument lights, flashlight?

....

....

....

13. The stall warning device, if installed, operates (electrically/mechanically).

....

14. If the electrical system of the aircraft totally fails (alternator not battery), which of the following items become inoperative. Mark them:

- Flap switch or lever
- landing gear switch or lever
- VHF-COM radio
- VHF-NAV radio
- ADF
- transponder
- rotating beacon
- taxi and landing lights
- flashlight
- ELT
- magnetos and engine ignition system

....

Flight Instruments

1. Name the flight instruments operated by the pitot-static system and know whether they use pitot pressure, static pressure or both.

....

....

....

2. Know the position of the pitot tube(s) and static vent(s), and any associated drains to eliminate water from the lines.

....

3. Is there electric pitot-heat to prevent ice forming on the pitot tube which would cause incorrect instrument indications?

....

4. Is there an alternate static source and, if so, where is it located? What is its purpose and what effect does it have on the instrument indications if the static source is changed by the pilot from normal to the alternate?

....

....

5. Name the gyroscopic flight instruments.

....

....

6. Name the flight instruments that are operated electrically.

....

....

7. Name the flight instruments that are operated by the vacuum system, if fitted, and know how the vacuum system works (venturi or vacuum pump) and the maximum/minimum suction required for correct operation.

....

....

8. The airspeed indicator is operated by _____ .

....

9. The attitude indicator (artificial horizon) is operated by_____ .

....

10. The altimeter is operated by _____ .

....

11. The vertical speed indicator is operated by _____ .

....

12. The heading indicator is operated by _____ . It (must/need not) be periodically realigned with the magnetic compass.

....

....

13. The turn coordinator (or turn indicator) is operated by _____ .

....

14. The clock is operated by _____ .

....

Radio Communication and Radio Navigation Aids

1. The aircraft (has/does not have) a VHF-COM set; it can be used with (cockpit speaker/headphones/either).

....

2. The aircraft (has/does not have) a VHF-NAV set which can be used to receive signals from an (NBD/VOR). It (has/does not have) D_____ M_____ E_____ (DME) capability.

....

3. The aircraft (has/does not have) A_____ D_____ F_____ (ADF), which can be tuned to a N____ D_____ B_____ (NDB).

....

4. The aircraft (has/does not have) a LORAN set.

....

5. The aircraft (has/does not have) G_____ P_____ S_____ (GPS) navigation receiver.

....

Fuel

1. The correct grade of fuel is _____ , colored _____ . What additives, if any, are permitted?

....

2. How many fuel tanks does your airplane have, where are they located, and what is their capacity in terms of usable fuel? How can you select fuel from each tank? Can you use fuel from both tanks simultaneously? Sketch from memory the fuel selector positions—OFF/LEFT/RIGHT/BOTH.

3. How can the airplane be fueled? Where are the filler caps and what precautions need be taken?

....

....

4. Is it advisable to fill the fuel tanks prior to parking the airplane overnight? Why?

....

....

5. Where are the fuel drains located and why are they used? When should fuel be drained?

....

....

6. Where are the fuel tank vents located and why are they important?

....

....

7. How can fuel quantity be measured, both on the ground and in flight? Is there a low-level warning?

....

....

8. Does the engine have a carburetor or a fuel injection system? How does it work?

....

9. Is the air that enters through the normal engine air intake filtered?

....

10. Is the air that passes into the carburetor when carburetor heat is *HOT* filtered?

....

11. Does the engine require priming prior to start-up and, if so, how is it done?

....

....

12. Does the airplane have fuel pumps and, if so, where are they located, what is their function, are they electrically or engine-driven, what are their maximum and minimum acceptable operating pressures, and when should they be used?

....

....

....

13. Know the correct fuel management procedures, such as which tank(s) to use for takeoff and landing, when to use fuel pumps if fitted, when and how to switch tanks.

....

....

....

Engine Oil

1. The correct engine oil for the airplane is _____ .

....

2. The engine oil is stored in a tank or sump which is located _____ .

....

3. Explain how oil quantity can be measured. How many oil quantity indicators does the aircraft have?

....

4. The minimum oil quantity prior to flight is _____ .

....

5. The maximum quantity of oil is _____ .

....

6. The oil is used to (lubricate/cool/both lubricate and cool) the engine.

....

The Engine

1. The make and model of the engine is _____ , and it can produce ___ horsepower. It has ___ cylinders, arranged (in-line/horizontally opposed/_____).

....

2. The engine is (air-cooled/water-cooled).

....

3. Cooling of the engine can be increased by opening the cowl flaps. (yes/no)

....

4. The cockpit gauges used to monitor engine operation are _____ , _____ , _____ , _____ .

....

....

5. The normal and the maximum rpm are ____ .

....

6. If the airplane is fitted with a fixed-pitch propeller, rpm is controlled with the _____ .

....

7. If the airplane is fitted with a constant speed propeller, rpm is controlled with the _____ and manifold pressure is controlled with the _____ .

....

8. The minimum and maximum oil pressures are ____ .

....

9. The normal oil pressure is approximately ____ .

....

10. The minimum and maximum oil temperatures are ____ .

....

11. Normal oil temperature is approximately ____ .

....

12. The airplane (is/is not) fitted with a cylinder head temperature (CHT) gauge. If it is, the CHT limits are _____ .

....

13. During ground operations of the engine, it is usual to perform a magneto check, which should be done according to procedures specified by your training organization.

    (a) Specify the maximum acceptable rpm drop when one magneto is switched to OFF, the maximum difference between the separate magneto drops, and (if permitted) the significance of the *grounding check* when both magnetos are switched to OFF briefly.

    ....

    ....

    ....

    ....

    (b) What is the probable cause if the engine keeps running even though the magneto switch has been placed to OFF?

    ....

    ....

14. Specify the action to be taken if an engine fire occurs in flight.

    ....

    ....

    ....

    ....

15. The aircraft (has/does not have) a fire detection and warning system.

    ....

16. Specify the action to be taken if an engine fire occurs on the ground.

    ....

    ....

    ....

    ....

17. What equipment is no longer available if the engine fails in flight?

    ....

    ....

18. What instruments are rendered inoperative if the engine fails in flight?

    ....

    ....

19. Moving the throttle in and out will _____ .

    ....

20. Explain the functioning of the mixture control and how to operate it correctly. If an exhaust gas temperature gauge (EGT) is fitted, explain how to use it.

    ....

    ....

    ....

21. Under what conditions is it permissible to lean the mixture?

    ....

    ....

22. To lean the mixture, the mixture control should be moved (in/out).

    ....

23. To enrichen the mixture, the mixture control should be moved (in/out).

    ....

24. Explain how to lean the mixture.

    ....

    ....

    ....

25. The full *out* position of the mixture control is called the _____ position and is used to (stop/start) the engine.

    ....

26. What are the indications if ice forms in the carburetor? For an engine with a fixed-pitch propeller? For an engine with a constant speed propeller?

    ....

    ....

27. How do you melt carburetor ice and prevent it forming again?

....

....

28. What effect does applying carburetor heat have on the mixture? Does it lean, richen or not alter it?

....

29. Does the hot air used to eliminate carburetor ice pass through a filter?

....

30. Should you use carburetor heat when taxiing if it is not necessary?

....

31. Is the engine normally aspirated, or supercharged or turbocharged to boost its performance on takeoff and at high altitudes?

....

Ventilation and Heating

1. Know how to ventilate the cockpit adequately. What controls do you have?

....

2. Know how to heat the cockpit adequately. What controls do you have? Is there a cockpit temperature gauge?

....

....

3. Know how the heating system works and where the heated air comes from—for example, from over the exhaust muffs, allowing air to circulate near the exhaust system, thereby raising its temperature, before being channeled into the cabin.

....

4. Exhaust fumes from the engine contain a dangerous gas (oxygen/carbon monoxide), which is colorless and odorless and should therefore be excluded from the cockpit.

....

5. The presence of carbon monoxide in the cabin (may/will not) lead to unconsciousness.

....

6. What precautions would you take if you suspect the presence of carbon monoxide in the cabin?

....

....

7. What action would you take in the event of a fire occurring in the cabin?

....

....

8. Is supplemental oxygen available for high altitude flying? Where is it located, and how is it used. Information is found in the Pilot's Operating Handbook, Section ____ .

....

....

9. Can the cabin be pressurized? If so, what controls and indicators do you have in the cockpit? What actions would you take in the event of a sudden decompression at high altitude? An emergency descent procedure is found in the Pilot's Operating Handbook, Section ____ .

....

....

Hydraulic System

1. The aircraft (has/does not have) a hydraulic system. What equipment does it operate?

....

....

2. What controls and indicators for the hydraulic system are in the cockpit?

....

....

3. The hydraulic pumps are (electrically/engine) driven.

....

4. How is the hydraulic pressure regulated?

....

5. What are the hydraulic pressure limits?

....

Index